Cultural Conversations
The Presence of the Past

STEPHEN DILKS

University of Missouri–Kansas City

REGINA HANSEN

Boston University

MATTHEW PARFITT

Boston University

Bedford/St. Martin's   *Boston* ♦ *New York*

FOR BEDFORD/ST. MARTIN'S

Development Editor: John E. Sullivan III
Production Editors: Ara Salibian, Arthur Johnson
Production Supervisors: Cheryl Mamaril, Sarah Zwiebach
Marketing Manager: Brian Wheel
Editorial Assistants: Katherine Gilbert, Kristen Harvey, Caroline Thompson
Production Assistant: Kendra LeFleur
Copyeditor: Barbara G. Flanagan
Text Design: Jean Hammond
Cover Design: Donna Lee Dennison
Cover Art: Bach's Rocks (Bachs Steine)/ROCI BERLIN, 1990, acrylic and fabric collage on plywood panels. Robert Rauschenberg (American, born 1925). National Gallery of Art, Washington. Gift of the Robert Rauschenberg Foundation.
Composition: Pine Tree Composition, Inc.
Printing and Binding: RR Donnelley & Sons Company

President: Charles H. Christensen
Editorial Director: Joan E. Feinberg
Editor in Chief: Karen S. Henry
Director of Marketing: Karen Melton
Director of Editing, Design, and Production: Marcia Cohen
Managing Editor: Elizabeth M. Schaaf

Library of Congress Control Number: 00–106440

For information, write: Bedford/St. Martin's, 75 Arlington Street, Boston, MA 02116 (617-399-4000)

ISBN: 0–312–20157–5

Acknowledgments

Eric Gary Anderson. "Unsettling Frontiers: Billy the Kid and the Outlaw Southwest." From *American Indian Literature and the Southwest: Contexts and Dispositions* by Eric Gary Anderson, pp. 41–50. Copyright © 1999 by Eric Gary Anderson. Reprinted by permission of University of Texas Press.

Arnold Bennett. "Queen of the High-Brows." Review of *A Room of One's Own* by Virginia Woolf. From the *Evening Standard*, November 28, 1929. Reprinted by permission.

Acknowledgments and copyrights are continued at the back of the book on pages 655–59, which constitute an extension of the copyright page. It is a violation of the law to reproduce these selections by any means whatsoever without the written permission of the copyright holder.

Preface for Instructors

Cultural Conversations: The Presence of the Past is a new composition reader structured around the dialogue between influential texts of the past and important texts of the present. It has been designed to invite students to "compose" the relationship between the past and the present in their own writing, and to bring their reading of the past to bear on present-day concerns. The readings have been drawn from a range of academic disciplines, and they raise an equally wide range of social, intellectual, spiritual, and political concerns.

The essays of first-year college students are often expected to resemble in form and purpose the kinds of essays that academics and public intellectuals write as statements that contribute to academic or public conversations—yet composition readers rarely give students the materials and the means to develop meaningful statements of this kind. Students are required to read texts that may be models of fine prose, but they read them with only a thin sense of their context and so struggle to find their own voice and purpose for writing. Some composition readers present contemporary conversations apart from their historical roots; others present the historical texts apart from their contemporary relevance and meaning. *Cultural Conversations* aims to give students a stronger sense of participation in a dialogue that continues to unfold, and thus a more adequate basis for developing their own ideas, arguments, and styles. Public and academic conversations frequently assume some familiarity with the major statements of writers who have shaped today's thinking by defining a problem and establishing key terms and concepts for the conversation that ensued. Students are eager to read these writers, whose names they know and whose work they came to college to read. We can represent only a few such thinkers in this book; ultimately, what *Cultural Conversations* offers is a structure that models a way of gaining access to intellectual dialogue and debate. It juxtaposes past and present, and includes a range of voices within the present that transmute the past.

The body of the reader is divided into six chapters, each of which contains three sections. The first section in each chapter, Text, offers a selection from the work of a major thinker from the past hundred years, one whose impact on contemporary thinking has been extensive and profound: Virginia Woolf, W. E. B. Du Bois, Helen Keller, Sigmund Freud, Mahatma Gandhi, and Frederick Jackson Turner. The middle section in each chapter, Context, contains a set of materials—such as song lyrics, diary entries, book reviews, ads, photographs, portraits, drawings, poetry, and letters—designed to give students an initial sketch of the historical context, a glimpse into the world in which and for which the author was writing. The Context sections have been designed to make difficult reading more accessible, but also to give students a starting point for a more informed critical reading of a canonical text. The final section in each chapter, Contemporary Conversation, contains four or five readings that introduce the reader to a contemporary controversy, problem, or debate that relies on the canonical text either implicitly or explicitly. This structure not only dramatizes the relationship between past and present thinking in the conversations of the academy and of the culture at large, but it gives students the opportunity to participate in deep-rooted debates and to develop authoritative positions of their own.

As a whole, each chapter throws up a multitude of opportunities for critical thinking and writing, but each also reveals multiple directions for further research, for extending the work of the chapter by locating materials in the library and on the Internet. Thus each chapter initiates a conversation to which students are invited to contribute and which they can extend in their writing and research. We imagine the chapter as a structure that opens up a fourth section beyond itself, a section of student writing that has yet to be written. This design reflects the fact that college students can and should be full participants in intellectual conversations that have long and deep roots in history: no less than their teachers, students are entitled to utter the latest but not the final word in conversations that shape our culture.

In the course of a semester, an instructor could expect to work through one or two chapters, allowing students time to reread the core historical text several times and to write two or three essays on each chapter (perhaps one informal response paper, one more formal critical paper, and one research paper). The semester might end with an interdisciplinary essay, using one of the ideas for Extending Your Work that invites students to work across two or more different chapters. While *Cultural Conversations* is a reader rather than a rhetoric and does not attempt to lay out principles of composition or take the place of a writer's handbook, students will receive guidance from the editors' introduction as to how they can negotiate the problems of historical reading and writing.

Texts

We have selected these readings according to several criteria: we have considered their importance throughout the past hundred years, their relevance to readers in the first years of this century, and their suitability for undergraduates, in particular. Of course, a suitable reading does not always mean an easy reading; in fact, we have deliberately included a number of difficult essays as well as more accessible selections. Students will no doubt find some of these texts more challenging than others. We expect that students will need to read each text more than once, but this work will enable students to produce their own readings, which can become starting points for writing.

Above, we spoke of these texts as "canonical." We do not, of course, think of them as somehow the major texts of the last hundred years or even as representatives of a permanent and unchanging canon. Yet each is a major statement by an author whose name students will likely recognize: each text is frequently cited, has somehow helped to shape the world in which we live, and continues to influence readers and writers. These are texts that might be considered classics in the sense that they seem inexhaustibly rich, as each generation rereads them and understands them anew.

Contexts

Each of these sections begins with a brief introductory essay, followed by documentary images and texts—reviews, contemporary responses, a portrait of the writer, illustrations, diaries, newspaper clippings, and so forth. These brief items show the writer of the historical text working in response to the realities of his or her own time and place. The introductory essay provides necessary historical and cultural background but does not attempt to explain (or explain away) the items in the Context section or their relationship to the text; these are offered with little or no commentary, as in a scrapbook. The indefinite but suggestive relationships between juxtaposed elements in the Context section, and between the Context section and the historical text, have been left for students themselves to puzzle through, articulate, work with, quarrel with, make use of, and extend.

Contemporary Conversations

The contemporary readings (almost all from works written since 1980) are texts that have been made possible by the historical text but that take the conversation into new territory, often reshaping the old thought in the process. The contemporary readings will help to explicate the historical readings (students are often able to reread the historical text with new understanding after having worked through two or three of the contemporary readings) and students also will be able to see ideas "mutating"—being developed by later thinkers, and applied in unforeseeable ways to new fields, problems, and debates.

The Contemporary Conversation readings have not been selected with the intent of representing all sides in a contemporary debate; rather they give the reader access to the conversation, delineating its terms in ways that make a range of responses possible and suggest new questions and new directions. They function as springboards for student writing and research and provide suggestive models of what it can mean to read, write, and think critically.

Ideas for Rereading, Ideas for Writing, Ideas for Research, and Ideas for Working across Chapters

Ideas for Rereading and Ideas for Writing follow each of the Text, Context, and Contemporary Conversation sections. Ideas for Rereading encourage students to read actively, and focus on some particular theme or problem as they work through a text for the second or third time. Ideas for Writing suggest more in-depth projects for students to work through on paper. At the end of the chapter, an additional group of ideas for Extending Your Work includes Ideas for Research and Ideas for Working across Chapters. Many of these ideas afford the opportunity to work across disciplines and discourses, and to look at traditions in untraditional ways. We use the word *ideas* rather than *assignments* because we recognize that many instructors take these suggestions and reshape them to meet their own purposes, and that students are often encouraged to do something similar: to think of the Ideas for Writing as a springboard for their own thinking rather than a rigid directive. We have written out these ideas so that they can be used as they are or easily modified to be used in other ways. Some of them can be used as discussion starters; others are designed to be note-taking exercises; still others are traditional writing assignments. We have tried not to place limits around the sorts of relationships that students might find among these readings or the connections they might make between these readings and the world they know.

Each chapter represents an extended project; as students work backward and forward in a chapter and become more confident with the material, their reading, their writing, and their thinking will become more creative and assured. It certainly is not necessary to work through a chapter from beginning to end. Instructors may want to start work on a chapter by assigning one of the more provocative readings from the Contemporary Conversation section of a particular chapter, then work back to the Text and the Context sections, and then return to the contemporary readings. In some cases, working with the Context section before the historical text will help students through a difficult reading. There are many ways of working with the readings in this book; its basic design is simple enough and flexible enough to be used in first-year introductory courses as well as second- and third-year "researched writing" courses. In the Instructor's Manual we have included sample syllabi suggesting different ways of using *Cultural Conversations*.

Cultural studies requires historical inquiry because culture is as much a process as a product; concepts, assumptions, and even words can be understood only with reference to their histories. Meanings are transformed as the individuals who make meaning develop and change in response to personal and cultural forces. But historical inquiry also enables writing because the past is at once foreign to us and something that already belongs to us. When we take seriously the thinking of another time, we become freshly conscious of our own; history gives us a standpoint for thinking in new, critical ways about assumptions that we have always held dear or taken for granted. And therefore it gives us a tool or lever for becoming more conscious of our cultural blindnesses and contradictions. It is one thing to know this in theory, but actually working with relationships between the present and the past forces us to confront questions that we might otherwise dismiss. To take a simple example: when students read Frederick Jackson Turner's "The Significance of the Frontier in American History," they will notice that he rarely mentions Indians, and when he does he often describes them as "savages." Students will be quick to condemn this assumption of cultural superiority. But it takes a second and more imaginative reading to begin to work out why Turner might be able to write this way without disturbing the sensitivities of his immediate audience. What are his values? What's the difference between his view of "progress" and our own? What ideals did Turner's standpoint embody, though he failed to recognize the full humanity of the Indian peoples? What can Turner teach us about our own assumptions—about the costs of economic progress as we understand it today? These questions and others are ones that first-year students can raise and take seriously when they begin to consider the presence of the past in our cultural conversations.

The structure of these chapters provides models of critique as well as models of influence. To read major statements from the past "in context" means not only to read them in historical context in the narrow sense—to know something of their original motivation and reception—but also to know something of the uses to which they are being put, how they have come to be reunderstood in the culture of today. Their "meaning," in the full sense, includes their legacy in the present. Placing canonical texts in juxtaposition with contemporary texts not only reflects how the "great thoughts" have been used, extended, and revised, it also prevents them from being received uncritically.

Acknowledgments

We wish to thank the following reviewers for their helpful comments on this project: Patricia Bizzell, The College of the Holy Cross; John Champagne, Pennsylvania State University at Erie, The Behrend College; Pam Dane, Lane Community College; Joan Graham, University of Washington; Alfred Guy, New York University; Joseph Harris, Duke University; Ken Smith, Indiana University South Bend; and Kathleen Welsch, Clarion University. In addition, there were several very helpful reviewers who chose to remain anonymous. We thank them for their thoughtful insights and suggestions.

A number of colleagues have contributed to this project at various stages and with varying degrees of specificity. The editors wish to convey personal thanks to Kathleen Dixon and Elizabeth Hampsten at the University of North Dakota; Robert Murray at Thomas Aquinas University; Hugh English at Queen's College, New York; T. R. Johnson at the University of New Orleans; Kurt Spellmeyer at Rutgers University; Ken Smith at the University of Indiana–Bloomington; Jane Greer and Barbara Ryan at University of Missouri–Kansas City; and Millard Baublitz, Jean Garrison, Lauren Henry, Jenna Ivers, Sally Sommers-Smith, and Megan Sullivan at the College of General Studies, Boston University. We also wish to acknowledge the hard work of the staff of the Somerville Public Library, Massachusetts, and the Miller-Nichols Library at University of Missouri–Kansas City. The editors wish to give special thanks to Dawn Skorczewski of Emerson College for her help, encouragement, and inspiration throughout the project.

At Bedford/St. Martin's, Chuck Christensen and Joan Feinberg merit our thanks for guiding this project with imaginative vision, offering help at many points along the way. Steve Scipione worked with us during the initial stages of the project and kept a keen interest in it during development, offering much sage advice. Our editor, John Sullivan, has earned our gratitude for his insight and guidance over the last several years. Karen Melton and Brian Wheel deserve praise for their efforts in marketing the book. Ara Salibian and Arthur Johnson expertly guided the manuscript through the production process.

Copyeditor Barbara Flanagan did an excellent job of editing the text and sharpening the Ideas following the selections and the chapters. Lisa Whipple helped us greatly by researching information for headnotes. Editorial assistants Katherine Gilbert, Kristen Harvey, and Caroline Thompson kept track of numerous details.

Projects of this sort always depend on the patience, goodwill, advice, and encouragement of family members and friends. This project would not have been possible without Michael and Marie Cremin, Mary Cremin, Maureen Cremin, Donna Mennona Dilks and Sara-Jessica Mennona Dilks, Joan and Maurice Dilks, Michele Hansen, Deanne Harper, Brian, Dominic, and Angelina Kemmett, Frank and Cecilia Mennona, Mary and Tony Parfitt, and Jeff Welch.

Contents

CHAPTER 2

African American Identity: How Does Race Shape the Arts?   127

CHAPTER 4

The Unconscious: How Can We Understand Ourselves?   311

CHAPTER 5

Nonviolence: A Weapon of Peace?   443

CHAPTER 6

The Frontier: How Do We Imagine the West?   527

people of the United States have taken their tone from the incessant expansion which has not only been open but has even been forced upon them."

"As powerful and persistent as the fantasy that the West set Americans free from relying on the federal government was the fantasy that westward movement could set one free from the past."

"I cannot resolve the contradiction between my experience at the Buffalo Bill Historical Center . . . and my response to the shining figure of Buffalo Bill as it emerged from the pages of books — on the one hand a history of shame; on the other, an image of the heart's desire. But I have reached one conclusion that for a while will have to serve."

". . . we need . . . a radically new symbolic mode for relating to 'the fairest, frutefullest, and pleasauntest [land] of all the worlde'; we can no longer afford to keep turning 'America the Beautiful' into America the Raped."

"The American public has difficulty believing such injustice continues to be inflicted upon Indian people because Americans assume that the sympathy or tolerance they feel toward Indians is somehow felt or transferred to the government policy that deals with Indians. This is not the case."

"The oral tradition demands the greatest clarity of speech and hearing, the whole strength of memory, and an absolute faith in the efficacy of language. Every word spoken, every word heard, is the utterance of prayer."

Introduction

Cultural Conversations: The Presence of the Past

Cultural Conversations invites you to read, think, and write about relationships between the present and the past. We have designed the book to encourage you to explore the ways in which the past produces the present, and the present continually reinvents the past. This relationship between where we are now and where we have been is a many-voiced and continuing conversation, one that we hope you will join as you work with this text.

"The past is never dead. In fact, it isn't even past," says a character in one of William Faulkner's novels. Unlike much of the history course work you may have done in elementary and high school, the work you will do with this book is not finally about distant people in faraway times; it is about yourself. It is about how our understanding of who we are both originates from and creates the stories we tell about where we have been. To focus attention on the ways that the past shapes and is shaped by the present, each chapter in this book is divided into three sections: Text, Context, and Contemporary Conversation.

The Text section contains an influential selection by a writer whose name you are likely to recognize—Virginia Woolf, W. E. B. Du Bois, Helen Keller, Sigmund Freud, Mahatma Gandhi, Frederick Jackson Turner—writers who have had a lasting effect on subsequent thinkers within their own fields of inquiry and well beyond. Although most of them wrote generations ago, these writers continue to appear frequently on syllabi and reading lists. The Context section in each chapter offers short texts and visuals that provide a sketch of the cultural context in which the historical text was written and first read. The selections here suggest ways for you to imagine the historical text in its original time and place. The Contemporary Conversation section presents recent writings that suggest a number of ways the historical text continues to be a part of our thinking today. As you work within and among these three sections, you will begin to construct your own versions of the presence of the past.

1

What does it mean to speak of the "presence of the past"? How do cultural conversations reveal the presence of the past? An eighteen-year-old person, though an adult for the first time, is also the three-year-old, the four-year-old, and so on through the seventeen-year-old—the culmination and product of all those years of experience and development. She or he is not just a person *with* a past, but in a real sense a person shaped by and constructed out of the past. Likewise, but on a broader scale, a culture—its works, values, beliefs, ideas, assumptions, even its language—has undergone a process of formation and reformation, construction and reconstruction, that still continues and that each new generation inherits and reshapes.

Though we might often speak of our values, attitudes, and assumptions as though they were inventions of our own, if we stop to examine them we often find they are largely a legacy from those who lived before us. Take, for example, our ideas about disabled people. Few of us today would dispute that disabled people are capable of significant accomplishments and that the person is more than just his or her disability. But people did not always think this way. Helen Keller amazed her readers in the early twentieth century by revealing that a deaf and blind person could be in so many ways just like themselves. Since then, generations of readers have reflected on the story of Annie Sullivan tracing the letters into Helen's hand and thus beginning her journey toward speaking and writing. Contemporary ideas about what it means to be a disabled person have been profoundly influenced by Keller's story.

Looking back at how Keller changed the world's ideas about disabled people can help us understand the origins of our contemporary assumptions about disability, but it can also help us rethink those assumptions and even begin to transform them. The heightened awareness of ourselves and our cultures that we get from looking into the past helps us to imagine how our familiar world might be different. We take this familiar world for granted partly because we absorb its customs and assumptions unconsciously. For example, many Americans associate the color blue with boys and pink with girls, black with death and white with innocence. These associations might seem natural and inevitable until we learn that a hundred years ago there were no special colors to distinguish boy infants from girl infants, that until fairly recently pink and blue had no special gender significance. Then we might meet someone from, say, India who associates the color white with death and by conversing with this person we might realize that our own associations with the color white are largely conventional—and we might even begin to explore how the connotations of black and white in Western culture have reflected and contributed to a history of racial conflict.

While it is certainly possible to study culture without reference to history, such an approach fails to dig beneath the surface of current concerns and issues. We may not find easy answers by searching out the histories of these concerns, but we will acquire a much deeper and fuller understanding of ourselves and the contemporary world. Just as individuals have histories that explain who they are, so cultures have histories that explain them. In many ways, a culture is its history, the accumulated outcome of thinking and working and writing over many years. Freud argues that even our personal histories remain in large part hidden from view, shaping us in obscure ways. Our cultural histories shape us too, but they are even more remote from us; in this respect, we're like the amnesiac who suddenly finds himself in some strange place with no idea of how he got there. We must find out about our past in order to recover and better understand our identities.

Francis Bacon, a contemporary of William Shakespeare, urged the people of his time to reverse their view of history, arguing that they must learn to look at the past not with nostalgia and regret but with confidence, because they were in a position to improve on the wisdom of the ancients. While people in Bacon's time tended to think of the ancients as older and wiser than themselves, he insisted that really the ancients were younger: the latest generation is the oldest and potentially the wisest. In effect, his view of history faced toward the future. A generation later, the revolutionary mathematician Isaac Newton wrote, "If I have seen farther than others, it is because I was standing on the shoulders of giants." Such a statement exposes the fallacy of the "timeless classic," the notion that autonomous works of genius stand on nothing and can only be venerated; instead, it sees the thinking of the past as something that we can *use* in order to reimagine our own possibilities. E. H. Carr defined history as "the reconstruction and interpretation of the past." By reversing our view of history so that we stand at the beginning of a search to understand ourselves rather than at the end of a story, we empower ourselves to revise (literally, to re-see) the story of the past, to continually learn from it anew, and to reshape the future. Starting from the present and looking backward into the past, we are like someone who turns the pages of a photo album at a critical moment in life, asking, "Who am I really?" This book is intended not simply to *illustrate* a relationship between historical ideas and modern controversies, but rather to give you a way to participate in these conversations for yourself, by writing directly about the readings or by extending the work of the chapter through research. The three-part structure of the chapters thus opens up a fourth section beyond itself, a section which has yet to be written and will be made up of your own writing—the latest but not the final words in an unfolding conversation with long and deep roots in history.

It is this unfolding conversation that we think of when we refer to the "legacy" of writers like Gandhi, Woolf, Turner—a sense of their place in a continuing dialogue rather than a sense of them as ultimate authorities or simply (and reductively) "great thinkers." Culture—a set of values, assumptions, and expectations that define how we understand the world—is not only something we can acquire, it is also an inheritance, something that comes into our collective possession, almost unavoidably and largely unconsciously; but nevertheless it is something we become collectively responsible for. Writers like Keller, Freud, and Du Bois have contributed enormously to the shaping of the values and assumptions of today's Americans (and today's world) concerning human nature and human rights, racial identity and sexual identity, and a host of other values and ideas. These are not simply writers who lived and wrote a hundred years ago or more: their works are of the present perhaps even more than of the past.

The three-part structure of the chapters allows you to work out your own understanding of the relationship between a historical text, its context, and the cultural conversations of today. When we in our own time reread these texts, we reinterpret them: we understand them in new ways, perceive meanings that others had overlooked, bring their ideas to bear on new situations and contexts, depending on when and where we are reading, why we are reading, and who we are as individuals. What it meant for Woolf to argue in 1929 that a woman writer needs "a room of her own" was disputed by her peers. The reviews included in the Context section of Chapter 1 give a sense of these disputes. What Woolf's argument means after the women's liberation movement of the 1960s and 1970s differs from what it meant before these developments. And these developments have not influenced us all equally or in the same way. As Monique Wittig's essay in the Contemporary Conversation section demonstrates, the whole category of "women's writing" might need to be radically reexamined now that some women question whether one is "born a woman" at all. And as the essay by Patricia Williams suggests, the struggle for self-ownership has become a professional issue for a class of women much larger than the one Woolf imagined as her audience in the 1920s. The meaning of Woolf's work in 2001 is not quite what it was in 1970 or in 1929. When a new generation of readers rediscovers its meaning in a new historical context, it partially remakes its meaning; it extends its meaning into the present; it makes it live again, and not precisely as it ever lived before. Thus to read a text means not simply to understand the meaning of the words on the page in the exact sense that they had when they were written, but rather to understand what those words might mean for us here and now. These are "great" texts not because their meaning is fixed and unchanging, but because the conversation about what they mean, a conversation that attests to their continuing relevance, still goes on.

We read, necessarily, with an incomplete sense of the context. And this is one reason why experts continue to debate the meaning or meanings of texts that have been read thousands of times: their sense of the meaning grows with the growth of learning and shifts with the lapse of time. At first, this notion that a text has no single definitive meaning may seem troubling: we're accustomed to the idea, especially in classrooms, that someone (usually the instructor) understands the text and holds its meaning in store for us. But while experience and expertise might make it easier to work with a text, they don't make the problems of interpretation disappear or produce a single, unambiguous, and definitive sense of the text's meaning. If anything, the reverse is true. As readers become more experienced, they become more aware that a multiplicity of reasonable interpretations is possible, that reading can be a stimulating and sometimes hazardous process of negotiating among a wide range of possible meanings.

Thus our subtitle, *The Presence of the Past*, has another sense, one that challenges the notion that the past is over and done with, fixed in time. The way we understand the past is always changing, reshaped by our shifting concerns and values. History is dead only when we no longer use it in our conversations, when we cease to look to it for new ideas, and when we cease to rethink its meaning for us. This book invites you to consider different kinds of relationships among different kinds of texts and contexts, to negotiate and mediate among the historical text, the context, and the contemporary conversation. Further, it invites you to explore relationships between and among different chapters—to consider, for example, how Virginia Woolf's ideas about womanhood compare with Sigmund Freud's; or how W. E. B. Du Bois's ideas regarding the rights and hopes of the marginalized compare with those of Mahatma Gandhi or Helen Keller. Finally, since each chapter only sketches certain features of a conversation that has continued without interruption, it can be used as a jumping-off point for further exploration. This book invites you to conduct research of your own in the library or on the Internet to fill in some of the gaps.

Text

These historical readings have been selected according to several criteria: we have considered their importance in history, their relevance to readers at the present time, and their suitability as readings for an undergraduate composition course. These are powerful and provocative texts. Each of them is frequently cited, each continues to educate and stimulate readers, and each has somehow helped shape our world. In many cases, their ideas have lent such richness to our thinking that they have become "received ideas," ideas so thoroughly accepted into the culture that we habitually refer to them with a brief phrase like "nonviolent resistance" or "the Turner thesis" or "a room of one's own" or "unconscious drives." *Cultural Conversations* will enable you to form a deeper and fuller understanding of the ideas the modern world inherits from Gandhi, Turner, Woolf, Freud, and others—and to use these ideas in work of your own.

These are texts not only to read but to reread. You may find some of them challenging at first, but the experience of slowly getting firm control of the text through a second and third reading and of discovering that you can respond to the author, argue with his or her ideas, and put those ideas to work in the world can be exhilarating. And like other experiences that at first seem daunting—like riding a roller coaster or diving from a height—the experience of reading these texts changes as we do it again and again. These are readings that will stay with you, both because other writers refer to them frequently and because these readings are so rich in themselves. What's exciting about them in a writing course is not their status as tokens of cultural literacy, perhaps not even the insights they convey, but the way that they allow us to see ideas in formation, under construction, affording us with entrance points for a dialogue with them. In many of these historical texts, we are struck by how tentative and open-ended the "great thoughts" reveal themselves to be when we rediscover them in their original setting. This discovery richly repays the effort it takes to bridge the gulf between our own historical moment and the author's. We see how the writer's ideas are embedded in very particular stories, in human observations and circumstances: a deaf-blind woman struggles to explain her way of knowing the world to readers who can hear and see, a well-known novelist gives a talk on women and fiction and describes her sense of alienation and exclusion in the environs of the world's most famous university, a Viennese doctor describes how his "talking cure" works and fails to work. Often we gain access to these texts by identifying aspects of them that resonate with our own experience. (For example, you may not have experienced the kind of relationship that we see between Freud and Dora, but you may be able to compare that situation with one in which a friend or relative tried to interpret your mind or your dreams.) Once the "great thoughts" begin to shake off the rigor mortis that has come from canonization, a real conversation can begin. Sigmund Freud offers a way of reassessing our conception of the conscious and unconscious mind; Virginia Woolf opens new ways of thinking about today's struggles for equal access to education and professional development; Helen Keller allows us to see, hear, and articulate new approaches to physical abilities and disabilities. W. E. B. Du Bois gives us insight into the cultural and political forces that have shaped our own forms of expression.

Context

A good way to get better acquainted with a new friend might be to sit down with her and browse through a scrapbook or photo album, or perhaps look at the items displayed on a bulletin board in her room. Though you cannot share your friend's past, these materials, however fragmentary and incomplete, might help you to re-create aspects of this past in your imagination. Museum exhibits sometimes work like this, presenting materials that, when placed in juxtaposition, compose a sketch of the world in which the subject lived and worked. The Context sections function in this way: like a scrapbook or museum exhibit, they offer material to help readers see the text in historical perspective. Consider an example from Chapter 4, "The Unconscious: How Can We Understand Ourselves?" When we read recent criticism of Freud's psychoanalytic technique in "A Fragment of an Analysis of a Case of Hysteria," we may find ourselves persuaded by those who find Freud guilty of misogyny, heterosexism, false logic, or fact twisting. There may well be justice in these charges. But in the Context section, you will find pictures of electrotherapy instruments that were widely used to treat hysteria in the late 1800s, when Freud was developing his "talking cure." Contemplating these crude instruments and the pain they must have inflicted helps us to appreciate Freud's achievement in introducing a more humane—if still imperfect—approach to the treatment of psychological disturbance. This consideration may or may not induce you to reject the arguments of Freud's critics, but it should help you take a more balanced and historically informed view of the controversy. A different kind of example appears in Chapter 6: we may find Turner's argument about the American frontier convincing, but reading statements by American Indians opens a conversation about possible gaps in his argument.

The documents and illustrations in the Context sections sketch the world out of which the text emerged and into which it made its first appearance. You can expect to find samples of work to which the classic text was responding, book reviews that suggest how the text was received when it was first published, a portrait of the author, as well as other items that help to situate the text in its historical context. The philosopher Hans-Georg Gadamer has observed that "we can understand a text only when we understand the question to which it is an answer." Almost any text, even a fictional one, responds to a question that somehow mattered to the author and to his or her contemporaries. To arrive at an understanding of the text, readers must try to recover and understand the question. This takes imagination, no matter how much material you have at your disposal. The Context sections offer juxtaposed materials with very little commentary, materials that are necessarily incomplete and fragmentary, in order to stimulate your imaginative re-creation of the historical scene surrounding the text, without dictating precisely where and how your thoughts proceed. Relationships between items in the Context section, and between the Context section and the readings, have been left for you to discover (and articulate, use, refute, and extend).

Contemporary Conversation

The Contemporary Conversation sections are composed of readings (mostly published since 1980) that have been made possible by the chapter's historical text but that take its insights into new territory, often reshaping the old thought in the process. They are not "critical essays" in the narrow sense of simply analyzing or explicating the historical text; instead, you will be able to see ideas "mutating," being developed and reexamined by later thinkers and applied in unforeseen ways to new fields, problems, and debates.

Sometimes the readings respond directly to the historical text, quoting its words; in Chapter 4, for example, Carolyn Steedman and Janet Malcolm directly address Freud's controversial "A Fragment of an Analysis of a Case of Hysteria." Elsewhere the debt is less explicit: several of the essays in the Conversation section of Chapter 5 make no mention of Gandhi in their discussion of nonviolence, but nevertheless you can discern the debt. In still other cases the connection is based on an evolving concept or issue rather than a particular idea, and the debt may not even be conscious; for example, the essays in Chapter 3, without responding directly to Helen Keller, carry on her legacy by opening new ways of thinking about the rhetoric of disability. In each case, the Conversation texts demonstrate the presence of the historical work in the thinking of our time, exemplifying how writers build upon and argue with the writers who precede them, finding in their work powerful "ideas to think with." Many of these readings are written by scholars with a good deal of expertise in their subject. Such expertise develops only by listening carefully to the conversation, learning from it, and finally joining it with something fresh to say. This book invites you to add your voice to conversations that are alive today and will continue to unfold in the future.

To offer just one example of how this process works: W. E. B. Du Bois argues that the African American "sorrow songs" represent a genuine contribution to Western culture. In one of the Conversation readings, Alice Walker argues that to recover her heritage as a black woman artist she must be prepared to look in unlikely places. "We have constantly looked high, when we should have looked high—and low" (p. 169). She finds a rich legacy in a nameless woman's quilt, a laborer's singing, her own mother's garden. Walker reminds us that when Du Bois was making his argument, the sorrow songs too would have been considered "low" art—in the eyes of many Americans not really art at all and certainly not "fine" art. Yet these spirituals have begotten the whole tradition of American music, from blues and gospel to jazz and rock and more recently hip-hop and rap. These writers force us to reconsider the conventional distinction between high art and low art and perhaps to think seriously—and write insightfully—about our own relationship with music or the other arts.

One of the great achievements of the last century has been the enrichment of the world of ideas by perspectives that were formerly excluded from it. For many years, works by male writers and artists, mostly of European descent, dominated college syllabi. Today's readers notice this imbalance because one of the themes of our times has been the importance of redressing it, of recognizing the value of perspectives and experiences that in the past were too often neglected. While this book includes among its historical texts some of the "minority" voices that have contributed to our awareness of this need, it remains a fact that in the English-speaking world before the twentieth century, relatively few women, blacks, or Native Americans enjoyed the opportunity to become writers, scientists, or professionals of any kind. Although the process of inclusion is far from complete, the contemporary conversations in this book reflect the progress that has been made: here we find a rich array of spokespersons for critical perspectives that were once silent or marginalized. Often these spokespersons enrich the contemporary conversation with a critique of blindness or prejudice in works that still exert a powerful influence. Such critiques have now become an essential part of the conversations that unfold from the past.

A course based on *Cultural Conversations* will move fairly rapidly between texts that traditionally belong to different disciplines. It will show how ideas from one discipline infiltrate others — how, for example, a social historian like Carolyn Steedman can bring a surprising new perspective to bear on psychoanalysis — and thereby enrich and enliven the conversations that animate that discipline. This book aims above all to help you find ways of working with the kind of texts that you will be reading throughout your college career and, more specifically, ways of developing your own responses to these texts so that you can enter the conversations of the academy — in your writing and in oral discussion — and continue to reshape and redirect these conversations in the new century.

While many of the readings in this book are fine examples of "academic discourse" — the kind of writing produced by professional scholars — the concept of a conversation that continues to unfold also implies that this kind of discourse is constantly evolving. We find many of these writers revising, even reinventing, the language, purpose, and strategies of academic writing, and these experiments demonstrate that academic discourse is no more fixed than history or culture: it changes according to the work of those who participate in academic conversations. By providing ways for you to participate fully in the conversations of the academy, this book is also inviting you to reassess, revise, and reinvent academic discourse.

Ideas for Rereading and Writing, and Extending Your Work

You will find suggestions for rereading and writing throughout *Cultural Conversations*. Ideas for Rereading and Ideas for Writing follow each of the readings and each of the Context sections. A further group of suggestions, Extending Your Work, will be found at the end of the chapter; it includes Ideas for Research and Ideas for Working across Chapters. Some of the ideas can be used as discussion starters; others as paper topics; others in different ways. We call them "ideas" rather than assignments because the latter term suggests a single type of short formal paper topic, and we wanted instead to offer a range of ways of working with the readings in this book. These ideas are not meant to quiz you on the content of the readings, but rather to encourage you to work with the concepts, terms, and arguments of the readings — perhaps to work on a single reading, or to work between readings, or to respond from your own experience, or to take a stand in a debate, or to use a set of essential terms and concepts as a lens through which to examine another text or some aspect of the world, or to extend the work of others through research in the library or on the Internet. This kind of creative writing demands creative reading. That is, we urge you to read these texts *responsibly*—with careful attention to the authors' words and meaning—but we also want you to read *responsively*—with a lively sense of your own thoughts, questions, affirmations, doubts, and suspicions as they occur to you. Summary and paraphrase are certainly useful exercises on the way to more ambitious and personal responses to a text, but the purpose of your work with these texts will be not to master their content but to make something of them, to bring your own knowledge, experience, and convictions to bear on your reading. (In the next section we offer some techniques for reading responsively.) The Ideas for Rereading and Writing function as suggestions and springboards, but they do not prescribe exactly how you'll make use of these texts. Some of them are fairly long and suggest a number of possible directions to pursue in your writing. As we have suggested, to read a historical text means not simply to understand the meaning of the words on the page in their original sense but to understand what those words might mean for you here and now. Your point of view, your context, is unique. It is the creative event that occurs when a reader's context and a writer's context come into contact that produces interesting writing.

Many of these ideas can be used in sequence, enabling you to build toward a complex response to the readings. For example, you can use the concept of "double-consciousness" as defined by W. E. B. Du Bois as a lens for reconsidering Alice Walker's essay "In Search of Our Mothers' Gardens," Glenn Loury's "Free at Last?" and Joan Morgan's "From Fly-Girls to Bitches and Hos." Thus your writing will eventually mediate between various different contexts—your own and perhaps two or three others—and gain in complexity and sophistication over the course of several assignments.

Having developed a complex response to the essays in a single chapter, you can then make connections between this chapter and another, perhaps to consider how "double-consciousness" might be used in a reading of essays in Chapter 3, "Disabled Persons: How Do Individuals Form a Culture?" This kind of sequencing has been explicitly built into the book through the Ideas for Working across Chapters, but you'll notice other themes as well that recur from one chapter to another. We encourage you to notice, record, and develop these connections as you work with this book.

A word of caution here about conducting research on the Internet. All research requires attentive reading of your sources and careful evaluation of their credibility, but Web sites often require special scrutiny. The Web is an exciting and powerful research tool that puts a vast amount of material within easy reach. But as you may know, anyone can post a simple Web site, and publishing on the Internet involves none of the procedures for fact checking and peer review that govern the publication of scholarly books and articles. Hence, Web sites are more likely to contain errors, falsehoods, and tendentious arguments than the books in a college library. When working with a Web site, then, consider the following: Who is responsible for the site and what qualifications do they have? Does the Web site identify its sources clearly so that you can trace them? What is the site's purpose—simply to inform readers or to persuade them of the author's views? Does the site reveal bias? Of course, no source in any medium is infallible or wholly unbiased, and perhaps the hazards of Web research simply serve as a reminder that we need to evaluate all of our sources carefully, whether electronic or print. Our publisher has a number of resources that can help you do this, located at www.bedfordstmartins.com/composition.

An Arc of Interpretation

The work we have been describing, even if unfamiliar, is the kind of work your high school years have prepared you to do. But we would like to suggest how you might work responsively with these readings to craft a statement of your own. As the phrase "ideas for rereading" suggests, you will find that many of these texts need to be reread, perhaps several times, before you can begin to write about them with confidence. If we think of interpretation in its fullest sense, as beginning in reading and ending in a written response, we might speak of an "arc of interpretation." This is to think of reading and writing as a single prolonged process that includes a number of different phases, strategies, and activities but remains really one process. In practice, the process varies a good deal, but it typically unfolds something like this:

- It begins with a first reading that you may find a little perplexing and unsatisfactory, a reading which is often slow and sometimes difficult work. On this reading or perhaps the next, you mark your text, underline some key sentences, and write notes or marks in the margins. You might attempt a radial diagram (see p. 15) to help you gain better control over the text.
- After this first reading or perhaps a second, you begin to work out an initial response, however informal or sketchy. It might take the form of freewriting in a journal or a double-entry notebook (see p. 14). This writing isn't necessarily meant to be read by anyone else, as it is full of incomplete thoughts and false starts—and you need to feel free to explore without any sense of constraint. The point is simply to enable you to think through the ideas and questions that are swirling around in your head.
- You may feel the need to read through the text again at this point, and then perhaps return to your notebook to winnow out some ideas and develop others. This cycle might be repeated several times before you embark on the rough draft of an essay.
- This initial draft will be an "exploratory draft," one that feels its way toward a stronger sense of what you want to say. With luck, you may have a rewarding moment of recognition at some point: "Oh, yes, that's what I've been trying to say! At last I can put it into words."
- Now that your ideas are clearer, you must figure out how to structure your argument, to develop some workable form for your ideas.

Now you are no longer writing for yourself, but for an imagined reader—for what Robert Graves calls "the reader over your shoulder." Many writers choose to begin testing out their writing on trustworthy readers at this point, readers who will give them honest and helpful criticism.

- Finally, after the essay has taken shape—and this may involve several revisions—you will need to polish and correct and proofread. Some writers feel the temptation to tinker with their sentences endlessly, but few writers can afford to be extreme perfectionists. At this point, the paper is ready for an audience.

At what point in this process does a "reader" turn into a "writer"? Perhaps there's no definite point of transition. At every stage, the reader-writer is preparing a statement that responds to the statement of some previous reader-writer. In this way a conversation—a slow and thoughtful conversation, one that need have no beginning or end—unfolds.

Throughout this process there's a kind of creative rhythm that many have noticed and described. One of Virginia Woolf's friends, the poet T. S. Eliot, used the terms "surrender" and "recovery" to describe the process by which acts of reading become acts of writing. Writing to another friend, Stephen Spender, Eliot said:

> You don't really criticize any author to whom you have never surrendered yourself. . . . Even just the bewildering minute counts; you have to give yourself up, and then recover yourself, and the third moment is having something to say, before you have wholly forgotten both surrender and recovery. Of course the self recovered is never the same as the self that was given.

When, as readers, we surrender ourselves to the text, the distance between ourselves and the writer is the least we can make it, because we are trying to see the world through the eyes of the writer. We read charitably, attempting to understand not only what's on the page but even the writer's whole way of seeing the world. This can be difficult—"bewildering," as Eliot puts it—but we're trying to play the game that the writer wants to play, so we place our faith in the writer and follow where he or she leads. In essence, we experiment with the idea of total agreement, a real meeting of minds. But in the moment of "recovery" (which may occur after we've finished, but usually begins while we're still reading), we take some distance from the writer's point of view, detach ourselves from the text, and start to read a bit more skeptically. We ask ourselves, What may be missing from all this? Do I feel entirely comfortable with all aspects of this argument? Finally, the third moment, as Eliot says, is "having something to say," and this arises from a reflection on both the experience of surrender and the experience of recovery. It arises from the encounter of your own mind—which has its own context, experience, and personality—with the statements made by the author. An encounter that is articulate and verbal rather than vague and unformed is the point of the whole process of rereading, note taking, freewriting, and drafting. Intriguingly, the outcome is something Eliot mentions matter-of-factly: "the self recovered is never the same as the self that was given." Our reading, especially our attentive and active reading, educates us (in the root sense of leading us to somewhere different): it effects a lasting change in our own minds and in how we see the world, so that it's a subtly altered self that comes away from the experience. And, reciprocally, the writing or even talking that we do in response to our reading, by contributing to an ongoing conversation, shifts, adjusts, or extends that conversation into the present, so that the world too may be said to undergo an alteration—inevitably very small at first, but potentially great.

We previously mentioned the double-entry notebook. This is a simple and powerful note-taking technique that many writers find useful. (We owe it to writing teacher Anne Berthoff.) You simply divide a notebook page down the middle. On the left-hand side, you copy out phrases, sentences, or short passages from the text that seem important, puzzling, interesting, or in any other sense noteworthy. On the right, you respond to these quotations in any way that seems helpful. These responses may take the form of a simple punctuation mark—a question mark or exclamation point—or they may take the form of longer remarks, questions, and ideas. As you reread, you can rework the right-hand side of the page, clarifying, revising, and extending your ideas until you run out of space and your double-entry notebook pages become the jumping-off point for more extended linear prose—the first draft of an essay. A page of double-entry notes taken on Virginia Woolf's *A Room of One's Own* is reproduced on page 14.

A second technique you may find useful, especially when you are working with a long and complicated text, is something we call a "radial diagram." This is simply a way of constructing an organized one-page visual representation of the text's main elements. It is best to begin it on your second reading, as you'll need to have a rough sense of the text's main themes in order to get started. As you can see from the example on page 15, a complete radial diagram can be quite elaborate, but it begins very simply, with just a couple of boxes or circles and a few words. We began this one with a box containing the words "FREUD: A Fragment of an Analysis of a Case of Hysteria" and another containing the word "CURE." Eventually, we added a box for Dora's symptoms on the left and another on the right for the "keys" that led to Freud's solution of the case. As usual with radial diagrams of any complexity, we found that as we filled in details it became necessary to rearrange and revise the whole diagram once or twice. But these fresh starts were helpful; the point of the exercise is not really the diagram as a product, but the way that the activity of puzzling out the diagram helps us to grasp relationships among the text's innumerable details and eventually to locate all the main themes and organize them in our minds—in effect, to conduct an analysis of the text. It helps us to get control of a complicated text, and thus to discuss it and write about it.

WOOLF   7

[The Elizabethan woman]   Why not?
"History scarcely mentions   (Is this still true?)
her"

"What one wants, I   That is, (I think) she's
thought — and why does   encouraging her readers
not some brilliant student   to take on this
at Newnham or Girton   project.
supply it? — in a mass   This is
of information..."   central,
                                                     but
                                                     INDIRECT

"It would be ambitious   But of course — that's
beyond my daring,   what she is doing.
I thought, ... to suggest   (Good example of
to the students of   VW's irony?)
those famous colleges   She seems a little
that they should   coy about this. Why?
re-write history, though   ...
I own that it often   She's recording her
seems a little queer as   thoughts, like "stream
it is, unreal, lop-   of consciousness"?
sided; ..."
...   NB "lop-sided" history.

Joanna Baillie (?)   Who is this?
Mary Russell Mitford (?)   Ditto?

Whether you use a double-entry notebook or some other way of taking notes, the point, as we've been suggesting, is that writing and reading are not necessarily separate activities. If you can keep the difference to a minimum, you are far less likely to find yourself in that frustrating position of staring at a computer screen or a blank sheet of paper with nothing to say.

Our hope is that this book will give you ways of working with the kinds of texts that you'll be reading throughout your college career, ways of developing your own insights and responses to these texts, and ways of

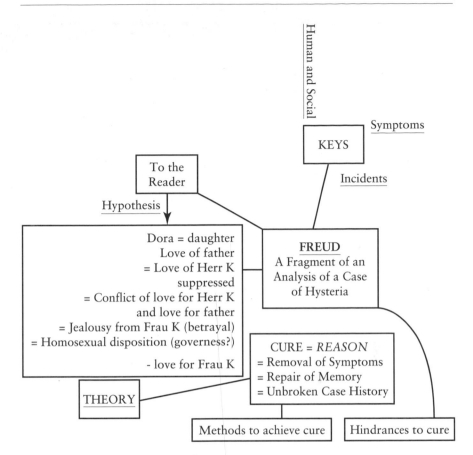

Human and Social

Symptoms

KEYS

Incidents

To the
Reader

Hypothesis

Dora = daughter
Love of father
= Love of Herr K
suppressed
= Conflict of love for Herr K
and love for father
= Jealousy from Frau K (betrayal)
= Homosexual disposition (governess?)

- love for Frau K

FREUD
A Fragment of an
Analysis of a Case
of Hysteria

CURE = *REASON*
= Removal of Symptoms
= Repair of Memory
= Unbroken Case History

THEORY

Methods to achieve cure

Hindrances to cure

"Radial diagram" in progress

articulating these ideas that are both satisfying and effective. One of the most valuable benefits of a college education is the opportunity to discuss ideas that have both a past and a future and to participate in the reshaping of these ideas for future generations. Whether or not your views find their way into print, your thoughts and your conversation will enrich, challenge, illuminate, and influence those around you, students like yourself who will transform these ideas yet again.

CHAPTER 1

Gender

Is One Born a Woman?

Biological differences between the sexes have deeply marked Western understandings of relations between men and women. And these understandings—of the nature of manhood and womanhood (and of what it means to be male/female, queer/straight, normal/perverted, strong/weak, feminine/masculine)—have profound influences on many aspects of our lives. But, except in the relatively rare case of hermaphrodism, where nature's sexual markers are ambiguous, biology presents us with a number of clear physical characteristics that indicate whether someone is a man or a woman: as Eve Kosofsky Sedgwick notes in this chapter, in gene science these physical markers are identified with two distinct chromosomal structures, XX and XY. When we focus on biological or chromosomal differences, as we often do in conversations about the natural roles of men and women, relations between men and women tend to become "essentialized"; that is, physical differences between the male of the species and the female of the species are reduced to their essence and become absolute, supposedly factual evidence that men and women are different in every way. By asking you to think about what it means to be a woman, this chapter also asks you to think about what it means to be a man. It invites you to think about sex, gender, and sexuality as problems, as the source of questions that have yet to be answered, as areas of exploration and discovery.

If it seems odd to ask the question "Is one born a woman?" you might think about the stages a female in your culture goes through before she becomes a woman: What kinds of things happen to create a sense of identity in an infant from birth to age three? What happens as she goes through girlhood from age four to age eleven or so? And what important social and cultural events define her as she moves through adolescence into womanhood? When do we know that someone has become a woman rather than a girl? What signs of girlishness remain? What, for you, are the most womanly behaviors, characteristics, and qualities? How do these aspects of womanliness differ from one generation to another (that is, what are the

17

differences between your ideas about women and your mother's or your grandmother's)? And how do different men and women in your generation identify the behaviors, characteristics, and qualities of a woman? What happens to the conversation about the identity of a woman when we include ideas about "good," "bad," "feminist," "lesbian," "manly," and "ultrafeminine" women?

When we shift away from questions of biology and physiology toward questions of socialization and culture, we shift from the subject of sex to the subject of gender. We move away from the basic physical essence of maleness and femaleness and turn instead to the ways in which individuals, societies, and cultures *imagine and define* sex and gender. It becomes necessary to put "woman," "man," and related words in quotation marks to indicate that we are working with open processes of definition rather than closed, unalterable categories. To ask "Is one born a woman?" is to ask what it has meant, what it means, and what it might mean to be a "woman." What does it mean—personally, professionally, politically— for a particular woman to be part of the social and cultural group defined by the collective name "women"? What are the social and cultural implications of scholarly work (like Monique Wittig's work included in this chapter) that treats "woman" as an open category, as something still to be defined? What happens when we suspend judgments based on biology and focus on gender-based expectations, experiences, and functions?

Virginia Woolf did not immediately concern herself with "the great problem of the true nature of woman" (p. 21). She was well aware that the long struggle for legal equality had left many gender-based problems unsolved. Women, even upper-middle-class women like Woolf, continued to experience domestic, economic, and educational deprivation. Reasons for confusion and anger remained. But Woolf chose not to align herself with the confused and angry; instead she adopted a tone that one reviewer in the Context section calls "the natural symbol of detachment and calm" (p. 61). However we read Woolf's tone—as a sign of elite self-confidence; as a sign of brilliant rhetorical control; as a sign that her "thesis is not apparently important to her" (p. 60)—it is undeniable that *A Room of One's Own* galvanized conversations about changes in the social and cultural condition of women at a time when "the change in the status of women" was "clearly and strongly defined among the distinctive features of our times," as Charlotte Perkins Gilman had put it six years earlier (p. 44).

The Contemporary Conversation readings in this chapter demonstrate the ongoing vibrancy of discussions about feminism, activism, self-possession, sexuality, and gender. bell hooks suggests that the word *feminism* has become a problem because it is now a catchall word with little specific meaning. Seeming to heed Audre Lorde's call for "the transformation of silence into language and action" (p. 80), hooks proposes that any serious move to overcome sexist oppression must turn the intellectual process of self-definition into political advocacy and activism. Patricia

Williams is also concerned with relationships between the personal and the political: in "Owning the Self in a Disowned World" she transforms a series of everyday personal experiences into a legal analysis of childbirth and a political analysis of the status of black professional women in the United States. Perhaps the most controversial essay in this chapter is Monique Wittig's "One Is Not Born a Woman." Juxtaposed with an essay in which Wittig asserts that "the category of sex . . . ordains slavery for women" (p. 104), this essay sets out to overturn an idea—"that women are a 'natural group'" (p. 105)—that most people in our culture assume as a given. The final selection in this chapter, Eve Kosofsky Sedgwick's "Sex and Gender," analyzes and defines how contemporary thinkers define sex, gender, and sexuality.

As you read the essays in this chapter, pay attention to the ways in which each writer defines herself. How does each writer use the word *woman*? In what ways does Woolf's argument about the need for a room of one's own underpin the work of the contemporary writers? To what extent does each of the recent thinkers confirm, complicate, or challenge Woolf's argument?

TEXT

VIRGINIA WOOLF

Virginia Woolf's reputation as a novelist and essayist has grown steadily since her death in 1941. She was singularly aware of what it meant to be a woman writer, of the special problems and possibilities that such a role entailed in her time. Partly as a result of an increasing interest in women's perspectives throughout the last fifty years, her work has gained an ever larger and more appreciative audience.

Woolf was born in London in 1882 into an intellectual, upper-middle-class family. Her father, Leslie Stephen, editor of the vast Dictionary of National Biography, *was a prominent writer and scholar. Although like most women of her time Virginia had little formal education, she read voraciously, wrote constantly, and learned a great deal from her father and the accomplished men and women who visited their household.*

After the death of her father in 1904, Virginia, her sister, Vanessa, and her brother, Thoby, moved into 46 Gordon Square in the Bloomsbury section of London. At Cambridge University, Thoby had become friends with a remarkable group of writers and artists who now began to gather regularly at their home. After Thoby's premature death in 1906, Virginia became the central figure in the "Bloomsbury Group" (as it has come to be known), a group that included the iconoclastic historian Lytton Strachey, the postimpressionist artists Roger Fry and Vanessa Bell (Virginia's sister), the economist J. M. Keynes, and the philosopher G. E. Moore. Writers such as T. S. Eliot and E. M. Forster are also associated with

*the group. Although its members shared no single philosophy of art or litera-
ture, they did insist on being frank and outspoken, and they scorned the prudish
social, sexual, and artistic conventions that prevailed in England before World
War I.*

*Woolf did not play an active role in the suffragist movement or the birth-
control movement, preferring to guard her independence as a writer and thinker.
She did not call herself a feminist, but Woolf's two nonfiction works on the place
of women in her society, A Room of One's Own (1929) and Three Guineas (1938),
exhibit both her deep insight and her deep feeling about the roots and the consequences of sexual inequality.*

*Many of Woolf's novels, including Mrs. Dalloway (1925), To the Lighthouse
(1927), and Orlando (1928), are bold experiments in form and voice, often employing a narrative method, sometimes called "stream of consciousness," that reveals the interior, moment-to-moment thoughts and feelings of the novel's
characters.*

*Though content to remain married to her husband, the writer Leonard Woolf,
from 1912 until her death, Woolf's friendship with the novelist Vita Sackville-West
was also one of the great love affairs of her life. With Leonard, she established the
Hogarth Press in 1917 at their home in Richmond and published not only her own
novels but also works by Katherine Mansfield, T. S. Eliot, and, in their first English
translation, the complete works of Sigmund Freud.*

*As you read A Room of One's Own think carefully about how Woolf uses
truth and fiction. Weigh the value of her statement that "Lies will flow from my
lips, but there may perhaps be some truth mixed up with them; it is for you to seek
out this truth" (p. 21). Identify passages that are, for you, "worth keeping" (p. 21)
and those that are not. Also pay close attention to Woolf's tone: what signals does
she give you about her level of anger, frustration, pleasure, confusion, and so on?
Underline specific words and phrases that give you a sense of her personality as a
writer and thinker. In what ways does Woolf's prose fit in with her celebration of
"the androgynous mind" (p. 37)?*

From *A Room of One's Own*

Chapter One

But, you may say, we asked you to speak about women and fiction —
what has that got to do with a room of one's own? I will try to explain.
When you asked me to speak about women and fiction I sat down on the
banks of a river and began to wonder what the words meant. They might
mean simply a few remarks about Fanny Burney; a few more about Jane
Austen; a tribute to the Brontës and a sketch of Haworth Parsonage under
snow; some witticisms if possible about Miss Mitford; a respectful allusion
to George Eliot; a reference to Mrs. Gaskell and one would have done. But
at second sight the words seemed not so simple. The title women and fiction might mean, and you may have meant it to mean, women and what
they are like; or it might mean women and the fiction that they write; or it
might mean women and the fiction that is written about them; or it might

mean that somehow all three are inextricably mixed together and you want me to consider them in that light. But when I began to consider the subject in this last way, which seemed the most interesting, I soon saw that it had one fatal drawback. I should never be able to come to a conclusion. I should never be able to fulfil what is, I understand, the first duty of a lecturer—to hand you after an hour's discourse a nugget of pure truth to wrap up between the pages of your notebooks and keep on the mantelpiece for ever. All I could do was to offer you an opinion upon one minor point—a woman must have money and a room of her own if she is to write fiction; and that, as you will see, leaves the great problem of the true nature of woman and the true nature of fiction unsolved. I have shirked the duty of coming to a conclusion upon these two questions—women and fiction remain, so far as I am concerned, unsolved problems. But in order to make some amends I am going to do what I can to show you how I arrived at this opinion about the room and the money. I am going to develop in your presence as fully and freely as I can the train of thought which led me to think this. Perhaps if I lay bare the ideas, the prejudices, that lie behind this statement you will find that they have some bearing upon women and some upon fiction. At any rate, when a subject is highly controversial—and any question about sex is that—one cannot hope to tell the truth. One can only show how one came to hold whatever opinion one does hold. One can only give one's audience the chance of drawing their own conclusions as they observe the limitations, the prejudices, the idiosyncrasies of the speaker. Fiction here is likely to contain more truth than fact. Therefore I propose, making use of all the liberties and licences of a novelist, to tell you the story of the two days that preceded my coming here—how, bowed down by the weight of the subject which you have laid upon my shoulders, I pondered it, and made it work in and out of my daily life. I need not say that what I am about to describe has no existence; Oxbridge is an invention; so is Fernham; "I" is only a convenient term for somebody who has no real being. Lies will flow from my lips, but there may perhaps be some truth mixed up with them; it is for you to seek out this truth and to decide whether any part of it is worth keeping. If not, you will of course throw the whole of it into the wastepaper basket and forget all about it.

Here then was I (call me Mary Beton, Mary Seton, Mary Carmichael or by any name you please—it is not a matter of any importance) sitting on the banks of a river a week or two ago in fine October weather, lost in thought. That collar I have spoken of, women and fiction, the need of coming to some conclusion on a subject that raises all sorts of prejudices and passions, bowed my head to the ground. To the right and left bushes of some sort, golden and crimson, glowed with the colour, even it seemed burnt with the heat, of fire. On the further bank the willows wept in perpetual lamentation, their hair about their shoulders. The river reflected whatever it chose of sky and bridge and burning tree, and when the undergraduate had oared his boat through the reflections they closed again, completely, as if he had never been. There one might have sat the clock round lost in thought. Thought—to call it by a prouder name than it deserved—had let its line down into the stream. It swayed, minute after minute, hither and thither among the reflections and the weeds, letting the water lift it and sink it, until—you know the little tug—the sudden conglomeration of an idea at the end of one's line: and then the cautious hauling of it in, and the careful laying of it out? Alas, laid on the grass how small, how insignificant this thought of mine looked; the sort of fish that a good fisherman puts back into the water so that it may grow fatter and be one day worth cooking and eating. I will not trouble you with that thought now, though if you look carefully you may find it for yourselves in the course of what I am going to say.

But however small it was, it had, nevertheless, the mysterious property of its kind—put back into the mind, it became at once very exciting, and important; and as it darted and sank, and flashed hither and thither, set up such a wash and tumult of ideas that it was impossible to sit still. It was thus that I found myself walking with extreme rapidity across a grass plot. Instantly a man's figure rose to intercept me. Nor did I at first understand that the gesticulations of a curious-looking object, in a cut-away coat and evening shirt, were aimed at me. His face expressed horror and indignation. Instinct rather than reason came to my help; he was a Beadle;* I was a woman. This was the turf; there was the path. Only the Fellows and Scholars are allowed here; the gravel is the place for me. Such thoughts were the work of a moment. As I regained the path the arms of the Beadle sank, his face assumed its usual repose, and though turf is better walking than gravel, no very great harm was done. The only charge I could bring against the Fellows and Scholars of whatever the college might happen to be was that in protection of their turf, which has been rolled for 300 years in succession, they had sent my little fish into hiding. . . .

[During her wanderings, the narrator attempts to gain access to one of the university's libraries. She is refused admission because, being a woman, she must be accompanied by a Fellow (a faculty member) of the College or must present a letter of introduction.]

That a famous library has been cursed by a woman is a matter of complete indifference to a famous library. Venerable and calm, with all its treasures safe locked within its breast, it sleeps complacently and will, so far as I am concerned, so sleep for ever. Never will I wake those echoes, never will I ask for that hospitality again, I vowed as I descended the steps

---

Beadle: A ceremonial officer at Oxford and Cambridge responsible for keeping order and maintaining discipline. Akin to a campus police officer.

in anger. Still an hour remained before luncheon, and what was one to do? Stroll on the meadows? sit by the river? Certainly it was a lovely autumn morning; the leaves were fluttering red to the ground; there was no great hardship in doing either. But the sound of music reached my ear. Some service or celebration was going forward. The organ complained magnificently as I passed the chapel door. Even the sorrow of Christianity sounded in that serene air more like the recollection of sorrow than sorrow itself; even the groanings of the ancient organ seemed lapped in peace. I had no wish to enter had I the right, and this time the verger might have stopped me, demanding perhaps my baptismal certificate, or a letter of introduction from the Dean. But the outside of these magnificent buildings is often as beautiful as the inside. Moreover, it was amusing enough to watch the congregation assembling, coming in and going out again, busying themselves at the door of the chapel like bees at the mouth of a hive. Many were in cap and gown; some had tufts of fur on their shoulders; others were wheeled in bath-chairs; others, though not past middle age, seemed creased and crushed into shapes so singular that one was reminded of those giant crabs and crayfish who heave with difficulty across the sand of an aquarium. As I leant against the wall the University indeed seemed a sanctuary in which are preserved rare types which would soon be obsolete if left to fight for existence on the pavement of the Strand. Old stories of old deans and old dons came back to mind, but before I had summoned up courage to whistle—it used to be said that at the sound of a whistle old Professor —— instantly broke into a gallop—the venerable congregation had gone inside. The outside of the chapel remained. As you know, its high domes and pinnacles can be seen, like a sailing-ship always voyaging never arriving, lit up at night and visible for miles, far away across the hills. Once, presumably, this quadrangle with its smooth lawns, its massive buildings, and the chapel itself was marsh too, where the grasses waved and the swine rooted. Teams of horses and oxen, I thought, must have hauled the stone in wagons from far countries, and then with infinite labour the grey blocks in whose shade I was now standing were poised in order one on top of another, and then the painters brought their glass for the windows, and the masons were busy for centuries up on that roof with putty and cement, spade and trowel. Every Saturday somebody must have poured gold and silver out of a leathern purse into their ancient fists, for they had their beer and skittles presumably of an evening. An unending stream of gold and silver, I thought, must have flowed into this court perpetually to keep the stones coming and the masons working; to level, to ditch, to dig and to drain. But it was then the age of faith, and money was poured liberally to set these stones on a deep foundation, and when the stones were raised, still more money was poured in from the coffers of kings and queens and great nobles to ensure that hymns should be sung here and scholars taught. Lands were granted; tithes were paid. And when the age of faith was over and the age of reason had come, still the same flow of gold and silver went on; fellowships were founded; lectureships endowed; only the gold and silver flowed now, not from the coffers of the king, but from the chests of merchants and manufacturers, from the purses of men who had made, say, a fortune from industry, and returned, in their wills, a bounteous share of it to endow more chairs, more lectureships, more fellowships in the university where they had learnt their craft. Hence the libraries and laboratories; the observatories; the splendid equipment of costly and delicate instruments which now stands on glass shelves, where centuries ago the grasses waved and the swine rootled. Certainly, as I strolled round the court, the foundation of gold and silver seemed deep enough; the pavement laid solidly over the wild grasses. Men with trays on their heads went busily from staircase to staircase. Gaudy blossoms flowered in window-boxes. The strains of the gramophone blared out from the rooms within. It was impossible not to reflect—the reflection whatever it may have been was cut short. The clock struck. It was time to find one's way to luncheon.

It is a curious fact that novelists have a way of making us believe that luncheon parties are invariably memorable for something very witty that was said, or for something very wise that was done. But they seldom spare a word for what was eaten. It is part of the novelist's convention not to mention soup and salmon and ducklings, as if soup and salmon and ducklings were of no importance whatsoever, as if nobody ever smoked a cigar or drank a glass of wine. Here, however, I shall take the liberty to defy that convention and to tell you that the lunch on this occasion began with soles, sunk in a deep dish, over which the college cook had spread a counterpane of the whitest cream, save that it was branded here and there with brown spots like the spots on the flanks of a doe. After that came the partridges, but if this suggests a couple of bald, brown birds on a plate you are mistaken. The partridges, many and various, came with all their retinue of sauces and salads, the sharp and the sweet, each in its order; their potatoes, thin as coins but not so hard; their sprouts, foliated as rosebuds but more succulent. And no sooner had the roast and its retinue been done with than the silent serving-man, the Beadle himself perhaps in a milder manifestation, set before us, wreathed in napkins, a confection which rose all sugar from the waves. To call it pudding and so relate it to rice and tapioca would be an insult. Meanwhile the wineglasses had flushed yellow and flushed crimson; had been emptied; had been filled. And thus by degrees was lit, halfway down the spine, which is the seat of the soul, not that hard little electric light which we call brilliance, as it pops in and out upon our lips, but the more profound, subtle and subterranean glow, which is the rich yellow flame of rational intercourse. No need to hurry. No need to sparkle. No need to be anybody but oneself. We are all going to heaven and Vandyck* is of the company—in other words, how good life seemed,

Vandyck: Sir Anthony Vandyck (or Van Dyck), 1599–1641. A Flemish-born painter famous for celebratory, elegant portraits of the aristocracy. He was court painter to Charles I of England from 1632 to 1641.

how sweet its rewards, how trivial this grudge or that grievance, how admirable friendship and the society of one's kind, as, lighting a good cigarette, one sunk among the cushions in the window-seat.

If by good luck there had been an ash-tray handy, if one had not knocked the ash out of the window in default, if things had been a little different from what they were, one would not have seen, presumably, a cat without a tail. The sight of that abrupt and truncated animal padding softly across the quadrangle changed by some fluke of the subconscious intelligence the emotional light for me. It was as if some one had let fall a shade. Perhaps the excellent hock was relinquishing its hold. Certainly, as I watched the Manx cat pause in the middle of the lawn as if it too questioned the universe, something seemed lacking, something seemed different. But what was lacking, what was different, I asked myself, listening to the talk. . . .

[The narrator travels from the men's college to Fernham, a college for women.]

The gardens of Fernham lay before me in the spring twilight, wild and open, and in the long grass, sprinkled and carelessly flung, were daffodils and bluebells, not orderly perhaps at the best of times, and now wind-blown and waving as they tugged at their roots. The windows of the building, curved like ships' windows among generous waves of red brick, changed from lemon to silver under the flight of the quick spring clouds. Somebody was in a hammock, somebody, but in this light they were phantoms only, half guessed, half seen, raced across the grass—would no one stop her?—and then on the terrace, as if popping out to breathe the air, to glance at the garden, came a bent figure, formidable yet humble, with her great forehead and her shabby dress—could it be the famous scholar, could it be J——— H——— herself? All was dim, yet intense too, as if the scarf which the dusk had flung over the garden were torn asunder by star or sword—the flash of some terrible reality leaping, as its way is, out of the heart of the spring. For youth———

Here was my soup. Dinner was being served in the great dining-hall. Far from being spring it was in fact an evening in October. Everybody was assembled in the big dining-room. Dinner was ready. Here was the soup. It was a plain gravy soup. There was nothing to stir the fancy in that. One could have seen through the transparent liquid any pattern that there might have been on the plate itself. But there was no pattern. The plate was plain. Next came beef with its attendant greens and potatoes—a homely trinity, suggesting the rumps of cattle in a muddy market, and sprouts curled and yellowed at the edge, and bargaining and cheapening, and women with string bags on Monday morning. There was no reason to complain of human nature's daily food, seeing that the supply was sufficient and coal-miners doubtless were sitting down to less. Prunes and custard followed. And if any one complains that prunes, even when mitigated by custard, are an uncharitable vegetable (fruit they are not), stringy as a miser's heart and exuding a fluid such as might run in misers' veins who have denied themselves wine and warmth for eighty years and yet not given to the poor, he should reflect that there are people whose charity embraces even the prune. Biscuits and cheese came next, and here the water-jug was liberally passed round, for it is the nature of biscuits to be dry, and these were biscuits to the core. That was all. The meal was over. Everybody scraped their chairs back; the swing-doors swung violently to and fro; soon the hall was emptied of every sign of food and made ready no doubt for breakfast next morning. Down corridors and up staircases the youth of England went banging and singing. And was it for a guest, a stranger (for I had no more right here in Fernham than in Trinity or Somerville or Girton or Newnham or Christchurch), to say, "The dinner was not good," or to say (we were now, Mary Seton and I, in her sitting-room), "Could we not have dined up here alone?" for if I had said anything of the kind I should have been prying and searching into the secret economies of a house which to the stranger wears so fine a front of gaiety and courage. No, one could say nothing of the sort. Indeed, conversation for a moment flagged. The human frame being what it is, heart, body and brain all mixed together, and not contained in separate compartments as they will be no doubt in another million years, a good dinner is of great importance to good talk. One cannot think well, love well, sleep well, if one has not dined well. The lamp in the spine does not light on beef and prunes. We are all *probably* going to heaven, and Vandyck is, we *hope*, to meet us round the next corner—that is the dubious and qualifying state of mind that beef and prunes at the end of the day's work breed between them. Happily my friend, who taught science, had a cupboard where there was a squat bottle and little glasses—(but there should have been sole and partridge to begin with)—so that we were able to draw up to the fire and repair some of the damages of the day's living. In a minute or so we were slipping freely in and out among all those objects of curiosity and interest which form in the mind in the absence of a particular person, and are naturally to be discussed on coming together again—how somebody has married, another has not; one thinks this, another that; one has improved out of all knowledge, the other most amazingly gone to the bad—with all those speculations upon human nature and the character of the amazing world we live in which spring naturally from such beginnings. While these things were being said, however, I became shamefacedly aware of a current setting in of its own accord and carrying everything forward to an end of its own. One might be talking of Spain or Portugal, of book or racehorse, but the real interest of whatever was said was none of those things, but a scene of masons on a high roof some five centuries ago. Kings and nobles brought treasures in huge sacks and poured it under the earth. This scene was for ever coming alive in my mind and placing itself by another of lean cows and a muddy market and withered greens and the stringy hearts of old men—these two pictures, disjointed and disconnected and nonsensical as they were, were for ever coming together and combating each other and had me entirely at their mercy. The best course, unless the whole talk was to be distorted, was to expose what was in my mind to the air, when with good luck it would fade and crumble like the head of the dead king when they opened the coffin at Windsor. Briefly, then, I told Miss Seton about the masons who had been all those years on the roof of the chapel, and about the kings and queens and nobles bearing sacks of gold and silver on their shoulders, which they shovelled into the earth; and then how the great financial magnates of our own time came and laid cheques and bonds, I suppose, where the others had laid ingots and rough lumps of gold. All that lies beneath the colleges down there, I said; but this college, where we are now sitting, what lies beneath its gallant red brick and the wild unkempt grasses of the garden? What force is behind the plain china off which we dined, and (here it popped out of my mouth before I could stop it) the beef, the custard and the prunes?

Well, said Mary Seton, about the year 1860—Oh, but you know the story, she said, bored, I suppose, by the recital. And she told me—rooms were hired. Committees met. Envelopes were addressed. Circulars were drawn up. Meetings were held; letters were read out; so-and-so has promised so much; on the contrary, Mr. ——— won't give a penny. The *Saturday Review* has been very rude. How can we raise a fund to pay for offices? Shall we hold a bazaar? Can't we find a pretty girl to sit in the front row? Let us look up what John Stuart Mill said on the subject. Can anyone persuade the editor of the ——— to print a letter? Can we get Lady ——— to sign it? Lady ——— is out of town. That was the way it was done, presumably, sixty years ago, and it was a prodigious effort, and a great deal of time was spent on it. And it was only after a long struggle and with the utmost difficulty that they got thirty thousand pounds together.[1] So obviously we cannot have wine and partridges and servants carrying tin dishes on their heads, she said. We cannot have sofas and separate rooms. "The amenities," she said, quoting from some book or other, "will have to wait."[2]

At the thought of all those women working year after year and finding it hard to get two thousand pounds together, and as much as they could do to get thirty thousand pounds, we burst out in scorn at the reprehensible poverty of our sex. What had our mothers been doing then that they had no wealth to leave us? Powdering their noses? Looking in at shop windows? Flaunting in the sun at Monte Carlo? There were some photographs on the mantel-piece. Mary's mother—if that was her picture—may have been a wastrel in her spare time (she had thirteen children by a minister of the church), but if so her gay and dissipated life had left too few traces of its pleasures on her face. She was a homely body; an old lady in a plaid shawl which was fastened by a large cameo; and she sat in a basket-chair, encouraging a spaniel to look at the camera, with the amused, yet strained expression of one who is sure that the dog will move directly the bulb is pressed. Now if she had gone into business; had become a manufacturer of artificial silk or a magnate on the Stock Exchange; if she had left two or three hundred thousand pounds to Fernham, we could have been sitting at our ease tonight and the subject of our talk might have been archaeology, botany, anthropology, physics, the nature of the atom, mathematics, astronomy, relativity, geography. If only Mrs. Seton and her mother and her mother before her had learnt the great art of making money and had left their money, like their fathers and their grandfathers before them, to found fellowships and lectureships and prizes and scholarships appropriated to the use of their own sex, we might have dined very tolerably up here alone off a bird and a bottle of wine; we might have looked forward without undue confidence to a pleasant and honourable lifetime spent in the shelter of one of the liberally endowed professions. We might have been exploring or writing; mooning about the venerable places of the earth; sitting contemplative on the steps of the Parthenon, or going at ten to an office and coming home comfortably at half-past four to write a little poetry. Only, if Mrs. Seton and her like had gone into business at the age of fifteen, there would have been—that was the snag in the argument—no Mary. What, I asked, did Mary think of that? There between the curtains was the October night, calm and lovely, with a star or two caught in the yellowing trees. Was she ready to resign her share of it and her memories (for they had been a happy family, though a large one) of games and quarrels up in Scotland, which she is never tired of praising for the fineness of its air and the quality of its cakes, in order that Fernham might have been endowed with fifty thousand pounds or so by a stroke of the pen? For, to endow a college would necessitate the suppression of families altogether. Making a fortune and bearing thirteen children—no human being could stand it. Consider the facts, we said. First there are nine months before the baby is born. Then the baby is born. Then there are three or four months spent in feeding the baby. After the baby is fed there are certainly five years spent in playing with the baby. You cannot, it seems, let children run about the streets. People who have seen them running wild in Russia say that the sight is not a pleasant one. People say, too, that human nature takes its shape in the years between one and five. If Mrs. Seton, I said, had been making money, what sort of memories would you have had of games and quarrels? What would you have known of Scotland, and its fine air and cakes and all the rest of it? But it is useless to ask these questions, because you would never have come into existence at all. Moreover, it is equally useless to ask what might have happened if Mrs. Seton and her mother and her mother before her had amassed great wealth and laid it under the foundations of college and library, because, in the first place, to earn money was impossible for them, and in the second, had it been possible, the law denied them the right to possess what money they earned. It is only for the last forty-eight years that Mrs. Seton has had a penny of her own. For all the centuries before that it would have been her husband's property—a thought which, perhaps, may have had its share in keeping Mrs. Seton and her mothers off the Stock Exchange. Every penny I earn, they may have said, will be taken from me and disposed of according to my husband's wisdom—perhaps to found a scholarship or to endow a fellowship in Balliol or Kings, so that to earn money, even if I could earn money, is not a matter that interests me very greatly. I had better leave it to my husband.

At any rate, whether or not the blame rested on the old lady who was looking at the spaniel, there could be no doubt that for some reason or other our mothers had mismanaged their affairs very gravely. Not a penny could be spared for "amenities"; for partridges and wine, beadles and turf, books and cigars, libraries and leisure. To raise bare walls out of the bare earth was the utmost they could do.

So we talked standing at the window and looking, as so many thousands look every night, down on the domes and towers of the famous city beneath us. It was very beautiful, very mysterious in the autumn moonlight. The old stone looked very white and venerable. One thought of all the books that were assembled down there; of the pictures of old prelates and worthies hanging in the panelled rooms; of the painted windows that would be throwing strange globes and crescents on the pavement; of the tablets and memorials and inscriptions; of the fountains and the grass; of the quiet rooms looking across the quiet quadrangles. And (pardon me the thought) I thought, too, of the admirable smoke and drink and the deep armchairs and the pleasant carpets: of the urbanity, the geniality, the dignity which are the offspring of luxury and privacy and space. Certainly our mothers had not provided us with anything comparable to all this—our mothers who found it difficult to scrape together thirty thousand pounds, our mothers who bore thirteen children to ministers of religion at St. Andrews.

So I went back to my inn, and as I walked through the dark streets I pondered this and that, as one does at the end of the day's work. I pondered why it was that Mrs. Seton had no money to leave us; and what effect poverty has on the mind; and what effect wealth has on the mind; and I thought of the queer old gentlemen I had seen that morning with tufts of fur upon their shoulders; and I remembered how if one whistled one of them ran; and I thought of the organ booming in the chapel and of the shut doors of the library; and I thought how unpleasant it is to be locked out; and I thought how it is worse perhaps to be locked in; and, thinking of the safety and prosperity of the one sex and of the poverty and insecurity of the other and of the effect of tradition and of the lack of tradition upon the mind of a writer, I thought at last that it was time to roll up the crumpled skin of the day, with its arguments and its impressions and its anger and its laughter, and cast it into the hedge. A thousand stars were flashing across the blue wastes of the sky. One seemed alone with an inscrutable society. All human beings were laid asleep—prone, horizontal, dumb. Nobody seemed stirring in the streets of Oxbridge. Even the door of the hotel sprang open at the touch of an invisible hand — not a boots* was sitting up to light me to bed, it was so late.

[In the following extract from chapter 3 of *A Room of One's Own* Woolf turns from recent experiences to history, seeking reasons for women's relative poverty in facts rather than opinions.]

. . . It is a perennial puzzle why no woman wrote a word of that extraordinary literature when every other man, it seemed, was capable of song or sonnet. What were the conditions in which women lived, I asked myself; for fiction, imaginative work that is, is not dropped like a pebble upon the ground, as science may be; fiction is like a spider's web, attached ever so lightly perhaps, but still attached to life at all four corners. Often the attachment is scarcely perceptible; Shakespeare's plays, for instance, seem to hang there complete by themselves. But when the web is pulled askew, hooked up at the edge, torn in the middle, one remembers that these webs are not spun in mid-air by incorporeal creatures, but are the work of suffering human beings, and are attached to grossly material things, like health and money and the houses we live in. . . .

I went, therefore, to the shelf where the histories stand and took down one of the latest, Professor Trevelyan's *History of England*. Once more I looked up Women, found "position of," and turned to the pages indicated. "Wife-beating," I read, "was a recognised right of man, and was practised without shame by high as well as low. . . . Similarly," the historian goes on, "the daughter who refused to marry the gentleman of her parents' choice was liable to be locked up, beaten and flung about the room, without any shock being inflicted on public opinion. Marriage was not an affair of personal affection, but of family avarice, particularly in the 'chivalrous' upper classes. . . . Betrothal often took place while one or both of the parties was in the cradle, and marriage when they were scarcely out of the nurses' charge." That was about 1470, soon after Chaucer's time. The next reference to the position of women is some two hundred years later, in the time of the Stuarts. "It was still the exception for women of the upper and middle class to choose their own husbands, and when the husband had been assigned, he was lord and master, so far at least as law and custom could make him. Yet even so," Professor Trevelyan concludes, "neither Shakespeare's women or those of authentic seventeenth-century memoirs, like the Verneys and the Hutchinsons, seem wanting in personality and character." Certainly, if we consider it, Cleopatra must have had a way

---

boots: Someone employed by male colleges at Oxford and Cambridge to clean the boots and shoes of teachers and students. The word is also used for a shoeshiner at a hotel.

with her; Lady Macbeth, one would suppose, had a will of her own; Rosalind, one might conclude, was an attractive girl. Professor Trevelyan is speaking no more than the truth when he remarks that Shakespeare's women do not seem wanting in personality and character. Not being a historian, one might go even further and say that women have burnt like beacons in all the works of all the poets from the beginning of time—Clytemnestra, Antigone, Cleopatra, Lady Macbeth, Phèdre, Cressida, Rosalind, Desdemona, the Duchess of Malfi, among the dramatists; then among the prose writers: Millamant, Clarissa, Becky Sharp, Anna Karenina, Emma Bovary, Madame de Guermantes—the names flock to mind, nor do they recall women "lacking in personality and character." Indeed, if woman had no existence save in the fiction written by men, one would imagine her a person of the utmost importance; very various; heroic and mean; splendid and sordid; infinitely beautiful and hideous in the extreme; as great as a man, some think even greater.[3] But this is woman in fiction. In fact, as Professor Trevelyan points out, she was locked up, beaten and flung about the room.

A very queer, composite being thus emerges. Imaginatively she is of the highest importance; practically she is completely insignificant. She pervades poetry from cover to cover; she is all but absent from history. She dominates the lives of kings and conquerors in fiction; in fact she was the slave of any boy whose parents forced a ring upon her finger. Some of the most inspired words, some of the most profound thoughts in literature fall from her lips; in real life she could hardly read, could scarcely spell, and was the property of her husband.

It was certainly an odd monster that one made up by reading the historians first and the poets afterwards—a worm winged like an eagle; the spirit of life and beauty in a kitchen chopping up suet. But these monsters, however amusing to the imagination, have no existence in fact. What one must do to bring her to life was to think poetically and prosaically at one and the same moment, thus keeping in touch with fact—that she is Mrs. Martin, aged thirty-six, dressed in blue, wearing a black hat and brown shoes; but not losing sight of fiction either—that she is a vessel in which all sorts of spirits and forces are coursing and flashing perpetually. The moment, however, that one tries this method with the Elizabethan woman, one branch of illumination fails; one is held up by the scarcity of facts. One knows nothing detailed, nothing perfectly true and substantial about her. History scarcely mentions her. And I turned to Professor Trevelyan again to see what history meant to him. I found by looking at his chapter headings that it meant—

"The Manor Court and the Methods of Open-field Agriculture . . . The Cistercians and Sheep-farming . . . The Crusades . . . The University . . . The House of Commons . . . The Hundred Years' War . . . The Wars of the Roses . . . The Renaissance Scholars . . . The Dissolution of the Monasteries . . . Agrarian and Religious Strife . . . The Origin of English Sea-power . . . The Armada . . ." and so on. Occasionally an individual woman is mentioned, an Elizabeth, or a Mary; a queen or a great lady. But by no possible means could middle-class women with nothing but brains and character at their command have taken part in any one of the great movements which, brought together, constitute the historian's view of the past. Nor shall we find her in any collection of anecdotes. Aubrey hardly mentions her. She never writes her own life and scarcely keeps a diary; there are only a handful of her letters in existence. She left no plays or poems by which we can judge her. What one wants, I thought—and why does not some brilliant student at Newnham or Girton supply it?—is a mass of information; at what age did she marry; how many children had she as a rule; what was her house like; had she a room to herself; did she do the cooking; would she be likely to have a servant? All these facts lie somewhere, presumably, in parish registers and account books; the life of the average Elizabethan woman must be scattered about somewhere, could one collect it and make a book of it. It would be ambitious beyond my daring, I thought, looking about the shelves for books that were not there, to suggest to the students of those famous colleges that they should re-write history, though I own that it often seems a little queer as it is, unreal, lopsided; but why should they not add a supplement to history? calling it, of course, by some inconspicuous name so that women might figure there without impropriety? For one often catches a glimpse of them in the lives of the great, whisking away into the background, concealing, I sometimes think, a wink, a laugh, perhaps a tear. And, after all, we have lives enough of Jane Austen....But what I find deplorable, I continued, looking about the bookshelves again, is that nothing is known about women before the eighteenth century. I have no model in my mind to turn about this way and that. Here am I asking why women did not write poetry in the Elizabethan age, and I am not sure how they were educated; whether they were taught to write; whether they had sitting-rooms to themselves; how many women had children before they were twenty-one; what, in short, they did from eight in the morning till eight at night. They had no money evidently; according to Professor Trevelyan they were married whether they liked it or not before they were out of the nursery, at fifteen or sixteen very likely. It would have been extremely odd, even upon this showing, had one of them suddenly written the plays of Shakespeare, I concluded, and I thought of that old gentleman, who is dead now, but was a bishop, I think, who declared that it was impossible for any woman, past, present, or to come, to have the genius of Shakespeare. He wrote to the papers about it. He also told a lady who applied to him for information that cats do not as a matter of fact go to heaven, though they have, he added, souls of a sort. How much thinking those old gentlemen used to save one! How the borders of ignorance shrank back at their approach! Cats do not go to heaven. Women cannot write the plays of Shakespeare.

Be that as it may, I could not help thinking, as I looked at the works of Shakespeare on the shelf, that the bishop was right at least in this; it would have been impossible, completely and entirely, for any woman to have written the plays of Shakespeare in the age of Shakespeare. Let me imagine,

since facts are so hard to come by, what would have happened had
Shakespeare had a wonderfully gifted sister, called Judith, let us say.
Shakespeare himself went, very probably—his mother was an heiress—to
the grammar school, where he may have learnt Latin—Ovid, Virgil and
Horace—and the elements of grammar and logic. He was, it is well
known, a wild boy who poached rabbits, perhaps shot a deer, and had,
rather sooner than he should have done, to marry a woman in the neighbourhood, who bore him a child rather quicker than was right. That es-
capade sent him to seek his fortune in London. He had, it seemed, a taste
for the theatre; he began by holding horses at the stage door. Very soon he
got work in the theatre, became a successful actor, and lived at the hub of
the universe, meeting everybody, knowing everybody, practising his art on
the boards, exercising his wits in the streets, and even getting access to the
palace of the queen. Meanwhile his extraordinarily gifted sister, let us suppose, remained at home. She was as adventurous, as imaginative, as agog
to see the world as he was. But she was not sent to school. She had no
chance of learning grammar and logic, let alone of reading Horace and
Virgil. She picked up a book now and then, one of her brother's perhaps,
and read a few pages. But then her parents came in and told her to mend
the stockings or mind the stew and not moon about with books and papers. They would have spoken sharply but kindly, for they were substantial
people who knew the conditions of life for a woman and loved their
daughter—indeed, more likely than not she was the apple of her father's
eye. Perhaps she scribbled some pages up in an apple loft on the sly, but
was careful to hide them or set fire to them. Soon, however, before she was
out of her teens, she was to be betrothed to the son of a neighbouring
wool-stapler. She cried out that marriage was hateful to her, and for that
she was severely beaten by her father. Then he ceased to scold her. He
begged her instead not to hurt him, not to shame him in this matter of her
marriage. He would give her a chain of beads or a fine petticoat, he said;
and there were tears in his eyes. How could she disobey him? How could
she break his heart? The force of her own gift alone drove her to it. She
made up a small parcel of her belongings, let herself down by a rope one
summer's night and took the road to London. She was not seventeen. The
birds that sang in the hedge were not more musical than she was. She had
the quickest fancy, a gift like her brother's, for the tune of the words. Like
him, she had a taste for the theatre. She stood at the stage door; she wanted
to act, she said. Men laughed in her face. The manager—a fat, loose-
lipped man—guffawed. He bellowed something about poodles dancing
and women acting—no woman, he said, could possibly be an actress. He
hinted—you can imagine what. She could get no training in her craft.
Could she even seek her dinner in a tavern or roam the streets at midnight?
Yet her genius was for fiction and lusted to feed abundantly upon the lives
of men and women and the study of their ways. At last—for she was very
young, oddly like Shakespeare the poet in her face, with the same grey eyes
and rounded brows—at last Nick Greene the actor-manager took pity on
her; she found herself with child by that gentleman and so—who shall

measure the heat and violence of the poet's heart when caught and tangled in a woman's body?—killed herself one winter's night and lies buried at some cross-roads where the omnibuses now stop outside the Elephant and Castle.

That, more or less, is how the story would run, I think, if a woman in Shakespeare's day had had Shakespeare's genius. But for my part, I agree with the deceased bishop, if such he was—it is unthinkable that any woman in Shakespeare's day should have had Shakespeare's genius. For genius like Shakespeare's is not born among labouring, uneducated, servile people. It is not born in England among the Saxons and the Britons. It is not born today among the working classes. How, then, could it have been born among women whose work began, according to Professor Trevelyan, almost before they were out of the nursery, who were forced to it by their parents and held to it by all the power of law and custom? Yet genius of a sort must have existed among women as it must have existed among the working classes. Now and again an Emily Brontë or a Robert Burns blazes out and proves its presence. But certainly it never got itself on to paper. When, however, one reads of a witch being ducked, of a woman possessed by devils, of a wise woman selling herbs, or even of a very remarkable man who had a mother, then I think we are on the track of a lost novelist, a suppressed poet, of some mute and inglorious Jane Austen, some Emily Brontë who dashed her brains out on the moor or mopped and mowed about the highways crazed with the torture that her gift had put her to. Indeed, I would venture to guess that Anon, who wrote so many poems without signing them, was often a woman. It was a woman Edward Fitzgerald, I think, suggested who made the ballads and the folk-songs, crooning them to her children, beguiling her spinning with them, or the length of the winter's night.

This may be true or it may be false—who can say?—but what is true in it, so it seemed to me, reviewing the story of Shakespeare's sister as I had made it, is that any woman born with a great gift in the sixteenth century would certainly have gone crazed, shot herself, or ended her days in some lonely cottage outside the village, half witch, half wizard, feared and mocked at. For it needs little skill in psychology to be sure that a highly gifted girl who had tried to use her gift for poetry would have been so thwarted and hindered by other people, so tortured and pulled asunder by her own contrary instincts, that she must have lost her health and sanity to a certainty. No girl could have walked to London and stood at a stage door and forced her way into the presence of actor-managers without doing herself a violence and suffering an anguish which may have been irrational—for chastity may be a fetish invented by certain societies for unknown reasons—but were none the less inevitable. Chastity had then, it has even now, a religious importance in a woman's life, and has so wrapped itself round with nerves and instincts that to cut it free and bring it to the light of day demands courage of the rarest. To have lived a free life in London in the sixteenth century would have meant for a woman who was poet and playwright a nervous stress and dilemma which might well have killed her. Had she survived, whatever she had written would have been twisted and deformed, issuing from a strained and morbid imagination. And undoubtedly, I thought, looking at the shelf where there are no plays by women, her work would have gone unsigned. That refuge she would have sought certainly. It was the relic of the sense of chastity that dictated anonymity to women even so late as the nineteenth century. Currer Bell, George Eliot, George Sand, all the victims of inner strife as their writings prove, sought ineffectively to veil themselves by using the name of a man. Thus they did homage to the convention, which if not implanted by the other sex was liberally encouraged by them (the chief glory of a woman is not to be talked of, said Pericles, himself a much-talked-of man), that publicity in women is detestable. Anonymity runs in their blood. The desire to be veiled still possesses them. They are not even now as concerned about the health of their fame as men are, and, speaking generally, will pass a tombstone or a sign-post without feeling an irresistible desire to cut their names on it, as Alf, Bert or Chas. must do in obedience to their instinct, which murmurs if it sees a fine woman go by, or even a dog, Ce chien est à moi. And, of course, it may not be a dog, I thought, remembering Parliament Square, the Sièges Allée and other avenues; it may be a piece of land or a man with curly black hair. It is one of the great advantages of being woman that one can pass even a very fine negress without wishing to make an Englishwoman of her.

That woman, then, who was born with a gift of poetry in the sixteenth century, was an unhappy woman, a woman at strife against herself. All the conditions of her life, all her own instincts, were hostile to the state of mind which is needed to set free whatever is in the brain. But what is the state of mind that is most propitious to the act of creation, I asked. Can one come by any notion of the state that furthers and makes possible that strange activity? . . .

Chapter Six

Next day the light of the October morning was falling in dusty shafts through the uncurtained windows, and the hum of traffic rose from the street. London then was winding itself up again; the factory was astir; the machines were beginning. It was tempting, after all this reading, to look out of the window and see what London was doing on the morning of the twenty-sixth of October 1928. And what was London doing? Nobody, it seemed, was reading *Antony and Cleopatra*. London was wholly indifferent, it appeared, to Shakespeare's plays. Nobody cared a straw—and I do not blame them—for the future of fiction, the death of poetry or the development by the average woman of a prose style completely expressive of her mind. If opinions upon any of these matters had been chalked on the pavement, nobody would have stooped to read them. The nonchalance of the hurrying feet would have rubbed them out in half on hour. Here came an errand-boy; here a woman with a dog on a lead. The fascination of the London street is that no two people are ever alike; each seems bound on some private affair of his own. There were the business-like, with their little bags; there were the drifters rattling sticks upon area railings; there were affable characters to whom the streets serve for clubroom, hailing men in carts and giving information without being asked for it. Also there were funerals to which men, thus suddenly reminded of the passing of their own bodies, lifted their hats. And then a very distinguished gentleman came slowly down a doorstep and paused to avoid collision with a bustling lady who had, by some means or other, acquired a splendid fur coat and a bunch of Parma violets. They all seemed separate, self-absorbed, on business of their own.

At this moment, as so often happens in London, there was a complete lull and suspension of traffic. Nothing came down the street; nobody passed. A single leaf detached itself from the plane tree at the end of the street, and in that pause and suspension fell. Somehow it was like a signal falling, a signal pointing to a force in things which one had overlooked. It seemed to point to a river, which flowed past, invisibly, round the corner, down the street, and took people and eddied them along, as the stream at Oxbridge had taken the undergraduate in his boat and the dead leaves. Now it was bringing from one side of the street to the other diagonally a girl in patent leather boots, and then a young man in a maroon overcoat; it was also bringing a taxi-cab; and it brought all three together at a point directly beneath my window; where the taxi stopped; and the girl and the young man stopped; and they got into the taxi; and then the cab glided off as if it were swept on by the current elsewhere.

The sight was ordinary enough; what was strange was the rhythmical order with which my imagination had invested it; and the fact that the ordinary sight of two people getting into a cab had the power to communicate something of their own seeming satisfaction. The sight of two people coming down the street and meeting at the corner seems to ease the mind of some strain, I thought, watching the taxi turn and make off. Perhaps to think, as I had been thinking these two days, of one sex as distinct from the other is an effort. It interferes with the unity of the mind. Now that effort had ceased and that unity had been restored by seeing two people come together and get into a taxi-cab. The mind is certainly a very mysterious organ, I reflected, drawing my head in from the window, about which nothing whatever is known, though we depend upon it so completely. Why do I feel that there are severances and oppositions in the mind, as there are strains from obvious causes on the body? What does one mean by "the unity of the mind," I pondered, for clearly the mind has so great a power of concentrating at any point at any moment that it seems to have no single state of being. It can separate itself from the people in the street, for example, and think of itself as apart from them, at an upper window looking down on them. Or it can think with other people spontaneously, as, for instance, in a crowd waiting to hear some piece of news read out. It can think back through its fathers or through its mothers, as I have said that a woman writing thinks back through her mothers. Again if one is a woman one is often surprised by a sudden splitting off of consciousness, say in walking down Whitehall, when from being the natural inheritor of that civilisation, she becomes, on the contrary, outside of it, alien and critical. Clearly the mind is always altering its focus, and bringing the world into different perspectives. But some of these states of mind seem, even if adopted spontaneously, to be less comfortable than others. In order to keep oneself continuing in them one is unconsciously holding something back, and gradually the repression becomes an effort. But there may be some state of mind in which one could continue without effort because nothing is required to be held back. And this perhaps, I thought, coming in from the window, is one of them. For certainly when I saw the couple get into the taxi-cab the mind felt as if, after being divided, it had come together again in a natural fusion. The obvious reason would be that it is natural for the sexes to co-operate. One has a profound, if irrational, instinct in favour of the theory that the union of man and woman makes for the greatest satisfaction, the most complete happiness. But the sight of the two people getting into the taxi and the satisfaction it gave me made me also ask whether there are two sexes in the mind corresponding to the two sexes in the body, and whether they also require to be united in order to get complete satisfaction and happiness. And I went on amateurishly to sketch a plan of the soul so that in each of us two powers preside, one male, one female; and in the man's brain, the man predominates over the woman, and in the woman's brain, the woman predominates over the man. The normal and comfortable state of being is that when the two live in harmony together, spiritually co-operating. If one is a man, still the woman part of the brain must have effect; and a woman also must have intercourse with the man in her. Coleridge perhaps meant this when he said that a great mind is androgynous. It is when this fusion takes place that the mind is fully fertilised and uses all its faculties. Perhaps a mind that is purely masculine cannot create, any more than a mind that is purely feminine, I thought. But it would be well to test what one meant by man-womanly, and conversely by woman-manly, by pausing and looking at a book or two.

Coleridge certainly did not mean, when he said that a great mind is androgynous, that it is a mind that has any special sympathy with women; a mind that takes up their cause or devotes itself to their interpretation. Perhaps the androgynous mind is less apt to make these distinctions than the single-sexed mind. He meant, perhaps, that the androgynous mind is resonant and porous; that it transmits emotion without impediment; that it is naturally creative, incandescent and undivided. In fact one goes back to Shakespeare's mind as the type of the androgynous, of the man-womanly mind, though it would be impossible to say what Shakespeare thought of women. And if it be true that it is one of the tokens of the fully developed mind that it does not think specially or separately of sex, how much harder it is to attain that condition now than ever before. Here I came to the books by living writers, and there paused and wondered if this fact were not at the root of something that had long puzzled me. No age can ever have been as stridently sex-conscious as our own; those innumerable books by men about women in the British Museum are a proof of it. The Suffrage campaign was no doubt to blame. It must have roused in men an extraordinary desire for self-assertion; it must have made them lay an emphasis upon their own sex and its characteristics which they would not have troubled to think about had they not been challenged. And when one is challenged, even by a few women in black bonnets, one retaliates, if one has never been challenged before, rather excessively. That perhaps accounts for some of the characteristics that I remember to have found here, I thought, taking down a new novel by Mr. A, who is in the prime of life and very well thought of, apparently, by the reviewers. I opened it. Indeed, it was delightful to read a man's writing again. It was so direct, so straightforward after the writing of women. It indicated such freedom of mind, such liberty of person, such confidence in himself. One had a sense of physical well-being in the presence of this well-nourished, well-educated, free mind, which had never been thwarted or opposed, but had had full liberty from birth to stretch itself in whatever way it liked. All this was admirable. But after reading a chapter or two a shadow seemed to lie across the page. It was a straight dark bar, a shadow shaped something like the letter "I." One began dodging this way and that to catch a glimpse of the landscape behind it. Whether that was indeed a tree or a woman walking I was not quite sure. Back one was always hailed to the letter "I." One began to be tired of "I." Not but what this "I" was a most respectable "I"; honest and logical; as hard as a nut, and polished for centuries by good teaching and good feeding. I respect and admire that "I" from the bottom of my heart. But—here I turned a page or two, looking for something or other—the worst of it is that in the shadow of the letter "I" all is shapeless as mist. Is that a tree? No, it is a woman. But . . . she has not a bone in her body, I thought, watching Phoebe, for that was her name, coming across the beach. Then Alan got up and the shadow of Alan at once obliterated Phoebe. For Alan had views and Phoebe was quenched in the flood of his views. And then Alan, I thought, has passions; and here I turned page after page very fast, feeling that the crisis was approaching, and so it was. It took place on the beach under the sun. It was done very openly. It was done very vigorously. Nothing could have been more indecent. But . . . I had said "but" too often. One cannot go on saying "but." One must finish the sentence somehow, I rebuked myself. Shall I finish it, "But—I am bored!" But why was I bored? Partly because of the dominance of the letter "I" and the aridity, which, like the giant beech tree, it casts within its shade. Nothing will grow there. And partly for some more obscure reason. There seemed to be some obstacle, some impediment of Mr. A's mind which blocked the fountain of creative energy and shored it within narrow limits. Being honest as the day and logical as the sun, there is only one thing he can do. And that he does, to do him justice, over and over (I said, turning the pages) and over again. And that, I added, aware of the awful nature of the confession, seems somehow dull. Shakespeare's indecency uproots a thousand other things in one's mind, and is far from being dull. But Shakespeare does it for pleasure; Mr. A, as the nurses say, does it on purpose. He does it in protest. He is protesting against the equality of the other sex by asserting his own superiority. He is therefore impeded and inhibited and self-conscious as Shakespeare might have been if he too had known Miss Clough and Miss Davies.* Doubtless Elizabethan literature would have been very different from what it is if the woman's movement had begun in the sixteenth century and not in the nineteenth.

What, then, it amounts to, if this theory of the two sides of the mind holds good, is that virility has now become self-conscious—men, that is to say, are now writing only with the male side of their brains. It is a mistake for a woman to read them, for she will inevitably look for something that she will not find. It is the power of suggestion that one most misses, I thought, taking Mr. B the critic in my hand and reading, very carefully and very dutifully, his remarks upon the art of poetry. Very able they were, acute and full of learning; but the trouble was, that his feelings no longer communicated; his mind seemed separated into different chambers; not a sound carried from one to the other. Thus, when one takes a sentence of Mr. B into the mind it falls plump to the ground—dead; but when one takes a sentence of Coleridge into the mind, it explodes and gives birth to all kinds of other ideas, and that is the only sort of writing of which one can say that it has the secret of perpetual life. . . .

Even so, the very first sentence that I would write here, I said, crossing over to the writing-table and taking up the page headed Women and Fiction, is that it is fatal for any one who writes to think of their sex. It is fatal to be a man or woman pure and simple; one must be woman-manly or man-womanly. It is fatal for a woman to lay the least stress on any grievance; to plead even with justice any cause; in any way to speak consciously as a woman. And fatal is no figure of speech; for anything written with that conscious bias is doomed to death. It ceases to be fertilised. Brilliant and effective, powerful and masterly, as it may appear for a day or two, it must wither at nightfall; it cannot grow in the minds of others. Some collaboration has to take place in the mind between the woman and the man before the act of creation can be accomplished. Some marriage of opposites has to be consummated. The whole of the mind must lie wide open if we are to get the sense that the writer is communicating his experience with perfect fullness. There must be freedom and there must be peace. Not a wheel must grate, not a light glimmer. The curtains must be close drawn. The writer, I thought, once his experience is over, must lie back and let his

---

Miss Clough and Miss Davies: Anne Jemima Clough (1820–1892) was a leader in the movement of higher education for women and became the first president of Newnham College when it was built in 1874. Emily Davies (1830–1921) was a cofounder of the Women's Suffrage Committee in 1858 and founded Girton College in 1873.

mind celebrate its nuptials in darkness. He must not look or question what is being done. Rather, he must pluck the petals from a rose or watch the swans float calmly down the river. And I saw again the current which took the boat and the undergraduate and the dead leaves; and the taxi took the man and the woman, I thought, seeing them come together across the street, and the current swept them away, I thought, hearing far off the roar of London's traffic, into that tremendous stream.

Here, then, Mary Beton ceases to speak. She has told you how she reached the conclusion—the prosaic conclusion—that it is necessary to have five hundred a year and a room with a lock on the door if you are to write fiction or poetry. She has tried to lay bare the thoughts and impressions that led her to think this. She has asked you to follow her flying into the arms of a Beadle, lunching here, dining there. . . . While she has been doing all these things, you no doubt have been observing her failings and foibles and deciding what effect they have had on her opinions. You have been contradicting her and making whatever additions and deductions seem good to you. That is all as it should be, for in a question like this truth is only to be had by laying together many varieties of error. And I will end now in my own person by anticipating two criticisms, so obvious that you can hardly fail to make them.

No opinion has been expressed, you may say, upon the comparative merits of the sexes even as writers. That was done purposely, because, even if the time had come for such a valuation—and it is far more important at the moment to know how much money women had and how many rooms than to theorise about their capacities—even if the time had come I do not believe that gifts, whether of mind or character, can be weighed like sugar and butter, not even in Cambridge, where they are so adept at putting people into classes and fixing caps on their heads and letters after their names. I do not believe that even the Table of Precedency which you will find in Whitaker's *Almanac* represents a final order of values, or that there is any sound reason to suppose that a Commander of the Bath will ultimately walk in to dinner behind a Master in Lunacy. All this pitting of sex against sex, of quality against quality; all this claiming of superiority and imputing of inferiority, belong to the private-school stage of human existence where there are "sides," and it is necessary for one side to beat another side, and of the utmost importance to walk up to a platform and receive from the hands of the Headmaster himself a highly ornamental pot. As people mature they cease to believe in sides or in Headmasters or in highly ornamental pots. At any rate, where books are concerned, it is notoriously difficult to fix labels of merit in such a way that they do not come off. Are not reviews of current literature a perpetual illustration of the difficulty of judgment? "This great book," "this worthless book," the same book is called by both names. Praise and blame alike mean nothing. No, delightful as the pastime of measuring may be, it is the most futile of all occupations, and to submit to the decrees of the measurers the most servile of attitudes. So long as you write what you wish to write, that is all that matters; and whether it matters for ages or only for hours, nobody can say. But to sacrifice a hair of the head of your vision, a shade of its colour, in deference to some Headmaster with a silver pot in his hand or to some professor with a measuring-rod up his sleeve, is the most abject treachery, and the sacrifice of wealth and chastity which used to be said to be the greatest of human disasters, a mere flea-bite in comparison.

Notes

1. "We are told that we ought to ask for £30,000 at least.... It is not a large sum, considering that there is to be but one college of this sort for Great Britain, Ireland and the Colonies, and considering how easy it is to raise immense sums for boys' schools. But considering how few people really wish women to be educated, it is a good deal." — Lady Stephen, *Life of Miss Emily Davies.*

2. Every penny which could be scraped together was set aside for building, and the amenities had to be postponed. — R. Strachey, *The Cause.*

3. "It remains a strange and almost inexplicable fact that in Athena's city, where women were kept in almost Oriental suppression as odalisques or drudges, the stage should yet have produced figures like Clytemnestra and Cassandra, Atossa and Antigone, Phèdre and Medea, and all the other heroines who dominate play after play of the 'misogynist' Euripides. But the paradox of this world where in real life a respectable woman could hardly show her face alone in the street, and yet on the stage woman equals or surpasses man, has never been satisfactorily explained. In modern tragedy the same predominance exists. At all events, a very cursory survey of Shakespeare's work (similarly with Webster, though not with Marlowe or Jonson) suffices to reveal how this dominance, this initiative of women, persists from Rosalind to Lady Macbeth. So too in Racine; six of his tragedies bear their heroines' names; and what male characters of his shall we set against Hermione and Andromaque, Bérénice and Roxane, Phèdre and Athalie? So again with Ibsen; what men shall we match with Solveig and Nora, Hedda and Hilda Wangel and Rebecca West?" — F. L. Lucas, *Tragedy in Relation to Aristotle's "Poetics"* (New York: Harcourt, c. 1928), 114–15.

Ideas for Rereading

1. Woolf's essay challenges readers because her style is deliberately relaxed, almost as though she is luxuriating in the fact of her own financial and spatial independence. Woolf frequently expects us to figure out for ourselves the full implications of what she is saying. Another way to put this is to say her meanings are often *implicit* rather than *explicit.* Apparent digressions often turn out to be related to her central theme, but we have to work out how they are related by paying close attention to meanings implicit in these digressions. As you reread *A Room of One's Own,* pay close attention to Woolf's use of digressions, noting the places where she tells us things explicitly and places where you are not sure what, exactly, she is doing or saying. Underline places where Woolf uses words that connect digressions to her main theme. Why does she so often make her argument indirectly, by implication?

2. Woolf writes: "What were the conditions in which women lived, I asked myself; for fiction, imaginative work that is, is not dropped like a pebble upon the ground, as science might be; fiction is like a spider's web, attached ever so lightly perhaps, but still attached to life at all four corners" (p. 30). In what ways is Woolf's essay "attached to life at all four corners"? As you reread the

essay, underline specific words, phrases, and passages that reveal the writer's social circumstances: What does *A Room of One's Own* tell you about Virginia Woolf's life? How is this life related to your own life? In what ways do you recognize, empathize with, or fail to understand the "real world" referred to in *A Room of One's Own*? Which specific "real-world" references are familiar to you? Which are only partly familiar? Which are entirely unfamiliar?

3. Woolf's essay depends on an elaborate rhetorical strategy, one that combines fiction and fact. Her statement in the first paragraph that "fiction here is likely to contain more truth than fact" (p. 21) implies that this approach is more than just decorative. What does Woolf's argument gain from her fictions? As you reread Woolf's essay, focus on one particular "fictional thread" (such as the descriptions of lunch and dinner; the conversation with Mary Seton; the life of Judith Shakespeare). Make notes about the main characters, settings, episodes, and plot of this fictional thread. Then make further notes suggesting how this particular story supports Woolf's argument. What does Woolf gain by using imagined, fictional examples rather than historical or nonfictional examples from experience or research?

Ideas for Writing

1. Write an essay in which you consider relationships between truth and fiction in *A Room of One's Own*. Begin by considering what Woolf says about truth and lies in the first paragraph. Then address specific passages that are, for you, "worth keeping" (p. 21), and passages that might be thrown away. Think about the ways in which Woolf uses digressions from her main point. Also pay attention to Woolf's use of a fictionalized narrator — "call me Mary Beton, Mary Seton, Mary Carmichael or by any name you please" (p. 21). What advantages does Woolf gain by distancing herself from the events described in *A Room of One's Own*? How does this use of distancing techniques contribute to her overall argument?

2. *A Room of One's Own* is in part concerned with the effects of poverty and wealth. On pages 26 and 27, Woolf imagines "two pictures," one filled with "treasure in huge sacks," the other of "lean cows and a muddy market and withered greens and the stringy hearts of old men." These pictures lead to "scorn at the reprehensible poverty of our sex" (p. 27) and to thoughts of "the urbanity, the geniality, the dignity which are the offspring of luxury and privacy and space" (p. 29).

Write an essay in which you respond to Woolf's contrasting pictures of the cultural status of men and women by using a situation from your own life in which you experienced limitations as a result of financial contraints or you experienced "luxury and privacy and space." Use specific parts of Woolf's essay — parts in which she addresses issues of poverty and wealth — to discuss, analyze, and critique the episode from your own experience. What did you learn from this episode? What kind of response does it enable you to make to Woolf's statement that a woman needs "money and a room of her own if she is to write fiction" (p. 21)? Using this episode as a starting point, engage in open conversation with Woolf on the relationship between material conditions and creative work.

CONTEXT

A Room of One's Own *began life as a lecture titled "Women and Fiction" at Cambridge University's two women's colleges. Woolf addressed the students at Newnham College on October 20, 1928, and at Girton College on October 26, 1928. Recent passage of the Equal Franchise Act had lowered the voting age of women from thirty to twenty-one; this meant that Woolf's entire audience would, for the first time in British history, be eligible to vote once they graduated. As Charlotte Perkins Gilman, author of* The Yellow Wallpaper *(1892) and* Herland *(1915), argued in 1923, there was a "new generation of women" who had made "marked and rapid" improvements in education.* A Room of One's Own *addresses these women.*

Woolf had just published her novel Orlando *(1928), a fictionalized biography of a man who transforms into a woman midway through a life that begins in the sixteenth and ends in the twentieth century. We have included the part of the novel where Orlando confronts what it means to be a woman who used to be a man. As the photograph from this section of the novel also indicates, Woolf used her friend and lover Vita Sackville-West as a model for the character of Orlando. When juxtaposed with the picture of "Orlando as a boy" and "Orlando about the year 1840," the photograph of "Orlando on her return to England" provides a useful context for the photograph of Virginia Woolf. An experimental modernist writer and an important influence on later postmodernist writing, Woolf presented* Orlando *as a biography rather than a novel, deliberately blurring the line between fact and fiction.*

Woolf revised and expanded her lecture extensively between writing "Women and Fiction" in 1928 and publishing A Room of One's Own *in October 1929. The cover of* A Room of One's Own *by Woolf's sister, Vanessa Bell, is representative of the kind of art valued by Woolf and the philosophers, writers, and artists in the Bloomsbury Group. (We encourage you to research this colorful and influential group; a few of the central figures are listed on p. 19.)*

The traditional ballad "The Four Marys," dating from about 1563 and of unknown authorship, appears to be the source for the Mary characters in A Room of One's Own. *The speaker in the ballad is Mary Hamilton; she, Mary Seaton, Mary Beaton, and Mary Carmichael, the "Four Marys," were ladies-in-waiting to a fifth Mary, Mary Queen of Scots, who was imprisoned and finally beheaded by Elizabeth I on a charge of conspiring against Elizabeth's life. The three Marys mentioned in the ballad are historical figures, though the speaker, Mary Hamilton, may not have been. We might interpret Woolf's adaptation of the fictive personae from "The Four Marys" not only as a way of deflecting direct criticism but also as a way of registering the dread involved in going public in an age when the book review industry was dominated by men hostile to feminism. The reviews of* A Room of One's Own *collected here suggest how successful Woolf was in anticipating criticism of her main line of reasoning; it is interesting, however, that even a positive review like Orlo Williams's from* The Criterion *begins by questioning "the wit of woman." Still, the reviews—Elisabeth Woodbridge's from* The Yale Review; *the brief, anonymous* Punch *review; Arnold Bennett's review from* Evening Standard, *titled "Queen of the High-Brows"; and an anonymous review from the* Times Literary Supplement—*together suggest that Woolf's greatest achievement is in the careful management of a highly volatile subject.*

CHARLOTTE PERKINS GILMAN

From *The New Generation of Women*   1923

Clearly and strongly defined among the distinctive features of our times stands the change in the status of women. Within scarcely more than a century from the first stir among advanced thinkers there has arisen in gathering force what has been known as "the woman's movement," more recently called "feminism," with results so swift and startling as to arouse alarm among the more conservative.

The very suddenness of this change, as well as the close intimacy of the relations involved, account for much that is unwelcome; but it is only within the last few years that any conspicuous new evils could be pointed out in the behavior of women. . . .

For a long time the movement was rightly called a revolt. Women lived under conditions of such glaring injustice that at first they demanded only "women's rights," such as equality before the law, equal opportunity in education, equal pay for equal work and an equal share in democracy.

Over the whole world, in proportion to its civilization, this stir is felt; the women of China have made swift advance, the women of Turkey are leaving off their veils, the women of Europe and America are showing in education, in industry, in the professions, in political ability, capacities which used to be thought quite beyond them.

The World War was a strong factor in the immediate past, calling upon women for unusual activities. The result of those activities astonished the world. But the war also brought other forces into play, acting both on men and women and leading to other results in many ways unfortunate.

. . . We must distinguish sharply between the general progress of the age, common to both men and women, and the special gain or loss of women in comparison with men.

Woman's Advance in Education

In education, for instance, the improvement is marked and rapid. In school, college and university, in popular literature and lectures, this improvement gives reason for mental progress in both sexes; but the gain of women is far greater in proportion. From being an almost uneducated class, supposed to have inferior brains, they have moved forward to such easy equality, in many cases to such superiority, that some now hold that the same courses of our college curricula, earlier considered beyond the powers of "the feminine mind," are now "too feminine."

This sudden advance in education must be further distinguished by its having been made under heavy opposition. A most interesting record could be made of this fact, as proving the weight of masculine prejudice, which so long placed every obstacle in the way of feminine progress.

There can be no longer any reasonable doubt as to the equality of the woman's mind with the man's in ability to learn. Whether this is accompanied by an equal ability to invent, to create, to make new steps in the world's advance, cannot be so swiftly established, on account of the conditional disadvantages of women. The man, married or single, is free to concentrate upon his specialty, and is, indeed, required to; while the woman if she is married carries upon her shoulders that group of primitive industries which we call "housework," in addition to the cares and untrained labors of child-culture. Motherhood itself would take some years from her professional life, though motherhood is not a disability, but a special power. A year's vacation should be taken with each baby.

The single woman, on the other hand, while freed from these complications, has not, as has the man, a home and a "help-mate" to strengthen and comfort her while she works. She is robbed of normal functioning as a mother and of the pleasures of family life; celibacy is an unnatural state for either sex.

But after allowing for all this, it may fairly be said that so far the woman's mind does not manifest in the same degree the qualities of individual initiative and of creative power that we are accustomed to consider peculiar to the man's. That some instances do exist, however, shows it is not a sex distinction. Perhaps another century or so must pass, with great development in "the belated trades" of the household and an ennobling specialization in child-culture, before it can be authoritatively stated that there is any essential difference in mental qualities; whether, in short, there is sex-distinction in the brain.

If the question arises as to whether there is any general revolt or protest by women against their previous status, this may be heartily answered in the affirmative. There are two lines of proof to be offered—one, the achievements established by women in so many lines of work, in so many new habits and customs of dress and behavior; the other in that inexorable record of passing events, current literature. The short story or novel gives a picture of its times. The blushing, weeping, swooning maiden of the past is wholly gone. Instead of fainting on Reginald's breast and crying "My preserver!" the heroine of today quite frequently preserves him.

Our previous judgments of women are being most rudely reversed in many directions. Women used to be called "conservative," especially in matters of religion, but now every new cult has its flocks of feminine followers, and the most widespread of them all has a woman prophet.[1] Here, at least, is no lack of initiative.

Too much must not be demanded, in measure of progress, from this newly emancipated class. They emerge from ages of domestic seclusion into a world already established and carried on by men—in short, into "a running concern." They cannot change it at once, even as far as they desire to, and much of their immediate behavior is mere reaction.

Notes

1. She is probably referring to Aimee Semple McPherson (1890–1944), who founded the International Church of the Foursquare Gospel.

VIRGINIA WOOLF

From *Orlando*   1928

She remembered how, as a young man, she had insisted that women must be obedient, chaste, scented, and exquisitely apparelled. "Now I shall have to pay in my own person for those desires," she reflected; "for women are not (judging by my own short experience of the sex) obedient, chaste, scented, and exquisitely apparelled by nature. They can only attain these graces, without which they may enjoy none of the delights of life, by the most tedious discipline. There's the hair-dressing," she thought, "that alone will take an hour of my morning; there's looking in the looking-glass, another hour; there's staying and lacing; there's washing and powdering; there's changing from silk to lace and from lace to paduasoy;* and there's being chaste year in year out. . . ." Here she tossed her foot impatiently, and showed an inch or two of calf. A sailor on the mast, who happened to look down at the moment, started so violently that he missed his footing and only saved himself by the skin of his teeth. "If the sight of my ankles means death to an honest fellow who, no doubt, has a wife and family to support, I must, in all humanity, keep them covered," Orlando thought. Yet her legs were among her chiefest beauties. And she fell to thinking what an odd pass we have come to when all a woman's beauty has to be kept covered, lest a sailor may fall from a mast-head. "A pox on them!" she said, realising for the first time, what, in other circumstances, she would have been taught as a child, that is to say, the sacred responsibilities of womanhood.

"And that's the last oath I shall ever be able to swear," she thought; "once I set foot on English soil. And I shall never be able to crack a man over the head, or tell him he lies in his teeth, or draw my sword and run him through the body, or sit among my peers, or wear a coronet, or walk in procession, or sentence a man to death, or lead an army, or prance down Whitehall on a charger, or wear seventy-two different medals on my

---

paduasoy: A rich, strong silk fabric used for ceremonial and highly formal garments of clothing.

breast. All I can do, once I set foot on English soil, is to pour out tea, and ask my lords how they like it. D'you take sugar? D'you take cream?" And mincing out the words, she was horrified to perceive how low an opinion she was forming of the other sex, the manly, to which it had once been her pride to belong. "To fall from a mast-head," she thought, "because you see a woman's ankles; to dress up like a Guy Fawkes* and parade the streets, so that women may praise you; to deny a woman teaching lest she may laugh at you; to be the slave of the frailest chit in petticoats, and yet to go about as if you were the Lords of creation.—Heavens!" she thought, "what fools they make of us—what fools we are!" And here it would seem from some ambiguity in her terms that she was censuring both sexes equally, as if she belonged to neither; and indeed, for the time being she seemed to vacillate; she was man; she was woman; she knew the secrets, shared the weaknesses of each. It was a most bewildering and whirligig state of mind to be in. The comforts of ignorance seemed utterly denied her. She was a feather blown on the gale. Thus it is no great wonder if, as she pitted one sex against the other, and found each alternately full of the most deplorable infirmities, and was not sure to which she belonged—it was no great wonder that she was about to cry out that she would return to Turkey and become a gipsy again when the anchor fell with a great splash into the sea; the sails came tumbling on deck, and she perceived (so sunk had she been in thought, that she had seen nothing for several days) that the ship was anchored off the coast of Italy. The Captain at once sent to ask the honour of her company ashore with him in the long boat.

When she returned the next morning, she stretched herself on her couch under the awning and arranged her draperies with the greatest decorum about her ankles.

"Ignorant and poor as we are compared with the other sex," she thought, continuing the sentence which she had left unfinished the other day, "armoured with every weapon as they are, while they debar us even from a knowledge of the alphabet" (and from these opening words it is plain that something had happened during the night to give her a push towards the female sex, for she was speaking more as a woman speaks than as a man, yet with a sort of content after all) "still—they fall from the mast-head—" Here she gave a great yawn and fell asleep. When she woke, the ship was sailing before a fair breeze so near the shore that towns on the cliffs' edge seemed only kept from slipping into the water by the interposition of some great rock or the twisted roots of some ancient olive tree. The scent of oranges wafted from a million trees, heavy with the fruit, reached her on deck. A score of blue dolphins, twisting their tails, leapt high now

---

Guy Fawkes: A Roman Catholic Englishman (1570–1606) executed for leading the Gunpowder Plot, an attempt in 1605 to blow up King James I and the Houses of Parliament. Guy Fawkes Day is celebrated on November 5 in England: effigies ("guys") of Fawkes are burned on bonfires, accompanied by fireworks.

and again into the air. Stretching her arms out (arms, she had learnt already, have no such fatal effects as legs) she thanked Heaven that she was not prancing down Whitehall on a war-horse, not even sentencing a man to death. "Better is it," she thought, "to be clothed with poverty and ignorance, which are the dark garments of the female sex; better to leave the rule and discipline of the world to others; better to be quit of martial ambition, the love of power, and all the other manly desires if so one can more

Detail of a painting showing one of the sons of the fourth earl of Dorset, used by Virginia Woolf to illustrate "Orlando as a boy"

Orlando on her return to England

Vita Sackville-West as "Orlando about the year 1840"

fully enjoy the most exalted raptures known to the human spirit, which are," she said aloud, as her habit was when deeply moved, "contemplation, solitude, love."

"Praise God that I'm a woman!" she cried, and was about to run into the extreme folly—than which none is more distressing in woman or man either—of being proud of her sex, when she paused over the singular word, which, for all we can do to put it in its place, has crept in at the end of the last sentence; Love. "Love," said Orlando. Instantly—such is its impetuosity—love took a human shape—such is its pride. For where other thoughts are content to remain abstract nothing will satisfy this one but to

Virginia Woolf, studio portrait, 1925

put on flesh and blood, mantilla and petticoats, hose and jerkin. And as all Orlando's loves had been women, now, through the culpable laggardry of the human frame to adapt itself to convention, though she herself was a woman, it was still a woman she loved; and if the consciousness of being of the same sex had any effect at all, it was to quicken and deepen those feelings which she had had as a man. For now a thousand hints and mysteries

Dust jacket for A Room of One's Own *by Vanessa Bell, Virginia Woolf's sister*

became plain to her that were then dark. Now, the obscurity, which divides the sexes and lets linger innumerable impurities in its gloom, was removed, and if there is anything in what the poet says about truth and beauty, this affection gained in beauty what it lost in falsity. At last, she cried, she knew Sasha as she was, and in the ardour of this discovery, and in the pursuit of all those treasures which were now revealed, she was so rapt and enchanted that it was as if a cannon ball had exploded at her ear when a man's voice said, "Permit me, Madam," a man's hand raised her to her feet; and the fingers of a man with a three-masted sailing ship tattooed on the middle finger pointed to the horizon.

The Four Marys

c. 1563

Last night there were four Marys
Tonight there'll be but three
There was Mary Seaton and Mary Beaton
And Mary Carmichael and me.

Oh, often have I dressed my queen
And put on her braw silk gown
But all the thanks I've got tonight
Is to be hanged in Edinborough Town.

Full often have I dressed my queen
Put gold upon her hair
But I have got for my reward
The gallows to be my share.

Oh little did my mother know
The day she cradled me
The land I was to travel in
The death I was to dee.

Oh, happy, happy is the maid
That's born of beauty free
Oh, it was my rosy dimpled cheeks
That's been the devil to me.

They'll tie a kerchief around my eyes
That I may not see to dee
And they'll never tell my father or mother
But that I'm across the sea.

(Sequenced by Barry Taylor)

ORLO WILLIAMS

From *The Criterion*   1929

Uniform Edition of the Works of Virginia Woolf.
  The Voyage Out, Jacob's Room, Mrs. Dalloway, The Common Reader, To the Lighthouse. (Hogarth Press). 5s. net each.

A Room of One's Own. By Virginia Woolf. (Hogarth Press). 5s. net.

This issue of a uniform and handy edition of Mrs. Woolf's works, of which the first four volumes have recently appeared, will be welcomed not only by British readers, but by foreign readers of Englisl. who find a considerable hindrance in the expense and bulk of new English books. Mrs. Woolf, the novelist, is becoming well known among intelligent readers on the Continent; even in Italy, where knowledge of modern English literature is still scanty, the name of "la Woolf" may be found collocated with those of Proust, Mr. Joyce, Mr. André Gide and Mr. Aldous Huxley, as an important example of later technique in fiction. Mrs. Woolf, the critic, or, rather, the composer of delightful *causeries* on other people's books, is probably not so well known, at all events, outside her own country. We may well hope that the pleasure to be found within the covers of *The Common Reader* may now become still more widely shared, and that her new book, *A Room of One's Own,* which is a remarkable discourse on the relation of women to literature, will awake echoes and discussions beyond, as well as within, the English-speaking countries.

This discourse, we are told, is based upon two papers read to literary societies at Newnham and Girton respectively; the subject suggested was, apparently, "Women and Fiction." What a subject! Every day of the week in Britain, in British Dominions and in the United States, a hundred fluffings and fidgettings with it must end in solemn resolutions and votes of thanks. And if to treat it without prejudice would be, so Mrs. Woolf suggests, beyond the practice of man, to treat it freshly might have seemed beyond the wit of woman. Mrs. Woolf has shown once more the revitalizing power of imagination. Here is nothing trite, and nothing typical but of the inimitable author. There is wit abundantly, but it pierces the surface; there is fancy, but it reaches conclusions; there is knowledge well-arranged, but used so artfully that it seems but a decoration. It may seem rash for a man, in face of Mrs. Woolf's scorn for men's lordly propensity to settle women's case, to say that she settles it unexceptionally; yet I am bold enough to assert that she does so, within the limits of her argument. Feminism—nobody can deny—is justified as a protest against an age-old masculinism, yet it defeats its own object by perpetuating the dissidence. For neither

Some references in the reviews are to the full text of *A Room of One's Own.*—Eds.

position is without truth; and if for instance, man's conception of woman has often been as ill-founded and petty as his treatment of her has been repressive, all those women, from Clytemnestra to Madame de Guermantes, whom Mrs. Woolf cites as having "burnt like beacons in all the works of all the poets from the beginning of time," somewhat restore the masculine balance. The contrast between the imaginative importance in which, down the ages, man has held woman and the insignificance to which he condemned her in practical life is not merely a curious fact, it is man's defence against a charge of unmitigated prejudice or ignorance. For, unless they disavow Desdemona, Rosalind, Millamant and the rest, pure feminists are driven to the somewhat arbitrary conclusion that, while man as poet understands and values woman, as father, husband, law-giver and professor he neither values nor understands her. Mrs. Woolf, for all the effective play she makes with the paradox of man's behaviour to woman, and for all the passion of her plea that woman's horizon must be completely unrestricted, sees beyond the dissidence.

At the conclusion of her brilliant argument she writes:

"Even so, the very first sentence that I would write here, I said, crossing over to the writing-table and taking up the page headed 'Women and Fiction' is that it is fatal for anyone who writes to think of their sex. It is fatal to be a man or woman pure and simple; one must be woman-manly or man-womanly. It is fatal for a woman to lay the least stress on any grievance; to plead even with justice any cause; in any way to speak consciously as a woman. And fatal is no figure of speech; for anything written with that conscious bias is doomed to death. It ceases to be fertilized. Brilliant and effective, powerful and masterly as it may appear for a day or two, it must wither at nightfall; it cannot grow in the minds of others. Some collaboration has to take place in the mind between the woman and the man before the art of creation can be accomplished. Some marriage of opposites has to be consummated."

I have laid stress on this aspect of *A Room of One's Own*, because it will be an antidote to certain nonsensical ideas, quite widely entertained, about the ultimate elimination of the masculine principle from the world. It is not, however, the main object of Mrs. Woolf to encourage the perfect co-operation of these two principles. She is more concerned with the handicaps and disabilities which have, up to recent times, hampered the emergence of woman poets and writers. Her fictitious Mary Beton or Seton, having partaken of a generous lunch — its description is a succulent poem — at a men's college, and having proceeded to a somewhat practical dinner, including prunes, at a women's college, asks herself why women have been too poor to endow colleges richly. She then goes back to London to work at her paper on "Women and Fiction" [and discovers] a mine of masculine absurdities, yet she charitably puts their prejudices down to a need for self-confidence. She has self-confidence too. What has given it her? A legacy of five hundred a year. She can think for herself and provide for herself, all her motions are untrammelled.

"Indeed my aunt's legacy unveiled the sky to me, and substituted for the large and imposing figure of a gentleman, which Milton recommended for my perpetual adoration, a view of the open sky."

She ruminates on the condition of Elizabethan woman and her failure to share in the outburst of Elizabethan song; she invents a grim story of what happened to Shakespeare's sister, gifted like him. Even in later ages the woman had no money and no room of her own; men proclaimed her intellectually inferior. "She was snubbed, slapped, lectured and generally exhorted. Her mind must have been strained and her vitality lowered by the need of opposing this, of disapproving that." In the next chapter — which in itself is a masterly critical *causerie* — Mrs. Woolf examines typical woman writers from Aphra Behn to Jane Austen and Charlotte Brontë, to bring out that almost inevitable lapse from the vital quality of "integrity" which was due to the women writers' consciousness of being always on the defensive. Moreover — and here Mrs. Woolf makes a critical point of extreme interest — a far greater difficulty faced them. "They had no tradition behind them, or one so short and partial that it was of little help." In two acute pages she amplifies the opinion that masculine models in literature — from verse-forms to sentences — were, and are, inappropriate to the motions of a woman's mind. In the future, the book, the poem, the sentence will be adapted to the body; there will be a feminine as well as a masculine tradition in a complete and legitimate sense.

But what of to-day? In Chapter V Mary Seton answers this question by criticizing with inimitable wit some first novel by some Mary Carmichael, all hot from the publishers. I will not spoil the reader's prospective pleasure by trying to summarise the happy acuteness with which she picks out Mary Carmichael's failing, enumerates the enormous field, symbolized by the sentence "Chloe liked Olivia," which remains for a woman writer of imagination to explore, and sums up her advantages at the moment. "Give her another hundred years, I concluded, reading the last chapter — people's noses and bare shoulders showed naked against a starry sky, for someone had twitched the curtain in the drawing-room — give her a room of her own and five hundred a year, let her speak her mind and leave out half that she now puts in, and she will write a better book one of these days. She will be a poet, I said . . . in another hundred years' time."

In the last chapter Mrs. Woolf introduces her theme of necessary bisexuality as a writer with an impressionistic picture from Mary Seton's window in London that is worthy of one of her (Mrs. Woolf's) novels. She complains that, to-day, men writers are protesting against the equality of the other sex by asserting their virility too self-consciously. The studied indecency of Mr. A. the novelist, the want of resonance in Mr. B. the critic, Mr. Kipling's officers, Mr. Galsworthy's Forsytes, fall dead upon a woman's ears. Not so Coleridge and Tennyson. With an epilogue in her own person she ends what might be termed a successful continuation of the effort which she ascribes in *The Common Reader* to George Eliot's heroines:

The ancient consciousness of woman, charged with suffering and sensibility, and for so many ages dumb, seems in them to have brimmed and overflowed and uttered a demand for something—they scarcely know what—for something that is perhaps incompatible with the facts of human existence.

Mrs. Woolf knows "what," and her demands, as she puts them, seem convincingly compatible with the facts of existence. And her art in putting them is the perfect proof of her argument.

ELISABETH WOODBRIDGE

From *The Yale Review*   1930

A Room of One's Own, by Virginia Woolf, Harcourt, Brace & Co.

Memory was the mother of all the muses, and distance of some sort is surely the mother of laughter. It may be only a flash of remoteness, swiftly alternating with pain or sympathy or indignation, but while we laugh the remoteness has intervened, bringing with it a new vision, and therefore refreshment. That, I suppose, is why, in Vaughn Moody's philosophy, victory is crowned with laughter—"laughter and rallying." That is why, in reading *A Room of One's Own*, its quiet, demure laughter is what one remembers with special delight. And that is why, as I finished, there floated into my mind those lovely, half-baffling lines from "The Fire-Bringer":

> Along the earth and up the sky
> The Fowler spreads his net . . .
>
> What sky is thine behind the sky,
> For refuge and for ecstasy?
> Why is each heaven twain . . .
>
> Behold, the net is empty, the cast is vain,
> And from thy circling in the other sky the lyric laughters rain!

Virginia Woolf, speaking for women—and she is frankly, in this delicious book, speaking for and about women as well as to them—has circled into that "other sky" whence laughter comes. And this, I think, is the most memorable thing about the book. I like to think of it beside Mary Wollstonecraft's *Vindication of the Rights of Women* and John Stuart Mill's grave and cogent *Subjection of Women*. Were it not for these and others, as well as for Aphra Behn and Jane Austen and the Brontës to whom she more explicitly pays her tribute, Virginia Woolf would not have written *Orlando* and *Mrs. Dalloway*. And of this she is fully aware. She is like a pilgrim—like Pilgrim* himself, looking back from the Delectable Mountains, and smiling as he remembers the lions, and the Slough, and the Giant.

I find myself thinking of it, too, along with another precious little book, Meredith's *Essay on Comedy*. For Virginia Woolf is the "Comic Spirit" incarnate, in Meredith's sense.

A Room of One's Own offers us, among other good things, a meditation, delicately whimsical and deeply true, on the writer-temperament, that inner drive to create in words, that is continually seeking expression, that is continually being frustrated, or partly frustrated, so that it rarely reaches the state of "incandescence" (inspired word!) in which creative activity is unhindered and free. Shakespeare reached it often, but Shakespeare's sister, a lovely creation of Mrs. Woolf's own "incandescent" imagination, died young, driven to despair by her own frustrated powers. This often happens to men. It must always have happened to women—must still happen until every woman has "a room of her own and 500 a year." This is Mrs. Woolf's demure "message" to women.

I feel sure we shall accept it in the spirit in which it is offered. We know that "incandescence" is easily missed. We know that divine carelessness when "the bolt is shot back"—

> And what we mean, we say,
> And what we would, we know,

could not come to women while they still felt repressed, or injured, or furtive, or apologetic, or defiant. We know that it is hard enough for a man to write a good book, and that it has been harder, because of circumstance, because of the "Zeitgeist" perhaps, for women. But I cannot help wondering whether Mrs. Woolf in her interpretation of the past, in her hope for the future, does not allow too much weight to "fortune and men's eyes," and too little to the fundamental and inescapable situation involved in being a woman. She does note in passing the "possibly relevant fact" that not one of the four great women novelists has a child. I think this fact is more than "possibly" relevant; I think it is quite certainly relevant.

One of the wisest of our philosophers once said to me that he thought genius might be accounted for as a *plus* of energy beyond the rest of mankind. If this should be so, and if it were also true that it takes more energy to be a woman than to be a man—more energy to be daughter, lover, wife, mother, aunt, than it does to be son, lover, husband, father, uncle—if this should all happen to be so—what then? It is perhaps a question we need not yet face. Women have unloaded so much weight from the pack that has bowed them down that they already run and are not weary. Some

---

Pilgrim: The central character in John Bunyan's *The Pilgrim's Progress* was actually called "Christian" but the reviewer refers to him as "Pilgrim." On his symbolic journey to the Promised Land, Christian suffers many trials and temptations, struggling through such metaphoric places as "the Slough of Despond" and "Castle Despair."

of them, like Virginia Woolf, are even mounting up on wings. We may then hope that some day the sister of Shakespeare "will put on the body she has so often laid down," and will carry it, and her genius, to success, with whatever added *plus* is needed to be a woman too.

ANONYMOUS

From *Punch*   1929

M*r. Pecksniff.* But, after all, your milestone or direction-post cannot possibly function both ways. It cannot stand sentry at the crucial corner and march in the right direction at the same time. And I believe there are ever so many excellent critics who are none the less excellent as critics for failing to carry out their counsels of perfection. Among these — and Ruskin on his own admission was one of them — I have the temerity to place Mrs. Virginia Woolf, whose inquiry into the conditions which should ultimately produce the feminine Shakespeare — they resolve themselves into *A Room of One's Own* (Hogarth Press) and five hundred a year — is one of the most accomplished, stout-hearted and right-minded pieces of criticism I have encountered for months. From the graceful and charitable banter of the beginning — where the amenities of a man's college luncheon at Oxbridge are contrasted with the lack of amenities in a women's college dining-hall — the chance of producing Shakespeare's imaginary sister from a comparatively "labouring, uneducated and servile race" are discerningly canvassed. Nothing is further from Mrs. Woolf's aim than to produce a feminist tract. She would not sacrifice at any price the unique and disciplined creative power of the woman who does not write or live like a man or look like a man. She would, if possible, release it. But there, of course, lies the difficulty — to release without destroying; and it cannot be said that Mrs. Woolf has solved it, though she has undoubtedly rendered first aid.

ARNOLD BENNETT

From "Queen of the High-Brows,"
Evening Standard   1929

I have often been informed by the elect that a feud exists between Virginia Woolf and myself, and I dare say that she has received the same tidings. Possibly she and I are the only two lettered persons unaware of this feud. True, she has written a book about me and a mythical Mrs. Brown. But I have not read the book (I don't know why). True, I always said, until she wrote *To the Lighthouse,* that she had not written a good novel. But I have said the same of lots of my novelist friends. True, she is the queen of the high-brows; and I am a low-brow. But it takes all sorts of brows to make a world, and without a large admixture of low-brows even Bloomsbury would be uninhabitable.

One thing I have said of her: she can write. *A Room of One's Own* is a further demonstration of this truth. . . . And I have said that you never know where you are in a book of hers. *A Room of One's Own* is a further demonstration of this truth also. It is stated to be based on two papers read to the Arts Society of Newnham and the One-Damned-Thing-After-Another Society at Girton. On p. 6 she refers to herself as a lecturer. On p. 6 she suggests that you may throw "it" into the waste-paper basket. Well, you can't throw a lecture into the waste-paper basket. You can only walk out from a lecture, or treat your ears as Ulysses treated the ears of his fellow-mariners.

The book has a thesis: namely, that "it is necessary to have five hundred a year and a room with a lock on it if you are to write fiction or poetry." With the implied corollary that women, being usually without five hundred a year of their very own, and liable to everlasting interruption, are at a serious disadvantage as novelists and poets.

The thesis is disputable. Dostoevsky wrote some of the greatest novels in the world while he was continually distracted by terrible extra-artistic anxieties. And I beg to state that I have myself written long and formidable novels in bedrooms whose doors certainly had no locks, and in the full dreadful knowledge that I had not five hundred a year of my own—nor fifty. And I beg to state further that from the moment when I obtained possession of both money and a lockable door all the high-brows in London conspired together to assert that I could no longer write.

However, Virginia Woolf's thesis is not apparently important to her, since she talks about everything but the thesis. If her mind was not what it is I should accuse her of wholesale padding. This would be unjust. She is not consciously guilty of padding. She is merely the victim of her extraordinary gift of fancy (not imagination). If I had to make one of those brilliant generalisations now so fashionable, defining the difference between men and women, I should say that whereas a woman cannot walk through a meadow in June without wandering all over the place to pick attractive blossoms, a man can. Virginia Woolf cannot resist the floral enticement.

Some will describe her book as a feminist tract. It is no such thing. It is a book a little about men and a great deal about women. But it is not "feminist." It is non-partisan. The author writes: "Women are hard on women. Women dislike women. Women—but are you not sick to death of the word? I can assure you that I am." Admirable attitude! And she comes to no satisfactory conclusion about the disparateness of men and women. Because nobody ever has and nobody could.

You may walk along Prince Consort Road, and through the open windows of the Royal College of Music hear the scrapings, the tinklings and the trillings of a thousand young people trying to make themselves professional musicians. And you may reflect that ten years hence nine-tenths of the girls among them will have abandoned all scraping, tinkling and trilling for love, domesticity and (perhaps) cradles. And you may think that you have discovered the origin and explanation of the disparateness of men and women. Not so! Great opera-singers have borne child after child, and remained great opera-singers.

ANONYMOUS
___

From *Times Literary Supplement*   1929

A Room of One's Own. By Virginia Woolf. (The Hogarth Press. 5s. net.)

How she was able to effect all this is surprising, for she had no separate study to repair to, and most of the work must have been done in the general sitting-room, subject to all kinds of casual interruptions." These unobtrusive words have grown familiar; Jane Austen, the surprising person, has emerged into what to her would have been an inconceivable fame. Mrs. Woolf quotes the sentence in her essay, and it must have suggested the image for her title. It seems, certainly, to make a room of one's own look superfluous. But though there may have been men of letters, and perhaps women, who have been unperturbed by the chatter of their families, they probably did not feel obliged to hide their writing from the eyes of servants or visitors as Jane Austen did. By a sort of pre-established harmony within her she achieved the perfect result; the chief wonder lying, as Mrs. Woolf observes, in the entire absence from her books of any signs of fear, protest or resentment aroused in her by doing something which it seemed not quite creditable to do. For "a room of one's own," like the *arrière-boutique* of Montaigne, seems the natural symbol of detachment and calm; and it will stand as well for the material minimum of freedom, means and opportunity which is essential to a writer.

But—to keep to the main path of a delightfully peripatetic essay— these necessaries, spiritual and material, have been long in coming within the reach of women. It is common knowledge, no doubt, but it sparkles into life again as Mrs. Woolf describes what might have happened to an imaginary gifted sister of Shakespeare; or how Lady Winchilsea turned bitter and Margaret of Newcastle a little mad; or Charlotte Brontë was warped by indignations. Women in her day were certainly allowed to write, but the assumptions and values were all against them. Still more does an old story light up with an amusing gleam as these pages depict the rule of men and their assured, confident sense of superiority, which women have for ages helped to sustain by holding up a magical enlarging mirror. "Let them tell us what we are to them"; one thinks of the aside at a critical moment in "The Egoist."* Since the lead is ours, the leaders must bow their heads to the sentence . . . let them tell us of their side of the battle." Well, here—on one point—is the lively and suggestive answer. But meanwhile the battle has shifted. What women can do now, in Mrs. Woolf's belief, is to tell us what women are to women. They can explore their creative gift without fear of "the opposing faction." And if this essay, lightly as it moves, gives a vivid sense of what that means to women: if, also, it wittily "enlarges" their side of the case a little, it may be because it has grown from two papers read to audiences of women.

But the most interesting, if less diverting, points are those in which it touches the art of writing. It is certainly of interest to find an artist who has (one is tempted to say) so masculine a sense of literary form as Mrs. Woolf remarking that women must devise a "sentence" of their own, as the weight and stride of a man's mind are too unlike theirs to be useful. And since "the book has somehow to be adapted to the body," theirs should perhaps be shorter and more concentrated than men's books. Their fiction, too, has counted for more than their poetry, even if the first impulse was poetic. Here, among other causes, may be the straits of poverty—one thinks of the tragic case of Charlotte Mew. However, in her work or Emily Dickinson's, as in the higher and more accomplished art of Christina Rossetti or Alice Meynell, a certain concentrated quality reappears. So it does in Katherine Mansfield's stories, where at times one feels the point is almost too exactly made. Perhaps such concentration in little is women's equivalent to masculine grasp. "Grasp" seems to imply both a wider surface and a trenchancy not so much of emotion as of brain.

But here it is a question of the imaginative reason. Coleridge, who said that he had known strong minds "with Cobbett-like manners" but never a great mind of that sort, believed that all great minds must be androgynous. And it is that thought of his which Mrs. Woolf persuasively develops. There is nothing very startling in the belief that, with artistic natures at least, the man's mind has a share of the feminine and the woman's of the masculine, and that the two elements must fuse with and fertilize each other to produce a complete creation. So to Mrs. Woolf Shakespeare seems the type of the androgynous unimpeded mind, "though it would be impossible to say what Shakespeare thought of women." It would be amusing, and at times perplexing, to go on with illustrations. Coleridge, for instance, pronounced Wordsworth to be "*all* man." But we can hardly suppose that he excluded him from the great minds in consequence. Mrs. Woolf may provoke some surprise when she says that Mr. Galsworthy has not a spark of the woman in him. But though we may dispute cases, the principle itself

---

"*The Egoist*": A London-based literary review that replaced a feminist magazine called *The New Freewoman* when Ezra Pound took it over in 1913. The review took a leading role in defining the literary movement known as modernism (of which Woolf is a part).

bridges those divisions of sex-consciousness which are disastrous to our age and have led men, in Mrs. Woolf's opinion, to write only with the male side of their minds. And her essay, while it glances in a spirited and good-tempered way over conflicts old and new, is really always bent on more intrinsic matters. These, one might say, are a love of life, a love of freedom and of letters; meeting in the conviction that if a writer does what he should he will bring us into the presence of reality.

Ideas for Rereading

1. How does the extract from *Orlando* influence your ways of seeing the photograph of Virginia Woolf and the three representations of Orlando? What relationships do you see between the description of Orlando's clothing and appearance and the ways in which Woolf is dressed? How do the three images of Orlando work alongside the description of Orlando as she approaches the Italian coast? What specific things indicate the gender identity of Woolf and the three versions of Orlando? It might help you to review Woolf's definitions of the "man-womanly" and the "woman-manly" in the final pages of *A Room of One's Own* (p. 37).

2. Charlotte Perkins Gilman's "The New Generation of Women" was written five years before Woolf began to draft the lecture that would become *A Room of One's Own*. Reread Gilman's essay by focusing on her use of direct statement. Underline the places where Gilman makes direct proposals about what should be done to improve material conditions for women. Notice where she writes sentences that depend on words such as *should* and *is*. Notice her use of the word *but* and her use of quotation marks around certain words.

3. The Context section includes five reviews of *A Room of One's Own*. For the most part these reviews are enthusiastic, despite the delicate and often controversial nature of Woolf's subject. What can you learn from these reviews about Woolf's achievement in handling her task? What do the reviewers see as praiseworthy in her work, and what seem to be their chief concerns and misgivings? Why do you think reviewers praise Woolf for her "quiet, demure laughter" (Woodbridge, p. 57), for her ability to see "beyond the dissidence" (Williams, p. 55), and for being "stout-hearted and right-minded" (*Punch*, p. 59)? What do such comments reveal about prevailing attitudes toward women's rights in Woolf's time?

Ideas for Writing

1. Write an essay that describes and analyzes the contemporary reception of Woolf's book. Speculate about the reasons the reviewers concentrate on the specific parts they choose to cite. Which parts do the reviewers miss? In other words, if you were to write a review of *A Room of One's Own*, which parts would *you* cite?

2. Write a review of *A Room of One's Own*. You might model your review on one or more of the reviews included here or you might write in the style of a re-

view published in a newspaper, magazine, or other source that you are familiar with. If you are most familiar with music or movie reviews, you may apply the method of those reviewers to Woolf's essay. Notice that reviewers tend to assume an audience of people who have not read or heard or seen what is being reviewed; also notice that reviewers tend to assume a particular point of view.

3. Use *Orlando* and "The New Generation of Women" to write an essay examining Woolf's suggestion that "the androgynous mind is resonant and porous; that it transmits emotion without impediment; that it is naturally creative, incandescent and undivided" (p. 37). In what ways does the description of Orlando's thoughts as she realizes what it means to be a woman help you to understand Woolf's point about the androgynous mind? In what ways does Gilman's use of direct statement resonate with Woolf's commentary on "the Suffrage campaign" (p. 38)? How does Gilman's discussion of improvements in women's material conditions compare with Orlando's recognition of the advantages and disadvantages of being a woman?

CONTEMPORARY CONVERSATION

BELL HOOKS

bell hooks (who deliberately uses lowercase letters for her name) is a teacher, social critic, and writer. Born Gloria Watkins in 1950, hooks has taught at Oberlin College and Yale University and is now a Distinguished Professor of English at City College in New York. She has published more than twenty books, including Ain't I a Woman: Black Women and Feminism *(1981);* Yearning: Race, Gender, and Cultural Politics *(1990); and* Teaching to Transgress: Education as the Practice of Freedom *(1994). hooks challenges readers to understand the interdependency of racism, sexism, and classism. Refusing to place herself along one axis of self-definition—as a "woman"—hooks is sometimes criticized for going against the grain of "mainstream" feminism: hooks claims that as a black woman from the working class, she enjoys no "natural" allegiance with white, middle-class women because race and class transform what it means—and even what it might mean—to be a woman. As this selection from* Feminist Theory: From Margin to Center *(1984) makes clear, hooks is interested in women's liberation only as a consensual and collectivist movement that eradicates the entire system of hierarchical oppression. In this essay, hooks considers different definitions of feminism as they depend on different racial and economic conditions. Specifically she concerns herself with why many women are uncomfortable calling themselves feminists (even when they have obviously benefited from the feminist movement) and with ways in which "bourgeois" feminism creates "pre-packaged" ways of being a woman that are entirely suited to the needs of "the present white supremacist capitalist, patriarchal state" (p. 68). Against this middle-class feminism hooks argues for the creation of a movement that emphasizes "political commitment" rather than "individual identity and lifestyle (p. 73).*

Feminism
A Movement to End Sexist Oppression

A central problem within feminist discourse has been our inability to either arrive at a consensus of opinion about what feminism is or accept definition(s) that could serve as points of unification. Without agreed upon definition(s), we lack a sound foundation on which to construct theory or engage in overall meaningful praxis. Expressing her frustrations with the absence of clear definitions in a recent essay, "Towards a Revolutionary Ethics," Carmen Vasquez comments:

> We can't even agree on what a "Feminist" is, never mind what she would believe in and how she defines the principles that constitute honor among us. In key with the American capitalist obsession for individualism and anything goes so long as it gets you what you want. Feminism in America has come to mean anything you like, honey. There are as many definitions of Feminism as there are feminists, some of my sisters say, with a chuckle. I don't think it's funny.[1]

It is not funny. It indicates a growing disinterest in feminism as a radical political movement. It is a despairing gesture expressive of the belief that solidarity between women is not possible. It is a sign that the political naiveté which has traditionally characterized woman's lot in male-dominated culture abounds.

Most people in the United States think of feminism or the more commonly used term "women's lib" as a movement that aims to make women the social equals of men. This broad definition, popularized by the media and mainstream segments of the movement, raises problematic questions. Since men are not equals in white supremacist, capitalist, patriarchal class structure, which men do women want to be equal to? Do women share a common vision of what equality means? Implicit in this simplistic definition of women's liberation is a dismissal of race and class as factors that, in conjunction with sexism, determine the extent to which an individual will be discriminated against, exploited, or oppressed. Bourgeois white women interested in women's rights issues have been satisfied with simple definitions for obvious reasons. Rhetorically placing themselves in the same social category as oppressed women, they were not anxious to call attention to race and class privilege.

Women in lower class and poor groups, particularly those who are non-white, would not have defined women's liberation as women gaining social equality with men since they are continually reminded in their everyday lives that all women do not share a common social status. Concurrently, they know that many males in their social groups are exploited and oppressed. Knowing that men in their groups do not have social, political, and economic power, they would not deem it liberatory to share their social status. While they are aware that sexism enables men in their respective groups to have privileges denied them, they are more likely to see exaggerated expressions of male chauvinism among their peers as stemming from the male's sense of himself as powerless and ineffectual in relation to ruling male groups, rather than an expression of an overall privileged social status. From the very onset of the women's liberation movement, these women were suspicious of feminism precisely because they recognized the limitations inherent in its definition. They recognized the possibility that feminism defined as social equality with men might easily become a movement that would primarily affect the social standing of white women in middle and upper class groups while affecting only in a very marginal way the social status of working class and poor women.

Not all the women who were at the forefront of organized women's movement shaping definitions were content with making women's liberation synonymous with women gaining social equality with men. On the opening pages of *Woman Power: The Movement for Women's Liberation,* Cellestine Ware, a black woman active in the movement, wrote under the heading "Goals":

> Radical feminism is working for the eradication of domination and elitism in all human relationships. This would make self-determination the ultimate good and require the downfall of society as we know it today.[2]

Individual radical feminists like Charlotte Bunch based their analyses on an informed understanding of the politics of domination and a recognition of the inter-connections between various systems of domination even as they focused primarily on sexism. Their perspectives were not valued by those organizers and participants in women's movement who were more interested in social reforms. The anonymous authors of a pamphlet on feminist issues published in 1976, *Women and the New World,* make the point that many women active in women's liberation movement were far more comfortable with the notion of feminism as a reform that would help women attain social equality with men of their class than feminism defined as a radical movement that would eradicate domination and transform society:

> Whatever the organization, the location or the ethnic composition of the group, all the women's liberation organizations had one thing in common: they all came together based on a biological and sociological fact rather than on a body of ideas. Women came together in the women's liberation movement on the basis that we were women and all women are subject to male domination. We saw all women as being our allies and all men as being the oppressor. We never questioned the extent to which American women accept the same materialistic and individualistic values as American men. We did not stop to think that American women are just as reluctant as American men to struggle for a new society based on new values of mutual respect, cooperation and social responsibility.[3]

It is now evident that many women active in feminist movement were interested in reform as an end in itself, not as a stage in the progression towards revolutionary transformation. Even though Zillah Eisenstein can optimistically point to the potential radicalism of liberal women who work for social reform in *The Radical Future of Liberal Feminism,* the process by which this radicalism will surface is unclear. Eisenstein offers as an example of the radical implications of liberal feminist programs the demands made at the government-sponsored Houston conference on women's rights issues which took place in 1978:

> The Houston report demands as a human right a full voice and role for women in determining the destiny of our world, our nation, our families, and our individual lives. It specifically calls for (1) the elimination of violence in the home and the development of shelters for battered women, (2) support for women's business, (3) a solution to child abuse, (4) federally funded nonsexist child care, (5) a policy of full employment so that all women who wish and are able to work may do so, (6) the protection of homemakers so that marriage is a partnership, (7) an end to the sexist portrayal of women in the media, (8) establishment of reproductive freedom and the end to involuntary sterilization, (9) a remedy to the double discrimination against minority women, (10) a revision of criminal codes dealing with rape, (11) elimination of discrimination on the basis of sexual preference, (12) the establishment of nonsexist education, and (13) an examination of all welfare reform proposals for their specific impact on women.[4]

The positive impact of liberal reforms on women's lives should not lead to the assumption that they eradicate systems of domination. Nowhere in these demands is there an emphasis on eradicating the politic of domination, yet it would need to be abolished if any of these demands were to be met. The lack of any emphasis on domination is consistent with the liberal feminist belief that women can achieve equality with men of their class without challenging and changing the cultural basis of group oppression. It is this belief that negates the likelihood that the potential radicalism of liberal feminism will ever be realized. Writing as early as 1967, Brazilian scholar Heleith Saffioti emphasized that bourgeois feminism has always been "fundamentally and unconsciously a feminism of the ruling class," that:

> Whatever revolutionary content there is in petty-bourgeois feminist praxis, it has been put there by the efforts of the middle strata, especially the less well off, to move up socially. To do this, however, they sought merely to expand the existing social structures, and never went so far as to challenge the status quo. Thus, while petty-bourgeois feminism may always have aimed at establishing social equality between the sexes, the consciousness it represented has remained utopian in its desire for and struggle to bring about a partial transformation of society; this it believed could be done without disturbing the foundations on which it rested. . . . In this sense, petty-bourgeois feminism is not feminism at all; indeed it has helped to consolidate class society by giving camouflage to its internal contradictions . . .[5]

Radical dimensions of liberal women's social protest will continue to serve as an ideological support system providing the necessary critical and analytical impetus for the maintenance of a liberalism that aims to grant women greater equality of opportunity within the present white supremacist capitalist, patriarchal state. Such liberal women's rights activism in its essence diminishes feminist struggle. Philosopher Mihailo Markovic discusses the limitations of liberalism in his essay "Women's Liberation and Human Emancipation":

> Another basic characteristic of liberalism which constitutes a formidable obstacle to an oppressed social group's emancipation is its conception of human nature. If selfishness, aggressiveness, the drive to conquer and dominate, really are among defining human traits, as every liberal philosopher since Locke tries to convince us, the oppression in civil society — i.e., in the social sphere not regulated by the state — is a fact of life and the basic civil relationship between a man and a woman will always remain a battlefield. Woman, being less aggressive, is then either the less human of the two and doomed to subjugation, or else she must get more power-hungry herself and try to dominate man. Liberation for both is not feasible.[6]

Although liberal perspectives on feminism include reforms that would have radical implications for society, these are the reforms which will be resisted precisely because they would set the stage for revolutionary transformation were they implemented. It is evident that society is more responsive to those "feminist" demands that are not threatening, that may even help maintain the status quo. Jeanne Gross gives an example of this co-optation of feminist strategy in her essay "Feminist Ethics from a Marxist Perspective," published in 1977:

> If we as women want change in all aspects of our lives, we must recognize that capitalism is uniquely capable of co-opting piecemeal change. . . . Capitalism is capable of taking our visionary changes and using them against us. For example, many married women, recognizing their oppression in the family, have divorced. They are thrown, with no preparation of protection, into the labor market. For many women this has meant taking their places at the row of typewriters. Corporations are now recognizing the capacity for exploitation in divorced women. The turnover in such jobs is incredibly high. "If she complains, she can be replaced."[7]

Particularly as regards work, many liberal feminist reforms simply reinforced capitalist, materialist values (illustrating the flexibility of capitalism) without truly liberating women economically.

Liberal women have not been alone in drawing upon the dynamism of feminism to further their interests. The great majority of women who have benefited in any way from feminist-generated social reforms do not want to be seen as advocates of feminism. Conferences on issues of relevance to women, that would never have been organized or funded had there not been a feminist movement, take place all over the United States and the participants do not want to be seen as advocates of feminism. They are either reluctant to make a public commitment to feminist movement or sneer at the term. Individual African-American, Native American Indian, Asian-American, and Hispanic American women find themselves isolated if they support feminist movement. Even women who may achieve fame and notoriety (as well as increased economic income) in response to attention given their work by large numbers of women who support feminism may deflect attention away from their engagement with feminist movement. They may even go so far as to create other terms that express their concern with women's issues so as to avoid using the term feminist. The creation of new terms that have no relationship to organized political activity tend to provide women who may already be reluctant to explore feminism with ready excuses to explain their reluctance to participate. This illustrates an uncritical acceptance of distorted definitions of feminism rather than a demand for redefinition. They may support specific issues while divorcing themselves from what they assume is feminist movement.

In a recent article in a San Francisco newspaper, "Sisters—Under the Skin," columnist Bob Greene commented on the aversion many women apparently have to the term feminism. Greene finds it curious that many women "who obviously believe in everything that proud feminists believe in dismiss the term 'feminist' as something unpleasant; something with which they do not wish to be associated." Even though such women often acknowledge that they have benefited from feminist-generated reform measures which have improved the social status of specific groups of women, they do not wish to be seen as participants in feminist movement:

> There is no getting around it. After all this time, the term "feminist" makes many bright, ambitious, intelligent women embarrassed and uncomfortable. They simply don't want to be associated with it.
>
> It's as if it has an unpleasant connotation that they want no connection with. Chances are if you were to present them with every mainstream feminist belief, they would go along with the beliefs to the letter—and even if they consider themselves feminists, they hasten to say no.[8]

Many women are reluctant to advocate feminism because they are uncertain about the meaning of the term. Other women from exploited and oppressed ethnic groups dismiss the term because they do not wish to be perceived as supporting a racist movement; feminism is often equated with white women's rights effort. Large numbers of women see feminism as synonymous with lesbianism; their homophobia leads them to reject association with any group identified as pro-lesbian. Some women fear the word "feminism" because they shun identification with any political movement, especially one perceived as radical. Of course there are women who do not wish to be associated with women's rights movement in any form so they reject and oppose feminist movement. Most women are more familiar with negative perspectives on "women's lib" than the positive significations of feminism. It is this term's positive political significance and power that we must now struggle to recover and maintain.

Currently feminism seems to be a term without any clear significance. The "anything goes" approach to the definition of the word has rendered it practically meaningless. What is meant by "anything goes" is usually that any woman who wants social equality with men regardless of her political perspective (she can be a conservative right-winger or a nationalist communist) can label herself feminist. Most attempts at defining feminism reflect the class nature of the movement. Definitions are usually liberal in origin and focus on the individual woman's right to freedom and self-determination. In Barbara Berg's *The Remembered Gate: Origins of American Feminism,* she defines feminism as a "broad movement embracing numerous phases of woman's emancipation." However, her emphasis is on women gaining greater individual freedom. Expanding on the above definition, Berg adds:

> It is the freedom to decide her own destiny; freedom from sex-determined role; freedom from society's oppressive restrictions; freedom to express her thoughts fully and to convert them freely into action. Feminism demands the acceptance of woman's right to individual conscience and judgment. It postulates that woman's essential worth stems from her common humanity and does not depend on the other relationships of her life.[9]

This definition of feminism is almost apolitical in tone; yet it is the type of definition many liberal women find appealing. It evokes a very romantic notion of personal freedom which is more acceptable than a definition that emphasizes radical political action.

Many feminist radicals now know that neither a feminism that focuses on woman as an autonomous human being worthy of personal freedom nor one that focuses on the attainment of equality of opportunity with men can rid society of sexism and male domination. Feminism is a struggle to end sexist oppression. Therefore, it is necessarily a struggle to eradicate the ideology of domination that permeates Western culture on various levels as well as a commitment to reorganizing society so that the self-development of people can take precedence over imperialism, economic expansion, and material desires. Defined in this way, it is unlikely that women would join feminist movement simply because we are biologically the same. A commitment to feminism so defined would demand that each individual participant acquire a critical political consciousness based on ideas and beliefs.

All too often the slogan "the personal is political" (which was first used to stress that woman's everyday reality is informed and shaped by politics and is necessarily political) became a means of encouraging women to think that the experience of discrimination, exploitation, or oppression automatically corresponded with an understanding of the ideological and institutional apparatus shaping one's social status. As a consequence, many women who had not fully examined their situation never developed a sophisticated understanding of their political reality and its relationship to that of women as a collective group. They were encouraged to focus on giving voice to personal experience. Like revolutionaries working to change the lot of colonized people globally, it is necessary for feminist activists to stress that the ability to see and describe one's own reality is a significant step in the long process of self-recovery; but it is only a beginning. When women internalized the idea that describing their own woe was synonymous with developing a critical political consciousness, the progress of feminist movement was stalled. Starting from such incomplete perspectives, it is not surprising that theories and strategies were developed that were collectively inadequate and misguided. To correct this inadequacy in past analysis, we must now encourage women to develop a keen, comprehensive understanding of women's political reality. Broader perspectives can only emerge as we examine both the personal that is political, the politics of society as a whole, and global revolutionary politics.

Feminism defined in political terms that stress collective as well as individual experience challenges women to enter a new domain—to leave behind the apolitical stance sexism decrees is our lot and develop political consciousness. Women know from our everyday lives that many of us rarely discuss politics. Even when women talked about sexist politics in the heyday of contemporary feminism, rather than allow this engagement with serious political matters to lead to complex, in-depth analysis of women's social status, we insisted that men were "the enemy," the cause of all our problems. As a consequence, we examined almost exclusively women's relationship to male supremacy and the ideology of sexism. The focus on "man as enemy" created, as Marlene Dixon emphasizes in her essay "The Rise and Demise of Women's Liberation: A Class Analysis," a "politics of psychological oppression" which evoked world views which "pit individual against individual and mystify the social basis of exploitation."[10] By repudiating the popular notion that the focus of feminist movement should be social equality of the sexes and emphasizing eradicating the cultural basis of group oppression, our own analysis would require an exploration of all aspects of women's political reality. This would mean that race and class oppression would be recognized as feminist issues with as much relevance as sexism.

When feminism is defined in such a way that it calls attention to the diversity of women's social and political reality, it centralizes the experiences of all women, especially the women whose social conditions have been least written about, studied, or changed by political movements. When we cease to focus on the simplistic stance "men are the enemy," we are compelled to examine systems of domination and our role in their maintenance and perpetuation. Lack of adequate definition made it easy for bourgeois women, whether liberal or radical in perspective, to maintain their dominance over the leadership of the movement and its direction. This hegemony continues to exist in most feminist organizations. Exploited and oppressed groups of women are usually encouraged by those in power to feel that their situation is hopeless, that they can do nothing to break the pattern of domination. Given such socialization, these women have often felt that our only response to white, bourgeois, hegemonic dominance of feminist movement is to trash, reject, or dismiss feminism. This reaction is in no way threatening to the women who wish to maintain control over the direction of feminist theory and praxis. They prefer us to be silent, passively accepting their ideas. They prefer us speaking against "them" rather than developing our own ideas about feminist movement.

Feminism is the struggle to end sexist oppression. Its aim is not to benefit solely any specific group of women, any particular race or class of women. It does not privilege women over men. It has the power to transform in a meaningful way all our lives. Most importantly, feminism is neither a lifestyle nor a ready-made identity or role one can step into. Diverting energy from feminist movement that aims to change society, many women concentrate on the development of a counter-culture, a woman-centered world wherein participants have little contact with men. Such attempts do not indicate a respect or concern for the vast majority of women who are unable to integrate their cultural expressions with the visions offered by alternative woman-centered communities. In *Beyond God the Father*, Mary Daly urged women to give up "the securities offered by the patriarchal system" and create new space that would be woman-centered. Responding to Daly, Jeanne Gross pointed to the contradictions that arise when the focus of feminist movement is on the construction of new space:

> Creating a "counterworld" places an incredible amount of pressure on the women who attempt to embark on such a project. The pressure comes from the belief that the only true resources for such an endeavor are ourselves. The past which is totally patriarchal is viewed as irredeemable. . . .
>
> If we go about creating an alternative culture without remaining in dialogue with others (and the historical circumstances that give rise to their identity) we have no reality check for our goals. We run the very real risk that the dominant ideology of the culture is re-duplicated in the feminist movement through cultural imperialism.[11]

Equating feminist struggle with living in a counter-cultural, woman-centered world erected barriers that closed the movement off from most women. Despite sexist discrimination, exploitation, or oppression, many women feel their lives as they live them are important and valuable. Naturally the suggestion that these lives could be simply left or abandoned for an alternative "feminist" lifestyle met with resistance. Feeling their life experiences devalued, deemed solely negative and worthless, many women responded by vehemently attacking feminism. By rejecting the notion of an alternative feminist "lifestyle" that can emerge only when women create a subculture (whether it is living space or even space like women's studies that at many campuses has become exclusive) and insisting that feminist struggle can begin wherever an individual woman is, we create a movement that focuses on our collective experience, a movement that is continually mass-based.

Over the past six years, many separatist-oriented communities have been formed by women so that the focus has shifted from the development of woman-centered space towards an emphasis on identity. Once woman-centered space exists, it can be maintained only if women remain convinced that it is the only place where they can be self-realized and free. After assuming a "feminist" identity, women often seek to live the "feminist" lifestyle. These women do not see that it undermines feminist movement to project the assumption that "feminist" is but another pre-packaged role women can now select as they search for identity. The willingness to see feminism as a lifestyle choice rather than a political commitment reflects the class nature of the movement. It is not surprising that the vast majority of women who equate feminism with alternative lifestyle are from middle class backgrounds, unmarried, college-educated, often students who are without many of the social and economic responsibilities that working class and poor women who are laborers, parents, homemakers, and wives confront daily. Sometimes lesbians have sought to equate feminism with lifestyle but for significantly different reasons. Given the prejudice and discrimination against lesbian women in our society, alternative communities that are woman-centered are one means of creating positive, affirming environments. Despite positive reasons for developing woman-centered space (which does not need to be equated with a "feminist" lifestyle), like pleasure, support, and resource-sharing, emphasis on creating a counter-culture has alienated women from feminist movement, for such space can be in churches, kitchens, etc.

Longing for community, connection, a sense of shared purpose, many women found support networks in feminist organizations. Satisfied in a personal way by new relationships generated in what was called a "safe," "supportive" context wherein discussion focused on feminist ideology, they did not question whether masses of women shared the same need for community. Certainly many black women as well as women from other ethnic groups do not feel an absence of community among women in their lives despite exploitation and oppression. The focus on feminism as a way to develop shared identity and community has little appeal to women who experience community, who seek ways to end exploitation and oppression in the context of their lives. While they may develop an interest in a feminist politic that works to eradicate sexist oppression, they will probably never feel as intense a need for a "feminist" identity and lifestyle.

Often emphasis on identity and lifestyle is appealing because it creates a false sense that one is engaged in praxis. However, praxis within any political movement that aims to have a radical transformative impact on society cannot be solely focused on creating spaces wherein would-be-radicals experience safety and support. Feminist movement to end sexist oppression actively engages participants in revolutionary struggle. Struggle is rarely safe or pleasurable.

Focusing on feminism as political commitment, we resist the emphasis on individual identity and lifestyle. (This should not be confused with the very real need to unite theory and practice.) Such resistance engages us in revolutionary praxis. The ethics of Western society informed by imperialism and capitalism are personal rather than social. They teach us that the individual good is more important than the collective good and consequently that individual change is of greater significance than collective change. This particular form of cultural imperialism has been reproduced in feminist movement in the form of individual women equating the fact that their lives have been changed in a meaningful way by feminism "as is" with a policy of no change need occur in the theory and praxis even if it has little or no impact on society as a whole, or on masses of women.

To emphasize that engagement with feminist struggle as political commitment we could avoid using the phrase "I am a feminist" (a linguistic structure designed to refer to some personal aspect of identity and self-definition) and could state "I advocate feminism." Because there has been undue emphasis placed on feminism as an identity or lifestyle, people usually resort to stereotyped perspectives on feminism. Deflecting attention away from stereotypes is necessary if we are to revise our strategy and direction. I have found that saying "I am a feminist" usually means I am plugged into preconceived notions of identity, role, or behavior. When I say "I advocate feminism" the response is usually "what is feminism?" A phrase like "I advocate" does not imply the kind of absolutism that is suggested by "I am." It does not engage us in the either/or dualistic thinking that is the central ideological component of all systems of domination in Western society. It implies that a choice has been made, that commitment to feminism is an act of will. It does not suggest that by committing oneself to feminism, the possibility of supporting other political movements is negated.

As a black woman interested in feminist movement, I am often asked whether being black is more important than being a woman; whether feminist struggle to end sexist oppression is more important than the struggle to end racism and vice-versa. All such questions are rooted in competitive either/or thinking, the belief that the self is formed in opposition to an other. Therefore one is a feminist because you are not something else. Most people are socialized to think in terms of opposition rather than compatibility. Rather than see anti-racist work as totally compatible with working to end sexist oppression, they are often seen as two movements competing for first place. When asked "Are you a feminist?" it appears that an affirmative answer is translated to mean that one is concerned with no political issues other than feminism. When one is black, an affirmative response is likely to be heard as a devaluation of struggle to end racism. Given the fear of being misunderstood, it has been difficult for black women and women in exploited and oppressed ethnic groups to give expression to their interest in feminist concerns. They have been wary of saying "I am a feminist." The shift in expression from "I am a feminist" to "I advocate feminism" could serve as a useful strategy for eliminating the focus on identity and lifestyle. It could serve as a way women who are concerned about feminism as well as other political movements could express their support while avoiding linguistic structures that give primacy to one particular group. It would also encourage greater exploration in feminist theory.

The shift in definition away from notions of social equality towards an emphasis on ending sexist oppression leads to a shift in attitudes in regard to the development of theory. Given the class nature of feminist movement so far, as well as racial hierarchies, developing theory (the guiding set of beliefs and principles that become the basis for action) has been a task particularly subject to the hegemonic dominance of white academic women. This has led many women outside the privileged race/class group to see the focus on developing theory, even the very use of the term, as a concern that functions only to reinforce the power of the elite group. Such reactions reinforce the sexist/racist/classist notion that developing theory is the domain of the white intellectual. Privileged white women active in feminist movement, whether liberal or radical in perspective, encourage black women to contribute "experiential" work, personal life stories. Personal experiences are important to feminist movement but they cannot take the place of theory. Charlotte Bunch explains the special significance of theory in her essay "Feminism and Education: Not By Degrees":

> Theory enables us to see immediate needs in terms of long-range goals and an overall perspective on the world. It thus gives us a framework for evaluating various strategies in both the long and the short run and for seeing the types of changes that they are likely to produce. Theory is not just a body of facts or a set of personal opinions. It involves explanations and hypotheses that are based on available knowledge and experience. It is also dependent on conjecture and insight about how to interpret those facts and experiences and their significance.[12]

Since bourgeois white women had defined feminism in such a way as to make it appear that it had no real significance for black women, they could then conclude that black women need not contribute to developing theory. We were to provide the colorful life stories to document and validate the prevailing set of theoretical assumptions.[13] Focus on social equality with men as a definition of feminism led to an emphasis on discrimination, male attitudes, and legalistic reforms. Feminism as a movement to end sexist oppression directs our attention to systems of domination and the inter-relatedness of sex, race, and class oppression. Therefore, it compels us to centralize the experiences and the social predicaments of women who bear the brunt of sexist oppression as a way to understand the collective social status of women in the United States. Defining feminism as a movement to end sexist oppression is crucial for the development of theory because it is a starting point indicating the direction of exploration and analysis.

The foundation of future feminist struggle must be solidly based on a recognition of the need to eradicate the underlying cultural basis and causes of sexism and other forms of group oppression. Without challenging and changing these philosophical structures, no feminist reforms will have a long range impact. Consequently, it is now necessary for advocates of feminism to collectively acknowledge that our struggle cannot be defined as a movement to gain social equality with men; that terms like "liberal feminist" and "bourgeois feminist" represent contradictions that must be resolved so that feminism will not be continually co-opted to serve the opportunistic ends of special interest groups.

Notes

1. Carmen Vasquez, "Towards a Revolutionary Ethics," p. 1.

2. Cellestine Ware, *Woman Power,* p. 3.

3. *Women and the New World,* p. 33.

4. Zillah Eisenstein, p. 232.

5. Heleith Saffioti, *Women in Class Society,* p. 223.

6. Mihailo Markovic, "Women's Liberation and Human Emancipation," pp. 145–67.

7. Jeanne Gross, "Feminist Ethics from a Marxist Perspective," pp. 52–56.

8. Bob Greene, "Sisters under the Skin," p. 3.

9. Barbara Berg, *The Remembered Gate.*

10. Marlene Dixon, "The Rise and Demise of Woman's Liberation: A Class Analysis," p. 61.

11. Gross, p. 54.

12. Charlotte Bunch, "Feminism and Education: Not By Degrees," pp. 7–18.

13. An interesting discussion of black women's responses to feminist movement may be found in the essay "Challenging Imperial Feminism" by Valerie Amos and Pratibha Parmar in the Autumn 1984 issue of *Feminist Review.*

Works Cited

Berg, Barbara. *The Remembered Gate: Origins of American Feminism.* New York: Oxford University Press, 1979.

Bunch, Charlotte. "Feminism and Education: Not By Degrees." *Quest,* Vol. V, No. 1 (Summer 1979), pp. 1–7.

Dixon, Marlene. *Women in Class Struggle.* San Francisco: Synthesis Publications, 1980.

Eisenstein, Zillah. *The Radical Future of Liberal Feminism.* New York: Longman, 1981.

Greene, Bob. "Sisters under the Skin," in *San Francisco Examiner* (San Francisco), May 15, 1983.

Gross, Jeanne. "Feminist Ethics from a Marxist Perspective," in *Radical Religion,* Vol. III, No. 2 (1977), pp. 52–56.

Markovic, Mihailo. "Women's Liberation and Human Emancipation," in *Women and Philosophy.* Eds. Carol Gould and Mary Wartofsky. New York: G. P. Putnam, 1976, pp. 145–67.

Saffioti, Heleith I. B. *Women in Class Society.* New York: Monthly Review Press, 1978.

Vasquez, Carmen. "Towards a Revolutionary Ethics," in *Coming Up,* January 1983, p. 11.

Ware, Cellestine. *Woman Power: The Movement for Women's Liberation.* New York: Tower Publications, 1970.

Women and the New World. Detroit: Advocators, 1976.

Ideas for Rereading

1. Academic writers use quotations for a variety of reasons. bell hooks is the most prolific user of long quotations in this book. Reread her essay, attending to her use of long quotations. Begin by numbering each of the indented quotations in hooks's essay. Write notes for each quotation that summarize the quotation. Then explain how each quotation functions in the essay. Why might hooks have chosen to include these specific quotations? What does each add to her essay? How does hooks's introduction and discussion of each quotation assist in your understanding of why hooks quotes these specific passages? How does she connect each quotation with her own writing?

2. Make a list of the writers that hooks cites to support the form of feminism that she advocates. Annotate the list by describing the exact position of each writer she quotes. Make further notes suggesting how the writers she agrees with differ from those she associates with liberal feminism. Which words and phrases give you the best way of understanding what hooks advocates and what she opposes? How does hooks's form of feminism promise to "eradicate systems of domination" (p. 67)? In what ways does the kind of feminism she opposes reinforce these systems? What criticisms does hooks direct at "liberal women's social protest" (p. 68)?

Ideas for Writing

1. Toward the end of her essay, hooks argues that "the shift in definition away from notions of social equality towards an emphasis on ending sexist oppression leads to a shift in attitudes in regard to the development of theory" (p. 75). In a way, then, "Feminism: A Movement to End Sexist Oppression" becomes an essay about the different ways in which "theory" contributes to feminist struggle; it becomes theoretical analysis of theory.

Use direct quotations and analysis of those quotations to write an essay in which you consider the value of "theories" (which we might define as "ways of thinking") in discussions of what it means, or might mean, to be a woman. Some of the following questions might help you draft your essay. How does hooks respond to and use other people's theories about feminism? What main theories does hooks summarize and how do these ways of thinking differ in terms of their perspectives, their ideas, and their definitions? How does each of these ways of thinking imagine interactions between and among everyday life, personal identity, political commitment, and theory? How does Charlotte Bunch contribute to hooks's ways of thinking about the role of theory?

2. Write an essay discussing how hooks uses quotations from scholars, theorists, and elsewhere. How do these source materials contribute to her ways of thinking about feminism? What different functions do these scholarly sources serve in hooks's essay? (You might think about this question by imagining what the essay would be like *without* the quotations.) As you begin to evaluate hooks's ways of thinking about feminism, you might consider how her theory reinforces, changes, challenges, or otherwise influences your own ways of thinking about feminism and sexism.

3. Write an essay applying hooks's essay to *A Room of One's Own*. In what ways does Woolf's book demonstrate hooks's opening argument that "a central problem within feminist discourse has been our inability to either arrive at a consensus of opinion about what feminism is or accept definition(s) that could serve as points of unification"? To you, does Woolf seem like someone "interested in reform as an end in itself" (p. 66)? Or are there ways in which her work points toward a "revolutionary transformation" (p. 67)? Pay attention to specific passages in Woolf and hooks, speculating on what hooks would think of Woolf. Which parts of Woolf would hooks be likely to criticize? Which parts might she applaud?

AUDRE LORDE

Born to West Indian parents, Audre Lorde (1934–1992) was a poet, novelist, essayist, and teacher. She dealt in much of her writing with her experience as a black woman and a lesbian. She published twelve volumes of poetry and was named the poet laureate of New York in 1991. Her writing is passionate, sometimes romantic, sometimes angry even to the point of fury. "I have a duty," she states in Black Women Writers (1950–1980): A Critical Evaluation, *"to speak the truth as I see it and to share not just my triumphs, not just the things that felt good, but the pain, the intense, often unmitigating pain."* The Cancer Journals, *a moving account of her struggle with the cancer to which she ultimately succumbed, bears out the depth of her commitment to this principle.* The Collected Poems of Audre Lorde *was published posthumously in 1997.*

In the 1960s, Lorde worked as a librarian; in 1970, she began a distinguished career as a teacher. She taught until 1979 in the English department at John Jay College of Criminal Justice and from 1980 to 1988 as professor of English at Hunter College of the City University of New York. "The Transformation of Silence into Language and Action," collected in Sister Outsider, *was originally presented as a lecture before an audience of professors and graduate students at the Modern Language Association's 1977 convention, in a panel called "The Lesbian and Literature."*

Whereas Woolf is careful to avoid using I *in a way that refers directly to herself, in this essay Lorde uses the word as an indicator of strictly personal, we might even say "private," experience. As you read the essay pay specific attention to the ways in which Lorde uses her own experiences as the basis of her argument. Notice how she uses other pronouns such as* you *and* we. *How does Lorde use personal and private experiences to create a sense of collective purpose?*

The Transformation of Silence into Language and Action

I have come to believe over and over again that what is most important to me must be spoken, made verbal and shared, even at the risk of having it bruised or misunderstood. That the speaking profits me, beyond any other effect. I am standing here as a Black lesbian poet, and the meaning of all that waits upon the fact that I am still alive, and might not have been. Less than two months ago I was told by two doctors, one female and one male, that I would have to have breast surgery, and that there was a 60 to 80 percent chance that the tumor was malignant. Between that telling and the actual surgery, there was a three-week period of the agony of an involuntary reorganization of my entire life. The surgery was completed, and the growth was benign.

But within those three weeks, I was forced to look upon myself and my living with a harsh and urgent clarity that has left me still shaken but much stronger. This is a situation faced by many women, by some of you here today. Some of what I experienced during that time has helped elucidate for me much of what I feel concerning the transformation of silence into language and action.

In becoming forcibly and essentially aware of my mortality, and of what I wished and wanted for my life, however short it might be, priorities and omissions became strongly etched in a merciless light, and what I most regretted were my silences. Of what had I *ever* been afraid? To question or to speak as I believed could have meant pain, or death. But we all hurt in so many different ways, all the time, and pain will either change or end. Death, on the other hand, is the final silence. And that might be coming quickly, now, without regard for whether I had ever spoken what needed to be said, or had only betrayed myself into small silences, while I planned someday to speak, or waited for someone else's words. And I began to recognize a source of power within myself that comes from the knowledge that while it is most desirable not to be afraid, learning to put fear into a perspective gave me great strength.

I was going to die, if not sooner then later, whether or not I had ever spoken myself. My silences had not protected me. Your silence will not protect you. But for every real word spoken, for every attempt I had ever made to speak those truths for which I am still seeking, I had made contact with other women while we examined the words to fit a world in which we all believed, bridging our differences. And it was the concern and caring of all those women which gave me strength and enabled me to scrutinize the essentials of my living.

The women who sustained me through that period were Black and white, old and young, lesbian, bisexual, and heterosexual, and we all shared a war against the tyrannies of silence. They all gave me a strength and concern without which I could not have survived intact. Within those weeks of acute fear came the knowledge—within the war we are all waging with the forces of death, subtle and otherwise, conscious or not—I am not only a casualty, I am also a warrior.

What are the words you do not yet have? What do you need to say? What are the tyrannies you swallow day by day and attempt to make your own, until you will sicken and die of them, still in silence? Perhaps for some of you here today, I am the face of one of your fears. Because I am woman, because I am Black, because I am lesbian, because I am myself—a

Black woman warrior poet doing my work—come to ask you, are you doing yours?

And of course I am afraid, because the transformation of silence into language and action is an act of self-revelation, and that always seems fraught with danger. But my daughter, when I told her of our topic and my difficulty with it, said, "Tell them about how you're never really a whole person if you remain silent, because there's always that one little piece inside you that wants to be spoken out, and if you keep ignoring it, it gets madder and madder and hotter and hotter, and if you don't speak it out one day it will just up and punch you in the mouth from the inside."

In the cause of silence, each of us draws the face of her own fear—fear of contempt, of censure, or some judgment, or recognition, of challenge, of annihilation. But most of all, I think, we fear the visibility without which we cannot truly live. Within this country where racial difference creates a constant, if unspoken, distortion of vision, Black women have on one hand always been highly visible, and so, on the other hand, have been rendered invisible through the depersonalization of racism. Even within the women's movement, we have had to fight, and still do, for that very visibility which also renders us most vulnerable, our Blackness. For to survive in the mouth of this dragon we call america, we have had to learn this first and most vital lesson—that we were never meant to survive. Not as human beings. And neither were most of you here today, Black or not. And that visibility which makes us most vulnerable is that which also is the source of our greatest strength. Because the machine will try to grind you into dust anyway, whether or not we speak. We can sit in our corners mute forever while our sisters and our selves are wasted, while our children are distorted and destroyed, while our earth is poisoned; we can sit in our safe corners mute as bottles, and we will still be no less afraid.

In my house this year we are celebrating the feast of Kwanza, the African-american festival of harvest which begins the day after Christmas and lasts for seven days. There are seven principles of Kwanza, one for each day. The first principle is Umoja, which means unity, the decision to strive for and maintain unity in self and community. The principle for yesterday, the second day, was Kujichagulia—self-determination—the decision to define ourselves, name ourselves, and speak for ourselves, instead of being defined and spoken for by others. Today is the third day of Kwanza, and the principle for today is Ujima—collective work and responsibility—the decision to build and maintain ourselves and our communities together and to recognize and solve our problems together.

Each of us is here now because in one way or another we share a commitment to language and to the power of language, and to the reclaiming of that language which has been made to work against us. In the transformation of silence into language and action, it is vitally necessary for each one of us to establish or examine her function in that transformation and to recognize her role as vital within that transformation.

For those of us who write, it is necessary to scrutinize not only the truth of what we speak, but the truth of that language by which we speak it. For others, it is to share and spread also those words that are meaningful to us. But primarily for us all, it is necessary to teach by living and speaking those truths which we believe and know beyond understanding. Because in this way alone we can survive, by taking part in a process of life that is creative and continuing, that is growth.

And it is never without fear—of visibility, of the harsh light of scrutiny and perhaps judgment, of pain, of death. But we have lived through all of those already, in silence, except death. And I remind myself all the time now that if I were to have been born mute, or had maintained an oath of silence my whole life long for safety, I would still have suffered, and I would still die. It is very good for establishing perspective.

And where the words of women are crying to be heard, we must each of us recognize our responsibility to seek those words out, to read them and share them and examine them in their pertinence to our lives. That we not hide behind the mockeries of separations that have been imposed upon us and which so often we accept as our own. For instance, "I can't possibly teach Black women's writing—their experience is so different from mine." Yet how many years have you spent teaching Plato and Shakespeare and Proust? Or another, "She's a white woman and what could she possibly have to say to me?" Or, "She's a lesbian, what would my husband say, or my chairman?" Or again, "This woman writes of her sons and I have no children." And all the other endless ways in which we rob ourselves of ourselves and each other.

We can learn to work and speak when we are afraid in the same way we have learned to work and speak when we are tired. For we have been socialized to respect fear more than our own needs for language and definition, and while we wait in silence for that final luxury of fearlessness, the weight of that silence will choke us.

The fact that we are here and that I speak these words is an attempt to break that silence and bridge some of those differences between us, for it is not difference which immobilizes us, but silence. And there are so many silences to be broken.

Ideas for Rereading

1. Lorde's prose style is rhythmic and poetic. As you reread her essay, pay close attention to the sounds and rhythms of words and phrases. Choose one paragraph or short passage that seems to you striking for its aural effects and write it out as though it were poetry. Analyze this passage of Lorde's prose in terms of its use of poetic techniques such as alliteration, metaphor, rhyme, and meter.

2. Respond in your notebook to this passage: "But primarily for us all, it is necessary to teach by living and speaking those truths which we believe and know beyond understanding. Because in this way alone we can survive, by taking part in a process of life that is creative and continuing, that is growth"

(p. 81). How do you understand these sentences? How might they apply to your own experience?

Ideas for Writing

1. Lorde's essay draws on personal experience, but she writes in a public voice that is directed outward, to a live audience. Write an essay in which you respond to Lorde's argument, but imitate the movement of her essay from personal to public. Move outward from personal experience to public voice, beginning with personal experiences but making them relevant to an audience of your peers. This assignment asks you to contemplate the transformative effects of experiences that have influenced how you think about the world or that have helped you define your relationship with a particular community. These may be experiences that you have come to understand only with hindsight and they should, somehow, become the basis of ways of thinking that are relevant not only to your present and future life but also to other people. In other words, you should describe and analyze personal or communal experiences with a view to showing what they have taught *you* and what they might teach other people.

2. Choose a passage from Lorde's essay and a passage from Woolf's *A Room of One's Own* that seem to work together in interesting ways, ones that seem interestingly connected or contrasting. The passages might be as brief as a phrase or as long as a page or two. You will need to choose the passages carefully. One way to proceed is to choose one passage that describes an experience and another that develops a specific way of thinking; or you might choose two passages that set out to define what women "must" do. Write an essay in which you discuss the relationship between the two passages you have chosen. What do you learn from placing them side by side?

Patricia Williams

Patricia Williams (b. 1951) is a law professor who specializes in commercial law. After graduating from Harvard Law School in 1975, Williams worked for three years in the Office of the City Attorney in Los Angeles and then became staff lawyer at the Western Center on Law and Poverty. Since 1980 she has taught at the University of Wisconsin, the City University of New York, and Golden Gate University School of Law. She now teaches at Columbia University. Williams has worked at Stanford's Institute for Research on Women and Gender and has published widely in both scholarly journals and the mainstream press in the areas of race, gender, and law and on other issues of legal theory and legal writing. Williams is the author of two collections of autobiographical essays, The Alchemy of Race and Rights: Diary of a Law Professor *(1993) and* The Rooster's Egg: On the Persistence of Prejudice *(1997). Her most recent publication is a long essay published as* Seeing a Color Blind Future: The Paradox of Race *(1998).*

The great-great-granddaughter of a slave and a white southern lawyer, Williams has built her career on the irrefutable assertion that "race" is a relatively recent, and entirely political and social, invention: there is no scientific, genetic basis for racial categorizations. In the 1997 BBC Reith Lectures that were published in revised form as Seeing a Color Blind Future, Williams set herself the following questions: "How precisely does the issue of color remain so powerfully determinative of everything from life circumstance to manner of death, in a world that is, by and large, officially 'color-blind'? What metaphors mask the hierarchies that make racial domination frequently seem so 'natural,' so invisible, indeed so attractive? How does racism continue to evolve, after slavery and after legislated equality, across such geographic, temporal, and political distance?" Herself a single African American mother, Williams in her recent work explodes the myth of the "black welfare queen" as both a symptom and a cause of current racist and sexist views of the welfare "problem." The fact that the majority of people receiving welfare are white women (many of whom have received the short end of a divorce settlement or are fugitives from abusive husbands) means nothing to those who "indulge in their masturbatory mulling about black welfare queens who purportedly reproduce like rabbits" in order to gain an extra two dollars a week from the government. Ultimately we might say that Williams contributes to contemporary moves away from absolute distinctions and toward theories of border-crossing. In a note at the end of The Alchemy of Race and Rights, Williams puts it thus:

> While being black has been the most powerful social attribution in my life, it is only one of a number of governing narratives or presiding fictions by which I am constantly reconfiguring myself in the world. Gender is another, along with ecology, pacifism, my peculiar brand of colloquial English, and Roxbury, Massachusetts. The complexity of role identification, the politics of sexuality, the infections of professionalized discourse—all prescribe and impose boundary in my life, even as they confound one another in unfolding spirals of confrontation, deflection, and dream. (256)

In this essay from The Alchemy of Race and Rights Williams uses personal experience as a platform for a series of observations about contemporary culture. The challenge in reading the first part of the essay comes from its use of jumps between subjects that are induced by Williams's temporary craziness, by channel-surfing on the television, and by skipping between newspaper stories. Even though Williams lets her thoughts spill onto the page as though unedited, a pattern emerges. As you read her essay try to identify this pattern. Take notes about what she explicitly says to connect her various subjects. Also take notes about connections that you see. Notice how she uses the word I in the essay. Also pay close attention to the places where she makes a parenthetical aside such as the one introduced with "Of course this won't work" (p. 88) and the one that begins "Yet, as a social statistic" (p. 93). What do these and other parenthetical remarks add to the essay? How does her use of quotation marks for specific words and phrases contribute to her essay?

Owning the Self in a Disowned World
(a menagerie of nightmares and hallucinations)

> Dr. Temple Grandin of the University of Illinois has shown that pigs like toys that dangle and people that are solicitous. In a five-week experiment, pigs with rubber hoses hanging in their pens were found to be less excitable. . . . The pigs did not get fatter any faster, but they were easier to

handle. They went through a narrow chute more willingly, which is useful at the slaughterhouse. Pigs in a panic can get bruised, and stress affects the texture and appearance of their meat.

Visits also pacify the pigs. In the same experiment, pigs that had been visited by a handler for only five minutes each week were less excitable and easier to handle than those that had been left alone. For the visit to count, a handler had to enter the pen; saying hello from an aisle was not enough. But such fraternizing can be overdone. One student spent so much time with her pigs that they refused to go through the chute to oblivion.[1]

It is early on a weekday afternoon. I sit at home watching a PBS children's program called *3–2–1 Contact*. A woman with a smarmy talking-down-for-children voice is conducting an interview of Frank Perdue at his chicken farm. The camera is panning the "plant room" where 250,000 chicks have hatched, all only a few hours old. They are placed on a long assembly line, packed on so that the black conveyor belt is yellow with densely piled chicks; human hands reach out at high speed and inoculate each fuzzy yellow chick by slamming it against an inoculator and throwing it back on the line. At the end of that line is a chute—and a shot of chicks scrambling for footing as they are dumped from a height onto yet another assembly line. Cute, catchy, upbeat music accompanies their tumbling, a children's song for the hurtling chicks.

"We deliver the little baby chicks in schoolbuses to the farms," says the voice of Frank Perdue. The interviewer laughs. "So it's like they're going off to kindergarten?" She holds a chick in her hand and strokes it like a pet. "You take really good care of them, don't you?" she says softly, as though to the chick. "We have to," says Frank Perdue. "It's our business." Fade to the farm: here they feed a million chicks a week. The farm is actually a huge factory building. The chickens never go outside. They are kept indoors all their lives, it is explained, because otherwise it would be "too unsanitary."

I switch channels. A soap-opera actress is the guest on some talk show. Her character has recently died on the soap opera, and the host shows a still photograph of that demise to the audience. The photo shows her body, crumpled in a twisted heap, bruised, abandoned in an alley, a trickle of blood seeping from her mouth. The talk host says in a hearty voice to the live studio audience, as well as to those of us viewers at home in the afterworld, "Remember that scene, guys? So how about a nice hand for the lovely . . ." and the audience applauds warmly.

I'm at home watching television in the middle of the afternoon because I don't feel well. I have a headache and think I'm going crazy. The world is filled with rumor and suspicion: Elvis has been reborn. I see the news in the *Midnight Sun* or the *Noonday Star,* some paper with a heavenly body in the name. Elsewhere there is a sighting of a whole tribe of Elvises, reborn in the Amazonian rain forest. They have been singing "Hound Dog" and beating on drums for an estimated five thousand years. The most amazing reincarnation of all, however, occurs on the Oprah Winfrey show, manifested in the body of a young black rap singer named L. D. Shore, rising to fame as "the Black Elvis." It is divinely parodic: Elvis, the white black man of a generation ago, reborn in a black man imitating Elvis.

I wonder, in my disintegration into senselessness, in whom I shall be reborn. What would "the white Pat Williams" look like? Have I yet given birth to myself as "the black Pat Williams"? I wonder about children, how I might be split in order to give life; I wonder how to go about inventing a child.

Recently, in Massachusetts, a woman who suffered a miscarriage in a drunk-driving accident was charged with vehicular homicide when the fetus was delivered stillborn.[2] I suppose this makes sense from the perspective of some litigation model in which mother "versus" fetus is the order of the day, in which the shell of a woman's body is assumed to be at cross-purposes with the heart within. It makes no sense from the perspective of a model in which woman and fetus are one, and in which the home of the body is also the site of sheer torment; it makes no sense from the sad seductive wisdom of self-destruction.

I edit myself as I sit before the television. I hold myself tightly and never spill into the world that hates brown spills. I'm afraid that everything I am will pour out onto the ground and be absorbed without a word. I may disappear. So I hold onto myself because I still have much left to say. I am brown by own invention, a crazy island, a suspicious hooded secret. One day I will give birth to myself, lonely but possessed. I organize my dreams in anticipation, combing out the frustration, ironing the pleats of my complications: soft empty complicated soft lonely. Dreaming all the time.

On TV, in between the chickens and the Amazon, there is a news snippet about a pregnant inmate in a Missouri prison who is suing the state on behalf of her unborn fetus, claiming that the thirteenth amendment prevents imprisonment of the fetus because it has not been tried, charged, and sentenced. The suit is premised on a Missouri antiabortion statute declaring that life begins at conception; the inmate is arguing that such a statute affords a fetus all the rights of personhood. "The fetus should not serve a sentence for the mother," says Michael Box, the Kansas City attorney representing the inmate.[3] Hearing about this case makes my head throb even harder, and my craziness advances several notches. Somewhere at the back of my head I remember having gone crazy before, only a few months ago, over a story about another pregnant woman, this one in Washington, D.C., who was put into prison by a judge to keep her off the streets and out of drug-temptation's way, ostensibly in order to *protect* her fetus.[4] In the litigation that followed, the underlying issue turned out to be similar to the one in the Missouri case: the living conditions for prisoners, whether pregnant or not, but epitomized by the lack of exercise, health care, and nutrition so necessary for prenatal nurture.

My head is throbbing because these cases don't make sense to me. I don't believe that a fetus is a separate person from the moment of conception; how could it be? It is interconnected, flesh-and-blood-bonded, completely a part of a woman's body. Why try to carve one from the other? Why is there no state interest in not simply providing for but improving the circumstances of the woman, whether pregnant or not? I'm not sure I believe that a child who has left the womb is really a separate person until sometime after the age of two. The entire life force is a social one, a process of grafting onto our surroundings and then growing apart and then grafting again, all in our own time and in all kinds of ways that defy biological timetables alone. (But I have been called extreme in this, and by my own mother, from whom I have not even yet moved fully apart.)

In both of these cases, it seems to me, the Idea of the child (the fetus) becomes more important than the actual Child (who will be reclassified as an adult in the flick of an eye in order to send him back to prison on his own terms), or the actual condition of the woman of whose body the real fetus is a part. In both cases the idea of the child is pitted against the woman; her body, and its need for decent health care, is suppressed in favor of a conceptual entity that is innocent, ideal, and all potential.

It seems only logical, I think while applying a cold compress to my brow, that in the face of a statute like Missouri's, pregnant women would try to assert themselves through their fetuses; that they would attempt to rejoin what has been conceptually pulled asunder. They would of course attempt to assert their own interests through the part of themselves that overlaps with some architecture of the state's interest, in order to recreate a bit of the habitable world within the womb of their protective-destructive prisons.

In bargaining this way, however, pregnant women trade in interests larger than the world of prisoners' rights. In having the fetus declared an other person, in allowing the separation in order to benefit the real mutuality, they enslave themselves to the state. They become partialized, moreover, in the commodification of that bargain, as a prostitute becomes seen only as a "cunt" and as pigs dressed for slaughter become only "hoof," "head," or "hide." Pregnant women become only their fetuses; they disguise and sacrifice the rest of themselves and their interests in deference to the state's willingness to see only a small part of their need. The fetus thus becomes an incorporation of the woman, a business fiction, an uncomfortable tapestry woven from rights-assertion-given-personhood. It is an odd, semiprivate, semipublic undertaking, in which an adversarial relationship is assumed between the public and the private.

What a cycle of absurdity, I think as the melting ice drips down my nose: protecting the fetus from the woman by putting her in jail, then protecting the fetus from jail by asserting the lack of due process accorded the fetus in placing it there. The state's paternalism in these cases is very like the nightmare of another woman I read about, named Melody Baldwin, who injected her baby with her own toxic antidepressant medication in order to protect the infant from the toxin of life's despair: it was a madperson's metaphor of maternalism.[5]

It's all enough to drive a person legally insane (but then of course the person would get thorazine).

After a while I turn off the television and pick up the newspaper. I think to find solace there, but the world gets weirder and weirder all the time. This particular day there's a story about a couple who deposited the husband's sperm in a bank and then some time later the wife came back to be artificially inseminated. In due time she gave birth to a child "whom she describes as black." (Did I forget to mention that the couple is white?) Though officials of the fertility clinic insist with the unflappable certitude of biological imperative and scientific imperialism that "the sperm that impregnated the woman and which resulted in the birth of her child did not come from this sperm bank," the woman charges the clinic with negligence and medical malpractice. She says that "her insemination 'became a tragedy and her life a nightmare.' " While stating that the child's "color has nothing to do with her anguish," the woman sued when the "racial taunting of her child became unbearable":

> [Her lawyer] said that she "loves her 3-year-old daughter very much."
>
> But he said the child was the repeated target of "racial teasing and embarrassment" and "she is determined that what happened to her and her daughter doesn't happen to any other couple."
>
> By contending that her daughter is a victim of prejudice, the woman is building a case for monetary damages.[6]

I ponder this case about the nightmare of giving birth to a black child who is tormented so that her mother gets to claim damages for emotional distress. I think about whether my mother shouldn't bring such a suit, both of us having endured at least the pain of my maturation in the racism of the Boston public school system. Do black mothers get to sue for such an outcome, or is it just white mothers? I wonder if this child can get damages of her own, for having been born to a litigation-happy white mother. I think about whether this might not be a nifty way of collecting reparations, this suit for racial deviance as breach of birthright, a broken warranty of merchantability in the forum of marketed actors.

I think about suing. This is not, mind you, the usual case of "wrongful life." In those cases a woman who thought she had been sterilized, for example, gives birth to triplets. The family sues for the cost of raising said children. Typically, at least an argument can be made, as one case put it, that

> the parents' suit for recovery of the child rearing costs is in no reasonable sense a signal to the child that the parents consider the child an unwanted burden. They obviously want to keep the child. The love, affection, and emotional support any child needs they are prepared to give. But these things do not bring with them the economic means that are also necessary

to feed, clothe, educate, and otherwise raise the child. That is what this suit is about, and we trust the child in the future will be well able to distinguish the two. Relieving the family of the economic costs of raising the child may well add to the emotional well-being of the entire family, including this child.[7]

Instead, this mother's is a suit for the emotional tragedy of a child's having been born into the pinnacle of her own unlove.

I try to concoct a suit out of my own life's circumstances. What mistake can I blame for having been born into an intolerant world? Whom can I charge with the damage that will not be healed for many generations?

On the bulletin board just outside my office, there hangs a notice from the department of obstetrics and gynecology of the University of Wisconsin. It offers fifty dollars for every semen specimen "we are able to use" in an artificial-insemination program. Donors must be under thirty-five years old and have a college degree. I wonder every time I enter my office at this market of selling sperm to women of the world desperately desiring to reproduce tall blond Nobel Prizewinners or, in the unavailability of that, then tall probably-blond college graduates.

And I think, in a technological age, guerrilla warfare must be redefined. I dream of the New Age manifesto: We must all unite, perhaps with the help of white male college graduates who are willing to smuggle small hermetically sealed vials of black sperm into the vaulted banks of unborn golden people; we must integrate this world from the inside out. We must smuggle not the biological code alone, but the cultural experience. We must shake up biological normativity; bring our cause down to particulars, to the real terms of what is at stake in the debate. We must be able to assert the battle from within, and in the most intimate terms conceivable. (Of course this won't work. We will end up with yet another generation of abandoned children, damaged in the manufacture, returned to the supplier, and sued for in the effort to undo their existence by the translation of the disaster of them into compensatory dollars and cents.)

I suggest guerrilla insemination to challenge the notion of choice, to complicate it in other contexts: the likelihood that white women would choose black characteristics if offered the supermarket array of options of blond hair, blue-green eyes, and narrow upturned noses. What happens if it is no longer white male seed that has the prerogative of dropping noiselessly and invisibly into black wombs, swelling ranks and complexifying identity? Instead it will be disembodied black seed that will swell white bellies; the symbolically sacred vessel of the white womb will bring the complication home to the guarded intimacy of white families, and into the madonna worship of the larger culture.

I suppose I'd better disclaim this as a serious exhortation, lest people start actually doing it and I get arrested in this brave new world for inciting reproductive riot. But it is interesting to examine the image it evokes, the vision of white mothers rushing to remedy the depreciation of their offspring in suits about the lost property of their children's bodies—this is the gut of why such a prospect would be terrifying to so many women, why such a child would be hard to love, even when one's very own. How profound the hatred, how deep the bigotry that lives beneath the skin, that wakens in this image of black life blooming within white. It becomes an image not of encompassment but of parasitism. It is an image that squeezes racism out from the pores of people who deny they are racist, or who say it's not racism that makes them fear blacks but the high crime rate or some such.

I am overwhelmed by this image: the vault of sperm banks. The clean container of white wombs. The swift messenger, the hermetic fire of white phallic power. The material principia of semen, sperm, paternity. From dross into capital. The daughter's born blackness as accident, as awful, as "fault" that must be rehabilitated and deterred by adequate compensation (although the mother in this case rather coyly refused to reveal exactly how much she was seeking in damages).

In Missouri a man named Steven Goodwin is an inmate in a federal prison. He and his wife are suing to allow him to father a child by artificial insemination. "The Federal Bureau of Prisons has refused this request, saying the process involved would interfere with orderly operation of the correction system." The case is now before the U.S. Court of Appeals for the Seventh Circuit. The Goodwins' attorney contends: "There is a body of law that says no matter who you are, you are allowed to have children. . . . The prison comes along and says they have a right to prevent conjugal visits. But we aren't questioning that. All we are asking for is a clean container and a swift messenger."[8]

There are 650,000 young black men in the U.S. penal system today, or approximately 23 percent of all black men between the ages of twenty and twenty-nine.[9] The increasing majority of them are there for drug-related offenses. Only 450,000 young black men are enrolled in U.S. colleges today; all the rest, we must conclude, are thus ineligible to deposit their sperm in the elite vaults of the University of Wisconsin's department of obstetrics and gynecology.

Instinct and extinction. The markers between life and death, black and white, male and female, sense and sensibility. The boundary between jail and the wide open plain. The threshold of childbearing, the lost generation. Old age, if it ever comes.

I think back to the black child whose white mother is suing over the breach of such divisions—what will happen if the mother wins this suit? What will she buy with the money? Into what exactly will this compensation be transformed? What will be the manifestation of pecuniary healing, the remedial token to mend the mirage of belonging? In some central way, this child is the icon of our entire civilization. The pure child, the philosopher's child, the impossible union of elements, forged in a crucible of torment, rattling the bars of her model prison, to wit, the schoolyards and the quiet streets of small "safe" white American towns; the black daughter's very integration at the heart of her duality. Trapped in racial circumstance; a little Frankenstein of ingredients, intolerably fearsome even to her creator, this monster child's racial hermaphrodism, the unpropertied guerrilla birth of herself, like a condensation, a rain of isolated social confrontations, like a prayer without answer.

It is the next day and I have more or less put myself back together. I am at a reading group on race/gender/class and critical legal thought. The topic is Harvard Law School professor Derrick Bell's new book *And We Are Not Saved* (1987). The chapter being discussed is called "The Race-Charged Relationship of Black Men and Black Women." The chapter deals generally with the social construction of antimiscegenation laws; forced sterilization and castration; the structure of the black family; teenage pregnancy; and the disproportionate number of black men in U.S. prisons. But the precise subject within the chapter that has caught everyone's attention is a surprising parable, "The Chronicle of the Twenty-Seventh-Year Syndrome." The Chronicle is structured as an interiorized dream had by Bell; he then tells it to an exteriorized dream-vision-anima figure named Geneva Crenshaw. In the dream, Twenty-Seventh-Year Syndrome is an affliction affecting only young black professional women: if they are not married to, or have not yet received a marriage proposal from, a black man by their twenty-seventh year, they fall into a deep coma from which they awaken only after several weeks, physically intact but having lost all their professional skills.

This story has scared everyone in the room, including me, to death. The conversation is very, very anxious and abstract. Big words rush through the air, careening dangerously close to my head. Defining feminism. Undefining feminism. Women/men. Black/white. Biology/social construction. Male creation/control of sexuality. Challenge/structure. Post-legal-realist feminist/feminist. Identify/define/understand. Privilege of white womanhood/self-flagellation. Problematic/useful. Critique of patriarchy/pervasive abstracted universal wholeness. Actual/historical pathways to possibility/perversion. And the cabbagehead of hegemony.

Sitting quietly in the vortex, I try to recall the last time I heard such definitional embattlement. Suddenly a sharp voice cuts through all the rest and states: "But look, we have One right here—a single black female over the age of twenty-seven, from whom we haven't heard anything—let's give her a chance to speak!" A hush falls over the room. I look up from my musings to find every head in the room turned toward me.

The world is full of black women who have never really been heard from. Take Maxine Thomas, for example. According to one version, Los Angeles Municipal Court Judge Maxine Thomas' nervous breakdown was inexplicable. ("'I thought Maxine was a lady of unlimited potential.' said Reginald Dunn, of the Los Angeles City Attorney's office."[10]) She was as strong a black woman as ever conjured—a celebrated, savvy judge who presided over hundreds of mostly white male judges. Yet one day she just snapped and had to be carted from her chambers, helpless as a baby. ("Clerk Richard Haines found Thomas—the first black woman to head the Municipal Court and a role model for young blacks in Los Angeles—slumped in her leather chair. The 40-year-old judge's head was bowed, and she wept uncontrollably.")

Another version has it that Judge Thomas was overcommitted. She had bitten off more than she could chew; she had too many irons in the fire; and she just wasn't competent or skillful enough to handle it all. ("'She's a small, frail person,' said Johnnie L. Cochran Jr., a prominent attorney and longtime Thomas friend. 'A human being breaks. . . . All these things turned in on her.'")

Some said that she was manic-depressive and that her endless politicking was nothing less than shamelessly irresponsible self-promotion, clearly the sign of an unbalanced black woman. ("Pampered, emotionally immature and unforgiving on one hand, she could also be seductively charming, selflessly kind. In public, she could inspire children with her speeches on how to succeed. In private, faced with disappointment or dissension, she could resort to temper tantrums.")

Others said she was a woman who, like many women, thought of herself through other people. A woman who drained others in search of herself. A woman who criticized others into conformity; who used others as substitutes for herself, as self-extenders, screens, crutches, and statements. A woman who was nothing without others. ("'I think that all along there was a perception of her by a not unsubstantial group of people that there was more form than substance, that there was a lot of razzle-dazzle and not a lot to back it up,' said one of [her] critics. Like several others, this judge asked not to be identified to avoid further rancor on the court.")

A woman who had forgotten her roots. ("The only child of a janitor and a sometime domestic worker, Thomas grew up in the heart of South-Central Los Angeles in a nondescript frame house. . . . She was adored as a child, coddled as an adult. . . . 'Maxine never had to do anything. She wasn't the type of girl who ever had to clean up her room,' said actress Shirley Washington, Thomas' closest friend and confidante for the past 16 years.")

A woman who exploited her blackness. ("Attorney Cochran, who now represents Thomas, characterizes her as having 'reached almost heroine status in the black community.' . . . 'She was a very friendly young lawyer with a great future,' said Atty. Gen. John K. Van de Kamp, who first met Thomas in the early 1970's. 'It was a time for strong and able black women.'")

A woman who was too individualistic. ("'I think she thought the job carried a certain power it just doesn't carry,' said retired Municipal Judge Xenophon Lang Sr. 'You're certainly not the boss of other judges. . . . You're not a king of anything or queen of anything.'")

A woman who couldn't think for herself. ("'She wasn't able to function very well,' said Justice Joan Dempsey Klein, who reviewed Thomas' performance.")

A woman who had the perfect marriage. ("Her career in chaos, Thomas focused on her private life and a new romantic interest. He was Donald Ware, a never-married cardiologist who admired her 'fighting spirit.' It seemed the perfect match, and after only a few months, Ware bought her a 4-carat diamond engagement ring.")

A woman who had no marriage at all. ("There was only one glitch in the fairy tale scenario. The wedding wasn't legal. The couple weren't married. They had no valid marriage license, and for that Ware blames Thomas. Thomas blames Ware.")

A woman who overpowered her men and assaulted their manhood. ("In all, the honeymoon trip lasted three weeks, the volcanic 'marriage' about four. . . . 'The girl wanted everything, my money and my income,' Ware said afterward. 'Our personal life has been a tragedy. She's got a lot of problems and wanted to give me problems.'")

A woman who was too emotional. ("'She wasn't professional,' said one judge who observed Thomas at work. 'I remember her clapping her hands when there was a settlement. . . . The way she would exclaim her glee was not very judgelike.'")

A woman who needed to loosen up. ("'People were afraid, truly afraid to confront her . . . because of a reputation, right or wrong, of vindictiveness . . . ,' one judge said. 'She probably came on the court with more political power than probably any of the other judges.'")

A woman who took her profession too seriously. ("'Here's a girl who was basically a straight-A student all her life, who never knew what rejection was, never knew what failure was until she decided to run for Superior Court,' Washington said. '. . . After the election, I went over there and had to pull her out of bed. All she was saying, "It isn't fair; it's not fair."'")

A woman who didn't take her profession seriously enough. ("She launched a night version of small claims court and then joined her judicial colleague Richard Adler in promoting a program to process short civil cases at night and in opening a special small claims court for visitors to the 1984 Olympics. Thomas was written up in the newspapers, not part of the routine for most Municipal Court judges. There was rumbling among some of the judges, and in private the more critical of them began deriding her, questioning where she was trying to go with her splashy programs and complaining that she was neglecting the nitty-gritty work of the court.")

My mother's most consistent message to me, growing up, was that I must become a professional woman. My only alternative, as she presented it, was to "die in the gutter." There was no in-between. My mother was a gritty realist, a chess player always on the verge of checkmate, cagey, wary, protective. And so I became a professional woman.

According to the best statistics available, I am the perfect average black professional woman. Single, never married—"For black career women single at age 30, the chances of marriage are only 8 percent. By age 35 it has dropped to 2.4 percent and by age 40, 0.7 percent."[11]—having bred a statistically negligible number of children. I supposed I should be miserable, but it's not the end of the world. The very existence of such a statistical category is against all the odds, is company enough for me. I feel no inclination to marry myself off just because I'm single. I like being single. (Yet, as a social statistic, sometimes I feel less like I'm single than socially widowed. Sometimes when I walk down the street and see some poor black man lying over a heating vent, I feel as if I'm looking into the face of my companion social statistic, my lost mate—so passionate, original, creative, fine-boned, greedy, and glorious—lying in the gutter, as my mother envisioned, lost, tired, drunk, howling.) Nor do I feel the obligation to have children just because engineering social statisticians say I am "better able" to parent than the vast majority of black women who, being lower-class, are purportedly "least able" to parent.[12] (Yet sometimes I wonder what denial of the death all around me, what insistence on the holy grail of a certain promised form of life, keeps me from taking into my arms the companions to my sorrow—real orphans, black and brown children who languish in institutional abandon, children born of desperate caring, unions of explosive love, with lives complicated at a more intimate level than I can know by guttered hopes and homelessness.)

It is early morning, the day after the seminar on race, gender, and class. In the next room my mother, who is visiting me, rises and prepares to greet the day. She makes several little trips to the bathroom, in developing stages of undress and dress. Back and forth, from bedroom to bath, seeking and delivering small things: washcloth, eyeliner, stockings, lipstick. The last trip to the bathroom is always the longest because it is then that she does her face and hair. Next door I can hear the anxiety of her preparations: the creaking of the floorboards as she stands closer then farther from the mirror; the lifting and replacing of infinite bottles and jars on the shelves; the click of her closing a compact of blush; the running of water over her hairbrush; an anonymous fidgety frequency of sounds. She is a constancy of small motions, clatters, soft rattles and bumps. When she leaves the bathroom at last, she makes one final trip to the bedroom, then goes downstairs, completely composed, with quick brave steps.

When I get up in the morning I stare in the mirror and stick on my roles: I brush my teeth, as a responsibility to my community. I buff my nails, paving the way for my race. I comb my hair in the spirit of pulling myself up by the bootstraps. I dab astringent on my pores that I might be a role model upon whom all may gaze with pride. I mascara my eyelashes that I may be "different" from all the rest. I glaze my lips with the commitment to deny pain and "rise above" racism.

I gaze in the mirror and realize that I'm very close to being Maxine. When I am fully dressed, my face is hung with contradictions; I try not to wear all my contradictions at the same time. I pick and choose among them; like jewelry, I hunt for this set of expectations that will go best with that obligation. I am just this close.

Judge Maxine Thomas' job as black female judge was to wear all the contradictions at the same time, to wear them well and reconcile them. She swallowed all the stories, all the roles, opening wide to all the expectations. Standing in the mirror, I understand the logic of her wild despair, the rationality of her unbounded rage. I understand the break she made as necessary and immediate. Her impatient self-protection was the incantation of an ancient and incomprehensible restlessness. Knowing she was to be devoured by life, she made herself inedible, full of thorns and sharp edges.

She split at the seams and returned to the womb. She lay huddled in a wilderness of meaning, lost, a speechless child again, her accommodative language heard as babble, the legacy of KKK and Nigger spilling from her heart, words and explanations seeping from her. Giving birth to a thousand possibilities, she exploded into fragments of intelligence and scattered wisdom. Her clerk found her curled into fetal position, crying in her chambers. She was singing her small songs, magic words, soothsayings of comfort and the inky juice of cuttlefish. She was singing the songs of meadow saffron and of arbor vitae, of eel serum and marking nut, snowberry, rue-bitterwort, and yew. She had—without knowing, yet feeling the way of power—invoked sea onion, shepherd's purse, red clover. In her desperation, she had called upon divinations larger than herself: pinkroot, aquilegia, jambol seeds, thornapple, and hedge-hyssop.

Her bailiff turned her in. (He, the taskmaster of the threshold world, the marker of the order of things. The tall protector of the way that things must be, a fierce border guard, bulldog-tough in his guarding of the gate, whose reward was not the scrap of salary but the satisfaction, the deep, solid warmth that comes from making-safe. How betrayed he must have felt when this warm-brown woman rose over her needled rim and rebuked him; told him, in her golden madness, above all to mix, mix it all up. Such conscientious, sacrilegious mockery of protective manhood.)

Once over the edge, once into the threshold world, another sober archangel, her attorney and spokesperson, announced to the public that not only was it unlikely she would ever be able to rejoin the ranks of the judiciary, but she would probably never be able to rejoin the ranks of practicing lawyers. Needing so much to be loved, and lacking the professionalism to intercede on behalf of those less fortunate than she, it is unlikely she will ever be heard from again.

It is two days after the seminar, and I am finally able to think directly about Derrick Bell's Chronicle of the Twenty-Seventh-Year Syndrome—this thorn of a story, a remarkable gauntlet cast into sadness and confusion.

Here, finally, are my thoughts on the matter. Giving it every benefit of the doubt, Bell's story is about gender relations as a political issue. The issue in the twenty-seventh year is not only the behavior or lack of political black mates; the issue is also the hidden, unmentionable secret between us—the historic white master-mate. Romantic love is the fantasy bridge across this silent chasm. The wider the chasm, the more desperately passionate the structuring of our compensatory vision.

The deep sleep into which the women of the twenty-seventh year fall is an intellectual castration—they are cut off from black community as well as from all their knowledge and talent and training. The acquisition of professionalism is sexualized: its assertion masculinizes as well as whitens. Professionalism, according to this construction, is one of several ways to get marooned in an uncomprehending white and patriarchal society; thus it sets women up to be cut off and then lost in the profundity of that world's misunderstanding and shortcoming.

The blackness of black people in this society has always represented the blemish, the uncleanliness, the barrier separating individual and society. Castration from blackness becomes the initiatory tunnel, the portal through which black people must pass if they are not to fall on their faces in the presence of society, paternity, and hierarchy. Once castrated they have shed their horrid mortality, the rapacious lust of lower manhood, the raucous, mother-witted passion of lower womanhood, and opened themselves up to participation in the pseudo-celestial white community. Intellectual castration is for blacks a sign of suffering for the Larger Society's love; and a sign to others, as in the Chronicle of the Twenty-Seventh-Year Syndrome, of membership in the tribe of those who need to be loved best.

For most blacks, however, this passage from closure to openness turns out not to be a passage from mortality to divine revelation—but openness in the opposite direction: openness as profane revelation. Not communion, but exposure, vulnerability, the collapse of boundary in the most assaultive way. White society takes the place of the blinding glory of Abraham's God: Pharaoh, not Yahweh.

Another thought I have about this Chronicle is Bell's use of the imaginary Geneva Crenshaw: throughout *And We Are Not Saved* Geneva Crenshaw, this witchy, dream-filled wishing-woman, is his instrument by which to attack the monolithism of white patriarchal legal discourse. She is an anti–Founding Father, wandering across time to the Constitutional Convention and back again, a source of aboriginal wisdom and intent. She is the word creation by which he legitimizes his own critique, as he delegitimizes the limits of the larger body of law's literature. She is the fiction who speaks from across the threshold to the powerful unfiction of the legal order; he argues with her, but he owns her, this destroyer of the rational order. Yet the Chronicle of the Twenty-Seventh Year is the only one of all the Chronicles in *And We Are Not Saved* that is not of her telling, that Bell owns by himself. In a reversal of roles, she receives *his* story and critiques it; from this "outside position," it is easy to forget that Geneva Crenshaw is not a real, objective third person, but part of the author. She is an extension of Bell, no less than the doctrines of precedent and of narrow constructionism are extensions of the judges who employ them. She is an opinion, no less than any judge's opinion, an invention of her author; an outgrowth of the text; a phantom.

I remember that my father used to use my sister and me in this way. He would write poems of extraordinary beauty and interest; he wanted to publish them but did not. He gave them to us instead. That way he could resolve his need for audience in safety; with his daughters as judges, he was assured a kind and gloating reception. Fears of failure or success or exposure motivated him, I suppose; but it placed my sister and me — or me, in any event — in a remarkably authoritative position. I was powerful. I knew what I was expected to say and I did my duty. The fact that I meant it didn't matter. What I did was a lie, no matter how much I believed or not in the talent of his poetry. My power was in living the lie that I was all audiences. My power was in the temptation to dissemble, either out of love or disaffection. This is blacks' and women's power, I used to think, the power to lie while existing in the realm of someone else's fantasy. It is the power to refrain from exerting the real, to shift illusion, while serving as someone else's weaponry, nemesis, or language club.

After meeting my new sisters, these inventions of Derrick Bell's mind, I began to wonder what would happen if I told my father the truth. What would happen if I were to cut through the fantasy and really let him know that I am not an extension of his pen; what if I were to tell him that I like his writing (or not), but in my own words and on my own terms?

By the same token, what would happen if the victims of Twenty-Seventh-Year Syndrome were to awaken from their coma, no longer merely derivative of the black or white male experience but sharper-tongued than ever? Whose legitimacy would be at risk? Theirs? Bell's? Geneva Crenshaw's? The twenty-seven-year-olds who can't shake the sleep from their eyes?

Or is there any risk at all?

[An undated entry from my computer files written sometime after the seminar:

A dream. I am in an amphitheater, creeping around the back wall. I am not supposed to be there — it is after hours, the theater is not open to the general public. On the stage, dead center, surrounded by a circle of friends, spotlighted in the quiet dark of the theater, is a vision, a version of myself. I am wearing my hair in an exaggerated beehive (a style I affected only once, fresh from an application of the hotcomb, at the age of twelve) and a sequined low-cut red dress (a dress I actually wore, once again, at the liberated age of twenty-three). There I am with that hair and that ridiculous cowgirl dress: it is an eye scorcher of a sparkling evening gown, my small breasts stuffed into it and uplifted in a way that resembles cleavage.

The me-that-is-on-stage is laughing loudly and long. She is extremely vivacious, the center of attention. She is, just as I have always dreamed of being, fascinating: showy yet deeply intelligent. She is not beautiful in any traditional sense, as I am not in real life — her mouth and teeth are very large, her nose very long, like a claymation model of myself — but her features are riveting. And she is radiantly, splendidly good-natured. She is lovely in the oddest possible combination of ways. I sit down in the small circle of friends-around-myself, to watch myself, this sparkling homely woman, dressed like a moment lost in time. I hear myself speaking: *Voices lost in the chasm speak from the slow eloquent fact of the chasm. They speak and speak and speak, like flowing water.*

From this dream, into a complicated world, a propagation of me's awakens, strong, single-hearted, and completely refreshed.]

Notes

1. "Tales of the Farmyard," *Economist,* July 8, 1989, p. 75.

2. Christopher Daly, "Woman Charged in Death of Own Fetus in Accident," *Washington Post,* November 25, 1989, p. A4.

3. "Missouri Fetus Unlawfully Jailed, Suit Says," *New York Times,* August 11, 1989, p. B5.

4. Victoria Churchville, "D.C. Judge Jails Woman as Protection for Fetus," *Washington Post,* July 23, 1988, p. 1.

5. "Proposal for Woman's Sterilization Draws Protest," *New York Times,* September 26, 1988, p. 30.

6. Ronald Sullivan, "Mother Accuses Sperm Bank of a Mixup," *New York Times,* March 9, 1990, p. B1.

7. *Marciniak v. Lundborg,* Wisc. Sup. Ct., No. 88–0088, 58 U.S.L.W. 2460, February 13, 1990.

8. William Robbins, "Court to Decide Missouri Prisoner's Right to Father Child," *New York Times,* February 20, 1990, p. A19.

9. *International Herald Tribune,* February 28, 1990, p. 1.

10. All quotes about Maxine Thomas from Roxane Arnold and Terry Pristin, "The Rise and Fall of Maxine Thomas," *Los Angeles Times,* May 6, 1988, part 2, pp. 1–3.

11. Dorothy Gilliam, "Mixed Rewards of Success," *Washington Post,* December 30, 1986, p. 1. Despite persistent public images to the contrary, black birth rates "declined from 153.5 per 1000 women in 1960, to 81.4 per 1000 women in 1984." T. B. Edsell, "Race in Politics," *New York Review of Books,* December 22, 1988, p. 24.

12. This representation is made so often that it has entered the stratosphere of needing-no-citation, but here is a random sample: "One factor [accounting for the decreasing numbers of black men enrolled in college] is the growing number of black families that are headed by young, impoverished, semiliterate single women, poor role models for daughters and no model at all for sons." "Blacks on Campus," *Los Angeles Times,* February 13, 1989, part 2, p. 4.

Ideas for Rereading

1. Think about the full title of "Owning the Self in a Disowned World (a menagerie of nightmares and hallucinations)." As you reread the essay, make notes about Williams's examples of "disownership." You might respond to some of the following questions (or you might use these questions as a way of formulating your own). What does Williams mean by saying that we live in "a disowned world" and how does she propose to achieve self-possession? What do you make of the various ideas Williams has for transforming "disintegration into senselessness" (p. 85) into ways of owning the self? Think, for example, of how she uses everyday activities such as watching television and reading

a newspaper, news stories about birth and babies, "guerrilla insemination" (p. 88), and personal thoughts about makeup and professionalism.

2. About halfway through the essay, Williams recounts "The Chronicle of the Twenty-Seventh-Year Syndrome" from Derrick Bell's *And We Are Not Saved*. She briefly describes the conversation of her reading group concerning this story in a paragraph that is full of "big words"—terms replete with capital letters and hyphens and slashes and "isms." Now that you have read her essay through, go back to this paragraph (p. 90) and try to make sense of these terms. You may need to look up some of these terms in a dictionary. What is their connection to the "Chronicle"? How do you imagine that the "Chronicle" might have evoked them? Jot down your thoughts, however speculative, in your notebook. As a next step, turn to the story of Maxine Thomas, the Los Angeles Municipal Court judge who suffers a "nervous breakdown" (p. 90). Williams embeds this story between "The Chronicle of the Twenty-Seventh-Year Syndrome" and her direct reflections on the "Chronicle." Reread the story of Maxine Thomas and consider its relation to the "Chronicle." Why, in your view, does Williams situate the story here? What is its significance in relation to the "Chronicle"? Nestled within the story of Maxine Thomas is another story: the brief description of Williams and her mother preparing their faces and their hair for the day (p. 93). What relations do you see between this story about Williams's domestic life and the story about Thomas? Between this story and the "Chronicle"? Finally, turn to the account of the dream with which Williams ends the essay. What relations and connections can you discern or suggest between this dream and the foregoing stories? In your notebook, work out your own interpretation or reading of this second half of the essay, one that takes into account its several episodes and threads.

Ideas for Writing

1. Choose a passage, story, or example from Williams's essay and consider how it relates to and helps to explain the title, "Owning the Self in a Disowned World (a menagerie of nightmares and hallucinations)." Then choose an episode from your own experience that relates to the title. Write an essay on the meaning of Williams's title, drawing on Williams's essay and your own experience as support for your argument.

2. Examine at least one passage from Woolf and one from Williams in which the writers discuss the challenges and obstructions faced by professional women in a patriarchal society. How does each writer present these challenges and obstructions? In what ways do their views differ and in what ways do they overlap or meet? To what would you attribute the differences: social circumstances? personality? historical setting? geographical setting? You might find many points of relationship between Woolf and Williams—one starting place might be their ways of imagining what it means to be independent; another might be the ways in which they imagine the function of writing in professional life.

3. Write an essay about "professional women" using examples from Williams and from magazines that give advice to professional women about how to be a

professional. *Vogue, Glamour, Harper's Bazaar, Working Women,* and *Ebony* might be good places to start. You may choose to work with electronic magazines published on the World Wide Web. (In either case, you should attach copies of the relevant articles and images to your essay.) Your goal should be to develop your own ways of thinking about how professional women are expected to dress, act, speak, write, and live. Incorporate at least three visual images into your essay and respond to at least two articles geared toward the "working woman."

MONIQUE WITTIG

Monique Wittig was born in 1934 in Alsace, a region on the borders of Germany, France, and Switzerland that has been a site of regional contention for many centuries. Wittig was educated at the University of Paris, Sorbonne, and now lives in New York. A writer of avant-garde novels including Les Guerilleres *(1969),* The Lesbian Body *(1975), and* Across the Acheron *(1987), she is widely celebrated as an experimental, postmodernist feminist. As Christine Froula put it in the* Women's Review of Books, *"Monique Wittig stations herself at the front in the war against women's domination by male culture. Her weapon, her technology, is language."*

The two essays selected here are taken from The Straight Mind and Other Essays *(1992). In them Wittig takes dialectical reasoning to an extreme with the express purpose of "destroying . . . the category of sex" by defining "a materialist feminist approach to women's oppression" (p. 105). She argues that the battle of the sexes is a battle between a higher and a lower class. Women, subordinated by a society that favors men, suffer physical deformation of the body. The problem is that the "deformed body" (plucked, shaved, thinned, surgically altered) is conventionally regarded as a product of natural forces, of forces that are an essential part of what it means to be a woman. Going against this conventional view, Wittig argues that "our bodies as well as our minds are the product of [political] manipulation" (p. 105), charging that the political forces at work on the female mind and body are "totalitarian," dictatorial. Wittig develops a strategy for combating totalitarian notions of sexual difference. The first essay, "The Category of Sex" (1976/1982), argues that "the category of sex is the category that ordains slavery for women, and it works specifically, as it did for black slaves, through an operation of reduction, by taking the part for the whole, a part (color, sex) through which the whole human group has to pass" (p. 104). The second essay, "One Is Not Born a Woman" (1981), rejects biological and other ways of understanding the oppression of women, arguing that "what we take for the cause of origin of oppression is in fact only the* mark *imposed by the oppressor" (p. 106). Wittig thus sees essentialist differences between men and women as coincident with patriarchal oppression; the eradication of essentialism is crucial to liberatory feminism.*

Wittig's essays make a series of moves that are both surprising and compelling: her writing leads the reader from bold statements to subtle, increasingly complex proofs; her argument tests readers because it is multilayered and provocative. But patient, step-by-step analysis can reward us with insights into a highly original rejection of the category of sex.

As you read Wittig notice the ways in which her argument challenges conventional uses of the words nature, natural, *and* naturalize. *Another word crucial to her essay is* ideology *(which refers to the spectrum of dominant ideas that a given society takes for granted, ideas that are accepted without question)—her main example of an ideological assumption is heterosexuality, a mode of sexual relations assumed to be natural. Focus on Wittig's attempt to turn ideas conventionally regarded as natural into ideas that she wants us to see as the product of political ideology. Pay particular attention to Wittig's discussion of the word* feminism *and the idea of "woman" (pp. 107–8).*

From *The Straight Mind and Other Essays*

The Category of Sex

> O. expresses a virile idea. Virile or at least masculine. At last a woman who admits it! Who admits what? Something that women have always till now refused to admit (and today more than ever before). Something that men have always reproached them with: that they never cease obeying their nature, the call of their blood, that everything in them, even their minds, is sex.
>
> —JEAN PAULHAN, "Happiness in Slavery,"
> preface to *The Story of O*, by Pauline de Réage

> In the course of the year 1838, the peaceful island of Barbados was rocked by a strange and bloody revolt. About two hundred Negroes of both sexes, all of whom had recently been emancipated by the Proclamation of March, came one morning to beg their former master, a certain Glenelg, to take them back into bondage. . . . I suspect . . . that Glenelg's slaves were in love with their master, that they couldn't bear to be without him.
>
> —JEAN PAULHAN, "Happiness in Slavery"

> What should I be getting married for? I find life good enough as it is. What do I need a wife for? . . . And what's so good about a woman?—A woman is a worker. A woman is a man's servant.—But what would I be needing a worker for?—That's just it. You like to have others pulling your chestnuts out of the fire. . . .—Well, marry me off, if that's the case.
>
> — IVAN TURGENEV, *The Hunting Sketches*

The perenniality of the sexes and the perenniality of slaves and masters proceed from the same belief, and, as there are no slaves without masters, there are no women without men. The ideology of sexual difference functions as censorship in our culture by masking, on the ground of nature, the social opposition between men and women. Masculine/feminine, male/female are the categories which serve to conceal the fact that social differences always belong to an economic, political, ideological order. Every system of domination establishes divisions at the material and economic level. Furthermore, the divisions are abstracted and turned into concepts by the masters, and later on by the slaves when they rebel and start to struggle. The masters explain and justify the established divisions as a result of natural differences. The slaves, when they rebel and start to struggle, read social oppositions into the so-called natural differences.

For there is no sex. There is but sex that is oppressed and sex that oppresses. It is oppression that creates sex and not the contrary. The contrary would be to say that sex creates oppression, or to say that the cause (origin) of oppression is to be found in sex itself, in a natural division of the sexes preexisting (or outside of) society.

The primacy of difference so constitutes our thought that it prevents turning inward on itself to question itself, no matter how necessary that may be to apprehend the basis of that which precisely constitutes it. To apprehend a difference in dialectical terms is to make apparent the contradictory terms to be resolved. To understand social reality in dialectical materialist terms is to apprehend the oppositions between classes, term to term, and make them meet under the same copula (a conflict in the social order), which is also a resolution (an abolition in the social order) of the apparent contradictions.

The class struggle is precisely that which resolves the contradictions between two opposed classes by abolishing them at the same time that it constitutes and reveals them as classes. The class struggle between women and men, which should be undertaken by all women, is that which resolves the contradictions between the sexes, abolishing them at the same time that it makes them understood. We must notice that the contradictions always belong to a material order. The important idea for me is that before the conflict (rebellion, struggle) there are no categories of opposition but only of difference. And it is not until the struggle breaks out that the violent reality of the oppositions and the political nature of the differences become manifest. For as long as oppositions (differences) appear as given, already there, before all thought, "natural" — as long as there is no conflict and no struggle — there is no dialectic, there is no change, no movement. The dominant thought refuses to turn inward on itself to apprehend that which questions it.

And, indeed, as long as there is no women's struggle, there is no conflict between men and women. It is the fate of women to perform three-quarters of the work of society (in the public as well as in the private domain) plus the bodily work of reproduction according to a preestablished rate. Being murdered, mutilated, physically and mentally tortured and abused, being raped, being battered, and being forced to marry is the fate of women. And fate supposedly cannot be changed. Women do not know that they are totally dominated by men, and when they acknowledge the fact, they can "hardly believe it." And often, as a last recourse before the bare and crude reality, they refuse to "believe" that men dominate them with full knowledge (for oppression is far more hideous for the oppressed than for the oppressors). Men, on the other hand, know perfectly well that they are dominating women ("We are the masters of women," said André Breton[1]) and are trained to do it. They do not need to express it all the time, for one can scarcely talk of domination over what one owns.

What is this thought which refuses to reverse itself, which never puts into question what primarily constitutes it? This thought is the dominant thought. It is a thought which affirms an "already there" of the sexes, something which is supposed to have come before all thought, before all society. This thought is the thought of those who rule over women.

> The ideas of the ruling class are in every epoch the ruling ideas, i.e., the class which is the ruling material force of society, is at the same time its ruling intellectual force. The class which has the means of material production at its disposal, has control at the same time over the means of mental production, so that thereby, generally speaking, the ideas of those who lack the means of mental production are subject to it. The ruling ideas are nothing more than the ideal expression of the dominant material relationships, the dominant material relationships grasped as ideas: hence of the relationships which make the one class the ruling one, therefore, the ideas of its dominance. (Marx and Engels, *The German Ideology*)[2]

This thought based on the primacy of difference is the thought of domination.

Dominance provides women with a body of data, of givens, of a prioris, which, all the more for being questionable, form a huge political construct, a tight network that affects everything, our thoughts, our gestures, our acts, our work, our feelings, our relationships.

Dominance thus teaches us from all directions:

— that there are before all thinking, all society, "sexes" (two categories of individuals born) with a constitutive difference, a difference that has ontological consequences (the metaphysical approach),

— that there are before all thinking, all social order, "sexes" with a "natural" or "biological" or "hormonal" or "genetic" difference that has sociological consequences (the scientific approach),

— that there is before all thinking, all social order, a "natural division of labor in the family," a "division of labor [that] was originally nothing *but* the division of labor in the sexual act" (the Marxist approach).

Whatever the approach, the idea remains basically the same. The sexes, in spite of their constitutive difference, must inevitably develop relationships from category to category. Belonging to the natural order, these relationships cannot be spoken of as social relationships. This thought which impregnates all discourses, including common-sense ones (Adam's rib or

Adam *is,* Eve is Adam's rib), is the thought of domination. Its body of discourses is constantly reinforced on all levels of social reality and conceals the political fact of the subjugation of one sex by the other, the compulsory character of the category itself (which constitutes the first definition of the social being in civil status). The category of sex does not exist a priori, before all society. And as a category of dominance it cannot be a product of natural dominance but of the social dominance of women by men, for there is but social dominance.

The category of sex is the political category that founds society as heterosexual. As such it does not concern being but relationships (for women and men are the result of relationships), although the two aspects are always confused when they are discussed. The category of sex is the one that rules as "natural" the relation that is at the base of (heterosexual) society and through which half of the population, women, are "heterosexualized" (the making of women is like the making of eunuchs, the breeding of slaves, of animals) and submitted to a heterosexual economy. For the category of sex is the product of a heterosexual society which imposes on women the rigid obligation of the reproduction of the "species," that is, the reproduction of heterosexual society. The compulsory reproduction of the "species" by women is the system of exploitation on which heterosexuality is economically based. Reproduction is essentially that work, that production by women, through which the appropriation by men of all the work of women proceeds. One must include here the appropriation of work which is associated "by nature" with reproduction, the raising of children and domestic chores. This appropriation of the work of women is effected in the same way as the appropriation of the work of the working class by the ruling class. It cannot be said that one of these two productions (reproduction) is "natural" while the other one is social. This argument is only the theoretical, ideological justification of oppression, an argument to make women believe that before society and in all societies they are subject to this obligation to reproduce. However, as we know nothing about work, about social production, outside of the context of exploitation, we know nothing about the reproduction of society outside of its context of exploitation.

The category of sex is the product of a heterosexual society in which men appropriate for themselves the reproduction and production of women and also their physical persons by means of a contract called the marriage contract. Compare this contract with the contract that binds a worker to his employer. The contract binding the woman to the man is in principle a contract for life, which only law can break (divorce). It assigns the woman certain obligations, including unpaid work. The work (housework, raising children) and the obligations (surrender of her reproduction in the name of her husband, cohabitation by day and night, forced coitus, assignment of residence implied by the legal concept of "surrender of the conjugal domicile") mean in their terms a surrender by the woman of her physical person to her husband. That the woman depends directly on her husband is implicit in the police's policy of not intervening when a husband beats his wife. The police intervene with the specific charge of assault and battery when one citizen beats another citizen. But a woman who has signed a marriage contract has thereby ceased to be an ordinary citizen (protected by law). The police openly express their aversion to getting involved in domestic affairs (as opposed to civil affairs), where the authority of the state does not have to intervene directly since it is relayed through that of the husband. One has to go to shelters for battered women to see how far this authority can be exercised.

The category of sex is the product of heterosexual society that turns half of the population into sexual beings, for sex is a category which women cannot be outside of. Wherever they are, whatever they do (including working in the public sector), they are seen (and made) sexually available to men, and they, breasts, buttocks, costume, must be visible. They must wear their yellow star, their constant smile, day and night. One might consider that every woman, married or not, has a period of forced sexual service, a sexual service which we may compare to the military one, and which can vary between a day, a year, or twenty-five years or more. Some lesbians and nuns escape, but they are very few, although the number is growing. Although women are very visible as sexual beings, as social beings they are totally invisible, and as such must appear as little as possible, and always with some kind of excuse if they do so. One only has to read interviews with outstanding women to hear them apologizing. And the newspapers still today report that "two students and a woman," "two lawyers and a woman," "three travelers and a woman" were seen doing this or that. For the category of sex is the category that sticks to women, for only they cannot be conceived of outside of it. Only *they* are sex, *the* sex, and sex they have been made in their minds, bodies, acts, gestures; even their murders and beatings are sexual. Indeed, the category of sex tightly holds women.

For the category of sex is a totalitarian one, which to prove true has its inquisitions, its courts, its tribunals, its body of laws, its terrors, its tortures, its mutilations, its executions, its police. It shapes the mind as well as the body since it controls all mental production. It grips our minds in such a way that we cannot think outside of it. This is why we must destroy it and start thinking beyond it if we want to start thinking at all, as we must destroy the sexes as a sociological reality if we want to start to exist. The category of sex is the category that ordains slavery for women, and it works specifically, as it did for black slaves, through an operation of reduction, by taking the part for the whole, a part (color, sex) through which the whole human group has to pass as through a screen. Notice that in civil matters color as well as sex still must be "declared." However, because of the abolition of slavery, the "declaration" of "color" is now considered discriminatory. But that does not hold true for the "declaration" of "sex," which not even women dream of abolishing. I say: it is about time to do so.[3]

One Is Not Born a Woman

A materialist feminist[4] approach to women's oppression destroys the idea that women are a "natural group": "a racial group of a special kind, a group perceived *as natural,* a group of men considered as materially specific in their bodies."[5] What the analysis accomplishes on the level of ideas, practice makes actual at the level of facts: by its very existence, lesbian society destroys the artificial (social) fact constituting women as a "natural group." A lesbian society[6] pragmatically reveals that the division from men of which women have been the object is a political one and shows that we have been ideologically rebuilt into a "natural group." In the case of women, ideology goes far since our bodies as well as our minds are the product of this manipulation. We have been compelled in our bodies and in our minds to correspond, feature by feature, with the *idea* of nature that has been established for us. Distorted to such an extent that our deformed body is what they call "natural," what is supposed to exist as such before oppression. Distorted to such an extent that in the end oppression seems to be a consequence of this "nature" within ourselves (a nature which is only an *idea*). What a materialist analysis does by reasoning, a lesbian society accomplishes practically: not only is there no natural group "women" (we lesbians are living proof of it), but as individuals as well we question "woman," which for us, as for Simone de Beauvoir, is only a myth. She said: "One is not born, but becomes a woman. No biological, psychological, or economic fate determines the figure that the human female presents in society: it is civilization as a whole that produces this creature, intermediate between male and eunuch, which is described as feminine."[7]

However, most of the feminists and lesbian-feminists in America and elsewhere still believe that the basis of women's oppression *is biological as well as* historical. Some of them even claim to find their sources in Simone de Beauvoir.[8] The belief in mother right and in a "prehistory" when women created civilization (because of a biological predisposition) while the coarse and brutal men hunted (because of a biological predisposition) is symmetrical with the biologizing interpretation of history produced up to now by the class of men. It is still the same method of finding in women and men a biological explanation of their division, outside of social facts. For me this could never constitute a lesbian approach to women's oppression, since it assumes that the basis of society or the beginning of society lies in heterosexuality. Matriarchy is no less heterosexual than patriarchy: it is only the sex of the oppressor that changes. Furthermore, not only is this conception still imprisoned in the categories of sex (woman and man), but it holds onto the idea that the capacity to give birth (biology) is what defines a woman. Although practical facts and ways of living contradict this theory in lesbian society, there are lesbians who affirm that "women and men are different species or races (the words are used interchangeably): men are biologically inferior to women; male violence is a biological inevitability . . ."[9] By doing this, by admitting that there is a "natural" division between women and men, we naturalize history, we assume that "men" and "women" have always existed and will always exist. Not only do we naturalize history, but also consequently we naturalize the social phenomena which express our oppression, making change impossible. For example, instead of seeing giving birth as a forced production, we see it as a "natural," "biological" process, forgetting that in our societies births are planned (demography), forgetting that we ourselves are programmed to produce children, while this is the only social activity "short of war"[10] that presents such a great danger of death. Thus, as long as we will be "unable to abandon by will or impulse a lifelong and centuries-old commitment to childbearing as *the* female creative act,"[11] gaining control of the production of children will mean much more than the mere control of the material means of this production: women will have to abstract themselves from the definition "woman" which is imposed upon them.

A materialist feminist approach shows that what we take for the cause or origin of oppression is in fact only the *mark*[12] imposed by the oppressor: the "myth of woman,"[13] plus its material effects and manifestations in the appropriated consciousness and bodies of women. Thus, this mark does not predate oppression: Colette Guillaumin has shown that before the socioeconomic reality of black slavery, the concept of race did not exist, at least not in its modern meaning, since it was applied to the lineage of families. However, now, race, exactly like sex, is taken as an "immediate given," a "sensible given," "physical features," belonging to a natural order. But what we believe to be a physical and direct perception is only a sophisticated and mythic construction, an "imaginary formation,"[14] which reinterprets physical features (in themselves as neutral as any others but marked by the social system) through the network of relationships in which they are perceived. (They are seen as *black*, therefore they *are* black; they are seen as *women*, therefore, they *are* women. But before being *seen* that way, they first had to be *made* that way.) Lesbians should always remember and acknowledge how "unnatural," compelling, totally oppressive, and destructive being "woman" was for us in the old days before the women's liberation movement. It was a political constraint, and those who resisted it were accused of not being "real" women. But then we were proud of it, since in the accusation there was already something like a shadow of victory: the avowal by the oppressor that "woman" is not something that goes without saying, since to be one, one has to be a "real" one. We were at the same time accused of wanting to be men. Today this double accusation has been taken up again with enthusiasm in the context of the women's liberation movement by some feminists and also, alas, by some lesbians whose political goal seems somehow to be becoming more and more "feminine." To refuse to be a woman, however, does not mean that one has to become a man. Besides, if we take as an example the perfect "butch," the classic example which provokes the most horror, whom Proust would have called a woman/man, how is her alienation different from that of someone who wants to become a woman? Tweedledum and Tweedledee. At least for a woman, wanting to become a man proves that she has escaped her initial programming. But even if she would like to, with all her strength, she cannot become a man. For becoming a man would demand from a woman not only a man's external appearance but his consciousness as well, that is, the consciousness of one who disposes by right of at least two "natural" slaves during his life span. This is impossible, and one feature of lesbian oppression consists precisely of making women out of reach for us, since women belong to men. Thus a lesbian *has* to be something else, a not-woman, a not-man, a product of society, not a product of nature, for there is no nature in society.

The refusal to become (or to remain) heterosexual always meant to refuse to become a man or a woman, consciously or not. For a lesbian this goes further than the refusal of the *role* "woman." It is the refusal of the economic, ideological, and political power of a man. This, we lesbians, and nonlesbians as well, knew before the beginning of the lesbian and feminist movement. However, as Andrea Dworkin emphasizes, many lesbians recently "have increasingly tried to transform the very ideology that has enslaved us into a dynamic, religious, psychologically compelling celebration of female biological potential."[15] Thus, some avenues of the feminist and lesbian movement lead us back to the myth of woman which was created by men especially for us, and with it we sink back into a natural group. Having stood up to fight for a sexless society,[16] we now find ourselves entrapped in the familiar deadlock of "woman is wonderful." Simone de Beauvoir underlined particularly the false consciousness which consists of selecting among the features of the myth (that women are different from men) those which look good and using them as a definition for women. What the concept "woman is wonderful" accomplishes is that it retains for defining women the best features (best according to whom?) which oppression has granted us, and it does not radically question the categories "man" and "woman," which are political categories and not natural givens. It puts us in a position of fighting within the class "women" not as the other classes do, for the disappearance of our class, but for the defense of "woman" and its reenforcement. It leads us to develop with complacency "new" theories about our specificity: thus, we call our passivity "nonviolence," when the main and emergent point for us is to fight our passivity (our fear, rather, a justified one). The ambiguity of the term "feminist" sums up the whole situation. What does "feminist" mean? Feminist is formed with the word "femme," "woman," and means: someone who fights for women. For many of us it means someone who fights for women as a class and for the disappearance of this class. For many others it means someone who fights for woman and her defense—for the myth, then, and its reenforcement. But why was the word "feminist" chosen if it retains the least ambiguity? We chose to call ourselves "feminists" ten years ago, not in order to support or reenforce the myth of woman, nor to identify ourselves with the oppressor's definition of us, but rather to affirm that our movement had a history and to emphasize the political link with the old feminist movement.

It is, then, this movement that we can put in question for the meaning that it gave to feminism. It so happens that feminism in the last century could never resolve its contradictions on the subject of nature/culture, woman/society. Women started to fight for themselves as a group and rightly considered that they shared common features as a result of oppression. But for them these features were natural and biological rather than social. They went so far as to adopt the Darwinist theory of evolution. They did not believe like Darwin, however, "that women were less evolved than men, but they did believe that male and female natures had diverged in the course of evolutionary development and that society at large reflected this polarization."[17] "The failure of early feminism was that it only attacked the Darwinist charge of female inferiority, while accepting the foundations of this charge—namely, the view of woman as 'unique.'"[18] And finally it was women scholars—and not feminists — who scientifically destroyed this theory. But the early feminists had failed to regard history as a dynamic process which develops from conflicts of interests. Furthermore, they still believed as men do that the cause (origin) of their oppression lay within themselves. And therefore after some astonishing victories the feminists of this first front found themselves at an impasse out of a lack of reasons to fight. They upheld the illogical principle of "equality in difference," an idea now being born again. They fell back into the trap which threatens us once again: the myth of woman.

Thus it is our historical task, and only ours, to define what we call oppression in materialist terms, to make it evident that women are a class, which is to say that the category "woman" as well as the category "man" are political and economic categories not eternal ones. Our fight aims to suppress men as a class, not through a genocidal, but a political struggle. Once the class "men" disappears, "women" as a class will disappear as well, for there are no slaves without masters. Our first task, it seems, is to always thoroughly dissociate "women" (the class within which we fight) and "woman," the myth. For "woman" does not exist for us: it is only an imaginary formation, while "women" is the product of a social relationship. We felt this strongly when everywhere we refused to be called a "*woman's* liberation movement." Furthermore, we have to destroy the myth inside and outside ourselves. "Woman" is not each one of us, but the political and ideological formation which negates "women" (the product of a relation of exploitation). "Woman" is there to confuse us, to hide the reality "women." In order to be aware of being a class and to become a class we first have to kill the myth of "woman" including its most seductive aspects (I think about Virginia Woolf when she said the first task of a woman writer is to kill "the angel in the house"). But to become a class we do not have to suppress our individual selves, and since no individual can be reduced to her/his oppression we are also confronted with the historical necessity of constituting ourselves as the individual subjects of our history as well. I believe this is the reason why all these attempts at "new" definitions of woman are blossoming now. What is at stake (and of course not only for women) is an individual definition as well as a class definition. For once one has acknowledged oppression, one needs to know and experience the fact that one can constitute oneself as a subject (as opposed to an object of oppression), that one can become *someone* in spite of oppression, that one has one's own identity. There is no possible fight for someone deprived of an identity, no internal motivation for fighting, since, although I can fight only with others, first I fight for myself.

The question of the individual subject is historically a difficult one for everybody. Marxism, the last avatar of materialism, the science which has politically formed us, does not want to hear anything about a "subject." Marxism has rejected the transcendental subject, the subject as constitutive of knowledge, the "pure" consciousness. All that thinks per se, before all experience, has ended up in the garbage can of history, because it claimed to exist outside matter, prior to matter, and needed God, spirit, or soul to exist in such a way. This is what is called "idealism." As for individuals, they are only the product of social relations, therefore their consciousness can only be "alienated." (Marx, in *The German Ideology,* says precisely that individuals of the dominating class are also alienated, although they are the direct producers of the ideas that alienate the classes oppressed by them. But since they draw visible advantages from their own alienation they can bear it without too much suffering.) There exists such a thing as class consciousness, but a consciousness which does not refer to a particular subject, except as participating in general conditions of exploitation at the same time as the other subjects of their class, all sharing the same consciousness. As for the practical class problems—outside of the class problems as traditionally defined—that one could encounter (for example, sexual problems), they were considered "bourgeois" problems that would disappear with the final victory of the class struggle. "Individualistic," "subjectivist," "petit bourgeois," these were the labels given to any person who had shown problems which could not be reduced to the "class struggle" itself.

Thus Marxism has denied the members of oppressed classes the attribute of being a subject. In doing this, Marxism, because of the ideological and political power this "revolutionary science" immediately exercised upon the workers' movement and all other political groups, has prevented all categories of oppressed peoples from constituting themselves historically as subjects (subjects of their struggle, for example). This means that the "masses" did not fight for themselves but for *the* party or its organizations. And when an economic transformation took place (end of private property, constitution of the socialist state), no revolutionary change took place within the new society, because the people themselves did not change.

For women, Marxism had two results. It prevented them from being aware that they are a class and therefore from constituting themselves as a class for a very long time, by leaving the relation "women/men" outside of the social order, by turning it into a natural relation, doubtless for Marxists the only one, along with the relation of mothers to children, to be seen this way, and by hiding the class conflict between men and women behind a natural division of labor (*The German Ideology*). This concerns the theoretical (ideological) level. On the practical level, Lenin, *the* party, all the communist parties up to now, including all the most radical political groups, have always reacted to any attempt on the part of women to reflect and form groups based on their own class problem with an accusation of divisiveness. By uniting, we women are dividing the strength of the people. This means that for the Marxists women *belong* either to the bourgeois class or to the proletariat class, in other words, to the men of these classes. In addition, Marxist theory does not allow women any more than other classes of oppressed people to constitute themselves as historical subjects, because Marxism does not take into account the fact that a class also consists of individuals one by one. Class consciousness is not enough. We must try to understand philosophically (politically) these concepts of "subject" and "class consciousness" and how they work in relation to our history. When we discover that women are the objects of oppression and appropriation, at the very moment that we become able to perceive this, we become subjects in the sense of cognitive subjects, through an operation of abstraction. Consciousness of oppression is not only a reaction to (fight against) oppression. It is also the whole conceptual reevaluation of the social world, its whole reorganization with new concepts, from the point of view of oppression. It is what I would call the science of oppression created by the oppressed. This operation of understanding reality has to be undertaken by every one of us: call it a subjective, cognitive practice. The movement back and forth between the levels of reality (the conceptual reality and the material reality of oppression, which are both social realities) is accomplished through language.

It is we who historically must undertake the task of defining the individual subject in materialist terms. This certainly seems to be an impossibility since materialism and subjectivity have always been mutually exclusive. Nevertheless, and rather than despairing of ever understanding, we must recognize the *need* to reach subjectivity in the abandonment by many of us to the myth "woman" (the myth of woman being only a snare that holds us up). This real necessity for everyone to exist as an individual, as well as a member of a class, is perhaps the first condition for the accomplishment of a revolution, without which there can be no real fight or transformation. But the opposite is also true; without class and class consciousness there are no real subjects, only alienated individuals. For women to answer the question of the individual subject in materialist terms is first to show, as the lesbians and feminists did, that supposedly "subjective," "individual," "private" problems are in fact social problems, class problems; that sexuality is not for women an individual and subjective expression, but a social institution of violence. But once we have shown that all so-called personal problems are in fact class problems, we will still be left with the question of the subject of each singular woman—not the myth, but each one of us. At this point, let us say that a new personal and subjective definition for all humankind can only be found beyond the categories of sex (woman and man) and that the advent of individual subjects demands first destroying the categories of sex, ending the use of them, and rejecting all sciences which still use these categories as their fundamentals (practically all social sciences).

To destroy "woman" does not mean that we aim, short of physical destruction, to destroy lesbianism simultaneously with the categories of sex, because lesbianism provides for the moment the only social form in which we can live freely. Lesbian is the only concept I know of which is beyond the categories of sex (woman and man), because the designated subject (lesbian) is *not* a woman, either economically, or politically, or ideologically. For what makes a woman is a specific social relation to a man, a relation that we have previously called servitude,[19] a relation which implies personal and physical obligation as well as economic obligation ("forced residence,"[20] domestic corvée, conjugal duties, unlimited production of children, etc.), a relation which lesbians escape by refusing to become or to stay heterosexual. We are escapees from our class in the same way as the American runaway slaves were when escaping slavery and becoming free. For us this is an absolute necessity; our survival demands that we contribute all our strength to the destruction of the class of women within which men appropriate women. This can be accomplished only by the destruction of heterosexuality as a social system which is based on the oppression of women by men and which produces the doctrine of the difference between the sexes to justify this oppression.

Notes

1. André Breton, *Le Premier Manifeste du Surréalisme*, 1924.

2. Karl Marx and Friedrich Engels, *The German Ideology*, Parts I and III, ed. Roy Pascal (New York: International Publishers, 1939, 1967).

3. Pleasure in sex is no more the subject of this paper than is happiness in slavery.

4. Christine Delphy, "Pour un féminisme matérialiste," *L'Arc* 61 (1975). Translated as "For a Materialist Feminism," *Feminist Issues* 1, no. 2 (Winter 1981).

5. Colette Guillaumin, "Race et Nature: Système des marques, idée de groupe naturel et rapports sociaux," *Pluriel*, no. 11 (1977). Translated as "Race and Nature: The System of Marks, the Idea of a Natural Group and Social Relationships," *Feminist Issues* 8, no. 2 (Fall 1988).

6. I use the word society with an extended anthropological meaning; strictly speaking, it does not refer to societies, in that lesbian societies do not exist completely autonomously from heterosexual social systems.

7. Simone de Beauvoir, *The Second Sex* (New York: Bantam, 1952), p. 249.

8. Redstockings, *Feminist Revolution* (New York: Random House, 1978), p. 18.

9. Andrea Dworkin, "Biological Superiority: The World's Most Dangerous and Deadly Idea," *Heresies* 6:46.

10. Ti-Grace Atkinson, *Amazon Odyssey* (New York: Links Books, 1974), p. 15.

11. Dworkin, op. cit.

12. Guillaumin, op. cit.

13. de Beauvoir, op. cit.

14. Guillaumin, op. cit.

15. Dworkin, op. cit.

16. Atkinson, p. 6: "If feminism has any logic at all, it must be working for a sexless society."

17. Rosalind Rosenberg, "In Search of Woman's Nature," *Feminist Studies* 3, no. 1/2 (1975): 144.

18. Ibid., p. 146.

19. In an article published in *L'Idiot International* (mai 1970), whose original title was "Pour un mouvement de libération des femmes" ("For a Women's Liberation Movement").

20. Christiane Rochefort, *Les stances à Sophie* (Paris: Grasset, 1963).

Ideas for Rereading

1. Consider "The Category of Sex" in terms of the three quotations Wittig uses as epigraphs. How do these quotations help you to decipher Wittig's argument? Why do you think she chooses these specific quotations? How do the sentiments expressed by Paulhan and Turgenev relate to Wittig's three statements about "dominance" on pages 102–3? How might these epigraphs help you to understand Wittig's rejection of "the primacy of difference" and her refusal to accept "natural" oppositions between "masculine/feminine" and "male/female"?

2. Carefully reread Wittig's conclusion that women "are escapees from our class in the same way as the American runaway slaves were when escaping slavery and becoming free" (p. 111). Note ways in which this conclusion follows from what Wittig says in the preceding sections of her essay about "the biologizing interpretation of history" (p. 105), the "myth of woman" (p. 106), the ambiguity of the word *feminist* (p. 108), the "question of the individual subject" (p. 109), "the science of oppression" (p. 110), and the need to "thoroughly dissociate 'women' (the class within which we fight) and 'woman,' the myth" (p. 108). In other words, make notes about each discrete section of "One Is Not Born a Woman" by assessing how it contributes to the argument that "our survival demands that we contribute all our strength to the destruction of the class of women within which men appropriate women" (p. 111).

Ideas for Writing

1. Write an essay based on the notes you compiled as you considered how each section of "One Is Not Born a Woman" contributes to Wittig's conclusion (question 2, Ideas for Rereading). Your essay should describe, interpret, and

critique how each part of Wittig's argument adds up to her "materialist feminist approach to women's oppression." Ultimately, you should develop a critical interpretation of Wittig's essay assessing how effective she is in arguing for the destruction of the "myth" that one is a woman by birth. At each stage of the writing process you should ask yourself, "Am I convinced by what she says? If so, what does she say that convinces me? If not, what doesn't she take into account?"

2. Write an essay analyzing an example from your own experiences and observations in terms of Wittig's assertion that "as long as there is no conflict and no struggle — there is no dialectic, there is no change, no movement" (p. 101). Focus on a situation where you experienced or observed conflict and struggle and suggest how Wittig's essays provide ways of thinking about the changes that resulted from the situation you describe. While you may address the ways in which Wittig's attitude to conflict and struggle illuminates and aids your understandings of gender identity, you may also apply her arguments about gender to a situation that involved other forms of personal, professional, or cultural identity.

3. Develop a reading of *A Room of One's Own* by applying the following quotation from Wittig:

> The category of sex is the product of a heterosexual society in which men appropriate for themselves the reproduction and production of women and also their physical persons by means of a contract called the marriage contract.

As you compose your essay focus on Woolf's definition of the "androgynous mind" in terms of "the man-womanly" and the "woman-manly" (pp. 36–40). Consider the ways in which Woolf's theory about androgyny confirms, complicates, and/or conflicts with Wittig's definition of "heterosexual society." Think beyond a strict idea of "the marriage contract," considering, for example, Woolf's assumption that there is much to be gained from a wedding of male and female qualities. Use material from the Context section to develop your essay — you may find the passage from *Orlando* particularly useful; the reviews of *A Room of One's Own* may be of assistance as you attempt to identify Woolf's assumptions about heterosexual relations and "the category of sex."

EVE KOSOFSKY SEDGWICK

Eve Kosofsky Sedgwick (b. 1951) is a Distinguished Professor of English at the City University of New York; previously she taught at Duke University. She is the author of Between Men: English Literature and Male Homosocial Desire *(1985) and* The Epistemology of the Closet *(1990). She has published a volume of poems entitled* Fat Art, Thin Art *(1994) and a psychological autobiography,* Dialogue on Love *(1999). Epistemology of the Closet, which proposed that questions of sexual definition are at the heart of twentieth-century thought and culture, was a groundbreaking work in queer theory, establishing Sedgwick's reputation as "the soft-spoken queen of gay studies" and the "mother of queer theory."*

In 1991, when she was forty, Sedgwick was diagnosed with breast cancer. After a mastectomy and six months of chemotherapy, she engaged in a course of psychotherapy that involved a protracted analysis of her own identity "as a woman." As she confesses in Dialogue on Love, *a series of postsession notes and poems interspersed with extracts from the therapist's notes, Sedgwick's understanding of her own sexuality is complex. Even though it is an academic piece written for the Modern Language Association (the main professional organization for scholars of language and literature), "Sex and Gender" is a testimony to Sedgwick's personal struggle to negotiate relationships between her intellectual theories about lesbianism and queerness (she defines herself as "queer") and her lived experience as a married woman for more than thirty years. The difficulty of the piece is a reflection of the difficulty we face when we try to define gender, sex, and sexuality, but it is also a reflection of Sedgwick's ambivalence about her own gender, sex, and sexuality.*

Before you read "Sex and Gender," jot down your own definition of each of the following words and phrases: gender studies, feminist studies, men's studies, sex, and sexuality. Give examples of what you think the three areas of study are concerned with and be as specific as you can in defining differences between sex and sexuality. Pay close attention to the places where these words and phrases overlap as well as to places where they are very distinct. As you read the essay make notes about Sedgwick's definitions of each of these words and phrases. How do your definitions compare with Sedgwick's? How does Sedgwick help you clarify, complicate, and/or refute your ways of thinking about sex and gender?

Sex and Gender

Gender criticism" sounds like a euphemism for something. In practice it is a euphemism for several things and more than that. One of its subtexts is gay and lesbian criticism. There can be no mystery about why that highly stigmatic label, though increasingly common, should be self-applied with care — however proudly — by those of us who do this scholarship. For instance, I almost never put "gay and lesbian" in the title of undergraduate gay and lesbian studies courses, though I always use the words in the catalog copy. To ask students to mark their transcripts permanently with so much as the name of this subject of study could have unpredictably disabling consequences for them in the future: The military, most churches, the CIA, and much of the psychoanalytic establishment, to mention only a few plausible professions, are still unblinking about wanting to exclude suspected lesbians and gay men, while in only a handful of places in the United States does anyone have even nominal legal protection against the routine denial of employment, housing, insurance, custody, or other rights on the basis of her or his perceived or supposed sexual orientation. Within and around academic institutions, as well, there can be similarly persuasive reasons for soft-selling the challenge to an oppression whose legal, institutional, and extrajudicial sanctions extend, uniquely, quite uninterruptedly up to the present.

Besides code-naming a range of gay- and lesbian-centered theoretical inquiries, "gender studies" also stands in a usably unmarked relation to another rubric, "feminist studies." Feminist studies might be defined as the study of the dynamics of gender definition, inequality, oppression, and change in human societies. To the extent that gender is thus at the definitional center of feminist studies, "gender studies" can sometimes be used as an alternative name for feminist studies, euphemistic only in not specifying, as the "feminist" label more than implicitly does, how far inequality, oppression, and struggle between genders may be seen as differentially constituting gender itself. Women's studies today is commonly defined, at least in practice, by the gender of its object of study (at my university, for instance, the women's studies program will not cross-list courses unless a majority of the texts read are by women). In contrast to women's studies, feminist studies, whose name specifies the angle of an inquiry rather than the sex of either its subject or its object, can make (and indeed has needed to make) the claim of having as privileged a view of male as of female cultural production.

What, then, can or does distinguish the project of gender studies from that of feminist studies? Sometimes, as I have suggested, "gender studies" is another, equally appropriate way of designating "feminist studies" — the reasons for offering the emollient name no more than tactical. In other instances, however, "gender studies" can mean "feminist studies" *minus* feminism or, in another version of the same deadening equation, "women's studies" (in the most positivist meaning of the term) *plus* some compensatory entity called "men's studies." Although they offer an illusion of enhanced inclusiveness, these are the arithmetics that can give "gender studies" a sinister sound to the very scholars most involved in active gender critique. The assumptions behind these usages are intellectually as well as politically stultifying. To assume that the study of gender can be definitionally detached from the analysis and critique of gender inequality, oppression, and struggle (that is, from some form of feminism) ignores, among other things, the telling fact that gender analysis per se became possible only under the pressure of the most pointed and political feminist demand. It ignores, that is to say, the degree to which the otherwise available analytic tools of Western culture had already been structured by precisely the need to naturalize or to deny, and hence to allow the continuance of, a gender inequality already assumed. To figure gender studies as a mere sum of women's studies plus something called "men's studies," meanwhile, reduces both women's studies and the supposedly symmetrical men's studies to static denominations of subject matter and reduces any understanding of relations between genders to something equally static and additive. That genders are constituted as such, not only in dialectical relation to each other but in relation to the oppression historically exercised by one over the other, is a knowledge repressed by this impulse toward the separate but equal. Things get even worse when the rationale for an additive gender studies agenda involves not a nominally depoliticized and positivist study of women as women and men as men but rather the conscious promotion of masculist viewpoints (under the men's studies rubric) as a remedial "balance" against feminist ones. One can only summon up the foundational feminist assertion that colleges don't need something called "men's studies" because so much of the rest of the curriculum already fulfills that function: the function, that is, not only of studying the cultural production of men but of furthering the interest many of them have in rationalizing, maintaining, or increasing their gender privilege over women.

It seems, then, that insofar as "gender studies" actually is the study of gender, its most substantive and intellectually respectable meanings make it coextensive with "feminist studies," and gender criticism coextensive with feminist criticism. Where, then, to look for the distinctive projects of gender criticism beyond its overlap with feminist criticism? In the context of this volume, where feminist criticism has its own topical assignment, distinct from this chapter, it seems particularly possible to insist on the question. And where, for that matter, to look for the already fecund connection of gender criticism with the agendas of gay- and lesbian-centered critique to which I began by alluding? *Homosexual* is not, after all, today understood as the name of a gender, though it alludes to and is defined by reference to gender. Nor has the feminist analysis of mutually constitutive relations and oppressions *between* genders proved to have an adequate purchase on how relations, identities, and oppressions are constituted, as in the exemplary gay instance, *within* genders. Yet so far the greatest success — institutionally as well as intellectually — of gender criticism per se has been specifically in gay and lesbian criticism.

For gender criticism not coextensive with feminist criticism, the most distinctive task may be not to do gender analysis but to explore what resists it: to ask, with respect to certain categories that can't be a priori disentangled from gender, nonetheless, *What isn't gender?* "Gender criticism" might here be taken to mean, then, not criticism *through* the categories of gender analysis but criticism *of* them, the mapping of the fractal borderlines between gender and its others. And if gay and lesbian criticism is so far the typifying site of such interrogations of gender analysis, then the first other of gender would seem to be, in this defining instance, sexuality.

Sex and Gender

Sex, gender, sexuality: three terms whose usage relations and analytical relations are almost irremediably slippery. The charting of a space between something called "sex" and something called "gender" has been one of the most influential and successful undertakings of feminist thought. For the purposes of that undertaking, *sex* has had the meaning of a certain group of irreducible, biological differentiations between members of the species *Homo sapiens* who have XX chromosomes and those who have XY chromosomes. These include (or are ordinarily thought to include) more or less marked dimorphisms of genital formation, hair growth (in populations that have body hair), fat distribution, hormonal function, and reproductive capacity. Sex in this sense—what I'll demarcate as "chromosomal sex"—is seen as the relatively minimal raw material on which is based the social construction of gender. Gender, then, is the far more elaborated, more fully and rigidly dichotomized social production and reproduction of male and female identities and behaviors—of male and female *persons*—in a cultural system for which "male-female" functions as a primary and perhaps model binarism affecting the structure and meaning of many other binarisms whose apparent connection to chromosomal sex may often be exiguous or nonexistent. Compared with chromosomal sex, which is seen (by these definitions) as tending to be immutable, immanent in the individual, and biologically based, gender is seen as culturally mutable and variable, highly relational (in the sense that each of the binarized genders is defined primarily by its relation to the other), and inextricable from a history of power differentials between genders. This feminist charting of what Gayle Rubin refers to as a "sex/gender system" ("Traffic" 159), the system by which chromosomal sex is turned into, and processed as, cultural gender, has tended to minimize the attribution of a person's various behaviors and identities to chromosomal sex and to maximize their attribution to socialized gender constructs. The purpose of that strategy has been to gain analytic and critical leverage on the female-disadvantaging social arrangements that prevail at a given time in a given society, by throwing into question their legitimate ideological grounding in biologically based narratives of the "natural."

Sex is, however, a term that extends indefinitely beyond chromosomal sex. That its history of usage often overlaps with what might now more properly be called "gender" is only one problem. ("I can only love someone of my own sex." Should *sex* be *gender* in such a sentence? "M. saw that the person who approached was of the opposite sex." Genders—insofar as there are two and they are defined in contradistinction to each other—may be said to be opposite; but in what sense is XX the opposite of XY?) Beyond chromosomes, however, the association of *sex,* precisely through the physical body, with reproduction and with genital activity and sensation keeps offering new challenges to the conceptual clarity or even possibility of sex-gender differentiation. A powerful argument can be made that a primary (or *the* primary) issue in gender differentiation and gender struggle is the question of who is to have control of women's (biologically) distinctive reproductive capability. Indeed, the intimacy of the association between several of the most signal forms of gender oppression and the "facts" of women's bodies and women's reproductive activity has led some radical feminists to question, more or less explicitly, the usefulness of insisting on a sex-gender distinction (see, e.g., MacKinnon, "Agenda"). For these reasons, even usages involving the sex-gender system within feminist theory are able to use *sex-gender* only to delineate a problematical space, rather than a crisp distinction. My loose usage here will be to denominate that problematized space of the sex-gender system, the whole package of physical and cultural distinctions between women and men, more simply under the rubric "gender." I adopt this terminology to reduce the likelihood of confusion between *sex* in the sense of the space of differences between male and female (what I'll group under *gender*) and *sex* in the sense of sexuality.

For meanwhile the whole realm of what modern culture refers to as "sexuality" and *also* calls "sex" — the array of acts, expectations, narratives, pleasures, identity formations, and knowledges, in both women and men, that tends to cluster most densely around certain genital sensations but is not adequately defined by them — is virtually impossible to situate on a map delimited by the feminist-defined sex-gender distinction. To the degree that *sexuality* has a center or starting point in certain physical sites, acts, and rhythms associated (however contingently) with procreation or the potential for it, the term in this sense may seem to be of a piece with *chromosomal sex:* a biological necessity for species survival, tending toward the individually immanent, the socially immutable, the given. But to the extent that, as Freud argued and Michel Foucault assumed, the distinctively sexual nature of human sexuality has to do precisely with its excess over or potential difference from the bare choreographies of procreation, sexuality might be the very opposite of what we originally referred to as chromosomal sex: it could occupy, instead, even more than gender the polar position of the relational, the social-symbolic, the constructed, the variable, the representational.

In "Thinking Sex," an influential essay published in 1984, Rubin hypothesizes that although the question of gender and the question of sexuality are inextricable in that each can be expressed only in the terms of the other, they are nonetheless not the same question. In twentieth-century Western culture, Rubin argues, gender and sexuality represent two analytic axes that one may productively imagine as being as distinct from each other as are, say, gender and class or class and race. Distinct, that is, no more than minimally but nonetheless usefully.

Under this hypothesis, just as one has learned to assume that no issue of racial meaning fails to be embodied through the specificity of a particular class position — and no issue of class, for instance, through the specificity of a particular gender position — so no issue of gender would fail to be embodied through the specificity of a particular sexuality, and vice versa; but nonetheless, there could be use in keeping the analytic axes distinct.

An objection to this analogy might be that gender is *definitionally* built into determinations of sexuality, in a way that neither gender nor sexuality is definitionally intertwined with, for instance, determinations of class or race. Without a concept of gender there could be, quite simply, no concept of homo- or heterosexuality. But many other dimensions of sexual choice (auto- or alloerotic; within or between generations, species, etc.) have no such distinctive, explicit definitional connection with gender; indeed some dimensions of sexuality might be tied not to gender but *instead* to differences or similarities of race or class. The definitional narrowing in this century of sexuality as a whole to a binarized calculus of homo- or heterosexuality is a weighty but an entirely historical fact. To use that fait accompli as a reason for analytically conflating sexuality per se with gender obscures the degree to which the fact itself requires explanation. It also, I think, risks obscuring yet again the extreme intimacy with which all these available analytic axes do after all mutually constitute one another: to assume the distinctiveness of the intimacy between sexuality and gender might well risk assuming too much about the definitional separability of either of them from determinations of, say, class or race.

It may also be, as Judith Butler argues in *Gender Trouble,* that a damaging bias toward heterosocial or heterosexist assumptions inheres unavoidably in the very concept of gender. This bias would be built into any gender-based analytic perspective to the extent that gender definition and gender identity are necessarily relational between genders—to the extent, that is, that in any gender system, female identity or definition is constructed by analogy, supplementarity, or contrast to male, or vice versa. Although many gender-based forms of analysis do involve accounts, sometimes fairly rich ones, of intragender behaviors and relations, the ultimate definitional appeal in any gender-based analysis must necessarily be to the diacritical frontier between different genders. This necessity gives heterosocial and heterosexual relations a conceptual privilege of incalculable consequence. Undeniably, residues, markers, tracks, signs referring to that diacritical frontier between genders are everywhere, as well, internal to and determinative of the experience of each gender and its intragender relations; gender-based analysis can never be dispensed with in even the most purely intragender context. Nevertheless, it seems predictable that the analytic bite of a purely gender-based account will grow less incisive and direct as the distance of its subject from a social interface between different genders increases. It is unrealistic to expect a close, textured analysis of same-sex relations through an optic calibrated in the first place to the coarser stigmata of gender difference (see King; de Lauretis, "Sexual Indifference"). The development of an alternative analytic axis—call it sexuality—must be, therefore, if anything a peculiarly central project to gay-lesbian and antihomophobic inquiry.

The gravity of gender division and gender oppression does have, however, the consequence that one can never take for granted how much women's same-sex relations will have analytically or experientially in common with men's; the sense of talking about "gay-lesbian" critique at all is itself always, and with good reason, contested. Still, it does seem that the interpretive frameworks within which lesbian writers, readers, and interlocutors are likely to process male-centered reflections on homo- and heterosexual issues, and vice versa, are currently in a phase of destabilizing flux and promise.

Until recently the lesbian interpretive framework most readily available to critics and theorists was the separatist-feminist one that emerged from the 1970s. According to that framework, there were essentially no valid grounds of commonality between gay-male and lesbian experience and identity; on the contrary, women-loving women and men-loving men were thought to be at precisely opposite ends of the gender spectrum. The assumptions at work here were indeed radical ones: most important among them was the stunningly efficacious re-visioning, in female terms, of same-sex desire as being at the very definitional center of each gender, rather than as occupying a cross-gender or liminal position between genders. Thus, women who loved women were seen as more female, and men who loved men as quite possibly more male, than those whose desire crossed boundaries of gender; the self-identification of the virilized woman gave way, at least for many, to that of the "woman-identified woman." The axis of sexuality, in this view, was not only exactly coextensive with the axis of gender but expressive of its most heightened essence: Feminism is the theory, lesbianism is the practice. By analogy, male homosexuality could be, and often was, seen as the practice for which male supremacy was the theory (see, e.g., M. Frye 128–51; Irigaray 170–91). A particular reading of modern gender history was, of course, implicit in and then propelled by this gender-separatist framework. In accord with, for instance, Adrienne Rich's understanding of many aspects of women's bonds as constituting a "lesbian continuum" ("Compulsory Heterosexuality" 79), this history, found in its purest form in the work of Lilian Faderman, de-emphasized the definitional discontinuities and perturbations between more and less sexualized, more and less prohibited, and more and less gender-identity-bound forms of female same-sex bonding. Insofar as lesbian object choice was viewed as epitomizing a specificity of female experience and resistance, insofar as a symmetrically opposite understanding of gay male object choice also obtained, and insofar also as feminism necessarily posited male and female experiences and interests as different and opposed, the implication was that an understanding of male homo- or heterosexual definition could offer little or no affordance or interest for any lesbian theoretical project. Indeed, the powerful impetus of a gender-polarized feminist ethical schema made it possible for a profoundly antihomophobic reading of lesbian desire (as a quintessence of the female) to fuel a correspondingly homophobic reading of gay male desire (as a quintessence of the male).

Since the late 1970s, however, there have been a variety of challenges to this understanding of how lesbian and gay male desires and identities might be mapped against each other. Each development has led many theorists to a refreshed sense that lesbians and gay men may share important though contested aspects of their histories, cultures, identities, politics, and destinies. These new perspectives have emerged from the "sex wars" within feminism over pornography and sadomasochism, which seemed to many pro-sex feminists to expose a devastating continuity between a certain, theretofore privileged feminist understanding of a resistant female identity, on the one hand, and, on the other, repressive nineteenth-century bourgeois constructions of a sphere of pure femininity. Such challenges arose as well from the reclamation and relegitimation of a courageous history of lesbian transgender role-playing and identification (see E. Newton; Nestle; Hollibaugh and Moraga; Case; de Lauretis, "Sexual Indifference"). Along with this new historical making-visible of self-defined mannish lesbians came a new salience of the many ways in which male and female homosexual identities had in fact been constructed through and in relation to each other over the last century—by the variously homophobic discourses of professional expertise but also and just as actively by many lesbians and gay men (see Grahn). The irrepressible, relatively class-nonspecific popular culture in which James Dean has been as numinous an icon for lesbians as Garbo or Dietrich has been for gay men seems resistant to a purely feminist theorization (see Golding; Dyer). It is in these contexts that calls for a theorized axis of sexuality as distinct from gender have developed. And after the antisadomasochism, antipornography liberal-feminist move toward labeling and stigmatizing particular sexualities joined its energies with those of the much longer established conservative sanctions against all forms of sexual "deviance," it remained only for the terrible accident of the HIV epidemic, and the terrifying societal threats constructed around it, to reconstruct a category of the pervert capacious enough to admit homosexuals of any gender. The newly virulent homophobia of the past decade, directed alike against women and men even though logically its medical pretext ought, if anything, to give a relative exemptive privilege to lesbians,[1] reminds ungently that it is more to our friends than to our enemies that sexually nonconforming women and men are perceptible as distinct groups. At the same time, however, the internal perspective of the gay movements shows women and men increasingly, though far from uncontestingly and far from equally, working together on mutually antihomophobic agendas (see, e.g., Winnow). The contributions brought by lesbians to current gay and AIDS activism are weighty, not despite but because of the intervening lessons of feminism. Feminist perspectives on medicine and health-care issues, on civil disobedience, and on the politics of class and race as well as of sexuality, for instance, have been centrally enabling for the recent waves of AIDS activism, while the extensive repertoire of intellectual strategies amassed and tested by feminism has been of incalculable benefit to emergent gay and lesbian theory. What these developments return to the lesbians involved in them may include a more richly pluralized range of imaginings of lines of gender and sexual identification.

Note

1. I do not, of course, intend to suggest that lesbians are less likely than persons of any other sexuality to contract HIV infection when they engage in the (quite common) acts that can transmit the virus with a person (and there are many, including lesbians) who already carries it. In this particular paradigm clash between a discourse of sexual identity and a discourse of sexual acts, the former alternative is uniquely damaging. No one should wish to reinforce the myth that the epidemiology of AIDS is a matter of discrete "risk groups" rather than of particular acts that can call for particular forms of prophylaxis. That myth is dangerous to self-

identified or publicly identified gay men and drug users because it scapegoats them, and it is dangerous to everyone else because it discourages those outside the "risk groups" from protecting themselves and their partners. But for a variety of reasons, the incidence of AIDS among lesbians has indeed been lower than that among many other groups.

Works Cited

Butler, Judith. *Gender Trouble: Feminism and the Subversion of Identity*. New York: Routledge, 1989.

Case, Sue-Ellen. "Toward a Butch-Femme Aesthetic." *Making a Spectacle: Feminist Essays on Contemporary Women's Theatre*. Ed. Lynda Hart. Ann Arbor: U of Michigan P, 1989. 282–99.

de Lauretis, Teresa. "Sexual Indifference and Lesbian Representation." *Theatre Journal* 40 (1988): 155–77.

Dyer, Richard. "Seen to Be Believed: Some Problems in the Representation of Gay People as Typical." *Studies in Visual Communication* 9.2 (1983): 2–19.

Faderman, Lilian. *Surpassing the Love of Man*. New York: Morrow, 1982.

Foucault, Michel. *Discipline and Punish*. Trans. Alan Sheridan. New York: Vintage, 1979.

Freud, Sigmund. *The Complete Psychological Works of Sigmund Freud: Standard Edition*. Ed. James Strachey. 24 vols. London: Hogarth, 1953–1974.

Frye, Marilyn. *The Politics of Reality: Essays in Feminist Theory*. Trumansburg: Crossing, 1983.

Golding, Sue. "James Dean: The Almost-Perfect Lesbian Hermaphrodite." *On Our Backs* (Winter 1988): 18–19, 39–44.

Grahn, Judy. *Another Mother Tongue: Gay Words, Gay Worlds*. Boston: Beacon, 1984.

Hollibaugh, Amber, and Cherrie Moraga. "What We're Rollin' Around in Bed With." *Heresies* 12.3 (1981): 58–62.

Irigaray, Luce. *This Sex Which Is Not One*. Trans. Catherine Porter, with Carolyn Burke. Ithaca: Cornell UP, 1985.

King, Katie. "The Situation of Lesbianism as Feminism's Magical Sign: Contests for Meaning and the U.S. Women's Movement, 1968–72." *Feminist Critiques of Popular Culture*. Ed. Paula Treichler and Ellen Wartella. Spec. issue of *Communication* 9 (1986): 65–91.

MacKinnon, Catherine A. "Feminism, Marxism, Method, and the State: An Agenda for Theory." *Signs* 7 (1982): 515–44.

Nestle, Joan. "Butch-Fem Relationships." *Heresies* 2.3 (1981): 21–24.

Newton, Esther. "The Mythic Mannish Lesbian: Radclyffe Hall and the New Woman." *The Lesbian Issue: Essays from* Signs. Ed. Estelle B. Freedman et al. Chicago: U of Chicago P, 1985. 7–25.

Rich, Adrienne. "Compulsory Heterosexuality and Lesbian Experience." *Women, Sex, and Sexuality*. Ed. Catharine R. Stimpson and Ethel Spector Person. Chicago: U of Chicago P, 1980. 62–91.

Rubin, Gayle. "Thinking Sex: Notes for a Radical Theory of the Politics of Sexuality." Vance 267–319.

——. "The Traffic in Women: Notes on the 'Political Economy' of Sex." *Toward an Anthropology of Women*. Ed. Rayna R. Reiter. New York: Monthly Review, 1975. 157–210.

Vance, Carole S., ed. *Pleasure and Danger: Exploring Female Sexuality*. Boston: Routledge, 1984.

Winnow, Jackie. "Lesbians Working on AIDS: Assessing the Impact on Health Care for Women." *Out/look: National Lesbian and Gay Quarterly* 5 (1989): 10–18.

Ideas for Rereading

1. Sedgwick's contribution to this chapter might be called a "definitional essay," an essay in which key terms are defined in relation to one another. Beginning with the academic debate over naming that creates programs in "women's studies," "gender studies," "feminist studies," "gay and lesbian studies," and "men's studies," Sedgwick's main emphasis is on "sex, gender, sexuality: three terms whose usage relations and analytical relations are almost irremediably slippery" (p. 116). As you reread "Sex and Gender," use quotations from Sedgwick to develop your own definitions of "sex," "gender," and "sexuality."

2. Use a radial diagram for one or more of the terms that Sedgwick sets out to define in "Sex and Gender" (see p. 15 for an illustration of a radial diagram). For example, put the word *sex* in the center of a blank sheet of paper and draw lines to different areas of the page that define *sex* in different ways. You might, for example, use the following categories suggested by Sedgwick: "chromosomal sex," "sex in the sense of sexuality," "sex" as distinct from "gender," "sex" in the sense of "sexual deviance." Each of these category areas might then branch out into definitional subgroups: "chromosomal sex" might have a branch for "male" and another for "female," each with a list of physical characteristics; "sex in the sense of sexuality" might have branches for "gay men," "lesbians," "straight men," "straight women," "bisexual." Note the places where you need to connect different areas of your diagram, where different categories overlap and otherwise interact.

Ideas for Writing

1. Choose two of the three terms that Sedgwick defines as "almost irremediably slippery" ("sex, gender, sexuality," p. 116). After rereading Sedgwick's discussion of these terms, develop your own account of some of the relationships between the two terms. If possible, introduce examples from your own experiences and observations. Now choose another essay in this chapter (Woolf, hooks, Lorde, Williams, Wittig) that helps to illustrate or illuminate relationships between the terms. Write an essay, drawing on Sedgwick and the example you have chosen from another writer, that explores the "almost irremediably slippery" relationships between the two key terms.

2. Write an essay about the implications of Sedgwick's discussion of "sex and gender" for men. You might begin with her reference to "the foundational feminist assertion that colleges don't need something called 'men's studies' because so much of the rest of the curriculum already fulfills that function" (p. 116). Some of the following questions might stimulate your work on this essay. In what ways might men benefit from increasingly complex understandings of sex, gender, and sexuality? How does Sedgwick's work with definitions of these terms and with "code-naming" fit with your own experiences with men or as a man? To what extent does "the definitional narrowing in this century of sexuality as a whole" (p. 119) seem helpful, normal, or harmful to your life with men or as a man? How important, irrelevant, or reasonable does it seem, to you, to make decisions about such problems as pornography, sado-

masochism, gender identity, gay-lesbian critique, homophobia? In what ways do these problems impact on your life as a man or with men?

EXTENDING YOUR WORK

Ideas for Research

1. Woolf several times suggests projects for the students of Newnham and Girton Colleges to undertake. On page 32, Woolf writes, "What one wants, I thought . . . is a mass of information" about women in the past. Choose an important woman who lived (at least mostly) before Woolf published *A Room of One's Own* (1929). You might begin your research with a good encyclopedia, but eventually you should try to locate and read more detailed sources, such as biographies and historical studies about this woman's life and work. If possible, try to locate and read several primary sources as well — sources that date from the subject's lifetime and provide direct evidence about her life and work, such as diaries, letters, and contemporary newspaper articles. What does your research reveal about the material conditions experienced by the subject? Were they exceptional or normal? What does your research reveal about the way this woman was regarded in her own time? How has her reputation changed over the years? Was her work taken seriously and appreciated during her own lifetime, or do you find evidence to the contrary?

This kind of analysis will help you form an idea of how researchers have gone about the task of uncovering women's lives, feelings, thoughts, and accomplishments. Now return to Woolf with these ideas in mind and consider how the life you have researched compares with the lives described in Woolf's essay. In what ways can Woolf help you understand the differences between the treatment of women and the treatment of men and between the opportunities faced by women and those faced by men? Also, consider the situation of women today. In what ways does *A Room of One's Own* seem outmoded? In what ways is its argument still relevant? What parts of Woolf's argument might you change to make it more relevant to today's social conditions?

2. In the library, find a representative selection of Audre Lorde's poems, either in a volume of poems written by Lorde or in an anthology. Using "The Transformation of Silence into Language and Action" as a framework, write an essay on the way the essay and the poems illuminate one another. How do the poems help us understand what Lorde means by "transforming silence into language"? How do they illuminate terms in the essay such as "warrior poet"? How does the essay help you read and appreciate the poems?

3. Choose two or three quotations from the other writers that bell hooks uses in "Feminism: A Movement to End Sexist Oppression." In the library, find the books or articles that hooks used as the source of these quotations. Then read the entire chapter or article — the "source-text" — from which each quotation was taken. Write an essay considering hooks's use of quotations in the light of where she found the quotations. In what ways does it help you read the full context of these quotations? How does hooks's "extraction" of quotations change their meaning? Which parts of the source-text could hooks also have

quoted? Which parts of the source-texts say things differently than those selected by hooks? You might extend your essay by comparing hooks's use of source-texts with the use of source-texts by another writer in this chapter, after searching the library for the sources of specific quotations used in Woolf, Lorde, Williams, Wittig, or Sedgwick.

4. Patricia Williams bases her essay on a number of contemporary cases picked up from watching television and reading the newspaper. Follow up on her work with these examples by using her footnoted citations to find one of her sources. Once you have located the specific text that Williams refers to, use its details about names, locations, and dates to find related articles. You might, for example, search for other material in the *Washington Post* from the days and weeks both before and after the report called "Woman Charged in Death of Own Fetus in Accident." Or you might look to coverage of this case in newspapers from Massachusetts and elsewhere. Once you have gathered a number of reports, write an essay developing your own interpretation and analysis of this particular case study. In what ways does your fuller sense of this example help you revise your understanding of Williams's work with the example in "Owning the Self in a Disowned World"? How does your extended research into this case study contribute to your ongoing sense of what it means to "own the self in a disowned world"? And how does your work with this example revise your answers to the question "Is one born a woman?"

5. Monique Wittig is associated with a tradition that adopts a "materialist feminist approach to women's oppression" (p. 105). In her two essays she refers to a number of peers and colleagues who work in this tradition. She also suggests how materialist feminism operates when she refers to the marriage contract, the sexualized body, and childbearing as evidence of the ways in which "the myth of woman" has perpetuated heterosexual oppression. Conduct research into the history of a specific aspect of feminism by focusing on a historic change in legislation that affected the material conditions of women as a class. First locate the law, amendment, or decision that changed the legal status of women; then locate documents written during the period when the legislation was debated and changed.

For example, if you focus on woman suffrage, locate and examine articles and essays in newspapers and magazines written between 1915 and 1925; if you focus on *Roe v. Wade,* locate and examine documents from the period 1966–1976; if you focus on women's attendance at federally funded military academies, locate and examine documents from 1990 to 1999. What do you learn about "feminism" and "women" by studying these documents? How do these documents perpetuate, challenge, or reimagine "the myth of woman"? What are the practical consequences of the change in legislation?

6. Search the Internet for Web sites associated with the various programs of study that Sedgwick names at the beginning of her essay: "women's studies," "gender studies," "feminist studies," "gay and lesbian studies," and "men's studies." Write an evaluative report about programs of the sort discussed by Sedgwick. How do the participants in these various programs define their mission? What kinds of work do these programs accomplish? Do these programs seem to be mainly academic (restricted to teaching and scholarship in colleges) or do they engage in community outreach? What kinds of work does each program emphasize? In what ways does each program engage with issues of "sex,"

"gender," and "sexuality"? How are these terms used in documents defining and publicizing each program?

An alternative might be to focus on a specific program at your own college or at a nearby college: find out about the history of the program by studying its publicity documents (Web pages, leaflets, course descriptions in catalogs, syllabi, newsletters). You might also interview participants in the program. Begin with questions that emerge from your reading of Sedgwick—you might, for example, ask for definitions of "sex," "gender," and "sexuality." You might also ask someone to interpret a part of Sedgwick that you find particularly tricky, interesting, or objectionable.

Ideas for Working across Chapters

1. Sigmund Freud (see Chapter 4) and Virginia Woolf both work by telling stories. While they tell stories in different ways and for different purposes, the art of storytelling allows each of them to reveal various truths about lived experience. Write an essay focusing on one story, one specific example, or one episode from each of their essays. Consider carefully the ways in which Freud and Woolf use stories to convey their truths. How does each story further the writer's main argument? Identify and reread passages where Freud and Woolf discuss their own methods as writers. How do these discussions help you appreciate the storytelling methods of each writer? (How, for example, does each writer make a coherent narrative out of apparently unrelated events?)

2. Both Freud and Woolf sought to effect real-world change. Freud was a medical doctor trying to help a suffering patient; Woolf was a writer and publisher seeking to alleviate some of the conditions that impede women writers. How does fiction help, complicate, or hinder practice-based work? How do Freud and Woolf use material facts (statistics, lived experiences, physical realities, biology, money, laws) and how do their uses of material facts interact with their imaginative ways of thinking (their stories and theories)? How, for example, does Freud's factual account of Dora's illness assist, confuse, or prevent your understanding of his interpretation of this factual account? How does Woolf's historical account of women's literary contributions interact with her interpretations of this historical account? Write an essay on the relation between fact and fiction in the work of these two writers. Consider, for example, the ways in which each writer teaches us to read relations between fact and fiction. Consider the ways in which the implied relation between fact and fiction is different for each writer. And consider their uses of fact and fiction in light of what you know about their "human and social circumstances" (p. 317).

3. Consider the ways in which Wittig's rejection of essentialism might affect issues besides "the woman question." Picking up on what she says at the end of "The Category of Sex" and interpreting her statement that "matriarchy is no less heterosexual than patriarchy" (p. 105), apply Wittig's overall way of thinking to examples from other parts of Cultural Conversations. How, for example, does her rejection of "dialectics" help you think about the Dora case (Chapter 4), or about Gandhi's strategies of peace (Chapter 5), or about Du Bois's argument about "double-consciousness" (Chapter 2)?

CHAPTER 2

African American Identity
How Does Race Shape the Arts?

Personal identity—the way we see ourselves—is often at odds with the way we are perceived by other people. At the beginning of the twentieth century, W. E. B. Du Bois suggested that this conflict was especially real to his fellow African Americans. Du Bois cited a "double-consciousness, this sense of always looking at one's self through the eyes of others, of measuring one's soul by the tape of a world that looks on in amused contempt and pity" (p. 132). To varying degrees, the history of African Americans and the arts bears out this conflict between the right and desire to define one's personal and cultural identity and the attempts of the outside world to stereotype based on race, class, and gender. This conflict is especially evident to artists, whose personal identity must be shared and expressed in order to make art, to be part of the creative process.

The vast African American contribution to the literary, visual, and performing arts is an undeniable fact of American history. Arts that are considered distinctly American—particularly musical forms such as jazz, rock, soul, and hip-hop; textile arts such as quilt making; and dance, including tap dancing—were in large part, and often exclusively, originated by African Americans. Even where black people did not create an art form—film, fiction, theater—their work and their influence have still had a huge impact on that art form's development and character in the United States. The larger American community—especially white America—has admired, even emulated, black artists and performers. Yet, at the same time, Americans not of African descent have often found it hard to see the integral part black people have played in the foundation and development of American art forms and of American culture in its broadest sense. Even where many Americans have to a degree acknowledged the history of black people's artistic contributions, the arts, along with sports, are often unfairly seen as the only areas of society where African Americans hold an important place.

Moreover, the arts have often formed and promulgated the very stereotypes that impede black people's desire to be seen and known as they see and know themselves. The performing arts—from the early proliferation of so-called minstrel shows to film depictions of African Americans as servants, criminals, or victims—have been particularly guilty in this regard. The practitioners of these art forms have even employed black people themselves in the service of racially biased stereotypes.

Each of the essays collected in this chapter explores some aspect of African American self-definition and its relation to the arts. Starting with Du Bois, the writers all discuss the problems of finding a personal and creative voice in the face of demeaning, elitist, or racist interpretations of what it is to be an African American. At the same time, the essays explore the extent to which artistic endeavor can and should reflect a particular cultural identity, putting forth the conflict between individuality and identification with a group—or two groups, American and black. While Du Bois's "Of Our Spiritual Strivings" deals specifically with concepts of identity, its companion piece here, "The Sorrow Songs," relates the issue of identity to the history and critique of the unique art form known as the "Negro spiritual." In the Contemporary Conversation section, Alice Walker and Glenn Loury both use the art form of the personal essay to explore questions of identity, while Walker deals specifically with neglected expressions of black female creativity such as quilt making, poetry, and gardening. Hazel Carby and Joan Morgan analyze the work of contemporary artists. In looking at the film personae and career of black actor Danny Glover, Carby posits an image of black male identity created by white filmmakers to serve white American concerns and desires. In contemporary rap and hip-hop, Morgan finds troubling expressions of sexism and even racism, but she argues that hip-hop is able "to articulate the pain our community is in" and can therefore be used to help "create a redemptive, healing space" (p. 203).

As you read these selections by Du Bois and other writers, note the variety of ways the authors assert their own right to self-definition, as well as that of their fellow African Americans. What is the significance of the arts as both aid and impediment to that process of self-definition? Where do you see tensions between calls for the expression of personal identity and calls for identification with a larger group or culture? Where do you notice yourself embracing or resisting what these writers say?

TEXT

W. E. B. DU BOIS

African American writer and critic Cornel West has referred to W. E. B. Du Bois as "the towering black scholar of the twentieth century," and indeed this may be true. A writer, teacher, editor, and social activist, Du Bois wrote in almost every imaginable genre—from journalism to literary criticism to fiction to children's stories. His writings, including The Souls of Black Folk *and* Dusk of Dawn, *as well as his* twenty-four-year tenure as editor of the NAACP journal The Crisis, *celebrate black people's unique and invaluable contribution to American culture while maintaining and insisting upon African American social and political equality. Du Bois's career and activism have influenced almost every African American scholar, and his ideas—even when questioned—are still considered relevant today in both the black community and the larger community of thinking Americans.*

William Edward Burghardt Du Bois was born in the small Massachusetts town of Great Barrington on February 23, 1868—as he would later note, this was five years after the Emancipation Proclamation. Du Bois was one of only a handful of black people living in Great Barrington and attending the town's small high school. Graduating the sole black person in his class, he was sent on scholarship to Fisk University in Nashville, Tennessee, where he found himself "thrilled to be for the first time among people of [his] own color." From Fisk, Du Bois continued to Harvard University, where he began writing outspoken articles about racial politics for the black newspaper The Boston Courant. He would eventually become the first black person to receive a doctorate from Harvard, and his dissertation, "The Suppression of the African Slave Trade in the United States of America 1638–1870," remains in print to this day as the first volume of the university's series of important historical studies.

While he isolated himself from the almost exclusively white student community at Harvard, Du Bois's subsequent years of study in Europe led him to believe that racial inequality and segregation were not inevitable but simply an example of "American narrowness." It was also during his time in Europe that Du Bois came to believe in the concept of Pan-Africanism. He wrote that while black people were indeed Americans by "political ideals . . . language . . . religion," they were as importantly "Negroes, members of a vast historic race . . . the first fruits of this new nation." Du Bois's belief in the unity and dignity of black people as both Americans and people of African descent was put forth eloquently in The Souls of Black Folk (1903). In this collection of essays, Du Bois illustrates his concept of the "veil" that separates his fellow "Negroes" from both white America and their own Africanness. Du Bois's admiration for uniquely African American culture, religion, and art—particularly the music of the Negro spiritual—and his insistence that black Americans not succumb to white expectations and bigotry were revolutionary ideas in the early twentieth century. Du Bois's book was an implicit—at times more than implicit—rejection of the pioneering black educator Booker T. Washington's nonconfrontational approach to the development of legal protection and social equality for blacks. Discussion and critique over the differences between Du Bois and Washington continue to this day.

Du Bois's social activism and his drive to be a leader among African Americans are evident in his commitment to organizing his people politically—first in the short-lived Niagara Movement of the early 1900s and later, most enduringly, as one of the founders of the NAACP (National Association for the Advancement of Colored People). He was the only black person elected to the NAACP's original board in 1910, and for the next twenty-four years, as founding editor of The Crisis, he would record and comment upon not only the ongoing struggles and triumphs of black Americans but his own ever-evolving political and social views. Du Bois would evince an increasing interest in Pan-Africanism as well as a belief in the centrality of the class struggle to the issue of human equality. Though his actual association with any socialist party was minimal, in later years his support of perceived socialist causes would lead him into difficulty with the United States government, especially the cold war–era FBI, which saw Du Bois's position as chair of the Peace

Information Center (1950–51) as an example of his Communist and Soviet sympathies. At the height of the 1950s "Red scare," because of his work with the Peace Information Center, Du Bois was investigated by the FBI and indicted with four others for failing to register as an agent of the Soviet Union.

At least partially because of his treatment by the FBI, Du Bois's influence in the American black community seemed for a time to fade near the end of his life. Yet abroad, particularly in Africa, his reputation was that of a great leader and scholar—so much so that in 1960 Kwame Nkrumah, the first president of Ghana, invited the ninety-one-year-old Du Bois to move to that country to begin work on The Encyclopedia Africana. *Du Bois would spend the remainder of his days as a Ghanian citizen at the center of an illustrious collection of African writers and leaders. After his death on August 27, 1963—one day before the March on Washington and Martin Luther King's historic "I Have a Dream" speech—Du Bois was given a state funeral by his adopted country. Five years later, on the one hundredth anniversary of Du Bois's birth, King would say of this "Father of Africa": "He saw and loved progressive humanity in all its hues, black, white, yellow, red and brown. . . . Dr. Du Bois has left us but he has not died. The spirit of freedom is not buried in the grave of the valiant."*

The following selections were originally published separately as individual essays and then collected, with other essays, into a single volume, The Souls of Black Folk, *which remains one of Du Bois's most read works. If Du Bois is the "towering"—the most historically important and influential—African American intellectual, where do we see his influence in today's society? Where have his ideas been put to use; where and how modified or rejected? How are his ideas still meaningful or relevant to issues of racial or cultural identity in the twenty-first century? In their discussions of the African American identity and the arts, how do the contemporary authors in this chapter reflect Du Bois's thinking and concerns?*

From *The Souls of Black Folk*

Of Our Spiritual Strivings

O water, voice of my heart, crying in the sand,
* All night long crying with a mournful cry,*
As I lie and listen, and cannot understand
*   The voice of my heart in my side or the voice of the sea,*
* O water, crying for rest, is it I, is it I?*
* All night long the water is crying to me.*

Unresting water, there shall never be rest
* Till the last moon droop and the last tide fail,*
And the fire of the end begin to burn in the west;
*   And the heart shall be weary and wonder and cry like the sea,*
* All life long crying without avail,*
*   As the water all night long is crying to me.*

—Arthur Symons

Between me and the other world there is ever an unasked question: unasked by some through feelings of delicacy; by others through the difficulty of rightly framing it. All, nevertheless, flutter round it. They approach me in a half-hesitant sort of way, eye me curiously or compassionately, and then, instead of saying directly, How does it feel to be a problem? they say, I know an excellent colored man in my town; or, I fought at Mechanicsville;* or, Do not these Southern outrages make your blood boil? At these I smile, or am interested, or reduce the boiling to a simmer, as the occasion may require. To the real question, How does it feel to be a problem? I answer seldom a word.

And yet, being a problem is a strange experience,—peculiar even for one who has never been anything else, save perhaps in babyhood and in Europe. It is the early days of rollicking boyhood that the revelation first bursts upon one, all in a day, as it were. I remember well when the shadow swept across me. I was a little thing, away up in the hills of New England, where the dark Housatonic* winds between Hoosac and Taghkanic to the sea. In a wee wooden schoolhouse, something put it into the boys' and girls' heads to buy gorgeous visiting-cards—ten cents a package—and exchange. The exchange was merry, till one girl, a tall newcomer, refused my card,—refused it peremptorily, with a glance. Then it dawned upon me with a certain suddenness that I was different from the others; or like, mayhap, in heart and life and longing, but shut out from their world by a vast veil. I had thereafter no desire to tear down that veil, to creep through; I held all beyond it in common contempt, and lived above it in a region of blue sky and great wandering shadows. That sky was bluest when I could beat my mates at examination-time, or beat them at a foot-race, or even beat their stringy heads. Alas, with the years all this fine contempt began to fade; for the worlds I longed for, and all their dazzling opportunities, were theirs, not mine. But they should not keep these prizes, I said; some, all, I would wrest from them. Just how I would do it I could never decide: by reading law, by healing the sick, by telling the wonderful tales that swam in my head,—some way. With other black boys the strife was not so fiercely sunny: their youth shrunk into tasteless sycophancy, or into silent hatred of the pale world about them and mocking distrust of everything white; or wasted itself in a bitter cry, Why did God make me an outcast and a stranger in mine own house? The shades of the prison-house closed round about us all: walls strait and stubborn to the whitest, but relentlessly narrow, tall, and unscalable to sons of night who must plod darkly on in resignation, or beat unavailing palms against the stone, or steadily, half hopelessly, watch the streak of blue above.

Mechanicsville: A town near Richmond, Virginia. It was the site of a particularly bloody battle during the Civil War. The Confederate army suffered overwhelming casualties.
Housatonic: A river in Massachusetts that flows near Great Barrington, the childhood home of Du Bois.

After the Egyptian and Indian, the Greek and Roman, the Teuton and Mongolian, the Negro is a sort of seventh son, born with a veil, and gifted with second-sight in this American world,—a world which yields him no true self-consciousness, but only lets him see himself through the revelation of the other world. It is a peculiar sensation, this double-consciousness, this sense of always looking at one's self through the eyes of others, of measuring one's soul by the tape of a world that looks on in amused contempt and pity. One ever feels his two-ness,—an American, a Negro; two souls, two thoughts, two unreconciled strivings; two warring ideals in one dark body, whose dogged strength alone keeps it from being torn asunder.

The history of the American Negro is the history of this strife,—this longing to attain self-conscious manhood, to merge his double self into a better and truer self. In this merging he wishes neither of the older selves to be lost. He would not Africanize America, for America has too much to teach the world and Africa. He would not bleach his Negro soul in a flood of white Americanism, for he knows that Negro blood has a message for the world. He simply wishes to make it possible for a man to be both a Negro and an American, without being cursed and spit upon by his fellows, without having the doors of Opportunity closed roughly in his face.

This, then, is the end of his striving: to be a co-worker in the kingdom of culture, to escape both death and isolation, to husband and use his best powers and his latent genius. These powers of body and mind have in the past been strangely wasted, dispersed, or forgotten. The shadow of a mighty Negro past flits through the tale of Ethiopia the Shadowy and of Egypt the Sphinx. Throughout history, the powers of single black men flash here and there like falling stars, and die sometimes before the world has rightly gauged their brightness. Here in America, in the few days since Emancipation, the black man's turning hither and thither in hesitant and doubtful striving has often made his very strength to lose effectiveness, to seem like absence of power, like weakness. And yet it is not weakness,—it is the contradiction of double aims. The double-aimed struggle of the black artisan—on the one hand to escape white contempt for a nation of mere hewers of wood and drawers of water, and on the other hand to plough and nail and dig for a poverty-stricken horde—could only result in making him a poor craftsman, for he had but half a heart in either cause. By the poverty and ignorance of his people, the Negro minister or doctor was tempted toward quackery and demagogy; and by the criticism of the other world, toward ideals that made him ashamed of his lowly tasks. The would-be black *savant* was confronted by the paradox that the knowledge his people needed was a twice-told tale to his white neighbors, while the knowledge which would teach the white world was Greek to his own flesh and blood. The innate love of harmony and beauty that set the rude souls of his people a-dancing and a-singing raised but confusion and doubt in the soul of the black artist; for the beauty revealed to him was the soul-beauty of a race which his larger audience despised, and he could not articulate the message of another people. This waste of double aims, this seeking to satisfy two unreconciled ideals, has wrought sad havoc with the courage and faith and deeds of ten thousand thousand people,—has sent them often wooing false gods and invoking false means of salvation, and at times has even seemed about to make them ashamed of themselves.

Away back in the days of bondage they thought to see in one divine event the end of all doubt and disappointment; few men ever worshipped Freedom with half such unquestioning faith as did the American Negro for two centuries. To him, so far as he thought and dreamed, slavery was indeed the sum of all villainies, the cause of all sorrow, the root of all prejudice; Emancipation was the key to a promised land of sweeter beauty than ever stretched before the eyes of wearied Israelites. In song and exhortation swelled one refrain—Liberty; in his tears and curses the God he implored had Freedom in his right hand. At last it came,—suddenly, fearfully, like a dream. With one wild carnival of blood and passion came the message in his own plaintive cadences:—

> "Shout, O children!
> Shout, you're free!
> For God has bought your liberty!"

Years have passed away since then,—ten, twenty, forty; forty years of national life, forty years of renewal and development, and yet the swarthy spectre sits in its accustomed seat at the Nation's feast. In vain do we cry to this our vastest social problem:—

> "Take any shape but that, and my firm nerves
> Shall never tremble!"

The Nation has not yet found peace from its sins; the freedman has not yet found in freedom his promised land. Whatever of good may have come in these years of change, the shadow of a deep disappointment rests upon the Negro people,—a disappointment all the more bitter because the unattained ideal was unbounded save by the simple ignorance of a lowly people.

The first decade was merely a prolongation of the vain search for freedom, the boon that seemed ever barely to elude their grasp,—like a tantalizing will-o'-the-wisp, maddening and misleading the headless host. The holocaust of war, the terrors of the Ku-Klux Klan, the lies of carpetbaggers, the disorganization of industry, and the contradictory advice of friends and foes, left the bewildered serf with no new watchword beyond the old cry for freedom. As the time flew, however, he began to grasp a new idea. The ideal of liberty demanded for its attainment powerful means, and these the Fifteenth Amendment* gave him. The ballot, which before he had looked upon as a visible sign of freedom, he now regarded as the chief

Fifteenth Amendment: Ratified on February 3, 1870, this amendment extended the right to vote to include black American men, including former slaves. It reads thus: "The right of citizens of the United States to vote shall not be denied or abridged by the United States or by any State on account of race, color, or previous condition of servitude."

means of gaining and perfecting the liberty with which war had partially endowed him. And why not? Had not votes made war and emancipated millions? Had not votes enfranchised the freedmen? Was anything impossible to a power that had done all this? A million black men started with renewed zeal to vote themselves into the kingdom. So the decade flew away, the revolution of 1876* came, and left the half-free serf weary, wondering, but still inspired. Slowly but steadily, in the following years, a new vision began gradually to replace the dream of political power,—a powerful movement, the rise of another ideal to guide the unguided, another pillar of fire by night after a clouded day. It was the ideal of "book-learning"; the curiosity, born of compulsory ignorance, to know and test the power of the cabalistic letters of the white man, the longing to know. Here at last seemed to have been discovered the mountain path to Canaan; longer than the highway of Emancipation and law, steep and rugged, but straight, leading to heights high enough to overlook life.

Up the new path the advance guard toiled, slowly, heavily, doggedly; only those who have watched and guided the faltering feet, the misty minds, the dull understandings, of the dark pupils of these schools know how faithfully, how piteously, this people strove to learn. It was weary work. The cold statistician wrote down the inches of progress here and there, noted also where here and there a foot had slipped or some one had fallen. To the tired climbers, the horizon was ever dark, the mists were often cold, the Canaan was always dim and far away. If, however, the vistas disclosed as yet no goal, no resting-place, little but flattery and criticism, the journey at least gave leisure for reflection and self-examination; it changed the child of Emancipation to the youth with dawning self-consciousness, self-realization, self-respect. In those sombre forests of his striving his own soul rose before him, and he saw himself,—darkly as through a veil; and yet he saw in himself some faint revelation of his power, of his mission. He began to have a dim feeling that, to attain his place in the world, he must be himself, and not another. For the first time he sought to analyze the burden he bore upon his back, that dead-weight of social degradation partially masked behind a half-named Negro problem. He felt his poverty; without a cent, without a home, without land, tools, or savings, he had entered into competition with rich, landed, skilled neighbors. To be a poor man is hard, but to be a poor race in a land of dollars is the very bottom of hardships. He felt the weight of his ignorance,— not simply of letters, but of life, of business, of the humanities; the accumulated sloth and shirking and awkwardness of decades and centuries shackled his hands and feet. Nor was his burden all poverty and ignorance. The red stain of bastardy, which two centuries of systematic legal defilement of

revolution of 1876: During the decade following the Civil War, American blacks experienced a period of relative freedom, but the "Revolution of 1876" put an end to this period of "Reconstruction." Regarded as a backward revolution, the defeat of Radical Republicans (also known as "Lincoln Republicans") and the election of a moderate Republican Congress under President Rutherford Hayes began a period during which federal protections of Southern blacks were steadily withdrawn. Jim Crow laws proliferated after 1876.

Negro women had stamped upon his race, meant not only the loss of ancient African chastity, but also the hereditary weight of a mass of corruption from white adulterers, threatening almost the obliteration of the Negro home.

A people thus handicapped ought not to be asked to race with the world, but rather allowed to give all its time and thought to its own social problems. But alas! while sociologists gleefully count his bastards and his prostitutes, the very soul of the toiling, sweating black man is darkened by the shadow of a vast despair. Men call the shadow prejudice, and learnedly explain it as the natural defence of culture against barbarism, learning against ignorance, purity against crime, the "higher" against the "lower" races. To which the Negro cries Amen! and swears that to so much of this strange prejudice as is founded on just homage to civilization, culture, righteousness, and progress, he humbly bows and meekly does obeisance. But before that nameless prejudice that leaps beyond all this he stands helpless, dismayed, and well-nigh speechless; before that personal disrespect and mockery, the ridicule and systematic humiliation, the distortion of fact and wanton license of fancy, the cynical ignoring of the better and the boisterous welcoming of the worse, the all-pervading desire to inculcate disdain for everything black, from Toussaint* to the devil,—before this there rises a sickening despair that would disarm and discourage any nation save that black host to whom "discouragement" is an unwritten word.

But the facing of so vast a prejudice could not but bring the inevitable self-questioning, self-disparagement, and lowering of ideals which ever accompany repression and breed in an atmosphere of contempt and hate. Whisperings and portents came borne upon the four winds: Lo! we are diseased and dying, cried the dark hosts; we cannot write, our voting is vain; what need of education, since we must always cook and serve? And the Nation echoed and enforced this self-criticism, saying: Be content to be servants, and nothing more; what need of higher culture for half-men? Away with the black man's ballot, by force or fraud,—and behold the suicide of a race! Nevertheless, out of the evil came something of good,—the more careful adjustment of education to real life, the clearer perception of the Negroes' social responsibilities, and the sobering realization of the meaning of progress.

So dawned the time of *Sturm und Drang:** storm and stress to-day rocks our little boat on the mad waters of the world-sea; there is within and without the sound of conflict, the burning of body and rending of soul; inspiration strives with doubt, and faith with vain questionings. The bright ideals of the past,—physical freedom, political power, the training of brains and the training of hands,—all these in turn have waxed and

---

Toussaint: François Dominique Toussaint L'Ouverture (1744–1803). Haitian patriot and martyr. He was freed from slavery shortly before a black slave rebellion in 1791. He joined the rebellion and became its leader, eventually challenging French imperial rule in Haiti. Toussaint died in prison before Haiti achieved independence from France.
Sturm und Drang: Du Bois translates this German phrase as "storm and stress."

waned, until even the last grows dim and overcast. Are they all wrong,—all false? No, not that, but each alone was over-simple and incomplete,—the dreams of a credulous race-childhood, or the fond imaginings of the other world which does not know and does not want to know our power. To be really true, all these ideals must be melted and welded into one. The training of the schools we need to-day more than ever,—the training of deft hands, quick eyes and ears, and above all the broader, deeper, higher culture of gifted minds and pure hearts. The power of the ballot we need in sheer self-defence,—else what shall save us from a second slavery? Freedom, too, the long-sought, we still seek,—the freedom of life and limb, the freedom to work and think, the freedom to love and aspire. Work, culture, liberty,—all these we need, not singly but together, not successively but together, each growing and aiding each, and all striving toward that vaster ideal that swims before the Negro people, the ideal of human brotherhood, gained through the unifying ideal of Race; the ideal of fostering and developing the traits and talents of the Negro, not in opposition to or contempt for other races, but rather in large conformity to the greater ideals of the American Republic, in order that some day on American soil two world-races may give each to each those characteristics both so sadly lack. We the darker ones come even now not altogether empty-handed: there are to-day no truer exponents of the pure human spirit of the Declaration of Independence than the American Negroes; there is no true American music but the wild sweet melodies of the Negro slave; the American fairy tales and folk-lore are Indian and African; and, all in all, we black men seem the sole oasis of simple faith and reverence in a dusty desert of dollars and smartness. Will America be poorer if she replace her brutal dyspeptic blundering with light-hearted but determined Negro humility? or her coarse and cruel wit with loving jovial good-humor? or her vulgar music with the soul of the Sorrow Songs?

Merely a concrete test of the underlying principles of the great republic is the Negro Problem, and the spiritual striving of the freedmen's sons is the travail of souls whose burden is almost beyond the measure of their strength, but who bear it in the name of an historic race, in the name of this the land of their fathers' fathers, and in the name of human opportunity.

And now what I have briefly sketched in large outline let me on coming pages tell again in many ways, with loving emphasis and deeper detail, that men may listen to the striving in the souls of black folk.

The Sorrow Songs

I walk through the churchyard
  To lay this body down;
I know moon-rise, I know star-rise;
I walk in the moonlight, I walk in the starlight;

I 'll lie in the grave and stretch out my arms,
I 'll go to judgment in the evening of the day,
And my soul and thy soul shall meet that day,
When I lay this body down.
— NEGRO SONG

They that walked in darkness sang songs in the olden days—Sorrow Songs—for they were weary at heart. And so before each thought that I have written in this book I have set a phrase, a haunting echo of these weird old songs in which the soul of the black slave spoke to men. Ever since I was a child these songs have stirred me strangely. They came out of the South unknown to me, one by one, and yet at once I knew them as of me and of mine. Then in after years when I came to Nashville I saw the great temple builded of these songs towering over the pale city. To me Jubilee Hall* seemed ever made of the songs themselves, and its bricks were red with the blood and dust of toil. Out of them rose for me morning, noon, and night, bursts of wonderful melody, full of the voices of my brothers and sisters, full of the voices of the past.

Little of beauty has America given the world save the rude grandeur God himself stamped on her bosom; the human spirit in this new world has expressed itself in vigor and ingenuity rather than in beauty. And so by fateful chance the Negro folk-song—the rhythmic cry of the slave—stands to-day not simply as the sole American music, but as the most beautiful expression of human experience born this side the seas. It has been neglected, it has been, and is, half despised, and above all it has been persistently mistaken and misunderstood; but notwithstanding, it still remains as the singular spiritual heritage of the nation and the greatest gift of the Negro people.

Away back in the thirties the melody of these slave songs stirred the nation, but the songs were soon half forgotten. Some, like "Near the lake where drooped the willow," passed into current airs and their source was forgotten; others were caricatured on the "minstrel" stage* and their memory died away. Then in war-time came the singular Port Royal experiment* after the capture of Hilton Head, and perhaps for the first time the

Jubilee Hall: The concert hall at Fisk University in Nashville, Tennessee, for which the Fisk Jubilee Singers are named.

"minstrel" stage: A reference to the use of theaters for a form of popular entertainment in the nineteenth century and well into the twentieth. White performers appeared in "blackface" makeup, dancing and singing songs in a style designed to imitate and parody black and slave culture.

Port Royal experiment: Begun soon after Union soldiers occupied the St. Helena Sea Island, off the coast of Georgia and South Carolina, early in the Civil War, the Port Royal experi-

North met the Southern slave face to face and heart to heart with no third witness. The Sea Islands of the Carolinas, where they met, were filled with a black folk of primitive type, touched and moulded less by the world about them than any others outside the Black Belt. Their appearance was uncouth, their language funny, but their hearts were human and their singing stirred men with a mighty power. Thomas Wentworth Higginson* hastened to tell of these songs, and Miss McKim* and others urged upon the world their rare beauty. But the world listened only half credulously until the Fisk Jubilee Singers sang the slave songs so deeply into the world's heart that it can never wholly forget them again.

There was once a blacksmith's son born at Cadiz, New York, who in the changes of time taught school in Ohio and helped defend Cincinnati from Kirby Smith.* Then he fought at Chancellorsville and Gettysburg and finally served in the Freedman's Bureau at Nashville. Here he formed a Sunday-school class of black children in 1866, and sang with them and taught them to sing. And then they taught him to sing, and when once the glory of the Jubilee songs passed into the soul of George L. White, he knew his life-work was to let those Negroes sing to the world as they had sung to him. So in 1871 the pilgrimage of the Fisk Jubilee Singers began. North to Cincinnati they rode, — four half-clothed black boys and five girl-women, — led by a man with a cause and a purpose. They stopped at Wilberforce, the oldest of Negro schools, where a black bishop blessed them. Then they went, fighting cold and starvation, shut out of hotels, and cheerfully sneered at, ever northward; and ever the magic of their song kept thrilling hearts, until a burst of applause in the Congregational Council at Oberlin revealed them to the world. They came to New York and Henry Ward Beecher* dared to welcome them, even though the metropolitan dailies sneered at his "Nigger Minstrels." So their songs conquered till they sang across the land and across the sea, before Queen and Kaiser, in

---

ment was an abolitionist's demonstration of the beneficial effects of freedom and education on a distinct community of Southern ex-slaves. The freed blacks cultivated and picked an especially lucrative variety of long-fibered cotton called Sea Island Cotton. The experiment, supported by the Union government, succeeded in convincing skeptical Northerners that African Americans deserved freedom at the same time that it filled Union coffers.

Thomas Wentworth Higginson: American author and Unitarian minister (1823–1911). He was the colonel of the first African American regiment and led them to battle against the Confederate army in the Civil War.

Miss McKim: Lucy McKim Garrison (1842–1877) was coauthor, with William Francis Allen and Charles Pickard Ware, of the classic 1867 anthology *Slave Songs of the United States.* The book represented the first systematic effort to collect and preserve songs sung by plantation slaves of the Old South. Giving the music and lyrics for over 130 songs, the book is arranged geographically.

Kirby Smith: Edmund Kirby Smith (1824–1893), Confederate general in the Civil War. He was the last Confederate general to surrender, May 26, 1865.

Henry Ward Beecher: (1813–1887) American preacher, orator and lecturer. Brother to Harriet Beecher Stowe, he was a leader in the antislavery movement.

Scotland and Ireland, Holland and Switzerland. Seven years they sang, and brought back a hundred and fifty thousand dollars to found Fisk University.

Since their day they have been imitated—sometimes well, by the singers of Hampton and Atlanta, sometimes ill, by straggling quartettes. Caricature has sought again to spoil the quaint beauty of the music, and has filled the air with many debased melodies which vulgar ears scarce know from the real. But the true Negro folk-song still lives in the hearts of those who have heard them truly sung and in the hearts of the Negro people.

What are these songs, and what do they mean? I know little of music and can say nothing in technical phrase, but I know something of men, and knowing them, I know that these songs are the articulate message of the slave to the world. They tell us in these eager days that life was joyous to the black slave, careless and happy. I can easily believe this of some, of many. But not all the past South, though it rose from the dead, can gainsay the heart-touching witness of these songs. They are the music of an unhappy people, of the children of disappointment; they tell of death and suffering and unvoiced longing toward a truer world, of misty wanderings and hidden ways.

The songs are indeed the siftings of centuries; the music is far more ancient than the words, and in it we can trace here and there signs of development. My grandfather's grandmother was seized by an evil Dutch trader two centuries ago; and coming to the valleys of the Hudson and Housatonic, black, little, and lithe, she shivered and shrank in the harsh north winds, looked longingly at the hills, and often crooned a heathen melody to the child between her knees, thus:

The child sang it to his children and they to their children's children, and so two hundred years it has travelled down to us and we sing it to our children, knowing as little as our fathers what its words may mean, but knowing well the meaning of its music.

This was primitive African music; it may be seen in larger form in the strange chant which heralds "The Coming of John":

"You may bury me in the East,
You may bury me in the West,
But I 'll hear the trumpet sound in that morning,"

—the voice of exile.

Ten master songs, more or less, one may pluck from this forest of melody—songs of undoubted Negro origin and wide popular currency, and songs peculiarly characteristic of the slave. One of these I have just mentioned. Another whose strains begin this book is "Nobody knows the trouble I 've seen." When, struck with a sudden poverty, the United States refused to fulfil its promises of land to the freedmen, a brigadier-general went down to the Sea Islands to carry the news. An old woman on the out-skirts of the throng began singing this song; all the mass joined with her, swaying. And the soldier wept.

The third song is the cradle-song of death which all men know,—"Swing low, sweet chariot,"—whose bars begin the life story of "Alexan-der Crummell." Then there is the song of many waters, "Roll, Jordan, roll," a mighty chorus with minor cadences. There were many songs of the fugitive like that which opens "The Wings of Atalanta," and the more fa-miliar "Been a-listening." The seventh is the song of the End and the Begin-ning—"My Lord, what a mourning! when the stars begin to fall"; a strain of this is placed before "The Dawn of Freedom." The song of groping—"My way's cloudy"—begins "The Meaning of Progress"; the ninth is the song of this chapter—"Wrestlin' Jacob, the day is a-breaking,"—a pæan of hopeful strife. The last master song is the song of songs—"Steal away,"—sprung from "The Faith of the Fathers."

There are many others of the Negro folk-songs as striking and charac-teristic as these, . . . and others I am sure could easily make a selection on more scientific principles. There are, too, songs that seem to me a step re-moved from the more primitive types: there is the maze-like medley, "Bright sparkles," one phrase of which heads "The Black Belt"; the Easter carol, "Dust, dust and ashes"; the dirge, "My mother's took her flight and gone home"; and that burst of melody hovering over "The Passing of the First-Born"—"I hope my mother will be there in that beautiful world on high."

These represent a third step in the development of the slave song, of which "You may bury me in the East" is the first, and songs like "March on" . . . and "Steal away" are the second. The first is African music, the second Afro-American, while the third is a blending of Negro music with the music heard in the foster land. The result is still distinctively Negro and the method of blending original, but the elements are both Negro and Cau-casian. One might go further and find a fourth step in this development, where the songs of white America have been distinctively influenced by the slave songs or have incorporated whole phrases of Negro melody, as "Swa-nee River" and "Old Black Joe." Side by side, too, with the growth has gone the debasements and imitations—the Negro "minstrel" songs, many of the "gospel" hymns, and some of the contemporary "coon" songs,—a mass of music in which the novice may easily lose himself and never find the real Negro melodies.

In these songs, I have said, the slave spoke to the world. Such a message is naturally veiled and half articulate. Words and music have lost each other and new and cant phrases of a dimly understood theology have displaced the older sentiment. Once in a while we catch a strange word of an unknown tongue, as the "Mighty Myo," which figures as a river of death; more often slight words or mere doggerel are joined to music of singular sweetness. Purely secular songs are few in number, partly because many of them were turned into hymns by a change of words, partly because the frolics were seldom heard by the stranger, and the music less often caught. Of nearly all the songs, however, the music is distinctly sorrowful. The ten master songs I have mentioned tell in word and music of trouble and exile, of strife and hiding; they grope toward some unseen power and sigh for rest in the End.

The words that are left to us are not without interest, and, cleared of evident dross, they conceal much of real poetry and meaning beneath conventional theology and unmeaning rhapsody. Like all primitive folk, the slave stood near to Nature's heart. Life was a "rough and rolling sea" like the brown Atlantic of the Sea Islands; the "Wilderness" was the home of God, and the "lonesome valley" led to the way of life. "Winter'll soon be over," was the picture of life and death to a tropical imagination. The sudden wild thunderstorms of the South awed and impressed the Negroes,— at times the rumbling seemed to them "mournful," at times imperious:

"My Lord calls me,
He calls me by the thunder,
The trumpet sounds it in my soul."

The monotonous toil and exposure is painted in many words. One sees the ploughmen in the hot, moist furrow, singing:

"Dere 's no rain to wet you,
Dere 's no sun to burn you,
Oh, push along, believer,
I want to go home."

The bowed and bent old man cries, with thrice-repeated wail:

"O Lord, keep me from sinking down,"

and he rebukes the devil of doubt who can whisper:

"Jesus is dead and God 's gone away."

Yet the soul-hunger is there, the restlessness of the savage, the wail of the wanderer, and the plaint is put in one little phrase:

My soul wants some thing that's new, that's new

Over the inner thoughts of the slaves and their relations one with another the shadow of fear ever hung, so that we get but glimpses here and
there, and also with them, eloquent omissions and silences. Mother and
child are sung, but seldom father; fugitive and weary wanderer call for pity
and affection, but there is little of wooing and wedding; the rocks and the
mountains are well known, but home is unknown. Strange blending of love
and helplessness sings through the refrain:

> "Yonder 's my ole mudder,
> Been waggin' at de hill so long;
> 'Bout time she cross over,
> Git home bime-by."

Elsewhere comes the cry of the "motherless" and the "Farewell, farewell,
my only child."

Love-songs are scarce and fall into two categories—the frivolous
and light, and the sad. Of deep successful love there is ominous silence,
and in one of the oldest of these songs there is a depth of history and
meaning:

Poor Ro - sy, poor gal; Poor Ro - sy,
poor gal; Ro - sy break my poor heart.
Heav'n shall - a - be my home.

A black woman said of the song, "It can't be sung without a full heart and
a troubled sperrit." The same voice sings here that sings in the German
folk-song:

> "Jetz Geh i' an's brunele, trink' aber net."

Of death the Negro showed little fear, but talked of it familiarly and
even fondly as simply a crossing of the waters, perhaps—who knows?—
back to his ancient forests again. Later days transfigured his fatalism, and
amid the dust and dirt the toiler sang:

"Dust, dust and ashes, fly over my grave,
But the Lord shall bear my spirit home."

The things evidently borrowed from the surrounding world undergo characteristic change when they enter the mouth of the slave. Especially is this true of Bible phrases. "Weep, O captive daughter of Zion," is quaintly turned into "Zion, weep-a-low," and the wheels of Ezekiel are turned every way in the mystic dreaming of the slave, till he says:

"There 's a little wheel a-turnin' in-a-my heart."

As in olden time, the words of these hymns were improvised by some leading minstrel of the religious band. The circumstances of the gathering, however, the rhythm of the songs, and the limitations of allowable thought, confined the poetry for the most part to single or double lines, and they seldom were expanded to quatrains or longer tales, although there are some few examples of sustained efforts, chiefly paraphrases of the Bible. Three short series of verses have always attracted me,—the one that heads this chapter, of one line of which Thomas Wentworth Higginson has fittingly said, "Never, it seems to me, since man first lived and suffered was his infinite longing for peace uttered more plaintively." The second and third are descriptions of the Last Judgment,—the one a late improvisation, with some traces of outside influence:

"Oh, the stars in the elements are falling,
And the moon drips away into blood,
And the ransomed of the Lord are returning unto God,
Blessed be the name of the Lord."

And the other earlier and homelier picture from the low coast lands:

"Michael, haul the boat ashore,
Then you 'll hear the horn they blow,
Then you 'll hear the trumpet sound,
Trumpet sound the world around,
Trumpet sound for rich and poor,
Trumpet sound the Jubilee,
Trumpet sound for you and me."

Through all the sorrow of the Sorrow Songs there breathes a hope—a faith in the ultimate justice of things. The minor cadences of despair change often to triumph and calm confidence. Sometimes it is faith in life, sometimes a faith in death, sometimes assurance of boundless justice in some fair world beyond. But whichever it is, the meaning is always clear: that sometime, somewhere, men will judge men by their souls and not by their skins. Is such a hope justified? Do the Sorrow Songs sing true?

The silently growing assumption of this age is that the probation of races is past, and that the backward races of to-day are of proven inefficiency and not worth the saving. Such an assumption is the arrogance of peoples irreverent toward Time and ignorant of the deeds of men. A thousand years ago such an assumption, easily possible, would have made it difficult for the Teuton to prove his right to life. Two thousand years ago such dogmatism, readily welcome, would have scouted the idea of blond races ever leading civilization. So wofully unorganized is sociological knowledge that the meaning of progress, the meaning of "swift" and "slow" in human doing, and the limits of human perfectability, are veiled, unanswered sphinxes on the shores of science. Why should Æschylus have sung two thousand years before Shakespeare was born? Why has civilization flourished in Europe, and flickered, flamed, and died in Africa? So long as the world stands meekly dumb before such questions, shall this nation proclaim its ignorance and unhallowed prejudices by denying freedom of opportunity to those who brought the Sorrow Songs to the Seats of the Mighty?

Your country? How came it yours? Before the Pilgrims landed we were here. Here we have brought our three gifts and mingled them with yours: a gift of story and song—soft, stirring melody in an ill-harmonized and unmelodious land; the gift of sweat and brawn to beat back the wilderness, conquer the soil, and lay the foundations of this vast economic empire two hundred years earlier than your weak hands could have done it; the third, a gift of the Spirit. Around us the history of the land has centred for thrice a hundred years; out of the nation's heart we have called all that was best to throttle and subdue all that was worst; fire and blood, prayer and sacrifice, have billowed over this people, and they have found peace only in the altars of the God of Right. Nor has our gift of the Spirit been merely passive. Actively we have woven ourselves with the very warp and woof of this nation,—we fought their battles, shared their sorrow, mingled our blood with theirs, and generation after generation have pleaded with a headstrong, careless people to despise not Justice, Mercy, and Truth, lest the nation be smitten with a curse. Our song, our toil, our cheer, and warning have been given to this nation in blood-brotherhood. Are not these gifts worth the giving? Is not this work and striving? Would America have been America without her Negro people?

Even so is the hope that sang in the songs of my fathers well sung. If somewhere in this whirl and chaos of things there dwells Eternal Good, pitiful yet masterful, then anon in His good time America shall rend the Veil and the prisoned shall go free. Free, free as the sunshine trickling down the morning into these high windows of mine, free as yonder fresh young voices welling up to me from the caverns of brick and mortar below—swelling with song, instinct with life, tremulous treble and darkening bass. My children, my little children, are singing to the sunshine, and thus they sing:

Let us cheer the wea - ry trav-el - ler,

Cheer the wea - ry trav - el - ler, Let us

cheer the wea - ry trav - el - ler   A

- long the heav - en - ly way,

And the traveller girds himself, and sets his face toward the Morning, and goes his way.

Ideas for Rereading

1. "How does it feel to be a problem?"(p. 131). Du Bois addresses this question to his fellow "Negroes" early on in "Of Our Spiritual Strivings." Throughout the essay, Du Bois posits a solution to the "Negro Problem" that must come from both outside black culture and within the hearts and minds of black people themselves. As you read, make notes on the way Du Bois frames his solution. List and classify the components of that solution.

2. In "Of Our Spiritual Strivings," Du Bois describes his perception of African American "double-consciousness, this sense of always looking at one's self

through the eyes of others" (p. 132). How does Du Bois elaborate on this concept of "double-consciousness"? As you reread the essay, mark passages relating to "double-consciousness" with an aim to developing the fullest possible understanding of what Du Bois means by the term. Pay attention to, and comment on, related phrases (for example, *two-ness, double aims, warring*) that pick up on the "double-consciousness" idea.

3. In "Of Our Spiritual Strivings," Du Bois writes, "After the Egyptian and Indian, the Greek and Roman, the Teuton and Mongolian, the Negro is a sort of seventh son, born with a veil, and gifted with second-sight in this American world" (p. 131). Du Bois is making use of a common superstition—that a child born "with a veil" (that is, still within the amniotic sack) will have the ability to see beyond the material world, even into the future. Throughout the essay, consider the way Du Bois both sustains the metaphor of "second sight" and modifies it to fit his rhetorical purpose. Are there ways in which Du Bois's depiction of the "veil" and "second sight" differ from the commonly held meanings of those terms?

4. As you reread Du Bois's essays, look for clues concerning the conditions of black Americans at the time that Du Bois was writing. What can you infer about the economic situation, the social conditions, and the intellectual and spiritual life of African Americans in 1903? Record your inferences in your notebook.

5. The essay "The Sorrow Songs" is partially a literary and musical critique of a uniquely African American art form—the spiritual—and partly a social and political statement. Consider Du Bois's interpretation of the lyrics of the spirituals and note how he uses those lyrics to serve his larger argument. In your notebook, identify key images and metaphors from the lyrics. How do these images and metaphors work together to give meaning and hope to the oppressed? Now look back to "Of Our Spiritual Strivings" and examine the images and metaphors that Du Bois uses there. How do these images and metaphors contribute to his purpose in that chapter? What is the significance of the Sorrow Songs for the social problems of Du Bois's time?

6. Du Bois himself never experienced slavery, nor was he the son of former slaves. He was also privileged, relative to many of his fellow African Americans, in terms of education and social connection. Thus his description of the Negro spirituals or Sorrow Songs is coming from a very specific point of view, one arguably different from that of the majority of black people in the early twentieth century. As you read "The Sorrow Songs," note the ways in which Du Bois's particular perspective may have affected his depiction and critique of the spirituals. Imagine also the perspective of black people closer to the experience of slavery.

7. Du Bois argues that a "primitive" essence lingers in the Sorrow Songs and that it can be recovered. Yet at the same time he argues that the Negro must take his rightful place in "civilized" America. At first, these values might appear to be in tension with one another. How does Du Bois work with them? How does he attempt to reconcile them in his claims about the gifts of the "Negro race" to America? What does Du Bois's rhetoric reveal about his own assumptions and the assumptions of his time? Take detailed notes on what you discover, and develop your views about the role of these two values—the primitive and the civilized—in Du Bois's text.

Ideas for Writing

1. Review your notes on Du Bois's references to "double-consciousness" in "Of Our Spiritual Strivings" (question 2, Ideas for Rereading). Beginning with a comprehensive understanding of the concept, ask yourself whether there are situations other than that described by Du Bois in which one might experience a sense of "double-consciousness." Are there situations in which you have experienced or might experience a sort of "double-consciousness" as Du Bois defines it? Keeping in mind Du Bois's point of view, write an essay exploring such a situation.

2. Review your notes on the concept of "double-consciousness" as Du Bois presents it in "Of Our Spiritual Strivings" (question 2, Ideas for Rereading). Now reread both chapters included here, with the following questions in mind: Is "double-consciousness" a feature of Du Bois's own text? Or has he transcended or escaped from "double-consciousness," perhaps even reunified his consciousness? Write an essay that presents your view, including both a careful discussion of the meaning of the phrase "double-consciousness" as presented by Du Bois and detailed reference to the text to support your main argument.

3. Reread "The Sorrow Songs," taking note of Du Bois's method of analyzing the spirituals as well as the conclusions he draws about that art form's meaning and importance. (You may have already done this for question 4, Ideas for Rereading.) Find a recording of one of the spirituals mentioned in "The Sorrow Songs," and write your own analysis of both the words and the music. In what ways does your interpretation parallel that of Du Bois? In what ways do you and Du Bois differ? Consider how hearing the song performed affects your analysis.

CONTEXT

Although his early years were spent in rural Great Barrington, Massachusetts, separated from the experience of the majority of African Americans of his time, W. E. B. Du Bois came of intellectual age in a thriving African American social and artistic climate. As editor of The Crisis, *he was in the thick of that explosion of black art, music, and culture known as the Harlem Renaissance. The poet Langston Hughes and scholar, poet, and folklorist James Weldon Johnson were contemporaries and friends. Johnson shared Du Bois's love of the Negro spiritual, pulling together many of the most important songs into what remains a definitive collection, while Hughes's poetry reflected a shared interest in uniquely black culture and Pan-Africanism. Upon Du Bois's death in 1963, Hughes would rededicate to him "The Negro Speaks of Rivers," one of the poet's most famous works.*

One of Du Bois's most illustrious contemporaries was the somewhat older ex-slave Booker T. Washington, founder of the Tuskegee Institute and promoter — among other accomplishments — of vocational education and opportunity for black people. While The Souls of Black Folk *includes a grateful acknowledgment of Washington's unique contribution to African American advancement ("Of Mr. Booker T. Washington and Others"), it also sternly criticizes the "accommodation-*

ist" ideas expressed in Washington's "Atlanta Exposition Address" of 1895, also known as the "Atlanta Compromise" because of its tone of rapprochement toward white people. Washington wrote that black agitation for social equality was "extremest folly," an idea that the more militant Du Bois could not abide. While Du Bois would later part ways with Washington completely, Du Bois was himself also criticized for a lack of militancy, most notably by Jamaican-born Marcus Garvey, head of the Universal Negro Improvement Association, a would-be rival organization to the NAACP. Garvey, who was dark-skinned, accused the light-skinned Du Bois of bias toward light-skinned black people. In an editorial letter to his own New York–based periodical, The Negro World, *Garvey wrote, "Du Bois represents a group that hates the Negro blood in their veins, and has been working subtly to build up a caste aristocracy that would socially divide the race."*

While Du Bois and other African American writers of the time are justifiably famous and influential even today, Du Bois himself was slow to recognize the unique experience of black women and their important part in the work toward equality and self-definition for African Americans. Scholars have only recently begun to rediscover the compelling work of Du Bois's black female contemporaries such as the novelist Anna Julia Cooper and her predecessor, the poet Frances E. W. Harper. Examples of both women's work — the introduction to Cooper's A Voice from the South *and Harper's poem "Ethiopia"—appear in this section alongside writings by Hughes, Washington, and Garvey. Also included are the original* New York Times *review of* The Souls of Black Folk; *part of an editorial by Du Bois from* The Crisis, *"Criteria of Negro Art"; and a reprint of the spiritual "Go Down Moses" as collected by James Weldon Johnson.*

LANGSTON HUGHES

The Negro Speaks of Rivers   1921

I've known rivers:
I've known rivers ancient as the world and older than the
    flow of human blood in human veins.

My soul has grown deep like the rivers.

I bathed in the Euphrates when dawns were young.
I built my hut near the Congo and it lulled me to sleep.
I looked upon the Nile and raised the pyramids above it.
I heard the singing of the Mississippi when Abe Lincoln
    went down to New Orleans, and I've seen its muddy
    bosom turn all golden in the sunset.

I've known rivers:
Ancient, dusky rivers.

My soul has grown deep like the rivers.

W. E. B. Du Bois
National Portrait Gallery. Smithsonian Institution, Washington, D.C.

BOOKER T. WASHINGTON

The Atlanta Exposition Address   *1895*

Mr. President and Gentlemen of the Board of Directors and Citizens.

One-third of the population of the South is of the Negro race. No enterprise seeking the material, civil, or moral welfare of this section can disregard this element of our population and reach the highest success. I but convey to you, Mr. President and Directors, the sentiment of the masses of my race when I say that in no way have the value and manhood of the American Negro been more fittingly and generously recognized than by the managers of this magnificent Exposition at every stage of its progress. It is a recognition that will do more to cement the friendship of the two races than any occurrence since the dawn of our freedom.

Not only this, but the opportunity here afforded will awaken among us a new era of industrial progress. Ignorant and inexperienced, it is not strange that in the first years of our new life we began at the top instead of at the bottom; that a seat in Congress or the state legislature was more sought than real estate or industrial skill; that the political convention or stump speaking had more attractions than starting a dairy farm or truck garden.

A ship lost at sea for many days suddenly sighted a friendly vessel. From the mast of the unfortunate vessel was seen a signal, "Water, water; we die of thirst!" The answer from the friendly vessel at once came back, "Cast down your bucket where you are." A second time the signal, "Water, water; send us water!" ran up from the distressed vessel, and was answered, "Cast down your bucket where you are." And a third and fourth signal for water was answered, "Cast down your bucket where you are." The captain of the distressed vessel, at last heeding the injunction, cast down his bucket, and it came up full of fresh, sparkling water from the mouth of the Amazon River. To those of my race who depend on bettering their condition in a foreign land or who underestimate the importance of cultivating friendly relations with the Southern white man, who is their next-door neighbour, I would say: "Cast down your bucket where you are" — cast it down in making friends in every manly way of the people of all races by whom we are surrounded.

Cast it down in agriculture, mechanics, in commerce, in domestic service, and in the professions. And in this connection it is well to bear in mind that whatever other sins the South may be called to bear, when it comes to business, pure and simple, it is in the South that the Negro is given a man's chance in the commercial world, and in nothing is this Exposition more eloquent than in emphasizing this chance. Our greatest danger is that in the great leap from slavery to freedom we may overlook the fact that the masses of us are to live by the productions of our hands, and fail to keep in mind that we shall prosper in proportion as we learn to dignify and glorify common labour and put brains and skill into the common occupations of life; shall prosper in proportion as we learn to draw the line between the superficial and the substantial, the ornamental gewgaws of life and the useful. No race can prosper till it learns that there is as much dignity in tilling a field as in writing a poem. It is at the bottom of life we must begin, and not at the top. Nor should we permit our grievances to overshadow our opportunities.

To those of the white race who look to the incoming of those of foreign birth and strange tongue and habits for the prosperity of the South, were I permitted I would repeat what I say to my own race, "Cast down your bucket where you are." Cast it down among the eight millions of Negroes whose habits you know, whose fidelity and love you have tested in days when to have proved treacherous meant the ruin of your firesides. Cast down your bucket among these people who have, without strikes and labour wars, tilled your fields, cleared your forests, builded your railroads and cities, and brought forth treasures from the bowels of the earth, and helped make possible this magnificent representation of the progress of the South. Casting down your bucket among my people, helping and encouraging them as you are doing on these grounds, and to education of head, hand, and heart, you will find that they will buy your surplus land, make blossom the waste places in your fields, and run your factories. While doing this, you can be sure in the future, as in the past, that you and your families will be surrounded by the most patient, faithful, law-abiding, and unresentful people that the world has seen. As we have proved our loyalty to you in the past, in nursing your children, watching by the sick-bed of your mothers and fathers, and often following them with tear-dimmed eyes to their graves, so in the future, in our humble way, we shall stand by you with a devotion that no foreigner can approach, ready to lay down our lives, if need be, in defence of yours, interlacing our industrial, commercial, civil, and religious life with yours in a way that shall make the interests of both races one. In all things that are purely social we can be as separate as the fingers, yet one as the hand in all things essential to mutual progress.

There is no defence or security for any of us except in the highest intelligence and development of all. If anywhere there are efforts tending to curtail the fullest growth of the Negro, let these efforts be turned into stimulating, encouraging, and making him the most useful and intelligent citizen. Effort or means so invested will pay a thousand per cent interest. These efforts will be twice blessed—"blessing him that gives and him that takes."

There is no escape through law of man or God from the inevitable:

> *The laws of changeless justice bind*
>   *Oppressor with oppressed;*
> *And close as sin and suffering joined*
>   *We march to fate abreast.*

Nearly sixteen millions of hands will aid you in pulling the load upward, or they will pull against you the load downward. We shall constitute one-third and more of the ignorance and crime of the South, or one-third its intelligence and progress; we shall contribute one-third to the business and industrial prosperity of the South, or we shall prove a veritable body of death, stagnating, depressing, retarding every effort to advance the body politic.

Gentlemen of the Exposition, as we present to you our humble effort at an exhibition of our progress, you must not expect overmuch. Starting thirty years ago with ownership here and there in a few quilts and pumpkins and chickens (gathered from miscellaneous sources), remember the path that has led from these to the inventions and production of agricultural implements, buggies, steam-engines, newspapers, books, statuary, carving, paintings, the management of drugstores and banks, has not been trodden without contact with thorns and thistles. While we take pride in what we exhibit as a result of our independent efforts, we do not for a moment forget that our part in this exhibition would fall far short of your expectations but for the constant help that has come to our educational life, not only from the Southern states, but especially from Northern philanthropists, who have made their gifts a constant stream of blessing and encouragement.

The wisest among my race understand that the agitation of questions of social equality is the extremest folly, and that progress in the enjoyment of all the privileges that will come to us must be the result of severe and constant struggle rather than of artificial forcing. No race that has anything to contribute to the markets of the world is long in any degree ostracized. It is important and right that all privileges of the law be ours, but it is vastly more important that we be prepared for the exercises of these privileges. The opportunity to earn a dollar in a factory just now is worth infinitely more than the opportunity to spend a dollar in an opera-house.

In conclusion, may I repeat that nothing in thirty years has given us more hope and encouragement, and drawn us so near to you of the white race, as this opportunity offered by the Exposition; and here bending, as it were, over the altar that represents the results of the struggles of your race and mine, both starting practically empty-handed three decades ago, I pledge that in your effort to work out the great and intricate problem which God has laid at the doors of the South, you shall have at all times the patient, sympathetic help of my race; only let this be constantly in mind, that, while from representations in these buildings of the product of field, of forest, of mine, of factory, letters, and art, much good will come, yet far above and beyond material benefits will be that higher good, that, let us pray God, will come, in a blotting out of sectional differences and racial animosities and suspicions, in a determination to administer absolute justice, in a willing obedience among all classes to the mandates of law. This, this, coupled with our material prosperity, will bring into our beloved South a new heaven and a new earth.

MARCUS GARVEY

Motive of the NAACP Exposed   1923

The observant members of our race must have noticed within recent years great hostility between the National Association for the Advancement of "Colored" People and the Universal "Negro" Improvement Association, and must have wondered why Du Bois writes so bitterly against Garvey and vice versa. Well, the reason is plainly to be seen after the following explanation:

Du Bois represents a group that hates the Negro blood in their veins, and has been working subtly to build up a caste aristocracy that would socially divide the race into two groups: One the superior because of color caste, and the other the inferior, hence the pretentious work of the National Association for the Advancement of "Colored" People. The program of deception was well arranged and under way for success when Marcus Garvey arrived in America, and he, after understudying the artful doctor and the group he represented, fired a "bomb" into the camp by organizing the Universal "Negro" Improvement Association to cut off the wicked attempt of race deception and distinction, and to in truth build up a race united in spirit and ideal with the honest desire of adjusting itself to its own moral-social pride and national self-respect. When Garvey arrived in America and visited the office of the National Association for the Advancement of "Colored" People to interview Du Bois, who was regarded as a leader of the Negro people and who had recently visited the West Indies, he was dumbfounded when, on approach to the office but for Mr. Dill and Dr. Du Bois himself and the office boy, he could not tell whether he was in a white office or that of the National Association for the Advancement of "Colored" People. The whole staff was either white or very near white, and thus Garvey got his first shock of the advancement hypocrisy. There was no representation of the race there that anyone could recognize. The advancement meant that you had to be as near white as possible, otherwise there was no place for you as stenographer, clerk or attendant in the office of the National Association for the Advancement of "Colored" People. After a short talk with Du Bois, Garvey became so disgusted with the man and his principles that the thought he never contemplated entered his m[i]nd—that of remaining in America to teach Du Bois and his group what real race pride meant. . . .

The National Association for the Advancement of "Colored" People is a scheme to destroy the Negro Race, and the leaders of it hate Marcus Garvey because he has discovered them at their game and because the Universal Negro Improvement Association, without any prejudice to color or caste, is making headway in bringing all the people together for their common good. They hate Garvey because the Universal Negro Improvement

Association and the Black Star Line employed every shade of color in the race, according to ability and merit, and put the N.A.A.C.P. to shame for employing only the "lightest" of the race. They hate Garvey because he forced them to fill Shilady's place with a Negro. They hate Garvey because they had to employ "black" Pickens to cover up their scheme after Garvey had discovered it; they hate Garvey because they have had to employ brown-skin "Bob" Bagnall to make a showing to the people that they were doing the "right" thing by them; they hate Garvey because he has broken up the "Pink Tea Set"; they hate Garvey because they have been forced to recognize mulatto, brown and black talent in the association equally with the lighter element; they hate Garvey because he is teaching the unity of race, without color superiority or prejudice. The gang thought that they would have been able to build up in America a buffer class between the white and the Negro, and thus in another fifty years join with the powerful race and crush the blood of their mothers, as is being done in South Africa and the West Indies.

The imprisonment of Garvey is more than appears on the surface, and the National Association for the Advancement of Colored People knows it. Du Bois and those who lead the Association are skillful enough to be using the old method of getting the "other fellow" to destroy himself, hence the activities of "brown-skin" Bagnall and "black" Pickens. Walter White, whom we can hardly tell from a Southern gentleman and who lives with a white family in Brooklyn, is kept in the background, but dark Bagnall, Pickens, and Du Bois are pushed to the front to make the attack, so that there would be no suspicion of the motive. They are to drive hard and hot, and then the silent influence would bring up the rear, hence the slogan, "Garvey must go!" and the vicious attacks in the different magazines by Pickens, Du Bois and Bagnall.

Gentlemen, you are very smart, but Garvey has caught your tune. The conspiracy to destroy the Negro race is so well organized that the moment anything interferes with their program there springs up a simultaneous action on the part of the leaders. . . .

The people who are directing the affairs of the National Association for the Advancement of "Colored" People are keen observers and wise leaders. It takes more than ordinary intelligence to penetrate their motive, hence you are now warned.

All the "gas" about anti-lynching and "social equality" will not amount to a row of pins; in fact, it is only a ruse to raise money to capitalize the scheme and hide the real motive. Negroes, watch your step and save yourselves from deception and subsequent extermination. With best wishes for your success, I have the honor to be, Your obedient servant,

MARCUS GARVEY
President General
Universal Negro Improvement Association

Anna Julia Cooper

Our Raison d'Être   1892

In the clash and clatter of our American Conflict, it has been said that the South remains Silent. Like the Sphinx she inspires vociferous disputation, but herself takes little part in the noisy controversy. One muffled strain in the Silent South, a jarring chord and a vague and uncomprehended cadenza has been and still is the Negro. And of that muffled chord, the one mute and voiceless note has been the sadly expectant Black Woman,

> An infant crying in the night,
> An infant crying for the light;
> And with *no language—but a cry.*

The colored man's inheritance and apportionment is still the sombre crux, the perplexing *cul de sac* of the nation,—the dumb skeleton in the closet provoking ceaseless harangues, indeed, but little understood and seldom consulted. Attorneys for the plaintiff and attorneys for the defendant, with bungling *gaucherie* have analyzed and dissected, theorized and synthesized with sublime ignorance or pathetic misapprehension of counsel from the black client. One important witness has not yet been heard from. The summing up of the evidence deposed, and the charge to the jury have been made—but no word from the Black Woman.

It is because I believe the American people to be conscientiously committed to a fair trial and ungarbled evidence, and because I feel it essential to a perfect understanding and an equitable verdict that truth from *each* standpoint be presented at the bar,—that this little Voice has been added to the already full chorus. The "other side" has not been represented by one who "lives there." And not many can more sensibly realize and more accurately tell the weight and the fret of the "long dull pain" than the open-eyed but hitherto voiceless Black Woman of America.

The feverish agitation, the perfervid energy, the busy objectivity of the more turbulent life of our men serves, it may be, at once to cloud or color their vision somewhat, and as well to relieve the smart and deaden the pain for them. Their voice is in consequence not always temperate and calm, and at the same time radically corrective and sanatory.* At any rate, as our Caucasian barristers are not to blame if they cannot *quite* put themselves in the dark man's place, neither should the dark man be wholly expected fully and adequately to reproduce the exact Voice of the Black Woman.

Delicately sensitive at every pore to social atmospheric conditions, her calorimeter may well be studied in the interest of accuracy and fairness in

---

sanatory: Related to the words *sanative* and *sanatorium,* "sanatory" means healing of, or tending to, physical or moral health. A near synonym is "curative."

diagnosing what is often conceded to be a "puzzling" case. If these broken utterances can in any way help to a clearer vision and a truer pulse-beat in studying our Nation's Problem, this Voice by a Black Woman of the South will not have been raised in vain.

FRANCES E. W. HARPER

Ethiopia   1854

Yes! Ethiopia yet shall stretch
   Her bleeding hands abroad;
Her cry of agony shall reach
   The burning throne of God.

The tyrant's yoke from off her neck,
   His fetters from her soul,
The mighty hand of God shall break,
   And spurn the base control.

Redeemed from dust and freed from chains,
   Her sons shall lift their eyes;
From cloud-capt hills and verdant plains
   Shall shouts of triumph rise.

Upon her dark, despairing brow,
   Shall play a smile of peace;
For God shall bend unto her wo,
   And bid her sorrows cease.

'Neath sheltering vines and stately palms
   Shall laughing children play,
And aged sires with joyous psalms
   Shall gladden every day.

Secure by night, and blest by day,
   Shall pass her happy hours;
Nor human tigers hunt for prey
   Within her peaceful bowers.

Then, Ethiopia! stretch, oh! stretch
   Thy bleeding hands abroad;
Thy cry of agony shall reach
   And find redress from God.

ANONYMOUS

Review of *The Souls of Black Folk,*
New York Times 1903

It is generally conceded that Booker T. Washington represents the best hope of the negro in America, and it is certain that of all the leaders of his people he has done the most for his fellows with the least friction with the whites who are most nearly concerned, those of the South. Here is another negro "educator," to use a current term, not brought up like Washington among the negroes of the South and to the manner of the Southern negro born, but one educated in New England—one who never saw a negro camp-meeting till he was grown to manhood and went among the people of his color as a teacher. Naturally he does not see everything as Booker Washington does; probably he does not understand his own people in their natural state as does the other; certainly he cannot understand the Southern white's point of view as the principal of Tuskegee does. Yet it is equally certain that "The Souls of Black Folk" throws much light upon the complexities of the negro problem, for it shows that the key note of at least some negro aspiration is still the abolition of the social color line. For it is the Jim Crow car,* and the fact that he may not smoke a cigar and drink a cup of tea with the white man in the South, that most galls William E. Burghardt Du Bois of the Atlanta College for Negroes. That this social color line must in time vanish like the mists of the morning is the firm belief of the writer, as the opposite is the equally firm belief of the Southern white man; but in the meantime he admits the "hard fact" that the color line is, and for a long time must be.

The book is of curious warp and woof, and the poetical form of the title is the index to much of its content and phraseology. To a Southerner who knows the negro race as it exists in the South, it is plain that this negro of Northern education is, after all, as he says, "bone of the bone and flesh of the flesh" of the African race. Sentimental, poetical, picturesque, the acquired logic and the evident attempt to be critically fair-minded is strangely tangled with these racial characteristics and the racial rhetoric. After an eloquent appeal for a fair hearing in what he calls his "Forethought," he goes in some detail into the vexed history of the Freedman's Bureau and the work it did for good and ill; for he admits the ill as he insists upon the good. A review of such a work from the negro point of view, even the Northern negro's point of view, must have its value to any unprejudiced student—still more, perhaps, for the prejudiced who is yet willing to be a student. It is impossible here to give even a general idea of the impression that will be gained from reading the text, but the underlying idea seems to

---

Jim Crow car: The train car reserved for black people. The term refers to the post–Civil War "Jim Crow" laws passed to maintain racial segregation in the American South.

be that it was impossible for the negro to get justice in the Southern courts just after the war, and "almost equally" impossible for the white man to get justice in the extra judicial proceeding of the Freedman's Bureau officials which largely superseded the courts for a time. Much is remembered of these proceedings by older Southerners—much picturesque and sentimental fiction, with an ample basis of truth, has been written about them by Mr. Thomas Nelson Page and others. Here we have the other side.

While the whole book is interesting, especially to a Southerner, and while the self-restraint and temperateness of the manner of stating even things which the Southerner regards as impossibilities, deserve much praise and disarm harsh criticism, the part of the book which is more immediately concerned with an arraignment of the present plans of Booker T. Washington is for the present the most important.

In this matter the writer, speaking, as he says, for many educated negroes, makes two chief objections—first, that Washington is the leader of his race not by the suffrage of that race, but rather by virtue of the support of the whites, and, second, that, by yielding to the modern commercial spirit and confining the effort for uplifting the individual to practical education and the acquisition of property and decent ways, he is after all cutting off the negro from those higher aspirations which only, Du Bois says, make a people great. For instance, it is said that Booker Washington distinctly asks that black people give up, at least for the present, three things:

First, political power;

Second, insistence on civil rights;

Third, higher education for negro youth, and concentrate all their energies on industrial education, the accumulation of wealth, and the conciliation of the South. This policy has been courageously and insistently advocated for over fifteen years, and has been triumphant for perhaps ten years. As a result of this tender of the palm branch what has been the return? In these years there have occurred:

1. The disfranchisement of the negro.

2. The legal creation of a distinct status of civil inferiority for the negro.

3. The steady withdrawal of aid from institutions for the higher training of the negro.

These movements are not, to be sure, direct results of Washington's teachings, but his propaganda has, without a shadow of doubt, helped their speedier accomplishment.

The writer admits the great value of Booker Washington's work. However, he does not believe so much in the gospel of the lamb, and does think that a bolder attitude, one of standing firmly upon rights guaranteed by the war amendments, and alluded to in complimentary fashion in the Declaration of Independence, is both more becoming to a race such as he conceives the negro race to be, and more likely to advance that race. "We feel in conscience bound," he says, "to ask three things: 1, The right to vote; 2, Civic equality; 3, The education of youth according to ability" and he is especially insistent on the higher education of the negro—going into some statistics to show what the negro can do in that way. The value of these arguments and the force of the statistics can best be judged after the book is read.

Many passages of the book will be very interesting to the student of the negro character who regards the race ethnologically and not politically, not as a dark cloud threatening the future of the United States, but as a peculiar people, and one, after all, but little understood by the best of its friends or the worst of its enemies outside of what the author of "The Souls of Black Folk" is fond of calling the "Awful Veil." Throughout it should be recalled that it is the thought of a negro of Northern education who has lived long among his brethren of the South yet who cannot fully feel the meaning of some things which these brethren know by instinct — and which the Southern-bred white knows by a similar instinct; certain things which are by both accepted as facts — not theories — fundamental attitudes of race to race which are the product of conditions extending over centuries, as are the somewhat parallel attitudes of the gentry to the peasantry in other countries.

W. E. B. Du Bois

From *Criteria of Negro Art*   1926

Suppose the only Negro who survived some centuries hence was the Negro painted by white Americans in the novels and essays they have written. What would people in a hundred years say of black Americans? Now turn it around. Suppose you were to write a story and put in it the kind of people you know and like and imagine. You might get it published and you might not. And the "might not" is still far bigger than the "might." The white publishers catering to white folk would say, "It is not interesting" — to white folk, naturally not. They want Uncle Toms, Topsies,* good "darkies" and clowns. I have in my office a story with all the earmarks of truth. A young man says that he started out to write and had his stories accepted. Then he began to write about the things he knew best about, that is, about his own people. He submitted a story to a magazine which said, "We are sorry, but we cannot take it." "I sat down and revised my story, changing the color of the characters and the locale and sent it under an assumed name with a change of address and it was accepted by the same magazine that had refused it, the editor promising to take anything else I might send in providing it was good enough."

We have, to be sure, a few recognized and successful Negro artists; but they are not all those fit to survive or even a good minority. They are but

---

Uncle Toms, Topsies: Uncle Tom was the title character of Harriet Beecher Stowe's antislavery novel *Uncle Tom's Cabin.* Topsy was another character in this novel. Both became synonymous with subservience and obsequiousness to whites.

the remnants of that ability and genius among us whom the accidents of education and opportunity have raised on the tidal waves of chance. We black folk are not altogether peculiar in this. After all, in the world at large, it is only the accident, the remnant, that gets the chance to make the most of itself; but if this is true of the white world it is infinitely more true of the colored world. It is not simply the great clear tenor of Roland Hayes that opened the ears of America. We have had many voices of all kinds as fine as his and America was as deaf as she was for years to him. Then a foreign land heard Hayes and put its imprint on him and immediately America with all its imitative snobbery woke up. We approved Hayes because London, Paris, and Berlin approved him and not simply because he was a great singer.

Thus it is the bounden duty of black America to begin this great work of the creation of beauty, of the preservation of beauty, of the realization of beauty, and we must use in this work all the methods that men have used before. And what have been the tools of the artist in times gone by? First of all, he has used the truth—not for the sake of truth, not as a scientist seeking truth, but as one upon whom truth eternally thrust itself as the highest handmaid of imagination, as the one great vehicle of universal understanding. Again artists have used goodness—goodness in all its aspects of justice, honor, and right—not for sake of an ethical sanction but as the one true method of gaining sympathy and human interest.

The apostle of beauty thus becomes the apostle of truth and right not by choice but by inner and outer compulsion. Free he is but his freedom is ever bounded by truth and justice; and slavery only dogs him when he is denied the right to tell the truth or recognize an ideal of justice.

Thus all art is propaganda and ever must be, despite the wailing of the purists. I stand in utter shamelessness and say that whatever art I have for writing has been used always for propaganda for gaining the right of black folk to love and enjoy. I do not care a damn for any art that is not used for propaganda. But I do care when propaganda is confined to one side while the other is stripped and silent.

In New York we have two plays: "White Cargo" and "Congo." In "White Cargo" there is a fallen woman. She is black. In "Congo" the fallen woman is white. In "White Cargo" the black woman goes down further and further and in "Congo" the white woman begins with degradation but in the end is one of the angels of the Lord.

You know the current magazine story: a young white man goes down to Central America and the most beautiful colored woman there falls in love with him. She crawls across the whole isthmus to get to him. The white man says nobly, "No." He goes back to his white sweetheart in New York.

In such cases, it is not the positive propaganda of people who believe white blood divine, infallible, and holy to which I object. It is the denial of a similar right of propaganda to those who believe black blood human, lovable, and inspired with new ideals for the world. White artists themselves suffer from this narrowing of their field. They cry for freedom in dealing with Negroes because they have so little freedom in dealing with whites. DuBose Heywood writes "Porgy" and writes beautifully of the black Charleston underworld. But why does he do this? Because he cannot do a similar thing for the white people of Charleston, or they would drum him out of town. The only chance he had to tell the truth of pitiful human degradation was to tell it of colored people. I should not be surprised if Octavius Roy Cohen had approached the *Saturday Evening Post* and asked permission to write about a different kind of colored folk than the monstrosities he has created; but if he has, the *Post* has replied, "No. You are getting paid to write about the kind of colored people you are writing about."

In other words, the white public today demands from its artists, literary and pictorial, racial prejudgment which deliberately distorts truth and justice, as far as colored races are concerned, and it will pay for no other.

On the other hand, the young and slowly growing black public still wants its prophets almost equally unfree. We are bound by all sorts of customs that have come down as second-hand soul clothes of white patrons. We are ashamed of sex and we lower our eyes when people will talk of it. Our religion holds us in superstition. Our worst side has been so shamelessly emphasized that we are denying we have or ever had a worst side. In all sorts of ways we are hemmed in and our new young artists have got to fight their way to freedom.

The ultimate judge has got to be you and you have got to build yourselves up into that wide judgment, that catholicity of temper which is going to enable the artist to have his widest chance for freedom. We can afford the truth. White folk today cannot. As it is now we are handing everything over to a white jury. If a colored man wants to publish a book, he has got to get a white publisher and a white newspaper to say it is great; and then you and I say so. We must come to the place where the work of art when it appears is reviewed and acclaimed by our own free and unfettered judgment. And we are going to have a real and valuable and eternal judgment only as we make ourselves free of mind, proud of body and just of soul to all men.

And then do you know what will be said? It is already saying. Just as soon as true art emerges; just as soon as the black artist appears, someone touches the race on the shoulder and says, "He did that because he was an American, not because he was a Negro; he was born here; he was trained here; he is not a Negro—what is a Negro anyhow? He is just human; it is the kind of thing you ought to expect."

I do not doubt that the ultimate art coming from black folk is going to be just as beautiful, and beautiful largely in the same ways, as the art that comes from white folk, or yellow, or red; but the point today is that until the art of the black folk compels recognition they will not be rated as human. And when through art they compel recognition then let the world discover if it will that their art is as new as it is old and as old as new.

I had a classmate once who did three beautiful things and died. One of them was a story of a folk who found fire and then went wandering in the gloom of night seeking again the stars they had once known and lost; suddenly out of blackness they looked up and there loomed the heavens; and what was it that they said? They raised a mighty cry: "it is the stars, it is the ancient stars, it is the young everlasting stars!"

Go Down Moses

Go down Moses
'Way down in Egypt land,
Tell ole Pharoah,
To let my people go.

Go down Moses
'Way down in Egypt land,
Tell ole Pharoah,
To let my people go.

When Israel was in Egypt's land:
Let my people go,
Oppressed so hard they could not stand,
Let my people go.

"Thus spoke the Lord," bold Moses said;
Let my people go,
If not I'll smite your first born dead,
Let my people go.

Go down Moses
'Way down in Egypt land,
Tell ole Pharoah,
To let my people go.

Ideas for Rereading

1. While Du Bois had never been a slave, Booker T. Washington was an ex-slave and menial worker who struggled to attain his level of education and position in society. Reread Washington's "Atlanta Exposition Address" in light of his background. How might that background have informed Washington's "accommodationist" stance?

2. Booker T. Washington and Marcus Garvey were Du Bois's contemporaries and—more often than not—his rivals for the hearts and minds of African Americans. Read carefully the Washington and Garvey selections. Then reread both of Du Bois's essays, taking careful note of how Washington's and Garvey's ideas contextualize and deepen your understanding of Du Bois's work.

3. Anna Julia Cooper was a contemporary and an occasional correspondent of Du Bois. As you read "Our Raison d'Être," note the ways in which her writing style could be said to mirror Du Bois's work. Taking into account Cooper's accent on the voice of black women, outline the ways in which her perspective could add to Du Bois's thinking. If you wish, consider also the possible influence of Cooper's work on the black women writers presented in this chapter's Contemporary Conversation section.

Ideas for Writing

1. Read carefully the *New York Times* review of *The Souls of Black Folk*. How would you characterize the reviewer's language? What does that language reveal about his attitude toward Du Bois and his work—on its own and in connection with Booker T. Washington? How do you think the reviewer would perceive his own attitudes toward Du Bois and African Americans in general? With these ideas in mind, write a review of the review.

2. Reread Du Bois's "Of Our Spiritual Strivings" in the context of the views expressed by Garvey and Washington. (You may have already done this in question 2, Ideas for Rereading.) Write an essay analyzing, and perhaps comparing, the ideas and theories of the three writers. What is important to each man? How do each writer's ideas connect to and diverge from those of the other two? What in your view is the significance of these connections and divergences?

3. Reread your notes on Du Bois's critical interpretation of the Negro spirituals in "The Sorrow Songs" (question 5, Ideas for Rereading, p. 146). Then apply your ideas to a written analysis of "Go Down Moses." Where does your analysis of the song reflect Du Bois's ideas about the Sorrow Songs? Where do you diverge from Du Bois's point of view?

4. Frances E. W. Harper wrote before and during the Civil War (1861–1865); Langston Hughes was the leading poet of the Harlem Renaissance, which took place from 1920 to about 1930. Yet the works of these poets are both concerned with the connection between black Americans and their African roots. Read the poems carefully and write an essay examining the poets' depiction of Africa as concept, metaphor, symbol, and actual place. Make reference if you wish to Du Bois's figurative use of Africa in "Of Our Spiritual Strivings."

CONTEMPORARY CONVERSATION

ALICE WALKER

Alice Walker (b. 1944) is a major American novelist and poet, author of the Pulitzer Prize–winning The Color Purple *(1982), the controversial but critically praised* Possessing the Secret of Joy *(1992), and many other works of poetry, fiction, and nonfiction. Walker refers to herself not as a feminist but as a*

"Womanist," someone who appreciates women's culture, emotions, and character. The following is the title essay from her collection In Search of Our Mothers' Gardens: Womanist Prose *(1983). Here, her own mother's garden becomes a metaphor for a creative legacy that flourishes despite the combined hindrance of long-standing gender, race, and class prejudices. As you read this essay, pay careful attention to the metaphors and images through which Walker makes her argument. Consider also the special connotations of words that Walker capitalizes. Finally, consider Walker's motive in the essay: Why might Walker need to discover her heritage and share it with others in an essay that speaks of "our" mothers' gardens?*

In Search of Our Mothers' Gardens

> *I described her own nature and temperament. Told how they needed a larger life for their expression. . . . I pointed out that in lieu of proper channels, her emotions had overflowed into paths that dissipated them. I talked, beautifully I thought, about an art that would be born, an art that would open the way for women the likes of her. I asked her to hope, and build up an inner life against the coming of that day. . . . I sang, with a strange quiver in my voice, a promise song.*
>
> — *"Avey,"* JEAN TOOMER, *Cane*
> *The poet speaking to a prostitute who falls
> asleep while he's talking*

When the poet Jean Toomer walked through the South in the early twenties, he discovered a curious thing: black women whose spirituality was so intense, so deep, so *unconscious*, they were themselves unaware of the richness they held. They stumbled blindly through their lives: creatures so abused and mutilated in body, so dimmed and confused by pain, that they considered themselves unworthy even of hope. In the selfless abstractions their bodies became to the men who used them, they became more than "sexual objects," more even than mere women: they became "Saints." Instead of being perceived as whole persons, their bodies became shrines: what was thought to be their minds became temples suitable for worship. These crazy Saints stared out at the world, wildly, like lunatics—or quietly, like suicides; and the "God" that was in their gaze was as mute as a great stone.

Who were these Saints? These crazy, loony, pitiful women?

Some of them, without a doubt, were our mothers and grandmothers.

In the still heat of the post-Reconstruction South, this is how they seemed to Jean Toomer: exquisite butterflies trapped in an evil honey, toiling away their lives in an era, a century, that did not acknowledge them, except as "the *mule* of the world." They dreamed dreams that no one knew—not even themselves, in any coherent fashion—and saw visions no one could understand. They wandered or sat about the countryside crooning lullabies to ghosts, and drawing the mother of Christ in charcoal on courthouse walls.

They forced their minds to desert their bodies and their striving spirits sought to rise, like frail whirlwinds from the hard red clay. And when those frail whirlwinds fell, in scattered particles, upon the ground, no one mourned. Instead, men lit candles to celebrate the emptiness that remained, as people do who enter a beautiful but vacant space to resurrect a God.

Our mothers and grandmothers, some of them: moving to music not yet written. And they waited.

They waited for a day when the unknown thing that was in them would be made known; but guessed, somehow in their darkness, that on the day of their revelation, they would be long dead. Therefore to Toomer they walked, and even ran, in slow motion. For they were going nowhere immediate, and the future was not yet within their grasp. And men took our mothers and grandmothers, "but got no pleasure from it." So complex was their passion and their calm.

To Toomer, they lay vacant and fallow as autumn fields, with harvest time never in sight; and he saw them enter loveless marriages, without joy; and become prostitutes, without resistance; and become mothers of children, without fulfillment.

For these grandmothers and mothers of ours were not Saints, but Artists; driven to a numb and bleeding madness by the springs of creativity in them for which there was no release. They were Creators, who lived lives of spiritual waste, because they were so rich in spirituality—which is the basis of Art—that the strain of enduring their unused and unwanted talent drove them insane. Throwing away this spirituality was their pathetic attempt to lighten the soul to a weight their work-worn, sexually abused bodies could bear.

What did it mean for a black woman to be an artist in our grandmothers' time? In our great-grandmothers' day? It is a question with an answer cruel enough to stop the blood.

Did you have a genius of a great-great-grandmother who died under some ignorant and depraved white overseer's lash? Or was she required to bake biscuits for a lazy backwater tramp, when she cried out in her soul to paint watercolors of sunsets, or the rain falling on the green and peaceful pasturelands? Or was her body broken and forced to bear children (who were more often than not sold away from her)—eight, ten, fifteen, twenty children—when her one joy was the thought of modeling heroic figures of rebellion, in stone or clay?

How was the creativity of the black woman kept alive, year after year and century after century, when for most of the years black people have been in America, it was a punishable crime for a black person to read or write? And the freedom to paint, to sculpt, to expand the mind with action did not exist. Consider, if you can bear to imagine it, what might have been the result if singing, too, had been forbidden by law. Listen to the voices of Bessie Smith, Billie Holiday, Nina Simone, Roberta Flack, and Aretha Franklin, among others, and imagine those voices muzzled for life. Then you may begin to comprehend the lives of our "crazy," "Sainted" mothers and grandmothers. The agony of the lives of women who might have been poets, Novelists, Essayists, and Short-Story Writers (over a period of centuries), who died with their real gifts stifled within them.

And, if this were the end of the story, we would have cause to cry out in my paraphrase of Okot p'Bitek's great poem:

> O, my clanswomen
> Let us all cry together!
> Come,
> Let us mourn the death of our mother,
> The death of a Queen
> The ash that was produced
> By a great fire!
> O, this homestead is utterly dead
> Close the gates
> With *lacari* thorns,
> For our mother
> The creator of the Stool is lost!
> And all the young women
> Have perished in the wilderness!

But this is not the end of the story, for all the young women—our mothers and grandmothers, *ourselves*—have not perished in the wilderness. And if we ask ourselves why, and search for and find the answer, we will know beyond all efforts to erase it from our minds, just exactly who, and of what, we black American women are.

One example, perhaps the most pathetic, most misunderstood one, can provide a backdrop for our mothers' work: Phillis Wheatley, a slave in the 1700s.

Virginia Woolf, in her book *A Room of One's Own*, wrote that in order for a woman to write fiction she must have two things, certainly; a room of her own (with key and lock) and enough money to support herself.

What then are we to make of Phillis Wheatley, a slave, who owned not even herself? This sickly, frail black girl who required a servant of her own at times—her health was so precarious—and who, had she been white, would have been easily considered the intellectual superior of all the women and most of the men in the society of her day.

Virginia Woolf wrote further, speaking of course not of our Phillis, that "any woman born with a great gift in the sixteenth century [insert "eighteenth century," insert "black woman," insert "born or made a slave"] would certainly have gone crazed, shot herself, or ended her days in some lonely cottage outside the village, half witch, half wizard [insert "Saint"], feared and mocked at. For it needs little skill and psychology to be sure that a highly gifted girl who had tried to use her gift of poetry would have been so thwarted and hindered by contrary instincts [add "chains, guns, the lash, the ownership of one's body by someone else, submission to an alien religion"], that she must have lost her health and sanity to a certainty."

The key words, as they relate to Phillis, are "contrary instincts." For when we read the poetry of Phillis Wheatley — as when we read the novels of Nella Larsen or the oddly false-sounding autobiography of that freest of all black women writers, Zora Hurston — evidence of "contrary instincts" is everywhere. Her loyalties were completely divided, as was, without question, her mind.

But how could this be otherwise? Captured at seven, a slave of wealthy, doting whites who instilled in her the "savagery" of the Africa they "rescued" her from . . . one wonders if she was even able to remember her homeland as she had known it, or as it really was.

Yet, because she did try to use her gift for poetry in a world that made her a slave, she was "so thwarted and hindered by . . . contrary instincts, that she . . . lost her health. . . ." In the last years of her brief life, burdened not only with the need to express her gift but also with a penniless, friendless "freedom" and several small children for whom she was forced to do strenuous work to feed, she lost her health, certainly. Suffering from malnutrition and neglect and who knows what mental agonies, Phillis Wheatley died.

So torn by "contrary instincts" was black, kidnapped, enslaved Phillis that her description of "the Goddess" — as she poetically called the Liberty she did not have — is ironically, cruelly humorous. And, in fact, has held Phillis up to ridicule for more than a century. It is usually read prior to hanging Phillis's memory as that of a fool. She wrote:

The Goddess comes, she moves divinely fair,
Olive and laurel binds her *golden* hair.
Wherever shines this native of the skies,
Unnumber'd charms and recent graces rise. [My italics]

It is obvious that Phillis, the slave, combed the "Goddess's" hair every morning, prior, perhaps, to bringing in the milk, or fixing her mistress's lunch. She took her imagery from the one thing she saw elevated above all others.

With the benefit of hindsight we ask, "How could she?"

But at last, Phillis, we understand. No more snickering when your stiff, struggling, ambivalent lines are forced on us. We know now that you were not an idiot or a traitor; only a sickly little black girl, snatched from your home and country and made a slave; a woman who still struggled to sing the song that was your gift, although in a land of barbarians who praised you for your bewildered tongue. It is not so much what you sang, as that you kept alive, in so many of our ancestors, *the notion of song*.

Black women are called, in the folklore that so aptly identified one's status in society, "the *mule* of the world," because we have been handed the burdens that everyone else — *everyone* else — refused to carry. We have also been called "Matriarchs," "Superwomen," and "Mean and Evil Bitches." Not to mention "Castraters" and "Sapphire's Mama." When we have pleaded for understanding, our character has been distorted, when we have asked for simple caring, we have been handed empty inspirational appellations, then stuck in the farthest corner. When we have asked for love, we have been given children. In short, even our plainer gifts, our labors of fidelity and love, have been knocked down our throats. To be an artist and a black woman, even today, lowers our status in many respects, rather than raises it: and yet, artists we will be.

Therefore we must fearlessly pull out of ourselves and look at and identify with our lives the living creativity some of our great-grandmothers were not allowed to know. I stress *some* of them because it is well known that the majority of our great-grandmothers knew, even without "knowing" it, the reality of their spirituality, even if they didn't recognize it beyond what happened in the singing at church—and they never had any intention of giving it up.

How they did it—those millions of black women who were not Phillis Wheatley, or Lucy Terry or Frances Harper or Zora Hurston or Nella Larsen or Bessie Smith; or Elizabeth Catlett, or Katherine Dunham, either—brings me to the title of this essay, "In Search of Our Mothers' Gardens," which is a personal account that is yet shared, in its theme and its meaning, by all of us. I found, while thinking about the far-reaching world of the creative black woman, that often the truest answer to a question that really matters can be found very close.

In the late 1920s my mother ran away from home to marry my father. Marriage, if not running away, was expected of seventeen-year-old girls. By the time she was twenty, she had two children and was pregnant with a third. Five children later, I was born. And this is how I came to know my mother: she seemed a large, soft, loving-eyed woman who was rarely impatient in our home. Her quick, violent temper was on view only a few times a year, when she battled with the white landlord who had the misfortune to suggest to her that her children did not need to go to school.

She made all the clothes we wore, even my brothers' overalls. She made all the towels and sheets we used. She spent the summers canning vegetables and fruits. She spent the winter evenings making quilts enough to cover all our beds.

During the "working" day, she labored beside—not behind—my father in the fields. Her day began before sunup, and did not end until late at night. There was never a moment for her to sit down, undisturbed, to unravel her own private thoughts; never a time free from interruption—by work or the noisy inquiries of her many children. And yet, it is to my mother—and all our mothers who were not famous—that I went in search of the secret of what has fed that muzzled and often mutilated, but vibrant, creative spirit that the black woman has inherited, and that pops out in wild and unlikely places to this day.

But when, you will ask, did my overworked mother have time to know or care about feeding the creative spirit?

The answer is so simple that many of us have spent years discovering it. We have constantly looked high, when we should have looked high— and low.

For example: in the Smithsonian Institution in Washington, D.C., there hangs a quilt unlike any other in the world. In fanciful, inspired, and yet simple and identifiable figures, it portrays the story of the Crucifixion. It is considered rare, beyond price. Though it follows no known pattern of quilt-making, and though it is made of bits and pieces of worthless rags, it is obviously the work of a person of powerful imagination and deep spiritual feeling. Below this quilt I saw a note that says it was made by "an anonymous black woman in Alabama, a hundred years ago."

If we could locate this "anonymous" black woman from Alabama, she would turn out to be one of our grandmothers—an artist who left her mark in the only materials she could afford, and in the only medium her position in society allowed her to use.

As Virginia Woolf wrote further, in *A Room of One's Own:*

> Yet genius of a sort must have existed among women as it must have existed among the working class. [Change this to "slaves" and the "wives and daughters of sharecroppers."] Now and again an Emily Brontë or a Robert Burns [change this to "a Zora Hurston or a Richard Wright"] blazes out and proves its presence. But certainly it never got itself on to paper. When, however, one reads of a witch being ducked, of a woman possessed by devils [or "Sainthood"], of a wise woman selling herbs [our root workers], or even a very remarkable man who had a mother, then I think we are on the track of a lost novelist, a suppressed poet, or some mute and inglorious Jane Austen. . . . Indeed, I would venture to guess that Anon, who wrote so many poems without singing them, was often a woman. . . .

And so our mothers and grandmothers have, more often than not anonymously, handed on the creative spark, the seed of the flower they themselves never hoped to see: or like a sealed letter they could not plainly read.

And so it is, certainly, with my own mother. Unlike "Ma" Rainey's songs, which retained their creator's name even while blasting forth from Bessie Smith's mouth, no song or poem will bear my mother's name. Yet so many of the stories that I write, that we all write, are my mother's stories. Only recently did I fully realize this: that through years of listening to my mother's stories of her life, I have absorbed not only the stories themselves, but something of the manner in which she spoke, something of the urgency that involves the knowledge that her stories—like her life—must be recorded. It is probably for this reason that so much of what I have written is about characters whose counterparts in real life are so much older than I am.

But the telling of these stories, which came from my mother's lips as naturally as breathing, was not the only way my mother showed herself as an artist. For stories, too, were subject to being distracted, to dying without conclusion. Dinners must be started, and cotton must be gathered before the big rains. The artist that was and is my mother showed itself to me only after many years. This is what I finally noticed.

Like Mem, a character in *The Third Life of Grange Copeland,** my mother adorned with flowers whatever shabby house we were forced to live in. And not just your typical straggly country stand of zinnias, either. She planted ambitious gardens—and still does—with over fifty different varieties of plants that bloom profusely from early March until late November. Before she left home for the fields, she watered her flowers, chopped up the grass, and laid out new beds. When she returned from the fields she might divide clumps of bulbs, dig a cold pit, uproot and replant roses, or prune branches from her taller bushes or trees—until night came and it was too dark to see.

Whatever she planted grew as if by magic, and her fame as a grower of flowers spread over three counties. Because of her creativity with her flowers, even my memories of poverty are seen through a screen of blooms—sunflowers, petunias, roses, dahlias, forsythia, spirea, delphiniums, verbena . . . and on and on.

And I remember people coming to my mother's yard to be given cuttings from her flowers; I hear again the praise showered on her because whatever rocky soil she landed on, she turned into a garden. A garden so brilliant with colors, so original in its design, so magnificent with life and creativity, that to this day people drive by our house in Georgia—perfect strangers and imperfect strangers—and ask to stand or walk among my mother's art.

I notice that it is only when my mother is working in her flowers that she is radiant, almost to the point of being invisible—except as Creator: hand and eye. She is involved in work her soul must have. Ordering the universe in the image of her personal conception of Beauty.

Her face, as she prepares the Art that is her gift, is a legacy of respect she leaves to me, for all that illuminates and cherishes life. She has handed down respect for the possibilities—and the will to grasp them.

For her, so hindered and intruded upon in so many ways, being an artist has still been a daily part of her life. This ability to hold on, even in very simple ways, is work black women have done for a very long time.

This poem is not enough, but it is something, for the woman who literally covered the holes in our walls with sunflowers.

> They were women then
> My mama's generation
> Husky of voice—Stout of
> Step

The Third Life of Grange Copeland: A 1970 novel by Alice Walker that narrates the life of a poor black sharecropper who selfishly flees destitute conditions in Georgia to start anew in New York. After his "second life" fails, Grange returns to Georgia and, through the discovery of selfless love, enters a "third life," a life of generosity and altruistic heroism.

With fists as well as
Hands
How they battered down
Doors
And ironed
Starched white
Shirts
How they led
Armies
Headragged Generals
Across mined
Fields
Booby-trapped
Kitchens
To discover books
Desks
A place for us
How they knew what we
Must know
Without knowing a page
Of it
Themselves

Guided by my heritage of a love of beauty and a respect for strength—in search of my mother's garden, I found my own.

And perhaps in Africa over two hundred years ago, there was just such a mother; perhaps she painted vivid and daring decorations in oranges and yellows and greens on the walls of her hut; perhaps she sang—in a voice like Roberta Flack's—*sweetly* over the compounds of her village; perhaps she wove the most stunning mats or told the most ingenious stories of all the village storytellers. Perhaps she was herself a poet—although only her daughter's name is signed to the poems that we know.

Perhaps Phillis Wheatley's mother was also an artist.

Perhaps in more than Phillis Wheatley's biological life is her mother's signature made clear.

Ideas for Rereading

1. In the second half of her essay, Walker uses the example of her own mother's garden to illustrate the physical, emotional, and—most important—creative endurance of black women. She writes, "How they did it [that is, how their creativity endured] . . . brings me to the title of this essay, 'In Search of Our Mothers' Gardens,' which is a personal account that is yet shared, in its theme and its meaning, by all of us" (p. 168). As you reread the essay, identify the manifestations of the symbolic "garden" in the lives and work of the women Walker describes.

2. Walker writes that "these grandmothers and mothers of ours were not Saints, but Artists." What is the difference? Take careful notes as you reread

the first section of the essay, in order to work out with some precision the special sense that she gives to each of these words. How do these terms help to introduce the rest of her argument?

3. What does Walker learn from her own mother's garden? What does the garden come to stand for on the personal and on the social level? In your notes, develop your ideas concerning this larger meaning and how it inflects the sense of the essay's title.

4. In reference to the Negro spirituals, Du Bois writes, "They that walked in darkness sang songs in the olden days — Sorrow Songs — for they were weary at heart" (p. 137). How would Walker react to Du Bois's notion of the inherent sadness of this uniquely African American art form? As you reread Walker's essay, apply this idea of "sorrow" to the creative efforts of black women. Mark places in the text where Walker's perspective conforms to that of Du Bois and where their perspectives diverge. Consider how Walker's femaleness — and that of her subjects — might affect her perspective.

Ideas for Writing

1. In describing the usual efforts to locate in history the creative spirit of black women, Walker suggests, "we have . . . looked high, when we should have looked high — and low" (p. 169). She offers examples of folk art and craft, such as gardens and quilts, as examples of looking "low." Look around you for an example of anonymous creativity — a quilt in a museum, graffiti, a particularly beautiful local house garden. The important thing is that you not know the identity of the work's creator. Consider the individual humanity of the anonymous creator. Write an essay profiling your image of that creator based on his or her work.

2. Throughout the essay, Walker uses and redefines religious vocabulary — words such as *saint* and *shrine*. Take careful note of these religious terms and write an essay that considers the ways in which Walker plays with, extends, and complicates their commonly accepted meanings. Consider her purpose in doing this. (Remember that the concept of the "garden" has its own religious connotations.)

GLENN LOURY

Glenn Loury (b. 1948) is a professor of economics at Boston University and consultant to the Federal Trade Commission and has been a visiting lecturer at colleges and universities in the United States and abroad. His writings include One by One, From the Inside Out: Essays and Reviews on Race and Responsibility in America *(1995), which won a* Christianity Today *Book Award. Loury has said, "As a black intellectual making my living in the academic establishment during a period of growing racial conflict in our society, I have often experienced some dissonance between my self-concept and the socially imputed definition of who I am supposed to be." He describes this experience of dissonance in the following personal essay, taken from Gerald Early's collection* Lure and Loathing: Essays on Race, Identity, and the Ambivalence of Assimilation *(1993).*

Free at Last? A Personal Perspective on Race and Identity in America

> *Then Peter opened his mouth and said, Of a truth I perceive that God is no respecter of persons: But in every nation he that feareth him, and worketh righteousness, is accepted with him.*
>
> —Acts 10:34–35

A formative experience of my growing-up on the South Side of Chicago in the 1960s occurred during one of those heated, earnest political rallies so typical of the period. I was about eighteen at the time. Woody, who had been my best friend since Little League, suggested that we attend. Being political neophytes, neither of us knew many of the participants. The rally was called to galvanize our community's response to some pending infringement by the white power structure, the exact nature of which I no longer remember. But I can still vividly recall how very agitated about it we all were, determined to fight the good fight, even to the point of being arrested if it came to that. Judging by his demeanor, Woody was among the most zealous of those present.

Despite this zeal, it took courage for Woody to attend that meeting. Though he often proclaimed his blackness, and though he had a Negro grandparent on each side of his family, he nevertheless looked to all the world like your typical white boy. Everyone, on first meeting him, assumed as much. I did, too, when we began to play together nearly a decade earlier, just after I had moved into the middle-class neighborhood called Park Manor, where Woody's family had been living for some time.

There were a number of white families on our block when we first arrived; within a couple of years they had all been replaced by aspiring black families like our own. I often wondered why Woody's parents never moved. Then I overheard his mother declare to one of her new neighbors, "We just wouldn't run from our own kind," a comment that befuddled me at the time. Somewhat later, while we were watching the movie *Imitation of Life* on television, my mother explained how someone could be black though he or she looked white. She told me about people like that in our own family—second cousins living in a fashionable suburb on whom one would never dare simply to drop in, because they were "passing for white." This was my earliest glimpse of the truth that racial identity in America is inherently a social and cultural, not simply a biological construct—that it necessarily involves an irreducible element of choice.

From the moment I learned of it I was at once intrigued and troubled by this idea of passing. I enjoyed imagining my racial brethren surreptitiously infiltrating the citadels of white exclusivity. It allowed me to believe that, despite appearances and the white man's best efforts to the contrary, we blacks were nevertheless present, if unannounced, *everywhere* in American society. But I was disturbed by an evident implication of the practice of passing—that denial of one's genuine self is a necessary concomitant of a black person's making it in this society. What "passing" seemed to say about the world was that if one were both black and ambitious it was necessary to choose between racial authenticity and personal success. Also, and ironically, it seemed grossly unfair to my adolescent mind that, however problematic it might be, this passing option was, because of my relatively dark complexion, not available to me!

It dawned on me after this conversation with my mother that Woody's parents must have been passing for white in preintegration Park Manor. The neighborhood's changing racial composition had confronted them with a moment of truth. They had elected to stay and to raise their children among "their own kind." This was a fateful decision for Woody, who, as he matured, became determined not simply to live among blacks but, perhaps in atonement for his parents' sins, unambiguously to become one. The young men in the neighborhood did not make this easy. Many delighted in picking fights with him, teasing him about being a "white boy," and refusing to credit his insistent, often repeated claim: "I'm a brother, too!"

The fact that some of his relatives were passing made Woody's racial-identity claims more urgent for him, but less compelling to others. He desperately wanted to be black, but his peers in the neighborhood would not let him. Because he had the option to be white—an option he radically rejected at the time—those without the option could not accept his claim to a shared racial experience. I knew Woody well. We became good friends, and I wanted to accept him on his own terms. But even I found myself doubting that he fully grasped the pain, frustration, anger, and self-doubt many of us felt upon encountering the intractability of American racism. However much he sympathized with our plight, he seemed to experience it only vicariously.

So there we were, at this boisterous, angry political rally. A critical moment came when the leaders interrupted their speech making to solicit input from "the people." Woody had an idea, and enthusiastically raised his voice above the murmur to be heard. He was cut short before finishing his first sentence by one of the dashiki-clad brothers-in-charge, who demanded to know how a "white boy" got the authority to have an opinion about what black people should be doing. That was one of our problems, the brother said, we were always letting white people "peep our hole card," while we were never privy to their deliberations in the same way.

A silence then fell over the room. The indignant brother asked if anyone could "vouch for this white boy." More excruciating silence ensued. Now was *my* moment of truth; Woody turned plaintively toward me, but I would not meet his eyes. To my eternal disgrace, I refused to speak up for him. He was asked to leave the meeting, and did so without uttering a word in his own defense. Subsequently, neither of us could bear to discuss the incident. I offered no apology or explanation, and he asked for none. However, though we continued to be friendly, our relationship was forever changed. I was never again to hear Woody exclaim: "I'm a brother, too."

I recall this story about Woody because his dilemma, and mine, tell us something important about race and personal identity in American society. His situation was made so difficult by the fact that he embraced a self-definition dramatically inconsistent with the identity reflexively and stubbornly imputed to him by others. This lack of social confirmation for his subjective sense of self left him uncertain, at a deep level, about who he really was. Ultimately there seemed to be no way for him to avoid living fraudulently—either as a black passing for white, or as a white trying (too hard) to be black. As his close friend and frequent companion I had become familiar with, and occasionally shared in, the pitfalls of this situation. People would assume when they saw us together both that he was white, and that I was "the kind of Negro who hangs out with white boys." I resented that assumption.

Since then, as a black intellectual making my living in the academic establishment during a period of growing racial conflict in our society, I have often experienced this dissonance between my self-concept and the socially imputed definition of who I am supposed to be. I have had to confront the problem of balancing my desire not to disappoint the expectations of others—both whites and blacks, but more especially blacks—with my conviction that one should strive to live life with integrity. This does not make me a heroic figure; I eschew the libertarian ideologue's rhetoric about the glorious individual who, though put upon by society, blazes his own path. I acknowledge that this opposition between individual and society is ambiguous, in view of the fact that the self is inevitably shaped by the objective world, and by other selves. I know that what one is being faithful to when resisting the temptation to conform to others' expectations by "living life with integrity" is always a socially determined, if subjectively experienced, vision of the self.

Still, I see this incident of a quarter-century ago as a kind of private metaphor for the ongoing problem of living in good faith, particularly as it relates to my personal identity as a black American. I have since lost contact with Woody. I suspect that, having tired of his struggle against society's presumptions about him, he is now passing. But that moment of truth in that South Side church basement, and my failure in the face of it, have helped me understand the depth of my own need to be seen by others as "black enough."

Upon reflection, my refusal to stand up for Woody exposed the tenuous quality of my personal sense of racial authenticity. The fact is, I willingly betrayed someone I had known for a decade, since we began to play stickball together in the alley that ran between our homes, a person whom I loved and who loved me, in order to avoid the risk of being rejected by strangers. In a way, at that moment and often again later in my life, I was "passing" too—hoping to be mistaken for something I was not. I had feared that to proclaim before the black radicals in the audience that this "white boy" at my side was in fact our "brother" would have compromised my own chance of being received among them as a genuine colleague, too. Who, after all, was there to vouch for me, had I been dismissed by one of the "brothers" as an Uncle Tom?

This was not an unfounded concern, for at that meeting, as at so many others of the period, people with insufficiently militant views were berated as self-hating, shuffle-along, "house nigger" types, complicit with whites in the perpetuation of racial oppression. Then, as now, blacks who befriended (or, heaven forbid, married) whites, who dressed or talked or wore their hair a certain way, who listened to certain kinds of music, read certain books, or expressed certain opinions were laughed at, ostracized and generally demeaned as inauthentic by other, more righteous (as in "self-righteous") blacks. The indignant brother who challenged Woody's right to speak at that rally was not merely imposing a racial test (only blacks are welcome here), he was mainly applying a loyalty test (are you truly with us or against us?) and this was a test that anyone present could fail through a lack of conformity to the collective definition of what it meant to be genuinely black. I feared that speaking up for Woody would have marked me as a disloyal Tom among the blacker-than-thou crowd. This was a fate, in those years, the thought of which I could not bear.

I now understand how this desire to be regarded as genuinely black, to be seen as a "regular brother," has dramatically altered my life. It narrowed the range of my earliest intellectual pursuits, distorted my relationships with other people, censored my political thought and expression, informed the way I dressed and spoke, and shaped my cultural interests. Some of this was inevitable and not all of it was bad, but in my experience the need to be affirmed by one's racial peers can take on a pathological dimension. Growing into intellectual maturity has been, for me, largely a process of becoming free of the need to have my choices validated by "the brothers." After many years I have come to understand that until I became willing to risk the derision of the crowd I had no chance to discover the most important truths about myself or about life—to know and accept my "calling," to perceive what I really value, what goals are most worth striving toward. In a perverse extension of the lesson from *Imitation of Life,* I have learned that one does not have to live surreptitiously as a Negro among whites in order to be engaged in a denial of one's genuine self for the sake of gaining social acceptance. This is a price that blacks often demand of each other as well.

I used to think about the irony in the idea of some blacks seeking to excommunicate others for crimes against the race, given that the external factors that affect us all are unaffected by the distinctions that so exercised the blacker-than-thou crowd. I would relish the seeming contradiction: I was still a "nigger" to the working-class toughs waiting to punish with their fists my trespass onto their white turf, yet I could not be a "brother" to the middle-class radicals with whom I shared so much history and circumstance. My racial identity in the larger white society was in no way conditional upon the espousal of particular beliefs or values (whatever my political views or cultural interests, I would always be black in white America), yet my standing among other blacks could be made conditional upon my fidelity to the prevailing party line of the moment. I would ponder this paradox, chafing at the restraint of an imposed racial uniformity, bemoaning the unfairness that I should have to face a threat of potential ostracism as punishment for the sin of being truthful to myself. In short, I would wallow in self-pity, which is always a waste of time. These days I am less given to, if not entirely free of, such inclinations.

Underlying my obsession with this paradox was a premise which I now believe to be mistaken—that being an authentic black person involves in some elemental way seeing oneself as an object of mistreatment by white people, while participating in a collective consciousness of that mistreatment with other black people. As long as I believed that my personal identity as a black American was necessarily connected to our country's history of racial violation, and derived much of its content from my sharing with other blacks in a recollection of and struggle against this violation, I was destined to be in a bind. For, as my evolving understanding of our history began to clash with the black consensus, and my definition of the struggle took on a different, more conservative form from that popular among other black intellectuals, I found myself cut off from the group, my racial bona fides in question. I was therefore forced to choose between my intellectual integrity and my access to that collective consciousness of racial violation and shared experience of struggle which I saw as essential to my black identity. Like Woody, lacking social confirmation of my subjective sense of self, I was left uncertain about who I really was.

I no longer believe that the camaraderie engendered among blacks by our collective experience of racism constitutes an adequate basis for any person's self-definition. Even if I restrict attention to the question "Who am I as a black American at the end of the twentieth century?," these considerations of historical victimization and struggle against injustice do not take me very far toward finding an answer. I am made "black" only in the most superficial way by virtue of being the object of a white racist's hate. The empathetic exchange of survivors' tales among "brothers," even the collective struggle against the clear wrong of racism, does not provide a tapestry sufficiently rich to give meaning and definition to the totality of my life. I am so much more than the one wronged, misunderstood, underestimated, derided, or ignored by whites. I am more than the one who has struggled against this oppression and indifference; more than a descendant of slaves now claiming freedom; more, that is, than either a "colored person" (as seen by the racist) or a "person of color" (as seen by the antiracist).

Who am I, then? Foremost, I am a child of God, created in his image, imbued with his spirit, endowed with his gifts, set free by his grace. The most important challenges and opportunities that confront me derive not from my racial condition, but rather from my human condition. I am a husband, a father, a son, a teacher, an intellectual, a Christian, a citizen. In none of these roles is my race irrelevant, but neither can racial identity alone provide much guidance for my quest to adequately discharge these responsibilities. The particular features of my social condition, the external givens, merely set the stage of my life, they do not provide a script. That script must be internally generated, it must be a product of a reflective deliberation about the meaning of this existence for which no political or ethnic program could ever substitute.

Or, to shift the metaphor slightly, the socially contingent features of my situation—my racial heritage and family background, the prevailing attitudes about race and class of those with whom I share this society—these are the building blocks, the raw materials, out of which I must construct the edifice of my life. The expression of my individual personality is to be found in the blueprint that I employ to guide this project of construction. The problem of devising such a plan for one's life is a universal problem, which confronts all people, whatever their race, class, or ethnicity. By facing and solving this problem we grow as human beings, and give meaning and substance to our lives. In my view, a personal identity wholly dependent on racial contingency falls tragically short of its potential because it embraces too parochial a conception of what is possible, and of what is desirable.

Thus, and ironically, to the extent that we individual blacks see ourselves primarily through a racial lens, we sacrifice possibilities for the kind of personal development that would ultimately further our collective, racial interests. We cannot be truly free men and women while laboring under a definition of self derived from the perceptual view of our oppressor, confined to the contingent facts of our oppression. In *A Portrait of the Artist as a Young Man* James Joyce says of Irish nationalism: "When the soul of a man is born in this country there are nets flung at it to hold it back from flight. You talk to me of nationality, language, religion. I shall try to fly by these nets. . . . Do you know what Ireland is? . . . Ireland is the old sow that eats her farrow." It seems to me that, too often, a search for some mythic authentic blackness works similarly to hold back young black souls from flight into the open skies of American society. Of course there is the constraint of racism also holding us back. But the trick, as Joyce knew, is to turn such "nets" into wings, and thus to fly by them. One cannot do that if one refuses to see that ultimately it is neither external constraint nor expanded opportunity but rather an indwelling spirit that makes this flight possible.

Last winter, on a clear, cold Sunday afternoon, my three-year-old son and I were walking in the woods near our New England home. We happened upon a small pond, which, having frozen solid, made an ideal skating rink. Dozens of men, ranging in age from late teens to early thirties, were distributed across the ice in clusters of ten or so, playing, or preparing to play hockey. They glided over the pond's surface effortlessly, skillfully passing and defending, stopping and turning on a dime, moving with such power, speed, and grace that we were spellbound as we watched them. Little Glenn would occasionally squeal with delight as he marveled at one astounding feat after another, straining against my grip, which alone prevented him from running out onto the ice to join in the fun.

All of these men were white—every last one of them. Few took notice of us at the pond's edge, and those who did were not particularly generous with their smiles, or so, at least, it seemed to me. I sensed that we were interlopers, that if we had come with sticks and skates we would not necessarily have been welcome. But this may be wrong; I do not really know what they thought of our presence; no words were exchanged. I do know that my son very much enjoyed watching the game, and I thought to myself at the time that he would, someday too soon, come asking for a pair of skates, and for his dad to teach him how to use them. I found myself consciously dreading that day.

The thought of my son's playing hockey on that frozen pond did not sit well with me. I much preferred to think of him on a basketball court. Hockey, we all know, is a white man's game. Who was the last "brother" to play in the NHL? Of course, I immediately sensed that this thought was silly and illegitimate, and attempted to banish it from my mind. But it kept coming back. I could not avoid the feeling that something important was at stake here. So I decided to discuss it with my wife, Linda.

We had carefully considered the implications for our children of our decision to buy a house in a predominantly white suburb. We joined and became active in a church with many black families like our own, in part so that our boys would be provided with suitable racial peers. We are committed to ensuring that their proper education about black history and culture, including their family history, is not left to chance. We are ever vigilant concerning the effect on their developing psyches of racial messages that come across on television, in their books, at their nursery school, and so on. On all of this Linda and I are in full accord. But she thought my concerns about hockey were taking things a bit too far.

I now believe that she was right, and I think I have learned something important from our conversations about this issue. My aversion to the idea of my son's involvement in that Sunday-afternoon ritual we witnessed was rooted in my own sense of identity, as a black American man who grew up when and where I did, who has had the experiences I have had. Because *I* would not have felt comfortable there, I began to think that *he* should not want to be a part of that scene either. I was inclined to impose upon my son, in the name of preserving his authentic blackness, a limitation of his pursuits deriving from my life but not really relevant to his. It is as if I were to insist that he study Swahili instead of Swedish because I could not imagine myself being interested in speaking Swedish!

The fact is that, given the class background of our children and the community in which we have chosen to make our lives, it is inevitable that their racial sensibilities will be quite different from ours. Moreover, it is impossible to predict just what self-definition they will settle upon. This can be disquieting to contemplate for those of our generation concerned about retaining a "genuinely black" identity in the face of the social mobility we have experienced within our lifetimes. But it is not, I think, to be feared.

The alternative seems much more frightening to me—stifling the development of our children's personalities by imposing upon them an invented ethnicity. I have no doubt that my sons will be black men of the twenty-first century, but not by their singing of racial anthems peculiar to our time. Theirs will be a blackness constructed yet again, out of the external givens of their lives, not mine, shaped by a cultural inheritance that I am responsible to transmit but expressed in their own voices, animated by a Spirit whose basis lies deeper than the color of any man's skin, and whose source is "no respecter of persons."

Ideas for Rereading

1. Loury starts his essay with a biblical quotation. What is the meaning of this quotation for Loury? How does he work with that meaning throughout the essay? Develop your observations and ideas in your notebook.

2. Of his youthful experience at the political meeting, Loury writes, "I see this incident of a quarter-century ago as a kind of private metaphor for the ongoing problem of living in good faith, particularly as it relates to my personal identity as a black American" (p. 175). How is Loury's experience a metaphor? As you reread Loury, consider how he establishes his metaphor and then sustains it throughout the essay. In what ways do this experience and its consequences exemplify Du Bois's concept of "double-consciousness"?

3. Although Loury's main focus is racial and cultural identity in the broad sense rather than strictly in relation to the arts, it is important to note that he refers to significant works of art at key moments to make his argument—for example, Douglas Sirk's 1959 film *Imitation of Life* and James Joyce's 1916 novel *A Portrait of the Artist as a Young Man*. As you reread, take note of such references. What might these references, and the way that Loury works with them in his essay, suggest about the role played by the arts in our effort to understand and grapple with problems of racial and cultural identity?

Ideas for Writing

1. Loury has chosen to discuss the issue of identity through the form of the personal essay. He has used an experience from his youth as a way into exploring self-identity and cultural identity among African Americans. Find a particularly compelling, identity-shaping anecdote from your past, and use that anecdote to explore the conflict and confluence between personal and group (ethnic, cultural) identity.

2. Reread Alice Walker's essay "In Search of Our Mothers' Gardens," taking careful note of the autobiographical elements of the essay. In a short critical essay, explore the different ways Loury and Walker employ the personal essay form. Explain and illustrate connections and divergences in the ways these authors use autobiography toward a broader purpose.

3. Loury writes, "From the moment I learned of it I was at once intrigued and troubled by this idea of passing. . . . What 'passing' seemed to say about the world was that if one were both black and ambitious it was necessary to choose between racial authenticity and personal success" (pp. 173–74). Among African Americans today, what might be the temptations to "pass"? What might be the deterrents? What about during Loury's youth? Du Bois's youth? Write an essay in which you consider what you know about each of those three periods in history, keeping in mind what Du Bois and Loury have suggested in their essays. Consider and illustrate the evolution of the concept of "passing" and potential individual and community responses to it.

4. Ice hockey probably cannot be included among the arts, but it certainly belongs to culture, and it may be that Loury's expectation that his son will soon want to play ice hockey pertains to questions about racial identity and the arts. If we treat the story metaphorically, what can it tell us about the cultural legacy that one generation can pass on to the next? Write an essay exploring your experience of an art form, sport, mode of dress, or any other cultural expression that is not seen as "belonging" to — or being authentically part of — your social, racial, gender, or other group. How might your experience relate to Loury's concerns about his son and ice hockey? How does it differ?

5. View Douglas Sirk's 1959 film *Imitation of Life*. (You may also want to study the film through the book *Imitation of Life* in the Rutgers Films in Print series [ed. Lucy Fischer, Rutgers UP, 1991].) Write an essay on the relationship between the film's themes and Loury's discussion of racial, ethnic, and cultural identity.

HAZEL CARBY

Hazel Carby (b. 1948) is a literary and social critic and professor of African American studies at Yale University. Her work reflects a keen understanding of the many complicated intersections of gender and race in American culture. In Reconstructing Womanhood: The Emergence of the Afro-American Woman Novelist *(1987), she finds in the work of early black female writers, like Frances E. W. Harper, the roots of the black woman's literary movement that continues in the writing of Toni Morrison, Gwendolyn Brooks, and others. Focusing on the largely ignored lives and works of the early writers, Carby argues that in their challenge to traditions of sexual inequality, as well as their refutation of the white, middle-class bias of the woman suffrage movement, these underappreciated African American women created a distinctive voice, both black and female, that resonates today in the work of their modern counterparts.*

In Race Men: The W. E. B. Du Bois Lectures *(1998), Carby turns her attention to African American manhood and its conflicting images within, and relationship to, the dominant white male culture. She does so through a series of biographical critiques of black male intellectuals and artists — including W. E. B. Du Bois, actor and activist Paul Robeson, musician Miles Davis, and actor Danny Glover. The Glover essay is included here. Like many works of cultural criticism, this is an essay that takes popular culture seriously — to a degree that some readers will find surprising. It is unusual, however, in that, rather than examining any single work in depth, it examines a persona, one that remains consistent in certain key respects from film to film, despite superficial differences between the characters that Glover plays. You will need to keep an attentive eye on the main thread of Carby's argument as she studies key scenes from a number of different films.*

Lethal Weapons and City Games

> *I'm an innocent bystander . . .*
> *Send lawyers, guns and money*
> *The shit has hit the fan.*
> — WARREN ZEVON

As *Grand Canyon* opens, a blank screen is all that can be seen. Out of the darkness gradually comes the pulsating sound of chopper blades.[1] Like so many others of my generation, I am used to connecting this sweep of mechanical wings with a particular place and history because, for more than twenty years, the sound of low-flying helicopters was used by film and television studios to signify the presence of Americans in the war zones of Southeast Asia.

Peter Markle used exactly the same cinematic effect, a blank screen and steady beat of helicopter blades, as the opening sequence of his 1988 Vietnam film, *Bat 21*.[2] By borrowing the opening of *Bat 21* for *Grand Canyon* in 1991, director Lawrence Kasdan brings the Vietnam war to the city of Los Angeles.[3] The strategy employed by Kasdan and other Hollywood filmmakers to equate these particular killing fields with the streets of Los Angeles is complex and contradictory and will haunt this chapter. The dramatic effect, however, is startling. Although ignorant of the subject of *Grand Canyon* when I started to watch it, the unmistakable sound of those blades alerted me to expect, post-Vietnam, the symbolic landscape of a black urban neighborhood.

Throughout the 1980s, Southeast Asia was presented in the popular culture of the United States as *the* primary site of the national nightmare: a landscape through which North American men crept under the constant surveillance of a subhuman population of menacing "gooks." The "enemy" masqueraded as ordinary men, women, and children by day but, within the heart of the nightmare, these people were never ordinary, never innocent, and barely human. Since then, this vision has been supplanted in the popular cultural and political imagination by images of black inner-city neighborhoods.

For contemporary Hollywood filmmakers, the black neighborhoods of Los Angeles have become important sites not just for the representation of death and destruction but for the enactment of racialized social and political confrontations that to them constitute a national crisis. Indeed, these neighborhoods are now, for bankers and studios alike, as fascinating in their exoticism, their potential for violent masculine confrontations, and therefore their commercial marketability, as was Vietnam. These neighborhoods have become the sites for the current enactment of the national nightmares of the white suburban bourgeoisie—these nightmares which are inscribed upon the bodies of young, urban black males and patrolled by the "Bloods" and the "Crips."

I am intrigued by Kasdan's *Grand Canyon* because it exemplifies Hollywood's fascination with the black inner city as the symbolic space of suburban anxiety. No matter how multiracial and multicultural our inner-city neighborhoods actually are, they are reduced in most Hollywood movies to an essentialist terrain of black and white male confrontation and resolution.

Grand Canyon conceals through its plot how, in a general way, it encourages white fear of black aggression. On the surface, the film appears merely to confirm what its target audience already understands, the material reality of the threat from young black men. But *Grand Canyon* also creates a utopian and somewhat magical racial relationship between two mature men, one black, one white, which acts as a possible imaginative resolution to the fears and anxieties of white suburban residents. The promotional material which accompanies the home video describes it as follows: "*Grand Canyon* is director Lawrence Kasdan's powerful and uplifting film about real life and real miracles... and about how, after the millions of choices we make in life, one chance encounter can change it all."[4]

At the beginning of the film Mack, an immigration lawyer played by Kevin Kline, looks for a way to avoid the heavy traffic leaving the Los Angeles Forum after a Lakers' game. He strays into a black neighborhood that is so alien to him that he will later categorically assure his family, "You have *never been* where I broke down."[5] What happens to Mack is evocative of the modernist journey into the "heart of darkness," a journey originally conceived in the context of European imperialism in Joseph Conrad's novel of that name, and recreated by Hollywood in Francis Ford Coppola's postmodern fantasy of war in Southeast Asia, *Apocalypse Now*. As Mack peers anxiously out of his windscreen at the unfamiliar and, to him, menacing black residential neighborhood, Warren Zevon's music plays in his car.

Music is important to Kasdan, and the Warren Zevon soundtrack, "Lawyers, Guns, and Money," establishes a background for his protagonist. Clearly, the repetition of the plea to "send lawyers, guns, and money" increases the tension of the moment and emphasizes the risk of imminent danger, but the song also acts to situate Mack in history. Zevon's music is a product of the seventies, of white, yuppie, southern California culture.

Mack's familiarity with the words and apparent nostalgia for the song places him within the liberal politics and culture of this time. The music provides the character with a social location and particular history.[6] Kasdan also uses music to signal the distance between modernist conceptions of history and subjectivity, such as those at work in Conrad's novel, and his own postmodern vision of the fragmentation of social and political positionality. In Kasdan's editing room the Zevon soundtrack was integrated into the film not only in order to register with the audience the potential threat to his protagonist but to prepare them for his making music the very ground of social and political conflict.

The words of "Lawyers, Guns, and Money" evoke, with a wry liberal irony, memories of the Cold War, of danger to Americans trespassing in exotic locales, and of covert intervention in other countries. The song also establishes the liberal credentials of the character of Mack, creates a mood of empathy for his mistake (his drive is intercut with scenes from the family home, complete with beautiful wife and handsome teenage son—all this he stands to lose), and alerts the audience to the gravity of his situation. As Mack's anxiety grows, Kasdan multiplies his visual and aural strategies for creating and maintaining anxiety, and increasing the sense of panic and foreboding in his audience.

Mack abruptly switches off his stereo in order to concentrate more effectively on finding his way home and, like a mouse in a laboratory maze, turns his car around in a futile effort to escape.[7] As Mack drives ever closer toward the "horror" that awaits, he passes the shells of cars and the skeletons of abandoned buildings. The landscape he drives through increasingly resembles a war zone, and Mack begins to sing Zevon's words himself as if to seek comfort in their meaning. But, as Mack mutters "send lawyers, guns, and money," his words are overwhelmed by the taunting voice of Ice Cube, "ruthless, plenty of that and much more," emanating from a white BMW that slows down and drives beside him like an animal stalking its prey. At this moment music becomes *the* prime vehicle for representing a cultural war which has encoded within it the political potential for a larger civil war. The rap group NWA (Niggaz with Attitude) is pitted against Zevon in a symbolic enactment of Kasdan's narrative of race and nation which is about to unfold: a liberal white suburban male confronts a "posse" of young black urban males. The musical battle both produces and accompanies the wider class and racialized meanings of the scene, meanings which in turn both produce and confirm contemporary ideological beliefs about the "problem" of the inner city, of what is wrong with America.

The skewed perspective of this cinematic confrontation is revealed in the unequal editing of the musical "war." In contrast to the verbal and musical fragments of NWA's "Quiet on the Set," the audience hears coherent narrative selections from the Zevon lyrics. We do not hear sequential sections of a verse, or even complete sentences, of the NWA lyrics; the narrative coherence of "Quiet on the Set" has been deliberately disrupted. The voice of Ice Cube fades in and out of the cat-and-mouse game as it is played out on the screen, and the words we can make out, "ruthless, plenty of that and much more," are intended only to confirm the menacing intentions of the occupants of the BMW, five young black males who take careful note of the interloper in their territory.

Mack responds to their presence by singing:

I'm an innocent bystander . . .
Send lawyers, guns and money
The shit has hit the fan.

His car coughs, splutters, stalls, and finally stops, and Mack becomes a man under siege. He uses his car phone in a desperate attempt to get help, but isn't sure just where he is. "I dunno . . . let's say . . . Inglewood," he decides, without conviction, as the car phone itself crackles and dies. Having run to a public telephone outside a convenience store, Mack continues to find it difficult, if not impossible, to describe his location exactly or, to continue the military analogy, to give his coordinates. "Buckingham, yes," he pants, "but remember it's about half a mile west, I guess, of there." Mack is not only lost; he is in alien territory, and his very survival is at stake.

Kasdan carefully and deliberately recreates film narratives of Vietnam for his narrative of Los Angeles. Here again, he appears to be influenced by Markle's *Bat 21*, in which Gene Hackman finds himself alone in enemy territory. In that movie Hackman plays the part of a man who shouldn't be in the situation in which he finds himself; he is a missile intelligence expert who has had to bail out from an unarmed plane on a reconnaissance mission. His only chance of survival is at the other end of his communications device and depends upon providing his exact coordinates. The camera work of these parallel scenes, in which Hackman and Kline run and hide from their enemies, desperate to find a safe place from which to call for help, is too similar to be coincidental, but, even more importantly, the Vietnam narrative is present in Kasdan's decision to cast the same actor to play the part of the heroic rescuer.

Roadside assistance tells Mack that it will take forty-five minutes to get to him. He replies that he understands but warns, "if it takes that long I might be like, ah, dead." (In the Vietnam movie, the Hackman character is also told that it is not possible to send help straight away and has a similar reaction.) Both Hackman and Kline remain under enemy surveillance. In *Grand Canyon* the NWA soundtrack changes to include fragments of "F*** the Police," signifying the imminence of the moment of confrontation. Mack returns to his car to wait for help and the BMW pulls up behind him.

What follows is a filmic moment in which language, sound, and image coalesce to evoke intense emotions of danger and fear in the audience, reminding it of the feelings of an American soldier coming down in enemy territory. Through his personal distress Mack gives voice to the anxieties of a constituency of the white suburban middle class, whose greatest fear is being stranded in a black urban neighborhood at night. The young black men advance, framed by the rear windscreen. The camera then focuses on Mack's face. His eyes, seen in the rearview mirror, flicker as he breathes a final distress call: "Mayday, Mayday. We're coming down."

What Kasdan excludes from his audience in this scene is an irony that only those who know the lyrics of "Quiet on the Set" and "F*** the Police" would perceive. In fact, I would argue that Kasdan depends upon the ignorance of his target audience. For those who aren't familiar with the album *Straight Outta Compton,* "Quiet on the Set" is about the power of performance, specifically, the potential power that a successful rap artist can gain over his audience.[8] Power is, quite explicitly, the power of words over the body. For example, "ruthless, plenty of that and much more" is about controlling the movements of people, particularly women, on a dance floor, and about the power to create "a look that keeps you staring and wondering why I'm invincible." This invincibility is entirely the result of being able to persuade with words: "when you hear my rhyme it's convinceable." Kasdan, however, disrupts NWA's intended narrative structure and lines like "I'm a walking threat" and "I wanna earn respect" are used to reinforce a contemporary image of the disobedient and dangerous black male who believes that respect is only gained through the possession of a gun (this is spelled out at the end of the confrontation). Perhaps the greatest irony of all is that the NWA song even predicts such misinterpretation and misuse of their words. Near the end of the rap, in a section excised from the film, an interesting dialogue occurs between Ice Cube and an unidentified voice that mimics the supposedly dispassionate, analytic tone of the sociologist or ethnographer. Ice Cube asserts that he can create "lyrics to make everybody say," and the academic voice responds: "They can be cold and ruthless, there's no doubt about that but, sometimes, it's more complicated." Ice Cube concludes: "You think I'm committing a crime, instead of making a rhyme."

A tow-truck driver comes to Mack's rescue at the height of his confrontation with the "gang" (in a similar way, in the rescue scene in *Bat 21,* a flyer heads toward Hackman at the last moment). Mack has been forced out of the safety of his car and is being directly threatened, when a blaze of oncoming headlights announces that he will be saved. The camera tantalizes the audience as it hesitates to reveal the identity of the man who climbs out of the truck. The lens tracks from the truck to Mack, flanked by the young black men in various poses of aggression, and then back again to the tow-truck driver's boots and slowly pans upwards. Here Kasdan reproduces the same low-angled shot he used moments before to stress the menacing nature of the black male faces that lean toward Mack in his car, a shot identical to one used in *Bat 21* as Hackman cowers away from the feet and legs of passing Viet Cong. Mack's rescuer is revealed to be a black man, armed with an enormous steel crowbar, a possible weapon, the size of which is exaggerated by the low camera angle. Before the audience can fully identify him, however, the tow-truck driver bends into the cab to reach for a cap.

This moment of uncertainty places in doubt the possible allegiance of the driver: is he really there to rescue Mack, as is implied by the change in the music, a signal upon which the audience has come to rely as a measure of mood? Or is the arrival of yet another black man an additional menace, as implied by the lingering of the camera over a body whose identity it is reluctant to reveal? The hesitation is only momentary, but it is sufficient to register ambiguity and doubt. Once the figure is revealed to be that of the actor, Danny Glover, the final threads of the complex Vietnam/Los Angeles web are woven in place. For Glover carries with him a built-in reference system from his previous roles, a filmic genealogy, if you will, that resolves any hesitation on the part of the audience about his possible allegiance. Indeed, Kasdan can toy so successfully with the audience's expectations because he can rely on the fact that Glover's appearance will instantly produce both the recognition and the assurance that he is a "good guy," a good black man:[9] after all, he was the heroic flyer who rescued Gene Hackman in *Bat 21* and the L.A.P.D.'s stalwart Sgt. Roger Murtaugh, whose partnership with Mel Gibson, in *Lethal Weapon,* has become a very profitable Hollywood legend.

The figure of Danny Glover as the tow-truck driver, Simon, is an important mechanism for the movie's resolution of the dilemma inherent in one of our most dominant contemporary narratives—a dilemma captured in the cinematic hesitation I have already described—how, exactly, can the white middle class distinguish between the good and the bad black male? The moment of Mack's rescue is a good point at which to interrupt the action in order to speculate about Kasdan's manipulation of black masculinity in his choice of Glover to play Simon.[10] It is through an analysis of the multiple ways in which the "good guy" genealogy has been formulated and established for Glover, a genealogy which film directors know exists in the popular imagination, that we can observe a particular narrative of race, nation, and masculinity at work.

Danny Glover's cinematic career blossomed during the conservative years of Reaganism and Reaganomics, but the particular projection of black manhood that Glover has come to embody is anticipated in interesting ways by the actor Canada Lee. In 1947, in Robert Rossen's *Body and Soul,* Canada Lee stars with John Garfield in a film about the corruption and violence present in the boxing world.[11] Garfield plays the part of a young and talented challenger to the title of world champion held by Ben Chaplin (Canada Lee). Both boxers are virtually owned by a gambler and boxing financier called Roberts, played by Lloyd Goff, who betrays Chaplin when it is profitable for him to do so. Chaplin is severely injured in a fight which leaves him with a blood clot on his brain. While encouraging Chaplin to fight Davis, assuring him that Davis will go easy on him, Roberts tells Davis, who remains ignorant of Chaplin's injury, to be brutal. When Chaplin is roughly defeated by Davis he is rushed to a hospital, and Davis discovers Roberts's betrayal. Contrite, Charlie Davis employs Ben Chaplin as his trainer, but Ben becomes much more: he becomes a voice of wisdom, an adviser, and a friend who, in contrast to Roberts, always has Charlie's interests at heart. He is not only a black man defeated and in a servile role; he is also proud, independent, and occupies the moral high ground. Chaplin is the only incorruptible man in the film, and when he dies, it is only his body that has gone; the moral and ethical superiority of his soul increases in power. In a number of scenes saturated by the music of "Body and Soul," Davis is finally persuaded to live up to the example of Ben Chaplin. When the ethical soul of the black man enters the white man's body, it ensures a return to honesty, integrity, and the familial social order.

This type of black male/white male partnership returns during the Reagan years, a period in which the partnership is elaborated into a complex social, political, and emotional as well as ethical unit. In *Bat 21,* Danny Glover's voice and his words of wisdom and advice are crucial to the eventual survival of the man he has to rescue. Like the character played by Canada Lee, Glover becomes obsessed with saving Hackman. He returns to fly over his position constantly, night and day, to the point of exhaustion and potential sacrifice of his own life. The words spoken by Glover through the radio become a literal lifeline, offering comfort against feelings of vulnerability and bringing encouragement, warmth, and hope to counter Hackman's despair. Again, like Canada Lee, Glover is portrayed as the man who can help the hero save himself from his enemies and, most importantly, save himself from his own weaknesses and fears. Danny Glover's film performances are a very significant elaboration of this portrayal of black manhood and constitute a complex, if contradictory, referential history of contemporary meanings of race and masculinity.

Danny Glover made his first movie appearance in the 1979 *Escape from Alcatraz,* in which he played one of many anonymous black male convicts.[12] In 1981 he was cast in *Chu Chu and the Philly Flash* as a member of a group of homeless men and women who lived in San Francisco's ferry terminal.[13] In this screwball comedy, Glover's black masculinity is rendered harmless as he forms part of an inept team whose antics resemble those of the Keystone Cops. The following year Glover appeared in the avant garde film *Out!,* aka *Deadly Drifter.*[14] Though in *Out!* Glover has the part of an urban revolutionary, complete with black leather coat and a stick of dynamite, he is not cast as a member of a threateningly dangerous black revolutionary army. On the contrary, Glover is, again, the only black member of a white collective and, toward the end of the film, is partnered with Peter Coyote in a mildly comic relationship. The film is an absurdist dismantling of revolutionary aims and methods through an existential journey across the United States. The desire for revolution is transformed into a New Age meditation on the moral and ethical superiority of native peoples and whales.

In 1984, however, Glover moves away from the syndrome of black male as criminal/outcast in his role of a laboratory assistant, Loomis, in Fred Schepisi's *Iceman.*[15] Though Loomis is a minor role, this is Glover's first opportunity to perform the part of a black male with a heart. The Iceman is a Neanderthal found frozen in the ice and brought back to life by a team of scientists; he is then kept under observation in an artificial habitat as if he were a specimen in a cage. In a brief but significant scene, the Glover character allies himself with the people who condemn this captivity on moral grounds and unlocks the door to let the Iceman escape, thus prefiguring his many later roles as a savior.

The role of Mose in Robert Benton's *Places in the Heart,* 1984, provides one of the keys to the development of Glover's cinematic genealogy as a good, trustworthy black man.[16] At the beginning of *Places in the Heart,* set in Texas in 1935 at the height of the Depression, Mose is a hobo and petty thief who steals the silver of a newly widowed young woman (Sally Field) while claiming to be looking for work. Field's husband and provider, the town sheriff, has recently been shot and killed by a drunken young black man, so the threat to the white family from lawless black men has multiple dimensions. Indeed, Glover's character could be described as a "deadly drifter," one who steals what little of value is owned by Field and her children, who are struggling to keep their farm from falling into the hands of a bank that wants to foreclose on its mortgage. When the thief is arrested, however, and returned to her house for identification, Field lies, claiming that Mose carries her silver with her permission in order to sell it for her. This generous action transforms the black man into an absolutely loyal bondsman and deliverer of a white family. This loyalty is supplemented by seemingly unlimited expressions of sacrifice and nobility, as Mose works to save the family in spite of tremendous opposition. He becomes their archetypal male provider, savior, and defender against all threats from the institutional forces of the dominant society, represented by the Bank and the Cotton Gin.

However, while Mose can successfully perform as the brains and the brawn hidden behind the skirts of a white woman, he fails to establish his patriarchal equality as a black man confronting white men. When threatened by the manager of the bank and the owner of the cotton gin, in their guise as leaders of the local Klan, Mose is forced to flee for his life. Ultimately, the black male ends as he began, without a place in this community—a figure of nobility but apart. In addition, the sense of worth of the black man is not gained through self-knowledge or self-respect but is granted from the outside. Mose's black masculinity gains its masculinity, as humanity, through white recognition: in the closing moments of the film, before he has to leave the town forever, Field acts like a queen bestowing a knighthood when she acknowledges Mose's loyalty and achievements: "Remember, you did this." It is this act of acknowledgment that remains with the character of Mose (and the audience). In the absence of a reward in the form of material goods, profit, or a social role in the community, these words are meant to sustain and comfort Mose. Recognition is his only consolation for his necessary racial exclusion from the family and the community for whose survival he is responsible.

In this sense, the resolution of *Places in the Heart* reproduces the resolution of Harriet Beecher Stowe's *Uncle Tom's Cabin,* an ideological paradigm that still appears to govern the Hollywood creation of the trustworthy black man. Each narrative genealogy of race and nation works in a structurally similar fashion: the imagining of the good black is dependent upon the rejection and removal of the alien black presence. Black saviors have to return to "Africa" or go to heaven. Though "Africa" as a literal reference point no longer functions in the same way that it did for Stowe, as a possible metaphoric and material place for disposing of an alien element that threatens to disrupt national unity, contemporary film directors do not have to explain to their audiences where black males are headed when they disappear from the screen. Hollywood can rely on the existence of the prison and the ghetto to function as equivalent spaces of exclusion in our contemporary political imagination.

As Glover walked out of a place in the heart of a Texas community, he walked into his first role as a police officer in *Witness* in 1985.[17] In this film Glover was still being cast in an ambiguous role. His character, McFee, is simultaneously inside of and outside of the law, a member of a police conspiracy to steal two and a half million dollars in drug money, and a cop who kills his fellow officers. Such ambiguity in relation to the law is resolved and ultimately transcended in *Lethal Weapon* and the series that followed.

A much more significant development in Glover's increasingly complex cinematic persona is his appearance, that same year, in Lawrence Kasdan's *Silverado,* a Western, in which he stars with Kevin Kline, Kevin Costner, and Scott Glenn.[18] At first *Silverado* looks as if it is going to merely reproduce elements from Glover's previous characterizations. Like Sally Field, Glenn and Kline win Glover's loyalty after they do him a favor, saving him from arrest by a racist town sheriff played, most incongruously, by John Cleese. Glover's character later has occasion to accuse Kline of a lack of moral and ethical commitment when it appears that Kline's self-interest is steering him to support the wrong side in a battle between settlers and the evil cattle barons who have purchased the protection of the local, and extremely corrupt, law enforcement officials. Glover occupies the moral high ground and eventually persuades his white buddy to defend the settlers. A close friendship develops between them, a partnership that prefigures the relation between Kline and Glover in *Grand Canyon* and Mel Gibson and Glover in the *Lethal Weapon* series.

While Glover's Vietnam roles establish the historical source of the modern black male/white male partnership, *Silverado* brings out the homosocial and at times homoerotic nature of the relationship between white and black men—a homoeroticism that will eventually come to characterize much of the humor of the *Lethal Weapon* films. The "special" nature of the friendship between Kline and Glover in *Silverado* is established primarily through editing—the cross cutting of shot and counter-shot of glances or lingering looks, the creation of frequent eye-contact intended to suggest more than is spoken in words. The film is also homosocial and frequently phallocentric in many of its general techniques and effects. The mise-en-scene for the development of the relationship among all four men, as they travel across country, is a landscape replete with phallic imagery, a terrain that both evokes and sustains their commonality.

The cinematic chronology of Glover's fictional black masculinity advances another step toward patriarchal power in the role of Albert Johnson (Mister) in Steven Spielberg's film based on Alice Walker's novel, *The Color Purple* (1985).[19] Glover is a glowering, threatening patriarchal presence as a husband and father. Incapable of expressing emotion toward other men, not even for his own son and father, Mister represents the constant threat of violence against women. But this black patriarchal power and rage reign only over black women and younger black men, not over whites. However, the character Glover plays has to be capable of transformation as he ages alone, and has to persuade the audience that he atones. Clearly, Glover's experience with his previous film personifications, plus his talent, make this transformation convincing, and *The Color Purple* confirms that Glover can play both the brutal and the sensitive black man.[20]

Between 1987 and 1992, Danny Glover starred in a number of films which reproduced the ideological terms within which the utopian dimensions of Hollywood's contemporary interracial masculine romance are imagined and secured. The historical experience of Vietnam is evoked as the source of this romance—a partnership which establishes equality in the shared experience of war and defeat. In Glover's own film genealogy, his role as Captain Bartholomew Clark in *Bat 21* (1988), as Sergeant Roger Murtaugh in the *Lethal Weapon* series (1987, 1989, and 1992), and as Frank "Dookie" Camparelli in *Flight of the Intruder* (1990) provide substantial examples of the cinematic black and white masculine partnerships that transcend racialization.

Flight of the Intruder, in which Glover stars with Willem Dafoe and Brad Johnson, elaborates on the persona Glover plays in *Bat 21.*[21] As Captain of a U.S. Navy aircraft carrier off the coast of Vietnam in September 1972, Glover plays the part of an authoritarian but nurturing parental male toward the younger men in his charge. A strict but caring disciplinarian, Glover wins the respect and love of his subordinates. "Christ, all we've really got is each other," he teaches them. The armed forces are represented as an all-male substitute or equivalent for the family, a unit which excludes women. In this homosocial order race is not *the* important issue; the principal concern is with ways of bonding. For example, in *Flight* Frank Camparelli identifies himself, and is characterized by others, as a Mafia boss. The reference to the Mafia, confirmed by his surname, evokes an alternative and familial structure of patriarchal allegiance, power, and control. This kind of homosocial partnership has become of increasing importance to male Hollywood film directors in developing an explicitly antifeminist male culture.

Richard Donner's *Lethal Weapon* series exemplifies this interracial male alliance against women.[22] Considered together, the three films document the development of a close and increasingly intimate partnership between an older black and a younger white male. But the origin of this phenomenon does not lie in the history of the movement to gain civil rights. It is the history of the desegregation of the United States armed forces and the "policing" of Southeast Asia that enables the relationship of equality between Martin Riggs and Roger Murtaugh. Men become buddies not in a movement for liberation but in a shared experience as oppressors, and their friendships are born outside the continental United States. What Riggs and Murtaugh share is the experience of Vietnam, which is the ground of their apparent equality and the basis for their mutual respect.

Lethal Weapon, the first in the series, forges Riggs and Murtaugh into an unbeatable fighting team as they defeat a rogue group of special forces mercenaries against a Los Angeles landscape that increasingly resembles Vietnam as the film progresses. Like Kasdan, Donner recreates Vietnam within Los Angeles. "We're gonna get bloody on this one, Roger. . . . You'll just have to trust me," Riggs declares. Both Murtaugh and Riggs are captured and tortured and have to learn that all they can trust, all they can rely on is each other. In the closing moment of the film, the rain-soaked muddy fields of Vietnam are explicitly evoked as Riggs is involved in hand to hand combat on Murtaugh's front lawn, which is being drenched by a burst hydrant.[23]

In *Lethal Weapon 2,* the national significance of their partnership is established in a battle to save the nation from a drug cartel run by South African diplomats. Riggs and Murtaugh's partnership and friendship also advance in this film. When the diplomats call Riggs a "Kaffir-lover,"* his antiracist credentials are secured. In *Lethal Weapon 3,* Los Angeles and Vietnam are again fused in the landscape as the two heroes wage war against a home-grown enemy who has declared war on the entire L.A.P.D., a police force which at this stage of the series is on the front line of a battle to save the nation.

The Murtaugh-Riggs partnership does not so much exclude women as relegate them to their proper sphere. In the first *Lethal Weapon,* when each man is still rather wary of the other, they share a joke about Trish Murtaugh's (Darlene Love) cooking. In the sequel Riggs and Murtaugh virtually share in the fruits of Trish's domestic labor. "Where does Trish keep my laundry, man?" queries Riggs, and they both agree that if only the bad guys had planted their bomb in Trish's stove rather than in the Murtaughs' bathroom, "they could have ended a lot of needless suffering right there."

The relationship between Riggs and Murtaugh has an explicitly homoerotic dimension which seems both to attract and repel Richard Donner. The film constantly flirts with homoeroticism and parodies it in a homo-

---

Kaffir: A member of a South African tribal group that is part of the Bantu family. The word became a derogatory term used by white South Africans to refer to black servants.

phobic manner. In the first film, "What are you, a fag?" shouts Riggs, in response to Murtaugh's jumping on top of him to try to extinguish the flames that engulf his body. *Lethal Weapon 2* has a series of running jokes that spin out of a scene in which Murtaugh is trapped, sitting on a toilet rigged to explode if he should stand up. In *Lethal Weapon 3* the homoeroticism is somewhat more mature and less directly inspired by anal humor. But at the same time Donner is clearly fascinated by the representation of homosexual attraction. As *Lethal Weapon 2* ends, Riggs is in Murtaugh's arms, possibly fatally injured. Their verbal exchange condenses the conflicted and contradictory aura of homoeroticism. "You're not dead until I tell you," insists Murtaugh, "now breathe!" Riggs's response is, "Did anyone ever tell you, you really are a beautiful man? Give us a kiss before they come." "Where did that bullet hit you anyway?" Murtaugh wants to know. The ambiguity of this exchange is left unresolved and perhaps even heightened by Donner's choice of closing music, George Harrison's "Cheer Down." As the credits roll Harrison sings,

> There's no tears to be shed
> Gonna love you instead
> I want you around
> Cheer down.[24]

In *Grand Canyon*, however, Kasdan deliberately distances his male characters from the homoeroticism that permeates the *Lethal Weapon* series. When the noise of the helicopter which opens the film fades, a basketball net appears, surrounded by black hands reaching upward. In a black-and-white opening sequence on an urban basketball court, the camera wanders over the bodies of the black players, torsos, legs, hands, and feet. There is a clear visual analogy with the second half of the credit sequence, which takes place in the Forum and is filmed in color. However, the force of the analogy is not established in the black-white commonality of the basketball court, a site which is reserved for the safe portrayal of interracial intimacy among men; rather, the analogy works through the gaze of the camera over black male bodies in the first sequence and the sexually predatory gaze of Mack across the court at the women who walk by. In this part of the credit sequence again the camera lingers over parts of bodies, particularly the torsos and bouncing breasts of the women as they walk in rhythm to the music.

Certainly Mack's blatant stare of sexual desire at these passing female bodies is intended to emphasize his heterosexuality and to prevent any misinterpretation of his later feelings for Simon. But these opening sequences and the confrontation scene that follows do establish the cultural spaces the film designates as safe. Safe spaces are cultural sites in which whites can be in close proximity to, intimate with, and gaze at black bodies. The two opening sequences, the neighborhood basketball court and the Forum game, prefigure the nature of the close relationship that develops between

Simon and Mack; a friendship that comes to a cinematic climax when they play basketball with each other in Mack's driveway.

In *Lethal Weapon 3,* one particular scene highlights the relationship between Martin Riggs and Roger Murtaugh. This scene thoroughly dissects the terms and conditions of their friendship, attempting to cast it in the mythical dimensions of the relationship between Huck and Jim on their raft in Mark Twain's 1885 novel, *Adventures of Huckleberry Finn.*[25] Riggs and Murtaugh face a crisis as partners and as friends, a crisis as serious as that faced by Huck and Jim when they missed the entry into the Ohio River and sailed ever deeper into the slave states of the South. In Mark Twain's novel, this mistake clinched the historical terms and conditions of Jim's existence and his dependence on Huck Finn: as a black male, in order to survive he had to "belong" to someone.

In *Lethal Weapon 3,* in a similar fashion, Donner reworks the contemporary terms and conditions of the relationship between his white and black male protagonists. The crisis has been precipitated by two events: Murtaugh is agonizing over the fact that in an armed confrontation he shot and killed a fifteen-year-old young black male whom he discovered to be his son's best friend; Riggs is distraught because their partnership is about to be dissolved when Murtaugh retires from the force in just three days.

This long, eight-minute segment explores the complex and contradictory possibilities for expressing interracial male intimacy, and while the scene is, at times, intensely homoerotic, it also closes off, both visually and verbally, the possibility that this intimacy could encompass a homosexual relation. As Huck and Jim's navigational error determined the public nature of their relation to each other, so Donner opens this scene in a way that determines what follows.

Riggs goes to find Murtaugh, who is hiding out on his boat drinking whiskey. He finds Murtaugh drunk and apparently out of control. Murtaugh holds a gun to Riggs's head and, in clichéd terms, threatens to harm the best friend he ever had. Why would Murtaugh betray his friend, his "brother" who has clearly demonstrated his loyalty to him? The moment is fraught with the tension of Riggs's agony and the betrayal he feels at Murtaugh's imminent retirement. This tension creates and reproduces on the screen a contemporary political anxiety: that black America, having demanded and gained equality, has somehow betrayed the white and middle-class America that graciously acceded to these demands. The political effect is that when Riggs shouts at Murtaugh, "You selfish bastard," a large segment of white male America makes the same accusation.

The accusation of the betrayal of white America by an aggressive black America informs and shapes the work of a number of contemporary liberal political analysts. Andrew Hacker, in *Two Nations: Black and White, Separate, Hostile and Unequal,* addresses this anxiety and argues that the processes of equalization and nationalization imagined to be inherent in the social consensus to grant civil rights were, indeed, only imaginary. He concludes that such a consensus no longer exists and that America must be regarded as two separate nations confronting each other. Hacker situates his discussion of the liberal anxiety evident in this political crisis in the context of the black urban rebellions of the late 1960s.

> After those disturbances, race relations never returned to their former plane. Whites ceased to identify black protests with a civil rights movement led by students and ministers. Rather, they saw a resentful and rebellious multitude, intent on imposing its presence on the rest of society. Blacks were seen as trying to force themselves into places and positions where they were not wanted or for which they lacked the competence. As the 1970s started, so came a rise in crimes, all too many of them with black perpetrators. By that point, many white Americans felt they had been betrayed. Worsening relations between the races were seen as largely due to the behavior of blacks, who had abused the invitations to equal citizenship white America had been tendering.[26]

Hacker's belief that white Americans have lost all sympathy for black Americans shapes his political agenda.

Belief in this apparent lack of sympathy also influences Donner's decision to locate the source for his characters' mutual respect in Southeast Asia rather than in the history of the struggle for civil rights. Hacker attempts to regain this host sympathy through an extraordinary performance of intellectual blackface. In a chapter called "Being Black in America," in which he imagines what it would be like to be black, he reveals an intense masculine anxiety about black male bodies.

Hacker is only one of many political critics who are busily constructing genealogies of race and nation that are centrally concerned with white male anxiety, particularly liberal anxiety, about relationships with black men. His argument that white men feel betrayed by actually or potentially rebellious black men is echoed in Thomas Edsall's very influential book, *Chain Reaction: The Impact of Race, Rights, and Taxes on American Politics,* in which such betrayal is used to explain the alienation of white Democratic [male] voters from the special-interest politics of racial injustice.[27] In the popular cultural imagination such anxiety is most frequently paired with the nightmarish landscape of urban crisis.

What *Grand Canyon,* the *Lethal Weapon* series, and a number of other contemporary Hollywood films have in common is their unspoken attempt to resolve and overcome a national, racialized crisis through an intimate interracial male partnership. What Danny Glover's cinematic career illustrates is a sequence of performances of black manhood which embodies all the ethical codes of white middle-class America. What Kasdan incorporates into *Grand Canyon* and Donner utilizes in the *Lethal Weapon* series is the national embodiment of the perfect black male: a sensitive black father and relentless seeker of justice. The Danny Glover persona has become the lethal weapon that is wielded by Hollywood directors to fight representations of black men that they define and create as dangerous. The cultural construction of the bad guy is a direct political response to the national bourgeois dilemma: how to distinguish the good from the bad black men.[28]

In *Grand Canyon* Kasdan grants Simon the moral authority to deny common humanity to the rebellious "gang" of five young men. This moral authority is acquired gradually and in a number of ways. First, Simon manages to extricate Mack and himself from the clutches of the young men without resorting to violence. He establishes who made the call for help and then continues to talk to Mack about the problem with the car as if the others weren't there. This behavior is quickly identified by the young men as a sign of disrespect. Next, Simon tries to persuade them that he is just doing his job. As the young men are unresponsive to the terms of the work ethic, Simon tries another tactic. He identifies the young man he supposes is the leader and takes him aside. He explains that he is responsible for the truck, Mack's car, and Mack himself and asks, as a favor' to be allowed to go on his way. This exchange is a very important moment because it establishes the ground upon which Simon's role as a mouthpiece for the philosophy of the film will be built. The young man asks: "Are you askin' me a favor as a sign of respect, or are you askin' me a favor 'cos I got the gun?" Simon pauses and then replies: "Man, the world ain't supposed to work like this, maybe you don't know that but this ain't the way it's supposed to be. I'm supposed to be able to do my job without asking you if I can. That dude is supposed to be able to wait with his car without you ripping him off. Everything is supposed to be different than what it is." The young man is clearly puzzled by this response and says, "So, what's your answer?" To which Simon replies, "You don't have the gun, we ain't having this conversation," which gets the response, "That's what I thought, no gun, no respect, that's why I always carry the gun."

Having made the point that Simon can voice the moral codes and ethics of the middle class and be streetwise at the same time, the Simon character is also used to dehumanize the young men. In a conversation with Mack that takes place back at the service station while waiting for the car to be fixed, Simon adopts a folksy persona, a persona from which many Americans seem to draw comfort, and compares the young men to predatory sharks. Simon explains to Mack that what happened to him was a matter of chance, that "one day, just one particular day you bump into the big shark." "Now the big shark don't hate you, he has no feelings for you at all, you look like food to him. . . . Those boys back there, they got nothing to lose. If you just happen to be swimming along and bump into them, well . . . It might not be worth worrying about; it's like being in a plane crash." Once he has dismissed these "boys" from the realm of humanity, they can be conveniently forgotten. They do not appear again in the film and presumably disappear into jail, say, or become urban homicide statistics. For do we really care or even think about what happens to sharks as long as they aren't preying upon us?

What inspires fear has been identified, given a body, but no name. The young black men presented as "gang" have served their purpose. This use of Glover to annihilate an aggressive black male force is even more explicit in *Predator 2,* in which the streets of Los Angeles have become "a slaughterhouse." Pitted against Jamaican drug lords, King Willie and his Voodoo posse, Glover also expels an extraterrestrial predator with long locks.

But in addition to playing a crucial role in the expulsion of an alien black presence in films like *Grand Canyon,* the *Lethal Weapon* series, *Dead Man Out* (1989), and more recent films like *The Saint of Fort Washington* (1993), Glover has performed another important role: that of father confessor and psychological counsellor to white men. In these films he acts as a sympathetic ear and a wise man, fostering the psychological healing of white men damaged by the stresses of postmodern life. Glover has become identified as the one who manages to persuade white men to recognize, understand, and express the truth about themselves to themselves. In his person Hollywood, in addition to producing the black male as an outcast who threatens to undermine the very foundations of America, adopts the black man as a sympathetic cypher, a means for white men to find meaning within themselves and discover the true meaning of their existence. On the one hand, these meanings are established for the audience of these films, but, on the other, they reflect the values of the producers and directors. In their minds and films reside myriad references, meanings, and relationships that can be endlessly drawn upon and recycled. Glover has come to occupy a particularly important position as a teller of stories that modern America needs to hear, an urban folk figure still in touch with the most important social values and ethics which a postmodern society is in danger of forgetting.

These intimate black and white male partnerships, which exclude women, project the black masculinity imagined by white male liberals in quest of perfect partners. Together and alone, these race men of Hollywood dreams promise to annihilate what ails this nation and resolve our contemporary crisis of race, of nation, and of manhood. If we are to expose the exploitative and oppressive nature of such dream-work, we must reclaim the political commitment of Paul Robeson* who challenged cultural workers, artists, and intellectuals to take a stand. Are we going to elect for freedom or slavery? Are we going to preserve this "threadbare" masculinity? Or are we going to burn it?

Notes

1. *Grand Canyon,* Panavision TCF, 1991, dir. Lawrence Kasdan.

2. *Bat 21,* Tri-Star, 1988, dir. Peter Markle.

3. It is clear that this association between the war zones of Southeast Asia and Los Angeles has been established incrementally. Of particular importance to this process are the three

Paul Robeson: American actor and singer (1898–1976) with a distinctively low, bass voice. The son of an escaped slave, he graduated from Columbia University law school. He was an advocate of many social causes and became notorious during the 1950s because of his left-wing sympathies. Robeson was a victim of Senator McCarthy's investigations into "un-American" activities.

Lethal Weapon films, which will be discussed later. *Lethal Weapon 3* is a culmination of the themes of the previous two: policing is indistinguishable from military intervention, and the burning of a housing complex is visually evocative of the burning of villages in Vietnam. Our reading of this scene of fire is, of course, directly influenced by *Apocalypse Now,* which reinforces my sense that Hollywood has and continues to mediate and inform this process of transition in the political imagination of the culture industry.

4. Promotional description, *Grand Canyon,* FoxVideo, 1992.

5. Emphasis as spoken.

6. This superficial way of locating Mack is of course a postmodern substitute for history. See Fredric Jameson, *Postmodernism, the Cultural Logic of Late Capitalism* (Durham: Duke University Press, 1991), pp. 6, 67–68.

7. This is a moment in which a scene of home is intercut into the nightmare journey.

8. NWA, *Straight Outta Compton,* Priority Records, 1988, CD 57102. I use the male pronoun here because the lyrics reference a very masculine performativity and sense of prowess.

9. I adopted the term "good guy" because of the following incident. When I was talking to a research assistant at the Video Library in Philadelphia who was helping me locate a copy of one of Danny Glover's early films, *Out,* he reacted with sharp surprise to my description of Glover's role in that film as an urban revolutionary. "But," he said in a shocked tone, "Danny Glover is a good guy!"

10. Perhaps it is crass to point to the biblical resonance of the choice of Simon as a name for Mack's rescuer, but it gains significance through the consistent religious references in the film, particularly its concern with spiritual and miraculous transformation. Kasdan's "gang" take pleasure not only in threatening physical harm but in taunting and mocking Mack. "And they spat upon him, and took the reed, and smote him on the head. And after that they mocked him, they took the robe off from him, and put his own raiment on him, and led him away to crucify him. And as they came out they found a man of Cyrene, Simon by name: him they compelled to bear his cross." Matthew 27, 30–32. Even if the biblical allusion works only at a subliminal level, it is important to recognize that Mack (and the white middle class) are being rescued from a possible crucifixion, a metaphor which has political and ideological meanings. In such a scenario, Mack (and the white middle class) are innocent victims of unjust persecution.

11. *Body and Soul,* Enterprise, 1947, dir. Robert Rossen.

12. *Escape from Alcatraz,* Paramount, 1979, dir. Don Siegel.

13. *Chu Chu and the Philly Flash,* Twentieth Century-Fox, 1981, dir. David Lowell Rich.

14. *Out!* (also known as *Deadly Drifter*), an independent production, 1982, dir. Eli Hollander.

15. *Iceman,* Universal, 1984, dir. Fred Schepisi.

16. *Places in the Heart,* Tri-Star, 1984, dir. Robert Benton.

17. *Witness,* Paramount, 1985, dir. Peter Weir.

18. *Silverado,* Columbia, 1985, dir. Lawrence Kasdan.

19. *The Color Purple,* Warner, 1985, dir. Steven Spielberg.

20. Danny Glover's roles as Nelson Mandela in *Mandela,* 1987, and as Micah Mangena in *Bopha!,* 1993, are not discussed, since these films address a very different set of political concerns from those I set out to cover in this book. Glover was also very active in anti-apartheid organizations.

21. *Flight of the Intruder,* Paramount, 1991, dir. John Milius.

22. *Lethal Weapon,* Warner, 1987, dir. Richard Donner; *Lethal Weapon 2,* Warner, 1989, dir. Richard Donner; *Lethal Weapon 3,* Warner, 1992, dir. Richard Donner.

23. See also n. 3.

24. George Harrison, "Cheer Down," Dark Horse Records, lyrics by George Harrison and Tom Petty.

25. I am grateful to Michael Denning for pointing out this literary parallel.

26. Andrew Hacker, *Two Nations: Black, White, Separate, Hostile and Unequal* (New York: Macmillan, 1992), p. 19.

27. Thomas Byrne Edsall, with Mary D. Edsall, *Chain Reaction: The Impact of Race, Rights, and Taxes on American Politics* (New York: Norton, 1992).

28. I have excluded *To Sleep with Anger,* Metro, 1990, dir. Charles Burnett, as being outside of the Hollywood circuit of representations of black men. This fine film, in which Danny Glover not only stars as Harry Mention but also acts as executive producer, explores complexities of black subjectivity far beyond Hollywood's limited imagination. His participation in production and his efforts to help finance Spike Lee's *Get on the Bus,* Forty Acres and a Mule, 1996, are evidence of Glover's attempts to move beyond the genealogy that Hollywood has created for him.

Ideas for Rereading

1. Early in her essay, Carby writes of the way the film *Grand Canyon* uses Vietnam War imagery, such as the noise of helicopter blades, to depict urban racial conflict. She writes, "The strategy employed by Kasdan [the film's director] . . . to equate these particular killing fields with the streets of Los Angeles is complex and contradictory and will haunt this chapter" (p. 182). As you reread Carby, consider how this "haunting" occurs. List Carby's suggestions about the artistic and social meaning behind the use of this imagery. What is your reaction to these suggestions?

2. Carby writes of actor Danny Glover's "cinematic genealogy as a good trustworthy black man (p. 189). As you reread the essay, trace that genealogy as Carby portrays it. If you have seen any of Glover's films, think about your own reaction to the characters the actor plays, as well as to Carby's impression of those characters. Do you agree with Carby's assessment? Why or why not?

3. Reread Du Bois's explanation of "double-consciousness" in "Of Our Spiritual Strivings." Then reread Carby, taking into account that her essay was originally collected in a volume subtitled *The W. E. B. Du Bois Lectures.* How might Carby be using Glover's image as either an illustration or a critique of the concept of "double-consciousness"? Explain the evidence for such an interpretation.

4. Carby uses three closely related but distinct terms in her analysis of the friendship between black and white male characters in Hollywood films: *homosocial, homoerotic,* and *homosexual.* As you reread her essay, note Carby's use of these terms. Judging from the etymology of these words (as given in a dictionary) and their context in Carby's essay, determine as precisely as you can the distinct connotations of each term. How do these terms function in Carby's argument?

Ideas for Writing

1. Consider Carby's assertion about Glover's "cinematic genealogy as a good trustworthy black man." Then see one of the films she critiques—*Grand Canyon, Lethal Weapon,* or another. What is your own experience of the film, particularly the character played by Glover? Now view at least one—

preferably several—of Glover's major film performances that Carby does not specifically discuss. Do these performances support the idea of Glover's "cinematic genealogy" (p. 189) that Carby puts forth in her discussion of *Grand Canyon, Lethal Weapon,* and so on? Write an essay that both analyzes Glover's performance and his characterization in the film and responds to Carby's assertions about Glover's role.

2. Carby suggests that for white filmmakers—and perhaps white America as a whole—Danny Glover represents "the national embodiment of the perfect black male: a sensitive black father and relentless seeker of justice" (p. 195). Review the selections by Morgan and Walker in this chapter, paying special attention to their discussion of white images and stereotypes of black women. Do these authors posit a nonblack person's "national embodiment" or stereotype of the perfect black woman? Keeping in mind Morgan's and Walker's ideas, as well as artistic (literary, film, and so on) depictions of black women, write an essay exploring what such a "national embodiment" or stereotype might entail.

3. Carby attempts to expose the fears and stereotypes at work in Hollywood films of the 1970s and 1980s. How do these fears and stereotypes compare with those that Du Bois identified in post-Emancipation America? What shifts, if any, have taken place in the intervening half-century? What shifts have taken place since the 1980s, if any? Write an essay exploring these questions. To help illustrate your argument, you may wish to view relevant films (such as the *Lethal Weapon* series, or perhaps work in the 1990s by directors such as Quentin Tarantino—*Pulp Fiction* and *Jackie Brown*—and by actors such as Eddie Murphy—*Trading Places*). You might also want to consider representations by Spike Lee—*School Daze* and *Jungle Fever.*

JOAN MORGAN

Joan Morgan (b. 1964) has written for Essence, The Village Voice, *and* Vibe. *Her book* When Chickenheads Come Home to Roost: My Life As a Hip-Hop Feminist *(1999) is a collection of provocative and often irreverent essays that aim to redefine feminism for a new generation of women, in particular African American women. A 1999 article in* Essence *magazine quotes her as saying: "Whenever feminist discourse came up, the eyes of many young women—and even my peers—glazed over.... It's important for us to stop complaining and get involved. I want the book to be a catalyst for conversation. If it's that, then I feel like I've done my job." Morgan disowns what she describes as "the myth of the Strong Black woman," urging her contemporaries instead to claim their right to "imperfections and vulnerability." The term* chickenheads *refers to women who "effectively work their erotic power," but her title also plays on Malcolm X's famous use of the expression "the chickens come home to roost" in the speech that announced his break with the Nation of Islam.*

In this essay Morgan makes the case for "black-on-black love" in the context of examples that reveal the erosion of such love. She does so by suggesting that the sexism expressed in hip-hop is "really the complex mask African-Americans often wear both to hide and to express the pain" (p. 200). As you read the essay under-

line the parts where Morgan identifies the power of black women and the illness of black men. What proposals does she make for ways to survive and heal the destructive illness of internalized racism and sexism? How does her story about the "sixty-year-old self-declared non-feminist" contribute to her argument? Why does Morgan advocate listening to hip-hop?

From Fly-Girls to Bitches and Hos

I guess it all depends on how you define the f-word. My feminism places the welfare of black women and the black community on its list of priorities. It also maintains that black-on-black love is essential to the survival of both.

We have come to a point in our history, however, when black-on-black love—a love that's survived slavery, lynching, segregation, poverty, and racism—is in serious danger. The stats usher in this reality like taps before the death march: According to the U.S. Census Bureau, the number of black two-parent households has decreased from 74 percent to 48 percent since 1960. The leading cause of death among black men ages fifteen to twenty-four is homicide. The majority of them will die at the hands of other black men.[1]

Women are the unsung victims of black-on-black crime. A while back, a friend of mine, a single mother of a newborn (her "babyfather"—a brother—abdicated responsibility before their child was born) was attacked by a pit bull while walking her dog in the park. The owner (a brother) trained the animal to prey on other dogs and the flesh of his fellow community members.

A few weeks later my moms called, upset, to tell me about the murder of a family friend. She was a troubled young woman with a history of substance abuse, aggravated by her son's murder two years ago. She was found beaten and burned beyond recognition. Her murderers were not "skinheads," "The Man," or "the racist white power structure." More likely than not, they were brown men whose faces resembled her own.

Clearly, we are having a very difficult time loving one another.

Any feminism that fails to acknowledge that black folks in nineties America are living and trying to love in a war zone is useless to our struggle against sexism. Though it's often portrayed as part of the problem, rap music is essential to that struggle because it takes us straight to the battlefield.

My decision to expose myself to the sexism of Dr. Dre, Ice Cube, Snoop Dogg, or the Notorious B.I.G. is really my plea to my brothers to tell me who they are. I need to know why they are so angry at me. Why is disrespecting me one of the few things that make them feel like men? What's the haps, what are you going through on the daily that's got you acting so foul?

As a black woman and a feminist I listen to the music with a willingness to see past the machismo in order to be clear about what I'm *really* dealing with. What I hear frightens me. On booming track after booming track, I hear brothers talking about spending each day high as hell on malt liquor and Chronic. Don't sleep. What passes for "40 and a blunt" good times in most of hip-hop is really alcoholism, substance abuse, and chemical dependency. When brothers can talk so cavalierly about killing each other and then reveal that they have no expectation to see their twenty-first birthday, that is straight-up depression *masquerading* as machismo.

Anyone curious about the processes and pathologies that form the psyche of the young, black, and criminal-minded needs to revisit our dearly departed Notorious B.I.G.'s first album, *Ready to Die*. Chronicling the life and times of the urban "soldier," the album is a blues-laden soul train that took us on a hustler's life journey. We boarded with the story of his birth, strategically stopped to view his dysfunctional, warring family, his first robbery, his first stint in jail, murder, drug-dealing, getting paid, partying, sexin', rappin', mayhem, and death. Biggie's player persona might have momentarily convinced the listener that he was livin' phat without a care in the world but other moments divulged his inner hell. The chorus of "Everyday Struggle": *I don't wanna live no more/Sometimes I see death knockin' at my front door* revealed that "Big Poppa" was also plagued with guilt, regret, and depression. The album ultimately ended with his suicide.

The seemingly impenetrable wall of sexism in rap music is really the complex mask African-Americans often wear both to hide and express the pain. At the close of this millennium, hip-hop is still one of the few forums in which young black men, even surreptitiously, are allowed to express their pain.

When it comes to the struggle against sexism and our intimate relationships with black men, some of the most on-point feminist advice I've received comes from sistas like my mother, who wouldn't dream of using the term. During our battle to resolve our complicated relationships with my equally wonderful and errant father, my mother presented me with the following gems of wisdom, "One of the most important lessons you will ever learn in life and love, is that you've got to love people for what they are—not for who you would like them to be."

This is crystal clear to me when I'm listening to hip-hop. Yeah, sistas are hurt when we hear brothers calling us bitches and hos. But the real crime isn't the name-calling, it's their failure to love us—to be our brothers in the way that we commit ourselves to being their sistas. But recognize: Any man who doesn't truly love himself is incapable of loving us in the healthy way we need to be loved. It's extremely telling that men who can only see us as "bitches" and "hos" refer to themselves only as "niggas."

In the interest of our emotional health and overall sanity, black women have got to learn to love brothers realistically, and that means differentiating between who they are and who we'd like them to be. Black men are engaged in a war where the real enemies—racism and the white power structure—are masters of camouflage. They've conditioned our men to believe the enemy is brown. The effects of this have been as wicked as they've been debilitating. Being in battle with an enemy that looks just like you makes it hard to believe in the basics every human being needs. For too many black men there is no trust, no community, no family. Just self.

Since hip-hop is the mirror in which so many brothers see themselves, it's significant that one of the music's most prevalent mythologies is that black boys rarely grow into men. Instead, they remain perpetually post-adolescent or die. For all the machismo and testosterone in the music, it's frighteningly clear that many brothers see themselves as powerless when it comes to facing the evils of the larger society, accepting responsibility for their lives, or the lives of their children.

So, sista friends, we gotta do what any rational, survivalist-minded person would do after finding herself in a relationship with someone whose pain makes him abusive. We've gotta continue to give up the love but *from a distance that's safe*. Emotional distance is a great enabler of un-conditional love and support because it allows us to recognize that the at-tack, the "bitch, ho" bullshit—isn't personal but part of the illness.

And the focus of black feminists has got to change. We can't afford to keep expending energy on banal discussions of sexism in rap when sexism is only part of a huge set of problems. Continuing on our previous path is akin to demanding that a fiending, broke crackhead not rob you blind be-cause it's *wrong* to do so.

If feminism intends to have any relevance in the lives of the majority of black women, if it intends to move past theory and become functional it has to rescue itself from the ivory towers of academia. Like it or not, hip-hop is not only the dominion of the young, black, and male, it is also the world in which young black women live and survive. A functional game plan for us, one that is going to be as helpful to Shequanna on 142nd as it is to Samantha at Sarah Lawrence, has to recognize hip-hop's ability to ar-ticulate the pain our *community* is in and use that knowledge to create a redemptive, healing space.

Notice the emphasis on "community." Hip-hop isn't only instrumental in exposing black men's pain, it brings the healing sistas need right to the surface. Sad as it may be, it's time to stop ignoring the fact that rappers meet "bitches" and "hos" daily—women who reaffirm their depiction of us on vinyl. Backstage, the road, and the 'hood are populated with women who would do anything to be with a rapper sexually for an hour if not a night. It's time to stop fronting like we don't know who rapper Jeru the Damaja was talking about when he said:

> Now a queen's a queen but a stunt's a stunt
> You can tell who's who by the things they want

Sex has long been the bartering chip that women use to gain protec-tion, material wealth, and the vicarious benefits of power. In the black community, where women are given less access to all of the above, "trickin'" becomes a means of leveling the playing field. Denying the justi-fiable anger of rappers—men who couldn't get the time of day from these women before a few dollars and a record deal—isn't empowering or strategic. Turning a blind eye and scampering for moral high ground diverts our attention away from the young women who are being denied access to power and are suffering for it.

It might've been more convenient to direct our sistafied rage attention to "the sexist representation of women" in those now infamous Sir Mix-A-Lot videos, to fuss over *one* sexist rapper, but wouldn't it have been more productive to address the failing self-esteem of the 150 or so half-naked young women who were willing, unpaid participants? And what about how flip we are when it comes to using the b-word to describe each other? At one point we've all been the recipients of competitive, unsisterly, "bitchiness," particularly when vying for male attention.

Since being black and a woman makes me fluent in both isms, I sometimes use racism as an illuminating analogy. Black folks have finally gotten to the point where we recognize that we sometimes engage in oppressive behaviors that white folks have little to do with. Complexion prejudices and classism are illnesses which have their *roots* in white racism but the perpetrators are certainly black.

Similarly, sistas have to confront the ways we're complicit in our own oppression. Sad to say it, but many of the ways in which men exploit our images and sexuality in hip-hop is done with our permission and cooperation. We need to be as accountable to each other as we believe "race traitors" (i.e., 100 or so brothers in blackface cooning in a skinhead's music video) should be to our community. To acknowledge this doesn't deny our victimization but it does raise the critical issue of whose responsibility it is to end our oppression. As a feminist, I believe it is too great a responsibility to leave to men.

A few years ago, on an airplane making its way to Montego Bay, I received another gem of girlfriend wisdom from a sixty-year-old self-declared non-feminist. She was meeting her husband to celebrate her thirty-fifth wedding anniversary. After telling her I was twenty-seven and very much single, she looked at me and shook her head sadly. "I feel sorry for your generation. You don't know how to have relationships, especially the women." Curious, I asked her why she thought this was. "The women of your generation, you want to be right. The women of my generation, we didn't care about being right. We just wanted to win."

Too much of the discussion regarding sexism and the music focuses on being right. We feel we're *right* and the rappers are wrong. The rappers feel it's their *right* to describe their "reality" in any way they see fit. The store owners feel it's their *right* to sell whatever the consumer wants to buy. The consumer feels it's his *right* to be able to decide what he wants to listen to. We may be the "rightest" of the bunch but we sure as hell ain't doing the winning.

I believe hip-hop can help us win. Let's start by recognizing that its illuminating, informative narration and its incredible ability to articulate our collective pain is an invaluable tool when examining gender relations. The information we amass can help create a redemptive, healing space for brothers and sistas.

We're all winners when a space exists for brothers to honestly state and explore the roots of their pain and subsequently their misogyny, sans judgment. It is criminal that the only space our society provided for the late Tupac Shakur to examine the pain, confusion, drug addiction, and fear that led to his arrest and his eventual assassination was in a prison cell. How can we win if a prison cell is the only space an immensely talented but troubled young black man could dare utter these words: "Even though I'm not guilty of the charges they gave me, I'm not innocent in terms of the way I was acting. I'm just as guilty for not doing things. Not with this case but with my life. I had a job to do and I never showed up. I was so scared of this responsibility that I was running away from it."[2] We have to do better than this for our men.

And we have to do better for ourselves. We desperately need a space to lovingly address the uncomfortable issues of our failing self-esteem, the ways we sexualize and objectify ourselves, our confusion about sex and love and the unhealthy, unloving, unsisterly ways we treat each other. Commitment to developing these spaces gives our community the potential for remedies based on honest, clear diagnoses.

As I'm a black woman, I am aware that this doubles my workload — that I am definitely going to have to listen to a lot of shit I won't like — but without these candid discussions, there is little to no hope of exorcising the illness that hurts and sometimes kills us.

Notes

1. Joan Morgan, "Real Love," *Vibe*, April 1996, p. 38.
2. Kevin Powell, "The Vibe Q: Tupac Shakur, Ready to Live," *Vibe*, April 11, 1995, p. 52.

Ideas for Rereading

1. Morgan claims that feminism must bridge the gap between the academy and "the majority of black women" and strive to become "functional" (p. 203). How does her own rhetoric as a "hip-hop feminist" enact such a bridge? As you reread, pay careful attention to the way she constructs her argument. Consider how she uses the language and speech patterns of the street in her writing in ways that are immediately striking. But also notice how she uses reasoning and evidence, including statistics and lyrics, to substantiate her claims. How do her style and her methods support her purpose in this essay?

2. As you reread Morgan's essay, make notes on her unique rhetorical strategy, specifically her use of "dialect" words such as *sista* and *moms*. What is her purpose in employing such words? At what points do you feel that this strategy succeeds best? At what points (if any) do you feel that it seems less effective? Explain in your notes.

Ideas for Writing

1. Morgan makes no explicit reference to W. E. B. Du Bois in her essay, and yet a reader might hear echoes in it of Du Bois's discussion of "double-consciousness." Du Bois writes: "Here in America, in the few days since Emancipation, the black man's turning hither and thither in hesitant and doubtful striving has often made his very strength to lose effectiveness, to seem like absence of power, like weakness. And yet it is not weakness,—it is the contradiction of double aims" (p. 132). Morgan exposes the weakness that underlies expressions of machismo in rap, but she recognizes that rap is often a necessary means of expressing pain and anger, even while it may help to perpetuate racist and sexist attitudes: "A functional game plan for us, one that is going to be as helpful to Shequanna on 142nd as it is to Samantha at Sarah Lawrence, has to recognize hip-hop's ability to articulate the pain our *community* is in and use that knowledge to create a redemptive, healing space" (p. 203). How might the language of rap, as observed by Morgan and as you have observed it in the rap lyrics you know, be considered to express a contemporary version of double-consciousness? How is this continuous with, and how is it different from, the double-consciousness that Du Bois describes? Beginning with a careful discussion of "double-consciousness" as explained in Du Bois's "Of Our Spiritual Strivings," write an essay that explores "double-consciousness" as a feature of both the racism and the sexism that Morgan identifies in rap music.

2. Morgan writes: "hip-hop is the mirror in which so many brothers see themselves" (p. 203). Reread W. E. B. Du Bois's "The Sorrow Songs," bearing in mind Morgan's discussion of hip-hop and "community." In what ways did the Sorrow Songs serve community? In what respects does their function resemble, or differ from, the function of hip-hop as presented by Morgan? Write an essay that examines the social function of the Sorrow Songs and hip-hop, taking into account the historical circumstances that produced them. Bring Morgan's perspective to bear on the Sorrow Songs, and bring Du Bois's perspective to bear on hip-hop.

3. Morgan argues for a "healing," "distanced," "sympathetic" way of reading hip-hop that understands the artists' pain and even anger. Select a hip-hop or rap album or song (one of those discussed by Morgan or another—but one that offers strong material for this essay) and develop an interpretation that meets Morgan's demands. Write an essay that presents a close reading, a detailed word-by-word and line-by-line analysis, of the work. Your essay should be an experiment in interpretation from the perspective offered by Morgan, but it should also work faithfully and thoughtfully with the particular words and music you have chosen.

Extending Your Work

Ideas for Research

1. Using both the Internet and traditional sources, conduct research into the origins and history of the Negro spiritual. Consider the place of the spiritual in African American culture and history. What were the purposes of this musical form? How has its influence been felt in later American music, including the blues, jazz, rock and roll, hip-hop, and rap? Write an essay reexamining Du Bois's essay "The Sorrow Songs" in light of the information you have gathered.

2. In "In Search of Our Mothers' Gardens," Alice Walker alludes to the customary distinction between "high art" and "low art." How do dominant cultural institutions help to preserve this distinction and what are its consequences for the prevailing attitudes toward "folk art"? What is the significance of this distinction for Du Bois's argument about the Sorrow Songs? Using the Internet and traditional sources, seek out some reviews of "low" or "folk" art exhibitions — quilt shows, flower shows, and so on. Then compare those reviews to reviews of "high" or "fine" art, such as painting. If possible, try to attend some exhibitions yourself. Are there differences in the language used to describe each exhibition? What are the attitudes of the critics toward each exhibition? To what extent can you apply Du Bois's and Walker's arguments to your analysis?

3. What does Hazel Carby's analysis of Danny Glover's films suggest about her beliefs about white filmmakers' depictions of black men? What does the analysis say about her beliefs about issues of gender and race in general? View a series of films starring an individual black actor or actress. Write an essay exploring how Carby might react to these films and the actors' performances in them.

Ideas for Working across Chapters

1. In "Of Our Spiritual Strivings," Du Bois says about the African American of his day: "This, then, is the end of his striving: to be a co-worker in the kingdom of culture . . . to husband and use his best powers and his latent genius. These powers of body and mind have in the past been strangely wasted, dispersed, or forgotten" (p. 132). For Du Bois, what role does education play in making black people co-workers in the "kingdom of culture"? With Du Bois's statement in mind, read the essay by Virginia Woolf in Chapter 1. Write an essay considering both Du Bois's insistence on education for black people and Woolf's plea for equal education for women. What reasons do the two writers give for this need for education? In what ways do the arguments seem similar? Different? How do you account for those similarities and differences? How do the authors characterize the situation, needs, and character of the people for whom they speak? What do they see as the role of education in the move toward self-consciousness? What in their tone and language is suggested about their attitude toward those people — African Americans and women?

2. In "In Search of Our Mothers' Gardens," Alice Walker quotes extensively from Virginia Woolf's *A Room of One's Own*, adapting Woolf's ideas to a

particular rhetorical purpose. Read the Woolf selections in this book (Chapter 1), carefully taking note of the ways in which Woolf's perspective, opinions, and purposes meet and diverge with Walker's. Consider the cultural, ethnic, and historical differences between the authors: What attracts Walker to Woolf's ideas? How might Woolf respond to Walker's rhetorical use of *A Room of One's Own*? Write an essay imagining the potential dialogue between these two women.

3. Consider Glenn Loury's essay and its concern with the idea of "passing." Then read Simi Linton's discussion of disabled people's passing for nondisabled (in Chapter 3). What are the connections between the two writers' depictions of passing? Using works by Linton and Lane (Chapter 3) as well as Loury's essay and outside sources, write an essay envisioning the similarities and differences between the African American and the disabled experience of "passing."

Disabled Persons
How Do Individuals Form a Culture?

Throughout history, people with disabilities have been both stigmatized and romanticized—often simultaneously. In her biography of Helen Keller, Dorothy Herrmann notes the ancient tendency to regard blindness as a punishment for sin, either our own or those of our ancestors. A look at literature from Sophocles' *Oedipus Rex* and biblical depictions of St. Paul to modern horror films like *The Mummy* would lend credence to Herrmann's suggestion. At the same time, writers, especially since the nineteenth century, have tended to make saints and heroes out of disabled people—Dickens's "lame" Tiny Tim and even Tommy, the deaf and blind "pinball wizard" of the Who's 1970s rock opera, or Tom Hanks's Oscar-winning portrayal of Forrest Gump, a character referred to as "slow." As psychologist Harlan Lane suggests, what both these approaches lack—both stigmatizing and romanticizing—is the possibility for disabled people to define their own place in the world.

The past hundred years have witnessed, among many disabled people, not only the development of a sense of self-definition but a creation and insistence on the existence of a community of disabled people. This is most notable in the deaf community, a self-defined culture—with its own language (American Sign Language), customs, and methods of cultural transmission—many of whose members do not perceive themselves as disabled at all. Authors and disability rights activists, such as Simi Linton, have also sought to create and promote a discourse that places disabled people at the center of any talk of their needs and concerns, rather than allowing themselves to be defined by the medical profession—which they believe often portrays them not as human beings but as victims of "afflictions." Personal essays such as those by Georgina Kleege and Slackjaw portray individual disabled people in all their flawed humanity with little use for the imagery of victim or sainthood.

The life and work of Helen Keller can be seen as the beginning of the push toward self-awareness and community building among disabled people, at least in the twentieth century. Keller's public persona and myth often encouraged the nondisabled image of disabled people as heroic victims, not to mention the nondisabled world's simultaneous fear of and fascination with disabled people. At the same time, however, Keller's autobiographical writings—especially *The World I Live In,* excerpted in this chapter—represent attempts at self-definition and the declaration of this one deaf and blind woman's humanity and individuality to a larger world. Keep both aspects of Keller's legacy in mind as you read her work and the work of the contemporary writers in this chapter, including Linton, Lane, Kleege, Slackjaw, and the neuroscientist Oliver Sacks.

TEXT

HELEN KELLER

"My whole desire," wrote Helen Keller, "has been to have my own door key, and go and come like people who can see."[1]

Helen Adams Keller was born on June 27, 1880, in Tuscumbia, Alabama. Deaf and blind from the age of nineteen months, she was, in her own words, "rescued" from a life of isolation and silence by her teacher Anne Mansfield Sullivan. The famous moment at the Keller family water pump when six-year-old Helen recognized the substance she was touching—both spelling the word into her teacher's hand and haltingly uttering "waa-waa"—has been told and retold in print (most notably in Keller's 1902 autobiography, The Story of My Life*), on the Broadway stage, and in at least two screen versions of William Gibson's play* The Miracle Worker. *If that moment can be seen as one of rescue, it was also the moment that began the public life and thus the public myth of Helen Keller.*

Under the guidance of her teacher, Keller would not only learn to communicate through the deaf-blind hand alphabet, but to read and write in Braille and even—though never as well as she hoped—to speak. At the age of twenty, she entered Radcliffe College, and with Sullivan translating almost every lecture into her hand, Keller would eventually graduate with honors in English. Throughout her life she would work tirelessly on behalf of blind people, helping to found the Massachusetts Commission for the Blind and raising more money for the American Foundation for the Blind than any other person. She was a sought-after lecturer, and for a time even had a popular vaudeville act in which she told jokes while demonstrating her senses of smell and touch to appreciative crowds.

Her most lasting impact, however, may have been as a writer—particularly as a chronicler of her unique life experience. Her autobiography made her a celebrity with the American public as well as a best-selling author. In her subsequent book The World I Live In *(1909), Keller gives an account of what it is actually like to live without sight or hearing. The optimistic, uncomplaining tone of these and other of her autobiographical works—as well as the heroic and beatific manner in which she was portrayed both by the media and by those closest to her—created an image of Helen Keller that was almost that of a secular saint. Still, it is important to note that Keller was almost never photographed without being posed and that the beautiful eyes that many people believed contained such serenity and wisdom were, by Keller's middle age, made of glass.*

While Keller was admired and appreciated by many nondisabled people as a symbol of triumph over potentially catastrophic disability, some in the disabled community have seen her as an object of scorn, a cypher made palatable to the hearing and sighted world by her physical attractiveness and genteel social back-ground. In fact, as Keller biographer Dorothy Herrmann makes clear, Annie Sulli-van — a poor, unattractive Irish orphan, herself partially blind as a result of childhood illness — was never entirely accepted by the social circles that so em-braced her famous student. Even today many blind people evince an impatience with being compared with the ghost of Helen Keller. Moreover, although Annie Sullivan's teaching methods are still seen as innovative, even revolutionary, teachers of deaf-blind people today make every effort to avoid the exclusive, almost symbi-otic teacher-student relationship Sullivan had with Keller. In this way, it is argued, deaf-blind people today gain an independence and self-sufficiency that Keller never had but always desired.

Whatever criticism or praise surrounds the myth of Helen Keller, the woman herself was far more complicated than her image. Although her writing was often supervised by strict and exacting editors, including Annie Sullivan's husband, John Macy, Keller's books are widely acknowledged to be her own work, to derive from her own thoughts and ideas. She wrote on many subjects other than her disability and was always disappointed that the public wanted only to read her autobio-graphical work. She also had a fully developed desire for romance and sex in her life and is known to have had at least one full-fledged affair, leading to a failed elopement attempt. She said once that, if granted her sight, the first thing she would do would be "to marry." Keller's political views were well reasoned — and markedly leftist — and she held deep religious convictions stemming from her study of the Christian mystic Emanuel Swedenborg (1688–1772). At her death on July 1, 1968, she was remembered in a Swedenborgian ceremony.

The following selections from The World I Live In *are a mixture of autobiog-raphy and philosophical essay. As you read, consider the ways in which Keller's de-piction of her own situation — as well as her explanation of her philosophical beliefs — helped to shape her public image. Where does her writing contribute to the making of her myth? Where is she asserting an identity outside that myth, both for herself and for others like her?*

Note

1. Dorothy Herrmann, *Helen Keller: A Life* (New York: Knopf, 1988).

From *The World I Live In*

The Seeing Hand

I have just touched my dog. He was rolling on the grass, with pleasure in every muscle and limb. I wanted to catch a picture of him in my fingers, and I touched him as lightly as I would cob-webs; but lo, his fat body revolved, stiffened and solidified into an upright position, and his tongue gave my hand a lick! He pressed close to me, as if he were fain to crowd himself into my hand. He loved it with his tail, with his paw, with his tongue. If he could speak, I believe he would say with me that paradise is attained by touch; for in touch is all love and intelligence.

This small incident started me on a chat about hands, and if my chat is fortunate I have to thank my dog-star. In any case, it is pleasant to have something to talk about that no one else has monopolized; it is like making a new path in the trackless woods, blazing the trail where no foot has pressed before. I am glad to take you by the hand and lead you along an untrodden way into a world where the hand is supreme. But at the very outset we encounter a difficulty. You are so accustomed to light, I fear you will stumble when I try to guide you through the land of darkness and silence. The blind are not supposed to be the best of guides. Still, though I cannot warrant not to lose you, I promise that you shall not be led into fire or water, or fall into a deep pit. If you will follow me patiently, you will find that "there's a sound so fine, nothing lives 'twixt it and silence," and that there is more meant in things than meets the eye.

My hand is to me what your hearing and sight together are to you. In large measure we travel the same highways, read the same books, speak the same language, yet our experiences are different. All my comings and goings turn on the hand as on a pivot. It is the hand that binds me to the world of men and women. The hand is my feeler with which I reach through isolation and darkness and seize every pleasure, every activity that my fingers encounter. With the dropping of a little word from another's hand into mine, a slight flutter of the fingers, began the intelligence, the joy, the fullness of my life. Like Job, I feel as if a hand had made me, fashioned me together round about and molded my very soul.

In all my experiences and thoughts I am conscious of a hand. Whatever moves me, whatever thrills me, is as a hand that touches me in the dark, and that touch is my reality. You might as well say that a sight which makes you glad, or a blow which brings the stinging tears to your eyes, is unreal as to say that those impressions are unreal which I have accumulated by means of touch. The delicate tremble of a butterfly's wings in my hand, the soft petals of violets curling in the cool folds of their leaves or lifting sweetly out of the meadow-grass, the clear, firm outline of face and limb, the smooth arch of a horse's neck and the velvety touch of his nose — all these, and a thousand resultant combinations, which take shape in my mind, constitute my world.

Ideas make the world we live in, and impressions furnish ideas. My world is built of touch-sensations, devoid of physical color and sound; but without color and sound it breathes and throbs with life. Every object is associated in my mind with tactual qualities which, combined in countless ways, give me a sense of power, of beauty, or of incongruity: for with my hands I can feel the comic as well as the beautiful in the outward appearance of things. Remember that you, dependent on your sight, do not realize how many things are tangible. All palpable things are mobile or rigid, solid or liquid, big or small, warm or cold, and these qualities are variously modified. The coolness of a water-lily rounding into bloom is different from the coolness of an evening wind in summer, and different again from the coolness of the rain that soaks into the hearts of growing things and gives them life and body. The velvet of the rose is not that of a ripe peach or of a baby's dimpled cheek. The hardness of the rock is to the hardness of wood what a man's deep bass is to a woman's voice when it is low. What I call beauty I find in certain combinations of all these qualities, and is largely derived from the flow of curved and straight lines which is over all things.

"What does the straight line mean to you?" I think you will ask.

It *means* several things. It symbolizes duty. It seems to have the quality of inexorableness that duty has. When I have something to do that must not be set aside, I feel as if I were going forward in a straight line, bound to arrive somewhere, or go on forever without swerving to the right or to the left.

That is what it means. To escape this moralizing you should ask, "How does the straight line feel?" It feels, as I suppose it looks, straight— a dull thought drawn out endlessly. Eloquence to the touch resides not in straight lines, but in unstraight lines, or in many curved and straight lines together. They appear and disappear, are now deep, now shallow, now broken off or lengthened or swelling. They rise and sink beneath my fingers, they are full of sudden starts and pauses, and their variety is inexhaustible and wonderful. So you see I am not shut out from the region of the beautiful, though my hand cannot perceive the brilliant colors in the sunset or on the mountain, or reach into the blue depths of the sky.

Physics tells me that I am well off in a world which, I am told, knows neither color nor sound, but is made in terms of size, shape, and inherent qualities; for at least every object appears to my fingers standing solidly right side up, and is not an inverted image on the retina which, I understand, your brain is at infinite though unconscious labor to set back on its feet. A tangible object passes complete into my brain with the warmth of life upon it, and occupies the same place that it does in space; for, without egotism, the mind is as large as the universe. When I think of hills, I think of the upward strength I tread upon. When water is the object of my thought, I feel the cool shock of the plunge and the quick yielding of the waves that crisp and curl and ripple about my body. The pleasing changes of rough and smooth, pliant and rigid, curved and straight in the bark and branches of a tree give the truth to my hand. The immovable rock, with its juts and warped surface, bends beneath my fingers into all manner of grooves and hollows. The bulge of a watermelon and the puffed-up rotundities of squashes that sprout, bud, and ripen in that strange garden planted somewhere behind my finger-tips are the ludicrous in my tactual memory and imagination. My fingers are tickled to delight by the soft ripple of a baby's laugh, and find amusement in the lusty crow of the barnyard autocrat. Once I had a pet rooster that used to perch on my knee and stretch his neck and crow. A bird in my hand was then worth two in the — barnyard.

My fingers cannot, of course, get the impression of a large whole at a glance; but I feel the parts, and my mind puts them together. I move around my house, touching object after object in order, before I can form an idea of the entire house. In other people's houses I can touch only what is shown me — the chief objects of interest, carvings on the wall, or a curious architectural feature, exhibited like the family album. Therefore a house with which I am not familiar has for me, at first, no general effect or harmony of detail. It is not a complete conception, but a collection of object-impressions which, as they come to me, are disconnected and isolated. But my mind is full of associations, sensations, theories, and with them it constructs the house. The process reminds me of the building of Solomon's temple, where was neither saw, nor hammer, nor any tool heard while the stones were being laid one upon another. The silent worker is imagination which decrees reality out of chaos.

Without imagination what a poor thing my world would be! My garden would be a silent patch of earth strewn with sticks of a variety of shapes and smells. But when the eye of my mind is opened to its beauty, the bare ground brightens beneath my feet, and the hedge-row bursts into leaf, and the rose-tree shakes its fragrance everywhere. I know how budding trees look, and I enter into the amorous joy of the mating-birds, and this is the miracle of imagination.

Twofold is the miracle when, through my fingers, my imagination reaches forth and meets the imagination of an artist which he has embodied in a sculptured form. Although, compared with the life-warm, mobile face of a friend, the marble is cold and pulseless and unresponsive, yet it is beautiful to my hand. Its flowing curves and bendings are a real pleasure; only breath is wanting; but under the spell of the imagination the marble thrills and becomes the divine reality of the ideal. Imagination puts a sentiment into every line and curve, and the statue in my touch is indeed the goddess herself who breathes and moves and enchants.

It is true, however, that some sculptures, even recognized masterpieces, do not please my hand. When I touch what there is of the Winged Victory, it reminds me at first of a headless, limbless dream that flies toward me in an unrestful sleep. The garments of the Victory thrust stiffly out behind, and do not resemble garments that I have felt flying, fluttering, folding, spreading in the wind. But imagination fulfils these imperfections, and straightway the Victory becomes a powerful and spirited figure with the sweep of sea-winds in her robes and the splendor of conquest in her wings.

I find in a beautiful statue perfection of bodily form, the qualities of balance and completeness. The Minerva, hung with a web of poetical allusion, gives me a sense of exhilaration that is almost physical; and I like the luxuriant, wavy hair of Bacchus and Apollo, and the wreath of ivy, so suggestive of pagan holidays.

So imagination crowns the experience of my hands. And they learned that cunning from the wise hand of another which, itself guided by imagination, led me safely in paths that I knew not, made darkness light before me, and made crooked ways straight.

The Five-Sensed World

The poets have taught us how full of wonders is the night; and the night of blindness has its wonders, too. The only lightless dark is the night of ignorance and insensibility. We differ, blind and seeing, one from another, not in our senses, but in the use we make of them, in the imagination and courage with which we seek wisdom beyond our senses.

It is more difficult to teach ignorance to think than to teach an intelligent blind man to see the grandeur of Niagara. I have walked with people whose eyes are full of light, but who see nothing in wood, sea, or sky, nothing in city streets, nothing in books. What a witless masquerade is this seeing! It were better far to sail forever in the night of blindness, with sense and feeling and mind, than to be thus content with the mere act of seeing. They have the sunset, the morning skies, the purple of distant hills, yet their souls voyage through this enchanted world with a barren stare.

The calamity of the blind is immense, irreparable. But it does not take away our share of the things that count—service, friendship, humor, imagination, wisdom. It is the secret inner will that controls one's fate. We are capable of willing to be good, of loving and being loved, of thinking to the end that we may be wiser. We possess these spirit-born forces equally with all God's children. Therefore we, too, see the lightnings and hear the thunders of Sinai. We, too, march through the wilderness and the solitary place that shall be glad for us, and as we pass, God maketh the desert to blossom like the rose. We, too, go in unto the Promised Land to possess the treasures of the spirit, the unseen permanence of life and nature.

The blind man of spirit faces the unknown and grapples with it, and what else does the world of seeing men do? He has imagination, sympathy, humanity, and these ineradicable existences compel him to share by a sort of proxy in a sense he has not. When he meets terms of color, light, physiognomy, he guesses, divines, puzzles out their meaning by analogies drawn from the senses he has. I naturally tend to think, reason, draw inferences as if I had five senses instead of three. This tendency is beyond my control; it is involuntary, habitual, instinctive. I cannot compel my mind to say "I feel" instead of "I see" or "I hear." The word "feel" proves on examination to be no less a convention than "see" and "hear" when I seek for words accurately to describe the outward things that affect my three bodily senses. When a man loses a leg, his brain persists in impelling him to use what he has not and yet feels to be there. Can it be that the brain is so constituted that it will continue the activity which animates the sight and the hearing, after the eye and the ear have been destroyed?

It might seem that the five senses would work intelligently together only when resident in the same body. Yet when two or three are left un-aided, they reach out for their complements in another body, and find that they yoke easily with the borrowed team. When my hand aches from over-touching, I find relief in the sight of another. When my mind lags, wearied with the strain of forcing out thoughts about dark, musicless, colorless, de-tached substance, it recovers its elasticity as soon as I resort to the powers of another mind which commands light, harmony, color. Now, if the five senses will not remain disassociated, the life of the deaf-blind cannot be severed from the life of the seeing, hearing race.

The deaf-blind person may be plunged and replunged like Schiller's diver* into seas of the unknown. But, unlike the doomed hero, he returns triumphant, grasping the priceless truth that his mind is not crippled, not limited to the infirmity of his senses. The world of the eye and the ear be-comes to him a subject of fateful interest. He seizes every word of sight and hearing because his sensations compel it. Light and color, of which he has no tactual evidence, he studies fearlessly, believing that all humanly know-able truth is open to him. He is in a position similar to that of the as-tronomer who, firm, patient, watches a star night after night for many years and feels rewarded if he discovers a single fact about it. The man deaf-blind to ordinary outward things, and the man deaf-blind to the im-measurable universe, are both limited by time and space; but they have made a compact to wring service from their limitations.

The bulk of the world's knowledge is an imaginary construction. History is but a mode of imagining, of making us see civilizations that no longer ap-pear upon the earth. Some of the most significant discoveries in modern sci-ence owe their origin to the imagination of men who had neither accurate knowledge nor exact instruments to demonstrate their beliefs. If astronomy had not kept always in advance of the telescope, no one would ever have thought a telescope worth making. What great invention has not existed in the inventor's mind long before he gave it tangible shape?

A more splendid example of imaginative knowledge is the unity with which philosophers start their study of the world. They can never perceive the world in its entire reality. Yet their imagination, with its magnificent al-lowance for error, its power of treating uncertainty as negligible, has pointed the way for empirical knowledge.

Schiller's diver: Friedrich Von Schiller (1759–1805) was part of the German romantic move-ment. He was a poet, dramatist, and philosopher best known for his image of the thinker who relentlessly pursues the ideal of perfected nature. *Die Räuber* (1781) is a romantic tragedy about a hero who dies pursuing this ideal.

In their highest creative moments the great poet, the great musician cease to use the crude instruments of sight and hearing. They break away from their sense-moorings, rise on strong, compelling wings of spirit far above our misty hills and darkened valleys into the region of light, music, intellect.

What eye hath seen the glories of the New Jerusalem? What ear hath heard the music of the spheres, the steps of time, the strokes of chance, the blows of death? Men have not heard with their physical sense the tumult of sweet voices above the hills of Judea nor seen the heavenly vision; but millions have listened to that spiritual message through many ages.

Our blindness changes not a whit the course of inner realities. Of us it is as true as it is of the seeing that the most beautiful world is always entered through the imagination. If you wish to be something that you are not,—something fine, noble, good,—you shut your eyes, and for one dreamy moment you are that which you long to be.

Analogies in Sense Perception

I have not touched the outline of a star nor the glory of the moon, but I believe that God has set two lights in my mind, the greater to rule by day and the lesser by night, and by them I know that I am able to navigate my life-bark, as certain of reaching the haven as he who steers by the North Star. Perhaps my sun shines not as yours. The colors that glorify my world, the blue of the sky, the green of the fields, may not correspond exactly with those you delight in; but they are none the less color to me. The sun does not shine for my physical eyes, nor does the lightning flash, nor do the trees turn green in the spring; but they have not therefore ceased to exist, any more than the landscape is annihilated when you turn your back on it.

I understand how scarlet can differ from crimson because I know that the smell of an orange is not the smell of a grape-fruit. I can also conceive that colors have shades, and guess what shades are. In smell and taste there are varieties not broad enough to be fundamental; so I call them shades. There are half a dozen roses near me. They all have the unmistakable rose scent; yet my nose tells me that they are not the same. The American Beauty is distinct from the Jacqueminot and La France. Odors in certain grasses fade as really to my sense as certain colors do to yours in the sun. The freshness of a flower in my hand is analogous to the freshness I taste in an apple newly picked. I make use of analogies like these to enlarge my conceptions of colors. Some analogies which I draw between qualities in surface and vibration, taste and smell, are drawn by others between sight, hearing, and touch. This fact encourages me to persevere, to try to bridge the gap between the eye and the hand.

Certainly I get far enough to sympathize with the delight that my kind feel in beauty they see and harmony they hear. This bond between humanity and me is worth keeping, even if the ideas on which I base it prove erroneous.

Sweet, beautiful vibrations exist for my touch, even though they travel through other substances than air to reach me. So I imagine sweet, delightful sounds, and the artistic arrangement of them which is called music, and I remember that they travel through the air to the ear, conveying impressions somewhat like mine. I also know what tones are, since they are perceptible tactually in a voice. Now, heat varies greatly in the sun, in the fire, in hands, and in the fur of animals; indeed, there is such a thing for me as a cold sun. So I think of the varieties of light that touch the eye, cold and warm, vivid and dim, soft and glaring, but always light, and I imagine their passage through the air to an extensive sense, instead of to a narrow one like touch. From the experience I have had with voices I guess how the eye distinguishes shades in the midst of light. While I read the lips of a woman whose voice is soprano, I note a low tone or a glad tone in the midst of a high, flowing voice. When I feel my cheeks hot, I know that I am red. I have talked so much and read so much about colors that through no will of my own I attach meanings to them, just as all people attach certain meanings to abstract terms like hope, idealism, monotheism, intellect, which cannot be represented truly by visible objects, but which are understood from analogies between immaterial concepts and the ideas they awaken of external things. The force of association drives me to say that white is exalted and pure, green is exuberant, red suggests love or shame or strength. Without the color or its equivalent, life to me would be dark, barren, a vast blackness.

Thus through an inner law of completeness my thoughts are not permitted to remain colorless. It strains my mind to separate color and sound from objects. Since my education began I have always had things described to me with their colors and sounds by one with keen senses and a fine feeling for the significant. Therefore I habitually think of things as colored and resonant. Habit accounts for part. The soul sense accounts for another part. The brain with its five-sensed construction asserts its right and accounts for the rest. Inclusive of all, the unity of the world demands that color be kept in it, whether I have cognizance of it or not. Rather than be shut out, I take part in it by discussing it, imagining it, happy in the happiness of those near me who gaze at the lovely hues of the sunset or the rainbow.

My hand has its share in this multiple knowledge, but it must never be forgotten that with the fingers I see only a very small portion of a surface, and that I must pass my hand continually over it before my touch grasps the whole. It is still more important, however, to remember that my imagination is not tethered to certain points, locations, and distances. It puts all the parts together simultaneously as if it saw or knew instead of feeling them. Though I feel only a small part of my horse at a time,—my horse is nervous and does not submit to manual explorations,—yet, because I have many times felt hock, nose, hoof and mane, I can see the steeds of Phœbus Apollo* coursing the heavens.

Phœbus Apollo: The ancient Greek sun god equated with the sun itself. Keller is using a literary convention that equates the rays of the sun with horses pulling Phœbus Apollo.

With such a power active it is impossible that my thought should be vague, indistinct. It must needs be potent, definite. This is really a corollary of the philosophical truth that the real world exists only for the mind. That is to say, I can never touch the world in its entirety; indeed, I touch less of it than the portion that others see or hear. But all creatures, all objects, pass into my brain entire, and occupy the same extent there that they do in material space. I declare that for me branched thoughts, instead of pines, wave, sway, rustle, make musical the ridges of mountains rising summit upon summit. Mention a rose too far away for me to smell it. Straightway a scent steals into my nostril, a form presses against my palm in all its dilating softness, with rounded petals, slightly curled edges, curving stem, leaves drooping. When I would fain view the world as a whole, it rushes into vision — man, beast, bird, reptile, fly, sky, ocean, mountains, plain, rock, pebble. The warmth of life, the reality of creation is over all — the throb of human hands, glossiness of fur, lithe windings of long bodies, poignant buzzing of insects, the ruggedness of the steeps as I climb them, the liquid mobility and boom of waves upon the rocks. Strange to say, try as I may, I cannot force my touch to pervade this universe in all directions. The moment I try, the whole vanishes; only small objects or narrow portions of a surface, mere touch-signs, a chaos of things scattered at random, remain. No thrill, no delight is excited thereby. Restore to the artistic, comprehensive internal sense its rightful domain, and you give me joy which best proves the reality.

Before the Soul Dawn

Before my teacher came to me, I did not know that I am. I lived in a world that was a no-world. I cannot hope to describe adequately that unconscious, yet conscious time of nothingness. I did not know that I knew aught, or that I lived or acted or desired. I had neither will nor intellect. I was carried along to objects and acts by a certain blind natural impetus. I had a mind which caused me to feel anger, satisfaction, desire. These two facts led those about me to suppose that I willed and thought. I can remember all this, not because I knew that it was so, but because I have tactual memory. It enables me to remember that I never contracted my forehead in the act of thinking. I never viewed anything beforehand or chose it. I also recall tactually the fact that never in a start of the body or a heart-beat did I feel that I loved or cared for anything. My inner life, then, was a blank without past, present, or future, without hope or anticipation, without wonder or joy or faith.

> It was not night — it was not day,
>
>   . . . . . .
>
> But vacancy absorbing space,
> And fixedness, without a place;
> There were no stars — no earth — no time —
> No check — no change — no good — no crime.

My dormant being had no idea of God or immortality, no fear of death.

I remember, also through touch, that I had a power of association. I felt tactual jars like the stamp of a foot, the opening of a window or its closing, the slam of a door. After repeatedly smelling rain and feeling the discomfort of wetness, I acted like those about me: I ran to shut the window. But that was not thought in any sense. It was the same kind of association that makes animals take shelter from the rain. From the same instinct of aping others, I folded the clothes that came from the laundry, and put mine away, fed the turkeys, sewed bead-eyes on my doll's face, and did many other things of which I have the tactual remembrance. When I wanted anything I liked,—ice-cream, for instance, of which I was very fond,—I had a delicious taste on my tongue (which, by the way, I never have now), and in my hand I felt the turning of the freezer. I made the sign, and my mother knew I wanted ice-cream. I "thought" and desired in my fingers. If I had made a man, I should certainly have put the brain and soul in his finger-tips. From reminiscences like these I conclude that it is the opening of the two faculties, freedom of will, or choice, and rationality, or the power of thinking from one thing to another, which makes it possible to come into being first as a child, afterward as a man.

Since I had no power of thought, I did not compare one mental state with another. So I was not conscious of any change or process going on in my brain when my teacher began to instruct me. I merely felt keen delight in obtaining more easily what I wanted by means of the finger motions she taught me. I thought only of objects, and only objects I wanted. It was the turning of the freezer on a larger scale. When I learned the meaning of "I" and "me" and found that I was something, I began to think. Then consciousness first existed for me. Thus it was not the sense of touch that brought me knowledge. It was the awakening of my soul that first rendered my senses their value, their cognizance of objects, names, qualities, and properties. Thought made me conscious of love, joy, and all the emotions. I was eager to know, then to understand, afterward to reflect on what I knew and understood, and the blind impetus, which had before driven me hither and thither at the dictates of my sensations, vanished for ever.

I cannot represent more clearly than any one else the gradual and subtle changes from first impressions to abstract ideas. But I know that my physical ideas, that is, ideas derived from material objects, appear to me first in ideas similar to those of touch. Instantly they pass into intellectual meanings. Afterward the meaning finds expression in what is called "inner speech." When I was a child, my inner speech was inner spelling. Although I am even now frequently caught spelling to myself on my fingers, yet I talk to myself, too, with my lips, and it is true that when I first learned to speak, my mind discarded the finger-symbols and began to articulate. However, when I try to recall what some one has said to me, I am conscious of a hand spelling into mine.

It has often been asked what were my earliest impressions of the world in which I found myself. But one who thinks at all of his first impressions knows what a riddle this is. Our impressions grow and change unnoticed, so that what we suppose we thought as children may be quite different from what we actually experienced in our childhood. I only know that after my education began the world which came within my reach was all alive. I spelled to my blocks and my dogs. I sympathized with plants when the flowers were picked, because I thought it hurt them, and that they grieved for their lost blossoms. It was years before I could be made to believe that my dogs did not understand what I said, and I always apologized to them when I ran into or stepped on them.

As my experiences broadened and deepened, the indeterminate, poetic feelings of childhood began to fix themselves in definite thoughts. Nature—the world I could touch—was folded and filled with myself. I am inclined to believe those philosophers who declare that we know nothing but our own feelings and ideas. With a little ingenious reasoning one may see in the material world simply a mirror, an image of permanent mental sensations. In either sphere self-knowledge is the condition and the limit of our consciousness. That is why, perhaps, many people know so little about what is beyond their short range of experience. They look within themselves—and find nothing! Therefore they conclude that there is nothing outside themselves, either.

However that may be, I came later to look for an image of my emotions and sensations in others. I had to learn the outward signs of inward feelings. The start of fear, the suppressed, controlled tensity of pain, the beat of happy muscles in others, had to be perceived and compared with my own experiences before I could trace them back to the intangible soul of another. Groping, uncertain, I at last found my identity, and after seeing my thoughts and feelings repeated in others, I gradually constructed my world of men and of God. As I read and study, I find that this is what the rest of the race has done. Man looks within himself and in time finds the measure and the meaning of the universe.

Ideas for Rereading

1. Keller writes of a world experienced through touch, smell, and taste rather than the privileged senses of sight and hearing. This experience carries with it an aesthetic—an idea of beauty and ugliness that shapes how we experience and appreciate the world we live in—far different from that of most hearing and sighted people. As you reread these selections, list the unique elements of Keller's aesthetic values and observations. Note the places where Keller is aware of the uniqueness of her perspective and of her unusual sensitivity to, and appreciation for, particular experiences. In what ways are Keller's "disabilities" responsible for her unique passions and her unique ways of appreciating the world?

2. Keller makes constant reference to the concepts of light and darkness, despite not having experienced them herself. As you reread, mark passages where Keller uses the imagery of light and darkness. How do you make sense of this practice? Note the places where Keller seems to use visual images as a way of appealing to an audience of sighted readers. Do you find anything about her use of these terms and images that makes them especially meaningful in the context of her writing?

3. Throughout her writing, Keller stresses the importance of imagination and an inner life, at one point stating that "the bulk of the world's knowledge is an imaginary construction" (p. 216). As you reread these essays, consider which aspects of Keller's experience, as she defines it, would tend to encourage this privileging of the imagination. How might such a privileging in turn affect her understanding of the world? List your observations, using, when possible, Helen Keller's own impressions.

Ideas for Writing

1. In the chapter titled "Analogies in Sense Perception," Keller defends her right to use—and the rightness of using—visual and aural imagery in her writing, despite her post-infancy lack of direct experience in these areas. Write an analysis of Keller's argument, taking into account your own habitual or frequent uses of such imagery in your speech or your writing. To what extent are your uses of visual and aural imagery related to your own experiences with eyesight and hearing? Explore your own uses of "analogies in sense perception," paying particular attention to at least one sense perception that you tend to take for granted.

2. In the chapter "Before the Soul Dawn," Keller writes, "Before my teacher came to me, I did not know that I am" (p. 219). Keller goes on to narrate her self-remembered experience of intellectual and emotional "unconsciousness." Considering Keller's insistence on the primacy of the mind and imagination throughout *The World I Live In,* what is the possibility that Keller is imagining at least part of this experience of unconsciousness? Try to locate for yourself the moment when you first became conscious of your own existence. Using Keller as a model, write an essay describing that moment and the life before. Take into account the fact they you may be imagining these memories—but also recognize that personal histories are built from combinations of imagined and selected memories that change over time. How has your "first moment of self-awareness" changed in meaning as you have grown older?

3. In *The World I Live In,* Keller is, at least in part, attempting to speak to and of the experience of other similarly disabled people—to offer her experience as a way for the hearing and sighted to understand the lives of deaf and/or blind people in a general sense. How does Keller go about that project in her writing? Write an essay analyzing her goal in representing the experience of other deaf and/or blind people and her methods of achieving that goal.

CONTEXT

Helen Keller was actually the second deaf-blind woman to achieve a measure of American, even international, fame. In fact, it was after reading novelist Charles Dickens's description of Laura Bridgman, a deaf-blind girl living in Massachusetts, that Keller's parents decided to seek help for their daughter. Keller herself became known and admired by some of her most illustrious contemporaries, including Alexander Graham Bell—educator of deaf people and inventor of the telephone— who helped connect her with Annie Sullivan. Bell became a lifelong friend of Keller's, as did the author Samuel Clemens (Mark Twain), who even campaigned to raise funds for her Radcliffe education. Keller's friendship with Bell connects her to controversy, since Bell's dismissal of sign language and insistence on speech in teaching deaf people is said by many to have dealt a major blow to the deaf culture and education of the time. An excerpt from Bell's address to the National Academy of Sciences in 1883 is included in this Context section, along with one of Twain's fundraising letters and Charles Dickens's remarks on the situation of Laura Bridgman.

The conflicting instincts toward pity and admiration, fear and hagiography in the Twain and Dickens excerpts are evident in the media reaction to Keller's own writings and in artistic renderings of her story. This Context section contains both an advertisement and a New York Times *review for* The World I Live In *as well as three representations of what many have considered the defining moment in Keller's life, her recovery of the word* water *at the age of six. The representations include Keller's own narration of the event in her autobiography,* The Story of My Life, *followed by the text of the climactic "water pump" scene from William Gibson's play* The Miracle Worker *and a photograph of a performance of that scene. Finally, the Context section includes three of the hundreds of carefully posed photographs of Keller—with Annie Sullivan, with Alexander Graham Bell, and with the statue* Winged Victory *that Keller describes in* The World I Live In. *The section concludes with one unposed picture, the rarity of which suggests the care that was usually taken to uphold Keller as a symbol of serenity, beauty, and virtue.*

CHARLES DICKENS

Remarks upon Meeting Miss Laura Bridgman   1842

The thought occurred to me as I sat down in another room, before a girl, blind, deaf, and dumb; destitute of smell; and nearly so, of taste: before a fair young creature with every human faculty, and hope, and power of goodness and affection, inclosed within her delicate frame, and but one outward sense—the sense of touch. There she was, before me; built up, as it were, in a marble cell, impervious to any ray of light, or particle of sound; with her poor white hand peeping through a chink in the wall, beckoning to some good man for help, that an Immortal soul might be awakened.

Long before I looked upon her, the help had come. Her face was radiant with intelligence and pleasure. Her hair, braided by her own hands, was bound about a head, whose intellectual capacity and development were beautifully expressed in its graceful outline, and its broad open brow; her dress, arranged by herself, was a pattern of neatness and simplicity; the work she had knitted, lay beside her; her writing-book was on the desk she leaned upon.—From the mournful ruin of such bereavement, there had slowly risen up this gentle, tender, guileless, grateful-hearted being.

ALEXANDER GRAHAM BELL

Upon the Formation of a Deaf Variety of the Human Race   1883

The influence of selection in modifying our breeds of domestic animals is most marked, and it is reasonable to suppose that if we could apply selection to the human race we could also produce modifications or varieties of men.

But how can we ascertain the susceptibility of the human race to variation produced by selection? We cannot dictate to men and women whom they shall marry, and natural selection no longer influences mankind to any great extent.

We can see around us everywhere evidences of the transmission by heredity of characteristics, both desirable and undesirable, but at first sight no general selective influence appears to be at work to bring about the union in marriage of persons possessing the same congenital peculiarities. On the contrary, sexual attraction often appears to operate after the manner of magnetical attraction—"unlike poles attract, like poles repel." Strong, vigorous, and robust men naturally feel a tenderness for weak, delicate, and fragile women, and are generally repelled by physical strength and masculine traits in one of the opposite sex. Even in such characteristics as the color of the hair and eyes, it often appears that unlikes attract.

Certain diseases are known to be liable to transmission by heredity. But we do not find epileptics marrying epileptics, or consumptives* knowingly marrying consumptives. Even though persons afflicted with the same hereditary disease were to intermarry for a number of successive generations, it is doubtful whether any permanent variety of the race could be formed in this way, for the increased tendency to disease inherited by the

---

consumptives: Carriers of tuberculosis (TB). The disease is also known as "consumption" and is characterized by a wasting away of bodily tissue, particularly in the lungs.

offspring would probably cause a greater tendency to premature death and ultimately occasion the extinction of the variety.

On the other hand, it is reasonable to suppose that the continuous intermarriage of persons possessing congenital defects not associated with diminished vitality or vigor of constitution would result after a number of generations in the production of a vigorous but defective variety of the race. For instance, the absence of coloring matter from the skin and hair is a defect occasionally found among human beings, and we may learn from the success of attempts to propagate Albinism among animals, that we would probably produce a pink-eyed, white-haired variety of the human race by causing Albinos to marry one another; but this is only speculation. We cannot control the marriages of men as we can the breeding of animals, and at first sight there seems to be no way of ascertaining how far human beings are susceptible of variation by selection.

Such a conclusion, however, would be incorrect; and I desire to direct attention to the fact that in this country *deaf-mutes marry deaf-mutes*.

An examination of the records of some of our institutions for the deaf and dumb reveals the fact that such marriages are not the exception, but the rule. For the last fifty years there has been some selective influence at work which has caused, and is still causing, the continuous selection of the deaf by the deaf in marriage.

If the laws of heredity that are known to hold in the case of animals also apply to man, the intermarriage of congenital deaf-mutes through a number of successive generations should result in the formation of a deaf variety of the human race.

On the other hand, if it can be shown that congenitally deaf persons marry one another without any greater liability to the production of deaf offspring than is to be found among the people at large, then it will be evident that we cannot safely apply to man the deductions that have been drawn from experiments upon animals.

There are good grounds for the belief that a thorough investigation of the marriages of the deaf and the influence of these marriages upon the offspring will afford a solution of the problem, "To what extent is the human race susceptible of variation by selection?"

Although the statistics I have been able to collect are very incomplete, I have ventured to bring the subject to the attention of the Academy, in the hope that the publication of the results so far obtained may lead to the completion of the statistics.

MARK TWAIN

Letter on Behalf of Helen Keller   1896

For & in behalf
    of Helen Keller
        Stone blind & deaf, &
            formerly dumb.

Dear Mrs. Rogers,—Experience has convinced me that when one wishes to set a hard-worked man at something which he mightn't prefer to be bothered with, it is best to move upon him behind his wife. If she can't convince him it isn't worth while for other people to try.

Mr. Rogers will remember our visit with that astonishing girl at Laurence Hutton's house when she was fourteen years old. Last July, in Boston, when she was 16 she underwent the Harvard examination for admission to Radcliffe College. She passed without a single condition. She was allowed only the same amount of time that is granted to other applicants, & this was shortened in her case by the fact that the question-papers had to be *read* to her. Yet she scored an average of 90 as against an average of 78 on the part of the other applicants.

It won't *do* for America to allow this marvelous child to retire from her studies because of poverty. If she can go on with them she will make a fame that will endure in history for centuries. Along her special lines she is the most extraordinary product of all the ages. . . .

Mrs. Hutton's idea is to raise a permanent fund the interest upon which shall support Helen & her teacher & put them out of the fear of want. I shan't say a word against it, but she will find it a difficult and disheartening job, & meanwhile, what is to become of that miraculous girl?

No, for immediate and sound effectiveness, the thing is for you to plead with Mr. Rogers for this hampered wonder of your sex.

Advertisement for *The World I Live In,* *New York Times Saturday Review*   1908

Anonymous

Review of *The World I Live In,* *New York Times Book Review*   1908

In the Darkness

A unique and intensely interesting bit of autobiography is Helen Keller's "The World I Live In." (The Century Company, $1.20.) This little volume is composed of a number of brief essays which have appeared in the Century Magazine. In them Miss Keller tries to explain what the world is like to one who can apprehend it only through the senses of touch, taste and smell, in what manner her sensations come to her and what meaning they bear. It is a wonder-story, no less for its short and simple account of how she has reconstructed for herself in her own dark and silent isolation the world of her fellow-men than by reason of the optimism which leads her to find in her own fate such marvelous blessings. She tells how she "listens with her feet" and "hears" the pattering of her dog across the floor, or the soft thud of falling leaves, knows whether a stranger approaching her is old or young, recognizes people by the touch of their hands or their bodily odor; how she smells a coming storm long before those who trust to their sight are aware of its approach. The sensation of beauty comes to her mainly from "the flow of curved and straight lines which is over all things."

HELEN KELLER

From *The Story of My Life*   1902

The most important day I remember in all my life is the one on which my teacher, Anne Mansfield Sullivan, came to me. I am filled with wonder when I consider the immeasurable contrasts between the two lives which it connects. It was the third of March, 1887, three months before I was seven years old.

On the afternoon of that eventful day, I stood on the porch, dumb, expectant. I guessed vaguely from my mother's signs and from the hurrying to and fro in the house that something unusual was about to happen, so I went to the door and waited on the steps. The afternoon sun penetrated the mass of honeysuckle that covered the porch, and fell on my upturned face. My fingers lingered almost unconsciously on the familiar leaves and blossoms which had just come forth to greet the sweet southern spring. I did not know what the future held of marvel or surprise for me. Anger and bitterness had preyed upon me continually for weeks and a deep languor had succeeded this passionate struggle.

Have you ever been at sea in a dense fog, when it seemed as if a tangible white darkness shut you in, and the great ship, tense and anxious, groped her way toward the shore with plummet and sounding-line, and you waited with beating heart for something to happen? I was like that ship before my education began, only I was without compass or sounding-line, and had no way of knowing how near the harbour was. "Light! give me light!" was the wordless cry of my soul, and the light of love shone on me in that very hour.

I felt approaching footsteps. I stretched out my hand as I supposed to my mother. Some one took it, and I was caught up and held close in the arms of her who had come to reveal all things to me, and, more than all things else, to love me.

The morning after my teacher came she led me into her room and gave me a doll. The little blind children at the Perkins Institution had sent it and Laura Bridgman had dressed it; but I did not know this until afterward. When I had played with it a little while, Miss Sullivan slowly spelled into my hand the word "d-o-l-l." I was at once interested in this finger play and tried to imitate it. When I finally succeeded in making the letters correctly I was flushed with childish pleasure and pride. Running downstairs to my mother I held up my hand and made the letters for doll. I did not know that I was spelling a word or even that words existed; I was simply making my fingers go in monkey-like imitation. In the days that followed I learned to spell in this uncomprehending way a great many words, among them *pin, hat, cup* and a few verbs like *sit, stand* and *walk.* But my teacher had been with me several weeks before I understood that everything has a name.

One day, while I was playing with my new doll, Miss Sullivan put my big rag doll into my lap also, spelled "d-o-l-l" and tried to make me understand that "d-o-l-l" applied to both. Earlier in the day we had had a tussle over the words "m-u-g" and "w-a-t-e-r." Miss Sullivan had tried to impress it upon me that "m-u-g" is *mug* and that "w-a-t-e-r" is *water,* but I persisted in confounding the two. In despair she had dropped the subject for the time, only to renew it at the first opportunity. I became impatient at her repeated attempts and, seizing the new doll, I dashed it upon the floor. I was keenly delighted when I felt the fragments of the broken doll at my feet. Neither sorrow nor regret followed my passionate outburst. I had not loved the doll. In the still, dark world in which I lived there was no strong sentiment or tenderness. I felt my teacher sweep the fragments to one side of the hearth, and I had a sense of satisfaction that the cause of my discomfort was removed. She brought me my hat, and I knew I was going out into the warm sunshine. This thought, if a wordless sensation may be called a thought, made me hop and skip with pleasure.

We walked down the path to the well-house, attracted by the fragrance of the honeysuckle with which it was covered. Some one was drawing water and my teacher placed my hand under the spout. As the cool stream gushed over one hand she spelled into the other the word *water,* first slowly, then rapidly. I stood still, my whole attention fixed upon the motions of her fingers. Suddenly I felt a misty consciousness as of something forgotten—a thrill of returning thought; and somehow the mystery of language was revealed to me. I knew then that "w-a-t-e-r" meant the wonderful cool something that was flowing over my hand. That living word awakened my soul, gave it light, hope, joy, set it free! There were barriers still, it is true, but barriers that could in time be swept away.

I left the well-house eager to learn. Everything had a name, and each name gave birth to a new thought. As we returned to the home every object which I touched seemed to quiver with life. That was because I saw everything with the strange, new sight that had come to me. On entering the door I remembered the doll I had broken. I felt my way to the hearth and picked up the pieces. I tried vainly to put them together. Then my eyes filled with tears; for I realized what I had done, and for the first time I felt repentance and sorrow.

I learned a great many new words that day. I do not remember what they all were; but I do know that *mother, father, sister, teacher* were among them—words that were to make the world blossom for me, "like Aaron's rod, with flowers." It would have been difficult to find a happier child than I was as I lay in my crib at the close of that eventful day and lived over the joys it had brought me, and for the first time longed for a new day to come.

The Water-Pump Scene from William Gibson's The Miracle Worker   *1956*

ANNIE: Water, W, a, t, e, r. *Water.* It has a—name—(And now the miracle happens. HELEN drops the pitcher on the slab under the spout, it shatters. She stands transfixed. ANNIE freezes on the pump handle; there is a change in the sundown light, and with it a change in HELEN'S face . . . and her lips tremble, trying to remember something the muscles around them once knew, till at last it finds its way out, painfully, a baby sound buried under the debris of years of dumbness.)
HELEN: Wah. Wah.

Anne Bancroft and Patty Duke as Annie Sullivan and Helen Keller

Helen Keller and Annie Sullivan

Helen Keller (left), Annie Sullivan, and Alexander Graham Bell communicating in tactile sign language, 1894

Helen Keller with Winged Victory

Twelve-year-old Helen with John Hitz, Alexander Graham Bell's secretary, 1892

Ideas for Rereading

1. Images, such as photographs, are cultural artifacts that can be read and examined to discover the meaning, purpose, cultural significance of what they depict. Look carefully at—read—the photos of Helen Keller in this section, noting the distinction between the posed and unposed photographs. Consider and list your impressions of these images. Note the ways you think the posing and composition of these photos contribute to the public perception of Keller. How do these photos make an argument about Keller? What is the argument? How would the one unposed photo modify the public perception of Keller?

2. Reread the Dickens and Twain selections in praise and support of Bridgman and Keller, respectively. Imagine how these short selections might conform to the prevailing idea of these women during their lifetimes. What do you think Dickens's and Twain's depictions say about themselves as men of their time?

Ideas for Writing

1. Consider the photograph and excerpt of the water-pump scene from the play *The Miracle Worker* in light of Keller's depiction of the same event in *The*

Story of My Life. If possible, view the film version of *The Miracle Worker,* focusing on that pivotal scene. Write an essay examining the creation of Keller's public image and potential myth in the context of the depictions of this "miraculous" moment in her life. Keep in mind that Keller herself was well acquainted with both the play and film *The Miracle Worker,* and also keep in mind your own sense of how life-defining events often change meaning according to when and where we recount them.

2. The *New York Times* reviewer of *The World I Live In* calls Keller's book "a wonder-story." What does he or she mean by that term? Keeping in mind that *wonder story* or *tale* has often been used as a synonym for *fairy tale,* write an essay analyzing the fairy-tale elements of Keller's depiction of her life in *The World I Live In.* In what ways might Keller be interpreted as a fairy-tale character? In what ways does Keller's life, and Keller's account of that life, confirm, complicate, or defy such readings?

CONTEMPORARY CONVERSATION

OLIVER SACKS

New York Times *reviewer Michiko Kakutani refers to Oliver Sacks (b. 1933) as "a medical man in the old-fashioned humanist tradition." Sacks is a neurologist and professor as well as a popular, award-winning author. His observations on his patients and clinical work — recorded in such books as* Awakenings *(1973),* The Man Who Mistook His Wife for a Hat *(1986), and* An Anthropologist on Mars *(1995) — have been turned into feature films, stage plays, an opera, and a PBS documentary series. Sacks is known for listening to his patients, even helping them to develop their own treatments, as well as for his "constant amazed appreciation of how men and women afflicted with frustrating and terrifying handicaps can cope with them and even help themselves to master them" (Douglas Hill,* Toronto Globe and Mail*). In this selection from* Seeing Voices: A Journey into the World of the Deaf *(1990), Sacks brings his characteristic sense of wonder and appreciation to a discussion of the student protests at Gallaudet University, the country's only university for deaf people, and describes those protests as a manifestation of the vitality and uniqueness of deaf culture.*

Protest at Gallaudet

W*ednesday morning, March 9, 1988:* "Strike at Gallaudet," "Deaf Strike for the Deaf," "Students Demand Deaf President"—the media are full of these happenings today; they started three days ago, have been steadily building, and are now on the front page of *The New York Times.* It looks like an amazing story. I have been to Gallaudet University a couple of times in the past year, and have been steadily getting to know the place. Gallaudet is the only liberal arts college for the deaf in the world and is, moreover, the core of the world's deaf community—but, in all its 124 years, it has never had a deaf president.

I flatten out the paper and read the whole story: the students have been actively campaigning for a deaf president ever since the resignation last year of Jerry Lee, a hearing person who had been president since 1984. Unrest, uncertainty, and hope have been brewing. By mid-February, the presidential search committee narrowed the search to six candidates—three hearing, three deaf. On March 1, three thousand people attended a rally at Gallaudet to make it clear to the board of trustees that the Gallaudet community was strongly insisting on the selection of a deaf president. On March 5, the night before the election, a candlelight vigil was held outside the board's quarters. On Sunday, March 6, choosing between three finalists, one hearing, two deaf, the board chose Elisabeth Ann Zinser, Vice-Chancellor for Academic Affairs at the University of North Carolina at Greensboro—the hearing candidate.

The tone, as well as the content, of the board's announcement caused outrage: it was here that the chairman of the board, Jane Bassett Spilman, made her comment that "the deaf are not yet ready to function in the hearing world." The next day, a thousand students marched to the hotel where the board was cloistered, then the six blocks to the White House, and on to the Capitol. The following day, March 8, the students closed the university and barricaded the campus.

Wednesday afternoon: The faculty and staff have come out in support of the students and their four demands: (1) that a new, *deaf* president be named immediately; (2) that the chairman of the board, Jane Bassett Spilman, resign immediately; (3) that the board have a 51 percent majority of deaf members (at present it has seventeen hearing members and only four deaf); and (4) that there be no reprisals. At this point, I phone my friend Bob Johnson. Bob is head of the linguistics department at Gallaudet, where he has taught and done research for seven years. He has a deep knowledge of the deaf and their culture, is an excellent signer, and is married to a deaf woman. He is as close to the deaf community as a hearing person can be.[1] I want to know how he feels about the events at Gallaudet. "It's the most remarkable thing I've ever seen," he says. "If you'd asked me a month ago, I'd have bet a million dollars this couldn't happen in my lifetime. You've got to come down and see this for yourself."

When I had visited Gallaudet in 1986 and 1987, I found it an astonishing and moving experience. I had never before seen an entire community of the deaf, nor had I quite realized (even though I knew this theoretically) that Sign might indeed be a complete language—a language equally suitable for making love or speeches, for flirtation or mathematics. I had to see philosophy and chemistry classes in Sign; I had to see the absolutely silent mathematics department at work; to see deaf bards, Sign poetry, on the campus, and the range and depth of the Gallaudet theater; I had to see the wonderful social scene in the student bar, with hands flying in all directions as a hundred separate conversations proceeded[2]—I had to see all this for myself before I could be moved from my previous "medical" view of deafness (as a condition, a deficit, that had to be "treated") to a "cultural" view of the deaf as forming a community with a complete language and culture of its own. I had felt there was something very joyful, even Arcadian about Gallaudet—and I was not surprised to hear that some of the students were occasionally reluctant to leave its warmth and seclusion and protectiveness, the cosiness of a small but complete and self-sufficient world, for the unkind and uncomprehending big world outside.[3]

But there were also tensions and resentments under the surface, which seemed to be simmering, with no possibility of resolution. There was an unspoken tension between faculty and administration—a faculty in which many of the teachers sign and some are deaf. The faculty could, to some extent, communicate with the students, enter their worlds, their minds; but the administration (so I was told) formed a remote governing body, running the school like a corporation, with a certain "benevolent" caretaker attitude to the "handicapped" deaf, but little real feeling for them as a community, as a culture. It was feared by the students and teachers I talked to that the administration, if it could, would reduce still further the percentage of deaf teachers at Gallaudet and further restrict the teachers' use of Sign there.[4]

The students I met seemed animated, a lively group when together, but often fearful and diffident of the outside world. I had the feeling of some cruel undermining of self-image, even in those who professed "Deaf Pride." I had the feeling that some of them thought of themselves as children—an echo of the parental attitude of the board (and perhaps of some of the faculty). I had the feeling of a certain passivity among them, a sense that though life might be improved in small ways here and there, it was their lot to be overlooked, to be second-class citizens.[5]

Thursday morning, March 10: A taxi deposits me on Eighth Street opposite the college. The gates have been blocked off for forty-eight hours; my first sight is of a huge, excited, but cheerful and friendly crowd of hundreds barring the entrance to the campus, carrying banners and placards, and signing to one another with great animation. One or two police cars sit parked outside, watching, their engines purring, but they seem a benign presence. There is a good deal of honking from the traffic passing by—I am puzzled by this, but then spot a sign reading HONK FOR A DEAF PRESIDENT. The crowd itself is both strangely silent and noisy: the signing, the Sign speeches, are utterly silent; but they are punctuated by curious applause—an excited shaking of the hands above the head, accompanied by high-pitched vocalizations and screams.[6] As I watch, one of the students leaps up on a pillar and starts signing with much expression and beauty. I can understand nothing of what he says, but I feel the signing is pure and impassioned—his whole body, all his feelings, seem to flow into the signing. I hear a murmured name—Tim Rarus—and realize that this is one of the student leaders, one of the Four. His audience visibly hangs on every sign, rapt, bursting at intervals into tumultuous applause.

As I watch Rarus and his audience, and then let my gaze wander past the barricades to the great campus filled with passionate Sign, with passionate soundless conversation, I get an overwhelming feeling not only of another mode of communication but of another mode of sensibility, another mode of being. One has only to see the students—even casually, from the outside (and I felt quite as much an outsider as those who walked or drove casually by)—to feel that in their language, their mode of being, they *deserve* one of their own, that no one not deaf, not signing, could possibly understand them. One feels, intuitively, that interpretation can never be sufficient—that the students would be cut off from any president who was not one of them.

Innumerable banners and signs catch the brilliant March sun: DEAF PREZ NOW is clearly the basic one. There is a certain amount of anger—it could hardly be otherwise—but the anger, on the whole, is clothed in wit: thus a common sign is DR. ZINSER IS NOT READY TO FUNCTION IN THE DEAF WORLD, a retort to Spilman's malapropos statement about the deaf. Dr. Zinser's own comment on *Nightline* the night before ("A deaf individual, one day, will . . . be president of Gallaudet") had provoked many signs saying: WHY NOT MARCH 10, 1988, DR. ZINSER? The papers have spoken of "battle" or "confrontation," which gives a sense of a negotiation, an inching to and fro. But the students say: "Negotiation? We have forgotten the word. 'Negotiation' no longer appears in our dictionaries." Dr. Zinser keeps asking for a "meaningful dialogue," but this in itself seems a meaningless request, for there is no longer, there never has been, any intermediate ground on which "dialogue" could take place. The students are concerned with their identity, their survival, an all-or-none: they have four demands, and there is no place for "sometime" or "maybe."

Indeed Dr. Zinser is anything but popular. It is felt by many not only that she is peculiarly insensitive to the mood of the students—the glaring fact that they do not want her, that the university has been literally barricaded against her—but that she actively stands for and prosecutes an official "hard line." At first there was a certain sympathy for her: she had been duly chosen and she had no idea what she had been thrown into. But with the passing of each day this view grew less and less tenable, and the whole business began to resemble a contest of wills. Dr. Zinser's tough, "no-nonsense" stance reached a peak yesterday, when she loudly asserted that she was going to "take charge" of the unruly campus. "If it gets any further out of control," she said, "I'm going to have to take action to bring it under control." This incensed the students, who promptly burned her in effigy.

Some of the placards are nakedly furious: one says ZINSER—PUPPET OF SPILMAN, another WE DON'T NEED A WET NURSE, MOMMY SPILMAN. I begin to realize that this is the deaf's coming of age, saying at last, in a very loud voice: "We're no longer your children. We no longer want your 'care.'"[7]

I edge past the barricades, the speeches, the signs, and stroll onto the large and beautifully green campus, with its great Victorian buildings setting off a most un-Victorian scene. The campus is buzzing, visibly, with conversation—everywhere there are pairs or small groups signing. There is conversing everywhere, and I can understand none if it; *I* feel like the deaf, the voiceless one today—the handicapped one, the minority, in this great signing community. I see lots of faculty as well as students on the campus: one professor is making and selling lapel buttons ("Frau Zinser, Go Home!"), which are bought and pinned on as quickly as he makes them. "Isn't this great?" he says, catching sight of me. "I haven't had such a good time since Selma. It feels a little like Selma—and the sixties."

A great many dogs are on the campus—there must be fifty or sixty on the great greensward out front. Regulations on owning and keeping dogs here are loose; some are "hearing ear" dogs, but some are just . . . dogs. I see one girl signing to her dog; the dog, obediently, turns over, begs, gives a paw. This dog itself bears a white cloth sign on each side: I UNDERSTAND SIGN BETTER THAN SPILMAN. (The chairman of Gallaudet's board of trustees has occupied her position for seven years while learning hardly any Sign.)

Where there was a hint of something angry, tense, at the barricades, there is an atmosphere of calm and peacefulness inside; more, a sense of joy, and something like festivity. There are dogs everywhere, and babies and children too, friends and families everywhere, conversing volubly in Sign. There are little colored tents on the grass, and hot dog stands selling frankfurters and soda—dogs and hot dogs: it is rather like Woodstock, much more like Woodstock than a grim revolution.

Earlier in the week, the initial reactions to Elisabeth Ann Zinser's appointment were furious—and uncoordinated; there were a thousand individuals on the campus, milling around, tearing up toilet paper, destructive in mood. But all at once, as Bob Johnson said, "the whole consciousness changed." Within hours there seemed to emerge a new, calm, clear consciousness and resolution; a political body, two thousand strong, with a single, focused will of its own. It was the astonishing swiftness with which this organization emerged, the sudden precipitation, from chaos, of a unanimous, communal mind, that astonished everyone who saw it. And yet, of course, this was partly an illusion, for there were all sorts of preparations—and people—behind it.

Central to this sudden "transformation"—and central, thereafter, in organizing and articulating the entire "uprising" (which was far too dignified, too beautifully modulated, to be called an "uproar")—were the four remarkable young student leaders: Greg Hlibok, the leader of the student body, and his cohorts Tim Rarus, Bridgetta Bourne, and Jerry Covell. Greg Hlibok is a young engineering student, described (by Bob Johnson) as "very engaging, laconic, direct, but in his words a great deal of thought and judgment." Hlibok's father, who is also deaf, runs an engineering firm; his deaf mother, Peggy O'Gorman Hlibok, is active in lobbying for the educational use of ASL; and he has two deaf brothers, one a writer and actor, one a financial consultant, and a deaf sister, also a student at Gallaudet. Tim Rarus, also born deaf, and from a deaf family, is a perfect foil for Greg: he has an eager spontaneity, a passion, an intensity that nicely complement Greg's quietness. The four had already been elected before the uprising—indeed while Jerry Lee was still president—but have taken on a very special, unprecedented role since President Lee's resignation.

Hlibok and his fellow student leaders have not incited or inflamed students—on the contrary, they are calming, restraining, and moderating in their influence, but have been highly sensitive to the "feel" of the campus and, beyond this, of the deaf community at large, and have felt with them that a crucial time has arrived. They have organized the students to press for a deaf president, but they have not done this alone: behind them there has been the active support of alumni, and of deaf organizations and leaders all around the country. Thus, much calculation, much preparation, preceded the "transformation," the emergence of a communal mind. It is not an order appearing from total chaos (even though it might seem so). Rather, it is the sudden manifestation of a latent order, like the sudden crystallization of a super-saturated solution—a crystallization precipitated by the naming of Zinser as president on Sunday night. This is a qualitative transformation, from passivity to activity, and in the moral no less than in the political sense, it is a revolution. Suddenly the deaf are no longer passive, scattered, and powerless; suddenly they have discovered the calm strength of union.

In the afternoon I recruit an interpreter and with her help interview a couple of deaf students. One of them tells me:

> I'm from a hearing family . . . my whole life I've felt pressures, hearing pressures on me—"You can't *do* it in the hearing world, you can't *make* it in the hearing world"—and right now all that pressure is lifted from me. I feel free, all of a sudden, full of energy now. You keep hearing "you can't, you can't," but I *can* now. The words "deaf and dumb" will be destroyed forever; instead there'll be "deaf and able."

These were very much the terms Bob Johnson had used, when we first talked, when he spoke of the deaf as laboring under "an illusion of powerlessness," and of how, all of a sudden, this illusion had been shattered.

Many revolutions, transformations, awakenings, are in response to immediate (and intolerable) circumstances. What is so remarkable about the Gallaudet strike of 1988 is its historical consciousness, the sense of deep historical perspective that informs it. This was evident on campus; as soon as I arrived I spotted a picket saying: LAURENT CLERC WANTS DEAF PREZ. HE IS NOT HERE BUT HIS *SPIRIT* IS HERE. SUPPORT US. I overhead one journalist say, "Who the hell's Laurent Clerc?" but his name, his persona, unknown to the hearing world, are known to virtually everyone in the deaf world. He is a founding father, a heroic figure, in deaf history and culture. The *first* emancipation of the deaf—their achievement of education and literacy, of self-respect and the respect of their fellows—was largely inspired by the achievement and person of Laurent Clerc. It was immensely moving, then, to see this placard, and one could not help feeling that Laurent Clerc *was* here, on the campus, *was,* albeit posthumously, the authentic spirit and voice of the revolt—for he, above all, had laid the foundations of their education and culture.

When Clerc founded the American Asylum at Hartford with Thomas Gallaudet in 1817, he not only introduced Sign as the medium of all deaf schooling in the United States but also introduced a remarkable school system—one that has no exact parallel in the speaking world. Other residential schools for the deaf soon opened throughout the country, all using the Sign that had evolved at Hartford. Virtually all the teachers in these schools were educated at Hartford, and most had met the charismatic Clerc. They contributed their own indigenous signs and later spread an increasingly polished and generalized ASL in many parts of the country, and the standards and aspirations of the deaf continually rose.

The unique pattern of transmission of deaf culture relates equally to the deaf's language (Sign) and to their schools. These schools acted as foci for the deaf community, passing down deaf history and culture from one generation to the next. Their influence went well beyond the classroom: commonly, deaf communities would spring up around the schools, and graduates would often remain close to the school, or even take jobs working in the school. And crucially, most of these schools for the deaf were residential schools, as Carol Padden and Tom Humphries point out:[8]

> The most significant aspect of residential life is the dormitory. In the dormitories, away from the structured control of the classroom, deaf children are introduced to the social life of deaf people. In the informal dormitory environment, children not only learn sign language but the content of the culture. In this way, the schools become hubs of the communities that surround them, preserving for the next generation the culture of earlier generations. . . . This unique pattern of transmission lies at the heart of the culture.[9]

Thus, with great rapidity, in the years after 1817, there spread throughout the States not just a language and a literacy, but a body of shared knowledge, shared beliefs, cherished narratives and images, which soon constituted a rich and distinctive culture. Now, for the first time, there was an "identity" for the deaf, not merely a personal one, but a social, cultural one. They were no longer just individuals, with an individual's plights or triumphs; they were *a people,* with their own culture, like the Jews or the Welsh.[10]

By the 1850s it had become clear that higher education was also needed—the deaf, previously illiterate, now needed a college. In 1857,

Thomas Gallaudet's son, Edward, only twenty years old, but uniquely equipped through his background (his mother was deaf, and he learned Sign as a primary language), his sensibilities, and his gifts, was appointed principal of the Columbia Institution for the Instruction of the Deaf and the Dumb and the Blind,[11] conceiving and hoping from the start it could be transformed into a college with federal support. In 1864 this was achieved, and what was later to become Gallaudet College received its charter from Congress.

Edward Gallaudet's own full and extraordinary life[12] lasted well into the present century and spanned great (though not always admirable) changes in attitudes to deaf people and their education. In particular, gathering force from the 1860s and promoted to a large extent in the United States by Alexander Graham Bell was an attitude that opposed the use of signing, and sought to forbid its use in schools and institutions. Gallaudet himself fought against this, but was overborne by the climate of the times, and by a certain ferocity and intransigence of mind that he himself was too reasonable to understand.[13]

By the time of Gallaudet's death, his college was world famous and had shown once and for all that the deaf, given the opportunity and the means, could match the hearing in every sphere of academic activity—and for that matter, in athletic activity, too (the spectacular gym at Gallaudet, designed by Frederick Law Olmsted and opened in 1880, was one of the finest in the country; and the football huddle was actually invented at Gallaudet, for players to pass secret tactics among themselves). But Gallaudet himself was one of the last defenders of Sign in an educational world that had turned its back on signing, and with his death the college lost—and because the college had become the symbol and aspiration of the deaf all over the world, the deaf world also lost—its greatest and last proponent of Sign in education.

With this, Sign, which had been the dominant language at the college before, went underground and became confined to a colloquial use.[14] The students continued to use it among themselves, but it was no longer considered a legitimate language for formal discourse or teaching. Thus the century between Thomas Gallaudet's founding of the American Asylum and Edward Gallaudet's death in 1917 saw the rise and fall, the legitimation and delegitimation, of Sign in America.[15]

The suppression of Sign in the 1880s had a deleterious effect on the deaf for seventy-five years, not only on their education and academic achievements but on their image of themselves and on their entire community and culture. Such community and culture as did exist remained in isolated pockets—there was no longer the sense there had once been, at least the sense that was intimated in the "golden age" of the 1840s, of a nationwide (even worldwide) community and culture.

But the last thirty years have again seen a reversal—and indeed a relegitimation and resurrection of Sign as never before; and with this, and much else, a discovery or rediscovery of the cultural aspects of deafness—a strong sense of community and communication and culture, of a self-definition as a unique mode of being.

De l'Epée had immense admiration, but also reservations, about sign language: on the one hand, he saw it as a complete form of communication ("Every deaf-mute sent to us already has a language . . . with it, he expresses his needs, desires, pains, and so on, and makes no mistake when others express themselves likewise"), on the other, as lacking inner structure, a grammar (which he tried to inject, from French, with his "methodical signs"). This strange mixture of admiration and denigration continued for the next two hundred years, even among the deaf. But it is likely that, until William Stokoe came to Gallaudet in 1955, no linguist had really confronted the reality of Sign.

One may speak of "the revolution of 1988" and feel, as Bob Johnson did, as, in a sense, everyone did, that this was an astounding event, a transformation, that could hardly have been expected in our lifetimes. At one level, indeed, this is true; but at another level one must see that the movement, the many movements that flowed together to create the explosion of 1988, were many years in the gathering, and that the seeds of the revolution were planted thirty years ago (if not a hundred and fifty years ago). It will be a complex task to reconstruct the history of the past thirty years, specifically the new chapter of deaf history which may be considered to have started in 1960 with Stokoe's "bombshell" paper on *Sign Language Structure*, the first-ever serious and scientific attention paid to "the visual communication system of the American deaf."

I have spoken about this complex prehistory of the revolution, the complex and tangled skein of events and changing attitudes that preceded it, to many people: to the students at Gallaudet; to historians like Harlan Lane, and John Van Cleve (who compiled the enormous three-volume *Gallaudet Encyclopedia of Deaf People and Deafness*); to researchers like William Stokoe, Ursula Bellugi, Michael Karchmer, Bob Johnson, Hilde Schlesinger, and many others; and no two of them see it the same way.[16]

Stokoe's own passions were those of a scientist — but a scientist of language is a special sort of creature who needs to be as interested in human life, in human community and culture, as he is in the biological determinants of language. This doubleness of interest and approach led Stokoe, in his 1965 *Dictionary,* to include an appendix (by his deaf collaborator, Carl Croneberg) on "The Linguistic Community," the first description of the social and cultural characteristics of deaf people who used American Sign Language. Writing of the *Dictionary* fifteen years later, Padden saw it as a "landmark":[17]

It was unique to describe "Deaf people" as constituting a cultural group . . . it represented a break from the long tradition of "pathologizing" Deaf people. . . . In a sense the book brought official and public recognition of a deeper aspect of Deaf people's lives: their culture.

But though, in retrospect, Stokoe's works were seen as "bombshells" and "landmarks," and though, in retrospect, they can be seen as having had a major part in leading to the subsequent transformation of consciousness, they were all but ignored at the time. Stokoe himself, looking back, commented wryly:[18]

> Publication in 1960 [of *Sign Language Structure*] brought a curious local reaction. With the exception of Dean Detmold and one or two colleagues, the entire Gallaudet College faculty rudely attacked me, linguistics, and the study of signing as a language. . . . If the reception of the first linguistic study of a Sign Language of the deaf community was chilly at home, it was cryogenic in a large part of special education—at that time a closed corporation as hostile to Sign Language, as [it was] ignorant of linguistics.

There was certainly very little impact among his fellow linguists: the great general works on language of the 1960s make no reference to it—or indeed to Sign at all. Nor did Chomsky, the most revolutionary linguist of our time when, in 1966, he promised (in the preface to *Cartesian Linguistics*) a future book on "language surrogates . . . for example, the gesture language of the deaf"—a description that placed Sign below the category of real language.[19] And when Klima and Bellugi themselves turned to the study of Sign, in 1970, they had the feeling of virgin soil, of a totally new subject (this was partly a reflection of their own originality, the originality that makes every subject seem totally new).

More remarkable, in a sense, was the indifferent or hostile reaction of the deaf themselves, whom one might have thought would have been the first to see and welcome Stokoe's insights. There are intriguing descriptions of this—and of later "conversions"—provided by former colleagues of Stokoe, and others, all of whom were themselves native signers, either deaf or born of deaf parents. Would not a signer be the first to see the structural complexity of his own language? But it was precisely signers who were most uncomprehending, or most resistant to Stokoe's notions. Thus Gilbert Eastman (later to become an eminent Sign playwright, and a most ardent supporter of Stokoe's) tells us, "My colleagues and I laughed at Dr. Stokoe and his crazy project. It was impossible to analyze our Sign Language."

The reasons for this are complex and deep and may not have any parallel in the hearing-speaking world. For we (99.9 percent of us) take speech and spoken language for granted; we have no special interest in speech, we never give it a second thought, nor do we care whether it is analyzed or not. But it is profoundly different for the deaf and Sign. They have a special, intense feeling for their own language: they tend to extol it in tender, reverent terms (and have done so since Desloges, in 1779). The deaf feel Sign as a most intimate, indissociable part of their being, as something they depend on, and also, frighteningly, as something that may be taken from them at any time (as it was, in a way, by the Milan conference in 1880). They are, as Padden and Humphries say, suspicious of "the science of others," which they feel may overpower their own knowledge of Sign, a knowledge that is "impressionistic, global, and not internally analytic." Yet, paradoxically, with all this reverent feeling, they have often shared the hearing's incomprehension or depreciation of Sign. (One of the things that most impressed Bellugi, when she launched on her own studies, was that the deaf themselves, while native signers, often had no idea of the grammar or inner structure of Sign and tended to see it as pantomime.)

And yet, perhaps, this is not so surprising. There is an old proverb that fish are the last to recognize water. And for signers, Sign is their medium and water, so familiar and natural to them, as to need no explanation. The users of a language, above all, will tend to a naive realism, to see their language as a reflection of reality, not as a construct. "The aspects of things that are most important to us are hidden because of their simplicity and familiarity," Wittgenstein says. Thus it may take an outside view to show the native users of a language that their own utterances, which appear so simple and transparent to themselves, are, in fact, enormously complex and contain and conceal the vast apparatus of a true language. This is precisely what happened with Stokoe and the deaf—and it is put clearly by Louie Fant:[20]

> Like most children of deaf parents, I grew up with no conscious awareness that ASL was a language. It was not until my mid-thirties that I was relieved of this misconception. My enlightenment came from people who were not native users of ASL—who had come into the field of deafness with no preconceived notions, and bound to no points of view regarding deaf people and their language. They looked at the signed language of the deaf with fresh eyes.

Fant goes on to describe how despite working at Gallaudet and getting to know Stokoe well (and even himself writing a sign language primer using some of Stokoe's analysis), he still resisted the idea that it was a real language. When he left Gallaudet to become a founding member of the National Theater of the Deaf, in 1967, this attitude persisted among him and others—all productions were in signed English, because ASL was considered "bastardized English not fit for the stage." Once or twice Fant, and others, almost inadvertently used ASL in declaiming on stage, with electric effect, and this had a strange effect on them. "Somewhere in the recesses of my mind," Fant writes of this time, "was a growing awareness that Bill was right, and that what we called 'real Sign Language' was in fact ASL."

But it was only in 1970, when Fant met Klima and Bellugi, who asked him innumerable questions about "his" language, that the change occurred:

> As the conversation proceeded, my attitude underwent a complete conversion. In her warm, winning way, she [Bellugi] made me realize how little I really knew about Sign Language, even though I had known it from childhood. Her praise for Bill Stokoe and his work made me wonder if I was missing something.

And then, finally, a few weeks later:

> I became a convert. I ceased to resist the idea that ASL was a language, and submerged myself in studying it so that I could teach it as a language.

And yet—despite talk of "conversion"—deaf people have always known, intuitively, that Sign was a language. But perhaps it required a scientific confirmation before this knowledge could become conscious and explicit, and form the basis of a bold and new consciousness of their own language.

Artists (Pound reminds us) are the antennae of the race. And it was artists who first felt in themselves, and announced, the dawn of this new consciousness. Thus the first movement to stem from Stokoe's work was not educational, not political, not social, but artistic. The National Theater of the Deaf (NTD) was founded in 1967, just two years after the publication of the *Dictionary*. But it was only in 1973, six years later, that the NTD commissioned, and performed, a play in true Sign; up to that point, their productions had merely been transliterations, in signed English, of English plays. (Although during the 1950s and 1960s, George Detmold, dean of Gallaudet College, produced a number of plays in which he urged the actors to move away from signed English and perform in ASL.)[21] Once the resistance had been broken, and the new consciousness established, there was no stopping deaf artists of all sorts. There arose Sign poetry, Sign wit, Sign song, Sign dance—unique Sign arts that could not be translated into speech. A bardic tradition arose, or re-arose, among the deaf, with Sign bards, Sign orators, Sign storytellers, Sign narrators, who served to transmit and disseminate the history and culture of the deaf, and, in so doing, raise the new cultural consciousness yet higher. The NTD traveled, and still travels, all over the world, not only introducing deaf art and culture to the hearing but reaffirming the deaf's feeling of having a world community and culture.

Though art is art, and culture is culture, they may have an implicitly (if not an explicitly) political and educational function. Fant himself became a protagonist and teacher; his 1972 book *Ameslan: An Introduction to American Sign Language* was the first Sign primer on explicitly Stokoean lines; it was a force in assisting the return of signed language to education. In the early 1970s the exclusive oralism of ninety-six years began to be reversed, and "total communication" (the use of both signed and spoken language) was introduced (or reintroduced, as it had been common enough, in many countries, a hundred and fifty years before).[22] This was not accomplished without great resistance. Schlesinger tells us that when she advocated the reintroduction of signed languages in education, she received warnings and threatening letters, and that when her book *Sound and Sign* appeared in 1972, it caused controversy and tended to be "wrapped in a plain brown wrapper as if unacceptable." And even now the conflict still rages unresolved, and though signed language is now used in schools, *it is virtually always signed English and not Sign that is used.* Stokoe had said from the first that the deaf should be bilingual (and bicultural), should acquire the language of the dominant culture, but also and equally their own language, Sign.[23] But since Sign is still not used in schools, or in any institutions (except religious ones), it is still largely restricted, as seventy years ago, to a colloquial and demotic use. This is even the case at Gallaudet itself—indeed, it has been the university's official policy since 1982 that all signing and interpretation in class be conducted in signed English—and this constituted an important contributing reason for the revolt.

The personal and the political are always combined, and here both are combined with the linguistic too. Barbara Kannapell brings this out when she traces the influence of Stokoe, of the new consciousness, on herself and how she became aware of herself as a deaf person with a special linguistic identity—"my language is me"—and moved from this to seeing Sign as central to the communal identity of the deaf ("To reject ASL is to reject the deaf person . . . [for] ASL is a personal creation of deaf persons as a group . . . it is the only thing we have that belongs to deaf people completely"). Moved by these personal and social considerations, Kannapell founded Deaf Pride, an organization dedicated to deaf consciousness-raising, in 1972.

Deaf depreciation, deaf deference, deaf passivity, and even deaf shame were all too common before the early 1970s; one sees this, very clearly, in the 1970 novel by Joanne Greenberg, *In This Sign*—and it took Stokoe's dictionary, and the legitimation of Sign by linguists, to allow the beginnings of a movement in the opposite direction, a movement toward deaf identity and deaf pride.

This was essential, but, of course, not the only factor in the deaf movement since 1960: there were many other factors of equal force, and all flowed together to produce the revolution of 1988. There was the mood of the sixties, with its special feeling for the poor, the disabled, the minorities—the civil rights movement, the political activism, the varied "pride" and "liberation" movements; all this was afoot at the same time that Sign was slowly, and against much resistance, being legitimated scientifically, and while the deaf were slowly collecting a sense of self-esteem and hope, and fighting against the negative images and feelings that had dogged them for a century. There was an increasing tolerance, generally, for cultural diversity, an increasing sense that peoples could be profoundly different, yet all be valuable and equal to one another; an increasing sense, specifically, that the deaf *were* a "people," and not merely a number of isolated, abnormal, disabled individuals; a movement from the medical or pathological view to an anthropological, sociological, or ethnic view.[24]

Going along with this depathologizing was an increase in portrayals of deaf people in every medium, from documentaries to plays and novels—a portrayal increasingly sympathetic and imaginative. Changing social attitudes, and changing self-image, were both reflected in, and affected by, these: the image ceased to be that of the diffident and pathetic Mr. Singer in *The Heart Is a Lonely Hunter* and became the audacious heroine of

Children of a Lesser God; Sign was introduced on television, in such programs as "Sesame Street," and started to become a popular elective at
some schools. The entire country became more aware of the previously invisible and inaudible deaf; and they too became more aware of themselves,
of their increasing visibility and power in society. Deaf people, and those
who studied them, started to look back into the past — to discover (or create) a deaf history, a deaf mythology, a deaf heritage.[25]

Thus, within twenty years of Stokoe's paper, new awareness, new motives, new forces, of all sorts were combining — a new movement
was afoot, a confrontation was in the making. The 1970s saw the rise
not only of Deaf Pride but of Deaf Power. Leaders arose among the previously passive deaf. A new vocabulary arose, with such words as "self-
determination" and "paternalism" in it. The deaf, who had previously
accepted characterizations of themselves as "disabled" and "dependent" —
for this is how they had been regarded by the hearing — now started to
think of themselves as powerful, as an autonomous community.[26] Sooner
or later, it was clear, there would have to be a revolt, a striking political assertion of self-determination and independence, and a once-and-for-all repudiation of paternalism.

The accusation that the Gallaudet authorities were "deaf in the mind"
implies no malevolence, but rather a misdirected paternalism, which, deaf
people feel, is anything but benign — based as it is on pity and condescen-
sion, and on an implicit view of them as "incompetent," if not diseased.
Special objection has been made to some of the doctors involved in Gallaudet's affairs, who, it is felt, tend to see the deaf merely as having diseased ears and not as whole people adapted to another sensory mode. In
general, it is felt this offensive benevolence hinges on a value judgment by
the hearing, their saying: "We know what is best for you. Let *us* handle
things," whether this is in response to the choice of language (allowing, or
not allowing, Sign), or in judging capacities for education or jobs. It is still
sometimes felt, or again felt — after the more spacious opportunities offered in the mid-nineteenth century — that deaf people should be printers,
or work in the post office, do "humble" jobs and not aspire to higher education. The deaf, in other words, felt they were being dictated to, that they
were being treated as children. Bob Johnson told me a typical story:

> It's been my impression, after having been here for several years, that the
> Gallaudet faculty and staff treat students as pets. One student, for ex-
> ample, went to the Outreach office; they had announced there would be
> an opportunity to practice interviewing for jobs. The idea was to sign up
> for a genuine interview and learn how to do it. So he went and put his
> name on a list. The next day a woman from the Outreach office called
> and told him she had set up the interview, had found an interpreter, had
> set up the time, had arranged for a car to take him . . . and she couldn't
> understand why he got mad at her. He told her, "The reason I was doing
> this was so that I could learn how to call the person, and learn how to get

the car, and learn how to get the interpreter, and you're doing it for me. That's not what I want here." That's the meat of the issue.

Far from being childlike or incompetent, as they were "supposed" to be (and so often they supposed themselves to be), the students at Gallaudet showed high competence in managing the March revolt. This impressed me especially when I wandered into the communications room, the nerve-center of Gallaudet during the strike, with its central office filled with TTY-equipped telephones.[27] Here the deaf students contacted the press and television—invited them in, gave interviews, compiled news, issued press releases, round the clock—masterfully; here they raised funds for a "Deaf Prez Now" campaign; here they solicited, successfully, support from Congress, presidential candidates, unions leaders. They gained the world's ear, at this extraordinary time, when they needed it.

Even the administration listened—so that after four days of seeing the students as foolish and rebellious children who needed to be brought into line, Dr. Zinser was forced to pause, to listen, to reexamine her own long-held assumptions, to see things in a new light—and, finally, to resign. She did so in terms that were moving and seemed genuine, saying that neither she nor the board had anticipated the fervor and commitment of the pro-testers, or that their protest was the leading edge of a burgeoning national movement for deaf rights. "I have responded to this extraordinary social movement of deaf people," she said as she tendered her resignation on the night of March 10 and spoke of coming to see this as "a very special moment in time," one that was "unique, a civil rights moment in history for deaf people."

Friday, March 11: The mood on campus is completely transformed. A battle has been won. There is elation. More battles have to be fought. Placards with the students' four demands have been replaced with placards saying, "3½," because the resignation of Dr. Zinser only goes halfway toward meeting the first demand, that there be a deaf president immediately. But there is also a gentleness that is new, the tension and anger of Thursday have gone, along with the possibility of a drawn-out, humiliating defeat. A largeness of spirit is everywhere apparent—released now, I partly feel, by the grace and the words with which Zinser resigned, words in which she aligned herself with, and wished the best for, what she called an "extraordinary social movement."

Support is coming in from every quarter: three hundred deaf students from the National Technical Institute for the Deaf arrive, elated and exhausted, after a fifteen-hour bus ride from Rochester, New York. Deaf schools throughout the country are closed in total support. Deaf people flood in from every state—I see signs from Iowa and Alabama, from Canada, from South America, as well as from Europe, even from New Zealand. Events at Gallaudet have dominated the national press for forty-eight hours. Virtually every car going past Gallaudet honks now, and the streets are filled with supporters as the time for the march on the Capitol comes near. And yet, for all the honking, the speeches, the banners, the pickets, an extraordinary atmosphere of quietness and dignity prevails.

Noon: There are now about 2,500 people, a thousand students from Gallaudet and the rest supporters, as we start on a slow march to the Capitol. As we walk a wonderful sense of quietness grows, which puzzles me. It is not wholly physical (indeed, there is rather a lot of noise in a way—the ear-splitting yells of the deaf, as a start), and I decide it is, rather, the quietness of a moral drama. The sense of history in the air gives it this strange quietness.

Slowly, for there are children, babes-in-arms, and some physically disabled among us (some deaf-blind, some ataxic, and some on crutches)—slowly, and with a mixed sense of resolve and festivity, we walk to the Capitol, and there, in the clear March sun that has shone the entire week, we unfurl banners and raise pickets. One great banner says WE STILL HAVE A DREAM, and another, with the individual letters carried by fourteen people, simply says: HELP US CONGRESS.

We are packed together, but there is no sense of a crowd, rather of an extraordinary camaraderie. Just before the speeches start, I find myself hugged—I think it must be someone I know, but it is a student bearing a sign ALABAMA, who hugs me, punches my shoulder, smiles, as a comrade. We are strangers, but yet, at this special moment, we are comrades.

There are many speeches—from Greg Hlibok, from some of the faculty, from congressmen and senators. I listen for a while:

> It is an irony [says one, a professor at Gallaudet] that Gallaudet has never had a deaf chief executive officer. Virtually every black college has a black president, testimony that black people are leading themselves. Virtually every women's college has a woman as president, as testimony that women are capable of leading themselves. It's long past time that Gallaudet had a deaf president as testimony that deaf people are leading themselves.

I let my attention wander, taking in the scene as a whole: thousands of people, each intensely individual, but bound and united with a single sentiment. After the speeches, there is a break of an hour, during which a number of people go in to see congressmen. But most of the group, who have brought packed lunches in on their backs, now sit and eat and talk, or rather sign, in the great plaza before the Capitol—and this, for me, as for all those who have come or chanced to see it, is one of the most wonderful scenes of all. For here are a thousand or more people signing freely, in a public place—not privately, at home, or in the enclosure of Gallaudet—but openly and unself-consciously, and beautifully, before the Capitol.

The press has reported all the speeches, but missed what is surely equally significant. They failed to give the watching world an actual vision of the fullness and vividness, the unmedical life, of the deaf. And once more, as I wander among the huge throng of signers, as they chat over sandwiches and sodas before the Capitol, I find myself remembering the words of a deaf student at the California School for the Deaf, who had signed on television:

> We are a unique people, with our own culture, our own language—American Sign Language, which has just recently been recognized as a language in itself—and that sets us apart from hearing people.

I walk back from the Capitol with Bob Johnson. I myself tend to be apolitical and have difficulty even comprehending the vocabulary of politics. Bob, a pioneer Sign linguist, who has taught and researched at Gallaudet for years, says as we walk back:

> It's really remarkable, because in all my experience I've seen deaf people be passive and accept the kind of treatment that hearing people give them. I've seen them willing, or seem to be willing, to be "clients," when in fact they should be controlling things . . . now all at once there's been a transformation in the consciousness of what it means to be a deaf person in the world, to take responsibility for things. The illusion that deaf people are powerless—all at once, now, that illusion has gone, and that means the whole nature of things can change for them now. I'm very optimistic and extremely enthusiastic about what I'm going to see over the next few years.

"I don't quite understand what you mean by 'clients,'" I say.

> You know Tim Rarus [Bob explains]—the one you saw at the barricades this morning, whose signing you so admired as pure and passionate—well, he summed up in two words what this transformation is all about. He said, "It's very simple. No deaf president, no university," and then he shrugged his shoulders, looked at the TV camera, and that was his whole statement. That was the first time deaf people ever realized that a colonial client-industry like this can't exist without the client. It's a billion-dollar industry for hearing people. If deaf people don't participate, the industry is gone.

Saturday has a delightful, holiday air about it—it is a day off (some of the students have been working virtually nonstop from the first demonstration on Sunday evening), and a day for cookouts on the campus. But even here the issues are not forgotten. The very names of the foods have a satirical edge: the choice lies between "Spilman dogs" and "Board burgers." The campus is festive now that students and schoolchildren from a score of other states have come in (a little deaf black girl from Arkansas, seeing all the signers around her, says in Sign, "It's like a family to me today"). There has also been an influx of deaf artists from all over, some coming to document and celebrate this unique event in the history of the deaf.

Greg Hlibok is relaxed, but very vigilant: "We feel that we are in control. We are taking things easy. We don't want to go too far." Two days earlier, Zinser was threatening to "take control." What one sees today is self-control, that quiet consciousness and confidence that comes from an inner strength and certainty.

Sunday evening, March 13: The board met today, for nine hours. There were nine hours of tension, waiting . . . no one knowing what was to come. Then the door opened, and Philip Bravin, one of the four deaf board members and known to all the deaf students, appeared. His appearance— and not Spilman's—already told the story, before he made his revelations in Sign. He was speaking now, he signed, as chairman of the board, for Spilman had resigned. And his first task now, with the board behind him, was the happy one of announcing that King Jordan had been elected the new president.

King Jordan, deafened at the age of twenty-one, has been at Gallaudet for fifteen years; he is dean of the School of Arts and Sciences, a popular, modest, and unusually sane man, who at first supported Zinser when she was selected.[28] Greatly moved, Jordan, in simultaneous Sign and speech, says:

> I am *thrilled* to accept the invitation of the board of trustees to become the president of Gallaudet University. This is a historic moment for deaf people around the world. This week we can truly say that we together, united, have overcome our reluctance to stand for our rights. The world has watched the deaf community come of age. We will no longer accept limits on what we can achieve. The highest praise goes to the students of Gallaudet for showing us exactly even now how one can seize an idea with such force that it becomes a reality.

With this, the dam bursts, and jubilation bursts out everywhere. As everyone returns to Gallaudet for a final, triumphal meeting, Jordan says, "They know now that the cap on what they can achieve has been lifted. We know that deaf people can do anything hearing people can except hear." And Hlibok, hugging Jordan, adds, "We have climbed to the top of the mountain, and we have climbed together."

Monday, March 14: Gallaudet looks normal on the surface. The barricades have been taken down, the campus is open. The "uprising" has lasted exactly one week—from last Sunday evening, March 6th, when Dr. Zinser was forced on an unwilling university, to the happy resolution last night, that utterly different Sunday evening, when all was changed.

"It took seven days to create the world, it took us seven days to change it"—this was the joke of the students, flashed in Sign from one end of the campus to another. And with this feeling they took their spring break, going back to their families throughout the country, carrying the euphoric news and mood with them.

But objective change, historical change, does not happen in a week, even though its first prerequisite, "the transformation of consciousness," may happen, as it did, in a day. "Many of the students," Bob Johnson told me, "don't realize the extent and the time that are going to be involved in changing, though they do have a sense now of their strength and power. . . . The structure of oppression is so deeply engrained."

And yet there are beginnings. There is a new "image" and a new movement, not merely at Gallaudet but throughout the deaf world. News reports, especially on television, have made the deaf articulate and visible across the entire nation. But the profoundest effect, of course, has been on the deaf themselves. It has welded them into a community, a worldwide community, as never before.[29]

There has already been a deep impact, if only symbolic, upon deaf children. One of King Jordan's first acts, when the college reconvened after spring break, was to visit the grade school at Gallaudet and talk to the children there, something no president had ever done before. Such concern has to affect their perception of what they can become. (Deaf children sometimes think they will "turn into" hearing adults, or else be feeble, put-upon creatures if they do not.) Charlotte, in Albany, watched the events at Gallaudet on television with great excitement, donned a "Deaf Power" T-shirt, and practiced a "Deaf Power" salute. And two months after the revolt at Gallaudet I found myself attending the annual graduation at the Lexington School for the Deaf, which has been a stronghold of oral education since the 1860s. Greg Hlibok, an alumnus, had been invited as the guest speaker (signer); Philip Bravin was also invited; and all the commencement speeches, for the first time in one hundred and twenty years, were given in Sign. None of this would have been conceivable without the Gallaudet revolt.

All sorts of changes, administrative, educational, social, psychological, are already beginning at Gallaudet. But what is clearest at this point is the much-altered bearing of its students, a bearing that conveys a new, wholly unself-conscious sense of pleasure and vindication, of confidence and dignity. This new sense of themselves represents a decisive break from the past, which could not have been imagined just a few months ago.

But has all been changed? Will there be a lasting "transformation of consciousness"? Will deaf people at Gallaudet, and the deaf community at large, indeed find the opportunities they seek? Will we, the hearing, allow them these opportunities? Allow them to be themselves, a unique culture in our midst, yet admit them as co-equals, to every sphere of activity? One hopes the events at Gallaudet will be but the beginning.

Notes

1. One can be very close to (if not actually a member of) the deaf community without being deaf. The most important prerequisite besides a knowledge of and sympathy for deaf people is being a fluent user of Sign: perhaps the only hearing people who are ever considered full members of the deaf community are the hearing children of deaf parents for whom Sign is a native language. This is the case with Dr. Henry Klopping, the much-loved superintendent of the California School for the Deaf in Fremont. One of his former students, talking to me at Gallaudet, signed, "He is Deaf, even though he is hearing."

2. Different social conventions arise in the intercourse of signers, dictated in the first place by the differences of eye and ear. For vision is more specific than hearing—one can move one's eyes, one can focus them, one can (literally or metaphorically) shut them, whereas one cannot move or focus or shut one's ears. And signing, so to speak, is lasered in a narrow beam, to and fro, between signers, and does not diffuse in all directions, acoustically, like speaking. Thus one can have a dozen different people signing at a table, in six different conversations, each conversation clear and distinct, none of them necessarily disturbing the others. There is no "noise," no visual noise, in a room full of signers, because of the directionality of visual voices and of visual attention. By the same token (this was very clear at the huge student bar at Gallaudet, and I have seen it at large deaf banquets and conventions) one can easily sign to somebody at the other end of a large, crowded room; whereas yelling would be horrible and offensive.

There are many other (some, to the hearing, rather strange) points of Sign etiquette. One must be very conscious of eye-lines and visual contact; and avoid inadvertently walking between people and interrupting this contact. One is free to tap on shoulders and to point—not done in hearing circles. And if one finds oneself overlooking a room full of signers, with three hundred Sign conversations clearly in view, one makes a point of not "overseeing" or eavesdropping, of only seeing what one is meant to see.

At NTID in Rochester, which was built in 1968 for deaf students, one can see an architectural corollary to this. The moment one enters, one can see that this is a building for visual beings—it is designed so that signing can be seen at great distances, and sometimes between floors. One would not shout from one floor to another, but it is perfectly natural to sign from one to another.

3. The deaf world, like all subcultures, is formed partly by exclusion (from the hearing world), and partly by the formation of a community and a world around a different center—its own center. To the extent that the deaf feel excluded, they may feel isolated, set apart, discriminated against. To the extent that they form a deaf world, voluntarily, for themselves, they are at home in it, enjoy it, see it as a haven and a buffer. In this aspect the deaf world feels self-sufficient, not isolated—it has no wish to assimilate or be assimilated; on the contrary, it cherishes its own language and images, and wishes to protect them.

One aspect of this is the so-called diglossia of the deaf. Thus a group of deaf people, at Gallaudet or elsewhere, converse in Sign among themselves; but if a hearing person should enter, they at once switch to signed English (or whatever) for a time, returning to Sign as soon as he is gone. ASL [American Sign Language] is often treated as an intimate and highly personal possession, to be shielded from intrusive or foreign eyes. Barbara Kannapell has gone so far as to suggest that if we all learned Sign, this would destroy the deaf world:

> ASL has a unifying function, since deaf people are unified by their common language. But the use of ASL simultaneously separates deaf people from the hearing world. So the two functions are different perspectives on the same reality—one from inside the group which is unified, and the other from outside. The group is separated from the hearing world. This separatist function is a protection for deaf people. For example, we can talk about anything we want, right in the middle of a crowd of hearing people. They are not supposed to understand us.
>
> It is important to understand that ASL is the only thing we have that belongs to deaf people completely. It is the only thing that has grown out of the deaf group. Maybe we are afraid to share our language with hearing people. Maybe our group identity will disappear once hearing people know ASL (Kannapell, 1980, p. 112).

4. Even those teachers who sign tend, however, to use a form of signed English rather than ASL. Except in the mathematical faculty, where a majority of the teachers are deaf, only a minority of the faculty now at Gallaudet is deaf—whereas in Edward Gallaudet's day a majority were deaf. This, alas, is still the case generally with regard to the education of the deaf. There are very few deaf teachers of the deaf; and ASL, for the most part, is either not known to, or not used by, hearing teachers.

5. Over and above the general disadvantagedness of the deaf (not through their disability, but through *our* discrimination), there are all sorts of specific problems which arise from their use of a signed language—but these are only problems to the extent that *we* make them so. It is difficult for a deaf person, for example, to get adequate medical or legal care; there are a score of signing attorneys in the United States, but almost no signing physicians at all (and, as yet, very few paramedics or nurses who sign). There are scarcely any adequate emergency facilities for the deaf. If a deaf person becomes seriously ill, it is crucial to immobilize only one arm with IVs; to immobilize both arms may render him unable to talk. Similarly, it is often not realized that to handcuff a deaf signer is equivalent to gagging him.

6. Although the deaf are sometimes supposed to *be* silent, as well as to inhabit a world of silence, this may not be the case. They can, if they wish to, yell very loudly, and may do this to arouse the attention of others. If they speak, they may speak very loudly, and with very poor modulation, since they cannot monitor their own voices by ear. Finally, they may have unconscious and often very energetic vocalizations of various sorts—accidental or inadvertent movements of the vocal apparatus, neither intended nor monitored, tending to accompany emotion, exercise, and excited communication.

7. This resentment of "paternalism" (or "mommyism") is very evident in the special edition of the students' newspaper (*The Buff and Blue*) published on March 9, in which there is a poem entitled "Dear Mom." This starts:

> Poor mommy Bassett-Spilman
> How her children do rebel,
> If only they would listen
> To the story she would tell

and continues in this vein for thirteen verses. (Spilman had appeared on television, pleading for Zinser, saying, "Trust us—she will not disappoint you.") Copies of this poem had been reproduced by the thousands—one could see them fluttering all over campus.

8. Padden and Humphries, 1988, p. 6.

9. Such considerations should be taken into account in relation to the current controversies about "special" schools or "mainstreaming." Mainstreaming—educating deaf children with the nondeaf—has the advantage of introducing the deaf to others, the world-at-large (at least, this is the supposition); but it may also introduce an isolation of its own—and serve to cut the deaf off from their own language and culture. There is much pressure, in the United States, Canada, England, and elsewhere at this time, to shut down residential and other special schools for the deaf. Sometimes this is done under the aegis of civil rights for the handicapped, giving them the right to "equal access" or to the "least restrictive" educational environment. But the deaf—at least the profoundly and prelingually deaf, whose native and communal language is Sign—are in a very special, indeed unique, category. They cannot be compared with any other group of pupils. The deaf do not regard themselves as handicapped, but as a linguistic and cultural minority, who have the need, and indeed the right, to be together, to go to school together, to learn in a language which is accessible to them, and to live in the company and community of others of their kind.

Legislation for the handicapped, with its emphasis on equal access, takes no note of these special needs and requirements; even worse, it threatens the dissolution of a unique educational system which has also been fundamental in providing linguistic and cultural continuity for the deaf. Very recently (1989) the state of Connecticut threatened to close the American School for the Deaf, the Hartford Asylum which was founded by Clerc and Gallaudet in 1817, which was not only the founder, but has been the guardian of deaf education in the United States for 173 years. Fortunately what would have been a rash and irrevocable move was postponed at the very last moment—but similar actions continue to threaten residential schools across the country.

The deaf student population, of course, is not homogeneous: it includes many postlingually deaf pupils, who are not native signers, and who do not identify themselves with the deaf community or with Sign; pupils such as these may indeed prefer to be mainstreamed. But there will always be prelingually deaf students whose early education and enculturation will be best accomplished in residential schools, and who must have at least the option of going to such schools, and not be mainstreamed by force. But such schools, founded in the eighteenth and nineteenth centuries, may have an anachronistic, Dickensian atmosphere. They need to be preserved, one feels—but modified, made more open, made less Victorian. Thus, the old via Nomentana school in Rome, modified, is now enjoying a new lease of life, not only as a school, but as a club, an arts and theater center, and a research center for the deaf—and one to which, now, some hearing pupils and their parents also come (Pinna et al., 1990).

10. There is nothing quite equivalent, in the hearing world, to the crucial role of residential deaf schools, deaf clubs, etc.; for these, above all, are places where deaf people find a home. Deaf youngsters, sadly, may feel deeply isolated, even estranged, in their own families, in hearing schools, in the hearing world; but they can find a new family, a profound sense of homecoming, when they meet other deaf people. Schein (1984) cites these words from a young deaf man:

> My sister told me about the Maryland School for the Deaf. . . . My immediate reaction was one of anger and rejection—of myself. I reluctantly accompanied her to the School one day—and at long last began to come *home*. It was literally a love experience. For the first time, I felt less like a *stranger* in a strange land and more like a member of a community.

And Kyle and Woll (1985) cite a contemporary account of Clerc's visit to a deaf school in London in 1814:

> As soon as Clerc beheld this sight [the children at dinner] his face became animated: he was as agitated as a traveller of sensibility would be on meeting all of a sudden in distant regions, a colony of his countrymen. . . . Clerc approached them. He made signs and they answered him by signs. This unexpected communication caused a most delicious sensation in them and for us was a scene of expression and sensibility that gave us the most heartfelt satisfaction.

11. There was soon a division of the ways, with blind pupils being educated separately from the "deaf and dumb" (as the congenitally deaf, with little or no speech, used to be called). Among the two thousand deaf students at Gallaudet now, there are about twenty students who are both deaf and blind (most with Usher's syndrome [a genetic disorder that typically involves profound deafness at birth and a progressive loss of vision—Eds.]). These students, of course, must develop astonishing tactile sensibility and intelligence, as Helen Keller did.

12. See Gallaudet, 1983.

13. The protagonists in this struggle, Bell and Gallaudet—both the sons of deaf mothers (but mothers with completely different attitudes to their own deafness), each passionately devoted to the deaf in his own way, were about as different as two human beings can be (see Winefield, 1987).

14. There has been one realm where sign language always continued to be used, all over the world, despite the changed habits and proscriptions of educators—in religious services for the deaf. Priests and others never forgot the souls of their deaf parishioners, learned Sign (often from them), and conducted services in Sign, right through the endless wrangles over oralism and the eclipse of Sign in secular education. De l'Epée's* concern was religious in the first instance, and this concern, with its prompt perception of the "natural language" of the deaf,

---

De l'Epée: Charles-Michel abbé de l'Epée (1713–1789) was an eighteenth-century French priest who developed a system for spelling French words with a manual alphabet. His system also included simple signs for whole concepts and was the basis of the French Sign Language (FSL) and the precursor to the American Sign Language (ASL). He opened the first school for the deaf in Paris in 1754. Thomas Gallaudet introduced the system into America in 1816.

has remained steadfast despite secular vicissitudes for two hundred years. This religious use of Sign is discussed by Jerome Schein:

> That sign has a spiritual aspect should not surprise anyone, especially if one considers its use by silent religious orders and by priests in the education of deaf children. What must be seen to be fully appreciated, however, is its singular appropriateness for religious worship. The depth of expression that can be achieved by signing defies accurate description. The Academy Award won by Jane Wyman in 1948 for her portrayal of a deaf girl in *Johnny Belinda* undoubtedly owed much to her beautiful (and accurate) rendering of the Lord's Prayer in Ameslan [American Sign Language — Eds.].
>
> It is perhaps in the church service that the beauty of sign becomes most evident. Some churches have sign choirs. Watching the robed members sign in unison can be an awe-inspiring experience (Schein, 1984, pp. 144–145).

In October of 1989 I visited a deaf synagogue in Arleta, in Southern California, for the solemn Day of Atonement (Yom Kippur) services. More than 200 people had gathered there, some coming from hundreds of miles away. A few people spoke, but the entire service was in Sign; the rabbi, the choir, and the congregants all signed. At the reading of the Law — the Hebrew Torah is written on a scroll, and portions of this are read by different congregants — this "reading aloud" took the form of signing, a fluent translation of biblical Hebrew into Sign. Some extra, special prayers had been added to the service. At one point, where there is a communal atonement, of the form "We have done this, we have done that; we have sinned through doing this, we have sinned through doing that . . ." an extra "sin" was added: "We have sinned through being impatient with the hearing when they failed to understand us." And an extra prayer of thanksgiving was thrown in: "Thou hast given us hands, that we might create language."

The Sign choir was especially astonishing; I had never before seen such large sweeping signs, or signs in unison — nor had I seen signing not in the usual sign-space used for human, social discourse, but high up, above the shoulders, towards Heaven, to God. (There was an atmosphere of great devotion, although, just in front of me, there was a middle-aged woman gossiping on the hands with her daughter, nonstop, a Sign yenta who reminded me of the murmuring and nattering of synagogues at home.)

The congregants gathered long before the service, and stayed till long after — it was an important social and cultural, as well as religious, event. Such congregations are exceedingly rare, and I could not help wondering how it would be for a deaf child to be brought up in Montana or Wyoming, without a deaf church or deaf synagogue in thousands of miles.

15. This happened not only in the United States, but throughout the world — even de l'Epée's school, when I visited it in 1990, had become rigidly "oral" (de l'Epée, I felt, was surely turning in his grave).

16. I regret that I have not had a chance to discuss this with Carol Padden and Tom Humphries, who being themselves both deaf and scientists, are in a position to see these events both from the inside and the outside; they have provided, in their chapter on "A Changing Consciousness" in *Deaf in America,* the most insightful short account of changing attitudes to the deaf, and among the deaf, in the past thirty years.

17. Padden, 1980, p. 90.

18. Stokoe, 1980, pp. 266–267.

19. But Klima and Bellugi relate how, at a 1965 conference, when Chomsky spoke of language as "a specific sound-meaning correspondence," he was asked how he would consider the sign languages of the deaf (in terms of this characterization). He showed an open mind, said that he did not see why the sound part should be crucial, and rephrased his definition of language as a "signal-meaning correspondence" (Klima and Bellugi, 1979, p. 35).

20. Fant, 1980.

21. ASL lends itself extremely well to artistic use and transformation—far more so than any form of manually coded or signed English—partly because it is an original language, and therefore a language for original creation, for thought; and partly because its iconic and spatial nature especially allows comic, dramatic, and aesthetic accentuation (the last section of Klima and Bellugi's book is especially devoted to "The Heightened Use of Language" in Sign). In ordinary discourse, however, few deaf people speak in pure ASL—most will bring in and incorporate expressions, signs, neologisms from signed English, as suits the needs of communication. Even though, in linguistic and neurological terms, ASL and signed English are wholly distinct, there is for practical purposes a continuum, from forms of signed English at one extreme, through various forms of "pidgin" signed English (PSE), to pure or "deep" ASL at the other.

22. Teachers and others are now being encouraged to speak and sign simultaneously; this method ("Sim Com"), it is hoped, can secure the advantages of both—in practice, though, it fails to do this. Speaking itself tends to be slowed down artificially, in order to allow the signs to be made, but even so, the signing suffers, tends to be poorly performed, and may in fact omit crucial signs—so much so that those for whom it is designed, the deaf, may find it unintelligible. It should be added that it is scarcely possible to sign ASL and speak simultaneously, because the languages are totally different: it is hardly more possible than speaking English and writing Chinese at the same time—indeed, it may be neurologically impossible.

23. But there has not yet been in the United States any official attempt to provide deaf children with a bilingual education—there have only been small pilot experiments (like that reported by Michael Strong in Strong, 1988). And yet, in contrast, as Robert Johnson observes, there has been a widespread and successful use of bilingual education in Venezuela, where this is a national policy and increasing numbers of deaf adults are being recruited as aides and teachers (Johnson, personal communication). Venezuelan schools have daycare centers where deaf children and infants are sent as early as they are diagnosed, to be exposed to deaf signing adults until they are old enough to go to nursery and grade schools, where they are instructed bilingually. A similar system has been set up in Uruguay. Both of these South American programs have already achieved notable success and hold out great promise for the future—they are, unfortunately, as yet virtually unknown to American and European educators (but see Johnson, Liddell, and Erting, 1989). The only other countries with bilingual programs for the deaf are Sweden and Denmark—where the native sign languages are officially recognized as "mother tongues" of the deaf. All of these show very clearly that one can learn to read perfectly well without speaking and that "total communication" is not a necessary intermediate between oral education and bilingual education.

24. The sociolinguist James Woodward is especially concerned with this (see Woodward, 1982). This increasing sense of cultural diversity, rather than a single fixed "norm," with "deviance" to either side, goes back to a generous tradition of a century or more earlier; in particular to the viewpoint of Laurent Clerc (and this is another, even more fundamental reason why the students invoked his name, and felt that *his* was the spirit that guided the revolt).

Clerc's teachings, until his death, had the effect of widening the nineteenth-century view of "human nature," of introducing a relativistic and egalitarian sense of great natural range, not just a dichotomy of "normal" and "abnormal." We speak of our nineteenth-century forebears as rigid, moralistic, repressive, censorious, but the tone of Clerc's voice, and of those who listened to him, conveyed quite the opposite impression: that this was an age very hospitable to "the natural"—to the whole variety and range of natural proclivities—and not disposed (or at least less disposed than our own) to make moralizing or clinical judgments on what was "normal" and what was "abnormal."

This sense of the range of nature is apparent again and again in Clerc's brief *Autobiography* (which is excerpted in Lane, 1984a). "Every creature, every work of God, is admirably made. What we find fault in its kind turns to our advantage without our knowing it." Or, again, "We can only thank God for the rich diversity of his creation, and hope that in the future world the reason for it will be explained."

Clerc's concept of "God," "creation," "nature"—humble, appreciative, mild, unresentful—is perhaps rooted in his sense of himself, and other deaf people, as different but nonetheless complete beings. It is in great contrast to the half-terrible, half-Promethean fury of Alexander Graham Bell, who constantly sees deafness as a swindle and a privation and a tragedy, and is constantly concerned with "normalizing" the deaf, "correcting" God's blunders, and, in general, "improving on" nature. Clerc argues for cultural richness, tolerance, diversity. Bell argues for technology, for genetic engineering, hearing aids, telephones. The two types are wholly opposite but both, clearly, have their parts to play in the world.

25. A massive, illustrated *Deaf Heritage: A Narrative History of Deaf America* by Jack R. Gannon was published in 1981. Harlan Lane's books, from 1976 onwards, not only presented the history of the deaf in stirring, dramatic terms, but were themselves "political" events, serving to give the deaf an intense (perhaps partly mythical) sense of their own past and an urge to regain the best of the past in the future. Thus they not only recorded history, they helped to make it as well (just as Lane himself was not just a recorder, but an active participant, in the 1988 revolt).

26. So, at least, the matter seemed to outside observers—the deaf revolting against the label of "disabled." Those within the deaf community were inclined to put it differently, to assert that they had never seen themselves as disabled. Padden and Humphries are emphatic on this point:

> "Disabled" is a label that historically has not belonged to Deaf people. It suggests political self-representations and goals unfamiliar to the group. When Deaf people discuss their deafness, they use terms deeply related to their language, their past, and their community. Their enduring concerns have been the preservation of their language, policies for educating deaf children, and maintenance of their social and political organizations. The modern language of "access" and "civil rights," as unfamiliar as it is to Deaf people, has been used by Deaf leaders because the public understands these concerns more readily than ones specific to the Deaf community (Padden and Humphries, 1988, p. 44).

27. It should not be thought that even the most avid signer is against other modes of communication when necessary. Life for deaf people has been altered immensely by various technical devices in the past twenty years, such as closed captioned TV, and teletypewriters (TTY; now TDD, or telecommunication devices for the deaf)—devices that would have delighted Alexander Graham Bell (who had originally invented the telephone, partly, as an aid for the deaf). The 1988 strike at Gallaudet could hardly have got going without such devices, which the students exploited brilliantly.

And yet TTYs have a negative side, too. Before they were widely available, fifteen years ago, deaf people went to great lengths to meet each other—they would constantly visit each other's homes, and would go regularly to their local deaf club. These were the only chances to talk with other deaf people; this constant visiting or meeting at clubs formed vital links which bound the deaf community into a close physical whole. Now, with TTYs (in Japan, faxes are used), there is much less actual visiting among the deaf; deaf clubs are starting to be deserted and empty; and a new, worrying tenuity has set in. It may be that TTYs (and closed captions or signed programs on television) give deaf people the sense of being together in an electronic village—but an electronic village is not like a real one, and the downfall of visiting and going to clubs is not readily reversed.

28. Although the choice of King Jordan delighted almost everyone, one faction saw his election as a compromise (since he was postlingually deaf), and supported instead Harvey Corson, superintendent of the Louisiana School for the Deaf, and the third finalist, who is both prelingually deaf and a native signer.

29. Though the level of political and public awareness in Europe may not yet match that in the United States, there are other ways in which the European deaf communities are more advanced. European signers are far more experienced, and far more skilled, than their American

counterparts in establishing communication with deaf people from other countries—and this is the case not only between individuals, but at meetings where people with a dozen different sign languages may come together. There is an artificial, invented system of gestures and signs called Gestuno, on the analogy of Ido or Esperanto; but the real mode of communication is increasingly the so-called International Sign Language, which draws upon the vocabularies and patterns of everyone present, and is, so to speak, continually improvised and enriched between them. ISL has been evolving, becoming richer, more formalized, more language-like for three decades—although it is still, in essence, a contact language, a *lingua franca*. It should be stressed that such "interlingual" communication between the deaf, which can develop with remarkable rapidity and sophistication—far beyond anything which can occur with speakers of different tongues—is rather mysterious, and is a subject of intense investigation at this time.

Not only do European deaf people tend to travel a great deal—for they can overcome language barriers much more easily than the hearing do—they often marry deaf people from other countries, and thus much interlingual migration takes place. It would be improbable and difficult for a Welshman, say, to settle in Finland, or vice versa; but such migrations (at least within Europe) are not all that uncommon among deaf people. For the deaf community is a supranational one, not unlike the world community of Jews, or other ethnic and cultural groups. We may, in fact, be seeing the beginnings of a pan-European deaf community—a community which may well spread beyond Europe, because the deaf community spans the entire world.

This, indeed, became very evident at a remarkable international festival and conference of deaf people, the Deaf Way, held in July 1989 in Washington, D.C. This was attended by more than 5,000 deaf people, coming from more than eighty countries across the world. As one entered the vast lobby of the conference hotel, one could see dozens of different sign languages being used; yet, by the end of a week, communication among different nationalities was relatively easy—not the Babel which would surely have resulted with dozens of spoken languages. There were eighteen national theaters of the deaf—one could, if one wished, see *Hamlet* in Italian Sign, *Oedipus* in Russian Sign, or all sorts of new Sign plays in a dozen and a half different sign languages. An International Deaf Club was formed, and one saw the beginnings, or the emergence, of a global deaf community.

Selected Bibliography

Demographic surveys are usually dull, but Jerome Schein is incapable of being dull. *The Deaf Population of the United States,* by Jerome D. Schein and Marcus T. Delk, Jr., provides a vivid cross-section of the deaf population in the United States fifteen years ago, at a time when major changes were just starting to occur. Also recommended is Jerome D. Schein, *Speaking the Language of Sign: The Art and Science of Signing.*

It is interesting to compare and contrast the situation of the deaf and their Sign in Britain. A fine account is given by J. G. Kyle and B. Woll, in *Sign Language: The Study of Deaf People and Their Language.*

A splendid overview of the deaf community is *Sign Language and the Deaf Community: Essays in Honor of William C. Stokoe,* edited by Charlotte Baker and Robbin Battison. There is not a single essay in this volume that is less than fascinating—and there is also an important and moving looking-back by Stokoe himself.

An extraordinary book—the more so because its authors are deaf, and can speak from within (as well as about) the deaf community: its organization, its aspirations, its images, its beliefs, its arts, its language, etc.—is *Deaf in America: Voices from a Culture* by Carol Padden and Tom Humphries.

Also very accessible for the general reader and full of vivid interviews with members of the deaf community is Arden Neisser's *The Other Side of Silence: Sign Language and the Deaf Community in America.*

A real treasure for browsing (even if the volumes are a little too heavy to read in bed, and a little too costly to read in the bath) is the *Gallaudet Encyclopedia of Deaf People and Deafness,* edited by John Van Cleve. One of the delights of this encyclopedia (as of all the best encyclopedias) is that one can open it anywhere and find illumination and enjoyment.

Works Cited

Chomsky, Noam. 1966. *Cartesian Linguistics: A Chapter in the History of Rationalist Thought.* New York: Harper and Row.

Fant, Louie. 1980. "Drama and Poetry in Sign Language: A Personal Reminiscence." In *Sign Language and the Deaf Community,* ed. C. Baker and R. Battison. Silver Spring, Md.: National Association of the Deaf.

Gallaudet, Edward Miner. 1983. *History of the College for the Deaf, 1857–1907.* Washington, D.C.: Gallaudet College Press.

Johnson, Robert E.; Liddell, Scott K.; and Erting, Carol J. 1989. "Unlocking the Curriculum: Principles for Achieving Access in Deaf Education." Gallaudet Research Institute Working Paper 89–3.

Kannapell, Barbara. 1980. "Personal Awareness and Advocacy in the Deaf Community." In *Sign Language and the Deaf Community,* ed. C. Baker and R. Battison. Silver Spring, Md.: National Association of the Deaf.

Klima, Edward S., and Bellugi, Ursula. 1979. *The Signs of Language.* Cambridge, Mass.: Harvard University Press.

Kyle, J. G., and Woll, B. 1985. *Sign Language: The Study of Deaf People and Their Language.* Cambridge: Cambridge University Press.

Lane, Harlan. 1976. *The Wild Boy of Aveyron.* Cambridge, Mass.: Harvard University Press.

————. 1984a. *When the Mind Hears: A History of the Deaf.* New York: Random House.

————, ed. 1984b. *The Deaf Experience: Classics in Language and Education,* trans. Franklin Philip. Cambridge, Mass., and London: Harvard University Press.

Padden, Carol. 1980. "The Deaf Community and the Culture of Deaf People." In *Sign Language and the Deaf Community,* ed. C. Baker and R. Battison. Silver Spring, Md.: National Association of the Deaf.

Padden, Carol, and Humphries, Tom. 1988. *Deaf in America: Voices from a Culture.* Cambridge, Mass., and London: Harvard University Press.

Schein, Jerome D. 1984. *Speaking the Language of Sign.* Garden City, N.Y.: Doubleday.

Stokoe, William C. 1960. *Sign Language Structure.* Reissued, Silver Spring, Md.: Linstok Press.

————. 1980. Afterword. In *Sign Language and the Deaf Community,* ed. C. Baker and R. Battison. Silver Spring, Md.: National Association of the Deaf.

Strong, Michael. 1988. "A Bilingual Approach to the Education of Young Deaf Children: ASL and English." In *Language Learning and Deafness,* ed. M. Strong. Cambridge and New York: Cambridge University Press.

Winefield, Richard. 1987. *Never the Twain Shall Meet: Bell, Gallaudet, and the Communications Debate.* Washington, D.C.: Gallaudet University Press.

Woodward, James. 1982. *How You Gonna Get to Heaven If You Can't Talk with Jesus: On Depathologizing Deafness.* Silver Spring, Md.: T. J. Publications.

Ideas for Rereading

1. Oliver Sacks is a scientist and clinician, trained in the work of objective observation. At the same time, his writing often reveals a sense of emotional and aesthetic discovery. As you reread his text, mark sections where Sacks uses the language of a clinician and where his emotional and aesthetic senses are more evident. Take special note of any convergence between these two writing personas. What is the effect of combining these two kinds of discussion? What does Sacks achieve in doing so?

2. Reread, on its own, the middle section of Sacks's essay, detailing the history of deaf education and the suppression and reemergence of American Sign Language. As you read, record your reaction to this history. What, if anything, surprises you? Where do you see parallels to the histories and struggles of other cultural groups?

Ideas for Writing

1. In the central portion of this essay, describing the history of deaf education in the United States, Sacks writes of the "unique pattern of transmission of deaf culture" (p. 241). Consider that pattern, as elaborated by Sacks, in terms of the transmission of other kinds of culture—for instance, national or ethnic cultures such as the Irish or African Americans. How are other types of culture passed on? In what ways is the transmission of deaf culture really "unique"? Write an essay illustrating your findings. You may wish to refer to sociological or anthropological texts, or use your own observations.

2. Reread the Helen Keller selections with the aim of forming your own perspective on Keller's character and opinions. Then consider Sacks's characterization of the student protests at Gallaudet. Write an essay imagining these protests from Keller's perspective rather than that of Sacks. Take into account how Keller might experience the protests—both in a practical sense, as a deaf and blind woman, and in an emotional sense. What might her opinion of the protests be, and why?

HARLAN LANE

Psychologist Harlan Lane (b. 1936), though not deaf himself, is respected in and out of the deaf community as a leading chronicler and interpreter of deaf culture, as well as an eloquent advocate for deaf people. He earned his Ph.D. in psychology from Harvard University in 1960 and a second doctorate from the University of Paris, Sorbonne, in 1973. He teaches in the Department of Psychology at Northeastern University. Most recent among his numerous publications are A Journey into the Deaf World *(1996) and* The Mask of Benevolence: Disabling the Deaf Community *(1999), from which the following is excerpted.*

Lane is particularly interested in what he calls "the extrapolative error," the tendency for someone who is thoroughly acculturated to one way of living to judge what it might be like to live like someone else by imagining the absence of abilities crucial to his/her own culture. Those who fall into this error fail to see that the deaf are a "linguistic and cultural minority with a rich and unique heritage" because they only think about what is missing and do not understand the different "center" around which deaf culture thrives.

As you read Lane notice how he creates a contrast between the hearing and the deaf: How does his use of questions, quotation marks around words like special, center, and afflicted, and the phrase "But we've got it all wrong" contribute to his argument? Why does Lane tell us about deaf uses of the signs for "A-LITTLE HARD-OF-HEARING" and "VERY HARD-OF-HEARING"? How does his description of the annual convention of the Massachusetts State Association the Deaf change your ways of thinking about deaf culture? As you read the essay take some rough notes about situations in which you or people you know have thought about other people in terms that Lane would define as examples of the "extrapolative error." In these notes develop your own definition of the "extrapolative error."

Representations of Deaf People
The Infirmity and Cultural Models

A Different Center

On June 27, 1990, the United States Food and Drug Administration approved a proposal by the Cochlear Corporation to market a "bionic ear" for surgical insertion in deaf children over the age of two. More properly called a cochlear prosthesis, this device converts sound waves into electrical currents that are delivered to a wire implanted in the child's inner ear. With the headline "New Hope for Deaf Children: Implant Gives Them Hearing and Speech," *American Health* enthused: "Results promise to be even more dramatic for very young children [than they have been for adults]. The implants will actually allow them to speak."[1] The modern miracle of biotechnology, you say, as do the media, and yet the National Association of the Deaf has called the FDA approval "unsound scientifically, procedurally, and ethically."[2] Audiologists and otologists—those who measure hearing and those who treat it medically, experts who "have only the best interests of deaf children at heart"—proclaim a dramatic advance; yet the American deaf community, whose members could not love deaf children more, proclaim a dangerous setback to their interests.

Cochlear implantation is a surgical procedure, lasting about three and a half hours under general anesthesia, and it requires hospitalization for two to four days. A broad crescent-shaped incision is made behind the operated ear, and the skin flap is elevated. A piece of temporalis muscle is removed. A depression is drilled in the skull and reamed to make a seat for the internal electrical coil of the cochlear implant. A section of the mastoid bone is removed to expose the middle ear cavity. Further drilling exposes the membrane of the round window on the inner ear. Observing the procedure under a microscope, the surgeon pierces the membrane. A wire about 25 millimeters long is pushed through the opening. Sometimes the way is blocked by abnormal bone growth in the inner ear; the surgeon will generally drill through this but may have to settle in the end for only partial insertion of the wire. The wire seeks its own path as it moves around and up the coiled inner ear, shaped like a snail and called the cochlea, from the Latin for "snail." The exquisitely detailed microstructure of the inner ear is often ripped apart as the electrode weaves its way, crushing cells and perforating membranes; if there was any residual hearing in the ear, it is almost certainly destroyed. The auditory nerve itself is unlikely to be damaged, however, and the implant stimulates the auditory nerve directly. The internal coil is then sutured into place. Finally, the skin is sewn back over the coil.

Not long after the FDA gave the green light to surgeons to implant the Cochlear Corporation prosthesis in children, the manufacturer announced a promotional meeting in Boston and I attended. Two sets of satisfied parents and their implanted children were flown in for the occasion and seated center stage. "Barry," nine, had become deaf when he was six and a half; "June" was four and a half and born deaf. Both children had been using their implants for about a year, and both attended special programs for deaf children housed in ordinary public schools. Barry could understand much of what his teachers said, but June required a sign language interpreter. Both children spent several hours every day practicing listening and speaking, under their mothers' tutelage or that of therapists.

During the presentation, researchers from the Cochlear Corporation reported on their investigations with several hundred implanted children, and then the members of an implant team spoke in turn: first the surgeon, then an audiologist and a speech therapist, and finally a special educator. While the scholars held forth and the parents beside them listened attentively, I noticed the two children, half-screened from the audience behind their parents' backs, signing furiously to each other across the stage.

Will the typical deaf child, who was born deaf, like June, or who became so early in life, be able to understand ordinary conversation after undergoing the surgery and a lot of training? Probably not. Will he or she be able to speak intelligibly? Probably not. Will he learn English better than he would have without the implant? Probably not, but we do not know. Will he be able to succeed in an ordinary school with hearing children? Probably not. Will he then generally rely on vision rather than hearing? Yes.

Although the implanted deaf child will not move easily in the hearing world, it is unlikely that he will move easily in the deaf community either, unlikely that he will learn American Sign Language (ASL) fluently and make his own the fundamental values of that community. So there is a real danger that he will grow up without any substantive communication, spoken or signed. He may develop problems of personal identity, of emotional adjustment, even of mental health—this has not been studied. You may well ask: If the benefits are so small and the psychological and social risks so great, why did the FDA approve general marketing of the device and why do surgeons implant it?

Why indeed? Why would such heroic medicine be practiced on young deaf children? For this to be justified, the plight of the deaf child must be seen as truly desperate. But surely, you say, the plight of the deaf child *is* desperate. The child is unable to communicate with his mother and father—nine out of ten deaf children have hearing parents. He will receive a "special" education—in fact an especially unsuccessful education that commonly leads to underemployment. He will take a deaf spouse and be shut off from the world of his hearing parents and the mainstream of American society.

Most people who were born deaf or became so early in life, like the child we are discussing, and who grew up deaf as part of the deaf community have a different point of view. They see themselves as fundamentally visual people, with their own visual language, social organization, history, and mores—in short, with their own way of being, their own language and culture. Scholarly research since the 1970s in such fields as linguistics, anthropology, sociology, and history supports them in this claim. Yes, the deaf child faces many obstacles in life, but the lack of communication at home, inferior education in school, discrimination in employment, are obstacles placed in his way by hearing people who, if only they came to know the deaf community, could readily remove them.

In their book on American deaf culture, deaf authors Carol Padden and Tom Humphries say that hearing professionals who work with deaf people have a different "center" than their clients, which they illustrate with this observation: From a hearing point of view, it is better to be hard of hearing than deaf; someone who is "a little hard of hearing" is much less deaf than someone who is "very hard of hearing." Deaf people see things the other way around. When they sign that an acquaintance is A-LITTLE HARD-OF-HEARING,* they mean that the person has some of the ways of hearing people but basically is quite deaf. When they sign that someone is VERY HARD-OF-HEARING, they mean that the person is very much like hearing people, scarcely like deaf people at all. The same opposing points of view of the hearing benefactor and the deaf beneficiary are revealed in this observation: Members of the deaf community commonly condemn a deaf acquaintance who is ORAL—that is, who does not fully acknowledge that he is deaf. They say disparagingly that that person ALWAYS-PLANS actions for every situation, in order to pass acceptably in a hearing world. Hearing experts, however, do not understand why some deaf people condemn others who are oral and trying to pass; they use terms like "afflicted" for the first group, deaf people who do not speak, and applaud the efforts of those who try to.[3]

---

*English glosses for the signs in American Sign Language (ASL) are conventionally written in capital letters. Hyphens connect glosses that are one word in ASL. It is important to note that glosses omit most of the grammar of ASL. They are *not* translations.

Two cultures, two points of view, two different "centers." This book is an exploration of the gulf that separates these two vantage points.

Hearing Representations of Deaf People

What are deaf people like? There are at least three approaches to answering the question. You may, first, reflect on the social identity of deaf people; they belong to a category, and the category has attributes that are part of our popular culture, as a result of the treatment of deaf people in literature and in the media. Second, you may make an extrapolative leap and try to imagine what your world would be like if you were deaf. Most hearing people, if they are led to think about deaf people, soon make this extrapolative leap, for they have little else to guide them; they have not read about deaf language and culture, and extrapolation must stand in for real knowledge. If it happens that you know someone who is deaf, a third way of apprehending deafness is open; it takes on the characteristics of that particular deaf person, as in: "John understands me when I talk to him directly; therefore, deaf people can lip-read."

All of these approaches commonly lead hearing people to the same point of departure in their representations of deaf people: Deafness is a bad thing. In hearing society, deafness is stigmatized.

The sociologist Erving Goffman distinguishes three kinds of stigma: physical, characterological, and tribal.[4] "There is only one complete, unblushing male in America," he explains. "[He is] a young, married, white, urban northern heterosexual Protestant father of college education, fully employed, of good complexion, weight, and height, and a recent record in sports." Any deviation is likely to entail a stigma, and we tend to impute many stigmas when we find a single one. All three categories of stigma are ascribed to deaf people. Physically they are judged defective; this is commonly taken to give rise to undesirable character traits, such as concreteness of thought and impulsive behavior. Hearing people may also view deaf people as clannish—even, indeed, an undesirable world apart, social deviants like those Goffman lists: prostitutes, drug addicts, delinquents, criminals, jazz musicians, bohemians, gypsies, carnival workers, hoboes, winos, show people, full-time gamblers, beach dwellers, gays, and the urban unrepentant poor. But even if the American deaf community were known for what it is, a linguistic and cultural minority with a rich and unique heritage, it would still be subject to a tribal stigma, as is, for example, the Hispanic-American community.

Stigma is relational. In the deaf community, to be called ORAL, we have seen, is unacceptable. ORAL means you have made the wrong life choices, you have uncritically embraced alien values that place a premium on speech. Hearing people fail to see what is wrong with deaf people's being ORAL; articulateness is prized in American society; gesturing is not.[5]

In the hearing stereotype, deafness is the lack of something, not the presence of anything. Silence is emptiness. The deaf community, say

Padden and Humphries, recognizes that "silent" "is part of a way of viewing deaf people that is pervasive in hearing society; they accept it and use it as an easy way for others to recognize them." Thus the magazine published by the National Association of the Deaf (NAD) was long called *The Silent Worker*. But for hearing people, "silent" represents the dark side of deaf people. They must not have the orientation and security in their environment that we have; of course, they can't appreciate music, we tell ourselves; nor can they engage in conversation, hear announcements, use the telephone. The deaf person moves about, it seems to us, encapsulated; there's a barrier between us. Hence the deaf person is isolated. Ivan Turgenev's character Gerasim, for example, was "shut off by his affliction from the society of men," as was Carson McCullers's deaf protagonist in *The Heart Is a Lonely Hunter*.[6]

In the parlance of hearing people, ordinary deaf people can't really communicate; for them to attempt it is to engage in a *dialogue des sourds*—a deaf dialogue, meaning mutual incomprehension. Hearing people are called deaf, by metaphorical extension, when they refuse to listen, especially to moral advice. If great flourishes in English are associated with a refined mind, simple, awkward speech and gesticulation are associated with a simple mind. Because language and intellect are so linked in our representations of people (we are surprised to hear a towering intellect expressed—unless by deliberate intent—in a Southern drawl or in ungrammatical sentences), deafness seems a defect of intellect. The "dumb" or "deaf and dumb" appears to refer not only to muteness but to weakness of mind. Joanne Greenberg's deaf couple in *In This Sign*[7] are ignorant even about childbearing. Paradoxically, in a reaction formation, deafness may also seem ennobling: the very simplicity of mind, the childlikeness, bespeaks a pure soul, one free of the artifices of civilization. Dickens's Sophy seems to have descended from heaven; Maupassant's Gargan is speechless, an ignorant shepherd, but strong, upright, pure in his misery.[8]

In fact, we imagine two kinds of deafness. The more usual kind is linked in our minds with blue-collar jobs or even poverty. Eudora Welty's deaf couple in "The Key" are poor, naive, "afflicted," and childlike. A deaf person may sell cards inscribed with the finger alphabet; or work in the manual trades, say as a printer. But then there is the exceptional deaf person who can speak and lip-read—who is just like you and me, except for some slight difference. (What a relief!) This person does not sell cards or labor with his hands; he is not poor or even middle-class in our imagination, but distinguished, elegant. Henry Kisor, book editor at the Chicago *Sun-Times*, confirmed this comfortable image of the deaf person in his 1990 autobiography, *What's That Pig Outdoors*.[9] (The title was chosen to illustrate the perils of lip-reading.)

Our society is sufficiently rich and enlightened that we are prepared to sympathize with marginal people who endorse our norms but, for reasons beyond their control, cannot live up to them. The deaf actress Marlee Matlin won the admiration of many hearing people when she chose to speak aloud on national television, rather than through an interpreter, on receiving the Oscar for her role as a culturally deaf person in the film *Children of a Lesser God*. By the same act she incurred criticism from some members of the American deaf community. For them, in those few halting words she negated the principles of the story she had so brilliantly enacted; she chose symbolically not to accept the award as a member of the deaf community; and she seemed to endorse the view that any amount of English is better for deaf people than the most eloquent American Sign Language.

Late-deafened people who make an effort to speak English and lip-read, to overcome the hurdles of their handicap, are much less discomfiting to hearing people than the members of the deaf community, with their distinctly different ways and language. What is unforgivable is that members of the deaf community insist they are fine—for example, two-thirds of deaf adults interviewed in a 1988 survey thought their social life was better than hearing people's[10]—when in fact we can give them a thousand reasons why they can't be. Goffman points out that the stigmatized are expected to keep a bargain: "they should not test the limits of the acceptance shown them, nor make it the basis for still further demands."[11] Thus, the person who is disabled (in our eyes) is expected to *be* disabled; to accept his role as such as to conform, *grosso modo,* to our representation of him. In return we will class him not among the bad (prostitutes, drug addicts, delinquents) but among the sick. The sick and the infirm have a claim on our tolerance and, even more, on our "reasonable accommodation," our compassion, our help.

But we've got it all wrong. Come with me to the annual convention of the Massachusetts State Association of the Deaf, for example. Friends, frequently former schoolmates, embrace at the joy of seeing each other after long separation. There's a lot of catching up to do, and throughout the hotel there are groups of deaf people conversing intently in ASL. At the same time, there are workshops in various meeting rooms to explore issues of common concern, such as the political, social, and athletic program for the year; the governance of the association; outreach to hearing parents; wise personal investing; new technology of interest to deaf people; and deaf awareness—including the roles of various deaf organizations in community service like teaching ASL or counseling unemployed deaf people. At dinner, there will be a banquet speaker—the last time I attended, it was the deaf president of Gallaudet University, the world's premier institution of higher learning in the liberal arts for deaf students. Speakers commonly urge on the audience some course of organized social action—protests at the statehouse in behalf of funding for interpreters; activism in the schools in favor of ASL; letters to the networks to promote captioning—action to enhance the lives of deaf children and adults.

The pageant to choose Miss Deaf Massachusetts has been part of the annual convention in some years. Young women sponsored by various Massachusetts high schools (or high school programs) for deaf students are judged by a committee of deaf community notables for their knowledge of state and national deaf history, for their presentation of their background and career goals, and for the sheer delight of looking at them. The winner becomes a contestant in the national competition held during the convention of the National Association of the Deaf. It has been my pleasure to come to know Miss Deaf New Jersey of some years ago, now a colleague at my university, and Miss Deaf America of 1989, both extraordinarily keen and beautiful young women. When I left the packed auditorium where the 1989 winner was being selected, a deaf student leader hailed me and asked what I thought of the pageant. I told her I liked parts of it but felt a little uneasy at seeing young women displayed like so many pounds of beef on the hoof. "You've a lot to learn about deaf culture," she replied. "I think it's just fine!"

In the course of the state convention there may be events that the deaf clubs in towns and cities across the nation also feature traditionally: a theatrical performance, a raffle, games, a dance, a sporting match. The state convention ends with numerous awards in recognition of service to the deaf community. The master of ceremonies (the last one I recall was B. J. Wood, who directs the state Commission for the Deaf and Hard of Hearing) recounts the many achievements of each recipient, who is given a plaque and asked to say a few words—they're usually about how he (or she) could not have done it (organized a successful tournament, put on a show, conducted a fund-raiser, run the summer camp for deaf children, published the community newspaper) without the help of A, B, and C. The recognition of service and the warm congratulations all around continue for hours, until friends bid each other a reluctant good night.

So the members of the American deaf community are not characteristically isolated, or uncommunicative, or unintelligent, or childlike, or needy, or any of these things we imagine them to be. Why, then, do we think they are? This mistake arises from an extrapolative leap, an egocentric error. To imagine what deafness is like, I imagine my world without sound—a terrifying prospect, and one that conforms quite well with the stereotype we project onto members of the deaf community. I would be isolated, disoriented, uncommunicative, and unreceptive to communication. My ties to other people would be ruptured. I remember my parents censuring me with silence; it was bearable for four hours, and then I implored their forgiveness. I recall the "silent treatment" of offenders in the Army. The Tunisian novelist Albert Memmi, author of several sociological studies of oppression, observes in his book on dependency: "The person who refuses to communicate severs the psychological ties that connect him to the other person. In so doing he isolates the other person and can drive him to despair."[12] A world without sound would be a world without meaning.[13] What could be more fundamental to my sense of myself than my sensory milieu—unless it be my spoken language.

What motivates the extrapolative error in disinterested laymen is existential dread. There but for the grace of God go I. "Contact with someone afflicted with a disease is regarded as a mysterious malevolency," writes critic and author Susan Sontag.[14] Some of my hearing friends say they are uneasy around deaf people for a different reason, because they don't know how to communicate with them; but then I ask them if they give blind people a wide berth and look away from physically handicapped people, and they acknowledge that they do.[15] Each meeting with a person we perceive as handicapped is an invitation to make the extrapolation—and to experience dread. They are deserving of our sympathy because we are deserving of our sympathy. Nineteenth-century authors catered to such sentiments by idealizing their deaf characters. The American poet Lydia Sigourney sang of "the silent ecstasy refined" displayed by a pupil at the first school for deaf children in America, and Alfred de Musset's beautiful deaf Camille "had admirable purity and freshness."[16]

Mothers in one central African nation report that on discovering that their child was deaf, their first thought was to verify that their ancestors had been properly buried.[17] Mothers in many societies consider the cause of their child's deafness to be spirit aggression.[18] We are fragile and dependent beings, they seem to imply, and deafness can be retribution for a moral failing. So, too, American mothers experience inexplicable guilt on discovering that they have a deaf child. There is a persistent belief, Sontag notes, that illness reveals, and is a punishment for, moral laxity. It is somehow reassuring when contracting a disease like AIDS is the result of doing something "wrong"; that hemophiliacs contract it through no act of their own arouses our rage at an immoral universe. It would be better if there were a reason for contracting deafness, something we could do, or refrain from doing, to avoid it. Such a reason might also justify our holding deaf people at arm's length, even justify our treating them badly. But there generally isn't one; so deafness or some other physical handicap may happen to us, as it were, whimsically, and that is dreadful.

The hearing person's extrapolation to what deafness must be like—a world without sound, without facile communication—is not entirely without a counterpart in the real world, for each year thousands of people lose substantial hearing because of illness, trauma, or old age. A few may take steps to enter the deaf community, to learn ASL, make friends in that community, join deaf organizations, attend a deaf club, and so on; most do not.

Growing up deaf, as have most users of ASL, is quite another matter. To evaluate that world of the deaf community, extrapolation from the hearing world is of no use at all. Is it better to be deaf or is it better to be hearing? Anthropologist Richard Shweder asks, "Is it better to have three gods and one wife or one god and three wives?"[19] Of course, the question makes no sense except in relation to a cultural "frame." To know what it is to be a member of the deaf community is to imagine how you would think, feel, and react if you had grown up deaf, if manual language had been your main means of communication, if your eyes were the portals of your mind, if most of your friends were deaf, if you had learned that there were children who couldn't sign only after you had known dozens who could, if the people you admired were deaf, if you had struggled daily for as long as you can remember with the ignorance and uncommunicativeness of hearing people, if . . . if, in a word, you *were* deaf.

The extrapolative error is an error twice over: True representations of the members of another culture cannot be had without a change in frame of reference, which requires, at least, understanding and empathy.[20] It is naive to imagine otherwise, and it is self-defeating. There will be no successful relations between hearing and deaf people, no successful education of deaf children, until the extrapolative error is set aside.

Notes

1. G. Weiss (1990). New hope for deaf children: Implant gives them hearing and speech. *American Health, 9,* 17.

2. National Association of the Deaf, Cochlear Implant Task Force. Cochlear implants in children: A position paper of the National Association of the Deaf. February 2, 1991. Reprint: *The National Association of the Deaf Broadcaster, 13,* March 1991, p. 1.

3. C. Padden and T. Humphries (1988). *Deaf in America: Voices from a Culture.* Cambridge, MA: Harvard University Press. "THINK-HEARING is . . . just as insulting as ORAL but can be used to label any Deaf person, even those who are not ORAL. . . . HEARING is not just a category of people who hear; it is a category of those who are the opposite of what Deaf people are; e.g., students at schools for Deaf children sometimes call their football opponents HEARING even when the team is from another school for Deaf children" T. Humphries (1990). An introduction to the culture of deaf people in the United States: Content notes and reference materials for teachers. *Sign Language Studies, 72,* 209–40, p. 222.

4. E. Goffman (1963). *Stigma: Notes on the Management of Spoiled Identity.* Englewood Cliffs, NJ: Prentice-Hall.

5. C. Padden and T. Humphries (1988). *Deaf in America: Voices from a Culture.* Cambridge, MA: Harvard University Press.

6. C. McCullers (1967). *The Heart Is a Lonely Hunter.* Boston: Houghton Mifflin. Also see I. Turgenev, *Mumu.* Reprinted in T. Batson and E. Bergman (1985). *Angels and Outcasts: An Anthology of Deaf Characters in Literature,* 3rd ed. Washington, DC: Gallaudet University Press, p. 86.

7. J. Greenberg (1970). *In This Sign.* New York: Holt, Rinehart & Winston.

8. Charles Dickens's *Dr. Marigold* and Guy de Maupassant's *The Deaf-Mute* are reprinted in *Angels and Outcasts: An Anthology of Deaf Characters in Literature,* 3rd ed. Washington, DC: Gallaudet University Press.

9. H. Kisor (1990). *What's That Pig Outdoors?* New York: Hill and Wang.

10. J. G. Kyle and G. Pullen (1988). Cultures in contact: Deaf and hearing people. *Disability, Handicap and Society, 3,* 49–61, p. 56.

11. E. Goffman (1963). *Stigma: Notes on the Management of Spoiled Identity.* Englewood Cliffs, NJ: Prentice-Hall, p. 121.

12. A. Memmi (1984). *Dependence.* Boston: Beacon Press, p. 108.

13. C. Padden and T. Humphries (1988). *Deaf in America: Voices from a Culture.* Cambridge, MA: Harvard University Press.

14. S. Sontag (1989). *Illness as Metaphor and AIDS and Its Metaphors.* New York: Anchor.

15. Undergraduates studying education were asked, "How do you feel when you meet someone who is disabled?" The strongest reaction encountered was unease and uncertainty as to

how to behave, and therefore embarrassment. The next most common response was: It is not different from meeting anyone else when you get used to the situation. In third place by frequency came emotions such as pity, guilt, and "thank goodness it's not me." Students were disinclined to share a house with someone disabled, but living next door they found acceptable. From L. Barton, ed. (1988). *The Politics of Special Educational Needs*. Philadelphia: Falmer Press, p. 138.

16. L. H. Sigourney (1866). *Letters of Life*. New York: Appleton, pp. 222–33. Also see A. de Musset, *Pierre et Camille*, reprinted in T. Batson and E. Bergman (1985). *Angels and Outcasts: An Anthology of Deaf Characters in Literature*, 3rd ed. Washington, DC: Gallaudet University Press.

17. A. Naniwe (1991). *L'enfant sourd et la société burundaise*. Ph.D. dissertation, University of Brussels.

18. Cf. G. P. Murdock (1980). *Theories of Illness*. Pittsburgh: University of Pittsburgh Press.

19. R. Shweder (1984). Anthropology's romantic rebellion against the enlightenment. In R. Shweder and R. A. LeVine, eds., *Culture Theory* (pp. 27–66). New York: Cambridge University Press, p. 55.

20. Z. Vendler (1984). Understanding people. In R. Shweder and R. A. LeVine, eds., *Culture Theory* (pp. 200–13). New York: Cambridge University Press, p. 209. Also see C. Geertz (1984). "From the native's point of view." On the nature of anthropological understanding. In R. Shweder and R. A. LeVine, eds., *Culture Theory* (pp. 123–36). New York: Cambridge University Press, p. 135.

Ideas for Rereading

1. Lane argues, "Our society is sufficiently rich . . . that we are prepared to sympathize with marginal people who endorse our norms but, for reasons beyond their control, cannot live up to them" (p. 267). Keeping in mind the examples Lane uses to illustrate his point, outline his subsequent rejection of this kind of "tolerance."

2. Lane suggests that the hearing world's perspective on deaf people—as unfortunate victims of a terrible affliction—is motivated by "existential dread" (p. 269). As you reread this essay, take note of how Lane defines this dread and list examples of how it manifests itself.

3. What is the "extrapolative error" (p. 269)? As you reread the essay, outline Lane's explanation and critique of that error.

Ideas for Writing

1. Although Lane does not mention her, consider how Helen Keller might or might not fit the role of a sympathetic marginalized person, one who endorses but is unable to live up to society's norms. Write an essay analyzing Keller's *The World I Live In* (p. 212) in terms of Lane's depiction of society's marginalization and conditional acceptance of disabled people.

2. After considering Lane's evaluation of the "existential dread" (p. 269) experienced by hearing people when confronted with deaf and other disabled people, begin an examination of your own attitudes. Write an essay in which you explore your own experiences of proximity to and interaction with people

with disabilities. What were your feelings and perceptions? How do you judge yourself in light of Lane's discussion of the subject?

GEORGINA KLEEGE

"We are all blind, when we read," says novelist, essayist, and translator Georgina Kleege. Kleege's point is that reading requires us to blind ourselves to our immediate surroundings so as to move into an imaginative realm, a realm where what we "see" is a matter of words rather than things. In her recent book Sight Unseen *(1999), Kleege, who is legally blind, urges sighted people to "revise their image of blindness." In the following essay, first published in* Southwest Review *in 1998, Kleege critiques the suffering and saintly popular image of Helen Keller, an image Kleege sees as a sometime impediment to herself and other contemporary blind people.*

On one level Kleege's letter gives a glimpse into the everyday routine of a blind university professor. As this narrative unfolds you might notice how many times she lets things go, deflecting her frustration at a world designed for the sighted. While she eventually expresses her "rage" at all the hurdles she has to overcome as a direct result of her blindness, Kleege maintains a lighthearted tone throughout. As you read the letter underline places where she makes light of things that cause inner rage. How does Kleege achieve the effect of lightheartedness? Which specific words and phrases create this effect?

Eventually Kleege castigates Keller as the "first, original disability poster child" and as someone who set an "impossible standard": In what ways does this attack on Keller serve a therapeutic function? As you read the letter make rough notes about why Kleege is angry at Keller. Make a list of the things that Kleege, Keller, and other people referred to in the letter could gripe about—in what ways does griping act as therapy? What does Kleege tell you about Keller that changes your understanding of Keller's life and work?

Blind Rage
An Open Letter to Helen Keller

February 3, 1998

Dear Helen Keller:
I'm writing to you because I'm having a bad day. I could spare you the details. But the whole point of writing to a dead person is that you don't have to worry about boring your reader. And if this is to have the therapeutic effect I'm hoping for, I need to get it all out, exorcise everything. So indulge me. I'll make it worth your while.

It all began with snow. Slush to be exact, a heavy wet snow about ankle deep by the time I left for work. I have nothing against snow, in the abstract. All things being equal, I'm happy to live in a climate that has the occasional snowfall. Snow in the abstract is pretty. It makes the world fresh and silent. But snow in reality makes it harder to get around. Especially when you're blind. As far as I know, you didn't use a white cane. But I do, and let me tell you, a white cane in snow is something of an adventure. You can't feel the texture of the surface underfoot. You lose landmarks. You can begin to feel disoriented. On top of this, I discover my waterproof boots are not what you'd call water-tight. Every third step I feel water seeping through seams. When I get to the bus stop, my feet are soaked. Then the bus is extra crowded, because of the snow. Which is probably why the driver forgets to announce my stop. Once she remembers me, I have to backtrack four blocks to start my regular route to my office. So by the time I get here, I'm damp and nervy. But weather is weather. And it's not the first time a bus driver has forgotten to announce my stop.

Then I find a message on the machine from the student I was supposed to be meeting. He can't make it. His car won't start. Needless to say the thought of taking the bus never occurs to him. This is car culture. The only people who take the bus are people who can't afford a car or can't drive. Suggest the bus to anyone else, and they get insulted.

But I'm here—early, damp and nervy—but I'm here. And it's not as if there's nothing to do. So I turn on my computer to check my e-mail and discover its synthesized voice is on the fritz. I fiddle with it for a while. Then I make phone calls. I say, "There's something wrong with the voice output."

The guy says, "Your computer talks to you?"

I want to say, "I'm blind, buddy. Not schizophrenic," but I don't. He's entitled, I suppose. He says he has to "consult with a colleague." This means he covers the receiver with his hand and yells at another computer guy across the room. Then he tells me, "That's a hardware problem. That software is on your hard drive. That software is not on the network."

I knew this already. I'm blind, not stupid. And I'm usually not this cranky. It's just that my feet are wet. I sigh. Did I call the wrong office? No, this is the right office, just the wrong guy. I want the hardware guy and the hardware guy is out today. Because of the snow. Also, there's a backlog. He takes my name, but says it may be a while. I don't ask what "a while" means.

Then I get a call from one of my readers, and she tells me she's leaving, moving out of town to get married. I say, "That's wonderful," but inside I'm thinking, "Now what am I going to do?" Not that she's my only reader, of course. I have other readers and I can hire a new one. And it's not that I'm fussy either. I can listen to any reader, any kind of voice—I can tolerate the computer's voice after all. But I really like her voice. I like the way she phrases things. It somehow coincides with my own voice, or the voice in my head when I'm reading. Listening to her is effortless. I never have to blot out a vocal tick or a funny accent. I'll find another reader, but I'll never find a better fit.

Of course I don't say this. I say, "I'm so happy for you." In fact, I am happy for her, just sad for myself. I consider mailing her stuff, but it will take that much more time. And I doubt the Postal Service's "Free Matter for the Blind" is going to apply here.

While I'm debating the postal question, another one of my readers shows up. This is actually a good thing. He can read me my e-mail. This reader is hired by my department. He's an ADA [Americans with Disabilities Act] accommodation. He's good enough, though. We get along. We gripe about the weather for a while. His feet are also wet. And he's a graduate student so he generally has lots to gripe about. He tells me he's having trouble with the book I gave him to tape. The style makes it hard to read, he says.

"Don't worry about it," I say. I want to say, "You don't have to like it. All you have to do is read it into the tape recorder," but I don't. I mean, he doesn't get paid much for this.

I get him to read me my e-mail. I stop him mid-sentence and tell him to delete. He does it, but I sense it annoys him. It's as if he thinks I should hear the whole message since he's reading it aloud. Or else he finds the whole thing beneath him. I get a lot of stupid e-mail. Reading it aloud makes it seem all the stupider. But what can I do? I need to go through it to be sure there's nothing important. His attitude gets to me. He acts like he's doing me a favor. He thinks I should be more grateful. But I let it go. I let him go home early. On account of the snow.

Then it's time for class. Half of them are not there. Did I mention it's snowing? And the ones who are there are lackluster and cranky. I suspect they have not done the reading. I sense they feel *Pride and Prejudice* is not as relevant to their everyday lives as *The X Files*. I could give them a pop quiz but it would only make them surly. And I just let my reader go home early, so I'd have to wait until tomorrow to read it.

One of them comes back to my office after class to complain about the grade on his last paper. I gave him a B and he thinks it should be an A. He always got A's in high school. I tell him this isn't high school but he doesn't buy it. I've ruined his perfect GPA, and he seems ready to argue with me all afternoon. Why go out in the snow when he can stay here and make my life miserable? I make him read the paper aloud to me. I stop him sentence by sentence, telling him everything that's wrong. I say, "Hear that? That sentence doesn't make any sense."

He says, "But you get what I mean."

"I get what you mean because I read it five times," I say. I'm beginning to think a B was a gift. But I don't say this. I tell him he has a chance to redeem himself on his next paper. Then I clam up. He is sulky and dissatisfied. He thinks I'm being arbitrary and capricious. As he leaves he grumbles something under his breath that I'm not supposed to understand, but I am supposed to hear. I'm supposed to hear his dissatisfaction. He leaves a bad taste in my mouth. Do I need this, on a day like today?

Which brings me to the present moment, and to you, Helen Keller. I know what you're thinking. What's all this to you? And you're right in a way. You don't know me. You don't owe me anything, certainly not a sympathetic ear (so to speak). You think I should consider myself lucky to have a job like this, and all these wonderful things—white canes, waterproof boots, public transit, free mail for the blind, readers paid by my employer, computer voice interface, e-mail, the internet, braille printers. For you a typewriter was a big deal. I know. You don't have to tell me, again, how lucky I am. I'm lucky to be educated, lucky to have a job at all, lucky to live in these advanced times with all this technology, lucky that able-bodied people at least pay lip service to notions of equality, equal opportunity, accessibility, and the rest of it. I should be grateful, cheerful in the face of such minimal inconveniences. I should adjust my attitude, put on a smiley face and get over it.

This is precisely why I'm writing to you Helen. (Mind if I call you Helen?) You've been saying this to me all my life. Not you in person, of course, but you in effect. People have been saying it in your stead. "Things could be worse," they say. "Think about Helen Keller. Yes, you're blind, but she was deaf too. And no one ever heard her complain."

Save your breath. I know how good I have it. And it's not as if I feel I've been singled out for suffering. Everyone has bad days. When it snows it snows on everyone. People miss appointments. People make annoying demands. People and things you rely on fail. And there are worse things too—disappointment, betrayal, illness, death, despair. But I'm talking about something else here. I'm talking about the fact that most of what's wrong with this day has to do with being blind, and this is what leaves me raging. I rage at myself, my body, my eyes, tears welling up in them, reminding me how useless they are. I rage against the world for being inaccessible to me. I rage against technology for offering the promise of access and then breaking down, being cumbersome, leaving me stranded.

So what I'd like you to tell me is this. What did you do with the rage, Helen? Because you must have felt it. There must have been days when you woke up and all you wanted to do was pull the covers over your head and say, "Chuck it. Fuck it all. What am I trying to prove here? I surrender. Someone please take care of me." There must have been days when you wanted to shred the sheets with your teeth.

I can't believe there weren't such days. I mean for God's sake Helen, when you read page proofs of your books, it meant someone had to spell the text letter by letter into your hand. Tell me that didn't make you grind your teeth and tear your hair. But you never let it show, Helen. I scan your writing for even a sign of ire or irritation. The most you ever express is the occasional nervous unease. But then you follow up with flowery praise for all the wonderful, kind people who did so much to help you, utterly effacing both the difficulty and your effort. Because you did this, you left a legacy behind for the rest of us—the likes of me. "Why can't you be more like Helen Keller, especially since you're really nowhere near as bad off as she was?" You set an impossible standard. You with your cheerfulness, your stiff upper lip, your valiant smile in the face of adversity. So those who came after you feel a moral imperative to fight back the tears, to minimize the trouble, to avoid asking for help.

And for what, Helen? Sure, when we emulate your plucky, chirpy self-reliance, the able-bodied find us tolerable. They gush, "You're so patient, so persevering. How ever do you manage?" But what are they really thinking? I'm talking about the doubt, Helen. You know about the doubt. It's that nagging uncertainty at the back of your mind whenever anything good happens. You're in school and you wonder, "Is the A on this paper a gift? Would a normal student get an A for this?" You get a job, but you wonder, "Do they really think I'm qualified or is this just some sort of affirmative action quota?"

The doubt, Helen. I know you felt it. I know, for instance that you were discouraged by the reception your writing received. Your volumes of memoirs about your life and your disabilities got a lot of play. But on the rare occasions when you published something on other topics—women's suffrage, socialism, religion—the general assumption was that some member of your entourage, Anne Sullivan or her husband, John Macy, ghost-wrote it for you. "Write what you know," someone told you. They thought what you knew was nothing but deafness and blindness. They couldn't imagine that you knew anything else, that you could tell them anything else worth knowing.

A bad day, Helen. Cast your mind back. Surely you remember a few. For instance, there was that day when you were eleven and you were accused of plagiarism. You were not only accused, but essentially put on trial by the faculty of the Perkins Institution where you were in school. Eleven years old—plagiarism. The sheer lunacy of the charge should have been enough to trigger a tantrum. If it were me, I would have sat on my hands and refused to dignify their questions with answers. But you answered all their questions earnestly, eager to clear your name, anxious to get back into their good graces. You were exonerated, but doubt lingered, in you and others. Later, you wrote about how the incident shook your faith in your writing. Afterwards you always questioned the provenance of every idea. When words came to you too easily you feared you were remembering them from something you'd read, and started over. When words come too easily to other writers they call it inspiration and keep at it. "Forget dinner. I'm on a roll!"

And there were other bad days for you. Admit it. Remember that man who asked you to marry him, who signed the marriage license with you, but then your own mother and Anne Sullivan made him go away. Because even they had doubts about you. They did not believe you had the wherewithal to make that kind of decision on your own, to live that kind of life. They worried about the children you might have, and your ability to care for them. They may have been right about the man. Perhaps his intentions were not honorable. Perhaps they even convinced you of that. But their intervention, the imposition of their judgment over yours, must have hurt, Helen, must have hit the rawest nerve of all.

There's more. I could go on, Helen. I guess you could say I've made something of a study of your life. But I don't want to badger you. I'm not here to make you squirm. All I want to know is what you did with the feelings of betrayal, injustice, the rage, Helen? How did you get over it—shrug your shoulders and swallow hard? How did you get it down without choking? I only wish you could have let it show, just once. If you could have let the mask slip for a minute, Helen—one lousy sneer of derision, one tear of rage. It would have made it better for the rest of us, a little easier. What's more, it just might have let them see you as human.

But they might just as well have scorned you for it. Or worse. "If you can't stand the heat, get out of the kitchen. If all you can do is make a fuss, well, there are places for people like you." Is that the message, Helen? Did you keep that smile glued to your lips because you knew it was the only thing that stood between you and the institution, the asylum, the freak show?

Say it then. Speak to me. I wish you could get word to me somehow. E-mail? How about it Helen? hkeller.627@afterlife.com. Not that I really think you would tell me anything I want to know.

"Hi," you'd probably write. "Sorry to hear about your bad day. Try to look at the bright side. At least you've got your health. Buck up. Turn that frown upside down, and smile! Smile!! Smile!!!"

I don't know why I bother. I don't know what I expect from you. And maybe—take this as a concession, Helen—you couldn't help yourself. Once you figured out that the only way your words would be read by anyone was if you took on the role of the first, original disability poster child. So you vowed to be the best damn poster child the world has ever known. I guess I can't blame you if the insipid, feel-good aphorisms got to be a habit. But level with me, Helen. Give me something I can use. "Get with the program," you could say. "Show them your weakness and they'll put you away in the blink of an eye. You're here by sufferance. They'll only tolerate you as long as you keep up the front. Nobody likes a grumpy cripple."

I know this already. That's the thing about doubt. There you are, talking to a student and all the while you're wondering whether or not he's thinking, "This woman is blind. How can she judge me, my work? How can she presume?" And if he goes to complain to another professor or to my chair, would that person look sympathetic and say, "Well you know, son, people like that feel they need to be tougher than normal people. It's over-compensation. You can put up with it. Noblesse oblige."

I know a graduate student here who is in a wheelchair. He's someone who doesn't seem to suffer doubts about his value. In other words, he really knows how to complain. At the rate my luck has been running today, he'll be in here any minute, to complain about the snow, about the Handivan being late, about the elevator in the library not working, about the construction they're doing outside his dorm and how it blocks his usual route, and whatever else may be going on. He complains because before he was here he went to school in California, where it not only never snows, but where they have better services for people with disabilities. I admit, when this guy starts in on things, even I roll my eyes at times. In the back of my mind I'm thinking, "When I was in school there was none of this, no adaptive technologies, no services for disabled students, no legislative mandates." And yet, this guy is right. Do we have to put up with all this stuff and smile about it too? The squeaky wheel gets the oil. Rattle the bars of the cage loud enough and someone will unlock the door just to shut you up.

Progress, is this what you're telling me, Helen? It's the sort of thing you'd say. It's a part of that American can-do attitude everyone loved you for. "I blazed this path," you're telling me. "If there are still bumps in the road you've got to deal with them yourself." You couldn't complain because the risks were too great. What are the risks for me? True, for me, institutionalization has never been a real threat. And no one ever tried to mess with my love life. Though raise the issue of reproductive rights for disabled people and all the ugly eugenics arguments still rise to the surface. But change doesn't happen overnight, or even over a century or two. And for now, I should quit apologizing for being blind. If my blindness slows me down, or makes me do things differently, I still have something to contribute. If they don't believe me, let them say it to my face.

A bad day, Helen. It makes me lose perspective, so to speak. It puts me on the defensive. Tomorrow will be better. And that's not just Helen Keller-ish optimism talking. In fact, things could improve any minute. Another student could come in and tell me how though I gave him a B—no, a C—on his paper, my comments were so helpful, he's inspired to do better. The computer could hiccup and the voice could come back on all by itself. The sun could come out and melt all the snow. Miracles happen. Or even without miracles, ninety-nine percent of my days are just fine. I get up, I go to work, I teach, I read, I write. The fact that I use aids and assistants to do some of these things is not really central to my consciousness. When everything works, I consider myself "normal." My blindness is just a fact of life, not an insurmountable obstacle blocking my path. I work around it. I ignore it. On a lot of days, it matters less than the weather.

I don't know, Helen. I sense there's more you would tell me if you could. Feel free to elaborate. A word, a sign, a dream vision, a shudder of recognition—whatever means you have at your disposal. I'd really appreciate it. Hell, I'll even be grateful.

Excuse me if I close with the language of the oppressor, but you know how that goes. I look forward to hearing from you soon.

Sincerely,

GK

Ideas for Rereading

1. Georgina Kleege published "Blind Rage: An Open Letter to Helen Keller" in 1998—long after Helen Keller's death. Clearly, then, the letter is also addressed to a wider audience—presumably a sighted audience. As you reread, consider why Kleege chose to use this strategy and what she aims to achieve in this essay. Why would it be useful or important for people to understand that Keller might have bad days and feel "rage" and "doubt"—or to imagine that she might have?

2. What do you learn from Kleege's letter about the day-to-day life of a professional woman who is blind? Take notes on the details of Kleege's day that you find surprising or unexpected or illuminating.

Ideas for Writing

1. Kleege imagines how Helen Keller might respond to this angry letter. Considering what you have read of Keller's work, imagine Keller's response to Kleege. Write Keller's answering letter, imagining her response to each of Kleege's assertions about her.

2. In part, this chapter asks you to see disability as only one aspect of the personality and experience of any human being. While Kleege and Keller are both disabled, they are also both women, though living in different historical periods. Reread Keller's and Kleege's writing in an attempt to discern how the culture's expectations for women in these different periods affected these women—both as women and as people with disabilities. What does their work tell you about the different expectations for women, especially disabled women, during their respective time periods? How did these expectations help to shape their experiences as disabled persons? Write an essay that presents your conclusions.

SIMI LINTON

Simi Linton is a disability rights scholar, a professor of psychology in the Division of Education at Hunter College, and a consultant on disability issues to arts organizations, museums, and film, theater, and television producers. She is also a disabled woman and an activist. According to Linton, her latest book, Claiming Disability *(1998), describes "how the errors embedded in our intellectual traditions have a direct impact on disabled people's social positioning." The excerpt from* Claiming Disability *presented here deals with the part that language plays in the construction of our attitude toward disability and disabled people.*

Linton addresses the issue of disabilities by working with definitions of key terms including ableism, *variants on* disability, physically challenged, special, *and* cripple. *Obviously these and other words and phrases have specific connotations and purposes that have a profound effect on the lives of individuals in contemporary culture, in the broadest form of American culture that includes all cultural, political, and social groupings regardless of ability, class, gender, race, religion, and sexuality.*

As you read Linton write a list of the words and phrases she discusses, making notes about how each word and phrase functions. Why do some people choose to use this particular word or phrase? What do you notice about differences between the ways people intend to use specific words and phrases and the ways others (particularly those being referred to) understand the hidden implications of these labels? How does Linton's discussion of labels connect with her discussion of "passing" and "overcoming"? In what ways do standard and mainstream uses of specific words and phrases create ideas about what is "normal" and "abnormal"? And how do these dominant ideas about normalcy and abnormalcy contribute to perceptions of "the disabled"? Why is it important to focus on such apparently insignificant parts of speech as the prefixes in (in invalid) and dis (in disability)? What do conventional uses of these prefixes tell us about our attitudes toward people who are different than the imagined ideal (which Linton defines in terms of "the white, the male, and the heterosexual positions . . . [of] privilege and power" [p. 296])?

Reassigning Meaning

The present examination of disability has no need for the medical language of symptoms and diagnostic categories. Disability studies looks to different kinds of signifiers and the identification of different kinds of syndromes for its material. The elements of interest here are the linguistic conventions that structure the meanings assigned to disability and the patterns of response to disability that emanate from, or are attendant upon, those meanings.

The medical meaning-making was negotiated among interested parties who packaged their version of disability in ways that increased the ideas' potency and marketability. The disability community has attempted to wrest control of the language from the previous owners, and reassign meaning to the terminology used to describe disability and disabled people. This new language conveys different meanings, and, significantly, the shifts serve as metacommunications about the social, political, intellectual, and ideological transformations that have taken place over the past two decades.

Naming Oppression

It has been particularly important to bring to light language that reinforces the dominant culture's views of disability. A useful step in that process has been the construction of the terms *ableist* and *ableism,* which can be used to organize ideas about the centering and domination of the nondisabled experience and point of view. *Ableism* has recently landed in the *Reader's Digest Oxford Wordfinder* (Tulloch 1993), where it is defined as "discrimination in favor of the able-bodied." I would add, extrapolating from the definitions of *racism* and *sexism,* that *ableism* also includes the idea that a person's abilities or characteristics are determined by disability or that people with disabilities as a group are inferior to nondisabled people. Although there is probably greater consensus among the general public on what could be labeled racist or sexist language than there is on what might be considered ableist, that may be because the nature of the oppression of disabled people is not yet as widely understood.

Naming the Group

Across the world and throughout history various terminologies and meanings are ascribed to the types of human variations known in contemporary Westernized countries as disabilities. Over the past century the term *disabled* and others, such as *handicapped* and the less inclusive term *crippled,* have emerged as collective nouns that convey the idea that there is something that links this disparate group of people. The terms have been used to arrange people in ways that are socially and economically convenient to the society.

There are various consequences of the chosen terminology and variation in the degree of control that the named group has over the labeling process. The terms *disability* and *disabled people* are the most commonly used by disability rights activists, and recently policy makers and health care professionals have begun to use these terms more consistently. Although there is some agreement on terminology, there are disagreements about what it is that unites disabled people and whether disabled people should have control over the naming of their experience.

The term *disability,* as it has been used in general parlance, appears to signify something material and concrete, a physical or psychological condition considered to have predominantly medical significance. Yet it is an arbitrary designation, used erratically both by professionals who lay claim to naming such phenomena and by confused citizens. A project of disability studies scholars and the disability rights movement has been to bring into sharp relief the processes by which *disability* has been imbued with the meaning(s) it has and to reassign a meaning that is consistent with a sociopolitical analysis of disability. Divesting it of its current meaning is no small feat. As typically used, the term *disability* is a linchpin in a complex web of social ideals, institutional structures, and government policies. As a result, many people have a vested interest in keeping a tenacious hold on the current meaning because it is consistent with the practices and policies that are central to their livelihood or their ideologies. People may not be driven as much by economic imperatives as by a personal investment in their own beliefs and practices, in metaphors they hold dear, or in their own professional roles. Further, underlying this tangled web of needs and beliefs, and central to the arguments presented in this book is an epistemological structure that both generates and reflects current interpretations.[1]

A glance through a few dictionaries will reveal definitions of disability that include incapacity, a disadvantage, deficiency, especially a physical or mental impairment that restricts normal achievement; something that hinders or incapacitates, something that incapacitates or disqualifies. Legal definitions include legal incapacity or disqualification. *Stedman's Medical Dictionary* (1976) identifies *disability* as a "medicolegal term signifying loss of function and earning power," whereas *disablement* is a "medicolegal term signifying loss of function without loss of earning power" (400). These definitions are understood by the general public and by many in the academic community to be useful ones. *Disability* so defined is a medically derived term that assigns predominantly medical significance and meaning to certain types of human variation.

The decision to assign medical meanings to *disability* has had many and varied consequences for disabled people. One clear benefit has been the medical treatments that have increased the well-being and vitality of many disabled people, indeed have saved people's lives. Ongoing attention by the medical profession to the health and well-being of people with disabilities and to prevention of disease and impairments is critical. Yet, along with these benefits, there are enormous negative consequences that will take a large part of this book to list and explain. Briefly, the medicalization of disability casts human variation as deviance from the norm, as pathological condition, as deficit, and, significantly, as an individual burden and personal tragedy. Society, in agreeing to assign medical meaning to *disability,* colludes to keep the issue within the purview of the medical establishment, to keep it a personal matter and "treat" the condition and the person with the condition rather than "treating" the social processes and policies that constrict disabled people's lives. The disability studies' and disability rights movement's position is critical of the domination of the medical definition and views it as a major stumbling block to the reinterpretation of *disability* as a political category and to the social changes that could follow such a shift.

While retaining the term *disability,* despite its medical origins, a premise of most of the literature in disability studies is that *disability* is best understood as a marker of identity. As such, it has been used to build a coalition of people with significant impairments, people with behavioral or anatomical characteristics marked as deviant, and people who have or are suspected of having conditions, such as AIDS or emotional illness, that make them targets of discrimination.[2] As rendered in disability studies scholarship, disability has become a more capacious category, incorporating people with a range of physical, emotional, sensory, and cognitive conditions. Although the category is broad, the term is used to designate a specific minority group. When medical definitions of *disability* are dominant, it is logical to separate people according to biomedical condition through the use of diagnostic categories and to forefront medical perspectives on human variation. When disability is redefined as a social/political category, people with a variety of conditions are identified as *people with disabilities* or *disabled people,* a group bound by common social and political experience. These designations, as reclaimed by the community, are used to identify us as a constituency, to serve our needs for unity and identity, and to function as a basis for political activism.

The question of who "qualifies" as disabled is as answerable or as confounding as questions about any identity status. One simple response might be that you are disabled if you say you are. Although that declaration won't satisfy a worker's compensation board, it has a certain credibility with the disabled community. The degree and significance of an individual's impairment is often less of an issue than the degree to which someone identifies as disabled. Another way to answer the question is to say that disability "is mostly a social distinction . . . a marginalized status" and the status is assigned by "the majority culture tribunal" (Gill 1994, 44). But the problem gets stickier when the distinction between disabled and nondisabled is challenged by people who say, "Actually, we're all disabled in some way, aren't we?" (46). Gill says the answer is no to those whose difference "does *not* significantly affect daily life and the person does not [with some consistency] present himself/herself to the world at large as a disabled person" (46). I concur with Gill; I am not willing or interested in erasing the line between disabled and nondisabled people, as long as disabled people are devalued and discriminated against, and as long as naming the category serves to call attention to that treatment.

Over the past twenty years, disabled people have gained greater control over these definitional issues. *The disabled* or *the handicapped* was replaced in the mid-70s by *people with disabilities* to maintain disability as a characteristic of the individual, as opposed to the defining variable. At the time, some people would purposefully say *women and men with disabilities* to provide an extra dimension to the people being described and to deneuter the way *the disabled* were traditionally described. Beginning in the early 90s *disabled people* has been increasingly used in disability studies and disability rights circles when referring to the constituency group. Rather than maintaining disability as a secondary characteristic, *disabled* has become a marker of the identity that the individual and group wish to highlight and call attention to.

In this book, the terms *disabled* and *nondisabled* are used frequently to designate membership within or outside the community. Disabled is centered, and nondisabled is placed in the peripheral position in order to look at the world from the inside out, to expose the perspective and expertise that is silenced. Occasionally, *people with disabilities* is used as a variant of *disabled people*. The use of *nondisabled* is strategic: to center disability. Its inclusion in this chapter is also to set the stage for postulating about the nondisabled position in society and in scholarship in later chapters. This action is similar to the strategy of marking and articulating "whiteness." The assumed position in scholarship has always been the male, white, nondisabled scholar; it is the default category. As recent scholarship has shown, these positions are not only presumptively hegemonic because they are the assumed universal stance, as well as the presumed neutral or objective stance, but also undertheorized. The nondisabled stance, like the white stance, is veiled. "*White* cannot be said quite out loud, or it loses its crucial position as a precondition of vision and becomes the object of scrutiny" (Haraway 1989, 152). Therefore, centering the disabled position and labeling its opposite nondisabled focuses attention on both the structure of knowledge and the structure of society.

Nice Words

Terms such as *physically challenged,* the *able disabled, handicapable,* and *special people/children* surface at different times and places. They are rarely used by disabled activists and scholars (except with palpable irony). Although they may be considered well-meaning attempts to inflate the value of people with disabilities, they convey the boosterism and do-gooder mentality endemic to the paternalistic agencies that control many disabled people's lives.

Physically challenged is the only term that seems to have caught on. Nondisabled people use it in conversation around disabled people with no hint of anxiety, suggesting that they believe it is a positive term. This phrase does not make much sense to me. To say that I am physically challenged is to state that the obstacles to my participation are physical, not social, and that the barrier is my own disability. Further, it separates those of us with mobility impairments from other disabled people, not a valid or useful partition for those interested in coalition building and social change. Various derivatives of the term *challenged* have been adopted as a description used in jokes. For instance, "vertically challenged" is considered a humorous way to say short, and "calorically challenged" to say fat. A review of the Broadway musical *Big* in the *New Yorker* said that the score is "melodically challenged."

I observed a unique use of *challenged* in the local Barnes and Noble superstore. The children's department has a section for books on "Children with Special Needs." There are shelves labeled "Epilepsy" and "Down Syndrome." A separate shelf at the bottom is labeled "Misc. Challenges," indicating that it is now used as an organizing category.

The terms *able disabled* and *handicapable* have had a fairly short shelf life. They are used, it seems, to refute common stereotypes of incompetence. They are, though, defensive and reactive terms rather than terms that advance a new agenda.

An entire profession, in fact a number of professions, are built around the word *special.* A huge infrastructure rests on the idea that *special children* and *special education* are valid and useful structuring ideas. Although dictionaries insist that *special* be reserved for things that surpass what is common, are distinct among others of their kind, are peculiar to a specific person, have a limited or specific function, are arranged for a particular purpose, or are arranged for a particular occasion, experience teaches us that *special* when applied to education or to children means something different.

The naming of disabled children and the education that "is designed for students whose learning needs cannot be met by a standard school curriculum" (*American Heritage Dictionary* 1992) as *special* can be understood only as a euphemistic formulation, obscuring the reality that neither the children nor the education are considered desirable and that they are not thought to "surpass what is common."

Labeling the education and its recipients special may have been a deliberate attempt to confer legitimacy on the educational practice and to prop up a discarded group. It is also important to consider the unconscious feelings such a strategy may mask. It is my feeling that the nation in general responds to disabled people with great ambivalence. Whatever antipathy and disdain is felt is in competition with feelings of empathy, guilt, and identification. The term *special* may be evidence not of a deliberate maneuver but of a collective "reaction formation," Freud's term for the unconscious defense mechanism in which an individual adopts attitudes and behaviors that are opposite to his or her own true feelings, in order to protect the ego from the anxiety felt from experiencing the real feelings.

The ironic character of the word *special* has been captured in the routine on *Saturday Night Live,* where the character called the "Church Lady" declares when she encounters something distasteful or morally repugnant, "Isn't that special!"

Nasty Words

Some of the less subtle or more idiomatic terms for disabled people such as *cripple, vegetable, dumb, deformed, retard,* and *gimp* have generally been expunged from public conversation but emerge in various types of discourse. Although they are understood to be offensive or hurtful, they are still used in jokes and in informal conversation.

Cripple as a descriptor of disabled people is considered impolite, but the word has retained its metaphoric vitality, as in "the exposé in the newspaper crippled the politician's campaign." The term is also used occasionally for its evocative power. A recent example appeared in *Lingua Franca* in a report on research on the behaviors of German academics. The article states that a professor had "documented the postwar careers of psychiatrists and geneticists involved in gassing thousands of cripples and schizophrenics" (Allen 1996, 37). *Cripple* is used rather loosely here to describe people with a broad range of disabilities. The victims of Nazi slaughter were people with mental illness, epilepsy, chronic illness, and mental retardation, as well as people with physical disabilities. Yet *cripple* is defined as "one that is partially disabled or unable to use a limb or limbs" (*American Heritage Dictionary* 1992) and is usually used only to refer to people with mobility impairments. Because *cripple* inadequately and inaccurately describes the group, the author of the report is likely to have chosen this term for its effect.

Cripple has also been revived by some in the disability community who refer to each other as "crips" or "cripples." A performance group with disabled actors call themselves the "Wry Crips." "In reclaiming 'cripple,' disabled people are taking the thing in their identity that scares the outside world the most and making it a cause to revel in with militant self-pride" (Shapiro 1993, 34).

A recent personal ad in the *Village Voice* shows how "out" the term is:

> **TWISTED CRIP:** Very sexy, full-figured disabled BiWF artist sks fearless, fun, oral BiWF for hot, no-strings nights. Wheelchair, tattoo, dom. Shaved a + N/S. No men/sleep-overs.

Cripple, gimp, and *freak* as used by the disability community have transgressive potential. They are personally and politically useful as a means to comment on oppression because they assert our right to name experience.

Speaking about Overcoming and Passing

The popular phrase *overcoming a disability* is used most often to describe someone with a disability who seems competent and successful in some way, in a sentence something like "She has overcome her disability and is a great success." One interpretation of the phrase might be that the individual's disability no longer limits her or him, that sheer strength or willpower has brought the person to the point where the disability is no longer a hindrance. Another implication of the phrase may be that the person has risen above society's expectation for someone with those characteristics. Because it is physically impossible to *overcome* a disability, it seems that what is *overcome* is the social stigma of having a disability. This idea is reinforced by the equally confounding statement "I never think of you as disabled." An implication of these statements is that the other members of the group from which the individual has supposedly moved beyond are not as brave, strong, or extraordinary as the person who has *overcome* that designation.

The expression is similar in tone to the phrase that was once more commonly used to describe an African American who was considered exceptional in some way: "He/she is a credit to his/her race." The implication of this phrase is that the "race" is somehow discredited and needs people with extraordinary talent to give the group the credibility that it otherwise lacks. In either case, talking about the person who is African American or talking about the person with a disability, these phrases are often said with the intention of complimenting someone. The compliment has a double edge. To accept it, one must accept the implication that the group is inferior and that the individual is unlike others in that group.

The ideas imbedded in the *overcoming* rhetoric are of personal triumph over a personal condition. The idea that someone can *overcome* a disability has not been generated within the community; it is a wish fulfillment generated from the outside. It is a demand that you be plucky and resolute, and not let the obstacles get in your way. If there are no curb cuts at the corner of the street so that people who use wheelchairs can get across, then you should learn to do wheelies and jump the curbs. If there are no sign language interpreters for deaf students at the high school, then you should study harder, read lips, and stay up late copying notes from a classmate. When disabled people internalize the demand to "overcome" rather than demand social change, they shoulder the same kind of exhausting and self-defeating "Super Mom" burden that feminists have analyzed.

The phrase *overcome a disability* may also be a shorthand version of saying "someone with a disability overcame many obstacles." Tremblay (1996) uses that phrase when describing behaviors of disabled World War II veterans upon returning to the community: "[T]heir main strategies were to develop individualized strategies to overcome the obstacles they found in the community" (165). She introduces this idea as a means to describe how the vets relied on their own ingenuity to manage an inaccessible environment rather than demand that the community change to include them.

In both uses of *overcome,* the individual's responsibility for her or his own success is paramount. If we, as a society, place the onus on individuals with disabilities to work harder to "compensate" for their disabilities or to "overcome" their condition or the barriers in the environment, we have no need for civil rights legislation or affirmative action.

Lest I be misunderstood, I don't see working hard, doing well, or striving for health, fitness, and well-being as contradictory to the aims of the disability rights movement. Indeed, the movement's goal is to provide greater opportunity to pursue these activities. However, we shouldn't be impelled to do these because we have a disability, to prove to some social overseer that we can perform, but we should pursue them because they deliver their own rewards and satisfactions.

A related concept, familiar in African American culture as well as in lesbian and gay culture, is that of *passing.* African Americans who pass for white and lesbians and gays who pass for straight do so for a variety of personal, social, and often economic reasons. Disabled people, if they are able to conceal their impairment or confine their activities to those that do not reveal their disability, have been known to pass. For a member of any of these groups, passing may be a deliberate effort to avoid discrimination or ostracism, or it may be an almost unconscious, Herculean effort to deny to oneself the reality of one's racial history, sexual feelings, or bodily state. The attempt may be a deliberate act to protect oneself from the loathing of society or may be an unchecked impulse spurred by an internalized self-loathing. It is likely that often the reasons entail an admixture of any of these various parts.

Henry Louis Gates, Jr. (1996), spoke of the various reasons for passing in an essay on the literary critic Anatole Broyard. Broyard was born in New Orleans to a family that identified as "Negro." His skin was so light that for his entire career as "one of literary America's foremost gatekeepers" (66) the majority of people who knew him did not know this. His children, by then adults, learned of his racial history shortly before he died. Sandy Broyard, Anatole's wife, remarked that she thought that "his own personal history continued to be painful to him. . . . In passing, you cause your family great anguish, but I also think conversely, do we look at the anguish it causes the person who is passing? Or the anguish that it was born out of?" (75).

When disabled people are able to pass for nondisabled, and do, the emotional toll it takes is enormous. I have heard people talk about hiding a hearing impairment to classmates or colleagues for years, or others who manage to conceal parts of their body, or to hide a prosthesis. These actions, though, may not result in a family's anguish; they may, in fact, be behaviors that the family insists upon, reinforces, or otherwise shames the individual into. Some disabled people describe how they were subjected to numerous painful surgeries and medical procedures when they were young not so much, they believe, to increase their comfort and ease of mobility as to fulfill their families' wish to make them appear "more normal."

Even when a disability is obvious and impossible to hide on an ongoing basis, families sometimes create minifictions that disabled people are forced to play along with. Many people have told me that when family pictures were taken as they were growing up, they were removed from their wheelchairs, or they were shown only from the waist up, or they were excluded from pictures altogether. The messages are that this part of you, your disability or the symbol of disability, your wheelchair, is unacceptable, or, in the last case, you are not an acceptable member of the family.

I was recently in an elementary school when class pictures were taken, and I learned that it is the custom for all the children who use wheelchairs to be removed from their chairs and carried up a few steps to the auditorium stage and placed on folding chairs. I spoke with people at the school who said they have thought about raising money to build a ramp to the stage, but in the meantime this was the solution. I wondered, of course, why they have to take pictures on the stage when it is inaccessible. The families of these children or the school personnel might even persist with this plan, believing that these actions have a positive effect on children, that they demonstrate that the disabled child is "just like everybody else." But these fictions are based more clearly on the projections of the adults than on the unadulterated feelings of the child. The message that I read in this action: You are like everyone else, but only as long as you hide or minimize your disability.

Both passing and overcoming take their toll. The loss of community, the anxiety, and the self-doubt that inevitably accompany this ambiguous social position and the ambivalent personal state are the enormous cost of declaring disability unacceptable. It is not surprising that disabled people also speak of "coming out" in the same way that members of the lesbian and gay community do. A woman I met at a disability studies conference not long ago said to me in the course of a conversation about personal experience: "I'm five years old." She went on to say that despite being significantly disabled for many years, she had really only recently discovered the disabled community and allied with it. For her, "coming out" was a process that began when she recognized how her effort to "be like every-one else" was not satisfying her own needs and wishes. She discovered other disabled people and began to identify clearly as disabled, and then purchased a motorized scooter, which meant she didn't have to expend enormous energy walking. She told this tale with gusto, obviously pleased with the psychic and physical energy she had gained. Stories such as hers provide evidence of the personal burdens many disabled people live with. Shame and fear are personal burdens, but if these tales are told, we can demonstrate how the personal is indeed the political. And further, that the unexamined connections between the personal and political are the cur-ricular.

Normal/Abnormal

Normal and *abnormal* are convenient but problematic terms used to de-scribe a person or group of people. These terms are often used to distin-guish between people with and without disabilities. In various academic disciplines and in common usage, *normal* and *abnormal* assume different meanings. In psychometrics, *norm* or *normal* are terms describing individu-als or characteristics that fall within the center of the normal distribution on whatever variable is being measured. However, as the notion of *normal* is applied in social science contexts and certainly in general parlance, it im-plies its obverse—*abnormal*—and they both become value laden. Often, those who are not deemed normal are devalued and considered a burden or problem, or are highly valued and regarded as a potential resource. Two examples are the variables of height and intelligence. Short stature and low measured intelligence are devalued and labeled abnormal, and people with those characteristics are considered disabled. Tall people (particularly males) and high scores on IQ tests are valued, and, although not normal in the statistical sense, are not labeled abnormal or considered disabled.[3]

Davis (1995) describes the historical specificity of the use of *normal* and thereby calls attention to the social structures that are dependent on its use. "[T]he very term that permeates our contemporary life—the nor-mal—is a configuration that arises in a particular historical moment. It is part of a notion of progress, of industrialization, and of ideological consol-idation of the power of the bourgeoisie. The implications of the hegemony of normalcy are profound and extend into the very heart of cultural pro-duction" (49).

The use of the terms *abnormal* and *normal* also moves discourse to a high level of abstraction, thereby avoiding concrete discussion of specific characteristics and increasing ambiguity in communication. In interac-tions, there is an assumed agreement between speaker and audience of what is normal that sets up an aura of empathy and "us-ness." This process "enhances social unity among those who feel they are normal" (Freilich, Raybeck, and Savishinsky 1991, 22), necessarily excluding the other or abnormal group.

These dynamics often emerge in discussions about disabled people when comparisons are made, for instance, between "the normal" and "the hearing impaired," or "the normal children" and "the handicapped children." The first example contrasts two groups of people; one defined by an abstract and evaluative term (the normal), the other by a more specific, concrete, and nonevaluative term (the hearing impaired). In the second comparison, the "handicapped children" are labeled abnormal by default. Setting up these dichotomies avoids concrete discussion of the ways the two groups of children actually differ, devalues the children with disabilities, and forces an "us and them" division of the population.

The absolute categories *normal* and *abnormal* depend on each other for their existence and depend on the maintenance of the opposition for their meaning. Sedgwick (1990), in *Epistemology of the Closet,* comments on a similar pattern in the forced choice categories homosexual and heterosexual:

> [C]ategories presented in a culture as symmetrical binary oppositions — heterosexual/homosexual, in this case — actually subsist in a more unsettled and dynamic tacit relation according to which, first, term B is not symmetrical with but subordinated to term A; but, second, the ontologically valorized term A actually depends for its meaning on the simultaneous subsumption and exclusion of term B; hence, third, the question of priority between the supposed central and the supposed marginal category of each dyad is irresolvably unstable, an instability caused by the fact that term B is constituted as at once internal and external to term A. (9–10)

Despite the instability and the relational nature of the designations *normal* and *abnormal,* they are used as absolute categories. They have achieved their certainty by association with empiricism, and they suffer from empiricism's reductive and simplifying tendencies. Their power and reach are enormous. They affect individuals' most private deliberations about their worth and acceptability, and they determine social position and societal response to behavior. The relationship between abnormality and disability accords to the nondisabled the legitimacy and potency denied to disabled people. And, central to our concerns here, the reification of *normal* and *abnormal* structures curriculum. Courses with titles such as "Abnormal Psychology," "Sociology of Deviance," "Special Education," and "Psychopathology" assume the internal consistency of a curriculum focused on "the abnormal" and depend on the curriculum of the "normal" being taught elsewhere. In fact, this organization of knowledge implicitly suggests that the rest of the curriculum is "normal."

Rosemarie Garland Thomson (1997) has coined the term *the normate,* which, like *nondisabled,* is useful for marking the unexamined center. "This neologism names the veiled subject position of cultural self, the figure outlined by the array of deviant others whose marked bodies shore up the normate's boundaries. The term *normate* usefully designates the social figure through which people can represent themselves as definitive human beings" (8). By meeting *normal* on some of its own terms, *normate* inflects its root, and challenges the validity, indeed the possibility, of normal. At the same time, its ironic twist gives a more flavorful reading of the idea of normal.

Passivity Versus Control

Language that conveys passivity and victimization reinforces certain stereotypes when applied to disabled people. Some of the stereotypes that are particularly entrenched are that people with disabilities are more dependent, childlike, passive, sensitive, and miserable and are less competent than people who do not have disabilities. Much of the language used to depict disabled people relates the lack of control to the perceived incapacities, and implies that sadness and misery are the product of the disabling condition.

These deterministic and essentialist perspectives flourish in the absence of contradictory information. Historically, disabled people have had few opportunities to be active in society, and various social and political forces often undermine the capacity for self-determination. In addition, disabled people are rarely depicted on television, in films, or in fiction as being in control of their own lives — in charge or actively seeking out and obtaining what they want and need. More often, disabled people are depicted as pained by their fate or, if happy, it is through personal triumph over their adversity. The adversity is not depicted as lack of opportunity, discrimination, institutionalization, and ostracism; it is the personal burden of their own body or means of functioning.

Phrases such as *the woman is a victim of cerebral palsy* implies an active agent (cerebral palsy) perpetrating an aggressive act on a vulnerable, helpless "victim." The use of the term *victim,* a word typically used in the context of criminal acts, evokes the relationship between perpetrator and victim. Using this language attributes life, power, and intention to the condition and disempowers the person with the disability, rendering him or her helpless and passive. Instead, if there is a particular need to note what an individual's disability is, saying *the woman has cerebral palsy* describes solely the characteristic of importance to the situation, without imposing extraneous meaning.

Grover (1987) analyzes the word *victim* as used to describe people with AIDS. She notes that the term implies fatalism, and therefore "enable[s] the passive spectator or the AIDS 'spectacle' to remain passive." Use of the term may also express the unconscious wish that the people with AIDS may have been "complicit with, to have courted, their fate" (29), in which case the individual would be seen as a *victim* of her or his own drives. This is particularly apparent when the phrase *innocent victim* is used to distinguish those who acquire HIV from blood transfusions or other medical procedures from those who contract HIV from sexual contact or shared needles. This analysis is also pertinent to people with other disabilities because a number of belief systems consider disability, or some disabilities, as punishment for sin in this or a former life.

Disabled people are frequently described as *suffering from* or *afflicted with* certain conditions. Saying that someone is *suffering from* a condition implies that there is a perpetual state of suffering, uninterrupted by pleasurable moments or satisfactions. *Afflicted* carries similar assumptions. The verb *afflict* shares with *agonize, excruciate, rack, torment,* and *torture* the central meaning "to bring great harm or suffering to someone" (*American Heritage Dictionary* 1992, 30). Although some people may experience their disability this way, these terms are not used as descriptors of a verified experience but are projected onto disability. Rather than assume suffering in the description of the situation, it is more accurate and less histrionic to say simply that a person *has a disability.* Then, wherever it is relevant, describe the nature and extent of the difficulty experienced. My argument here isn't to eliminate descriptions of suffering but to be accurate in their appointment. It is interesting that AIDS activists intentionally use the phrase *living with AIDS* rather than *dying from AIDS,* not to deny the reality of AIDS but to emphasize that people are often actively engaged in living even in the face of a serious illness.

The ascription of passivity can be seen in language used to describe the relationship between disabled people and their wheelchairs. The phrases *wheelchair bound* or *confined to a wheelchair* are frequently seen in newspapers and magazines, and heard in conversation. A more puzzling variant was spotted in *Lingua Franca,* which described the former governor of Alabama, George Wallace, as the "slumped, wheelchair-ridden 'Guv'nah'" (Zalewski 1995, 19). The choice here was to paint the wheelchair user as *ridden,* meaning "dominated, harassed, or obsessed by" (*American Heritage Dictionary* 1992), rather than the rider in the wheelchair. The various terms imply that a wheelchair restricts the individual, holds a person prisoner. Disabled people are more likely to say that someone *uses a wheelchair.* The latter phrase not only indicates the active nature of the user and the positive way that wheelchairs increase mobility and activity but recognizes that people get in and out of wheelchairs for different activities: driving a car, going swimming, sitting on the couch, or, occasionally, for making love.

A recent oral history conducted with disabled Canadian World War II veterans and other disabled people who are contemporaries of the vets recounts their memories of the transition from hospital-style wicker wheelchairs used to transport patients to self-propelled, lighter-weight, folding chairs that were provided to disabled people, mostly to veterans, in the years following the war. Prior to the new chairs, one man recalls that "one was often confined to bed for long periods of time. . . . There were a few cerebral palsy chaps there. . . . If they transgressed any rule . . . they'd take their wheelchairs away from them and leave them in bed for two weeks" (Tremblay 1996, 153). In this and other interviews the value of wheelchairs is revealed. A vet described how the medical staff's efforts were geared toward getting veterans to walk with crutches, but when the vets discovered the self-propelled chairs they realized "it didn't make much sense spending all that energy covering a short distance [on crutches] . . . when you could do it quickly and easily with a wheelchair. . . . It didn't take long for people to get over the idea that walking was that essential" (158–59). Another veteran recalled how the staff's emphasis on getting the men to walk "delayed our rehabilitation for months and months" (159). The staff obviously understood the value of the wheelchair to disabled people; otherwise they would not have used it as a means of control, yet they resisted purchasing the new self-push chairs for some time after they were made available. It is that type of manipulation and control, along with architectural and attitudinal barriers, that confine people. It is not wheelchairs.

Multiple Meanings

Are *invalid*, with the emphasis on the first syllable, and *invalid*, with the emphasis on the second, synonyms or homonyms? Does the identical housing of *patient*, the adjective, and *patient*, the noun, conflate the two meanings? Did their conceptual relationship initially determine their uniform casing?

For instance, *invalid* is a designation used to identify some disabled people. The term is seen most prominently on the sides of vans used to transport people with mobility impairments. Disabled people, desperate for accessible transportation, must use vans with the dubious appellation "*Invalid Coach*" printed in bold letters on the side. Aside from this being a fertile source of jokes about the aptness of these notoriously bad transportation services being identified as "not factually or legally valid; falsely based or reasoned; faulty" (*American Heritage Dictionary* 1992), those on the inside of the bus suffer the humiliation of being written off so summarily. Both *invalid*s share the Latin root *invalidus*, which means weak. It could be argued that some disabilities do result in weakening of the body, or, more likely, parts of the body, but the totalizing noun, *invalid*, does not confine the weakness to the specific bodily functions; it is more encompassing.

The homonymic *patient/patient*, is, I think, not coincidental or irrelevant. The noun *patient* is a role designation that is always relational. A patient is understood to belong to a doctor or other health care professional, or more generally to an institution. As a noun, *patient* is a neutral description of the role of "one who receives medical attention, care, or treatment" (*American Heritage Dictionary* 1992). The adjective *patient* moves beyond the noun's neutral designation to describe a person who is capable of "bearing or enduring pain, difficulty, provocation, or annoyance with calmness" as well as "tolerant . . . persevering . . . constant . . . not hasty" (*American Heritage Dictionary* 1992). The "good" patient is one who does not challenge the authority of the practitioner or institution and who complies with the regimen set out by the expert, in other words a patient patient. Disabled people, who have often spent a great deal of time as patients, discuss the ways that we have been socialized in the medical culture to be compliant, and that has often undermined our ability to challenge authority or to function autonomously. Further, the description of disabled people as patients in situations where we are not, reinforces these ideas.[4]

Reflections on the *Dis* in *Disability*

Before discussing the prefix *dis*, let's examine a similar bound morpheme that conveys meaning and significantly modifies the words it is attached to. The suffix *ette*, when appended to nouns, forms words meaning small or diminutive, as in *kitchenette;* female, as in *usherette;* or imitation or inferior kind, as in *leatherette (American Heritage Dictionary* 1992). These various meanings of *ette* slip around in our minds to influence how we interpret other words with the same suffix. So, for instance, although the word *leatherette* is used to tell us it is not the real thing and an inferior version of leather, *usherette* becomes, by association, not only the female version of usher but denotes a poor imitation. *Usherette* becomes, like *kitchenette,* the diminutive version. These various meanings tumble into one another, propagating new meanings, unintended and imprecise. I recently met a woman who told me that she had been a Rockette at Radio City Music Hall in Rockefeller Center for twenty years. I realized that this string of high-kicking, synchronized dancing women are perpetually cast as the smaller, imitation, inferior and female counterparts of the great male barons, the Rockefellers.

The prefix *dis,* like the suffix *ette,* has similarly unchecked impulses. Although *ette* qualifies its base and reduces it to the more diminutive and less valid version, a relationship is maintained between the base and its amended version. However, the prefix *dis* connotes separation, taking apart, sundering in two. The prefix has various meanings such as not, as in *dissimilar;* absence of, as in *disinterest;* opposite of, as in *disfavor;* undo, do the opposite of, as in *disarrange;* and deprive of, as in *disfranchise.* The Latin root *dis* means apart, asunder. Therefore, to use the verb *disable* means, in part, to deprive of capability or effectiveness. The prefix creates a barrier, cleaving in two ability and its absence, its opposite. Disability is the "not" condition, the repudiation of ability.

Canguilhem (1991), in his explorations of the normal and the pathological, recognizes the way that prefixes signal their relationship to the words they modify. He asserts that

> the pathological phenomena found in living organisms are nothing more than quantitative variations, greater or lesser according to corresponding physiological phenomena. Semantically, the pathological is designated as departing from the normal not so much by *a-* or *dys-* as by *hyper-* or *hypo-*. . . . [T]his approach is far from considering health and sickness as qualitatively opposed, or as forces joined in battle. (42)

Ette, hyper and *hypo,* and *dis* have semantic consequences, but, more-over, each recapitulates a particular social arrangement. The suffix *ette* not only qualifies the meaning of the root word it is attached to but speaks of the unequal yet dynamic relationship between women and men, in which "woman was, as we see in the profoundly influential works of Aristotle, not the equal opposite of man but a failed version of the supposedly defining type" (Minnich 1990, 54). The medical prefixes *hyper* and *hypo* are typically attached to medical conditions that are temporary or circum-scribed. People with those conditions are not socially marked and sepa-rated as are those with the more pronounced, and long standing conditions known as disabilities. With *hyper* and *hypo* conditions, there is less seman-tic and social disjuncture. However, the construction of *dis/ability* does not imply the continuum approach Canguilhem finds in diagnostic categories. *Dis* is the semantic reincarnation of the split between disabled and nondis-abled people in society.

Yet *women and men with disabilities, disabled people,* and the *disabil-ity community* are terms of choice for the group. We have decided to reas-sign meaning rather than choose a new name. In retaining *disability* we run the risk of preserving the medicalized ideas attendant upon it in most people's idea of disability. What I think will help us out of the dilemma is the naming of the political category in which *disability* belongs. Women is a category of *gender,* and black or Latino/a are categories of *race/ethnicity,* and it is the recognition of those categories that has fostered understanding of the political meaning of *women* and *black.* Although *race* and *gender* are not perfect terms because they retain biological meanings in many quarters, the categories are increasingly understood as axes of oppression; axes along which power and resources are distributed. Although those of us within the disability community recognize that power is distributed along disability lines, the naming and recognition of the axis will be a sig-nificant step in gaining broader recognition of the issues. Further, it will enrich the discussion of the intersections of the axes of class, race, gender and sexual orientation, and disability.

Constructing the axis on which disabled and nondisabled fall will be a critical step in marking all points along it. Currently, there is increased at-tention to the privileged points on the continua of race, gender, and sexual orientation. There is growing recognition that the white, the male, and the heterosexual positions need to be noted and theorized. Similarly, it is im-portant to examine the nondisabled position and its privilege and power. It is not the neutral, universal position from which disabled people deviate, rather, it is a category of people whose power and cultural capital keep them at the center.

In this book, though, disabled people's perspectives are kept central and are made explicit, partly to comment on how marginal and obscure they typically are, and partly to suggest the disciplinary and intellectual transformation consequent on putting disability studies at the center.

Notes

1. Various authors have discussed issues related to definitions of *disability*. See Wendell (1996), Longmore (1985, 1987), and Hahn (1987), and also the June Isaacson Kailes (1995) monograph *Language Is More Than a Trivial Concern!* which is available from the Institute on Disability Culture, 2260 Sunrise Point Road, Las Cruces, New Mexico 88011.

2. The definition of *disability* under the Americans with Disabilities Act is consistent with the sociopolitical model employed in disability studies. A person is considered to have a disability if he or she:

- has a physical or mental impairment that substantially limits one or more of his or her major life activities;
- has a record of such an impairment; or
- is regarded as having such an impairment.

The last two parts of this definition acknowledge that even in the absence of a substantially limiting impairment, people can be discriminated against. For instance, this may occur because someone has a facial disfigurement or has, or is suspected of having, HIV or mental illness. The ADA recognizes that social forces, such as myths and fears regarding disability, function to substantially limit opportunity.

3. I am indebted to my colleague John O'Neill for his input on these ideas about the use of the term *normal*.

4. See June Isaacson Kailes's (1995) *Language Is More Than a Trivial Concern!* for a discussion on language use.

Works Cited

Allen, A. 1996. Open secret: A German academic hides his past—in plain sight. *Lingua Franca* 6(3): 28–41.

American Heritage Dictionary. 1992. 3d ed. Boston: Houghton Mifflin.

Canguilhem, G. 1991. *The normal and the pathological.* New York: Zone Books.

Davis, L. J. 1995. *Enforcing normalcy: Disability, deafness, and the body.* London: Verso.

Freilich, M., Raybeck, D., and Savishinsky, J. 1991. *Deviance: Anthropological perspectives.* New York: Bergin and Garvey.

Gates, H. L., Jr. 1996. White like me. *New Yorker* 72 (16): 66–81.

Gill, C. J. 1994. Questioning continuum. In B. Shaw, ed., *The ragged edge: The disability experience from the pages of the first fifteen years of "The Disability Rag,"* 42–49. Louisville, Ky.: Advocado Press.

Grover, J. Z. 1987. AIDS: Keywords. In Douglas Crimp, ed., *AIDS: Cultural analysis,* 17–30. Cambridge: MIT Press.

Hahn, H. 1987. Disability and capitalism: Advertising the acceptably employable image. *Policy Studies Journal* 15 (3): 551–70.

Haraway, D. 1989. *Primate visions: Gender, race, and nature in the world of modern science.* New York: Routledge.

Kailes, J. I. 1995. *Language is more than a trivial concern!* (Available from June Isaacson Kailes, Disability Policy Consultant, 6201 Ocean Front Walk, Suite 2, Playa del Rey, California 90293-7556)

Longmore, P. K. 1985. The life of Randolph Bourne and the need for a history of disabled people. *Reviews in American History* 586 (December): 581–87.

———. 1987. Uncovering the hidden history of people with disabilities. *Reviews in American History* 15 (3) (September): 355–64.

Minnich, E. K. 1990. *Transforming knowledge.* Philadelphia: Temple University Press.

Sedgwick, E. K. 1990. *Epistemology of the closet.* Berkeley: University of California Press.

Shapiro, J. P. 1993. *No pity: People with disabilities forging a new civil rights movement.* New York: Times Books.

Stedman's Medical Dictionary. 1976. 23d ed. Baltimore: Williams and Wilkins.

Thomson, R. G. 1997. *Extraordinary bodies: Figuring physical disability in American culture and literature.* New York: Columbia University Press.

Tremblay, M. 1996. Going back to civvy street: A historical account of the Everest and Jennings wheelchair for Canadian World War II veterans with spinal cord injury. *Disability and Society* 11 (2): 149–69.

Tulloch, S., ed. 1993. *The Reader's Digest Oxford wordfinder.* Oxford, Eng.: Clarendon Press.

Wendell, S. 1996. *The rejected body: Feminist philosophical reflections on disability.* New York: Routledge.

Zalewski, D. 1995. Unfriendly competition. *Lingua Franca* 5 (September/October): 19–21.

Ideas for Rereading

1. Linton writes, "The disability studies' and disability rights movement's position is critical of the domination of the medical definition [of *disability*] and views it as a major stumbling block to the reinterpretation of *disability* as a political category and to the social changes that could follow such a shift" (p. 283). As you reread Simi Linton's essay, outline her evaluation of the "medical definition" of *disability* as well as her advancement of the alternate definition "marker of identity." List the reasons such a distinction is important to Linton and other activists.

2. Linton studies the importance of language in the formation of identity among disabled people, as well as in the relationship between disabled people and society at large. As you reread the essay, note your reaction to the vocabulary Linton either supports or criticizes. Which of her choices surprise you? Are there any terms that you yourself have used? Has she persuaded you to continue or discontinue that use?

Ideas for Writing

1. Begin with a clear understanding of Linton's critique of the "medical definition" of disability, the image of disabled people based on their symptoms. Why does Linton prefer to see disability as a "marker of identity" (p. 283)? What does she mean by that term? Write an essay exploring the issues inherent in the distinction between disability as a medical condition and disability as a marker of identity. Apply the terms and concepts employed by Linton to your own analysis.

2. Linton places considerable emphasis on the language that is used for disability. Write an essay that responds to her argument. To what extent does language reflect and reinforce harmful and negative attitudes? To what extent can a reformed language produce social change?

SLACKJAW

Slackjaw is a pen name for Jim Knipfel, a staff writer and columnist for the New York Press. *Knipfel's blindness—which developed over many years—is due to a genetic condition known as retinitis pigmentosa, which causes photoreceptor cells in the eye to degenerate. Early in his recently published memoir, Knipfel recalls an encounter with an older, similarly affected relative at a family funeral: "Uncle Tom looked down at me sitting there on that chair with the scratchy floral-patterned seat and didn't say hello, didn't say anything except 'You better start learning braille now.'" Knipfel's struggle to come to terms with the meaning of his Uncle Tom's words and with his own growing blindness is the subject of* Slackjaw: You Better Start Learning Braille Now *(1999), in which the chapter excerpted here appears.*

"Getting Hip to the Lights-Out Way" is largely about "matters of pride and self-sufficiency" (p. 303). As you read Slackjaw's story make a list of the things that happen to make him realize he should become more public about the fact of his blurry vision. Why does the simple act of using a cane transform him from "a crippled lamb" into "the one in control" (p. 302)? Notice the ways in which Slackjaw's attitudes about what it means to be proud and self-sufficient change during the course of his essay—throughout the piece he is motivated by pride and self-sufficiency, but what it means for him to be proud and self-sufficient changes. What does not change, however, is his opinion that "Blindness is a big pain in the ass": make notes about the main reasons that Slackjaw gives for this opinion. What, for Slackjaw, is the main problem with being blind?

Getting Hip to the Lights-Out Way

Despite the training, and the past injuries and humiliations, I found it difficult to get into the habit of pulling my cane out when I needed it. *I can handle this,* I would think when confronted with a darkened street. I continued thinking that way until I got into trouble again.

I was stumbling home late one night, my vision even blurrier than normal. I was proud of myself after slowing down enough to maneuver without incident around a bunch of voices blocking the sidewalk. I was proud of myself for maintaining my balance after hooking my leg on a gate someone had left open. Pride was what kept me from pulling the cane out. I could handle things just fine without any props to declare my cripplehood to the world. Then I stepped on something.

The dog—it sounded like a big dog, too—let out a yelp and jerked its leg from beneath my shoe.

"Christ, didn't you see it?" an old man, the dog's owner, shouted at me.

I stopped, thought about my situation, then turned in the direction of the voice.

"Jeez, I'm very sorry . . . fact is, I *didn't* see it."

"It's a big damn dog!"

"I'm sure it is. I'm sorry. Y'see, this is my fault, see, I have"—I flipped my bag open and reached inside—"I have this red-and-white cane here that I really should be using." I took the cane out and held it for the man to see. "I'm blind, sir. I didn't see the dog, and it was my fault."

"Oh my God. I'm sorry." The anger was gone from his voice, and he touched my arm lightly. "I . . . I didn't know."

"It's okay. There's no way you could've known. If I'd been using the cane the way I was supposed to, you would have, and this wouldn't have happened."

"I'm so sorry." He started to cry, quietly. I felt like a shit.

I squeezed his hand, apologized again, repeated that it was all right, then slid the cane into my bag and shuffled down the last block home, where my cats would know well enough to get the hell out of my way.

A few weeks later, I was in a similar incident. I was supposed to meet some people at a bar after work. They were coming from various parts of the city, and I decided to grab a table early and wait for them. I'd never met some of them before, and I was nervous. It was a reasonably well lit bar when the sun was out, which is why I chose it. That and the fact that the bartenders knew me.

When I walk in from the street, no matter how well lit a place is, my eyes take a few minutes to adjust. And despite the windows, there was a spot of perpetual darkness in the middle of this bar that always gave me trouble. Upon entering, I put my head down and started shoving my way to the back. It seemed pretty empty. Then I stepped on something. Again I heard a yelp. Again I'd stepped on a dog, again a big one.

"Didn't you see him? Open your fucking eyes!" a woman sitting at the bar growled.

Nearly the same exchange followed as with the old man, except that this woman was not at all forgiving. "Watch where you're fucking walking."

"Fine," I muttered as I turned away. I continued muttering as I stomped to a table in the rear, where I slapped my bag down and yanked out my cane and laid it in front of me. I jammed a smoke in my mouth and sat down to calm myself before going to get a beer.

I was half pissed at her for yelling at me and for letting her dog sprawl across the floor. But I was also half pissed at myself for fucking up again.

As I sat there stewing, the bartender quietly explained the situation to the woman. When I got up and felt my way to the bar, the woman leaned in my direction and apologized.

"It's okay," I told her. "You didn't know."

Then she kept apologizing. When I went to the bar to order a beer. When she passed me on her way to the bathroom. When she passed me on her way back from the bathroom. This went on a long time.

She's been in the bar since then, always with some large beast, and every time I walk past she tugs the creature out of my path.

"See, I pulled him out of your way," she says.

"Thank you, that's very kind. Appreciate it."

When I run into people, or step on their pets, or slam into garbage cans, stoplights, or I-beams on subway platforms, people who see me must assume that I'm intoxicated. Of course they do. Without my cane flopping around, what other explanation could there be?

"Don't laugh at me."

I knew it wasn't coming out loud enough for her to hear me. I didn't care. I stood at the corner, waiting for the light to change, quivering with an old hatred, muttering blood.

"Don't laugh at me."

It was an accident, and a simple one at that. Could happen to anyone; unfortunately, it usually happened to me. I was walking home, it was a reasonably early winter evening, and I bumped into her. Some big woman blocking most of the sidewalk, yapping with some big friend of hers.

I stopped and immediately apologized. It was reflex now. "Excuse me, I'm terribly sorry," I said, trying to look in her general direction, "but I don't see very well."

There was silence, as I shuffled the few yards to the corner. The walk sign was never with me when I needed it. With that sixth sense we blind folk develop, I could feel her tiny eyes on me. I wanted to get away.

The woman started laughing at me. The cruel, subhuman laughter of a junior high schooler. Her friend joined in. They were enjoying my predicament.

I stood on the corner, coward that I was, muttering, "Don't laugh at me," knowing they would never hear over the passing traffic. A few days after the fact, it might be no big deal, but at the time it could only trigger bad memories. I remembered one fall night a few years earlier in particular.

I was in Manhattan, on my way to a club where I was supposed to sing with a band, when a hipster walking a few steps behind me began tossing out insults. I'm not sure why. I tried to ignore him. I had to get to the club, and he wasn't worth it. But it was late and I hadn't taken my anticonvulsive. His comments burrowed into my flesh. I felt tension building in my head, and without any calming intervention, it would probably lead to a seizure.

His insults continued as we reached the middle of the block. I turned on him and threw a roundhouse his way, which caught him on the side of the head but glanced off uselessly. He backed off, stepped around me, and kept walking. I stood in the middle of the cold sidewalk, my rage all but dissipated with that one foul swing.

I could see that he was expecting me at the corner, staring at me as I stood motionless and waited for the fire to go out before I went on to the club. I don't know how long I stood there. Finally the cold started getting to me, and I had to move on. He was still waiting. There was no avoiding it. When I got up to him, I made an even greater mistake.

"Sorry about that," I said. "About punching you in the head."

"Man, I don't get that at all." He chuckled.

He moved on down the street, and I stood there, feeling filthy for having been the coward. First for not doing more damage, and then for apologizing for the damage I had done.

Since then I've had the seizures under control, as long as I remember to gobble my pills. The night those women laughed at me, I almost ran home, away from their mocking laughter, hating them, hating everyone else who had ever laughed at me. I muttered loud enough that folks on the dark sidewalk cleared a path.

Throughout my life, I realize, I've recognized things in myself that were worth mocking. I started mocking them before anybody else had the chance. What's more, my own mockery was much crueler and colder and funnier than anything anyone else would ever dare say.

That made things much easier for everybody.

I never could stand to be laughed at. That's why my encounter with those two women got to me the way it did. They didn't know me, had not read any of my stories, had no clue as to what the score was, or that I would gladly laugh at myself before they had the chance. This was a simple misencounter, the sort of thing that happened to me every day, and I made a kind and quick apology for having failed again. And they laughed at me anyway.

I had had enough.

Everybody I dealt with, myself included, thought it would take a major event to make me use my cane the way I should. Maybe a broken leg or another concussion. Blood would have to be spilled. Instead, all it took was two middle-aged, porcine gargoyles laughing at me on a darkened street corner. The night after that incident, I slipped my cane out of my bag to help me find the way home from the subway, and I've done so since.

I've kicked myself on an almost nightly basis for not having done this before. Using the cane, the very cane I went through six weeks of training to learn how to use, was the best damn idea I'd had in a long time, and for a very simple reason.

By pulling the cane out of the bag and letting it flubbity-flop open, I changed the nature of the game entirely. I inverted the rules. For the past several years, I had been shuffling down the street with all the grace of a crippled lamb, always on the defensive, afraid of what each step would slam me headlong into. I dodged shadows, but plowed straight over garbage cans. I stepped on animals, I stepped on people, and then had to explain why. I was yelled at, I was laughed at. All because my pride kept me from admitting that I needed to use a tool. I was refusing to use a hammer to pound nails, insisting that my forehead did the job just fine, thanks.

But now, ha, now once the cane comes out, I'm the one in control. Tapping home from work just three or four nights after deciding to use the cane, I stumbled hard into three people before I even got to the subway and *they* apologized to *me*. Suddenly everybody wanted to be nice to me, either by getting out of my way or by offering assistance (which I tend to decline politely).

One day I was crossing a street in the rain and heard two voices nearby. I wasn't sure they were talking to me until they repeated themselves.

"Hold there. Puddle! Big puddle in front of you!"

It was an Australian couple. I hesitated before taking another step.

"Go to your left a bit," they suggested, so I did. "There's still a puddle there, but it's not so big."

I could sense them standing there, cheering me on, afraid to simply reach out and lead me around the damn thing. Maybe they were afraid they might catch whatever I had.

"There you go, straight ahead now. Step up!"

I, of course, dropped my foot into the middle of the smaller puddle, but that was okay. Once on the curb, I started to turn the corner.

"Whoa there, look out! You want to go straight? It's over here."

"No, that's okay." I gestured with the cane. "I'm just going into this bar here. There is a bar here, isn't there?"

I thanked them and waved in what I believed their general direction before going inside.

I had been talking to friends about this decision of mine, this next step in accepting the present and the inevitable. Discussing matters of pride and self-sufficiency. For a long time, friends had been telling me that it was something I had better start doing. Still, as pigheaded as I am, it was a decision I had to make for myself.

All these months and years, I simply stopped listening to them when the question came up. Once I made the decision to use the cane, however, I could start listening again, happy with myself all the while.

"You talk about pride in making it around without it," one of my friends said, "but there is also a certain pride that must come with using it."

"Everybody parts in front of me like the fucking Red Sea, that's for damn sure."

"Yeah, it's like walking through a crowd with a shotgun."

"Except with a cane, all I can really do is whack 'em around the knees and ankles."

After the *New York Press* offices moved from SoHo to Chelsea, I was forced to walk down Twenty-third Street every morning to get to work. And every morning I would encounter three or four other blind folk. I passed by the Associated Blind building, an apartment complex designed specifically for people who can't see at all. I am told it's a hotbed for carnal rutting-about of every variety. Great orgies of the blind, I hear. And when I see these people tapping down the sidewalk or being led by their guide dogs, I can't help thinking, as I try to envision these orgies, that it's a good thing these people are blind. It's funny how many of them end up looking exactly the same: short, squat, bad bowl haircuts, puffy down jackets, puffier pasty faces. None of them I saw wore shades; I suppose they were content to face the world with their creepy blind stares.

I noted the various cane styles these folks used: they scraped their canes lightly this way and then maybe that, slid along walls, missed beats, simply didn't put their canes to any real, worthwhile use at all. Each person with his own style, but each style too sloppy.

Of course, if they were getting around okay, that was all that mattered, I suppose. Maybe my newfound pride had me working a little arrogant. They should be wielding their canes with determination and cold viciousness, I thought, each tap an announcement that something mean was coming through, so clear a path. Use the thing as if it had a silver wolf's-head handle, and walk tall. These people shuffled down the street the way I used to without a cane, afraid of what every step might bring.

I still feel uncomfortable around the blind. Not horribly uncomfortable, but vaguely so. Not nearly as uncomfortable as I felt around the deaf or the retarded, though. They have always made me nervous. I should know better. But it seems a normal, visceral human reaction to cripples, regardless of the fact that I was one of them.

One night as I was leaving work, I stopped, as I usually did, outside the doors of the office building to light a smoke. I heard a voice next to me.

"You wanna give me a little room, or what?" It was a woman's voice, and it startled me.

"I'm sorry, ma'am." I reached into my bag and grabbed my cane, then let it flop open. "But I didn't see you there."

"Goodness sakes, look at you. You carry yourself just like a sighted person. I think that's great."

"Thank you, ma'am," I said, before heading off down the sidewalk. I took it as a tremendous compliment. Perhaps I shouldn't have. I spent most of my life sighted, or reasonably so, and never had anything but trouble.

"Veer to your right a little."

I recognized the voice by now. This was the third night in a row that I'd heard it. Each time I was tapping my way to the subway after work, and each time it offered some helpful information. Whoever was speaking—it was a man, that's all I know—never stopped, never introduced himself, never spoke more than a sentence, always kept walking.

The first night it was, "You're crossing Twenty-fifth Street."

"Thank you," I said, as we went in opposite directions. By now I was used to people offering helpful bits of information to me. But this guy kept popping up.

The next night it was, "Hurry, the light's going to change at any second."

"Thank you," I said again. And again, I thought nothing of it. It wasn't until after the third night, when he said, "Veer to the right a little," that I came to expect him, and started to find it all very funny and peculiar.

I can't get to the train these days without having one person, and usually more, offer assistance in some way. Whether it's the old woman who
told me the light had changed, but to watch out for "those goddamn cab
drivers," or the Puerto Rican midget who helped me cross for six straight
blocks, or the bum who, goodness exploding from his tattered insane
heart, grabbed my arm and dragged me across the street after I told him I
didn't need any help, me stumbling over my own feet, the cane catching
every bump in the road and finishing in a puddle, the bum furious because
I wasn't moving fast enough. Well, I wasn't moving fast enough because
the wind was howling that night, and along with handling the cane, I was
trying to keep my hat from flying away and to balance a smoke with my
free hand as he yanked me between the cars.

In the midst of all these other voices, there has been this singularly
kind and accurate one. Even if I didn't need it, even if I knew very well that
I had to veer to the right a little, I appreciated it.

The phone rang in the middle of the afternoon one Tuesday in March.
"Jim?"
"Yeah." I recognized the voice; it was my caseworker from the Commission for the Blind.
"I was concerned," she said. "Jack from the Lighthouse said he's been
trying to get hold of you, but you weren't returning his calls. And when he
called the paper, whoever answered the phone told him you were just a
free-lancer."
"That was him? Yeah, that was me who told him that. He never told
me who he was, so I never told him who I was."
"He says he has some computer software tips for you."
"Yeah, well, I'll tell you, when he stopped by the office, oh, what?
about eight months ago now, he said he'd get back to me the next day.
Never heard a peep out of him, till now. I've since taken care of most of
that stuff for myself."
"What did you get?"
I ran through the list. Not too much, but more than the Lighthouse
had been able to help with.
"And it's working okay?"
"Yeah, fine."
"Good, then. It sounds like things are going pretty well for you. It
sounds like you're doing just fine."
"Guess so," I told her.
"Super. In that case, I think I'm going to close your file. I think we've
taken care of everything."
"Yeah, great," I said. "Go ahead."
"Great."
Before she hung up, though, before she could slap a sticker across my
folder, happy to have foisted another self-sufficient blind man onto the
streets of New York City, no burden on anyone anymore, I stopped her.

"Hey, before you go."

"Yes?"

"Thanks for the help."

"No problem." End of conversation, and I went back to work.

In one of the newsletters I received regularly from the Lighthouse, someone suggested, as a helpful New Year's resolution, "Update your will." I wasn't sure how to take that when I first read it. I thought it was funny, in a sick way. I still do.

Going blind is itself a sick and funny business. Especially going blind slowly, over thirty years. I got used to the notion as the lights dimmed. It may have taken me a long time to learn to do things, learn to use the cane for instance, but I finally did learn. And I finally did use it.

Blindness, without question, changes a lot of things, despite what all the Blind Man Trainers in the world would like to say. Life becomes much more structured, much more organized, much smaller, at least if you live alone. You can't go out and take a long, aimless stroll through the city on a carefree Sunday afternoon. Okay, you could, but probably not without dire consequences. You can't hop a bus and ride to a town you've never visited, simply because you've never visited that town before. Even the notion of moving into a different apartment, for me at least, is ridiculous. Every object around you must remain cemented in place except while in use. Out of necessity, the blind become in a sense not only agoraphobic but obsessive-compulsive as well.

People who are involved in the blind industry, the trainers, the social workers, the self-righteous types, don't care to hear things like this. But I prefer being honest.

Blindness is a big pain in the ass. If I had a choice, of course I wouldn't be blind. It would be stupid to choose blindness. Given that I don't have a choice in the matter, given that I am in it now, and in it for good, I have to decide where to go from here. Suicide no longer interests me. Nor do I have any interest in being one of those overcompensatory types who learns how to ski and sky-dive. Nor am I interested in joining the blind subculture, full of blind people talking about blind things all the time, wasting their days wallowing in memories of sight.

There is another route, somewhere between denying and wallowing. Despite everything, going blind hasn't bothered me so much, except for those times when I fall or unduly burden someone. It's another thing to deal with, like madness or drunkenness or crime or poverty or the realization that I've hurt people around me over the years. All of those things, in one way or another, will be with me forever, near the surface. Going blind, curiously, has been my salvation from many of these things — or my karmic retribution. The blindness will be *on* the surface, of course, affecting everything I do.

It's just one more float in the weirdness parade I have been marching in my whole life. I know there is more weirdness along the way, around the corner in front of me, so I will trudge along as I have all these years. I'm anxious to see what's coming next. And what's coming will be interesting, that's for damn sure, because I'll keep fucking up. I know I will. It's what I do best.

Ideas for Rereading

1. In his essay, Slackjaw often refers to himself and other disabled people as "cripples." As you reread the essay, note your response to his use of this word. Extend your response by analyzing his use of the word *cripple* in terms of Simi Linton's discussion of the word.

2. Consider Slackjaw's use of humor to portray his situation, his acceptance of inevitable blindness. Note his stated reasons for such humor. What effect does this rhetorical strategy have on your perception of Slackjaw? On your perception of his disability? How does his use of humor affect your perception of blind people in general?

3. Reread Simi Linton's essay, focusing first on the disabled community's will to self-definition and then on her discussion of the perils of "passing" for nondisabled. Then reread Slackjaw's essay, noting the passages in which he attempts to define his own character. In what ways does Slackjaw's self-definition run up against Linton's critique of "passing"? Take into account Slackjaw's self-confessed desire to be different from the blind people with whom he is in contact and his self-confessed aversion to other disabled people.

Ideas for Writing

1. Slackjaw writes about the process of acceptance of his blindness and of the moment when that acceptance took final shape—symbolized by his decision to use the white cane. Write about a time when you made the decision to accept an undesirable circumstance. What event spurred you to that decision? What were the effects of that acceptance? Was your experience in any way analogous to Slackjaw's? How? How not?

2. Unlike Helen Keller, who had no memory of ever seeing, Slackjaw spent his youth as a sighted person. Reread the Keller and Slackjaw selections, and consider how these biographical facts affect the writers' attitudes, the way they present and understand their experiences as blind persons. Write an essay discussing Keller's and Slackjaw's work in terms of this difference.

EXTENDING YOUR WORK

Ideas for Research

1. Georgina Kleege refers to Keller as the "original disability poster child" (p. 278). While Kleege does not mean this as a compliment, the poster child is still a common fundraising tool among organizations purporting to serve disabled people. Conduct research into the use of poster children to promote the cause of people with disabilities. What are the roots of this practice? Can you relate the idea to Keller's own fundraising for the American Federation for the Blind? Write an essay examining some aspect of this history.

2. Focusing on Georgina Kleege's fruitless search for signs of the "rage" she believes Keller must have stifled during her life, conduct your own research into Keller's life—analyze the myth and what you can discover about the reality. Look at biographies, letters, photos, and examples of her writing. Then, in a paper try to construct a picture of Keller that goes beyond her public myth and perhaps even hints at the rage Kleege is unable to discover.

3. Using the Internet and traditional sources, review the promotional materials of at least three organizations for disabled people—for instance, Amvets, the Muscular Dystrophy Association, the American Federation for the Blind. In what ways do these materials reflect a rhetoric that empowers disabled people? Which materials might be termed, in Simi Linton's phrase, "ableist"? Which materials might Linton, Harlan Lane, and others perceive as perpetuating a victimology of disabled people? Write an essay considering the intended audience for the research materials you have located. Assess the positions of the authors by analyzing them in terms of Linton's discussion of definitions. Which words and phrases best reveal the attitude of your sources?

4. Harlan Lane begins his essay with a discussion of the controversy surrounding the cochlear implant. Conduct your own research into the controversy with an aim to developing an informed opinion on the subject. (On the Internet, you may wish to visit www.cici.org, the Cochlear Implant Club International.) Illustrate that opinion in a well-reasoned essay.

Ideas for Working across Chapters

1. Use examples from the Contemporary Conversation for the Woolf chapter to develop at least two working definitions of the terms *culture* and *community*. Use these definitions to consider the examples of deaf culture and community put forward by Sacks and Lane. In what ways does the discussion of gender identity assist you in your understanding of the cultures of disability? In what ways do considerations of gender identity lead us into "extrapolative errors" when it comes to blindness and deafness?

2. Refer to W. E. B. Du Bois's definition of *double-consciousness* in Chapter 2. Then reread the personal essays in this chapter—those by Keller, Slackjaw,

and Kleege. Is it possible for disabled people to experience a double-consciousness parallel to that described by Du Bois? Using at least one of the works suggested, write an essay exploring areas where the writer may be evincing a sort of double-consciousness. To what extent is he or she aware of that double-consciousness and participating in its critique?

CHAPTER 4

The Unconscious
How Can We Understand Ourselves?

Euro-American culture assumes Sigmund Freud's work as part of its indelible fabric of ideas: narcissism, repression, slips of the tongue, Oedipus and Electra complexes, dream analysis, anal retention, subconsciousness, phallic imagery, and countless other phrases and ideas have become central to the ways in which we understand ourselves as socio-sexual beings. These phrases and ideas, which constitute the discipline of psychoanalysis, develop out of Freud's persistent effort to understand human motivations, desires, and behaviors: they are all part of Freud's effort to understand, and to name, the contents of the unconscious mind.

Psychoanalysis is founded on a basic principle: human beings are driven by unconscious forces. For the psychoanalyst, understanding the unconscious mind begins with the creation of conditions that allow expression of repressed ideas and experiences, traumatic phenomena that have been pushed into parts of the brain inaccessible to the conscious mind. The whole point of psychoanalysis is to bring unconscious ideas into consciousness: once they are in the open these ideas can be untangled, deciphered, understood. This is far from being just an intellectual exercise. The assumption behind Freud's method is that repressed ideas and experiences are responsible for physical and behavioral problems, for problems that cause individuals all manner of pain and distress. Exposed and interpreted through various techniques of the sort demonstrated in "A Fragment of an Analysis of a Case of Hysteria," a case study of a Viennese woman born in 1882, the contents of the unconscious mind become understandable; and with understanding comes healing.

Because the path to wellness is trodden with speech, Freud's method is sometimes referred to as the "talking cure." It has entered the popular imagination of Europeans and Americans in ways that shape our everyday lives and experiences: Oprah Winfrey, Geraldo Rivera, Woody Allen, and countless others have made careers by capitalizing on the pervasiveness of Freudian ways of thinking. A quick sense of the history of hysteria should suggest how Freud's methods advanced our understanding of the human mind. Dora—Freud's name for Ida Bauer, the patient analyzed in "A Fragment of an Analysis of a Case of Hysteria"—was diagnosed with hysteria and had already been treated unsuccessfully with electrotherapy, hydrotherapy, and other methods before being referred to Freud. When she terminated her treatment after narrating the second dream, which we include, Dora was essentially cured.

When "A Fragment of an Analysis of a Case of Hysteria" was published in 1905, treatments of hysteria were largely based on the assumption that it was caused by physical abnormalities. One of the oldest recorded medical diagnoses—a piece of Egyptian papyrus from 1900 B.C.—identifies "hysteria." The word itself comes from the Sanskrit for "stomach" and the Greek word for "uterus"—hysteria was long thought to be caused by a dislocation of the uterus. We get a glimpse into the way the ancient Greeks understood hysteria from Plato's argument in the *Timaeus:*

> The womb is an animal which longs to generate children. When it remains barren too long after puberty, it is distressed and sorely disturbed, and straying about in the body and cutting off the passages of the breath, it impedes respiration and brings the sufferer into the extremest anguish and provokes all manner of diseases besides.

This understanding of hysteria as a disease with a physical cause led the ancient Greeks to treat the disease by fumigating the uterus, tightly wrapping the abdomen, and prescribing regular sexual intercourse in the marriage bed. Although Roman doctors later had enough dissection-based knowledge to dispel theories about wandering wombs, they still saw hysteria as a product of the female anatomy and as something to be cured through marriage and heterosexual sex.

After the rise of Christianity, with its fundamental assumption that all human pain is the result of sin and evil, hysteria was understood as the female manifestation of satanic possession. If rituals of prayer, chanting, penance, and exorcism failed to rid women of Satan, they were treated as "witches" and burned. Between the Renaissance in the sixteenth century and the end of the eighteenth century, practitioners emphasized medical pathology: hysteria was increasingly regarded as a complex physical ailment with a number of emotional causes. Instead of being burned, those diagnosed with hysteria were treated as lunatics and were thrown into asylums. At the same time, major advances in understanding the nervous system led to the development of what Mark Micale, author of *Approaching Hysteria: Disease and Its Interpretations,* calls "the first neuropsychological model of the disease." Seventeenth-century neurologists such as Thomas Sydenham argued that the disease was so comprehensive that it mimicked many other diseases *and* that it was observable in men as well as women.

Interestingly enough, the next phase in the history of hysteria again emphasized connections between hysteria and female sexuality. But now doctors theorized that hysteria was the result of an overactive sex life. During the eighteenth and nineteenth centuries doctors developed techniques to control female sexuality with physical interventions: in mild cases this involved douches and the application of pressure; in the most extreme cases, sexual organs were removed. In the entire history of hysteria up to this point, in the one area medicine concerned with what we now refer to as "the unconscious mind," no one had imagined that the psyche, the mind, might be a source of physical and behavioral ailments: the mind itself was regarded as a physical thing, as something indistinguishable from the brain; ideas were produced through physical processes, good and bad, or they were derived from an external agent, divine or satanic.

When Freud began to study bodily ailments that did not respond to established medical treatments and that had no obvious physical cause, the main influence was the French physician Jean-Martin Charcot. Charcot was based at the Salpêtrière, a clinic and teaching hospital in Paris that attracted students from across Europe. Freud studied with Charcot for five months in 1885 and 1886. A charismatic figure, Charcot defined hysteria as a neurological phenomenon with hereditary and environmental causes. He became famous for theatrical performances in which female patients would display symptoms in response to prodding with a baton, but he did little to develop cures because he saw the illness as a product of innate physiological disorders. The movement away from neurological explanations for hysteria, explanations based on analysis of the nervous system, coincides with the development of theories of the unconscious mind. The most important of these developments were all made by students of Charcot. For example, Hippolyte Bernheim and Pierre Janet, two French doctors based at the Salpêtrière, experimented with hypnotherapy and magnetotherapy; but it was Freud who demonstrated how a theory of the unconscious could be used to cure hysteria. Freud earned his place in history because, at the same time that his theories shifted emphasis from physiology to psychology, from physical symptoms to the unconscious causes of those symptoms, his practice actually cured people.

When Freud began his work with patients diagnosed as hysterical, hypnosis, electrotherapy (application of localized electric shocks), and hydrotherapy (blasting the body with jets of alternately hot and cold water) were widely practiced. Janet had suggested a way forward by moving to magnetotherapy, a technique that uses magnets held at a slight distance from the site of any given symptom: he had thus eliminated direct physical contact between the doctor's instruments and the patient's body. Freud turned his entire attention to the psyche, transforming the entire interaction between patient and doctor into talk. The cure for hysteria became a matter of talking and analyzing: physical manipulation of the patient's body gave way to psychological engagement with the patient's mind.

This chapter uses long extracts from "The Clinical Picture" of "A Fragment of an Analysis of a Case of Hysteria" to give a detailed sense of how Freud's "talking cure" works. We have included the full text of Freud's interpretations of Dora's "Second Dream" to provide a hands-on example of how he understood the main conscious product of the unconscious mind: the dream. The Context selections give a sense of the state of medicine immediately before Freud, some idea of Freud's reflections on his work with Dora, and a glimpse into the immediate European and American response to the publication of the Dora case study. The four Conversation texts contextualize and complicate Freud's legacy. Michel Foucault's "Scientia Sexualis" takes a historical view, showing how voluntary and forced confessions and personal narratives have become part of scientific practice. Foucault puts Freud's work in the context of the traditions of Asian and Western erotic art and Christian acts of confession and contrition. In "Woman's Place in Man's Life Cycle," Carol Gilligan places Freud in a twentieth-century tradition of male-centered psychology that has "tried to fashion women out of a masculine cloth" (p. 391). Gilligan's interest is in overcoming psychological models of human development that have tended to treat women and girls as failures: while she does not directly address the case of Dora, Gilligan should help you see the observational bias at work in Freud's analysis of Dora's stories. Both Carolyn Steedman and Janet Malcolm make direct reference to "A Fragment of an Analysis of a Case of Hysteria," exposing and challenging its ways of thinking about its subject. Steedman's "Histories" puts Dora's case in the context of the story of an eight-year-old girl who sold watercress on the streets of London in 1849. Different as the stories are in terms of social and economic conditions, they both demonstrate Steedman's argument that "the compulsions of scientific inquiry" led "middle-aged men" to induce women and young girls to tell stories that were then shown to fail as narratives (p. 411). Taking a different tack in a review of a book about "A Fragment of an Analysis of a Case of Hysteria," Malcolm suggests that the only benefit of psychoanalysis is that "the patient leaves the analysis older, and wiser about analysis" (p. 422).

As you read the selections in this chapter, pay close attention to the ways in which storytelling operates. How does each writer address the subject of storytelling? How does each writer evaluate the cultural usefulness of personal narration and confession? And how does each writer understand the process through which the messy raw material of everyday life is transformed into stories that can be interpreted and analyzed?

TEXT

SIGMUND FREUD

Sigismundo Schlomo Freud was born in Freiburg, Moravia, on May 6, 1856. After initially considering the study of law, he enrolled at Vienna University as a medical student in 1873. Freud was interdisciplinary from the start: his 1881 graduation from medical school was long overdue because he was more interested in research and a variety of courses across the humanities than he was in becoming a practicing doctor. In 1882, however, he began work in an internlike position at Vienna General Hospital. His on-the-job training was supplemented in 1885 by study with the famous Paris-based neurologist Jean-Martin Charcot. On returning to Vienna in 1886 Freud was a fully qualified doctor and set up a private practice. While he invested most of his start-up money in tools designed to treat physical ailments with electric shocks, he also incorporated Charcot's techniques of hypnosis.

By 1892 Freud no longer used water and electricity as part of his repertoire of therapeutic methods and was moving away from hypnosis; he had begun to develop "the talking cure." In 1894 he published "The Neuro-Psychoses of Defense," explaining the sexual causes of hysterical symptoms; in 1896 he published "Heredity and the Aetiology of the Neuroses," coining the word psychoanalysis *to describe his innovative method for using a patient's stories to develop a diagnosis and cure. During the next decade Freud wrote and published his most important and controversial works:* The Interpretation of Dreams *(1900) and* Three Essays on the Theory of Sexuality *(1905) established the field of psychoanalysis. With the publication of "A Fragment of an Analysis of a Case of Hysteria" in 1905, Freud provided an extended demonstration of how the talking cure works in practice. The Dora case is one of the foundational texts in the field of psychotherapy.*

From 1905 until 1939, when Freud died in London after his 1938 escape from Hitlerist anti-Semitism, Freud refined his theory, applying it in ever-widening spheres by using it to study the general questions of anxiety (in Inhibitions, Symptoms, and Anxiety, *1926), civilization (in* Civilization and Its Discontents, *1930), and religion (most famously in* Moses and Monotheism, *1938).*

As you read "The Clinical Picture" and "The Second Dream" pay attention to the ways in which Freud establishes his position as a doctor. What does he say that is specifically designed to convince you that you should take him seriously? What, exactly, does he do that you recognize as the work of a doctor? Also pay attention to the ways in which he positions Dora as a patient. What specific details does he provide about her illness? What, exactly, did she suffer from? Identify specific passages where Freud discusses the content of Dora's unconscious mind. How does he understand this content? As you make notes, distinguish between the places where Freud summarizes Dora's situation and the places where he offers interpretations of this situation.

From *A Fragment of an Analysis of a Case of Hysteria*

The Clinical Picture

In my *Interpretations of Dreams*,[1] published in 1900, I showed that dreams in general can be interpreted, and that after the work of interpretation has been completed they can be replaced by perfectly correctly constructed thoughts which can be assigned a recognizable position in the chain of mental events. I wish to give an example in the following pages of the only practical application of which the art of interpreting dreams seems to admit. . . . The dream is one of the roads along which consciousness can be reached by psychical material which, on account of the opposition aroused by its content, has been cut off from consciousness and repressed, and has thus become pathogenic. The dream, in short, is one of the *détours by which repression can be evaded*; it is one of the principal means employed by what is known as the indirect method of representation in the mind. The following fragment from the history of the treatment of a hysterical girl is intended to show the way in which the interpretation of dreams plays a part in the work of analysis. . . .

If I were to begin by giving a full and consistent case history, it would place the reader in a very different situation from that of the medical observer. The reports of the patient's relatives—in the present case I was given one by the eighteen-year-old girl's father—usually afford a very indistinct picture of the course of the illness. I begin the treatment, indeed, by asking the patient to give me the whole story of his life and illness, but even so the information I receive is never enough to let me see my way about the case. The first account may be compared to an unnavigable river whose stream is at one moment choked by masses of rock and at another divided and lost among shallows and sandbanks. I cannot help wondering how it is that the authorities can produce such smooth and precise histories in cases of hysteria. As a matter of fact the patients are incapable of giving such reports about themselves. They can, indeed, give the physician plenty of coherent information about this or that period of their lives; but it is sure to be followed by another period as to which their communications run dry, leaving gaps unfilled, and riddles unanswered; and then again will come yet another period which will remain totally obscure and unilluminated by even a single piece of serviceable information. The connections—even the ostensible ones—are for the most part incoherent, and the sequence of different events is uncertain. Even during the course of their story patients will repeatedly correct a particular or a date, and then perhaps, after wavering for some time, return to their first version. The patients' inability to give an ordered history of their life in so far as it coincides with the history of their illness is not merely characteristic of the neurosis.[2] It also possesses great theoretical significance. For this inability has the following grounds. In the first place, patients consciously and intentionally keep back part of what they ought to tell—things that are perfectly well known to them—because they have not got over their feelings of timidity and shame (or discretion, where what they say concerns other people); this is the share taken by *conscious* disingenuousness. In the second place, part of the anamnestic knowledge, which the patients have at their disposal at other times, disappears while they are actually telling their story, but without making any deliberate reservations: the share taken by *unconscious* disingenuousness. In the third place, there are invariably true amnesias—gaps in the memory into which not only old recollections but even quite recent ones have fallen—and paramnesias, formed secondarily so as to fill in those gaps.[3] When the events themselves have been kept in mind, the purpose underlying the amnesias can be fulfilled just as surely by destroying a connection, and a connection is most surely broken by altering the chronological order of events. The latter always proves to be the most vulnerable element in the store of memory and the one which is most easily subject to repression. Again, we meet with many recollections that are in what might be described as the first stage of repression, and these we find surrounded with doubts. At a later period the doubts would be replaced by a loss or a falsification of memory.[4]

That this state of affairs should exist in regard to the memories relating to the history of the illness is *a necessary correlate of the symptoms and one which is theoretically requisite.* In the further course of the treatment the patient supplies the facts which, though he had known them all along, had been kept back by him or had not occurred to his mind. The paramnesias prove untenable, and the gaps in his memory are filled in. It is only towards the end of the treatment that we have before us an intelligible, consistent, and unbroken case history. Whereas the practical aim of the treatment is to remove all possible symptoms and to replace them by conscious thoughts, we may regard it as a second and theoretical aim to repair all the damages to the patient's memory. These two aims are coincident. When one is reached, so is the other; and the same path leads to them both.

It follows from the nature of the facts which form the material of psycho-analysis that we are obliged to pay as much attention in our case histories to the purely human and social circumstances of our patients as to the somatic data and the symptoms of the disorder. Above all, our interest will be directed towards their family circumstances—and not only, as will be seen later, for the purpose of enquiring into their heredity.

The family circle of the eighteen-year-old girl who is the subject of this paper included, besides herself, her two parents and a brother who was one and a half years her senior. Her father was the dominating figure in this circle, owing to his intelligence and his character as much as to the circumstances of his life. It was those circumstances which provided the framework for the history of the patient's childhood and illness. At the time at which I began the girl's treatment her father was in his late forties, a man of rather unusual activity and talents, a large manufacturer in very comfortable circumstances. His daughter was most tenderly attached to him, and for that reason her critical powers, which developed early, took all the more offence at many of his actions and peculiarities.

Her affection for him was still further increased by the many severe illnesses he had been through since her sixth year. At that time he had fallen ill with tuberculosis and the family had consequently moved to a small town in a good climate, situated in one of our southern provinces. There his lung trouble rapidly improved; but, on account of the precautions which were still considered necessary, both parents and children continued for the next ten years or so to reside chiefly in this spot, which I shall call B——. When her father's health was good, he used at times to be away, on visits to his factories. During the hottest part of the summer the family used to move to a health-resort in the hills.

When the girl was about ten years old, her father had to go through a course of treatment in a darkened room on account of a detached retina. As a result of this misfortune his vision was permanently impaired. His gravest illness occurred some two years later. It took the form of a confusional attack, followed by symptoms of paralysis and slight mental disturbances. A friend of his (who plays a part in the story with which we shall be concerned later on [see p. 351, *n.* 13] persuaded him, while his condition had scarcely improved, to travel to Vienna with his physician and come to me for advice. I hesitated for some time as to whether I ought not to regard the case as one of tabo-paralysis, but I finally decided upon a diagnosis of a diffuse vascular affection; and since the patient admitted having had a specific infection before his marriage, I prescribed an energetic course of anti-luetic treatment, as a result of which all the remaining disturbances passed off. It is no doubt owing to this fortunate intervention of mine that four years later he brought his daughter, who had meanwhile grown unmistakably neurotic, and introduced her to me, and that after another two years he handed her over to me for psychotherapeutic treatment.

I had in the meantime also made the acquaintance in Vienna of a sister of his, who was a little older than himself. She gave clear evidence of a severe form of psychoneurosis without any characteristically hysterical symptoms. After a life which had been weighed down by an unhappy marriage, she died of a marasmus which made rapid advances and the symptoms of which were, as a matter of fact, never fully cleared up. An elder brother of the girl's father, whom I once happened to meet, was a hypochondriacal bachelor.

The sympathies of the girl herself, who, as I have said, became my patient at the age of eighteen, had always been with the father's side of the family, and ever since she had fallen ill she had taken as her model the aunt who has just been mentioned. There could be no doubt, too, that it was from her father's family that she had derived not only her natural gifts and her intellectual precocity but also the predisposition to her illness. I never made her mother's acquaintance. From the accounts given me by the girl and her father I was led to imagine her as an uncultivated woman and above all as a foolish one, who had concentrated all her interests upon domestic affairs, especially since her husband's illness and the estrangement to which it led. She presented the picture, in fact, of what might be called the "housewife's psychosis." She had no understanding of her children's more active interests, and was occupied all day long in cleaning the house with its furniture and utensils and in keeping them clean—to such an extent as to make it almost impossible to use or enjoy them. This condition, traces of which are to be found often enough in normal housewives, inevitably reminds one of forms of obsessional washing and other kinds of obsessional cleanliness. But such women (and this applied to the patient's mother) are entirely without insight into their illness, so that one essential characteristic of an "obsessional neurosis" is lacking. The relations between the girl and her mother had been unfriendly for years. The daughter looked down on her mother and used to criticize her mercilessly, and she had withdrawn completely from her influence.[5]

During the girl's earlier years, her only brother (her elder by a year and a half) had been the model which her ambitions had striven to follow. But in the last few years the relations between the brother and sister had grown more distant. The young man used to try so far as he could to keep out of the family disputes; but when he was obliged to take sides he would support his mother. So that the usual sexual attraction had drawn together the father and daughter on the one side and the mother and son on the other.

The patient, to whom I shall in future give the name of "Dora,"[6] had even at the age of eight begun to develop neurotic symptoms. She became subject at that time to chronic dyspnoea with occasional accesses in which the symptom was very much aggravated. The first onset occurred after a short expedition in the mountains and was accordingly put down to overexertion. In the course of six months, during which she was made to rest and was carefully looked after, this condition gradually passed off. The family doctor seems to have had not a moment's hesitation in diagnosing the disorder as purely nervous and in excluding any organic cause for the dyspnoea; but he evidently considered this diagnosis compatible with the aetiology of over-exertion.

The little girl went through the usual infectious diseases of childhood without suffering any lasting damage. As she herself told me—and her words were intended to convey a deeper meaning—her brother was as a rule the first to start the illness and used to have it very slightly, and she would then follow suit with a severe form of it. When she was about twelve she began to suffer from unilateral headaches in the nature of a migraine, and from attacks of nervous coughing. At first these two symptoms always appeared together, but they became separated later on and ran different courses. The migraine grew rarer, and by the time she was sixteen she had quite got over it. But attacks of *tussis nervosa,* which had no doubt been started by a common catarrh, continued to occur over the whole period. When, at the age of eighteen, she came to me for treatment, she was again coughing in a characteristic manner. The number of these attacks could not be determined; but they lasted from three to five weeks, and on one occasion for several months. The most troublesome symptom during the first half of an attack of this kind, at all events in the last few years, used to be a complete loss of voice. The diagnosis that this was once more a nervous complaint had been established long since; but the various methods of treatment which are usual, including hydrotherapy and the local application of electricity, had produced no result. It was in such circumstances as these that the child had developed into a mature young woman of very independent judgement, who had grown accustomed to laugh at the efforts of doctors, and in the end to renounce their help entirely. Moreover, she had always been against calling in medical advice, though she had no personal objection to her family doctor. Every proposal to consult a new physician aroused her resistance, and it was only her father's authority which induced her to come to me at all.

I first saw her when she was sixteen, in the early summer. She was suffering from a cough and from hoarseness, and even at that time I proposed giving her psychological treatment. My proposal was not adopted, since the attack in question, like the others, passed off spontaneously, though it had lasted unusually long. During the next winter she came and stayed in Vienna with her uncle and his daughters after the death of the aunt of whom she had been so fond. There she fell ill of a feverish disorder which was diagnosed at the time as appendicitis.[7] In the following autumn, since her father's health seemed to justify the step, the family left the health-resort of B—— for good and all. They first moved to the town where her father's factory was situated, and then, scarcely a year later, settled permanently in Vienna.

Dora was by that time in the first bloom of youth—a girl of intelligent and engaging looks. But she was a source of heavy trials for her parents. Low spirits and an alteration in her character had now become the main features of her illness. She was clearly satisfied neither with herself nor her family; her attitude towards her father was unfriendly, and she was on very bad terms with her mother, who was bent upon drawing her into taking a share in the work of the house. She tried to avoid social intercourse, and employed herself—so far as she was allowed to by the fatigue and lack of concentration of which she complained—with attending lectures for women and with carrying on more or less serious studies. One day her parents were thrown into a state of great alarm by finding on the girl's writing-desk, or inside it, a letter in which she took leave of them because, as she said, she could no longer endure her life.[8] Her father, indeed, being a man of some perspicacity, guessed that the girl had no serious suicidal intentions. But he was none the less very much shaken; and when one day, after a slight passage of words between him and his daughter, she had a first attack of loss of consciousness[9]—an event which was subsequently covered by an amnesia—it was determined, in spite of her reluctance, that she should come to me for treatment.

No doubt this case history, as I have so far outlined it, does not upon the whole seem worth recording. It is merely a case of *"petite hystérie"* with the commonest of all somatic and mental symptoms: dyspnoea, *tussis nervosa,* aphonia, and possibly migraines, together with depression, hysterical unsociability, and a *taedium vitae* which was probably not entirely genuine. More interesting cases of hysteria have no doubt been published, and they have very often been more carefully described; for nothing will be found in the following pages on the subject of stigmata of cutaneous sensibility, limitation of the visual field, or similar matters. I may venture to remark, however, that all such collections of the strange and wonderful phenomena of hysteria have but slightly advanced our knowledge of a disease which still remains as great a puzzle as ever. What is wanted is precisely an elucidation of the *commonest* cases and of their most frequent and typical symptoms. I should have been very well satisfied if the circumstances had allowed me to give a complete elucidation of this case of *petite hystérie*. And my experiences with other patients leave me in no doubt that my analytic method would have enabled me to do so. . . .

In Dora's case, thanks to her father's shrewdness which I have remarked upon more than once already, there was no need for me to look about for points of contact between the circumstances of the patient's life and her illness, at all events in its most recent form. Her father told me that he and his family while they where at B—— had formed an intimate friendship with a married couple who had been settled there for several years. Frau K. had nursed him during his long illness, and had in that way, he said, earned a title to his undying gratitude. Herr K. had always been most kind to Dora. He had gone walks with her when he was there, and had made her small presents; but no one had thought any harm of that. Dora had taken the greatest care of the K.'s two little children, and been almost a mother to them. When Dora and her father had come to see me two years before in the summer, they had been just on their way to stop with Herr and Frau K., who were spending the summer on one of our lakes in the Alps. Dora was to have spent several weeks at the K.'s, while her father had intended to return home after a few days. During that time Herr K. had been staying there as well. As her father was preparing for his departure the girl had suddenly declared with the greatest determination that she was going with him, and she had in fact put her decision into effect. It was not until some days later that she had thrown any light upon her strange behaviour. She had then told her mother—intending that what she said should be passed on to her father—Herr K. had had the audacity to make her a proposal while they were on a walk after a trip upon the lake. Herr K. had been called to account by her father and uncle on the next occasion of their meeting, but he had denied in the most emphatic terms having on his side made any advances which could have been open to such a construction. He had then proceeded to throw suspicion upon the girl, saying that he had heard from Frau K. that she took no interest in anything but sexual matters, and that she used to read Mantegazza's *Physiology of Love* and books of that sort in their house on the lake. It was most likely, he had added, that she had been over-excited by such reading and had merely "fancied" the whole scene she had described.

"I have no doubt," continued her father, "that this incident is responsible for Dora's depression and irritability and suicidal ideas. She keeps pressing me to break off relations with Herr K. and more particularly with Frau K., whom she used positively to worship formerly. But that I cannot do. For, to begin with, I myself believe that Dora's tale of the man's immoral suggestions is a phantasy that has forced its way into her mind; and besides I am bound to Frau K. by ties of honourable friendship and I do not wish to cause her pain. The poor woman is most unhappy with her husband, of whom, by the by, I have no very high opinion. She herself has suffered a great deal with her nerves, and I am her only support. With my state of health I need scarcely assure you that there is nothing wrong in our relations. We are just two poor wretches who give one another what comfort we can by an exchange of friendly sympathy. You know already that I get nothing out of my own wife. But Dora, who inherits my obstinacy, cannot be moved from her hatred of the K.'s. She had her last attack after a conversation in which she had again pressed me to break with them. Please try and bring her to reason."

Her father's words did not always quite tally with this pronouncement; for on other occasions he tried to put the chief blame for Dora's impossible behaviour on her mother—whose peculiarities made the house unbearable for every one. But I had resolved from the first to suspend my judgement of the true state of affairs till I had heard the other side as well.

The experience with Herr K.—his making love to her and the insult to her honour which was involved—seems to provide in Dora's case the psychical trauma which Breuer and I declared long ago[10] to be the indispensable prerequisite for the production of a hysterical disorder. But this new case also presents all the difficulties which have since led me to go beyond that theory,[11] besides an additional difficulty of a special kind. For, as so often happens in histories of cases of hysteria, the trauma that we know of as having occurred in the patient's past life is insufficient to explain or to determine the *particular character* of the symptoms; we should understand just as much or just as little of the whole business if the result of the trauma had been symptoms quite other than *tussis nervosa*, aphonia, depression, and *taedium vitae*. But there is the further consideration that some of these symptoms (the cough and the loss of voice) had been produced by the patient years before the time of the trauma, and that their earliest appearances belong to her childhood, since they occurred in her eighth year. If, therefore, the trauma theory is not to be abandoned, we must go back to her childhood and look about there for any influences or impressions which might have had an effect analogous to that of a trauma. Moreover, it deserves to be remarked that in the investigation even of cases in which the first symptoms had not already set in in childhood I have been driven to trace back the patients' life history to their earliest years.[12]

When the first difficulties of the treatment had been overcome, Dora told me of an earlier episode with Herr K., which was even better calculated to act as a sexual trauma. She was fourteen years old at the time. Herr K. had made an arrangement with her and his wife that they should meet him one afternoon at his place of business in the principal square of B—— so as to have a view of a church festival. He persuaded his wife, however, to stay at home, and sent away his clerks, so that he was alone when the girl arrived. When the time for the procession approached, he asked the girl to wait for him at the door which opened on to the staircase leading to the upper story, while he pulled down the outside shutters. He then came back, and, instead of going out by the open door, suddenly clasped the girl to him and pressed a kiss upon her lips. This was surely just the situation to call up a distinct feeling of sexual excitement in a girl of fourteen who had never before been approached. But Dora had at that moment a violent feeling of disgust, tore herself free from the man, and hurried past him to the staircase and from there to the street door. She nevertheless continued to meet Herr K. Neither of them ever mentioned the little scene; and according to her account Dora kept it a secret till her confession during the treatment. For some time afterwards, however, she avoided being alone with Herr K. The K.'s had just made plans for an expedition which was to last for some days and on which Dora was to have accompanied them. After the scene of the kiss she refused to join the party, without giving any reason.

In this scene—second in order of mention, but first in order of time—the behaviour of this child of fourteen was already entirely and completely hysterical. I should without question consider a person hysterical in whom an occasion for sexual excitement elicited feelings that were preponderantly or exclusively unpleasurable; and I should do so whether or no the person were capable of producing somatic symptoms. The elucidation of the mechanism of this *reversal of affect* is one of the most important and at the same time one of the most difficult problems in the psychology of the neuroses. In my own judgement I am still some way from having achieved this end; and I may add that within limits of the present paper I shall be able to bring forward only a part of such knowledge on the subject as I do possess.

In order to particularize Dora's case it is not enough merely to draw attention to the reversal of affect; there has also been a *displacement* of sensation. Instead of the genital sensation which would certainly have been felt by a healthy girl in such circumstances, Dora was overcome by the unpleasurable feeling which is proper to the tract of mucous membrane at the entrance to the alimentary canal—that is by disgust. The stimulation of her lips by the kiss was no doubt of importance in localizing the feeling at that particular place; but I think I can also recognize another factor in operation.[13]

The disgust which Dora felt on that occasion did not become a permanent symptom, and even at the time of the treatment it was only, as it were, potentially present. She was a poor eater and confessed to some disinclination for food. On the other hand, the scene had left another consequence behind it in the shape of a sensory hallucination which occurred from time to time and even made its appearance while she was telling me her story. She declared that she could still feel upon the upper part of her body the pressure of Herr K.'s embrace. In accordance with certain rules of symptom-formation which I have come to know, and at the same time taking into account certain other of the patient's peculiarities, which were otherwise inexplicable,—such as her unwillingness to walk past any man whom she saw engaged in eager or affectionate conversation with a lady, — I have formed in my own mind the following reconstruction of the scene. I believe that during the man's passionate embrace she felt not merely his kiss upon her lips but also the pressure of his erect member against her body. This perception was revolting to her; it was dismissed from her memory, repressed, and replaced by the innocent sensation of pressure upon her thorax, which in turn derived an excessive intensity from its repressed source. Once more, therefore, we find a displacement from the lower part of the body to the upper.[14] On the other hand, the compulsive piece of behaviour which I have mentioned was formed as though it were derived from the undistorted recollection of the scene: she did not like walking past any man who she thought was in a state of sexual excitement, because she wanted to avoid seeing for a second time the somatic sign which accompanies it.

It is worth remarking that we have here three symptoms — the disgust, the sensation of pressure on the upper part of the body, and the avoidance of men engaged in affectionate conversation — all of them derived from a single experience, and that it is only taking into account the interrelation of these three phenomena that we can understand the way in which the formation of the symptoms came about. The disgust is the symptom of repression in the erotogenic oral zone, which . . . had been over-indulged in Dora's infancy by the habit of sensual sucking. The pressure of the erect member probably led to an analogous change in the corresponding female organ, the clitoris; and the excitation of this second erotogenic zone was referred by a process of displacement to the simultaneous pressure against the thorax and became fixed there. Her avoidance of men who might possibly be in a state of sexual excitement follows the mechanism of a phobia, its purpose being to safeguard her against any revival of the repressed perception.

In order to show that such a supplement to the story was possible, I questioned the patient very cautiously as to whether she knew anything of the physical signs of excitement in a man's body. Her answer, as touching the present, was "Yes," but, as touching the time of the episode, "I think not." From the very beginning I took the greatest pains with this patient not to introduce her to any fresh facts in the region of sexual knowledge; and I did this, not from any conscientious motives, but because I was anxious to subject my assumptions to a rigorous test in this case. Accordingly, I did not call a thing by its name until her allusions to it had became so unambiguous that there seemed very slight risk in translating them into direct speech. Her answer was always prompt and frank: she knew about it already. But the question of *where* her knowledge came from was a riddle which her memories were unable to solve. She had forgotten the source of all her information on this subject.[15]

If I may suppose that the scene of the kiss took place in this way, I can arrive at the following derivation for the feelings of disgust.[16] Such feelings seem originally to be a reaction to the smell (and afterwards also to the sight) of excrement. But the genitals can act as a reminder of the excretory functions; and this applies especially to the male member, for that organ performs the function of micturition as well as the sexual function. Indeed, the function of micturition is the earlier known of the two, and the *only* one known during the pre-sexual period. Thus it happens that disgust becomes one of the means of affective expression in the sphere of sexual life. The Early Christian Father's *"inter urinas et faeces nascimur"** clings to sexual life and cannot be detached from it in spite of every effort at idealization. I should like, however, expressly to emphasize my opinion that the problem is not solved by the mere pointing out of this path of association. The fact that this association *can* be called up does not show that it actually *will* be called up. And indeed in normal circumstances it will not be. A knowledge of the paths does not render less necessary a knowledge of the forces which travel along them.[17]

I did not find it easy, however, to direct the patient's attention to her relations with Herr K. She declared that she had done with him. The uppermost layer of all her associations during the sessions, and everything of which she was easily conscious and of which she remembered having been conscious the day before, was always connected with her father. It was quite true that she could not forgive her father for continuing his relations with Herr K. and more particularly with Frau K. But she viewed those relations in a very different light from that in which her father wished them to appear. In her mind there was no doubt that what bound her father to this young and beautiful woman was a common love-affair. Nothing that could help to confirm this view had escaped her perception, which in this connection was pitilessly sharp; *here there were no gaps to be found in her memory*. Their acquaintance with the K.'s had begun before her father's serious illness; but it had not become intimate until the young woman had officially taken on the position of nurse during that illness, while Dora's mother had kept away from the sick-room. During the first summer holidays after his recovery things had happened which must have opened every one's eyes to the true character of this "friendship." The two families had taken a suite of rooms in common at the hotel. One day Frau K. had announced that she could not keep the bedroom which she had up till then shared with one of her children. A few days later Dora's father had given up his bedroom, and they had both moved into new rooms—the end rooms, which were only separated by the passage, while the rooms they had given up had not offered any such security against interruption. Later on, whenever she had reproached her father about Frau K., he had been in the habit of saying that he could not understand her hostility and that, on the contrary, his children had every reason for being grateful to Frau K. Her mother, whom she had asked for an explanation of this mysterious remark, had told her that her father had been so unhappy at that time that he had made up his mind to go into the wood and kill himself, and that

---

"inter urinal et faeces nascimur": We are born among urine and excrement.

Frau K., suspecting as much, had gone after him and had persuaded him by her entreaties to preserve his life for the sake of his family. Of course, Dora went on, she herself did not believe this story; no doubt the two of them had been seen together in the wood, and her father had thereupon invented this fairy tale of his suicide so as to account for their rendezvous.[18]

When they had returned to B——, her father had visited Frau K. every day at definite hours, while her husband was at his business. Everybody had talked about it and had questioned her about it pointedly. Herr K. himself had often complained bitterly to her mother, though he had spared her herself any allusions to the subject — which she seemed to attribute to delicacy of feeling on his part. When they had all gone for walks together, her father and Frau K. had always known how to manage things so as to be alone with each other. There could be no doubt that she had taken money from him, for she spent more than she could possibly have afforded out of her own purse or her husband's. Dora added that her father had begun to make handsome presents to Frau K., and in order to make these less conspicuous had at the same time become especially liberal towards her mother and herself. And, while previously Frau K. had been an invalid and had even been obliged to spend months in a sanatorium for nervous disorders because she had been unable to walk, she had now become a healthy and lively woman.

Even after they had left B—— for the manufacturing town, these relations, already of many years' standing, had been continued. From time to time her father used to declare that he could not endure the rawness of the climate, and that he must do something for himself; he would begin to cough and complain, until suddenly he would start off to B——, and from there write the most cheerful letters home. All these illnesses had only been pretexts for seeing his friend again. Then one day it had been decided that they were to move to Vienna and Dora began to suspect a hidden connection. And sure enough, they had scarcely been three weeks in Vienna when she heard that the K.'s had moved there as well. They were in Vienna, so she told me, at that very moment, and she frequently met her father with Frau K. in the street. She also met Herr K. very often, and he always used to turn round and look after her; and once when he had met her out by herself he had followed her for a long way, so as to make sure where she was going and whether she might not have a rendezvous.

On one occasion during the course of the treatment her father again felt worse, and went off to B—— for several weeks; and the sharp-sighted Dora had soon unearthed the fact that Frau K. had started off to the same place on a visit to her relatives there. It was at this time that Dora's criticisms of her father were the most frequent: he was insincere, he had a strain of falseness in his character, he only thought of his own enjoyment, and he had a gift for seeing things in the light which suited him best.

I could not in general dispute Dora's characterization of her father; and there was one particular respect in which it was easy to see that her reproaches were justified. When she was feeling embittered she used to be overcome by the idea that she had been handed over to Herr K. as the price of his tolerating the relations between her father and his wife; and her rage at her father's making such a use of her was visible behind her affection for him. At other times she was quite well aware that she had been guilty of exaggeration in talking like this. The two men had of course never made a formal agreement in which she was treated as an object for barter; her father in particular would have been horrified at any such suggestion. But he was one of those men who know how to evade a dilemma by falsifying their judgement upon one of the conflicting alternatives. If it had been pointed out to him that there might be danger for a growing girl in the constant and unsupervised companionship of a man who had no satisfaction from his own wife, he would have been certain to answer that he could rely upon his daughter, that a man like K. could never be dangerous to her, and that his friend was himself incapable of such intentions, or that Dora was still a child and was treated as a child by K. But as a matter of fact things were in a position in which each of the two men avoided drawing any conclusions from the other's behaviour which would have been awkward for his own plans. It was possible for Herr K. to send Dora flowers every day for a whole year while he was in the neighbourhood, to take every opportunity of giving her valuable presents, and to spend all his spare time in her company, without her parents noticing anything in his behaviour that was characteristic of love-making.

When a patient brings forward a sound and incontestable train of argument during psycho-analytic treatment, the physician is liable to feel a moment's embarrassment, and the patient may take advantage of it by asking: "This is all perfectly correct and true, isn't it? What do you want to change now that I've told it you?" But it soon becomes evident that the patient is using thoughts of this kind, which the analysis cannot attack, for the purpose of cloaking others which are anxious to escape from criticism and from consciousness. A string of reproaches against other people leads one to suspect the existence of a string of self-reproaches with the same content. All that need be done is to turn back each particular reproach on to the speaker himself. There is something undeniably automatic about this method of defending oneself against a self-reproach by making the same reproach against some one else. A model of it is to be found in the *tu quoque* arguments of children; if one of them is accused of being a liar, he will reply without an instant's hesitation: "You're another." A grown-up person who wanted to throw back abuse would look for some really exposed spot in his antagonist and would not lay the chief stress upon the same content being repeated. In paranoia the projection of a reproach on to another person without any alteration in its content and therefore without any consideration for reality becomes manifest as the process of forming delusions.

Dora's reproaches against her father had a "lining" or "backing" of self-reproaches of this kind with a corresponding content in every case, as I

shall show in detail. She was right in thinking that her father did not wish
to look too closely into Herr K.'s behaviour to his daughter, for fear of
being disturbed in his own love-affair with Frau K. But Dora herself had
done precisely the same thing. She had made herself an accomplice in the
affair, and had dismissed from her mind every sign which tended to show
its true character. It was not until after her adventure by the lake [p. 321]
that her eyes were opened and that she began to apply such a severe standard to her father. During all the previous years she had given every possible assistance to her father's relations with Frau K. She would never go to
see her if she thought her father was there; but, knowing that in that case
the children would have been sent out, she would turn her steps in a direction where she would be sure to meet them, and would go for a walk with
them. There had been some one in the house who had been anxious at an
early stage to open eyes to the nature of her father's relations with Frau K.,
and to induce her to take sides against her. This was her last governess, an
unmarried woman, no longer young, who was well-read and of advanced
views.[19] The teacher and her pupil were for a while upon excellent terms,
until suddenly Dora became hostile to her and insisted on her dismissal. So
long as the governess had any influence she used it for stirring up feeling
against Frau K. She explained to Dora's mother that it was incompatible
with her dignity to tolerate such an intimacy between her husband and another woman; and she drew Dora's attention to all the obvious features of
their relations. But her efforts were vain. Dora remained devoted to
Frau K. and would hear of nothing that might make her think ill of her relations with her father. On the other hand she very easily fathomed the
motives by which her governess was actuated. She might be blind in one direction, but she was sharp-sighted enough in the other. She saw that the
governess was in love with her father. When he was there, she seemed to be
quite another person: at such times she could be amusing and obliging.
While the family were living in the manufacturing town and Frau K. was
not on the horizon, her hostility was directed against Dora's mother, who
was then her more immediate rival. Up to this point Dora bore her no ill-
will. She did not become angry until she observed that she herself was a
subject of complete indifference to the governess, whose pretended affection for her was really meant for her father. While her father was away
from the manufacturing town the governess had no time to spare for her,
would not go for walks with her, and took no interest in her studies. No
sooner had her father returned from B——— than she was once more ready
with every sort of service and assistance. Thereupon Dora dropped her.

The poor woman had thrown a most unwelcome light on a part of
Dora's own behaviour. What the governess had from time to time been to
Dora, Dora had been to Herr K.'s children. She had been a mother to
them, she had taught them, she had gone for walks with them, she had offered them a complete substitute for the slight interest which their own
mother showed in them. Herr K. and his wife had often talked of getting a
divorce; but it never took place, because Herr K., who was an affectionate

father, would not give up either of the two children. A common interest in the children had from the first been a bond between Herr K. and Dora. Her preoccupation with his children was evidently a cloak for something else that Dora was anxious to hide from herself and from other people.

The same inference was to be drawn both from her behaviour towards the children, regarded in the light of the governess's behaviour towards herself, and from her silent acquiescence in her father's relations with Frau K.—namely, that she had all these years been in love with Herr K. When I informed her of this conclusion she did not assent to it. It is true that she at once told me that other people besides (one of her cousins, for instance—a girl who had stopped with them for some time at B——) had said to her: "Why you're simply wild about that man!" But she herself could not be got to recollect any feelings of the kind. Later on, when the quantity of material that had come up had made it difficult for her to persist in her denial, she admitted that she might have been in love with Herr K. at B——, but declared that since the scene by the lake it had all been over.[20] In any case it was quite certain that the reproaches which she made against her father of having been deaf to the most imperative calls of duty and of having seen things in the light which was most convenient from the point of view of his own passions—these reproaches recoiled on her own head.[21]

Her other reproach against her father was that his ill-health was only a pretext and that he exploited it for his own purposes. This reproach, too, concealed a whole section of her own secret history. One day she complained of a professedly new symptom, which consisted of piercing gastric pains. "Whom are you copying now?" I asked her, and found I had hit the mark. The day before she had visited her cousins, the daughters of the aunt who had died. The younger one had become engaged, and this had given occasion to the elder one for falling ill with gastric pains, and she was to be sent off to Semmering.[22] Dora thought it was all just envy on the part of the elder sister; she always got ill when she wanted something, and what she wanted now was to be away from home so as not to have to look on at her sister's happiness.[23] But Dora's own gastric pains proclaimed the fact that she identified herself with her cousin, who, according to her, was a malingerer. Her grounds for this identification were either that she too envied the luckier girl her love, or that she saw her own story reflected in that of the elder sister, who had recently had a love-affair which had ended unhappily. But she had also learned from observing Frau K. what useful things illnesses could become. Herr K. spent part of the year in traveling. Whenever he came back, he used to find his wife in bad health, although, as Dora knew, she had been quite well only the day before. Dora realized that the presence of the husband had the effect of making his wife ill, and that she was glad to be ill so as to be able to escape the conjugal duties which she so much detested. At this point in the discussion Dora suddenly brought in an allusion to her own alternations between good and bad health during the first years of her girlhood at B——; and I was thus driven to suspect that her states of health were to be regarded as depending upon something else, in the same way as Frau K.'s. (It is a rule of psycho-analytic technique that an internal connection which is still undisclosed will announce its presence by means of a contiguity—a temporal proxim-ity—of associations; just as in writing, if "a" and "b" are put side by side, it means that the syllable "ab" is to be formed out of them.) Dora had had a very large number of attacks of coughing accompanied by loss of voice. Could it be that the presence or absence of the man she loved had had an influence upon the appearance and disappearance of the symptoms of her illness? If this were so, it must be possible to discover some coincidence or other which would betray the fact. I asked her what the average length of these attacks had been. "From three to six weeks, perhaps." How long had Herr K.'s absences lasted? "Three to six weeks, too," she was obliged to admit. Her illness was therefore a demonstration of her love for K., just as his wife's was a demonstration of her *dislike*. It was only necessary to sup-pose that her behaviour had been the opposite of Frau K.'s and that she had been ill when he was absent and well when he had come back. And this really seemed to have been so, at least during the first period of the at-tacks. Later on it no doubt became necessary to obscure the coincidence between her attacks of illness and the absence of the man she secretly loved, lest its regularity should betray her secret. The length of the attacks would then remain as a trace of their original significance.

I remembered that long before, while I was working at Charcot's clinic [1885–86], I had seen and heard how in cases of hysterical mutism writing operated vicariously in the place of speech. Such patients were able to write more fluently, quicker, and better than others did or than they themselves had done previously. The same thing had happened with Dora. In the first days of her attacks of aphonia "writing had always come specially easy to her." No psychological elucidation was really required for this peculiarity, which was the expression of physiological substitutive function enforced by necessity; it was noticeable, however, that such an elucidation was eas-ily to be found. Herr K. used to write to her at length while he was travel-ling and to send her picture post-cards. It used to happen that she alone was informed as to the date of his return, and that his arrival took his wife by surprise. Moreover, that a person will correspond with an absent friend whom he cannot talk to is scarcely less obvious than that if he has lost his voice he will try to make himself understood in writing. Dora's aphonia, then, allowed of the following symbolic interpretation. When the man she loved was away she gave up speaking; speech had lost its value since she could not speak to *him*. On the other hand, writing gained in importance, as being the only means of communication with him in his absence.

Am I now going on to assert that in every instance in which there are peri-odical attacks of aphonia we are to diagnose the existence of a loved per-son who is at times away from the patient? Nothing could be further from my intention. The determination of Dora's symptoms is far too specific for

it to be possible to expect a frequent recurrence of the same accidental aetiology. But, if so, what is the value of our elucidation of the aphonia in the
present case? Have we not merely allowed ourselves to become the victims
of a *jeu d'esprit*? I think not. In this connection we must recall the question
which has so often been raised, whether the symptoms of hysteria are of
psychical or of somatic origin, or whether, if the former is granted, they are
necessarily *all* of them psychically determined. Like so many other questions to which we find investigators returning again and again without success, this question is not adequately framed. The alternatives stated in it do
not cover the real essence of the matter. As far as I can see, every hysterical
symptom involves the participation of *both* sides. It cannot occur without
the presence of a certain degree of *somatic compliance*[24] offered by some
normal or pathological process in or connected with one of the bodily organs. And it cannot occur more than once—and the capacity for repeating
itself is one of the characteristics of a hysterical symptom—unless it has a
psychical significance, a *meaning*. The hysterical symptom does not carry
this meaning with it, but the meaning is lent to it, soldered to it, as it were;
and in every instance the meaning can be a different one, according to the
nature of the suppressed thoughts which are struggling for expression.
However, there are a number of factors at work which tend to make less
arbitrary the relations between the unconscious thoughts and the somatic
processes that are at their disposal as a means of expression, and which
tend to make those relations approximate to a few typical forms. For therapeutic purposes the most important determinants are those given by the
fortuitous psychical material; the clearing-up of the symptoms is achieved
by looking for their psychical significance. When everything that can be
got rid of by psycho-analysis has been cleared away, we are in a position to
form all kinds of conjectures, which probably meet the facts, as regards the
somatic basis of the symptoms—a basis which is as a rule constitutional
and organic. Thus in Dora's case we shall not content ourselves with a
psycho-analytic interpretation of her attacks of coughing and aphonia; but
we shall also indicate the organic factor which was the source of the "somatic compliance" that enabled her to express her love for a man who was
periodically absent. And if the connection between the symptomatic expression and the unconscious mental content should strike us as being in
this case a clever *tour de force*, we shall be relieved to hear that it succeeds
in creating the same impression in every other case and in every other instance.

I am prepared to be told at this point that there is no very great advantage in having been taught by psycho-analysis that the clue to the problem
of hysteria is to be found not in "a peculiar instability of the molecules of
the nerves" or in a liability to "hypnoid states"—but in a "somatic compliance." But in reply to the objection I may remark that this new view has
not only to some extent pushed the problem further back, but has also to
some extent diminished it. We have no longer to deal with the *whole* problem, but only with the portion of it involving that particular characteristic

of hysteria *which differentiates it* from other psychoneuroses. The mental events in all psychoneuroses proceed for a considerable distance along the same lines before any question arises of the "somatic compliance" which may afford the unconscious mental processes a physical outlet. When this factor is not forthcoming, something other than a hysterical symptom will arise out of the total situation; yet it will still be something of an allied nature, a phobia, perhaps, or an obsession—in short, a psychical symptom. . . .

None of her father's actions seemed to have embittered her so much as his readiness to consider the scene by the lake as a product of her imagination. She was almost beside herself at the idea of its being supposed that she had merely fancied something on that occasion. For a long time I was in perplexity as to what the self-reproach could be which lay behind her passionate repudiation of this explanation of the episode. It was justifiable to suspect that there was something concealed, for a reproach which misses the mark gives no lasting offence. On the other hand, I came to the conclusion that Dora's story must correspond to the facts in every respect. No sooner had she grasped Herr K.'s intention than, without letting him finish what he had to say, she had given him a slap in the face and hurried away. Her behaviour must have seemed as incomprehensible to the man after she had left him as to us, for he must long before have gathered from innumerable small signs that he was secure of the girl's affections. In our discussion of Dora's second dream we shall come upon the solution of this riddle as well as upon the self-reproach which we have hitherto failed to discover.

As she kept on repeating her complaints against her father with a wearisome monotony, and as at the same time her cough continued, I was led to think that this symptom might have some meaning in connection with her father. And apart from this, the explanation of the symptom which I had hitherto obtained was far from fulfilling the requirements which I am accustomed to make of such explanations. According to a rule which I had found confirmed over and over again by experience, though I had not yet ventured to erect it into a general principle, a symptom signifies the representation—the realization—of a phantasy with a sexual content, that is to say, it signifies a sexual situation. It would be better to say that at least *one* of the meanings of a symptom is the representation of a sexual phantasy, but that no such limitation is imposed upon the content of its other meanings. Any one who takes up psycho-analytic work will quickly discover that a symptom has more than one meaning and serves to represent several unconscious mental processes simultaneously. And I should like to add that in my estimation a single unconscious mental process or phantasy will scarcely ever suffice for the production of a symptom.

An opportunity very soon occurred for interpreting Dora's nervous cough in this way by means of an imagined sexual situation. She had once again been insisting that Frau K. only loved her father because he was *"ein* *vermögender Mann"* ["a man of means"]. Certain details of the way in which she expressed herself (which I pass over here, like most other purely technical parts of the analysis) led me to see that behind this phrase its opposite lay concealed, namely, that her father was *"ein unvermögender Mann"* ["a man without means"]. This could only be meant in a sexual sense—that her father, as a man, was without means, was impotent.[25] Dora confirmed this interpretation from her conscious knowledge; whereupon I pointed out the contradiction she was involved in if on the one hand she continued to insist that her father's relation with Frau K. was a common love-affair, and on the other hand maintained that her father was impotent, or in other words incapable of carrying on an affair of such a kind. Her answer showed that she had no need to admit the contradiction. She knew very well, she said, that there was more than one way of obtaining sexual gratification. (The source of this piece of knowledge, however, was once more untraceable.) I questioned her further, whether she referred to the use of organs other than the genitals for the purpose of sexual intercourse, and she replied in the affirmative. I could then go on to say that in that case she must be thinking of precisely those parts of the body which in her case were in a state of irritation,—the throat and the oral cavity. To be sure, she would not hear of going so far as this in recognizing her own thoughts; and indeed, if the occurrence of the symptom was to be made possible at all, it was essential that she should not be completely clear on the subject. But the conclusion was inevitable that with her spasmodic cough, which, as is usual, was referred for its exciting stimulus to a tickling in her throat, she pictured to herself a scene of sexual gratification *per os*[*] between the two people whose love-affair occupied her mind so incessantly. A very short time after she had tacitly accepted this explanation her cough vanished—which fitted in very well with my view; but I do not wish to lay too much stress upon this development, since her cough had so often before disappeared spontaneously.

This short piece of the analysis may perhaps have excited in the medical reader—apart from the scepticism to which he is entitled—feelings of astonishment and horror; and I am prepared at this point to look into these two reactions so as to discover whether they are justifiable. The astonishment is probably caused by my daring to talk about such delicate and unpleasant subjects to a young girl—or, for that matter, to any woman who is sexually active. The horror is aroused, no doubt, by the possibility that an inexperienced girl could know about practices of such a kind and could occupy her imagination with them. I would advise recourse to moderation and reasonableness upon both points. There is no cause for indignation either in the one case or in the other. It is possible for a man to talk to girls and women upon sexual matters of every kind without doing them harm and without bringing suspicion upon himself, so long as, in the first

---

per os: Latin for "by mouth"; in context it refers to oral sex.

place, he adopts a particular way of doing it, and, in the second place, can make them feel convinced that it is unavoidable. A gynaecologist, after all, under the same conditions, does not hesitate to make them submit to uncovering every possible part of their body. The best way of speaking about such things is to be dry and direct; and that is at the same time the method furthest removed from the prurience with which the same subjects are handled in "society," and to which girls and women alike are so thoroughly accustomed. I call bodily organs and processes by their technical names, and I tell these to the patient if they—the names, I mean—happen to be unknown to her. *J'appelle un chat un chat.** I have certainly heard of some people—doctors and laymen—who are scandalized by a therapeutic method in which conversations of this sort occur, and who appear to envy either me or my patients the titillation which, according to their notions, such a method must afford. But I am too well acquainted with the respectability of these gentry to excite myself over them. I shall avoid the temptation of writing a satire upon them. But there is one thing that I will mention: often, after I have for some time treated a patient who had not at first found it easy to be open about sexual matters, I have had the satisfaction of hearing her exclaim: "Why, after all, your treatment is far more respectable than Mr. X.'s conversation!"

No one can undertake the treatment of a case of hysteria until he is convinced of the impossibility of avoiding the mention of sexual subjects, or unless he is prepared to allow himself to be convinced by experience. The right attitude is: *"pour faire une omelette il faut casser des œufs."** The patients themselves are easy to convince; and there are only too many opportunities of doing so in the course of the treatment. There is no necessity for feeling any compunction at discussing the facts of normal or abnormal sexual life with them. With the exercise of a little caution all that is done is to translate into conscious ideas what was already known in the unconscious; and, after all, the whole effectiveness of the treatment is based upon our knowledge that the affect attached to an unconscious idea operates more strongly and, since it cannot be inhibited, more injuriously than the affect attached to a conscious one. There is never any danger of corrupting an inexperienced girl. For where there is no knowledge of sexual processes even in the unconscious, no hysterical symptom will arise; and where hysteria is found there can no longer be any question of "innocence of mind" in the sense in which parents and educators use the phrase. With children of ten, of twelve, or of fourteen, with boys and girls alike, I have satisfied myself that the truth of this statement can invariably be relied upon.

As regards the second kind of emotional reaction, which is not directed against me this time, but against my patient—supposing that my view of her is correct—and which regards the perverse nature of her phantasies as horrible, I should like to say emphatically that a medical man has no busi-

---

J'appelle un chat un chat: A literal translation from French is "I call a cat a cat"; equivalent to the expression "I call a spade a spade," it means that he calls things by their proper name.
"pour faire une omelette il faut casser des œufs": To make an omelette one must break eggs.

ness to indulge in such passionate condemnation. I may also remark in passing that it seems to me superfluous for a physician who is writing upon the aberrations of the sexual instincts to seize every opportunity of inserting into the text expressions of his personal repugnance at such revolting things. We are faced by a fact; and it is to be hoped that we shall grow accustomed to it, when we have put our own tastes on one side. We must learn to speak without indignation of what we call the sexual perversions—instances in which the sexual function has extended its limits in respect either to the part of the body concerned or to the sexual object chosen. The uncertainty in regard to the boundaries of what is to be called normal sexual life, when we take different races and different epochs into account, should in itself be enough to cool the zealot's ardour. We surely ought not to forget that the perversion which is the most repellent to us, the sensual love of a man for a man, was not only tolerated by a people so far our superiors in cultivation as were the Greeks, but was actually entrusted by them with important social functions. The sexual life of each one of us extends to a slight degree—now in this direction, now in that— beyond the narrow lines imposed as the standard of normality. The perversions are neither bestial nor degenerate in the emotional sense of the word. They are a development of germs all of which are contained in the undifferentiated sexual disposition of the child, and which, by being suppressed or by being diverted to higher, asexual aims—by being "sublimated"[26]— are destined to provide the energy for a great number of our cultural achievements. When, therefore, any one has *become* a gross and manifest pervert, it would be more correct to say that he has *remained* one, for he exhibits a certain stage of *inhibited development.* All psychoneurotics are persons with strongly marked perverse tendencies, which have been repressed in the course of their development and have become unconscious. Consequently their unconscious *phantasies* show precisely the same content as the documentarily recorded *actions* of perverts—even though they have not read Krafft-Ebing's *Psychopathia Sexualis,* to which simple-minded people attribute such a large share of the responsibility for the production of perverse tendencies. Psychoneuroses are, so to speak, the *negative* of perversions. In neurotics their sexual constitution, under which the effects of heredity are included, operates in combination with any accidental influences in their life which may disturb the development of normal sexuality. A stream of water which meets with an obstacle in the river-bed is dammed up and flows back into old channels which had formerly seemed fated to run dry. The motive forces leading to the formation of hysterical symptoms draw their strength not only from repressed *normal* sexuality but also from unconscious perverse activities.[27] . . .

The interpretation . . . of Dora's throat symptoms may also give rise to a further remark. It may be asked how this sexual situation imagined by her can be compatible with our other explanation of the symptoms. That explanation, it will be remembered, was to the effect that the coming and going of the symptoms reflected the presence and absence of the man she was in love with, and, as regards his wife's behaviour, expressed the following thought: "If *I* were his wife, I should love him in quite a different way; I should be ill (from longing, let us say) when he was away, and well (from joy) when he was home again." To this objection I must reply that my experience in the clearing-up of hysterical symptoms has shown that it is not necessary for the various meanings of a symptom to be compatible with one another, that is, to fit together into a connected whole. It is enough that the unity should be constituted by the subject-matter which has given rise to all the various phantasies. In the present case, moreover, compatibility even of the first kind is not out of the question. One of the two meanings is related more to the cough, and the other to the aphonia and the periodicity of the disorder. A closer analysis would probably have disclosed a far greater number of mental elements in relation to the details of the illness.

We have already learnt that it quite regularly happens that a single symptom corresponds to several meanings *simultaneously*. We may now add that it can express several meanings *in succession*. In the course of years a symptom can change its meaning or its chief meaning, or the leading role can pass from one meaning to another. It is as though there were a conservative trait in the character of neuroses which ensures that a symptom that has once been formed shall if possible be retained, even though the unconscious thought to which it gave expression has lost its meaning. Moreover, there is no difficulty in explaining this tendency towards the retention of a symptom upon a mechanical basis. The production of a symptom of this kind is so difficult, the translation of a purely psychical excitation into physical terms—the process which I have called "conversion"[28]—depends on the concurrence of so many favourable conditions, the somatic compliance necessary for conversion is so seldom forthcoming, that an impulsion towards the discharge of an unconscious excitation will so far as possible make use of any channel for discharge which may already be in existence. It appears to be far more difficult to create a fresh conversion than to form paths of association between a new thought which is in need of discharge and the old one which is no longer in need of it. The current flows along these paths from the new source of excitation to the old point of discharge—pouring into the symptom, in the words of the Gospel, like new wine into an old bottle. These remarks would make it seem that the somatic side of a hysterical symptom is the more stable of the two and the harder to replace, while the psychical side is a variable element for which a substitute can more easily be found. Yet we should not try to infer anything from this comparison as regards the relative importance of the two elements. From the point of view of mental therapeutics the mental side must always be the more significant. . . .

I must now turn to consider a further complication to which I should certainly give no space if I were a man of letters engaged upon the creation of a mental state like this for a short story, instead of being a medical man engaged upon its dissection. The element to which I must now allude can only serve to obscure and efface the outlines of the fine poetic conflict which we have been able to ascribe to Dora. This element would rightly fall a sacrifice to the censorship of a writer, for he, after all, simplifies and abstracts when he appears in the character of a psychologist. But in the world of reality, which I am trying to depict here, a complication of motives, an accumulation and conjunction of mental activities—in a word, overdetermination—is the rule. For behind Dora's supervalent* train of thought which was concerned with her father's relations with Frau K. there lay concealed a feeling of jealousy which had that lady as its *object*—a feeling, that is, which could only be based upon an affection on Dora's part for one of her own sex. It has long been known and often been pointed out that at the age of puberty boys and girls show clear signs, even in normal cases, of the existence of an affection for people of their own sex. A romantic and sentimental friendship with one of her school-friends, accompanied by vows, kisses, promises of eternal correspondence, and all the sensibility of jealousy, is the common precursor of a girl's first serious passion for a man. Thenceforward, in favourable circumstances, the homosexual current of feeling often runs completely dry. But if a girl is not happy in her love for a man, the current is often set flowing again by the libido in later years and is increased up to a greater or lesser degree of intensity. If this much can be established without difficulty of healthy persons, and if we take into account what had already been said [p. 335] about the fuller development in neurotics of the normal germs of perversion, we shall expect to find in these latter too a fairly strong homosexual predisposition. It must, indeed, be so; for I have never yet come through a single psychoanalysis of a man or a woman without having to take into account a very considerable current of homosexuality. When, in a hysterical woman or girl, the sexual libido which is directed towards men has been energetically suppressed, it will regularly be found that the libido which is directed towards women has become vicariously reinforced and even to some extent conscious.

I shall not in this place go any further into this important subject, which is especially indispensable to an understanding of hysteria in men, because Dora's analysis came to an end before it could throw any light on this side of her mental life. But I should like to recall the governess, whom I have already mentioned [p. 328f.], and with whom Dora had at first enjoyed the closest interchange of thought, until she discovered that she was being admired and fondly treated not for her own sake but for her father's; whereupon she had obliged the governess to leave. She used also to dwell with noticeable frequency and a peculiar emphasis on the story of another estrangement which appeared inexplicable even to herself. She had always been on particularly good terms with the younger of her two cousins—the girl who had later on become engaged . . .—and had shared all sorts of

*supervalent: Freud describes a *supervalent* train of thought as one that the patient repeats over and over.

secrets with her. When, for the first time after Dora had broken off her stay by the lake, her father was going back to B——, she had naturally refused to go with him. This cousin had then been asked to travel with him instead, and she had accepted the invitation. From that time forward Dora had felt a coldness towards her, and she herself was surprised to find how indifferent she had become, although, as she admitted, she had very little ground for complaint against her. These instances of sensitiveness led me to inquire what her relations with Frau K. had been up till the time of the breach. I then found that the young woman and the scarcely grown girl had lived for years on a footing of the closest intimacy. When Dora stayed with the K.'s she used to share a bedroom with Frau K., and the husband used to be quartered elsewhere. She had been the wife's confidante and adviser in all the difficulties of her married life. There was nothing they had not talked about. Medea* had been quite content that Creusa should make friends with her two children; and she certainly did nothing to interfere with the relations between the girl and the children's father. How Dora managed to fall in love with the man about whom her beloved friend had so many bad things to say is an interesting psychological problem. We shall not be far from solving it when we realize that thoughts in the unconscious live very comfortably side by side, and even contraries get on together without disputes—a state of things which persists often enough even in the conscious.

When Dora talked about Frau K., she used to praise her "adorable white body" in accents more appropriate to a lover than to a defeated rival. Another time she told me, more in sorrow than in anger, that she was convinced the presents her father had brought her had been chosen by Frau K., for she recognized her taste. Another time, again, she pointed out that, evidently through the agency of Frau K., she had been given a present of some jewellery which was exactly like some that she had seen in Frau K.'s possession and had wished for aloud at the time. Indeed, I can say in general that I never heard her speak a harsh or angry word against the lady, although from the point of view of her supervalent thought she should have regarded her as the prime author of her misfortunes. She seemed to behave inconsequently; but her apparent inconsequence was precisely the manifestation of a complicating current of feeling. For how had this woman to whom Dora was so enthusiastically devoted behaved to her? After Dora had brought forward her accusation against Herr K., and her father had written to him and had asked for an explanation, Herr K. had replied in the first instance by protesting sentiments of the highest esteem for her and by proposing that he should come to the manufacturing town to clear up every misunderstanding. A few weeks later, when her father spoke to him at B——, there was no longer any question of esteem. On the

---

Medea: In Greek mythology, Medea fell in love with Jason, leader of the Argonauts, and assisted his taking of the Golden Fleece. Jason then betrayed her by marrying the daughter of the King of Corinth.

contrary, Herr K. spoke of her with disparagement, and produced as his trump card the reflection that no girl who read such books and was interested in such things could have any title to a man's respect. Frau K., therefore, had betrayed her and had calumniated her; for it had only been with her that she had read Mantegazza and discussed forbidden topics. It was a repetition of what had happened with the governess: Frau K. had not loved her for her own sake but on account of her father. Frau K. had sacrificed her without a moment's hesitation so that her relations with her father might not be disturbed. This mortification touched her, perhaps, more nearly and had a greater pathogenic effect than the other one, which she tried to use as a screen for it, — the fact that she had been sacrificed by her father. Did not the obstinacy with which she retained the particular amnesia concerning the sources of her forbidden knowledge [p. 324] point directly to the great emotional importance for her of the accusation against her upon that score, and consequently to her betrayal by her friend?

I believe, therefore, that I am not mistaken in supposing that Dora's supervalent train of thought, which was concerned with her father's relations with Frau K., was designed not only for the purpose of suppressing her love for Herr K., which had once been conscious, but also to conceal her love for Frau K., which was in a deeper sense unconscious. The supervalent train of thought was directly contrary to the latter current of feeling. She told herself incessantly that her father had sacrificed her to this woman, and made noisy demonstrations to show that she grudged her the possession of her father; and in this way she concealed from herself the contrary fact, which was that she grudged her father Frau K.'s love, and had not forgiven the woman she loved for the disillusionment she had been caused by her betrayal. The jealous emotions of a woman were linked in the unconscious with a jealousy such as might have been felt by a man. These masculine or, more properly speaking, *gynaecophilic* currents of feeling are to be regarded as typical of the unconscious erotic life of hysterical girls.

[The first dream told by Dora went like this: "A house was on fire. My father was standing beside my bed and woke me up. I dressed quickly. Mother wanted to stop and save her jewel-case; but Father said: 'I refuse to let myself and my two children be burnt for the sake of your jewel-case.' We hurried downstairs, and as soon as I was outside I woke up." Freud's interpretation of this dream hinges on the fact that, in German, the word for "jewel-case" (*Schmuckkästchen*) is a euphemism for the female genitals.]

The Second Dream

A few weeks after the first dream the second occurred, and when it had been dealt with the analysis was broken off. It cannot be made as completely intelligible as the first, but it afforded a desirable confirmation of an assumption which had become necessary about the patient's mental state, it filled up a gap in her memory, and it made it possible to obtain a deep insight into the origin of another of her symptoms.

Dora described the dream as follows: *"I was walking about in a town which I did not know. I saw streets and squares which were strange to me.*[29] *Then I came into a house where I lived, went to my room, and found a letter from Mother lying there. She wrote saying that as I had left home without my parents' knowledge she had not wished to write to me to say that Father was ill. 'Now he is dead, and if you like*[30] *you can come.' I then went to the station ['Bahnhof'] and asked about a hundred times: 'Where is the station?' I always got the answer: 'Five minutes.' I then saw a thick wood before me which I went into, and there I asked a man whom I met. He said to me: 'Two and a half hours more.'*[31] *He offered to accompany me. But I refused and went alone. I saw the station in front of me and could not reach it. At the same time I had the usual feeling of anxiety that one has in dreams when one cannot move forward. Then I was at home. I must have been travelling in the meantime, but I know nothing about that. I walked into the porter's lodge, and inquired for our flat. The maidservant opened the door to me and replied that Mother and the others were already at the cemetery ['Friedhof'].*"[32]

It was not without some difficulty that the interpretation of this dream proceeded. In consequence of the peculiar circumstances in which the analysis was broken off—circumstances connected with the content of the dream—the whole of it was not cleared up. And for this reason, too, I am not equally certain at every point of the order in which my conclusions were reached. I will begin by mentioning the subject-matter with which the current analysis was dealing at the time when the dream intervened. For some time Dora herself had been raising a number of questions about the connection between some of her actions and the motives which presumably underlay them. One of these questions was: "Why did I say nothing about the scene by the lake for some days after it had happened?" Her second question was: "Why did I then suddenly tell my parents about it?" Moreover, her having felt so deeply injured by Herr K.'s proposal seemed to me in general to need explanation, especially as I was beginning to realize that Herr K. himself had not regarded his proposal to Dora as a mere frivolous attempt at seduction. I looked upon her having told her parents of the episode as an action which she had taken when she was already under the influence of a morbid craving for revenge. A normal girl, I am inclined to think, will deal with a situation of this kind by herself. I shall thus present the material produced during the analysis of this dream in the somewhat haphazard order in which it recurs to my mind.

She was wandering about alone in a strange town, and saw streets and squares. Dora assured me that it was certainly not B——, which I had first hit upon, but a town in which she had never been. It was natural to suggest that she might have seen some pictures or photographs and have taken the dream-pictures from them. After this remark of mine came the addendum about the monument in one of the squares and immediately afterwards her recognition of its source. At Christmas she had been sent an album from a German health-resort, containing views of the town; and the very day before the dream she had looked this up to show it to some relatives who were stopping with them. It had been put in a box for keeping pictures in, and she could not lay her hands on it at once. She had therefore said to her mother: "Where is the box?"[33] One of the pictures was of a square with a monument in it. The present had been sent to her by a young engineer, with whom she had once had a passing acquaintance in the manufacturing town. The young man had accepted a post in Germany, so as to become sooner self-supporting; and he took every opportunity of reminding Dora of his existence. It was easy to guess that he intended to come forward as a suitor one day, when his position had improved. But that would take time, and it meant waiting.

The wandering about in a strange town was overdetermined. It led back to one of the exciting causes from the day before. A young cousin of Dora's had come to stay with them for the holidays, and Dora had had to show him round Vienna. This cause was, it is true, a matter of complete indifference to her. But her cousin's visit reminded her of her own first brief visit to Dresden. On that occasion she had been a stranger and had wandered about, not failing, of course, to visit the famous picture gallery. Another cousin of hers, who was with them and knew Dresden, had wanted to act as a guide and take her round the gallery. *But she declined, and went alone,* and stopped in front of the pictures that appealed to her. She remained *two hours* in front of the Sistine Madonna, rapt in silent admiration. When I asked her what had pleased her so much about the picture she could find no clear answer to make. At last she said: "The Madonna."

There could be no doubt that these associations really belonged to the material concerned in forming the dream. They contained portions which reappeared in the dream unchanged ("she declined, and went alone" and "two hours"). I may remark at once that "pictures" was a point of junction in the network of her dream-thoughts (the pictures in the album, the pictures at Dresden). I should also like to single out, with a view to subsequent investigation, the theme of the "Madonna," of the virgin mother. But what was most evident was that in this first part of the dream she was identifying herself with a young man. This young man was wandering about in a strange place, he was striving to reach a goal, but he was being kept back, he needed patience and must wait. If in all this she had been thinking of the engineer, it would have been appropriate for the goal to have been the possession of a woman, of herself. But instead of this it was — a station. Nevertheless, the relation of the question in the dream to the question which had actually been put allows us to substitute *"box"* for "station."[34] A box and a woman: the notions begin to agree better.

She asked quite a hundred times.... This led to another exciting cause of the dream, and this time to one that was less indifferent. On the previous evening they had had company, and afterwards her father had asked her to fetch him the brandy: he could not get to sleep unless he had taken some brandy. She had asked her mother for the key of the sideboard; but the latter had been deep in conversation, and had not answered her, until Dora had exclaimed with the exaggeration of impatience: "I've asked you *a hundred times* already where the key is." As a matter of fact, she had of course only repeated the question about *five times*.[35]

"Where is the *key*?" seems to me to be the masculine counterpart to the question "Where is the *box*?" They are therefore questions referring to — the genitals.

Dora went on to say that during this same family gathering some one had toasted her father and had expressed the hope that he might continue to enjoy the best of health for many years to come, etc. At this a strange quiver had passed over her father's tired face, and she had understood what thoughts he was having to keep down. Poor sick man! Who could tell what span of life was still to be his?

This brings us to the *contents of the letter* in the dream. Her father was dead, and she had left home by her own choice. In connection with this letter I at once reminded Dora of the farewell letter which she had written to her parents or had at least composed for their benefit. This letter had been intended to give her father a fright, so that he should give up Frau K.; or at any rate to take revenge on him if he could not be induced to do that. We are here concerned with the subject of her death and of her father's death. (Cf. "cemetery" later on in the dream.) Shall we be going astray if we suppose that the situation which formed the facade of the dream was a phantasy of revenge directed against her father? The feelings of pity for him which she remembered from the day before would be quite in keeping with this. According to the phantasy she had left home and gone among strangers, and her father's heart had broken with grief and with longing for her. Then she would be revenged. She understood very clearly what it was that her father needed when he could not get to sleep without a drink of brandy.[36] We will make a note of Dora's *craving for revenge* as a new element to be taken into account in any subsequent synthesis of her dream-thoughts.

But the contents of the letter must be capable of further determination. What was the source of the words "if you like"? It was at this point that the addendum of there having been a question-mark after the word "like" occurred to Dora, and she then recognized these words as a quotation out of the letter from Frau K. which had contained the invitation to L——, the place by the lake. In that letter there had been a question-mark placed, in a most unusual fashion, in the very middle of a sentence, after the intercalated words "if you would like to come."

So here we were back again at the scene by the lake and at the problems connected with it. I asked Dora to describe the scene to me in detail. At first she produced little that was new. Herr K.'s exordium had been somewhat serious; but she had not let him finish what he had to say. No sooner had she grasped the purport of his words than she had slapped him in the face and hurried away. I inquired what his actual words had been.

Dora could only remember one of his pleas: "You know I get nothing out of my wife."[37] In order to avoid meeting him again she had wanted to get back to L—— on foot, by walking round the lake, and *she had asked a man whom she met how far it was.* On his replying that it was *"Two and a half hours,"* she had given up her intention and had after all gone back to the ship, which left soon afterwards. Herr K. had been there too, and had come up to her and begged her to forgive him and not to mention the incident. But she had made no reply. — Yes. The *wood* in the dream had been just like the wood by the shore of the lake, the wood in which the scene she had just described once more had taken place. But she had seen precisely the same thick wood the day before, in a picture at the Secessionist exhibition. In the background of the picture there were *nymphs.*[38]

At this point a certain suspicion of mine became a certainty. The use of *"Bahnhof"* ["station"; literally, "railway-court"][39] and *"Friedhof"* ["cemetery"; literally, "peace-court"] to represent the female genitals was striking enough in itself, but it also served to direct my awakened curiosity to the similarly formed *"Vorhof"* ["vestibulum"; literally, "fore-court"] — an anatomical term for a particular region of the female genitals. This might have been no more than a misleading joke. But now, with the addition of "nymphs" visible in the background of a "thick wood," no further doubts could be entertained. Here was a symbolic geography of sex! "Nymphae,"[40] as is known to physicians though not to laymen (and even by the former the term is not very commonly used), is the name given to the labia minora, which lie in the background of the "thick wood" of the pubic hair. But any one who employed such technical names as "vestibulum" and "nymphae" must have derived his knowledge from books, and not from popular ones either, but from anatomical text-books or from an encyclopedia — the common refuge of youth when it is devoured by sexual curiosity. If this interpretation were correct, therefore, there lay concealed behind the first situation in the dream a phantasy of defloration, the phantasy of a man seeking to force an entrance into the female genitals."[41]

I informed Dora of the conclusions I had reached. The impression made upon her must have been forcible, for there immediately appeared a piece of the dream which had been forgotten: *"she went calmly to her room, and began reading a big book that lay on her writing-table."*[42] The emphasis here was upon the two details "calmly" and "big" in connection with "book." I asked whether the book was in encyclopaedia *format,* and she said it was. Now children never read about forbidden subjects in an encyclopaedia *calmly.* They do it in fear and trembling, with an uneasy look over their shoulder to see if some one may not be coming. Parents are very much in the way while reading of this kind is going on. But this uncomfortable situation had been radically improved, thanks to the dream's power of fulfilling wishes. Dora's father was dead, and the others had already gone to the cemetery. She might calmly read whatever she chose. Did not this mean that one of her motives for revenge was a revolt against her parents' constraint? If her father was dead she could read or love as she pleased.

At first she would not remember ever having read anything in an encyclopaedia; but she then admitted that a recollection of an occasion of the kind did occur to her, though it was of an innocent enough nature. At the time when the aunt she was so fond of had been so seriously ill and it had already been settled that Dora was to go to Vienna, a *letter* had come from another uncle, to say that they could not go to Vienna, as a boy of his, a cousin of Dora's therefore, had fallen dangerously ill with appendicitis. Dora had thereupon looked up in the encyclopaedia to see what the symptoms of appendicitis were. From what she had then read she still recollected the characteristic localization of the abdominal pain.

I then remembered that shortly after her aunt's death Dora had had an attack of what had been alleged to be appendicitis. Up till then I had not ventured to count that illness among her hysterical productions. She told me that during the first few days she had had high fever and had felt the pain in her abdomen that she had read about in the encyclopaedia. She had been given cold fomentations but had not been able to bear them. On the second day her period had set in, accompanied by violent pains. (Since her health had been bad, the periods had been very irregular.) At that time she used to suffer continually from constipation.

It was not really possible to regard this state as a purely hysterical one. Although hysterical fever does undoubtedly occur, yet it seemed too arbitrary to put down the fever accompanying this questionable illness to hysteria instead of to some organic cause operative at the time. I was on the point of abandoning the track, when she herself helped me along it by producing her last addendum to the dream: *"she saw herself particularly distinctly going up the stairs."*

I naturally required a special determinant for this. Dora objected that she would anyhow have had to go upstairs if she had wanted to get to her flat, which was on an upper floor. It was easy to brush aside this objection (which was probably not very seriously intended) by pointing out that if she had been able to travel in her dream from the unknown town to Vienna without making a railway journey she ought also to have been able to leave out a flight of stairs. She then proceeded to relate that after the appendicitis she had not been able to walk properly and had dragged her right foot. This state of things had continued for a long time, and on that account she had been particularly glad to avoid stairs. Even now her foot sometimes dragged. The doctors whom she had consulted at her father's desire had been very much astonished at this most unusual after-effect of an appendicitis, especially as the abdominal pains had not recurred and did not in any way accompany the dragging of the foot.[43]

Here, then, we have a true hysterical symptom. The fever may have been organically determined—perhaps by one of those very frequent attacks of influenza that are not localized in any particular part of the body. Nevertheless it was now established that the neurosis had seized upon this chance event and made use of it for an utterance of its own. Dora had therefore given herself an illness which she had read up about in the encyclopaedia, and she had punished herself for dipping into its pages. But she was forced to recognize that the punishment could not possibly apply to her reading the innocent article in question. It must have been inflicted as the result of a process of displacement, after another occasion of more guilty reading had become associated with this one; and the guilty occasion must lie concealed in her memory behind the contemporaneous innocent one.[44] It might still be possible, perhaps, to discover the nature of the subjects she had read about on that other occasion.

What, then, was the meaning of this condition, of this attempted simulation of a perityphlitis?[*] The remainder of the disorder, the dragging of one leg, was entirely out of keeping with perityphlitis. It must, no doubt, fit in better with the secret and possibly sexual meaning of the clinical picture; and if it were elucidated might in its turn throw light upon the meaning which we were in search of. I looked about for a means of approaching the puzzle. Periods of time had been mentioned in the dream; and time is assuredly never a matter of indifference in any biological event. I therefore asked Dora when this attack of appendicitis had taken place; whether it had been before or after the scene by the lake. Every difficulty was resolved at a single blow by her prompt reply: "Nine months later." The period of time is sufficiently characteristic. Her supposed attack of appendicitis had thus enabled the patient with the modest means at her disposal (the pains and the menstrual flow) to realize a phantasy of *childbirth*.[45] Dora was naturally aware of the significance of this period of time, and could not dispute the probability of her having, on the occasion under discussion, read up in the encyclopaedia about pregnancy and childbirth. But what was all this about her dragging her leg? I could now hazard a guess. That is how people walk when they have twisted a foot. So she had made a "false step": which was true indeed if she could give birth to a child nine months after the scene by the lake. But there was still another requirement upon the fulfilment of which I had to insist. I am convinced that a symptom of this kind can only arise where it has an *infantile* prototype. All my experience hitherto has led me to hold firmly to the view that recollections derived from the impressions of later years do not possess sufficient force to enable them to establish themselves as symptoms. I scarcely dared hope that Dora would provide me with the material that I wanted from her childhood, for the fact is that I am not yet in a position to assert the general validity of this rule, much as I should like to be able to do so. But in this case there came an immediate confirmation of it. Yes, said Dora, once when she was a child she had twisted the same foot; she had slipped on one of the steps as she was going *downstairs*. The foot— and it was actually the same one that she afterwards dragged—had swelled up and had to be bandaged and she had had to lie up for some weeks. This had been a short time before the attack of nervous asthma in her eighth year.

perityphlitis: Appendicitis.

The next thing to do was to turn to account our knowledge of the existence of this phantasy: "If it is true that you were delivered of a child nine months after the scene by the lake, and that you are going about to this very day carrying the consequences of your false step with you, then it follows that in your unconscious you must have regretted the upshot of the scene. In your unconscious thoughts, that is to say, you have made an emendation in it. The assumption that underlies your phantasy of childbirth is that on that occasion something took place,[46] that on that occasion you experienced and went through everything that you were in fact obliged to pick up later on from the encyclopaedia. So you see that your love for Herr K. did not come to an end with the scene, but that (as I maintained) it has persisted down to the present day—though it is true that you are unconscious of it."—And Dora disputed the fact no longer.[47]

The labour of elucidating the second dream had so far occupied two hours. At the end of the second sitting, when I expressed my satisfaction at the result, Dora replied in a depreciatory tone: "Why, has anything so very remarkable come out?" These words prepared me for the advent of fresh revelations.

She opened the third sitting with these words: "Do you know that I am here for the last time to-day?"—"How can I know, as you have said nothing to me about it?"—"Yes, I made up my mind to put up with it till the New Year.[48] But I shall wait no longer than that to be cured."—"You know that you are free to stop the treatment at any time. But for to-day we will go on with our work. When did you come to this decision?"—"A fortnight ago, I think."—"That sounds just like a maidservant or a governess—a fortnight's warning."—"There was a governess who gave warning with the K.'s, when I was on my visit to them that time at L——, by the lake."—"Really? You have never told me about her. Tell me."

"Well, there was a young girl in the house, who was the children's governess; and she behaved in the most extraordinary way to Herr K. She never said good morning to him, never answered his remarks, never handed him anything at table when he asked for it, and in short treated him like thin air. For that matter he was hardly any politer to her. A day or two before the scene by the lake, the girl took me aside and said she had something to tell me. She then told me that Herr K. had made advances to her at a time when his wife was away for several weeks; he had made violent love to her and had implored her to yield to his entreaties, saying that he got nothing from his wife, and so on."—"Why, those are the very words he used afterwards, when he made his proposal to you and you gave him the slap in his face."—"Yes. She had given way to him, but after a little while he had ceased to care for her, and since then she hated him."—"And this governess had given warning?"—"No. She meant to give warning. She told me that as soon as she felt she was thrown over she had told her parents what had happened. They were respectable people living in Germany somewhere. Her parents said that she must leave the house instantly; and, as she failed to do so, they wrote to her saying that they would have nothing more to do with her, and that she was never to come home again." — "And why had she not gone away?" — "She said she meant to wait a little longer, to see if there might not be some change in Herr K. She could not bear living like that any more, she said, and if she saw no change she should give warning and go away." — "And what became of the girl?" — "I only know that she went away." — "And she did not have a child as a result of the adventure?" — "No."

Here, therefore (and quite in accordance with the rules), was a piece of material information coming to light in the middle of the analysis and helping to solve problems which had previously been raised. I was able to say to Dora: "Now I know your motive for the slap in the face with which you answered Herr K.'s proposal. It was not that you were offended at his suggestions; you were actuated by jealousy and revenge. At the time when the governess was telling you her story you were still able to make use of your gift for putting on one side everything that is not agreeable to your feelings. But at the moment when Herr K. used the words "I get nothing out of my wife" — which were the same words he had used to the governess — fresh emotions were aroused in you and tipped the balance. 'Does he dare,' you said to yourself, 'to treat me like a governess, like a servant?' Wounded pride added to jealousy and to the conscious motives of common sense — it was too much.[49] To prove to you how deeply impressed you were by the governess's story, let me draw your attention to the repeated occasions upon which you have identified yourself with her both in your dream and in your conduct. You told your parents what happened — a fact which we have hitherto been unable to account for — just as the governess wrote and told *her* parents. You give me a fortnight's warning, just like a governess. The letter in the dream which gave you leave to go home is the counterpart of the governess's letter from her parents forbidding her to do so."

"Then why did I not tell my parents at once?"

"How much time did you allow to elapse?"

"The scene took place on the last day of June; I told my mother about it on July 14th."

"Again a fortnight, then — the time characteristic for a person in service. Now I can answer your question. You understood the poor girl very well. She did not want to go away at once, because she still had hopes, because she expected that Herr K.'s affections would return to her again. So that must have been your motive too. You waited for that length of time so as to see whether he would repeat his proposals; if he had, you would have concluded that he was in earnest, and did not mean to play with you as he had done with the governess."

"A few days after I had left he sent me a picture postcard."[50]

"Yes, but when after that nothing more came, you gave free rein to your feelings of revenge. I can even imagine that at that time you were still able to find room for a subsidiary intention, and thought that your accusation might be a means of inducing him to travel to the place where you were living." — "As he actually offered to do at first," Dora threw in. — "In that way your longing for him would have been appeased" — here she nodded assent, a thing which I had not expected — "and he might have made you the amends you desired."

"What amends?"

"The fact is, I am beginning to suspect that you took the affair with Herr K. much more seriously than you have been willing to admit so far. Had not the K.'s often talked of getting a divorce?"

"Yes, certainly. At first she did not want to, on account of the children. And now she wants to, but he no longer does."

"May you not have thought that he wanted to get divorced from his wife so as to marry you? And that now he no longer wants to because he has no one to replace her? It is true that two years ago you were very young. But you told me yourself that your mother was engaged at seventeen and then waited two years for her husband. A daughter usually takes her mother's love-story as her model. So you too wanted to wait for him, and you took it that he was only waiting till you were grown up enough to be his wife.[51] I imagine that this was a perfectly serious plan for the future in your eyes. You have not even got the right to assert that it was out of the question for Herr K. to have had any such intention; you have told me enough about him that points directly towards his having such an intention.[52] Nor does his behaviour at L—— contradict this view. After all, you did not let him finish his speech and do not know what he meant to say to you. Incidentally, the scheme would by no means have been so impracticable. Your father's relations with Frau K. — and it was probably only for this reason that you lent them your support for so long — made it certain that her consent to a divorce could be obtained; and you can get anything you like out of your father. Indeed, if your temptation at L—— had had a different upshot, this would have been the only possible solution for all the parties concerned. And I think that is why you regretted the actual event so deeply and emended it in the phantasy which made its appearance in the shape of the appendicitis. So it must have been a bitter piece of disillusionment for you when the effect of your charges against Herr K. was not that he renewed his proposals but that he replied instead with denials and slanders. You will agree that nothing makes you so angry as having it thought that you merely fancied the scene by the lake. I know now — and this is what you do not want to be reminded of — that you *did* fancy that Herr K.'s proposals were serious, and that he would not leave off until you had married him."

Dora had listened to me without any of her usual contradictions. She seemed to be moved; she said good-bye to me very warmly, with the heartiest wishes for the New Year, and — came no more. Her father, who called on me two or three times afterwards, assured me that she would come back again, and said it was easy to see that she was eager for the treatment to continue. But it must be confessed that Dora's father was never entirely straightforward. He had given his support to the treatment so long as he could hope that I should "talk" Dora out of her belief that there was something more than a friendship between him and Frau K. His interest faded when he observed that it was not my intention to bring about that result. I knew Dora would not come back again. Her breaking off so unexpectedly, just when my hopes of a successful termination of the treatment were at their highest, and her thus bringing those hopes to nothing—this was an unmistakable act of vengeance on her part. Her purpose of self-injury also profited by this action. No one who, like me, conjures up the most evil of those half-tamed demons that inhabit the human breast, and seeks to wrestle with them, can expect to come through the struggle unscathed. Might I perhaps have kept the girl under my treatment if I myself had acted a part, if I had exaggerated the importance to me of her staying on, and had shown a warm personal interest in her—a course which, even after allowing for my position as her physician, would have been tantamount to providing her with a substitute for the affection she longed for? I do not know. Since in every case a part of the factors that are encountered under the form of resistance remains unknown, I have always avoided acting a part, and have contented myself with practising the humbler arts of psychology. In spite of every theoretical interest and of every endeavour to be of assistance as a physician, I keep the fact in mind that there must be some limits set to the extent to which psychological influence may be used, and I respect as one of these limits the patient's own will and understanding.

Nor do I know whether Herr K. would have done any better if it had been revealed to him that the slap Dora gave him by no means signified a final "No" on her part, but that it expressed the jealousy which had lately been roused in her, while her strongest feelings were still on his side. If he had disregarded that first "No," and had continued to press his suit with a passion which left room for no doubts, the result might very well have been a triumph of the girl's affection for him over all her internal difficulties. But I think she might just as well have been merely provoked into satisfying her craving for revenge upon him all the more thoroughly. It is never possible to calculate towards which side the decisions will incline in such a conflict of motives: whether towards the removal of the repression or towards its reinforcement. Incapacity for meeting a *real* erotic demand is one of the most essential features of a neurosis. Neurotics are dominated by the opposition between reality and phantasy. If what they long for the most intensely in their phantasies is presented to them in reality, they none the less flee from it; and they abandon themselves to their phantasies the most readily where they need no longer fear to see them realized. Nevertheless, the barrier erected by repression can fall before the onslaught of a violent emotional excitement produced by a real cause; it is possible for a neurosis to be overcome by reality. But we have no general means of calculating through what person or what event such a cure can be effected.[53]

Notes

1. *The Interpretation of Dreams,* Chapter II [Standard Ed., 4, 100 ff.].

2. Another physician once sent his sister to me for psychotherapeutic treatment, telling me that she had for years been treated without success for hysteria (pains and defective gait). The short account which he gave me seemed quite consistent with the diagnosis. In my first hour with the patient I got her to tell me her history herself. When the story came out perfectly clearly and connectedly in spite of the remarkable events it dealt with, I told myself that the case could not be one of hysteria, and immediately instituted a careful physical examination. This led to the diagnosis of a not very advanced stage of tabes [progressive bodily wasting accompanying a chronic disease — Eds.], which was later on treated with Hg [mercury— Eds.] injections (Ol. cinereum) by Professor Lang with markedly beneficial results.

3. Amnesias and paramnesias stand in a complementary relation to each other. When there are large gaps in the memory there will be few mistakes in it. And conversely, paramnesias can at first glance completely conceal the presence of amnesias.

4. If patient exhibits doubts in the course of his narrative, an empirical rule teaches us to disregard such expressions of his judgement entirely. If the narrative wavers between two versions, we should incline to regard the first one as correct and the second as a product of repression. [Cf. a discussion of doubt in connection with dreams in *The Interpretation of Dreams,* 1900a (Chapter VII, Section A; Standard Ed., 5, 515 ff.). For the very different mechanism of doubt in obsessional neurosis, see the case history of the "Rat Man," 1909d (Part II, Section C).—Trans.]

5. I do not, it is true, adopt the position that heredity is the only aetiological factor in hysteria. But, on the other hand—and I say this with particular reference to some of my earlier publications, e.g. "Heredity and the Aetiology of the Neuroses" (1896a), in which I combated that view—I do not wish to give an impression of underestimating the importance of heredity in the aetiology of hysteria or of asserting that it can be dispensed with. In the case of the present patient the information I have given about her father and his brother and sister indicates a sufficiently heavy taint; and, indeed, if the view is taken that pathological conditions such as her mother's must also imply a hereditary predisposition, the patient's heredity may be regarded as a convergent one. To my mind, however, there is another factor which is of more significance in the girl's hereditary or, properly speaking, constitutional predisposition. I have mentioned that her father had contracted syphilis before his marriage. Now a *strikingly high* percentage of the patients whom I have treated psycho-analytically come of fathers who have suffered from tabes or general paralysis. In consequence of the novelty of my therapeutic method, I see only the *severest* cases, which have already been under treatment for years without success. In accordance with the Erb-Fournier theory, tabes or general paralysis in the male parent may be regarded as evidence of an earlier luetic infection; and indeed I was able to obtain direct confirmation of such an infection in a number of cases. In the most recent discussion on the offspring of syphilitic parents (Thirteenth International Medical Congress, held in Paris, August 2nd to 9th, 1900: papers by Finger, Tarnowsky, Jullien, etc.), I find no mention of the conclusion to which I have been driven by my experience as a neuro-pathologist— namely, that syphilis in the male parent is a very relevant factor in the aetiology of the neuropathic constitution of children.

6. [The determinants of Freud's choice of this pseudonym were discussed by him in Chapter XII, Example A (1), of his *Psychopathology of Everyday Life* (1901b).—Trans. Reprinted on p. 368 of this volume.—Eds.]

7. On this point see the analysis of the second dream [p. 339].

8. As I have already explained, the treatment of the case, and consequently my insight into the complex of events composing it, remained fragmentary. There are therefore many questions to which I have no solution to offer, or in which I can only rely upon hints and conjectures. This affair of the letter came up in the course of one of our sessions and the girl showed signs of astonishment. "How on earth . . . , she asked, "did they find the letter? It was shut up in

my desk." But since she knew that her parents had read this draft of a farewell letter, I conclude that she had herself arranged for it to fall into their hands.

9. The attack was, I believe, accompanied by convulsions and delirious states. But since this event was not reached by the analysis either, I have no trustworthy recollections on the subject to fall back upon.

10. [In their "Preliminary Communication" (Breuer and Freud, 1893*a*) — Trans.]

11. I have gone beyond that theory, but I have not abandoned it; that is to say, I do not to-day consider the theory incorrect, but incomplete. All that I have abandoned is the emphasis laid upon the so-called "hypnoid state," which was supposed to be occasioned in the patient by the trauma, and to be the foundation for all the psychologically abnormal events which followed. If, where a piece of joint work is in question, it is legitimate to make a subsequent division of property, I should like to take this opportunity of stating that the hypothesis of "hypnoid states" — which many reviewers were inclined to regard as the central portion of our work — sprang entirely from the initiative of Breuer. I regard the use of such a term as superfluous and misleading, because it interrupts the continuity of the problem as to the nature of the psychological process accompanying the formation of hysterical symptoms. — ["Hypnoid states" were referred to in the "Preliminary Communication," but they were discussed at greater length by Breuer in his contribution to the *Studies on Hysteria* (1895), Chapter III, Section IV. Freud enters into his theoretical disagreement with Breuer in more detail in the first section of his "History of the Psycho-Analytic Movement" (1914*d*). — Trans.]

12. Cf. my paper on "The Aetiology of Hysteria" (1896*c*).

13. The causes of Dora's disgust at the kiss were certainly not adventitious, for in that case she could not have failed to remember and mention them. I happen to know Herr K., for he was the same person who had visited me with the patient's father [p. 318], and he was still quite young and of prepossessing appearance.

14. The occurrence of displacements of this kind has not been assumed for the purpose of this single explanation; the assumption has proved indispensable for the explanation of a large class of symptoms. Since treating Dora I have come across another instance of an embrace (this time without a kiss) causing a fright. It was a case of a young woman who had previously been devotedly fond of the man she was engaged to, but had suddenly begun to feel a coldness towards him, accompanied by severe depression, and on that account came to me for treatment. There was no difficulty in tracing the fright back to an erection on the man's part, which she had perceived but had dismissed from her consciousness.

15. See the second dream [p. 339].

16. Here, as in all similar cases, the reader must be prepared to be met not by one but by several causes — by *overdetermination*. [Freud had mentioned this characteristic of hysterical symptoms in Section III of his chapter on the psychotherapy of hysteria in Breuer and Freud's *Studies on Hysteria*, 1895. It was also discussed by Breuer (with an acknowledgement to Freud) in Section III of his theoretical contribution to the same work. — Trans.]

17. All these discussions contain much that is typical and valid for hysteria in general. The subject of erection solves some of the most interesting hysterical symptoms. The attention that women pay to the outlines of men's genitals as seen through their clothing becomes, when it has been repressed, a source of the very frequent cases of avoiding company and of dreading society. — It is scarcely possible to exaggerate the pathogenic significance of the comprehensive tie uniting the sexual and the excremental, a tie which is at the basis of a very large number of hysterical phobias. [This topic recurs very frequently in Freud's writings. It appears, for instance, as early as 1897 in Draft K in the Fliess correspondence (Freud, 1950*a*), and as late as 1930 in the long footnote at the end of Chapter IV of *Civilization and Its Discontents* (1930*a*). — Trans.]

18. This is the point of connection with her own pretence at suicide [p. 320], which may thus be regarded as the expression of a longing for a love of the same kind.

19. This governess used to read every sort of book on sexual life and similar subjects, and talked to the girl about them, at the same time asking her quite frankly not to mention their

conversations to her parents, as one could never tell what line they might take about them. For some time I looked upon this woman as the source of all Dora's secret knowledge, and perhaps I was not entirely wrong in this.

20. Compare the second dream [p. 339].

21. The question then arises: If Dora loved Herr K., what was the reason for her refusing him in the scene by the lake? Or at any rate, why did her refusal take such a brutal form, as though she were embittered against him? And how could a girl who was in love feel insulted by a proposal which was made in the manner neither tactless nor offensive?

22. [A fashionable health resort in the mountains, about fifty miles south of Vienna. — Trans.]

23. An event of everyday occurrences between sisters.

24. [This seems to be Freud's earliest use of the term, which scarcely reappears in later works. (See the last words of his paper on psychogenic disturbances of vision, 1910i, and the discussion on masturbation, 1912f.) — Trans.]

25. ["Unvermögend" means literally "unable," and is commonly used in the sense of both "not rich" and "impotent." — Trans.]

26. [Cf. the second of Freud's Three Essays (1950d). — Trans.]

27. These remarks upon the sexual perversions had been written some years before the appearance of Bloch's excellent book (Beiträge zur Ätiologie der Psychopathia sexualis, 1902 and 1903). See also my Three Essays on the Theory of Sexuality, published this year [1905d, particularly the first essay, in which most of the points in the present paragraph are enlarged upon . . . — Trans.].

28. [The term "conversion" was introduced by Freud in Section 1 of his first paper on the neuro-psychoses of defence (1894a). — Trans.]

29. To this she subsequently made an important addendum: "I saw a monument in one of the squares."

30. To this came the addendum: "There was a question-mark after this word, thus: 'like?'"

31. In repeating the dream she said: "Two hours."

32. In the next sitting Dora brought me two addenda to this: "I saw myself particularly distinctly going up the stairs," and "After she had answered I went to my room, but not the least sadly, and began reading a big book that lay on my writing-table."

33. In the dream she said: "Where is the station?" The resemblance between the two questions led me to make an inference which I shall go into presently.

34. ["Schachtel," the word which was used for "box" by Dora in her question, is a depreciatory term for "woman." — Trans.]

35. In the dream the number five occurs in the mention of the period of "five minutes." In my book on the interpretation of dreams I have given several examples of the way in which numbers occurring in the dream-thoughts are treated by the dream. We frequently find them torn out of their true context and inserted into a new one.

36. There can be no doubt that sexual satisfaction is the best soporific, just as sleeplessness is almost always the consequence of lack of satisfaction. Her father could not sleep because he was debarred from sexual intercourse with the woman he loved. (Compare in this connection the phrase discussed below: "I get nothing out of my wife.")

37. These words will enable us to solve one of our problems.

38. Here for the third time we come upon "picture" (views of towns, the Dresden gallery), but in a much more significant connection. Because of what appears in the picture (the wood, the nymphs), the "Bild" ["picture"] is turned into a "Weibsbild" [literally, "picture of a woman" — a derogatory expression for "woman"].

39. Moreover, a "station" is used for purposes of "Verkehr" ["traffic," "intercourse," "sexual intercourse"]: this affords the psychological wrapping in many cases of railway phobia.

40. [In German the same word, "Nymphen," represents both "nymphs" and "nymphae." — Trans.]

41. The phantasy of defloration formed the second component of the situation. The emphasis upon the difficulty of getting forward and the anxiety felt in the dream indicated the stress which the dreamer was so ready to lay upon her virginity—a point alluded to in another place by means of the Sistine Madonna. These sexual thoughts gave an unconscious ground-colouring to the wishes (which were perhaps merely kept secret) concerned with the suitor who was waiting for her in Germany. We have already recognized the phantasy of revenge as the first component of the same situation in the dream. The two components do not coincide completely, but only in part. We shall subsequently come upon the traces of a third and still more important train of thought.

42. On another occasion, instead of "calmly" she said "not the least sadly." (See note 4)—I can quote this dream as fresh evidence for the correctness of an assertion which I made in my *Traumdeutung* (1900a, Seventh Edition, pp. 387 ff.) to the effect that those pieces of a dream which are at first forgotten and are only subsequently remembered are invariably the most important from the point of view of understanding the dream. In the same place I went on to the conclusion that the forgetting of dreams must also be explained as an effect of endo-psychic resistance.

43. We must assume the existence of some somatic connection between the painful abdominal sensations known as "ovarian neuralgia" and locomotor disturbances in the leg on the same side; and we must suppose that in Dora's case the somatic connection had been given an inter-pretation of a particularly specialized sort, that is to say, that it had been overlaid with and brought into the service of a particular psychological meaning. The reader is referred to my analogous remarks in connection with the analysis of Dora's symptom of coughing and with the relation between catarrh and anorexia.

44. This is quite a typical example of the way in which symptoms arise from exciting causes which appear to be entirely unconnected with sexuality.

45. I have already indicated that the majority of hysterical symptoms, when they have at-tained their full pitch of development, represent an imagined situation of sexual life—such as a scene of sexual intercourse, pregnancy, childbirth, confinement, etc.

46. The phantasy of defloration is thus found to have an application to Herr K., and we begin to see why this part of the dream contained material taken from the scene by the lake—the refusal, two and a half hours, the wood, the invitation to L——.

47. I may here add a few supplementary interpretations to those that have already been given: The *"Madonna"* was obviously Dora herself; in the first place because of the "adorer" who had sent her the pictures, in the second place because she had won Herr K.'s love chiefly by the moth-erliness she had shown towards his children, and lastly because she had had a child though she was still a girl (this being a direct allusion to the phantasy of childbirth). Moreover, the notion of the "Madonna" is a favourite counter-idea in the mind of girls who feel themselves oppressed by imputations of sexual guilt, —which was the case with Dora. A first suspicion of this con-nection came to me while I was working as a physician at the Psychiatric Clinic of the Univer-sity. I there came across a case of confusional insanity with hallucinations, in which the attack, which ran a rapid course, turned out to be a reaction to a reproach made against the patient by her *fiancé*. —If the analysis had been continued, Dora's maternal longing for a child would probably have been revealed as an obscure though powerful motive in her behaviour. —The nu-merous questions which she had been raising latterly seem to have been belated derivatives of questions inspired by the sexual curiosity which she had tried to gratify with the encyclopaedia. The subjects which she read up in it were presumably pregnancy, childbirth, virginity, and so on. —In reproducing the dream Dora had forgotten one of the questions which need to be in-serted into the course of the second situation in the dream. This question could only be: "Does Herr—— live here?" or "Where does Herr—— live?" There must have been some reason for her having forgotten this apparently innocent question, especially as she need not have brought it into the dream at all. This reason, it seems to me, lay in her surname itself, which also denoted an object and in fact more than one kind of object, and which could therefore be re-garded as an "ambiguous" word. Unluckily I cannot give the name and show how well designed it was to indicate something "ambiguous" and "improper." This interpretation was supported

by the discovery of a similar play upon words in another part of the dream, where the material was derived from Dora's recollections of her aunt's death ("they have already gone to the cemetery") and where there was similarly a play upon her aunt's name. These improper words seemed to point to a second and *oral* source of information, since the encyclopaedia would not cover them. I should not have been surprised to hear that this source had been Frau K. herself, Dora's calumniator. In that case she would have been the one person whom Dora generously spared, while she pursued the others with an almost malignant vindictiveness. Behind the almost limitless series of displacements which were thus brought to light, it was possible to divine the operation of a single simple factor—Dora's deep-rooted homosexual love for Frau K.

48. It was December 31st.

49. It is not a matter of indifference, perhaps, that Dora may have heard her father make the same complaint about his wife, just as I myself did from his own lips. She was perfectly well aware of its meaning.

50. Here is the point of contact with the engineer, who was concealed behind the figure of Dora herself in the first situation in the dream.

51. The theme of waiting till the goal is reached occurs in the content of the first situation in the dream. I recognize in this phantasy of waiting for a fiancée a portion of the third component of that situation. I have already alluded to the existence of this third component.

52. In particular there was a speech which he had made in presenting Dora with a letter-case for Christmas in the last year in which they lived together at B——.

53. I will add a few remarks upon the structure of this dream, though it is not possible to understand it thoroughly enough to allow of a synthesis being attempted. A prominent piece of the dream is to be seen in the phantasy of revenge against her father, which stands out like a façade in front of the rest. (She had gone away from home by her own choice; her father was ill, and then dead. . . . Then she went home; all the others were already at the cemetery. She went to her room, not the least sadly, and calmly began reading the encyclopaedia.) This part of the material also contained two allusions to her other act of revenge, which she had actually carried out, when she let her parents discover a farewell letter from her. (The letter—from her mother, in the dream—and the mention of the funeral of the aunt who had always been her model.)—Behind this phantasy lie concealed her thoughts of revenge against Herr K., for which she found an outlet in her behaviour to me. (The maidservant, the invitation, the wood, the two and a half hours—all these came from material connected with the events at L——.) Her recollection of the governess and of the latter's exchange of letters with her parents, is related, no less than her farewell letter, to the letter in the dream allowing her to come home. Her refusal to let herself be accompanied and her decision to go alone may perhaps be translated into these words: "Since you have treated me like a maidservant, I shall take no more notice of you, I shall go my own way by myself, and not marry." — Screened by these thoughts of revenge, glimpses can be caught in other places of material derived from tender phantasies based upon the love for Herr K. which still persisted unconsciously in Dora. ("I would have waited for you till I could be your wife"—defloration—childbirth.)—Finally, we can see the action of the fourth and most deeply buried group of thoughts—those relating to her love for Frau K.—in the fact that the phantasy of defloration is represented from the man's point of view (her identification of herself with her admirer who lived abroad) and in the fact that in two places there are the clearest allusions to ambiguous speeches ("Does Herr——— live here?") and to that source of her sexual knowledge which had not been oral (the encyclopaedia).—Cruel and sadistic tendencies find satisfaction in this dream.

List of Abbreviations

G.S.   =   Freud, *Gesammelte Schriften* (12 vols.), Vienna, 1924–34

G.W.   =   Freud, *Gesammelte Werke* (18 vols.), London, from 1940

C.P.   = Freud, *Collected Papers* (5 vols.), London, 1924–50

Standard Ed. = Freud, *Standard Edition* (24 vols.), London, from 1953

S.K.S.N. = *Sammlung kleiner Schriften zur Neurosenlehre* (5 vols.),
           Vienna, 1906–22

S.P.H.   = *Selected Papers on Hysteria and Other Psychoneuroses*,
           3rd. ed., New York, 1920

Works Cited

Bloch, I. (1902–3) *Beiträge zur Ätiologie der Psychopathia sexualis* (2 vols.), Dresden. (51, *n.* 1, 139, *n.* 2)

Breuer, J., and Freud, S. (1893) See Freud, S. (1893*a*) (1895) See Freud, S. (1895*d*)

Freud, S. (1893*a*) With Breuer, J., "Über den psychischen Mechanismus hysterischer Phänomene: Vorläufige Mitteilung', *G.S.*, **1**, 7; *G.W.*, **1**, 81. (127, 276 *n.*) [Trans.: "On the Psychical Mechanism of Hysterical Phenomena: Preliminary Communication," *C.P.*, **1**, 24; *Standard Ed.*, **2**.]

——. (1894*a*) "Die Abwehr-Neuropsychosen," *G.S.*, **1**, 290; *G.W.*, **1**, 57. (53*n.*, 276) [*Trans.:* "The Neuro-Psychoses of Defence," *C.P.*, **1**, 59; *Standard Ed.*, **3**.]

——. (1895*d*) With Breuer, J., *Studien über Hysterie*, Vienna. (*G.S.*, **1**; *G.W.*, **1**, 75. Omitting Breuer's contributions.) (7 *n.*, 12, 24, 27, *n.* 1, 31, *n.* 2, 117 *n.*, 164 *n.*, 248–9, 257, 272) [*Trans.: Studies on Hysteria, Standard Ed.*, **2**. Including Breuer's contributions.]

——. (1896*a*) "L'hérédité et l'étiologie des Névroses," *G.S.*, **1**, 388; *G.W.*, **1**, 405. (20 *n.*, 275, *n.* 2) [*Trans.:* "Heredity and the Aetiology of the Neuroses," *C.P.*, **1**, 138; *Standard Ed.*, **3**.]

——. (1896*c*) "Zur Ätiologie der Hysterie," *G.S.*, **1**, 404; *G.W.*, **1**, 423. (7 *n.*, 27, *n.* 2, 176, *n.* 1, 190, 257 *n.*, 273) [*Trans.:* "The Aetiology of Hysteria," *C.P.*, **1**, 183; *Standard Ed.*, **3**.]

——. (1900*a*) *Die Traumdeutung*, Vienna. (*G.S.*, **2–3**; *G.W.*, **2–3**.) (4, 10, 11, *n.* 1, 15, 17, *n.* 2, 29, *n.* 1, 56 *n.*, 67, 71 *nn.*, 85–6, 87 *n.*, 88 *n.*, 92 *n.*, 97, *n.* 2, 100, *n.* 2, 117 *n.*, 126–9, 184, *n.* 3, 192, *n.* 2, 201 *n.*, 226 *n.*, 227 *n.*, 250 *n.*, 252, 284 *n.*, 295 *n.*, 309, *n.* 1) [*Trans.: The Interpretation of Dreams*, London and New York, 1955; *Standard Ed.*, **4–5**.]

——. (1905*d*) *Drei Abhandlungen zur Sexualtheorie*, Vienna. (*G.S.*, **5**, 3; *G.W.*, **5**, 29.) (4–5, 50 *n.*, 51, *n.* 1, 52, *n.* 1, 56 *n.*, 74, *n.* 2, 81, *n.* 1, 113 *n.*, 275, *n.* 1, 276–7, 279, *n.* 2) [*Trans.: Three Essays on the Theory of Sexuality*, London, 1949; *Standard Ed.*, **7**, 125.]

—— (1909*d*) "Bemerkungen über einen Fall von Zwangsneurose," *G.S.*, **8**, 269; *G.W.*, **7**, 381. (13 *n.*, 17, *n.* 2, 155, *n.* 2, 226 *n.*, 248) [*Trans.:* "Notes on a Case of Obsessional Neurosis," *C.P.*, **3**, 293; *Standard Ed.*, **10**.]

——. (1910*i*) "Die psychogene Sehstörung in psychoanalytischer Auffassung," *G.S.*, **5**, 301; *G.W.*, **8**, 94. (40 *n.*) [*Trans.:* "The Psycho-Analytic View of Psychogenic Disturbance of Vision," *C.P.*, **2**, 105; *Standard Ed.*, **11**.]

——. (1912*f*) "Zur Onanie-Diskussion," *G.S.*, **3**, 324; *G.W.*, **8**, 332. (40 *n.*, 185, *n.* 1, 188, *n.* 2) [*Trans.:* "Contributions to a Discussion on Masturbation," *Standard Ed.*, **12**.]

——. (1914*d*) "Zur Geschichte der psychoanalytischen Bewegung," *G.S.*, **4**, 411; *G.W.*, **10**, 44. (5, 27, *n.* 1, 128 *n.*, 275, *n.* 1) [*Trans.:* "On the History of the Psycho-Analytic Movement," *C.P.*, **1**, 287; *Standard Ed.*, **14**.]

——. (1930*a*) *Das Unbehagen in der Kultur*, Vienna. (*G.S.*, **12**, 29; *G.W.*, **14**, 421.) (32 *n.*, 155, *n.* 2, 219 *n.*) [*Trans.: Civilization and Its Discontents*, London and New York, 1930; *Standard Ed.*, **21**.]

———. (1950a [1887–1902]) *Aus den Anfängen der Psychoanalyse,* London. Includes the "Entwurf einer Psychologie" (1895). (3–5, 32 *n.*, 43 *n.*, 55, *n.* 1, 78 *n.*, 126–9, 143 *n.*, 156, *n.* 2, 162, *n.* 1, 165, *n.* 2, 167, *n.* 2, 184, *n.* 3, 216 *n.*, 225, *n.* 3, 235 *n.*, 236 *n.*, 275 *nn.*) [*Trans.: The Origins of Psycho-Analysis,* London and New York, 1954. (Partly, including "A Project for a Scientific Psychology," in *Standard Ed.,* **1.**)]

Ideas for Rereading

1. Write a chronology of key events in Dora's life, annotating each of the events that Freud directly interprets. The chronology should include each of the incidents that Freud focuses on, including her father's illnesses, the family's visits to B——, Dora's encounters with Herr K., and her visits to Freud. You might also include a chronology of Freud's work with Dora, noting when he saw her, when he published her account, and when he commented on the choice of the name "Dora" (see p. 368 in the Context section).

2. What do you make of Freud's report that Dora's father initially asked Freud to "please try and bring her [Dora] to reason" (p. 322)? Identify and discuss the places where Freud's methods and practices are focused on bringing Dora to reason. What do you make of Freud's statement that *"pour faire une omelette il faut casser des œufs"* ("to make an omelette one must break eggs," p. 334)? How do you interpret Dora's reasons for quitting her treatment with Freud?

Ideas for Writing

1. Consider the importance of storytelling in Freud's methodology. In the absence of Dora's version of events from her childhood and from her visits to Freud, we can rely only on evidence from Freud's case history to build an understanding of what really happened with Dora. Working with the assumption that Freud's account is as accurate as possible, write an interpretation of the case history from Dora's point of view. Perhaps begin by imagining what Dora might have written to a friend after they had both seen the published version in 1905. Or you might imagine her penning a letter to Freud, Herr K., Frau K., or her father after Freud's report became public. Rather than quibbling with facts of the case, suggest how Dora's interpretations of these facts might have differed from Freud's: use specific quotations from Freud's analysis to develop your version of what Dora might have said in explaining her case history. Imagine that Dora has been completely cured so that she is now able "to give an ordered history of [her] life" (p. 316); you could then give Dora's version of how she came to terms with her illness and why she felt able to terminate her therapy.

2. In a preface that he wrote for "A Fragment of an Analysis of a Case of Hysteria" Freud stated that "What is new has always aroused bewilderment and resistance." In this preface he addressed different forms of resistance, bewilderment, incompletion, and difficulty experienced both by Dora and himself dur-

ing the three months of their meetings and during the years of writing the report. Freud also anticipated some of the confused and hostile responses by readers.

Write an essay about resistance, bewilderment, incompletion, and difficulty created by "A Fragment of an Analysis of a Case of Hysteria." While you might take into account Freud and Dora's problematic experiences, you should concentrate on your own reactions to "The Clinical Picture" and "The Second Dream." You might begin by addressing your own experiences as you read the piece for the first time. Which passages seemed the most outlandish, bizarre, or weird when you first read them? What makes these passages unacceptable, confusing, incomplete, and/or difficult? Which of Freud's ideas do you find bewildering? Which ideas do you resist? One way of focusing your response would be to analyze specific passages where Freud explains his methods and/or where he adopts a posture of self-defense, self-justification, and apology.

3. Write an essay reconsidering your notes about "The Clinical Picture" by taking into account Freud's work with "a symbolic geography of sex" (p. 343). Pay specific attention to the endnotes throughout "The Second Dream." How does the final note on page 354 contribute to your understanding of this case of hysteria? How does Freud's work with this dream help you to understand his methods?

CONTEXT

In the years before Freud developed "the talking cure," European doctors had depended on aggressive interventions in their patients' physical and emotional lives. Electrotherapy—shocking patients with electric current—and hypnosis were standard practices. Even the most progressive approaches to hysteria involved rather violent acts of public and private manipulation. Alongside the melodramatic picture of Jean-Martin Charcot's hypnotherapy of a hysterical patient, the pictures of instruments used to treat hysteria—an electric brush and probe, which were inserted into the patient's throat to apply current directly to her larynx—suggest how hysteria was treated when Freud began work in the field. There were, however, doctors and thinkers before Freud who looked for rational insight into "the hidden self." William James (1842–1910), an important philosopher and psychologist who helped found a uniquely American system of thought called pragmatism, summarizes the work of M. Pierre Janet (1859–1947), a student of Charcot who slightly predates Freud. This essay from the late 1880s provides a detailed sense of an approach that forms a bridge between Charcot and Freud.

The dramatic way in which Freud shifted the very setting in which hysteria was treated is evident from the photograph of Freud's consulting room: Charcot's public performances at the Salpêtrière* and Janet's use of magnets have been

---

Salpêtrière: Named after the gun-powder factory from which it was converted in 1656, this hospital functioned as a place of incarceration and experiment rather than a place for healing.

*This picture shows Jean-Martin Charcot with a hysterical patient and an audience
of doctors and students. It was taken in the mid-1880s at the Salpêtrière, a hospital
for the poor located in Paris.*

replaced by a room designed for the one-on-one exchange of stories and analyses.
The 1906 photograph gives an idea of what Freud looked like when he published
"A Fragment of an Analysis of a Case of Hysteria." In his definition of the psychoanalytic method, Fritz Wittels, one of Freud's students, gives us a good idea of what
was involved in the patient-doctor encounter: you may find yourself questioning
whether Wittels is accurate in his representation of the work of psychoanalysis as
demonstrated in the Dora case. You may also find yourself testing the idea that
Freud inaugurated "an artistic science" (p. 365).

In "Postscript to the Dora Case," Freud begins by confessing his failure to appreciate the importance of homosexuality in the case; he then goes on to say that a
return visit by Dora gave him the opportunity "to forgive her for having deprived
[him] of the satisfaction of affording her a far more radical cure for her troubles"
(p. 367). Juxtaposed with Freud's meditation on his choice of the name "Dora" in
the excerpt from "Determinism and Superstition," this retrospective account suggests the extent to which Freud engaged in critical self-analysis.

Ernest Jones (1879–1958), a Welsh psychoanalyst who corresponded regularly
with Freud from 1908 until 1938, published an authoritative biography between
1953 and 1957, The Life and Work of Sigmund Freud. The piece we include is
from the biography and it summarizes the reception of "A Fragment of an Analysis
of a Case of Hysteria," suggesting the widespread hostility among psychologists,
doctors, philosophers, and publishers. Finally, the 1909 excerpt from the New
York Times suggests that the New World was immediately more receptive to
Freud's thinking than was the Old World.

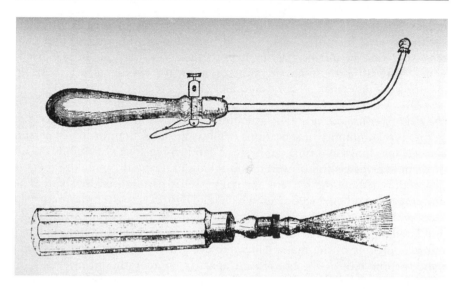

Electric brush and probe used to treat hysteria before Freud. Instruments such as these were inserted into Dora's throat and an electric current was applied through them to treat her cough and loss of voice.

WILLIAM JAMES

From *The Hidden Self*   *ca. 1890*

One of the most constant symptoms in persons suffering from hysteric disease in its extreme forms consists in alterations of the natural sensibility of various parts and organs of the body. Usually the alteration is in the direction of defect, or anaesthesia. One or both eyes are blind, or blind over one half of the field of vision, or the latter is extremely contracted, so that its margins appear dark, or else the patient has lost all sense for color. Hearing, taste, smell may similarly disappear, in part or in totality. Still more striking are the cutaneous anaesthesias. The old witch-finders, looking for the "devil's seals," well learned the existence of those insensible patches on the skin of their victims, to which the minute physical examinations of recent medicine have but lately attracted attention again. They may be scattered anywhere, but are very apt to affect one side of the body. Not infrequently they affect an entire lateral half, from head to foot, and the insensible skin of, say the left side, will then be found separated from the naturally sensitive skin of the right by a perfectly sharp line of demarcation down the middle of the front and back. Sometimes, most remarkable of all, the entire skin, hands, feet, face, everything, and the mucous membranes, muscles, and joints, so far as they can be explored, become *completely* insensible without the other vital functions being gravely disturbed. These anaesthesias and hemianaesthesias, in all their various grades, form the nucleus of M. Janet's observations and hypotheses. And, first of all, he has an hypothesis about the anaesthesia itself, which, like all provisional hypotheses, may do excellent service while awaiting the day when a better one shall take its place.

The original sin of the hysteric mind, he thinks, is the *contractions of the field of consciousness.* The attention has not sufficient strength to take in the normal number of sensations or ideas at once. If an ordinary person can feel ten things at a time, an hysteric can feel but five. Our minds are all of them like vessels full of water, and taking in a new drop makes another drop fall out; only the hysteric mental vessel is preternaturally small. The unifying or synthetizing power which the Ego exerts over the manifold facts which are offered to it is insufficient to do its full amount of work, and an ingrained habit is formed of neglecting or overlooking certain determinate portions of the mass. Thus one eye will be ignored, one arm and hand, or one half of the body. And apart from anaesthesia, hysterics are often extremely *distraites,* and unable to attend to two things at once. When talking with you they forget everything else. When Lucie* stopped conversing directly with anyone, she ceased to be able to hear anyone else. You might stand behind her, call her by name, shout abuse into her ears, without making her turn round; or place yourself before her, show her objects, touch her, etc., without attracting her notice. When finally she becomes aware of you, she thinks you have just come into the room again, and greets you accordingly. This singular forgetfulness makes her liable to tell all her secrets aloud, unrestrained by the presence of unsuitable auditors. This contracted mental field (or state of monoideism, as it has been called) characterizes also the hypnotic state of normal persons, so that in this important respect a waking hysteric is like a well person in the hypnotic trance. Both are wholly lost in their present idea, its normal "reductives" and correctives having lapsed from view.

The anaesthesias of the class of patients we are considering can be made to disappear more or less completely by various odd processes. It has been recently found that magnets, plates of metal, the electrodes of a battery, placed against the skin, have this peculiar power. And when one side is relieved in this way, the anaesthesia is often found to have transferred itself to the opposite side, which, until then, was well. Whether these strange effects of magnets and metals be due to their direct physiological action, or to a prior effect on the patient's mind ("expectant attention" or "suggestion") is still a mooted question.[1] A still better awakener of sensibility in most of these subjects is the *hypnotic state,* which M. Janet seems to have most easily induced by the orthodox "magnetic" method of "passes" made

---

Lucie: A patient of Janet's who suffered from a special kind of hysteria that Janet termed "automatism." Her case history is reported in *L'Automatisme psychologique (The Psychology of Automatism),* 1889.

Freud's consulting room in Vienna, 1938, photographed by Edmund Engelman

over the face and body. It was in making these passes that he first stumbled on one of the most curious facts recorded in his volume. One day, when the subject named Lucie was in the hypnotic state, he made passes over her again for half an hour, just as if she were not already "asleep." The result was to throw her into a sort of syncope* from which, after another half hour, she revived in a second somnambulic condition entirely unlike that which had characterized her hitherto—different sensibilities, a different memory, a different person, in short. In the waking state the poor young woman was anaesthetic all over, nearly deaf, and with a badly contracted field of vision. Bad as it was, however, sight was her best sense, and she used it as a guide in all her movements. With her eyes bandaged she was entirely helpless, and, like other persons of a similar sort whose cases have

syncope: Loss of consciousness.

Sigmund Freud, 1906, age 50

been recorded, she almost immediately fell asleep in consequence of the withdrawal of her last sensorial stimulus. M. Janet calls this waking or primary (one can hardly, in such a connection, say "normal") state by the name of Lucie 1. In Lucie 2, her first sort of hypnotic trance, the anaesthesias were diminished but not removed. In the deeper trance, "Lucie 3," brought about as just described, no trace of them remained. Her sensibility became perfect, and instead of being an extreme example of the "visual" type, she was transformed into what, in Professor Charcot's terminology, is known as a motor. That is to say, that whereas, when awake, she had thought in visual terms exclusively, and could imagine things only by remembering how they *looked*, now, in this deeper trance, her thoughts and memories seemed largely composed of images of movement and of touch—of course I state summarily here what appears in the book as an induction from many facts.

Having discovered this deeper trance in Lucie, M. Janet naturally became eager to find it in his other subjects. He found it in Rose, in Marie, and in Léonie; and, best of all, his brother, Dr. Jules Janet, who was *interne* at the Salpêtrière Hospital, found it in the celebrated subject Witt, whose trances had been studied for years by the various doctors of that institution without any of them having happened to awaken this very peculiar modification of the personality.

With the return of all the sensibilities in the deeper trance, the subjects are transformed, as it were, into normal persons.

Note

1. M. Janet seems rather to incline to the former view, though suggestion may at times be exclusively responsible, as when he produced what was essentially the same phenomenon by pointing an orange-peel held out on the end of a long stick at the parts!

FRITZ WITTELS

From *Veiling and Unveiling Psychotherapy*   1931

We want to educate the ambivalent to a "post-ambivalent" person. He ought to know what he wants and whether he still wants it, and must decide whether he is right in wanting it. We wish to show him that his weakness and his distress result from his ambivalence. He can no longer in the light of the secondary function say yes and no at the same time. The neurotic falls ill because he flees such decisions and in their place produces his pathological symptoms. He chooses neither of two possibilities, but a third. That would not be so bad in itself, did not the superego* protest against such evading of decision and produce in neurotics a feeling of illness which frequently becomes unbearable. The environment suffers from nervous characters, even if they themselves do not suffer. We need only to observe hysterical leaders and we notice immediately that undissolved conflicts are the sources of much harm, even if the hysteric is satisfied with himself. These people torment themselves and others with their restlessness. We know well that the progress of civilization depends upon discontent, but we recognize a difference between the sublimation of a conflict and neurotic reaction and we know that for one victor in a neurotic

---

superego: Freud imagined three parts of the human psyche, the id, the ego, and the superego. He defined the id as the base, animalistic drive for satisfaction; the ego as the more controlled drive to manipulate the world to satisfy oneself; and the superego as one's social conscience. The superego is formed through an internalization of parental and other standards of behavior: it produces feelings of guilt and shame.

conflict there are thousands of hopelessly languishing ambivalent cripples and masochists.

We endeavor with our methods of discovery to reach the sources of the disorder. Obsolete childish wishes have to be disinterred so that they can be forgotten. Feelings of guilt must be ejected through recognition of their origin and by either atoning for the wrong or otherwise expunging it from the record. Perverse impulses; feelings of inferiority; fixation upon parents and brothers and sisters in love and in hate; dangerous rhythms, which are forever leading to undesirable transferences; confusion of actuality and fantasy, that of to-day and of a remote past; confusion of fear and desire, of hatred and love—everything must come to light that it may be discharged. Let a scoundrel be a scoundrel, if he must, a saint a saint; but both should know what drives them to extremes, and above all the scoundrel must not deceive himself that he is a saint, nor the saint that he is a rogue.

Our patients do not want all this. They develop unconsciously and consciously violent resistance against the disillusioning method. Our patients run away if we tell them the truth without preparing them slowly and systematically for it. We have therefore learned a technique which is related to obstetrics. We wait and deliver the child when it has reached full term. Our patients are always seeking to compel us to go from the method of discovery to suggestion. They want us to play the role of stern father or tender mother or vice versa. They want solace instead of the truth. The primary function participates directly in comfort-giving, in stroking, while enlightenment demands the hard work of protracted thought, of acknowledgment of disagreeable facts, of final decision. The patients would like to debase the analyst to the level of a hypnotist, transfer their ego ideal upon him, with which for the analyst "is associated the temptation to assume toward the patient the role of prophet, savior of souls, redeemer" (Freud). No matter how much we defend ourselves against this attempt of the patients, we shall not be able to prevent the relationship of the child to authority from being constantly reestablished. We have to attribute to this tendency a vanishing success at the beginning of almost every curative psychoanalysis. This same tendency has to bear the blame for failures right at the beginning of our work. Persons who endure authority badly and are always bursting forth from such bonds, break off the analysis in the early stage. Many desert it because too much truth is disclosed before they are able to bear it. The majority of patients, however, feel wonderfully relieved; yet this is no reason for boasting of the success of the analysis but a bit of veiling suggestion which must be removed according to the rules of psychoanalysis. We analysts are in a bad way indeed when we consider how easy it is to play the role before our patients of the great man and the miracle worker. Our great final goal is from the start the unmasking of the truth—with technical limitations into which I will not enter here.

The fundamental rule of psychoanalysis is that the analysand is in duty bound "to tell everything which passes through his mind, even if it is unpleasant to him, even though it seems to him to be unimportant, irrelevant, or absurd" (Freud). This rule excludes any self-criticism. Besides, physical relaxation is necessary; the patient lies comfortably on a couch. The analyst withdraws to a place behind the patient, who is thus to a great degree diverted from the direction of his secondary function toward the primary function. The secondary function controls motor action; the patient's motor activity is cut off. The secondary function develops social restraints: clever and stupid, attractive and ugly, noble and petty—we put all that aside. There remain then as determinants those things which arise from the unconscious depths. It is therefore not to be wondered at that psychoanalysis was soon aware that its work only in part brought to light memories and thoughts which are clothed in words. A unity is created in the form of participation, called by Freud transference, out of the group of two in which psychoanalysis takes place, a unity that is first felt and afterward becomes understood.

Psychoanalysis is the experiencing (*das Erlebnis*) of one's own primary function in forms which can be psychoanalytically grasped and comprehended. One experiences one's own primary function in one's narcissistic, heterosexual and homosexual, sadistic, masochistic, anal, oral, phallic, and castrating tendencies. One cannot describe an experience (*Erlebnis*) in words. Psychoanalysis cannot therefore be learned from books; it must be felt. Rational memories succeeding one another afford an interesting biographical construction. But only in the transference can the primary function be felt and influenced, in so far as one human being can influence another.

We have just admitted that psychoanalysis is not to be learned from books—due to the peculiarities of the primary function which we have described. Likewise it must be acknowledged that psychoanalysis is not a pure science, but an artistic science. Many will see perhaps in an artistic science a *contradictio in adjecto* (contradiction in terms); in such case, I believe that we must dispense rather with the word science than with the word art. For there are analysts who have not had much instruction and who yet obtain good analytic results because of a native or early developed talent for introspection. There are also analysts who have gone into a deep study of psychoanalysis and its literature and submitted to an analysis, with an uncertain result—but they are unable to analyze. As far as I can see, a good analyst combines a measure of intuition, that is, immediate entrance into his own and therefore another's primary function, with the compulsive pertinacity of the methodical person, which prevents his being moved from his base, namely, from his learned fundamental principles.

SIGMUND FREUD

From *Postscript to Dora Case*   1905

The longer the interval of time[1] that separates me from the end of this analysis, the more probable it seems to me that the fault in my technique lay in this omission: I failed to discover in time and to inform the patient that her homosexual (gynaecophilic) love for Frau K. was the strongest unconscious current in her mental life. I ought to have guessed that the main source of her knowledge of sexual matters could have been no one but Frau K.—the very person who later on charged her with being interested in those same subjects. Her knowing all about such things and, at the same time, her always pretending not to know where her knowledge came from was really too remarkable. [Cf. p. 324.—Trans.] I ought to have attacked this riddle and looked for the motive of such an extraordinary piece of repression. If I had done this, the second dream would have given me my answer. The remorseless craving for revenge expressed in that dream was suited as nothing else was to conceal the current of feeling that ran contrary to it—the magnanimity with which she forgave the treachery of the friend she loved and concealed from every one the fact that it was this friend who had herself revealed to her the knowledge which had later been the ground of the accusations against her. Before I had learnt the importance of the homosexual current of feeling in psychoneurotics, I was often brought to a standstill in the treatment of my cases or found myself in complete perplexity.

It was not until fifteen months after the case was over and this paper composed that I had news of my patient's condition and the effects of my treatment. On a date which is not a matter of complete indifference, on the first of April (times and dates, as we know, were never without significance for her), Dora came to see me again: to finish her story and to ask for help once more. One glance at her face, however, was enough to tell me that she was not in earnest over her request. For four or five weeks after stopping the treatment she had been "all in a muddle," as she said. A great improvement had then set in; her attacks had become less frequent and her spirits had risen. In the May of that year one of the K.'s two children (it had always been delicate) had died. She took the opportunity of their loss to pay them a visit of condolence, and they received her as though nothing had happened in the last three years. She made it up with them, she took her revenge on them, and she brought her own business to a satisfactory conclusion. To the wife she said: "I know you have an affair with my father"; and the other did not deny it. From the husband she drew an admission of the scene by the lake which he had disputed, and brought the news of her vindication home to her father. Since then she had not resumed her relations with the family.

After this she had gone on quite well till the middle of October, when she had had another attack of aphonia which had lasted for six weeks. I was surprised at this news, and, on my asking her whether there had been any exciting cause, she told me that the attack had followed upon a violent fright. She had seen some one run over by a carriage. Finally she came out with the fact that the accident had occurred to no less a person than Herr K. himself. She had come across him in the street one day; they had met in a place where there was a great deal of traffic; he had stopped in front of her as though in bewilderment, and in his abstraction he had allowed himself to be knocked down by a carriage.[2] She had been able to convince herself, however, that he escaped without serious injury. She still felt some slight emotion if she heard any one speak of her father's affair with Frau K., but otherwise she had no further concern with the matter. She was absorbed in her work, and had no thoughts of marrying.

She went on to tell me that she had come for help on account of a right-sided facial neuralgia, from which she was now suffering day and night. "How long has it been going on?" "Exactly a fortnight."[3] I could not help smiling; for I was able to show her that exactly a fortnight earlier she had read a piece of news that concerned me in the newspaper. (This was in 1902.)[4] And this she confirmed.

Her alleged facial neuralgia was thus a self-punishment—remorse at having once given Herr K. a box on the ear, and at having transferred her feelings of revenge on to me. I do not know what kind of help she wanted from me, but I promised to forgive her for having deprived me of the satisfaction of affording her a far more radical cure for her troubles.

Years have again gone by since her visit. In the meantime the girl has married, and indeed—unless all the signs mislead me—she has married the young man who came into her associations at the beginning of the analysis of the second dream.[5] Just as the first dream represented her turning away from the man she loved to her father—that is to say, her flight from life into disease—so the second dream announced that she was about to tear herself free from her father and had been reclaimed once more by the realities of life.

Notes

1. [The Postscript was written in 1905, immediately prior to the publication of "A Fragment of an Analysis of a Case of Hysteria." It was published in a journal in two parts, in October and November: the English translation of the journal is called *Notes for Psychiatry and Neurology.*—Eds.]

2. We have here an interesting contribution to the problem of indirect attempts at suicide, which I have discussed in my *Psychopathology of Everyday Life.*

3. For the significance of this period of time and its relation to the theme of revenge, see the analysis of the second dream [p. 346 ff.].

4. [No doubt the news was of Freud's appointment to a Professorship in March of that year.—Trans.]

5. [In the editions of 1909, 1912, and 1921 the following footnote appeared at this point: "This, as I afterwards learnt, was a mistaken notion."—Trans.]

SIGMUND FREUD

From *Determinism and Superstition*   1901

If we give way to the view that a part of our physical functioning cannot be explained by purposive ideas, we are failing to appreciate the extent of determination[1] in mental life. Both here and in other spheres this is more far-reaching than we suspect. In an article in [the Vienna daily paper] *Die Zeit* by R. M. Meyer, the literary historian, which I came across in 1900, the view was put forward and illustrated by examples that it is impossible intentionally and arbitrarily to make up a piece of nonsense. I have known for some time that one cannot make a number occur to one at one's own free choice any more than a name. Investigation of a number made up in an apparently arbitrary manner—one, let us say, of several digits uttered by someone as a joke or in a moment of high spirits—reveals that it is strictly determined in a way that would really never have been thought possible. I will begin by briefly discussing an instance of an arbitrarily chosen first name. . . .

With a view to preparing the case history[2] of one of my women patients for publication I considered what first name I should give her in my account. There appeared to be a very wide choice; some names, it is true, were ruled out from the start—the real name in the first place, then the names of members of my own family, to which I should object, and perhaps some other women's names with an especially peculiar sound. But otherwise there was no need for me to be at a loss for a name. It might have been expected—and I myself expected—that a whole host of women's names would be at my disposal. Instead, one name and only one occurred to me—the name "Dora."

I asked myself how it was determined. Who else was there called Dora? I should have liked to dismiss with incredulity the next thought to occur to me—that it was the name of my sister's nursemaid; but I have so much self-discipline or so much practice in analysing that I held firmly to the idea and let my thoughts run on from it. At once there came to my mind a trivial incident from the previous evening which provided the determinant I was looking for. I had seen a letter on my sister's dining-room table addressed to "Fräulein Rosa W." I asked in surprise who there was of that name, and was told that the girl I knew as Dora was really called Rosa, but had had to give up her real name when she took up employment in the house, since my sister could take the name "Rosa" as applying to herself as well. "Poor people," I remarked in pity, "they cannot even keep their own names!" After that, I now recall, I fell silent for a moment and began to think of a variety of serious matters which drifted into obscurity, but which I was now easily able to make conscious. When next day I was looking for a name for someone *who could not keep her own*, "Dora" was the only one to occur to me. The complete absence of alternatives was here based on a solid association connected with the subject-matter that I was dealing with: for it was a person employed in someone else's house, a governess, who exercised a decisive influence on my patient's story, and on the course of the treatment as well.

Years later[3] this little incident had an unexpected sequel. Once, when I was discussing in a lecture the long since published case history of the girl now called Dora, it occurred to me that one of the two ladies in my audience had the same name Dora that I should have to utter so often in a whole variety of connections. I turned to my young colleague, whom I also knew personally, with the excuse that I had not in fact remembered that that was her name too, and added that I was very willing to replace it in my lecture by another name. I was now faced with the task of rapidly choosing another one, and I reflected that I must at all costs avoid selecting the first name of the other lady in the audience and so setting a bad example to my other colleagues, who were already well grounded in psychoanalysis. I was therefore very much pleased when the name "Erna" occurred to me as a substitute for Dora, and I used it in the lecture. After the lecture I asked myself where the name Erna could possibly have come from, and I could not help laughing when I noticed that the possibility I had been afraid of when I was choosing the substitute name had nevertheless come about, at least to some extent. The other lady's family name was Lucerna, of which Erna is a part.

Notes

1. [I.e. the degree to which the principle of determinism operates. — Trans.]

2. [This was the "Fragment of an Analysis of a Case of Hysteria." Though the greater part of this was written in January, 1901 (that is to say, before the present work appeared), Freud did not publish it till the autumn of 1905. — Trans. *Psychopathology of Everyday Life* was published in 1901. All but the Postscript to "A Fragment of an Analysis of a Case of Hysteria" was written in 1900–1901. The Postscript was written in 1905. — Eds.]

3. [This paragraph was added in 1907. — Trans.]

ERNEST JONES

Summary of Early Responses
to the Dora Analysis   *1953*

In the first years of the century Freud and his writings were either quietly ignored or else they would be mentioned with a sentence or two of disdain as if not deserving any serious attention. At the Congress of Mid-German Psychiatrists and Neurologists held at Halle in 1900 there was a symposium of the pathogenesis of hysteria, but Freud's name was not even mentioned by any of the speakers. When the same Congress met in 1904

Stegmann gave an account of cases he had treated by Freud's method and was severely castigated by Professor Binswanger of Jena, the author of the standard textbook on hysteria.

But after 1905 when the *Three Essays on the Theory of Sexuality* and the Dora analysis appeared this attitude of silence soon changed, and the critics took a more active line. If his ideas would not die by themselves they had to be killed. Freud was evidently relieved at this change of tactics. He remarked to one of his favorite patients—no other than the "Wolfman"*—that open opposition, and even abuse, was far preferable to being silently ignored. "It was a confession that they had to deal with a serious opponent with whom they had *nolens volens** to thrash matters out." He could at times laugh at the moral indignation displayed, such as when he told the same patient that a meeting at which his views had been decried as immoral ended by the audience relating the most obscene jokes among themselves.

Even in the first review of the Dora analysis Spielmeyer declaimed against the use of a method that he described as "mental masturbation." Bleuler protested that no one was competent to judge the method without testing it, but Spielmeyer in an angry retort overwhelmed him with moral indignation.

The first person to take independent action was Gustav Aschaffenburg. At a Congress in Baden-Baden in May 1906 he expressed himself vigorously and came to the conclusion that "Freud's method is wrong in most cases, objectionable in many and superfluous in all." It was an immoral method and anyhow was based only on auto-suggestion. Hoche joined in. According to him psychoanalysis was an evil method proceeding from mystical tendencies and full of dangers to the medical profession; it was wrong-headed and one-sided. Jung* replied to this outburst in the periodical that published Aschaffenburg's paper, but not very effectively.

In the same year Ostwald Bumke made great play of quoting the first devastating denunciation of Freud, which Rieger had published ten years previously on Freud's contribution to the theory of paranoia. According to Rieger Freud's views were such as "no alienist could read without feeling a real sense of horror." The ground of this horror lay in the way Freud treated as of the greatest importance a paranoid rigmarole with sexual allusions to purely accidental incidents which, even if not invented, were entirely indifferent. All that sort of thing could lead to nothing other than "a simply gruesome old-wives' psychiatry." This quotation was to be dug up

---

"Wolfman": Refers to Freud's case study, published in 1918, called "The Wolf Man." The case involves a dream analysis of a kind related to Dora's.

nolens volens: A literal translation from Latin is "unwilling willing." In context it means "whether willing or not."

Jung: Carl Gustav Jung (1875–1961). A Swiss-German psychoanalyst who was an early supporter of Freud but who later developed a non-Freudian theory of the unconscious. Rejecting Freud's emphasis on individual sexual trauma, Jung thought in terms of the collective unconscious and archetypes, positing universal sources for creativity, spirituality, and personality.

again in yet another ten years' time by Professor von Luschan of Berlin. Some years later Bumke extended his denunciation into a book, the second edition of which was to serve in Nazi times as a standard reference work on the subject.

In November of that year Jung and Hoche had a set-to at the Congress of South-West German Psychiatrists in Tübingen.

In the following year there was a more serious duel between Aschaffenburg and Jung at the First International Congress of Psychiatry and Neurology which took place in Amsterdam in September 1907.

Freud himself had been invited to take part in the symposium, but he had unhesitatingly refused. He wrote to Jung about it: "They were evidently looking forward to my having a duel with Janet, but I hate gladiator fights in front of the noble mob and find it hard to agree to an unconcerned crowd voting on my experiences." Nevertheless he had some misgiving later at the thought of how he was enjoying a pleasant holiday when someone was fighting on his behalf. So just before the Congress he wrote an encouraging letter to Jung: "I don't know whether you will be lucky or unlucky, but I should like to be with you just now, enjoying the feeling that I am no longer alone. If you needed any encouragement I could tell you about my long years of honorable, but painful, loneliness that began for me as soon as I got the first glimpse into the new world; of the lack of interest and understanding on the part of my nearest friends; of the anxious moments when I myself believed I was in error and wondered how it was going to be possible to follow such unconventional paths and yet support my family; of my gradually strengthening conviction, which clung to *The Interpretation of Dreams* as to a rock in the breakers; and of the calm certainty I finally compassed which bade me wait until a voice from beyond my ken would respond. It was yours!" Freud also predicted that Jung would come across some sympathizer at the Congress, a prediction my presence there unexpectedly fulfilled.

Jung could certainly do with any encouragement before such an ordeal. Aschaffenburg repeated his previous dictum about the untrustworthiness of Freud's method because of every single word being interpreted in a sexual sense. This was not only painful for the patient but often directly harmful. Then, striking his breast with a gesture of self-righteousness, he asseverated how he forbade his patients ever to mention any sexual topic. In the course of his address Aschaffenburg made this revealing slip of the tongue: "As is well known, Breuer and *I* published a book some years ago." He did not appear to have noticed it himself, and perhaps Jung and I were the only people to have done so, or at least to perceive its significance; we could only smile across at each other. Jung said in his address that he had found Freud's conclusions correct in every case of hysteria he had examined, and he remarked that the subject of symbolism, although familiar to poets and the makers of myths, was new to psychiatrists. Unfortunately he made the mistake of not timing his paper and also of refusing to obey the chairman's repeated signals to finish. Ultimately he was compelled to, whereupon with a flushed angry face he strode out of the room. I remember the unfortunate impression his behavior made on the impatient and already prejudiced audience, so that there could be no doubt about the issue of the debate. Both papers were subsequently published. Aschaffenburg was not able to be present on the following day when the discussion took place, but Konrad Alt and Karl Heilbronner seconded his attack in a fashion that made Jung feel it was useless to reply. Alt said that, apart from Freud's methods, it had always been known that sexual traumata influenced the genesis of hysteria. "Many hysterics had suffered severely from the prejudice of their relatives that hysteria can only arise on a sexual foundation. This widely spread prejudice we German neurologists have taken endless trouble to destroy. Now if the Freudian opinion concerning the genesis of hysteria should gain ground the poor hysterics will again be condemned as before. This retrograde step would do the greatest harm." Amid great applause he promised that no patient of his should ever be allowed to reach any of Freud's followers, with their conscienceless descent into absolute filth. The cheering was renewed when Ziehen rose to congratulate the speaker on the firm stand he had taken.

Jung was naturally extremely disgusted at the whole performance and very glad that Freud had not been present to be exposed to such contumely.

"Strangled Emotion," *New York Times*   *1909*

The theories of the German physician Freud are caviare even to the medical profession in this country, but they are being accepted by the leading specialists on hysteria, and are of public interest in their definition of its cause. A review of Freud's conception of this common ailment is presented by Dr. A. A. Brill in the current issue of *The Medical Record*. According to this conception all hysterics have at some time in their past history strangled or repressed their emotions. When Malcolm cried out to Macduff, who had listened to the story of Macbeth's savage slaughter of his wife and children,

> What, man! ne'er pull your hat upon
>   your brows,
> Give sorrow words: the grief that
>   does not speak
> Whispers the o'erfraught heart, and
>   bids it break,

he diagnosed a most serious manifestation of this tendency. In the usual cases it is not so dangerous, but leads to periodic excitements for which the patient is himself at a loss to account. Wounds to the feelings "act like foreign bodies in the consciousness, and even long after their occurrence continue to influence like new causative factors." If the patient can be brought to remember the original hurt—even occurring so far back as in childhood—and circumstantially to discuss the process, "giving free play to the effect" in the discussion, the hysterical symptoms disappear. Dr. Brill says:

> The reason for the strangulation of the emotion was because at the time of its occurrence it could not be adequately worked off. We all know that it is not always possible to give vent to our feelings, and that an insult retaliated leaves quite a different impression than one that has to be swallowed.

Usually the experience is one of which the patient has reason to be ashamed, and strives to forget. To persuade his patients to revive it Dr. Freud has to overcome a certain reluctance:

> Through my psychic work I had to overcome a psychic force in the patient which opposed the pathogenic idea from becoming conscious. The resistance was due to the fact that the ideas which had to be disinterred were all of a painful nature, adapted to provoke the effects of shame, reproach, mental pain, and the feeling of injury—they were altogether of that kind which one would not like to experience and prefers to forget.

Here "confession is good for the soul." And unless the victim of the strange fears, ties, and bodily contortions can in some way cleanse his stuffed bosom in the presence of a skilled and sympathetic confessor, they will continue to plague him. As in other things prevention of such experiences is simpler than the cure. The business man and the housewife who brood and bottle up their emotions instead of frankly living through their disagreeable experiences and taking counsel about them as they occur, are the ones who help swell the army of neurasthenics.

Ideas for Reading

1. In the extract from "The Hidden Self," James summarizes a theory familiar to Freud, M. Pierre Janet's theory of "monoideism" (p. 360). His references to Lucie, Rose, and Janet's other patients give you a sense of the methods that accompanied this theory. How does this theory and practice compare with, differ from, and otherwise relate to Freud's ways of thinking and working?

2. How does Fritz Wittels's version of psychoanalysis influence your understandings of Freud? In what senses might we say that Dora's problems are a result of her "undissolved conflicts" (p. 363)? How do you respond to Wittels's commitment to "the unmasking of the truth" (p. 364)? In what sense do you understand Wittels's description of psychoanalysis as "an artistic science" (p. 365)?

3. Initial reactions to Freud's theories were mixed, but they were mainly negative. To many—particularly those heavily invested in directly physical techniques, those convinced by Charcot's hypnotherapy, and those who preferred

matters of sexuality to remain behind closed doors—Freud's work was dismissed as "mental masturbation" and "gruesome old-wives' psychiatry" (p. 370). How does Jones's report of the hostile responses to Freud's theories influence your thoughts about the Dora case? And how does "Strangled Emotion," with its more positive assessment of Freud's theories as "caviare even to the medical profession in this country" (p. 372), help you to revise your work with the Dora case study?

Ideas for Writing

1. Write an essay addressing the ways in which Freud defends and justifies his work with Dora. Take into account the various reviews and other materials in the Context section, including Freud's comments on his choice of the name "Dora." Also take into account places in the body of "A Fragment of an Analysis of a Case of Hysteria" where Freud addresses those who might question or otherwise challenge his methods. Finally, consider the alternatives available to Freud in 1900. In what ways was Freud justified, mistaken, or wrong in his treatment of Dora? To what extent are you convinced by his defense of this treatment? In what ways was the publication of "A Fragment of an Analysis of a Case of Hysteria" beneficial, problematic, or unacceptable for Dora, for Freud's peers, for our contemporary culture, for you?

2. Write an essay analyzing Freud's methods in "A Fragment of an Analysis of a Case of Hysteria" in the context of the different techniques available to Freud when he consulted with Dora. How does the illustration of the equipment used for electrotherapy affect your reading of Freud's "talking cure"? How does the photograph influence your ways of seeing the pictures of Charcot with a patient and of Freud's consulting room? Consider the instruments, the Charcot picture, and the consulting room in light of the approaches to psychology represented in the selections from William James and Fritz Wittels. You might return to your essay after you have read Carol Gilligan's and Janet Malcolm's work in the Contemporary Conversation section, revising it in light of their implied and explicit criticisms of the "talking cure."

CONTEMPORARY CONVERSATION

MICHEL FOUCAULT

Famous in Europe and the United States as a historian of ideas and institutions, Paul-Michel Foucault (1926–1984) was born in Poitiers, France. Growing up in a family with an extensive pedigree of surgeons and doctors, Foucault was solidly part of the French bourgeoisie. After disruptions caused by World War II, during which his family lived in relative luxury in German-occupied Vichy France, Foucault was educated at the best schools in Paris. At the École Normale

Supérieure, a college designed to train elite teachers and professors, he mixed with the best-known postwar French intellectuals of the day, including Jean Hyppolite and Louis Althusser.

Foucault's first teaching appointment was in Lille, an industrial city in northern France. A strict Parisian in lifestyle, however, Foucault continued to live and study in the capital: from 1951 to 1981 he was a regular at the Bibliothèque Nationale. His first book, Madness and Civilization: A History of Insanity in the Age of Reason *(1961), was based on research conducted at the nation's main libraries in Paris. He had spent most of the previous years teaching at the University of Uppsala, Sweden (1954–1958), the University of Warsaw, Poland (1958–1959), and the Institut Français in Hamburg, Germany (1959–1960). In the period between 1960 and 1966, as a full professor at the University of Clermont-Ferrand, six hours from Paris, Foucault researched, wrote, and published four books including* The Birth of the Clinic *(1963) and* The Order of Things *(1966). Although written as a philosophical book for a specialized audience,* The Order of Things *nevertheless became a best-seller, establishing Foucault as a figure of national importance.*

While teaching at the University of Tunis in 1966–1968, Foucault wrote An Archaeology of Knowledge *(1969). He then returned to Paris to begin a professorship of philosophy at the University of Vincennes, an experimental college that was the first in France to open its doors to students without a high school diploma (a baccalauréat). Two years later Foucault was elected to the most prestigious academic institution in France, the Collège de France. In 1975 he published* Discipline and Punish, *a sometimes graphic argument about the prison system, and immediately began work on what was to be a three-volume study called* The History of Sexuality. *"Scientia Sexualis" is Part III of the introductory first volume.*

Foucault uses the term discourse *to refer to a particular way of using language that is special to a specific social and cultural group. A discourse community is a group of people, such as members of a professional organization or advocates of a particular political message, that shares a common set of terms and definitions, and that views the world through an identifiable perspective. As you read "Scientia Sexualis" make notes about each use of the words* discourse *and* discourses. *Define the characteristic perspective associated with the group referred to by these terms. How, for example, does Foucault characterize the "confessional discourse" (p. 381)? How does the discourse of the confession interact with the "discourse of science" (p. 382)?*

Scientia Sexualis

I suppose that the first two points will be granted me; I imagine that people will accept my saying that, for two centuries now, the discourse on sex has been multiplied rather than rarefied; and that if it has carried with it taboos and prohibitions, it has also, in a more fundamental way, ensured the solidification and implantation of an entire sexual mosaic. Yet the impression remains that all this has by and large played only a defensive role. By speaking about it so much, by discovering it multiplied, partitioned off, and specified precisely where one had placed it, what one was seeking essentially was simply to conceal sex: a screen-discourse, a dispersion-avoidance. Until Freud at least, the discourse on sex—the discourse of scholars and theoreticians—never ceased to hide the thing it was speaking about. We could take all these things that were said, the painstaking precautions and detailed analyses, as so many procedures meant to evade the unbearable, too hazardous truth of sex. And the mere fact that one claimed to be speaking about it from the rarefied and neutral viewpoint of a science is in itself significant. This was in fact a science made up of evasions since, given its inability or refusal to speak of sex itself, it concerned itself primarily with aberrations, perversions, exceptional oddities, pathological abatements, and morbid aggravations. It was by the same token a science subordinated in the main to the imperatives of a morality whose divisions it reiterated under the guise of the medical norm. Claiming to speak the truth, it stirred up people's fears; to the least oscillations of sexuality, it ascribed an imaginary dynasty of evils destined to be passed on for generations; it declared the furtive customs of the timid, and the most solitary of petty manias, dangerous for the whole society; strange pleasures, it warned, would eventually result in nothing short of death: that of individuals, generations, the species itself.

It thus became associated with an insistent and indiscreet medical practice, glibly proclaiming its aversions, quick to run to the rescue of law and public opinion, more servile with respect to the powers of order than amenable to the requirements of truth. Involuntarily naive in the best of cases, more often intentionally mendacious, in complicity with what it denounced, haughty and coquettish, it established an entire pornography of the morbid, which was characteristic of the *fin de siècle* society. In France, doctors like Garnier, Pouillet, and Ladoucette were its unglorified scribes and Rollinat its poet. But beyond these troubled pleasures, it assumed other powers; it set itself up as the supreme authority in matters of hygienic necessity, taking up the old fears of venereal affliction and combining them with the new themes of asepsis, and the great evolutionist myths with the recent institutions of public health; it claimed to ensure the physical vigor and the moral cleanliness of the social body; it promised to eliminate defective individuals, degenerate and bastardized populations. In the name of a biological and historical urgency, it justified the racisms of the state, which at the time were on the horizon. It grounded them in "truth."

When we compare these discourses on human sexuality with what was known at the time about the physiology of animal and plant reproduction, we are struck by the incongruity. Their feeble content from the standpoint of elementary rationality, not to mention scientificity, earns them a place apart in the history of knowledge. They form a strangely muddled zone. Throughout the nineteenth century, sex seems to have been incorporated into two very distinct orders of knowledge: a biology of reproduction, which developed continuously according to a general scientific normativity, and a medicine of sex conforming to quite different rules of formation. From one to the other, there was no real exchange, no reciprocal structuration; the role of the first with respect to the second was scarcely more than as a distant and quite fictitious guarantee: a blanket guarantee under cover of which moral obstacles, economic or political options, and traditional fears could be recast in a scientific-sounding vocabulary. It is as if a fundamental resistance blocked the development of a rationally formed discourse concerning human sex, its correlations, and its effects. A disparity of this sort would indicate that the aim of such a discourse was not to state the truth but to prevent its very emergence. Underlying the difference between the physiology of reproduction and the medical theories of sexuality, we would have to see something other and something more than an uneven scientific development or a disparity in the forms of rationality; the one would partake of that immense will to knowledge which has sustained the establishment of scientific discourse in the West, whereas the other would derive from a stubborn will to nonknowledge.

This much is undeniable: the learned discourse on sex that was pronounced in the nineteenth century was imbued with age-old delusions, but also with systematic blindnesses: a refusal to see and to understand; but further—and this is the crucial point—a refusal concerning the very thing that was brought to light and whose formulation was urgently solicited. For there can be no misunderstanding that is not based on a fundamental relation to truth. Evading this truth, barring access to it, masking it: these were so many local tactics which, as if by superimposition and through a last-minute detour, gave a paradoxical form to a fundamental petition to know. Choosing not to recognize was yet another vagary of the will to truth. Let Charcot's Salpêtrière serve as an example in this regard: it was an enormous apparatus for observation, with its examinations, interrogations and experiments, but it was also a machinery for incitement, with its public presentations, its theater of ritual crises, carefully staged with the help of ether or amyl nitrate, its interplay of dialogues, palpations, laying on of hands, postures which the doctors elicited or obliterated with a gesture or a word, its hierarchy of personnel who kept watch, organized, provoked, monitored, and reported, and who accumulated an immense pyramid of observations and dossiers. It is in the context of this continuous incitement to discourse and to truth that the real mechanisms of misunderstanding (*méconnaissance*) operated: thus Charcot's gesture interrupting a public consultation where it began to be too manifestly a question of "that"; and the more frequent practice of deleting from the succession of dossiers what had been said and demonstrated by the patients regarding sex, but also what had been seen, provoked, solicited by the doctors themselves, things that were almost entirely omitted from the published observations.[1] The important thing, in this affair, is not that these men shut their eyes or stopped their ears, or that they were mistaken; it is rather that they constructed around and apropos of sex an immense apparatus for producing truth, even if this truth was to be masked at the last moment. The essential point is that sex was not only a matter of sensation and pleasure, of law and taboo, but also of truth and falsehood, that the truth of sex became something fundamental, useful, or dangerous, precious or formidable: in short, that sex was constituted as a problem of truth. What needs to be situated, therefore, is not the threshold of a new rationality whose discovery was marked by Freud—or someone else—but the progressive formation (and also the transformations) of that "interplay of truth and sex" which was bequeathed to us by the nineteenth century, and which we may have modified, but, lacking evidence to the contrary, have not rid ourselves of. Misunderstandings, avoidances, and evasions were only possible, and only had their effects, against the background of this strange endeavor: to tell the truth of sex. An endeavor that does not date from the nineteenth century, even if it was then that a nascent science lent it a singular form. It was the basis of all the aberrant, naive, and cunning discourses where knowledge of sex seems to have strayed for such a long time.

Historically, there have been two great procedures for producing the truth of sex.

On the one hand, the societies—and they are numerous: China, Japan, India, Rome, the Arabo-Moslem societies—which endowed themselves with an *ars erotica*. In the erotic art, truth is drawn from pleasure itself, understood as a practice and accumulated as experience; pleasure is not considered in relation to an absolute law of the permitted and the forbidden, nor by reference to a criterion of utility, but first and foremost in relation to itself; it is experienced as pleasure, evaluated in terms of its intensity, its specific quality, its duration, its reverberations in the body and the soul. Moreover, this knowledge must be deflected back into the sexual practice itself, in order to shape it as though from within and amplify its effects. In this way, there is formed a knowledge that must remain secret, not because of an element of infamy that might attach to its object, but because of the need to hold it in the greatest reserve, since, according to tradition, it would lose its effectiveness and its virtue by being divulged. Consequently, the relationship to the master who holds the secrets is of paramount importance; only he, working alone, can transmit this art in an esoteric manner and as the culmination of an initiation in which he guides the disciple's progress with unfailing skill and severity. The effects of this masterful art, which are considerably more generous than the spareness of its prescriptions would lead one to imagine, are said to transfigure the one fortunate enough to receive its privileges: an absolute mastery of the body, a singular bliss, obliviousness to time and limits, the elixir of life, the exile of death and its threats.

On the face of it at least, our civilization possesses no *ars erotica*. In return, it is undoubtedly the only civilization to practice a *scientia sexualis;* or rather, the only civilization to have developed over the centuries procedures for telling the truth of sex which are geared to a form of knowledge-power strictly opposed to the art of initiations and the masterful secret: I have in mind the confession.

Since the Middle Ages at least, Western societies have established the confession as one of the main rituals we rely on for the production of truth: the codification of the sacrament of penance by the Lateran Council in 1215, with the resulting development of confessional techniques, the declining importance of accusatory procedures in criminal justice, the abandonment of tests of guilt (sworn statements, duels, judgments of God) and the development of methods of interrogation and inquest, the increased participation of the royal administration in the prosecution of infractions, at the expense of proceedings leading to private settlements, the setting up of tribunals of Inquisition: all this helped to give the confession a central role in the order of civil and religious powers. The evolution of the word *avowal* and of the legal function it designated is itself emblematic of this development: from being a guarantee of the status, identity, and value granted to one person by another, it came to signify someone's acknowledgment of his own actions and thoughts. For a long time, the individual was vouched for by the reference of others and the demonstration of his ties to the commonweal (family, allegiance, protection); then he was authenticated by the discourse of truth he was able or obliged to pronounce concerning himself. The truthful confession was inscribed at the heart of the procedures of individualization by power.

In any case, next to the testing rituals, next to the testimony of witness, and the learned methods of observation and demonstration, the confession became one of the West's most highly valued techniques for producing truth. We have since become a singularly confessing society. The confession has spread its effects far and wide. It plays a part in justice, medicine, education, family relationships, and love relations, in the most ordinary affairs of everyday life, and in the most solemn rites; one confesses one's crimes, one's sins, one's thoughts and desires, one's illnesses and troubles; one goes about telling, with the greatest precision, whatever is most difficult to tell. One confesses in public and in private, to one's parents, one's educators, one's doctor, to those one loves; one admits to oneself, in pleasure and in pain, things it would be impossible to tell to anyone else, the things people write books about. One confesses—or is forced to confess. When it is not spontaneous or dictated by some internal imperative, the confession is wrung from a person by violence or threat; it is driven from its hiding place in the soul, or extracted from the body. Since the Middle Ages, torture has accompanied it like a shadow, and supported it when it could go no further: the dark twins.[2] The most defenseless tenderness and the bloodiest of powers have a similar need of confession. Western man has become a confessing animal.

Whence a metamorphosis in literature: we have passed from a pleasure to be recounted and heard, centering on the heroic or marvelous narration of "trials" of bravery or sainthood, to a literature ordered according to the infinite task of extracting from the depths of oneself, in between the words, a truth which the very form of the confession holds out like a shimmering mirage. Whence too this new way of philosophizing: seeking the fundamental relation to the true, not simply in oneself—in some forgotten knowledge, or in a certain primal trace—but in the self-examination that yields, through a multitude of fleeting impressions, the basic certainties of consciousness. The obligation to confess is now relayed through so many different points, is so deeply ingrained in us, that we no longer perceive it as the effect of a power that constrains us; on the contrary, it seems to us that truth, lodged in our most secret nature, "demands" only to surface; that if it fails to do so, this is because a constraint holds it in place, the violence of a power weighs it down, and it can finally be articulated only at the price of a kind of liberation. Confession frees, but power reduces one to silence; truth does not belong to the order of power, but shares an original affinity with freedom: traditional themes in philosophy, which a "political history of truth" would have to overturn by showing that truth is not by nature free—nor error servile—but that its production is thoroughly imbued with relations of power. The confession is an example of this.

One has to be completely taken in by this internal ruse of confession in order to attribute a fundamental role to censorship, to taboos regarding speaking and thinking; one has to have an inverted image of power in order to believe that all these voices which have spoken so long in our civilization—repeating the formidable injunction to tell what one is and what one does, what one recollects and what one has forgotten, what one is thinking and what one thinks he is not thinking—are speaking to us of freedom. An immense labor to which the West has submitted generations in order to produce—while other forms of work ensured the accumulation of capital—men's subjection: their constitution as subjects in both senses of the word. Imagine how exorbitant must have seemed the order given to all Christians at the beginning of the thirteenth century, to kneel at least once a year and confess to all their transgressions, without omitting a single one. And think of that obscure partisan, seven centuries later, who had come to rejoin the Serbian resistance deep in the mountains; his superiors asked him to write his life story; and when he brought them a few miserable pages, scribbled in the night, they did not look at them but only said to him, "Start over, and tell the truth." Should those much-discussed language taboos make us forget this millennial yoke of confession?

From the Christian penance to the present day, sex was a privileged theme of confession. A thing that was hidden, we are told. But what if, on the contrary, it was what, in a quite particular way, one confessed? Suppose the obligation to conceal it was but another aspect of the duty to admit to it (concealing it all the more and with greater care as the confession of it was more important, requiring a stricter ritual and promising more decisive effects)? What if sex in our society, on a scale of several centuries, was something that was placed within an unrelenting system of confession? The transformation of sex into discourse, which I spoke of earlier, the dissemination and reinforcement of heterogeneous sexualities, are perhaps two elements of the same deployment: they are linked together with the help of the central element of a confession that compels individuals to articulate their sexual peculiarity—no matter how extreme. In Greece, truth and sex were linked, in the form of pedagogy, by the transmission of a precious knowledge from one body to another; sex served as a medium for initiations into learning. For us, it is in the confession that truth and sex are joined, through the obligatory and exhaustive expression of an individual secret. But this time it is truth that serves as a medium for sex and its manifestations.

The confession is a ritual of discourse in which the speaking subject is also the subject of the statement; it is also a ritual that unfolds within a power relationship, for one does not confess without the presence (or virtual presence) of a partner who is not simply the interlocutor but the authority who requires the confession, prescribes and appreciates it, and intervenes in order to judge, punish, forgive, console, and reconcile; a ritual in which the truth is corroborated by the obstacles and resistances it has had to surmount in order to be formulated; and finally, a ritual in which the expression alone, independently of its external consequences, produces intrinsic modifications in the person who articulates it: it exonerates, redeems, and purifies him; it unburdens him of his wrongs, liberates him, and promises him salvation. For centuries, the truth of sex was, at least for the most part, caught up in this discursive form. Moreover, this form was not the same as that of education (sexual education confined itself to general principles and rules of prudence); nor was it that of initiation (which remained essentially a silent practice, which the act of sexual enlightenment or deflowering merely rendered laughable or violent). As we have seen, it is a form that is far removed from the one governing the "erotic art." By virtue of the power structure immanent in it, the confessional discourse cannot come from above, as in the *ars erotica,* through the sovereign will of a master, but rather from below, as an obligatory act of speech which, under some imperious compulsion, breaks the bonds of discretion or forgetfulness. What secrecy it presupposes is not owing to the high price of what it has to say and the small number of those who are worthy of its benefits, but to its obscure familiarity and its general baseness. Its veracity is not guaranteed by the lofty authority of the magistery, nor by the tradition it transmits, but by the bond, the basic intimacy in discourse, between the one who speaks and what he is speaking about. On the other hand, the agency of domination does not reside in the one who speaks (for it is he who is constrained), but in the one who listens and says nothing; not in the one who knows and answers, but in the one who questions and is not supposed to know. And this discourse of truth finally takes effect, not in the one who receives it, but in the one from whom it is wrested. With these confessed truths, we are a long way from the learned initiations into pleasure, with their technique and their mystery. On the other hand, we belong to a society which has ordered sex's difficult knowledge, not according to the transmission of secrets, but around the slow surfacing of confidential statements.

The confession was, and still remains, the general standard governing the production of the true discourse on sex. It has undergone a considerable transformation, however. For a long time, it remained firmly entrenched in the practice of penance. But with the rise of Protestantism, the

Counter Reformation, eighteenth-century pedagogy, and nineteenth-century medicine, it gradually lost its ritualistic and exclusive localization; it spread; it has been employed in a whole series of relationships: children and parents, students and educators, patients and psychiatrists, delinquents and experts. The motivations and effects it is expected to produce have varied, as have the forms it has taken: interrogations, consultations, auto-biographical narratives, letters; they have been recorded, transcribed, as-sembled into dossiers, published, and commented on. But more important, the confession lends itself, if not to other domains, at least to new ways of exploring the existing ones. It is no longer a question simply of saying what was done—the sexual act—and how it was done; but of reconstructing, in and around the act, the thoughts that recapitulated it, the obsessions that accompanied it, the images, desires, modulations, and quality of the plea-sure that animated it. For the first time no doubt, a society has taken upon itself to solicit and hear the imparting of individual pleasures.

A dissemination, then, of procedures of confession, a multiple localiza-tion of their constraint, a widening of their domain: a great archive of the pleasures of sex was gradually constituted. For a long time this archive de-materialized as it was formed. It regularly disappeared without a trace (thus suiting the purposes of the Christian pastoral) until medicine, psychi-atry, and pedagogy began to solidify it: Campe, Salzmann, and especially Kaan, Krafft-Ebing, Tardieu, Molle, and Havelock Ellis carefully as-sembled this whole pitiful, lyrical outpouring from the sexual mosaic. Western societies thus began to keep an indefinite record of these people's pleasures. They made up a herbal of them and established a system of clas-sification. They described their everyday deficiencies as well as their oddi-ties or exasperations. This was an important time. It is easy to make light of these nineteenth-century psychiatrists, who made a point of apologizing for the horrors they were about to let speak, evoking "immoral behavior" or "aberrations of the genetic senses," but I am more inclined to applaud their seriousness: they had a feeling for momentous events. It was a time when the most singular pleasures were called upon to pronounce a dis-course of truth concerning themselves, a discourse which had to model it-self after that which spoke, not of sin and salvation, but of bodies and life processes—the discourse of science. It was enough to make one's voice tremble, for an improbable thing was then taking shape: a confessional sci-ence, a science which relied on a many-sided extortion, and took for its ob-ject what was unmentionable but admitted to nonetheless. The scientific discourse was scandalized, or in any case repelled, when it had to take charge of this whole discourse from below. It was also faced with a theo-retical and methodological paradox: the long discussions concerning the possibility of constituting a science of the subject, the validity of introspec-tion, lived experience as evidence, or the presence of consciousness to itself were responses to this problem that is inherent in the functioning of truth in our society: can one articulate the production of truth according to the old juridico-religious model of confession, and the extortion of confidential evidence according to the rules of scientific discourse? Those who believe

that sex was more rigorously elided in the nineteenth century than ever before, through a formidable mechanism of blockage and a deficiency of discourse, can say what they please. There was no deficiency, but rather an
excess, a redoubling, too much rather than not enough discourse, in any
case an interference between two modes of production of truth: procedures
of confession, and scientific discursivity.

And instead of adding up the errors, naivetés, and moralisms that
plagued the nineteenth-century discourse of truth concerning sex, we
would do better to locate the procedures by which that will to knowledge
regarding sex, which characterizes the modern Occident, caused the rituals
of confession to function within the norms of scientific regularity: how did
this immense and traditional extortion of the sexual confession come to be
constituted in scientific terms?

1. *Through a clinical codification of the inducement to speak.* Combining confession with examination, the personal history with the deployment
of a set of decipherable signs and symptoms; the interrogation, the exacting
questionnaire, and hypnosis, with the recollection of memories and free association: all were ways of reinscribing the procedure of confession in a
field of scientifically acceptable observations.

2. *Through the postulate of a general and diffuse causality.* Having to
tell everything, being able to pose questions about everything, found their
justification in the principle that endowed sex with an inexhaustible and
polymorphous causal power. The most discrete event in one's sexual behavior — whether an accident or a deviation, a deficit or an excess — was
deemed capable of entailing the most varied consequences throughout
one's existence; there was scarcely a malady or physical disturbance to
which the nineteenth century did not impute at least some degree of sexual
etiology. From the bad habits of children to the phthises of adults, the
apoplexies of old people, nervous maladies, and the degenerations of the
race, the medicine of that era wove an entire network of sexual causality to
explain them. This may well appear fantastic to us, but the principle of sex
as a "cause of any and everything" was the theoretical underside of a confession that had to be thorough, meticulous, and constant, and at the same
time operate within a scientific type of practice. The limitless dangers that
sex carried with it justified the exhaustive character of the inquisition to
which it was subjected.

3. *Through the principle of a latency intrinsic to sexuality.* If it was
necessary to extract the truth of sex through the technique of confession,
this was not simply because it was difficult to tell, or stricken by the taboos
of decency, but because the ways of sex were obscure; it was elusive by nature; its energy and its mechanisms escaped observation, and its causal
power was partly clandestine. By integrating it into the beginnings of a scientific discourse, the nineteenth century altered the scope of the confession;
it tended no longer to be concerned solely with what the subject wished to
hide, but with what was hidden from himself, being incapable of coming to

light except gradually and through the labor of a confession in which the questioner and the questioned each had a part to play. The principle of a latency essential to sexuality made it possible to link the forcing of a difficult confession to a scientific practice. It had to be exacted, by force, since it involved something that tried to stay hidden.

4. *Through the method of interpretation.* If one had to confess, this was not merely because the person to whom one confessed had the power to forgive, console, and direct, but because the work of producing the truth was obliged to pass through this relationship if it was to be scientifically validated. The truth did not reside solely in the subject who, by confessing, would reveal it wholly formed. It was constituted in two stages: present but incomplete, blind to itself, in the one who spoke, it could only reach completion in the one who assimilated and recorded it. It was the latter's function to verify this obscure truth: the revelation of confession had to be coupled with the decipherment of what it said. The one who listened was not simply the forgiving master, the judge who condemned or acquitted; he was the master of truth. His was a hermeneutic function. With regard to the confession, his power was not only to demand it before it was made, or decide what was to follow after it, but also to constitute a discourse of truth on the basis of its decipherment. By no longer making the confession a test, but rather a sign, and by making sexuality something to be interpreted, the nineteenth century gave itself the possibility of causing the procedures of confession to operate within the regular formation of a scientific discourse.

5. *Through the medicalization of the effects of confession.* The obtaining of the confession and its effects were recodified as therapeutic operations. Which meant first of all that the sexual domain was no longer accounted for simply by the notions of error or sin, excess or transgression, but was placed under the rule of the normal and the pathological (which, for that matter, were the transposition of the former categories); a characteristic sexual morbidity was defined for the first time; sex appeared as an extremely unstable pathological field: a surface of repercussion for other ailments, but also the focus of a specific nosography, that of instincts, tendencies, images, pleasure, and conduct. This implied furthermore that sex would derive its meaning and its necessity from medical interventions: it would be required by the doctor, necessary for diagnosis, and effective by nature in the cure. Spoken in time, to the proper party, and by the person who was both the bearer of it and the one responsible for it, the truth healed.

Let us consider things in broad historical perspective. Breaking with the traditions of the *ars erotica,* our society has equipped itself with a *scientia sexualis.* To be more precise, it has pursued the task of producing true discourses concerning sex, and this by adapting—not without difficulty—the ancient procedure of confession to the rules of scientific discourse. Paradoxically, the *scientia sexualis* that emerged in the nineteenth century kept as its nucleus the singular ritual of obligatory and exhaustive confession, which in the Christian West was the first technique for producing the truth of sex. Beginning in the sixteenth century, this rite gradually detached itself from the sacrament of penance, and via the guidance of souls and the direction of conscience—the *ars artium*—emigrated toward pedagogy, relationships between adults and children, family relations, medicine, and psychiatry. In any case, nearly one hundred and fifty years have gone into the making of a complex machinery for producing true discourses on sex: a deployment that spans a wide segment of history in that it connects the ancient injunction of confession to clinical listening methods. It is this deployment that enables something called "sexuality" to embody the truth of sex and its pleasures.

"Sexuality": the correlative of that slowly developed discursive practice which constitutes the *scientia sexualis*. The essential features of this sexuality are not the expression of a representation that is more or less distorted by ideology, or of a misunderstanding caused by taboos; they correspond to the functional requirements of a discourse that must produce its truth. Situated at the point of intersection of a technique of confession and a scientific discursivity, where certain major mechanisms had to be found for adapting them to one another (the listening technique, the postulate of causality, the principle of latency, the rule of interpretation, the imperative of medicalization), sexuality was defined as being "by nature": a domain susceptible to pathological processes, and hence one calling for therapeutic or normalizing interventions; a field of meanings to decipher; the site of processes concealed by specific mechanisms; a focus of indefinite causal relations; and an obscure speech (*parole*) that had to be ferreted out and listened to. The "economy" of discourses—their intrinsic technology, the necessities of their operation, the tactics they employ, the effects of power which underlie them and which they transmit—this, and not a system of representations, is what determines the essential features of what they have to say. The history of sexuality—that is, the history of what functioned in the nineteenth century as a specific field of truth—must first be written from the viewpoint of a history of discourses.

Let us put forward a general working hypothesis. The society that emerged in the nineteenth century—bourgeois, capitalist, or industrial society, call it what you will—did not confront sex with a fundamental refusal of recognition. On the contrary, it put into operation an entire machinery for producing true discourses concerning it. Not only did it speak of sex and compel everyone to do so; it also set out to formulate the uniform truth of sex. As if it suspected sex of harboring a fundamental secret. As if it needed this production of truth. As if it was essential that sex be inscribed not only in an economy of pleasure but in an ordered system of knowledge. Thus sex gradually became an object of great suspicion; the general and disquieting meaning that pervades our conduct and our existence, in spite of ourselves; the point of weakness where evil portents reach through to us; the fragment of darkness that we each carry within us: a general signification, a universal secret, an omnipresent cause, a fear that never ends. And so, in this "question" of sex (in both senses: as interrogation and problematization, and as the need for confession and integration into a field of rationality), two processes emerge, the one always conditioning the other: we demand that sex speak the truth (but, since it is the secret and is oblivious to its own nature, we reserve for ourselves the function of telling the truth of its truth, revealed and deciphered at last), and we demand that it tell us our truth, or rather, the deeply buried truth of that truth about ourselves which we think we possess in our immediate consciousness. We tell it its truth by deciphering what it tells us about that truth; it tells us our own by delivering up that part of it that escaped us. From this interplay there has evolved, over several centuries, a knowledge of the subject; a knowledge not so much of his form, but of that which divides him, determines him perhaps, but above all causes him to be ignorant of himself. As unlikely as this may seem, it should not surprise us when we think of the long history of the Christian and juridical confession, of the shifts and transformations this form of knowledge-power, so important in the West, has undergone: the project of a science of the subject has gravitated, in ever narrowing circles, around the question of sex. Causality in the subject, the unconscious of the subject, the truth of the subject in the other who knows, the knowledge he holds unbeknown to him, all this found an opportunity to deploy itself in the discourse of sex. Not, however, by reason of some natural property inherent in sex itself, but by virtue of the tactics of power immanent in this discourse.

Scientia sexualis versus *ars erotica,* no doubt. But it should be noted that the *ars erotica* did not disappear altogether from Western civilization; nor has it always been absent from the movement by which one sought to produce a science of sexuality. In the Christian confession, but especially in the direction and examination of conscience, in the search for spiritual union and the love of God, there was a whole series of methods that had much in common with an erotic art: guidance by the master along a path of initiation, the intensification of experiences extending down to their physical components, the optimization of effects by the discourse that accompanied them. The phenomena of possession and ecstasy, which were quite frequent in the Catholicism of the Counter Reformation, were undoubtedly effects that had got outside the control of the erotic technique immanent in this subtle science of the flesh. And we must ask whether, since the nineteenth century, the *scientia sexualis*—under the guise of its decent positivism—has not functioned, at least to a certain extent, as an *ars erotica.* Perhaps this production of truth, intimidated though it was by the scientific model, multiplied, intensified, and even created its own intrinsic pleasures. It is often said that we have been incapable of imagining any new pleasures. We have at least invented a different kind of pleasure: pleasure in the truth of pleasure, the pleasure of knowing that truth, of discovering and exposing it, the fascination of seeing it and telling it, of captivating and capturing others by it, of confiding it in secret, of luring it out in the open—the specific pleasure of the true discourse on pleasure.

The most important elements of an erotic art linked to our knowledge about sexuality are not to be sought in the ideal, promised to us by medicine, of a healthy sexuality, nor in the humanist dream of a complete and flourishing sexuality, and certainly not in the lyricism of orgasm and the good feelings of bio-energy (these are but aspects of its normalizing utilization), but in this multiplication and intensification of pleasures connected to the production of the truth about sex. The learned volumes, written and read; the consultations and examinations; the anguish of answering questions and the delights of having one's words interpreted; all the stories told to oneself and to others, so much curiosity, so many confidences offered in the face of scandal, sustained—but not without trembling a little—by the obligation of truth; the profusion of secret fantasies and the dearly paid right to whisper them to whoever is able to hear them; in short, the formidable "pleasure of analysis" (in the widest sense of the latter term) which the West has cleverly been fostering for several centuries: all this constitutes something like the errant fragments of an erotic art that is secretly transmitted by confession and the science of sex. Must we conclude that our *scientia sexualis* is but an extraordinarily subtle form of *ars erotica,* and that it is the Western, sublimated version of that seemingly lost tradition? Or must we suppose that all these pleasures are only the by-products of a sexual science, a bonus that compensates for its many stresses and strains?

In any case, the hypothesis of a power of repression exerted by our society on sex for economic reasons appears to me quite inadequate if we are to explain this whole series of reinforcements and intensifications that our preliminary inquiry has discovered: a proliferation of discourses, carefully tailored to the requirements of power; the solidification of the sexual mosaic and the construction of devices capable not only of isolating it but of stimulating and provoking it, of forming it into focuses of attention, discourse, and pleasure; the mandatory production of confessions and the subsequent establishment of a system of legitimate knowledge and of an economy of manifold pleasures. We are dealing not nearly so much with a negative mechanism of exclusion as with the operation of a subtle network of discourses, special knowledges, pleasures, and powers. At issue is not a movement bent on pushing rude sex back into some obscure and inaccessible region, but on the contrary, a process that spreads it over the surface of things and bodies, arouses it, draws it out and bids it speak, implants it in reality and enjoins it to tell the truth: an entire glittering sexual array, reflected in a myriad of discourses, the obstination of powers, and the interplay of knowledge and pleasure.

All this is an illusion, it will be said, a hasty impression behind which a more discerning gaze will surely discover the same great machinery of repression. Beyond these few phosphorescences, are we not sure to find once more the somber law that always says no? The answer will have to come out of a historical inquiry. An inquiry concerning the manner in which a knowledge of sex has been forming over the last three centuries; the manner in which the discourses that take it as their object have multiplied, and the reasons for which we have come to attach a nearly fabulous price to the truth they claimed to produce. Perhaps these historical analyses will end by dissipating what this cursory survey seems to suggest. But the postulate I started out with, and would like to hold to as long as possible, is that these deployments of power and knowledge, of truth and pleasures, so unlike those of repression, are not necessarily secondary and derivative; and further, that repression is not in any case fundamental and overriding. We need to take these mechanisms seriously, therefore, and reverse the direction of our analysis: rather than assuming a generally acknowledged repression, and an ignorance measured against what we are supposed to know, we must begin with these positive mechanisms, insofar as they produce knowledge, multiply discourse, induce pleasure, and generate power; we must investigate the conditions of their emergence and operation, and try to discover how the related facts of interdiction or concealment are distributed with respect to them. In short, we must define the strategies of power that are immanent in this will to knowledge. As far as sexuality is concerned, we shall attempt to constitute the "political economy" of a will to knowledge.

Notes

1. Cf., for example, Désiré Bourneville, *Iconographie photographique de la Salpêtrière* (1878–1881), pp. 110 ff. The unpublished documents dealing with the lessons of Charcot, which can still be found at the Salpêtrière, are again more explicit on this point than the published texts. The interplay of incitement and elision is clearly evident in them. A handwritten note gives an account of the session of November 25, 1877. The subject exhibits hysterical spasms; Charcot suspends an attack by placing first his hand, then the end of a baton, on the woman's ovaries. He withdraws the baton, and there is a fresh attack, which he accelerates by administering inhalations of amyl nitrate. The afflicted woman then cries out for the sex-baton in words that are devoid of any metaphor: "G. is taken away and her delirium continues."
2. Greek law had already coupled torture and confession, at least where slaves were concerned, and Imperial Roman law had widened the practice.

Ideas for Rereading

1. While Foucault observes that there were two "distinct orders of knowledge" about sex — "a biology of reproduction" and "a medicine of sex" (p. 376) — he argues that both were grounded in "a fundamental resistance . . . [to] a rationally formed discourse concerning human sex, its correlations, and its effects" (p. 377). The consequence is that "sex was constituted as a problem of truth" (p. 377) and that "Western man has become a confessing animal" (p. 379).

   As you reread "Scientia Sexualis," think about differences between biological and psychological treatments of sex. What kinds of facts are relevant to each area of study? What are the most important truths of each academic discipline? How do specialists in biology and psychology gather and publish information about their respective subjects? What kinds of things would you learn about sex in a biology class as different from a psychology class? As you map out differences between biology and psychology, you might think about the distinction between the natural sciences and the social sciences. You might also think about the differences between these forms of science, with their shared emphasis on truth, and a third area of academic work, the arts and humanities. Which parts of Foucault's essay fit into each of the three general areas of academic study?

2. Reread "Scientia Sexualis," taking notes about the ways in which Foucault's essay applies to Freud: How does Foucault characterize the Freudian discourse community? Make at least one reference to an example from Freud's "A Fragment of an Analysis of a Case of Hysteria" for each of Foucault's five points about how the discourse of sex functions "within the norms of scientific regularity" (p. 383).

Ideas for Writing

1. Write an essay analyzing "A Fragment of an Analysis of a Case of Hysteria" in terms of the five reasons Foucault gives for the constitution of the "sexual confession" in "scientific terms" (p. 383). You might begin by asking the following questions, all of which are based on quotations from Foucault's list of five characteristics that have transformed confessions into subjects for science: How does Freud use "clinical codification" (p. 383)? In what ways does he assume the "inexhaustible and polymorphous causal power" (p. 383) of Dora's experiences with sex? How does Freud work with the assumption that Dora's sexuality "involved something that tried to stay hidden" (p. 384)? What techniques does Freud use to frame his "decipherment" of Dora's story as a "scientific" project (p. 384)? In what ways does Freud treat Dora's "confessions" as "therapeutic operations" that become meaningful and necessary through his "medical interventions" (p. 384)? As you apply Foucault's observations to "A Fragment of an Analysis of a Case of Hysteria," cite and quote specific examples from Freud, reading those examples in the context of language borrowed from "Scientia Sexualis."

2. Write an essay about the strategies you have developed for reading and understanding Foucault's essay. Discuss specific passages from "Scientia Sexualis" that make sense to you, explaining not only what you think he is saying but also how you deciphered his meaning. Which ideas from Foucault strike you as the most accessible? Which parts are confusing to you? What are the differences among such passages? Explain the main lessons you take from Foucault by applying them to a situation that his ideas help you to understand.

CAROL GILLIGAN

Carol Gilligan is the Patricia Albjerg Graham Professor of Gender Studies in educational psychology and human development at Harvard University. Her work on women's development and psychological theory led to the book that established her national reputation as an educational psychologist, In a Different Voice: Psychological Theory and Women's Development *(1982). The essay reprinted here, "Woman's Place in Man's Life Cycle," introduces the thesis of this influential book.*

Ms. magazine's 1984 Woman of the Year, Gilligan is a founding member of the collaborative Harvard Project on Women's Psychology and Girls' Development and has coauthored a series of books reporting and extending the work of the project, including Between Voice and Silence: Women and Girls, Race and Relationship *(with Jill McLean Taylor and Amy M. Sullivan, 1995) and* Meeting at the Crossroads: Women's Psychology and Girls' Development *(with Lyn Mikel Brown, 1992). Gilligan received the Grawemeyer Award in Education in 1992 for her work on the Harvard Project and is the 1998 winner of the Heinz Award for work designed to strengthen healthy resistance and courage in girls.*

Gilligan began to study and reconsider women's development because of the lack of attention given to women and girls in psychological research. Her work in the early 1970s as a research assistant for the head of Educational Psychology at Harvard University, Professor Lawrence Kohlberg, convinced her that the social sciences were fundamentally oblivious to differences between men and women. Taking exception to the fact that Kohlberg's six stages of moral development were based on a twenty-year research project that did not include females, Gilligan asserted that Kohlberg's renowned theory was biased against women. Arguing that women scored lower than men on Kohlberg's moral reasoning test because women prefer the lower, care-based stages, while men tend toward abstract, justice-based judgments, Gilligan argued that the ethical basis in the female voice would lead to more nonviolent human relations.

Through research, Gilligan discovered that women are more concerned with the relational aspect; the consequence is that men and women frame and resolve moral problems differently, with women speaking of connection, peace, care, and response, while men speak of equality, reciprocity, justice, and rights. Assuming that differences in moral judgment stem primarily from internal differences between people, Gilligan does not insist that one way of speaking is better than the other; rather, she argues that harmonious human relations depend on a nonjudgmental, nonhierarchical gathering of different voices. As you read Gilligan's essay, take notes about the different kinds of observational bias that she identifies and analyzes.

Woman's Place in Man's Life Cycle

In the second act of *The Cherry Orchard*, Lopahin, a young merchant, describes his life of hard work and success. Failing to convince Madame Ranevskaya to cut down the cherry orchard to save her estate, he will go on in the next act to buy it himself. He is the self-made man who, in purchasing the estate where his father and grandfather were slaves, seeks to eradicate the "awkward, unhappy life" of the past, replacing the cherry orchard with summer cottages where coming generations "will see a new life." In elaborating this developmental vision, he reveals the image of man that underlies and supports his activity: "At times when I can't go to sleep, I think: Lord, thou gavest us immense forests, unbounded fields and the widest horizons, and living in the midst of them we should indeed be giants" — at which point, Madame Ranevskaya interrupts him, saying, "You feel the need for giants — They are good only in fairy tales, anywhere else they only frighten us."

Conceptions of the human life cycle represent attempts to order and make coherent the unfolding experiences and perceptions, the changing wishes and realities of everyday life. But the nature of such conceptions depends in part on the position of the observer. The brief excerpt from Chekhov's play suggests that when the observer is a woman, the perspective may be of a different sort. Different judgments of the image of man as giant imply different ideas about human development, different ways of imagining the human condition, different notions of what is of value in life.

At a time when efforts are being made to eradicate discrimination between the sexes in the search for social equality and justice, the differences between the sexes are being rediscovered in the social sciences. This discovery occurs when theories formerly considered to be sexually neutral in their scientific objectivity are found instead to reflect a consistent observational and evaluative bias. Then the presumed neutrality of science, like that of language itself, gives way to the recognition that the categories of knowledge are human constructions. The fascination with point of view that has informed the fiction of the twentieth century and the corresponding recognition of the relativity of judgment infuse our scientific understanding as well when we begin to notice how accustomed we have become to seeing life through men's eyes.

A recent discovery of this sort pertains to the apparently innocent classic *The Elements of Style* by William Strunk and E. B. White. A Supreme Court ruling on the subject of sex discrimination led one teacher of English to notice that the elementary rules of English usage were being taught through examples which counterposed the birth of Napoleon, the writings of Coleridge, and statements such as "He was an interesting talker. A man who had traveled all over the world and lived in half a dozen countries," with "Well, Susan, this is a fine mess you are in" or, less drastically, "He saw a woman, accompanied by two children, walking slowly down the road."

Psychological theorists have fallen as innocently as Strunk and White into the same observational bias. Implicitly adopting the male life as the norm, they have tried to fashion women out of a masculine cloth. It all goes back, of course, to Adam and Eve — a story which shows, among other things, that if you make a woman out of a man, you are bound to get into trouble. In the life cycle, as in the Garden of Eden, the woman has been the deviant.

The penchant of developmental theorists to project a masculine image, and one that appears frightening to women, goes back at least to Freud (1905), who built his theory of psychosexual development around the experiences of the male child that culminate in the Oedipus complex. In the 1920s, Freud struggled to resolve the contradictions posed for his theory by the differences in female anatomy and the different configuration of the young girl's early family relationships. After trying to fit women into his masculine conception, seeing them as envying that which they missed, he came instead to acknowledge, in the strength and persistence of women's pre-Oedipal attachments to their mothers, a developmental difference. He considered this difference in women's development to be responsible for what he saw as women's developmental failure.

Having tied the formation of the superego or conscience to castration anxiety, Freud considered women to be deprived by nature of the impetus for a clear-cut Oedipal resolution. Consequently, women's superego—the heir to the Oedipus complex—was compromised: it was never "so inexorable, so impersonal, so independent of its emotional origins as we require it to be in men." From this observation of difference, that "for women the level of what is ethically normal is different from what it is in men," Freud concluded that women "show less sense of justice than men, that they are less ready to submit to the great exigencies of life, that they are more often influenced in their judgments by feelings of affection or hostility" (1925, pp. 257–58).

Thus a problem in theory became cast as a problem in women's development, and the problem in women's development was located in their experience of relationships. Nancy Chodorow (1974), attempting to account for "the reproduction within each generation of certain general and nearly universal differences that characterize masculine and feminine personality and roles," attributes these differences between the sexes not to anatomy but rather to "the fact that women, universally, are largely responsible for early child care." Because this early social environment differs for and is experienced differently by male and female children, basic sex differences recur in personality development. As a result, "in any given society, feminine personality comes to define itself in relation and connection to other people more than masculine personality does" (pp. 43–44).

In her analysis, Chodorow relies primarily on Robert Stoller's studies which indicate that gender identity, the unchanging core of personality formation, is "with rare exception firmly and irreversibly established for both sexes by the time a child is around three." Given that for both sexes the primary caretaker in the first three years of life is typically female, the interpersonal dynamics of gender identity formation are different for boys and girls. Female identity formation takes place in a context of ongoing relationship since "mothers tend to experience their daughters as more like, and continuous with, themselves." Correspondingly, girls, in identifying themselves as female, experience themselves as like their mothers, thus fusing the experience of attachment with the process of identity formation. In contrast, "mothers experience their sons as a male opposite," and boys, in defining themselves as masculine, separate their mothers from themselves, thus curtailing "their primary love and sense of empathic tie." Consequently, male development entails a "more emphatic individuation and a more defensive firming of experienced ego boundaries." For boys, but not girls, "issues of differentiation have become intertwined with sexual issues" (1978, pp. 150, 166–67).

Writing against the masculine bias of psychoanalytic theory, Chodorow argues that the existence of sex differences in the early experiences of individuation and relationship "does not mean that women have 'weaker' ego boundaries than men or are more prone to psychosis." It means instead that "girls emerge from this period with a basis for 'empathy' built into their primary definition of self in a way that boys do not." Chodorow thus replaces Freud's negative and derivative description of female psychology with a positive and direct account of her own: "Girls emerge with a stronger basis for experiencing another's needs or feelings as one's own (or of thinking that one is so experiencing another's needs and feelings). Furthermore, girls do not define themselves in terms of the denial of preoedipal relational modes to the same extent as do boys. Therefore, regression to these modes tends not to feel as much a basic threat to their ego. From very early, then, because they are parented by a person of the same gender . . . girls come to experience themselves as less differentiated than boys, as more continuous with and related to the external object-world, and as differently oriented to their inner object-world as well" (p. 167).

Consequently, relationships, and particularly issues of dependency, are experienced differently by women and men. For boys and men, separation and individuation are critically tied to gender identity since separation from the mother is essential for the development of masculinity. For girls and women, issues of femininity or feminine identity do not depend on the achievement of separation from the mother or on the progress of individuation. Since masculinity is defined through separation while femininity is defined through attachment, male gender identity is threatened by intimacy while female gender identity is threatened by separation. Thus males tend to have difficulty with relationships, while females tend to have problems with individuation. The quality of embeddedness in social interaction and personal relationships that characterizes women's lives in contrast to men's, however, becomes not only a descriptive difference but also a developmental liability when the milestones of childhood and adolescent development in the psychological literature are markers of increasing separation. Women's failure to separate then becomes by definition a failure to develop.

The sex differences in personality formation that Chodorow describes in early childhood appear during the middle childhood years in studies of children's games. Children's games are considered by George Herbert Mead (1934) and Jean Piaget (1932) as the crucible of social development during the school years. In games, children learn to take the role of the other and come to see themselves through another's eyes. In games they learn respect for rules and come to understand the ways rules can be made and changed.

Janet Lever (1976), considering the peer group to be the agent of socialization during the elementary school years and play to be a major activity of socialization at that time, set out to discover whether there are sex differences in the games that children play. Studying 181 fifth-grade, white, middle-class children, ages ten and eleven, she observed the organization and structure of their playtime activities. She watched the children as they played at school during recess and in physical education class, and in addition kept diaries of their accounts as to how they spent their out-of-school time. From this study, Lever reports sex differences: boys play out of doors more often than girls do; boys play more often in large and age-heterogeneous groups; they play competitive games more often, and their games last longer than girls' games. The last is in some ways the most interesting finding. Boys' games appeared to last longer not only because they required a higher level of skill and were thus less likely to become boring, but also because, when disputes arose in the course of a game, boys were able to resolve the disputes more effectively than girls: "During the course of this study, boys were seen quarrelling all the time, but not once was a game terminated because of a quarrel and no game was interrupted for more than seven minutes. In the gravest debates, the final word was always, to 'repeat the play,' generally followed by a chorus of 'cheater's proof'" (p. 482). In fact, it seemed that the boys enjoyed the legal debates as much as they did the game itself, and even marginal players of lesser size or skill participated equally in these recurrent squabbles. In contrast, the eruption of disputes among girls tended to end the game.

Thus Lever extends and corroborates the observations of Piaget in his study of the rules of the game, where he finds boys becoming through childhood increasingly fascinated with the legal elaboration of rules and the development of fair procedures for adjudicating conflicts, a fascination that, he notes, does not hold for girls. Girls, Piaget observes, have a more "pragmatic" attitude toward rules, "regarding a rule as good as long as the game repaid it" (p. 83). Girls are more tolerant in their attitudes toward rules, more willing to make exceptions, and more easily reconciled to innovations. As a result, the legal sense, which Piaget considers essential to moral development, "is far less developed in little girls than in boys" (p. 77).

The bias that leads Piaget to equate male development with child development also colors Lever's work. The assumption that shapes her discussion of results is that the male model is the better one since it fits the requirements for modern corporate success. In contrast, the sensitivity and care for the feelings of others that girls develop through their play have little market value and can even impede professional success. Lever implies that, given the realities of adult life, if a girl does not want to be left dependent on men, she will have to learn to play like a boy.

To Piaget's argument that children learn the respect for rules necessary for moral development by playing rule-bound games, Lawrence Kohlberg (1969) adds that these lessons are most effectively learned through the opportunities for role-taking that arise in the course of resolving disputes. Consequently, the moral lessons inherent in girls' play appear to be fewer than in boys'. Traditional girls' games like jump rope and hopscotch are turn-taking games, where competition is indirect since one person's success does not necessarily signify another's failure. Consequently, disputes requiring adjudication are less likely to occur. In fact, most of the girls whom Lever interviewed claimed that when a quarrel broke out, they ended the game. Rather than elaborating a system of rules for resolving disputes, girls subordinated the continuation of the game to the continuation of relationships.

Lever concludes that from the games they play, boys learn both the independence and the organizational skills necessary for coordinating the activities of large and diverse groups of people. By participating in controlled and socially approved competitive situations, they learn to deal with competition in a relatively forthright manner—to play with their enemies and to compete with their friends—all in accordance with the rules of the game. In contrast, girls' play tends to occur in smaller, more intimate groups, often the best-friend dyad, and in private places. This play replicates the social pattern of primary human relationships in that its organization is more cooperative. Thus, it points less, in Mead's terms, toward learning to take the role of "the generalized other," less toward the abstraction of human relationships. But it fosters the development of the empathy and sensitivity necessary for taking the role of "the particular other" and points more toward knowing the other as different from the self.

The sex differences in personality formation in early childhood that Chodorow derives from her analysis of the mother-child relationship are thus extended by Lever's observations of sex differences in the play activities of middle childhood. Together these accounts suggest that boys and girls arrive at puberty with a different interpersonal orientation and a different range of social experiences. Yet, since adolescence is considered a crucial time for separation, the period of "the second individuation process" (Blos, 1967), female development has appeared most divergent and thus most problematic at this time.

"Puberty," Freud says, "which brings about so great an accession of libido in boys, is marked in girls by a fresh wave of *repression*," necessary for the transformation of the young girl's "masculine sexuality" into the specifically feminine sexuality of her adulthood (1905, pp. 220–21). Freud posits this transformation on the girl's acknowledgment and acceptance of "the fact of her castration" (1931, p. 229). To the girl, Freud explains, puberty brings a new awareness of "the wound to her narcissism" and leads her to develop, "like a scar, a sense of inferiority" (1925, p. 253). Since in Erik Erikson's expansion of Freud's psychoanalytic account, adolescence is the time when development hinges on identity, the girl arrives at this juncture either psychologically at risk or with a different agenda.

The problem that female adolescence presents for theorists of human development is apparent in Erikson's scheme. Erikson (1950) charts eight stages of psychosocial development, of which adolescence is the fifth. The task at this stage is to forge a coherent sense of self, to verify an identity that can span the discontinuity of puberty and make possible the adult capacity to love and work. The preparation for the successful resolution of the adolescent identity crisis is delineated in Erikson's description of the crises that characterize the preceding four stages. Although the initial crisis in infancy of "trust versus mistrust" anchors development in the experience of relationship, the task then clearly becomes one of individuation. Erikson's second stage centers on the crisis of "autonomy versus shame and doubt," which marks the walking child's emerging sense of separateness and agency. From there, development goes on through the crisis of "initiative versus guilt," successful resolution of which represents a further move in the direction of autonomy. Next, following the inevitable disappointment of the magical wishes of the Oedipal period, children realize that to compete with their parents, they must first join them and learn to do what they do so well. Thus in the middle childhood years, development turns on the crisis of "industry versus inferiority," as the demonstration of competence becomes critical to the child's developing self-esteem. This is the time when children strive to learn and master the technology of their culture, in order to recognize themselves and to be recognized by others as capable of becoming adults. Next comes adolescence, the celebration of the autonomous, initiating, industrious self through the forging of an identity based on an ideology that can support and justify adult commitments. But about whom is Erikson talking?

Once again it turns out to be the male child. For the female, Erikson (1968) says, the sequence is a bit different. She holds her identity in abeyance as she prepares to attract the man by whose name she will be known, by whose status she will be defined, the man who will rescue her from emptiness and loneliness by filling "the inner space." While for men, identity precedes intimacy and generativity in the optimal cycle of human separation and attachment, for women these tasks seem instead to be fused. Intimacy goes along with identity, as the female comes to know herself as she is known, through her relationships with others.

Yet despite Erikson's observation of sex differences, his chart of life-cycle stages remains unchanged: identity continues to precede intimacy as male experience continues to define his life-cycle conception. But in this male life cycle there is little preparation for the intimacy of the first adult stage. Only the initial stage of trust versus mistrust suggests the type of mutuality that Erikson means by intimacy and generativity and Freud means by genitality. The rest is separateness, with the result that development itself comes to be identified with separation, and attachments appear to be developmental impediments, as is repeatedly the case in the assessment of women.

Erikson's description of male identity as forged in relation to the world and of female identity as awakened in a relationship of intimacy with another person is hardly new. In the fairy tales that Bruno Bettelheim (1976) describes an identical portrayal appears. The dynamics of male adolescence are illustrated archetypically by the conflict between father and son in "The Three Languages." Here a son, considered hopelessly stupid by his father, is given one last chance at education and sent for a year to study with a master. But when he returns, all he has learned is "what the dogs bark." After two further attempts of this sort, the father gives up in disgust and orders his servants to take the child into the forest and kill him. But the servants, those perpetual rescuers of disowned and abandoned children, take pity on the child and decide simply to leave him in the forest. From there, his wanderings take him to a land beset by furious dogs whose barking permits nobody to rest and who periodically devour one of the inhabitants. Now it turns out that our hero has learned just the right thing: he can talk with the dogs and is able to quiet them, thus restoring peace to the land. Since the other knowledge he acquires serves him equally well, he emerges triumphant from his adolescent confrontation with his father, a giant of the life-cycle conception.

In contrast, the dynamics of female adolescence are depicted through the telling of a very different story. In the world of the fairy tale, the girl's first bleeding is followed by a period of intense passivity in which nothing seems to be happening. Yet in the deep sleeps of Snow White and Sleeping Beauty, Bettelheim sees that inner concentration which he considers to be the necessary counterpart to the activity of adventure. Since the adolescent heroines awake from their sleep, not to conquer the world, but to marry the prince, their identity is inwardly and interpersonally defined. For women, in Bettelheim's as in Erikson's account, identity and intimacy are intricately conjoined. The sex differences depicted in the world of fairy tales, like the fantasy of the woman warrior in Maxine Hong Kingston's (1977) recent autobiographical novel which echoes the old stories of Troilus and Cressida and Tancred and Chlorinda, indicate repeatedly that active adventure is a male activity, and that if a woman is to embark on such endeavors, she must at least dress like a man.

These observations about sex difference support the conclusion reached by David McClelland (1975) that "sex role turns out to be one of the most important determinants of human behavior; psychologists have found sex differences in their studies from the moment they started doing empirical research." But since it is difficult to say "different" without saying "better" or "worse," since there is a tendency to construct a single scale of measurement, and since that scale has generally been derived from and standardized on the basis of men's interpretations of research data drawn predominantly or exclusively from studies of males, psychologists "have tended to regard male behavior as the 'norm' and female behavior as some kind of deviation from that norm" (p. 81). Thus, when women do not conform to the standards of psychological expectation, the conclusion has generally been that something is wrong with the women.

What Matina Horner (1972) found to be wrong with women was the anxiety they showed about competitive achievement. From the beginning, research on human motivation using the Thematic Apperception Test (TAT) was plagued by evidence of sex differences which appeared to confuse and complicate data analysis. The TAT presents for interpretation an ambiguous cue—a picture about which a story is to be written or a segment of a story that is to be completed. Such stories, in reflecting projective imagination, are considered by psychologists to reveal the ways in which people construe what they perceive, that is, the concepts and interpretations they bring to their experience and thus presumably the kind of sense that they make of their lives. Prior to Horner's work it was clear that women made a different kind of sense than men of situations of competitive achievement, that in some way they saw the situations differently or the situations aroused in them some different response.

On the basis of his studies of men, McClelland divided the concept of achievement motivation into what appeared to be its two logical components, a motive to approach success ("hope success") and a motive to avoid failure ("fear failure"). From her studies of women, Horner identified as a third category the unlikely motivation to avoid success ("fear success"). Women appeared to have a problem with competitive achievement, and that problem seemed to emanate from a perceived conflict between femininity and success, the dilemma of the female adolescent who struggles to integrate her feminine aspirations and the identifications of her early childhood with the more masculine competence she has acquired at school. From her analysis of women's completions of a story that began, "after first term finals, Anne finds herself at the top of her medical school class," and from her observation of women's performance in competitive achievement situations, Horner reports that, "when success is likely or possible, threatened by the negative consequences they expect to follow success, young women become anxious and their positive achievement strivings become thwarted" (p. 171). She concludes that this fear "exists because for most women, the anticipation of success in competitive achievement activity, especially against men, produces anticipation of certain negative consequences, for example, threat of social rejection and loss of femininity" (1968, p. 125).

Such conflicts about success, however, may be viewed in a different light. Georgia Sassen (1980) suggests that the conflicts expressed by the women might instead indicate "a heightened perception of the 'other side' of competitive success, that is, the great emotional costs at which success achieved through competition is often gained—an understanding which, though confused, indicates some underlying sense that something is rotten in the state in which success is defined as having better grades than everyone else" (p. 15). Sassen points out that Horner found success anxiety to be present in women only when achievement was directly competitive, that is, when one person's success was at the expense of another's failure.

In his elaboration of the identity crisis, Erikson (1968) cites the life of George Bernard Shaw to illustrate the young person's sense of being co-opted prematurely by success in a career he cannot wholeheartedly endorse. Shaw at seventy, reflecting upon his life, described his crisis at the age of twenty as having been caused not by the lack of success or the absence of recognition, but by too much of both: "I made good in spite of myself, and found, to my dismay, that Business, instead of expelling me as the worthless imposter I was, was fastening upon me with no intention of letting me go. Behold me, therefore, in my twentieth year, with a business training, in an occupation which I detested as cordially as any sane person lets himself detest anything he cannot escape from. In March 1876 I broke loose" (p. 143). At this point Shaw settled down to study and write as he pleased. Hardly interpreted as evidence of neurotic anxiety about achievement and competition, Shaw's refusal suggests to Erikson "the extraordinary workings of an extraordinary personality [coming] to the fore" (p. 144).

We might on these grounds begin to ask, not why women have conflicts about competitive success, but why men show such readiness to adopt and celebrate a rather narrow vision of success. Remembering Piaget's observation, corroborated by Lever, that boys in their games are more concerned with rules while girls are more concerned with relationships, often at the expense of the game itself—and given Chodorow's conclusion that men's social orientation is positional while women's is personal—we begin to understand why, when "Anne" becomes "John" in Horner's tale of competitive success and the story is completed by men, fear of success tends to disappear. John is considered to have played by the rules and won. He has the *right* to feel good about his success. Confirmed in the sense of his own identity as separate from those who, compared to him, are less competent, his positional sense of self is affirmed. For Anne, it is possible that the position she could obtain by being at the top of her medical school class may not, in fact, be what she wants.

"It is obvious," Virginia Woolf says, "that the values of women differ very often from the values which have been made by the other sex" (1929, p. 76). Yet, she adds, "it is the masculine values that prevail." As a result, women come to question the normality of their feelings and to alter their judgments in deference to the opinion of others. In the nineteenth-century novels written by women, Woolf sees at work "a mind which was slightly pulled from the straight and made to alter its clear vision in deference to external authority." The same deference to the values and opinions of others can be seen in the judgments of twentieth-century women. The difficulty women experience in finding or speaking publicly in their own voices emerges repeatedly in the form of qualification and self-doubt, but also in intimations of a divided judgment, a public assessment and private assessment which are fundamentally at odds.

Yet the deference and confusion that Woolf criticizes in women derive from the values she sees as their strength. Women's deference is rooted not only in their social subordination but also in the substance of their moral concern. Sensitivity to the needs of others and the assumption of responsibility for taking care lead women to attend to voices other than their own and to include in their judgment other points of view. Women's moral weakness, manifest in an apparent diffusion and confusion of judgment, is thus inseparable from women's moral strength, an overriding concern with relationships and responsibilities. The reluctance to judge may itself be indicative of the care and concern for others that infuse the psychology of women's development and are responsible for what is generally seen as problematic in its nature.

Thus women not only define themselves in a context of human relationship but also judge themselves in terms of their ability to care. Women's place in man's life cycle has been that of nurturer, caretaker, and helpmate, the weaver of those networks of relationships on which she in turn relies. But while women have thus taken care of men, men have, in their theories of psychological development, as in their economic arrangements, tended to assume or devalue that care. When the focus on individuation and individual achievement extends into adulthood and maturity is equated with personal autonomy, concern with relationships appears as a weakness of women rather than as a human strength (Miller, 1976).

The discrepancy between womanhood and adulthood is nowhere more evident than in the studies on sex-role stereotypes reported by Broverman, Vogel, Broverman, Clarkson, and Rosenkrantz (1972). The repeated finding of these studies is that the qualities deemed necessary for adulthood—the capacity for autonomous thinking, clear decision-making, and responsible action—are those associated with masculinity and considered undesirable as attributes of the feminine self. The stereotypes suggest a splitting of love and work that relegates expressive capacities to women while placing instrumental abilities in the masculine domain. Yet looked at from a different perspective, these stereotypes reflect a conception of adulthood that is itself out of balance, favoring the separateness of the individual self over connection to others, and leaning more toward an autonomous life of work than toward the interdependence of love and care.

The discovery now being celebrated by men in mid-life of the importance of intimacy, relationships, and care is something that women have known from the beginning. However, because that knowledge in women has been considered "intuitive" or "instinctive," a function of anatomy coupled with destiny, psychologists have neglected to describe its development. In my research, I have found that women's moral development centers on the elaboration of that knowledge and thus delineates a critical line of psychological development in the lives of both of the sexes. The subject of moral development not only provides the final illustration of the reiterative pattern in the observation and assessment of sex differences in the literature on human development, but also indicates more particularly why the nature and significance of women's development has been for so long obscured and shrouded in mystery.

The criticism that Freud makes of women's sense of justice, seeing it as compromised in its refusal of blind impartiality, reappears not only in the work of Piaget but also in that of Kohlberg. While in Piaget's account (1932) of the moral judgment of the child, girls are an aside, a curiosity to whom he devotes four brief entries in an index that omits "boys" altogether because "the child" is assumed to be male, in the research from which Kohlberg derives his theory, females simply do not exist. Kohlberg's (1958, 1981) six stages that describe the development of moral judgment from childhood to adulthood are based empirically on a study of eighty-four boys whose development Kohlberg has followed for a period of over twenty years. Although Kohlberg claims universality for his stage sequence, those groups not included in his original sample rarely reach his higher stages (Edwards, 1975; Holstein, 1976; Simpson, 1974). Prominent among those who thus appear to be deficient in moral development when measured by Kohlberg's scale are women, whose judgments seem to exemplify the third stage of his six-stage sequence. At this stage morality is conceived in interpersonal terms and goodness is equated with helping and pleasing others. This conception of goodness is considered by Kohlberg and Kramer (1969) to be functional in the lives of mature women insofar as their lives take place in the home. Kohlberg and Kramer imply that only if women enter the traditional arena of male activity will they recognize the inadequacy of this moral perspective and progress like men toward higher stages where relationships are subordinated to rules (stage four) and rules to universal principles of justice (stages five and six).

Yet herein lies a paradox, for the very traits that traditionally have defined the "goodness" of women, their care for and sensitivity to the needs of others, are those that mark them as deficient in moral development. In this version of moral development, however, the conception of maturity is derived from the study of men's lives and reflects the importance of individuation in their development. Piaget (1970), challenging the common impression that a developmental theory is built like a pyramid from its base in infancy, points out that a conception of development instead hangs from its vertex of maturity, the point toward which progress is traced. Thus, a change in the definition of maturity does not simply alter the description of the highest stage but recasts the understanding of development, changing the entire account.

When one begins with the study of women and derives developmental constructs from their lives, the outline of a moral conception different from that described by Freud, Piaget, or Kohlberg begins to emerge and informs a different description of development. In this conception, the moral problem arises from conflicting responsibilities rather than from competing rights and requires for its resolution a mode of thinking that is contextual and narrative rather than formal and abstract. This conception of morality as concerned with the activity of care centers moral development around the understanding of responsibility and relationships, just as the conception of morality as fairness ties moral development to the understanding of rights and rules.

This different construction of the moral problem by women may be seen as the critical reason for their failure to develop within the constraints of Kohlberg's system. Regarding all constructions of responsibility as evidence of a conventional moral understanding, Kohlberg defines the highest stages of moral development as deriving from a reflective understanding of human rights. That the morality of rights differs from the morality of responsibility in its emphasis on separation rather than connection, in its consideration of the individual rather than the relationship as primary, is illustrated by two responses to interview questions about the nature of morality. The first comes from a twenty-five-year-old man, one of the participants in Kohlberg's study:

[*What does the word morality mean to you?*] Nobody in the world knows the answer. I think it is recognizing the right of the individual, the rights of other individuals, not interfering with those rights. Act as fairly as you would have them treat you. I think it is basically to preserve the human being's right to existence. I think that is the most important. Secondly, the human being's right to do as he pleases, again without interfering with somebody else's rights.

[*How have your views on morality changed since the last interview?*] I think I am more aware of an individual's rights now. I used to be looking at it strictly from my point of view, just for me. Now I think I am more aware of what the individual has a right to.

Kohlberg (1973) cites this man's response as illustrative of the principled conception of human rights that exemplifies his fifth and sixth stages. Commenting on the response, Kohlberg says: "Moving to a perspective outside of that of his society, he identifies morality with justice (fairness, rights, the Golden Rule), with recognition of the rights of others as these are defined naturally or intrinsically. The human's being right to do as he pleases without interfering with somebody else's rights is a formula defining rights prior to social legislation" (pp. 29–30).

The second response comes from a woman who participated in the rights and responsibilities study. She also was twenty-five and, at the time, a third-year law student:

[*Is there really some correct solution to moral problems, or is everybody's opinion equally right?*] No, I don't think everybody's opinion is equally right. I think that in some situations there may be opinions that are equally valid, and one could conscientiously adopt one of several courses of action. But there are other situations in which I think there are right and wrong answers, that sort of inhere in the nature of existence, of all individuals here who need to live with each other to live. We need to depend on each other, and hopefully it is not only a physical need but a need of fulfillment in ourselves, that a person's life is enriched by cooperating with other people and striving to live in harmony with everybody else, and to that end, there are right and wrong, there are things which promote that end and that move away from it, and in that way it is possible to choose in certain cases among different courses of action that obviously promote or harm that goal.

[*Is there a time in the past when you would have thought about these things differently?*] Oh, yeah, I think that I went through a time when I thought that things were pretty relative, that I can't tell you what to do and you can't tell me what to do, because you've got your conscience and I've got mine.

[*When was that?*] When I was in high school. I guess that it just sort of dawned on me that my own ideas changed, and because my own judgment changed, I felt I couldn't judge another person's judgment. But now I think even when it is only the person himself who is going to be affected, I say it is wrong to the extent it doesn't cohere with what I know about human nature and what I know about you, and just from what I think is true about the operation of the universe, I could say I think you are making a mistake.

[*What led you to change, do you think?*] Just seeing more of life, just recognizing that there are an awful lot of things that are common among people. There are certain things that you come to learn promote a better life and better relationships and more personal fulfillment than other things that in general tend to do the opposite, and the things that promote these things, you would call morally right.

This response also represents a personal reconstruction of morality following a period of questioning and doubt, but the reconstruction of moral understanding is based not on the primacy and universality of individual rights, but rather on what she describes as a "very strong sense of being responsible to the world." Within this construction, the moral dilemma changes from how to exercise one's rights without interfering with the rights of others to how "to lead a moral life which includes obligations to myself and my family and people in general." The problem then becomes one of limiting responsibilities without abandoning moral concern. When asked to describe herself, this woman says that she values "having other people that I am tied to, and also having people that I am responsible to. I have a very strong sense of being responsible to the world, that I can't just live for my enjoyment, but just the fact of being in the world gives me an obligation to do what I can to make the world a better place to live in, no matter how small a scale that may be on." Thus while Kohlberg's subject worries about people interfering with each other's rights, this woman worries about "the possibility of omission, of your not helping others when you could help them."

The issue that this woman raises is addressed by Jane Loevinger's fifth "autonomous" stage of ego development, where autonomy, placed in a context of relationships, is defined as modulating an excessive sense of responsibility through the recognition that other people have responsibility for their own destiny. The autonomous stage in Loevinger's account (1970) witnesses a relinquishing of moral dichotomies and their replacement with "a feeling for the complexity and multifaceted character of real people and real situations" (p. 6). Whereas the rights conception of morality that informs Kohlberg's principled level (stages five and six) is geared to arriving at an objectively fair or just resolution to moral dilemmas upon which all rational persons could agree, the responsibility conception focuses instead on the limitations of any particular resolution and describes the conflicts that remain.

Thus it becomes clear why a morality of rights and noninterference may appear frightening to women in its potential justification of indifference and unconcern. At the same time, it becomes clear why, from a male perspective, a morality of responsibility appears inconclusive and diffuse, given its insistent contextual relativism. Women's moral judgments thus elucidate the pattern observed in the description of the developmental differences between the sexes, but they also provide an alternative conception of maturity by which these differences can be assessed and their implications traced. The psychology of women that has consistently been described as distinctive in its greater orientation toward relationships and interdependence implies a more contextual mode of judgment and a different moral understanding. Given the differences in women's conceptions of self and morality, women bring to the life cycle a different point of view and order human experience in terms of different priorities.

The myth of Demeter and Persephone, which McClelland (1975) cites as exemplifying the feminine attitude toward power, was associated with the Eleusinian Mysteries celebrated in ancient Greece for over two thousand years. As told in the Homeric *Hymn to Demeter,* the story of Persephone indicates the strengths of interdependence, building up resources and giving, that McClelland found in his research on power motivation to characterize the mature feminine style. Although, McClelland says, "it is fashionable to conclude that no one knows what went on in the Mysteries, it is known that they were probably the most important religious ceremonies, even partly on the historical record, which were organized by and for women, especially at the onset before men by means of the cult of Dionysos began to take them over." Thus McClelland regards the myth as "a special presentation of feminine psychology" (p. 96). It is, as well, a life-cycle story par excellence.

Persephone, the daughter of Demeter, while playing in a meadow with her girlfriends, sees a beautiful narcissus which she runs to pick. As she does so, the earth opens and she is snatched away by Hades, who takes her to his underworld kingdom. Demeter, goddess of the earth, so mourns the loss of her daughter that she refuses to allow anything to grow. The crops that sustain life on earth shrivel up, killing men and animals alike, until Zeus takes pity on man's suffering and persuades his brother to return Persephone to her mother. But before she leaves, Persephone eats some pomegranate seeds, which ensures that she will spend part of every year with Hades in the underworld.

The elusive mystery of women's development lies in its recognition of the continuing importance of attachment in the human life cycle. Woman's place in man's life cycle is to protect this recognition while the developmental litany intones the celebration of separation, autonomy, individuation, and natural rights. The myth of Persephone speaks directly to the distortion in this view by reminding us that narcissism leads to death, that the fertility of the earth is in some mysterious way tied to the continuation of the mother-daughter relationship, and that the life cycle itself arises from an alternation between the world of women and that of men. Only when life-cycle theorists divide their attention and begin to live with women as they have lived with men will their vision encompass the experience of both sexes and their theories become correspondingly more fertile.

Works Cited

Bettelheim, Bruno. *The Uses of Enchantment*. New York: Alfred A. Knopf, 1976.

Blos, Peter. "The Second Individuation Process of Adolescence." In A. Freud, ed., *The Psychoanalytic Study of the Child*, vol. 22. New York: International Universities Press, 1967.

Broverman, I., Vogel, S., Broverman, D., Clarkson, F., and Rosenkrantz, P. "Sex-role Stereotypes: A Current Appraisal." *Journal of Social Issues* 28 (1972): 59–78.

Chekhov, Anton. *The Cherry Orchard* (1904). In *Best Plays by Chekhov*, trans. Stark Young. New York: The Modern Library, 1956.

Chodorow, Nancy. "Family Structure and Feminine Personality." In M. Z. Rosaldo and L. Lamphere, eds., *Woman, Culture and Society*. Stanford: Stanford University Press, 1974.

———. *The Reproduction of Mothering*. Berkeley: University of California Press, 1978.

Edwards, Carolyn P. "Societal Complexity and Moral Development: A Kenyan Study." *Ethos* 3 (1975): 505–27.

Erikson, Erik H. *Childhood and Society*. New York: W. W. Norton, 1950.

———. *Identity: Youth and Crisis*. New York: W. W. Norton, 1968.

Freud, Sigmund. *The Standard Edition of the Complete Psychological Works of Sigmund Freud*, trans. and ed. James Strachey. London: The Hogarth Press, 1961.

———. *Three Essays on the Theory of Sexuality* (1905). Vol. VII.

———. "Some Psychical Consequences of the Anatomical Distinction Between the Sexes" (1925). Vol. XIX.

———. "Female Sexuality" (1931). Vol. XXI.

Holstein, Constance. "Development of Moral Judgment: A Longitudinal Study of Males and Females." *Child Development* 47 (1976): 51–61.

Horner, Matina S. "Sex Differences in Achievement Motivation and Performance in Competitive and Noncompetitive Situations." Ph.D. Diss., University of Michigan, 1968. University Microfilms #6912135.

———. "Toward an Understanding of Achievement-related Conflicts in Women." *Journal of Social Issues* 28 (1972): 157–75.

Kingston, Maxine Hong. *The Woman Warrior*. New York: Alfred A. Knopf, 1977.

Kohlberg, Lawrence. "The Development of Modes of Thinking and Choices in Years 10 to 16." Ph.D. Diss., University of Chicago, 1958.

———. "Stage and Sequence: The Cognitive-Development Approach to Socialization." In D. A. Goslin, ed., *Handbook of Socialization Theory and Research*. Chicago: Rand McNally, 1969.

———. "Continuities and Discontinuities in Childhood and Adult Moral Development Revisited." In *Collected Papers on Moral Development and Moral Education*. Moral Education Research Foundation, Harvard University, 1973.

———. *The Philosophy of Moral Development*. San Francisco: Harper and Row, 1981.

Kohlberg, L., and Kramer, R. "Continuities and Discontinuities in Child and Adult Moral Development." *Human Development* 12 (1969): 93–120.

Lever, Janet. "Sex Differences in the Games Children Play." *Social Problems* 23 (1976): 478–87.

Loevinger, Jane, and Wessler, Ruth. *Measuring Ego Development*. San Francisco: Jossey-Bass, 1970.

McClelland, David C. *Power: The Inner Experience*. New York: Irvington, 1975.

Mead, George Herbert. *Mind, Self, and Society*. Chicago: University of Chicago Press, 1934.

Miller, Jean Baker. *Toward a New Psychology of Women.* Boston: Beacon Press, 1976.

Piaget, Jean. *The Moral Judgment of the Child* (1932). New York: The Free Press, 1965.

———. *Structuralism.* New York: Basic Books, 1970.

Sassen, Georgia. "Success Anxiety in Women: A Constructivist Interpretation of Its Sources and Its Significance." *Harvard Educational Review* 50 (1980): 13–25.

Simpson, Elizabeth L. "Moral Development Research: A Case Study of Scientific Cultural Bias." *Human Development* 17 (1974): 81–106.

Stoller, Robert J. "A Contribution to the Study of Gender Identity." *International Journal of Psycho-Analysis* 45 (1964): 220–26.

Strunk, William Jr., and White, E. B. *The Elements of Style* (1918). New York: Macmillan, 1958.

Woolf, Virginia. *A Room of One's Own.* New York: Harcourt, Brace and World, 1929.

Ideas for Rereading

1. Compose two lists, one noting the ways in which girls form ideas of gender identity and detailing the characteristics typically associated with girls (according to Gilligan), the other noting the ways in which boys form ideas of gender identity and detailing the characteristics typically associated with boys (again, according to Gilligan). Annotate these lists by indicating how specific traits tend to be regarded in a particular situation of your own choosing. You might, for example, choose to comment on the value attached to "empathy" by students in a chemistry class, by players in a professional hockey match, or on a daytime chat show like *Oprah.* You might then comment on the value attached to "separation and individuation" in the same situation. Do this for each of the ideas of gender identity and each characteristic noted and detailed in your lists.

2. Reread Gilligan's essay, developing an annotated list of the ways of thinking to which she refers. The list should include brief notes characterizing Gilligan's work with each writer she responds to in some detail (Chekhov, Freud, Chodorow, Lever, Piaget, Erikson, McClelland, Horner, Sassen, Woolf, Broverman et al., Loevinger). The following questions might help you with your annotations: Why does Gilligan refer to this particular writer? How does her reference to this writer contribute to her argument? Does she agree with, challenge, or refute the writer?

Ideas for Writing

1. Use two annotated lists of the sort described in question 1 of Ideas for Rereading as the basis for an essay responding to Gilligan's delineation of personality differences between females and males. Apply your understanding of the differences that Gilligan describes to a situation or event of your choosing. Describe and analyze your example in terms of ideas such as autonomy, competition, doubt, deviation, individuation, interpersonal relationships, flexibility, morality, and sensitivity. How is each of these ideas valued or devalued in the situation you describe? What changes have you experienced with regard to these ideas as you have developed them?

2. Develop an interpretive reading of Sigmund Freud's "The Second Dream" (p. 339) by applying Gilligan's statement "Conceptions of the human life cycle represent attempts to order and make coherent the unfolding experiences and perceptions, the changing wishes and realities of everyday life. But the nature of such conceptions depends in part on the position of the observer" (p. 390). In what ways does Freud's interpretation in "The Second Dream" depend on *his* position as he defines it in "The Clinical Picture" (p. 315)? What model of understanding, what framework of assumptions, does Freud bring to his inter-pretation of this dream? How does Gilligan's statement interact with Freud's opening remarks about Dora's dream? In what ways does Freud's interpreta-tion of Dora's dream connect with Gilligan's assertion about "attempts to order and make coherent" the "realities of everyday life"? You may wish to frame this essay in terms of your own interpretation of Dora's second dream: How does your interpretation depend on your position as an observer?

CAROLYN STEEDMAN

Born in England in 1948 in the aftermath of World War II, during the period when the British Labour Party established the "welfare state" by instituting a National Health Service and public ownership of essential utilities and industries, Carolyn Steedman worked as an elementary school teacher before becoming a professor at the University of Warwick. Associated with the Centre for the Study of Social History, Steedman has published a number of books about children and childhood, in-cluding The Tidy House: Little Girls Writing *(1982);* Childhood, Culture, and Class in Britain: Margaret McMillan, 1860–1931 *(1990); and* Strange Dislocations: Childhood and the Idea of Human Interiority, 1780–1930 *(1995).*

*Steedman's work as a social historian ranges from a close analysis of writing by three eight-year-olds (*The Tidy House*), to a dispassionate biography of Margaret McMillan, a socialist who dedicated her life to improving the lives and educations of working-class children in Victorian Britain, to a study of the Victo-rian obsession with waiflike girls (*Strange Dislocations*). Steedman has also pub-lished books on the history of English provincial police forces, the story of a radical soldier, and writing as a tool for autobiography and history.*

Throughout, Steedman writes history that breaks out of academic molds. Landscape for a Good Woman: A Story of Two Lives *(1986) melds personal expe-rience, academic scholarship, and cultural critique into what we might call an "academicultural" autobiography. In the excerpt printed here, "Histories," Steed-man puts Dora's story in the context of Henry Mayhew's 1850s account of "an eight-year-old street-trader in watercresses." Steedman writes that the essay is about "the relationship between the autobiographical account (the personal his-tory), case-history, and the construction and writing of history" (p. 409). She uses Dora and the watercress girl to explore childhood as "a landscape of feeling" that helps us to map childhood understandings of the self.*

Steedman's work with two class-marked representations of childhood demon-strates the technique of comparative analysis: using key quotations from Freud and Mayhew as evidence, she shows how cross-readings of texts open spaces for complex, well-substantiated theoretical interpretations.

Steedman focuses on storytelling as a way of thinking about the uncertain relationships between girlhood and womanhood and as a way of thinking about the failure of traditional ways of understanding the female mind. Focus on the ways in which she exposes areas of uncertainty. Notice her use of words and phrases that denote difficulties of definition and comprehension. As you move along in your reading, pay attention to what Steedman says about the failure of interpretation. How does she represent Freud's and Mayhew's accounts of interpretive failure? How does she explain this failure? How do economic factors contribute to Steedman's explanation?

Histories

Pointless stories are met with the withering rejoinder, "So what?" Every good narrator is continually warding off this question; when his narrative is over it should be unthinkable for a bystander to say "So what?"
—WILLIAM LABOV, *Language in the Inner City*[1]

I grew up in a culture and at a time when it was easy to place childhood on a developmental map. My mother, using both the transmitted child psychology of the 1950s and much older notions of what children could do or could be expected to do when they reached a certain age, knew when I stopped being a child. Understanding human development in this particular way is a fairly recent cultural achievement, and it is still somewhat shaky in its application after babyhood is passed, especially where female children are concerned, with little girls often seen to embody the physical virtues of the ideal woman: narcissism, containment, clarity of flesh, large eyes and slenderness. Little boys, by way of contrast, are frequently understood to possess an adult masculinity as soon as they emerge from infancy. Steven Marcus in "Freud and Dora: Story, History, Case-History" has pointed out that the late-nineteenth-century Viennese physician had a great deal of trouble in siting his eighteen-year-old hysterical patient in the tables of physiological and sexual growth:

> he is . . . utterly uncertain about where Dora is, or was developmentally. At one moment in the passage he calls her a "girl," at another a "child"—but in point of fact he treats her throughout as if this fourteen- sixteen- and eighteen-year-old adolescent had the capacities for sexual response of a grown woman.[2]

Examples of this uncertainty abound in all sociological and literary accounts of nineteenth-century girlhood.[3] William Thackeray, for example, addressed thus the *sixteen-year-old* daughter of an American acquaintance in the 1850s:

> If I were to come there now, I wonder should I be allowed to come and see you in your nightcap—I wonder even if you wear a nightcap? I should step up, take your little hand, which I daresay is lying outside the coverlet,

give it a little shake, and then sit down and talk all sorts of stuff and non-sense to you for half an hour.[4]

This uncertainty about development and sexuality also extended to very young girls—to children—and to those of the working class. Henry Mayhew, collecting material for a series of articles in the *Morning Chronicle* in 1849/50, and transcribing the conversations that were later to make up *London Labour and the London Poor,* interviewed an eight-year-old street-trader in watercresses and frankly recorded his confusion about her place on the developmental map: "the little watercress girl . . . although only eight years of age had already lost all childish ways, was indeed, in thoughts and manner, a woman. . . ."[5] The little girl herself knew that she occupied some place between childhood and adulthood, and told the social investigator that "I ain't a child, and I shan't be a woman till I'm twenty, but I'm past eight, I am." Mayhew mused on her status: "I did not know how to talk with her," he recorded; and Freud, after Dora's last visit, did "not know what kind of help she wanted from me";[6] both of them trans-fixed by the determinations of femininity, both seduced in spite of them-selves, the one moved by compassion, the other by the manipulations of hysteria.

Dora and the little watercress girl are of use here because they both told stories, that is, each of them had an autobiography to impart, and they did so through the agency of the interest and inquiry of two investigators of the human condition. They are divided by age, by class, by time and ge-ography, and the content of their stories seems different too, in so far as each represents a different social reality. They are held together, however, not only by the dichotomous nature of their two narratives and the way in which one illuminates the other, but by being young girls, occupying the contradictory and categorically diffuse place between infancy and woman-hood. Dora's and the little watercress girl's stories are used here because they are rare autobiographical accounts of femininity: the little watercress girl, in fact, presents an almost unique piece of evidence about working-class childhood. The two accounts taken together bring into focus certain themes of this book; and in the making of history what evidence presents itself must be used, in spite of the chronological disturbance it suggests (London in the 1850s, Vienna in the 1900s); the making of history might, in fact, be seen as the theorization of such disruption and dislocation. This final chapter, then, is concerned with the relationship between the autobio-graphical account (the personal history), case-history, and the construction and writing of history. It is about women's history, as indeed this book is, about the difficulties of writing it, the other stories that get in the way, and different kinds of narrative form.

Within this enterprise, childhood is at once revelatory and problem-atic. Working-class childhood is problematic because of the many ways in which it has been pathologized over the last century and a half.[7] In the ro-mantic construction of childhood, which propelled the earliest child-study and within which the psychoanalytic enterprise must place itself, the children of the poor are only a measure of what they lack as children: they are a falling-short of a more complicated and richly endowed "real" child; though that real child may suffer all the vicissitudes of neurosis. Child analysis was a late manifestation of the romantic quest to establish childhood as an area of experience lying within us all, not as a terrain abandoned, but as a landscape of feeling that might be continually reworked and reinterpreted.[8] The appropriation of these ideas—both romantic and literary, and technical—to general social understanding, has tended to de-historicize childhood, has allowed it to be seen as existing in and of itself. Yet childhood *is* a kind of history, the continually reworked and re-used personal history that lies at the heart of each present. What is brought forward for interpretation is structured by its own figurative devices, arranged according to the earliest perceptions of the entities in the real world that give us our metaphors, and the social reality and meaning that metaphor co-joins.

Henry Mayhew encountered the eight-year-old watercress-seller in the East End of London, probably in the Farringdon area, sometime in the winter of 1849/50. Of all the little girls he interviewed during this winter and over the next ten years, she was the one who touched him the most: he was puzzled by her, he pitied her, he felt affection for her; she was not like the children he knew, and yet she was a child. He was attracted by her, and repelled at the same time:

> There was something cruelly pathetic in hearing this infant, so young that her features had scarcely formed themselves, talking of the bitterest struggles of life, with the calm earnestness of one who has endured them all. At first I treated her as a child, speaking on childish subjects; so that I might, by being familiar with her, remove all shyness and get her to relate her life freely. . .

The method did not work; the child would not be treated as a child; "a look of amazement soon put an end to any attempt at fun" on Mayhew's part. However, the child did have a story to tell, and she eventually related it, moving back in time from her current position, after some preliminary remarks:

> I go about the street with watercresses, crying "Four bunches a penny, watercresses." I am just eight years old—that's all, and I've a big sister, and a brother, and a sister younger than I am. On and off I've been very near a twelvemonth on the streets. Before that I used to take care of a baby for my aunt. I . . . minded it for ever such a long time—till it could walk . . . Before I had the baby, I used to help mother, who was in the fur trade; and if there was any slits in the fur I'd sew them up. My mother learned me to needlework and knit when I was about five. I used to go to school too; but I wasn't there long. I've forgotten all about it now, it's such a long time ago . . .

From this sequentially accurate (though chronologically reversed) ac-count, the child selected certain themes—her relationship with her parents and siblings, the financial organization of her life, the questions of play and enjoyment that she had formerly denied—and elaborated on them for the benefit of her interlocutor.[9] These themes, which were central to the child's understanding of herself, will be returned to later.

Some fifty years later, in another European city, Freud encountered the upper-middle-class hysteric "Dora" (in reality, Ida Bauer) who was brought to him by her father at various points during her adolescence in the hope of curing her of coughing attacks, loss of voice, depression and various other nervous symptoms. The implicit expectation was also that the analyst would be able to cure her of a view of her social and sexual re-ality that did not suit her father, who was at this time and who had for sev-eral years past been adulterously involved with the wife of a family friend, called "Frau K." in the case-history.[10]

At several points during the four years before she started analysis with Freud, Dora had come to believe that there was a tacit agreement between her father and the husband of her father's mistress, to hand her over to Herr K. as the trade-off for the adulterous relationship. "When she was feeling embittered," recorded Freud

> she used to be overcome by the idea that she had been handed over to Herr K. as the price of his tolerating the relations between her father and his wife; and her rage at her father's making such a use of her was visible behind her affection for him. At other times she was quite aware that she had been guilty of exaggeration in talking like this. The two men had never of course made a formal agreement in which she was an object for barter.[11]

There are several accounts of the case-study available, and indeed, "Fragment of an Analysis of a Case of Hysteria" is one of the most widely read of Freud's works.[12] The account above, then, is the merest outline of the case itself, and what follows is not concerned with Dora's hysteria, nor with Freud's failure to cure it, nor with her relentless desire to present to her analyst the validity of her own version of events. It is rather concerned with the questions raised by the presentation of personal stories, the rela-tionship of those narratives to history, and above all with the question that Ida Bauer herself raised so explicitly eighty years ago, that of the exchange of women in modern Western society. If we are able to move the idea of the traffic in women through time, space and culture, move it from remote and pre-capitalist societies to our own, and see it as a valid label for subjec-tive experience, then this is largely to do with the evidence that Dora so clearly laid on the table, and that Freud interpreted for us.

Using these two accounts, we may suddenly see the nineteenth century peopled by middle-aged men who, propelled by the compulsions of scien-tific inquiry, demanded stories from young women and girls; and then ex-pressed their dissatisfaction with the form of the narratives they obtained.

Freud began his treatment of Dora by asking her "to give me the whole story of [her] life and illness."[13] It was the unsatisfactory nature of this first narrative that usually allowed the analyst to "see [his] way about the case": it was with the gaps, the inconclusive narrative connections, the hesitations and spontaneous revisions as to date, time and place, that the patient presented clues to where the true account lay:

> The patient comes with the story of his or her own life. The analyst listens; through an association something intrudes, disrupts, offers the "anarchic carnival" back into that history, the story won't quite do, and so the process starts again. You go back, and you make a new history.[14]

It has been suggested that in his writing of this particular case-study Freud implied that "everyone—that every life, every existence—has a story"; and that the story the hysteric tells presents dramatic shortcomings as narrative. "What we are forced at this juncture to conclude," remarks Steven Marcus

> is that a coherent story is in some manner connected with mental health . . . and that this in turn provides assumptions of the broadest and deepest kind about both the nature of coherence and the form and structure of human life. On this reading, human life is, ideally, a connected and coherent story, with all the details in explanatory order and with everything . . . accounted for, in its proper causal or other sequence.[15]

What a successful analyst might do is to give the analysand possession of her own story, and that possession would be "a final act of appropriation, the appropriation by oneself of ones' own history."[16]

Some of Freud's earliest efforts in his short treatment of Dora were directed towards demonstrating that she did not say what she meant, that she was in fact attracted by Herr K., but was unwilling to acknowledge her own desire. He concentrated particularly on an event that took place when the girl was sixteen and, out alone on a holiday walk with the man, was propositioned by him. She slapped his face, hurried away, and on telling her parents about the incident, was met with disbelief—or a kind of feigned and socially appropriate disbelief.[17] Freud recognized that what obsessed Dora was her father's apparent willingness to believe that this scene by the lake was just "a figment of her imagination. She was almost beside herself at the idea of its being supposed that she had merely fancied something on that occasion."[18]

Later, in his revision of the case-study for publication, Freud concluded that "Dora's story must correspond to the facts in every respect";[19] but it is not clear that he acknowledged its validity at the time. What Dora needed to do was to demonstrate to him that she had been right, and two years after her analysis terminated she returned to Freud's consulting room on the pretext of asking for further help, but in fact to tell him that she had extracted confessions of adultery from Frau K. and "an admission of the scene by the lake that [Herr K.] had disputed."[20]

The failure in narrative that it has been suggested Freud attributed to Dora was not in fact a failure of which he always accused his patients. Indeed, in a later case-study, that of the Wolf Man, there is a clear implication that narrative truth, order and sequence does not much signify in the eliciting of a life history, for it must remain the same story in the end, that is, the individual's account of how she got to be the way she is.[21] To concentrate on narrative sequence is to ignore the transactional nature of individual narratives. Narratives are a means of exchange. People may remember the past, and may verbalize their recollections, but to become a story what they say must "achieve a coherence and point which are the same for the hearer as the teller."[22] Dora's early accounts did not become stories because the point of the situation in which they were delivered was to present her with an account that was different from her own, to give her, in fact, Freud's story of Dora.

After the scene at the lake, two years before her analysis with Freud started, Dora had had a recurring dream which she later recounted to him:

> A house was on fire. My father was standing beside my bed and woke me up. I dressed myself quickly. Mother wanted to stop and save her jewel-case; but father said: "I refuse to let myself and my children be burnt for the sake of your jewel-case." We hurried downstairs, and soon as I was outside, I woke up.[23]

This dream of the 1890s has been taken through many interpretations that move far beyond the one that Freud originally made. An essential feature of all of them though, is the attention that Freud paid at the time to the connection between the German word for jewel-case (*Schmuckkästchen*) and its slang meaning, which is a name for the female genitals.[24] Some time before the "scene" and the dream, Herr K. had given Dora an expensive jewel-case. "Bring your mind back to the jewel-case," suggested Freud.

> You have there a starting point for a . . . line of thoughts in which Herr K. is to be put in the place of your father just as he was in the matter of standing beside your bed. He gave you a jewel-case; so now you are to give him your jewel-case . . . you are ready to give to Herr K. what his wife withholds from him.[25]

The role of the mother in the dream is problematic in Freud's analysis of it, as Maria Ramas has pointed out. In "Freud's Dora, Dora's Hysteria," she suggests that Frau Bauer, Ida's mother, saw heterosexuality as representative of contamination, in particular of venereal infection, and that her desire to save her jewel-case in her daughter's dream about the fire, was a repudiation of sexual intercourse and any man's gift—an understanding that Dora had appropriated and which she presented to Freud as her own.[26]

When he came to write his final version of the case-study, Freud was willing to admit social meaning and sociological reality to the narrative:

> It follows from the nature of the facts which form the material of psycho-analysis that we are obliged to pay as much attention in our case-histories to the purely human and social circumstances of our patients as to the somatic data and the symptoms of the disorder.[27]

He has been condemned for this in analytic terms[28] but it is entirely due to his recording of social detail and social interpretation that Ida Bauer's evidence can be used as historical evidence. Dora understood two things about her social and sexual worth. She knew that she was desired and that she might be thought of as an object of exchange between two men. She knew also, with great specificity, what it was that was the subject of exchange: not herself, but her genitals, not a person, but what that person possessed, which was her sex: an object, a valuable item, a thing to be bought and sold. The metaphor that Freud used for interpretation draws on no perceptible connection between genitals and jewel-cases, but rather on a highly specific and powerfully represented *connection* between middle- and upper-class women and their value on the market and in the social world. That, in time and place, was Dora's value, what she understood of herself because the world told her so (Freud too, as part of that world, told her this); and it was this knowledge that she tried to repudiate by her hysteria.[29]

The little watercress girl on the other hand, possessed nothing, except her labour, and her story, which was coherent, and ordered, though told in reverse sequence. Her interlocutor did not accuse her of narrative inconsistencies and lacunae, of denials and repressions (Mayhew was not listening for them); what Mayhew found fault with was not her story (for unlike Freud, who already knew Dora's story, Mayhew did not know the tale this child told) but herself, and the blank absence of childhood from her face. The child knew that there was a point to the tale she told (and Mayhew allowed her her point of view) and performed the device known among narratologists as "the *evaluation* of the narrative: the means used by the narrator to indicate the point of the narrative, its *raison d'être,* why it was told and what the narrator was getting at."[30] Within these strictly sociolinguistic terms, evaluation is to do with dramatization, that is, the eventual presentation of a dramatic *point* to the story, such as a fight. But the little watercress girl made the same gesture of evaluation in order to reach a different kind of conclusion: the point of her story was herself, and how that self had been made.

What the child chose to extract from her autobiographical narrative and to comment on was the financial ordering of her household, and the way in which her labour was managed and controlled by her mother. The personal relationships she described were all bound by this economic vision. She talked in some detail about a Saturday job that she did for a Jewish couple, and about her career as a baby-minder. She had in her short lifetime looked after a nephew or a niece, and was still engaged in looking after her baby sister. Child care represented paid employment, and even in looking after her sister she was performing a function that would have had cash laid out on it by her mother had she not existed.[31] The child understood herself to be in this way a worker, and described her working life with great exactitude:

> Sometimes I make a great deal of money. One day I took 1s 6d* and the cresses cost 6d,[32] but it isn't often that I make as much as that. I oftener make 3d or 4d than 1s; and then I'm at work crying "Cresses, four bunches a penny, cresses!" from six in the morning till about ten . . . The shops buys most of me. Some of 'em says "Oh, I ain't a goin to give a penny for these"; and they want them at the same price I buys 'em at. I always gives mother my money, she's so very good to me . . . She's very poor and goes out cleaning rooms sometimes, now she doesn't work at the fur.[33] I ain't got no father, he's a father in law. No, mother ain't married again—he's a father in law. He grinds scissors and he's very good to me. No; I don't mean by that that he says kind things to me for he never hardly speaks . . . I am a capital hand at bargaining . . . they can't take me in. If the woman tries to give me a small handful of cresses I says "I ain't a goin to have that for a ha'porth," and I goes to the next basket, and so on, all round. I know the quantities very well. For a penny I ought to have a full market hand . . . For 3d I has a lap full, enough to earn about a shilling; and for 6d I gets as many as crams my basket . . . When I've bought 3d of cresses, I ties 'em up into as many little bundles as I can. They must look biggish, or the people won't buy them.

It is clear that under the conditions of distress that her family experienced, she received the most praise and approbation from the adults around her when she made 4d profit out of a bundle of watercress. Her labour functioned as a description of herself—or rather, she used it as a description of what she knew herself to be—and the babies she minded show this metaphoric use she made of her own labour most clearly. In the little watercress girl's account, the baby was both a source of love and affection, a means of play and enjoyment (she spoke of the warmth of a small body in bed at night, the pleasurable weight of her baby sister on her hip, the smiles of infancy); and at the same time the baby was also a source of income and adult praise for earning that income. The baby represented economically what the watercress seller had been in her turn, when she was a baby, and what she was now to her mother: a worker, a good and helpful little girl, a source of income. In this situation her labour was not an attribute, nor a possession, but herself; that which she exchanged daily for the means of livelihood, for love, and food and protection. It was in the face of this integrity of being that Mayhew felt undone.

1s 6d: Before decimalization in 1970, the main unit of British currency, the pound, was divided into twenty shillings. There were twelve pennies in a shilling. A shilling is equivalent to five cents. A small *s* was used to abbreviate *shilling;* a small *d* was used to abbreviate *penny.* The child bought the cress for six pennies ("6d") and sold each bunch for a penny ("1d"). She "took" a shilling-and-a-half ("1s 6d"). A "ha'porth" is a half penny.

The child did possess something after all, she told the social investigator, quite late during the course of their conversation: some toys: "Oh yes; I've got some toys at home. I've a fireplace and a box of toys, and a knife and fork and two little chairs . . ." Perhaps presented by Mayhew for the purposes of demonstrating pathos (did she really have play-furniture, or was she, out of her confusion and deprivation, describing her family's limited stock of household goods?), toys, the possible symbols of easier childhoods, rest uneasily in a reading of the child's account. Toys belong to a world of things that we know immensely and conventionally about; the watercresses though, the pieces of fur with the slits to sew up, the pennies saved for clothes, are not only strange entities, but the connections made between them remain unrevealed by our reading.

It is generally recognized in literary accounts of metaphor, that the connective device on which metaphor turns, that is, on the perception of real similarities between entities in the real world, is often in actuality no more than the recognition of culturally highly specific contingent relations: we are used to comparing certain things with particular other things, and metaphor often works through this connection, rather than perceived similarity. Reading literature from unfamiliar cultures often serves to reveal the conventions of our own metaphoric system, for we do not have forty-three names for the eagle, nor a gradation of terms to describe the colour of snow. "There is scant physical basis for comparing women with swans," remarks Jonathan Culler on this point; but we are massively used to reading the comparison as metaphor.[34]

In Dora's account the contingencies of our understanding furnish almost everything (it is a world we know about, a real world, a big house, by a lake, or behind a gate: this story has been told before; it is *the* story). There are things (entities, relationships, people: names) and there is the placing of things in relationship to each other, which give them their meaning. When a thing is presented in Dora's story, it takes on a universe of meaning: a jewel-case, a reticule, a closed door, a pair of pearl ear-rings. In this way, the writing of case-history takes on the dimensions of story-telling: it works by telling us that something is about to be revealed—that the story is already there to tell.

But there is no story for the little watercress girl. The things she spoke to Mayhew about (pieces of fur, the bunches of cress, the scrubbed floor) still startle after 130 years, not because they are strange things in themselves, but because in our conventional reading, they are not held together in figurative relationship to each other. According to some authorities, both narrative and metaphor work by bringing together things that at first seem separate and distant, but which then, moved towards each other through logical space, make a new and pertinent sense. But this shift through space depends on our ability as listeners and readers to accept the new ordering of events and entities which have been made by the plot of a story, or by the use of a metaphor. Where there is not the vision that permits the understanding of these new connections, then a story cannot be told.

Those who have pointed to the social specificity of the personal accounts around which psychoanalysis constructed itself have also been talking about the conventions of story-telling and story-reading that have confined it. Jane Gallop has discussed the position of the maid, the nurse and the governess in classic psychoanalysis, the figure who relates the idealized and isolated family of the late-nineteenth-century case-histories to the economic world, but who has always been denied a place in them.[35] In *In Search of a Past,* an autobiography structured by psychoanalytic inquiry, Ronald Fraser replaces the servants in the manor house of his own childhood—in all the haunted houses—gives them a voice, fills the place that classic psychoanalysis cannot discuss.[36] But even with this replacement, the narrative continues to work in the same way, telling a story that we know already.

In the narrative terms that Freud can be seen to have laid down in "Fragment of an Analysis," the little watercress girl is a person in mental health, in possession of her story. But it is the story itself that does not fit: all its content and its imagery demonstrate its marginality to the central story, of the bourgeois household and the romances of the family and the fairy-tales that lie behind its closed doors: no different culture here, not a place where they have forty-three terms for the eagle and where a woman cannot be conceived of as a swan; but the arena outside the gate, the set of metaphors forged out of the necessary and contingent relationship between all the big houses and the Clerkenwell rooms in which the child grew up. The marginality of her story is what maintains the other's centrality; there is no kind of narrative that can hold the two together (though perhaps history can): an outsider's tale, held in oscillation by the relationships of class.

She was free, and she was not free. Her father didn't matter, he didn't represent any law: he was just a "father in law." The law, the distant functioning world, was the gentleman who stopped her once in the street, not to pity her, but to ask why she was out so early, and who gave her nothing. It was the inexorable nature of the market, the old women wholesalers, some kind, some not. She was free; she was hungry, meat made her feel sick, she was so unused to it. She had integrity; and she was very poor. Her matted and dirty hair stood out wildly from her head, she shuffled along to keep the carpet slippers on her feet; her life slipped away into the darkness, as she turned into the entrance of her Clerkenwell court.

Notes

1. William Labov, *Language in the Inner City,* University of Pennsylvania Press, Philadelphia, 1972, pp. 370–71.

2. Steven Marcus, "Freud and Dora: Story, History, Case-History," in *Representations: Essays on Literature and Society,* Macmillan, 1976, pp. 247–310.

3. Carolyn Steedman, *The Tidy House: Little Girls Writing,* Virago, 1982, pp. 61–84, 113–23.

4. William Thackeray, *Thackeray's Letters to an American Family*, introduced by Lucy W. Baxter, Smith, Elder, 1904, p. 32.

5. Henry Mayhew, *London Labour and the London Poor* (4 vols.), vol. 1, George Woodfall and Sons, 1851, pp. 151–52. The following extracts from the watercress-seller's narrative are all taken from this two-page transcript of 1851.

6. Sigmund Freud, "Fragment of an Analysis of a Case of Hysteria (Dora)" (1905), The Pelican Freud Library, vol. 8, *Case Histories I*, Penguin, 1977, pp. 27–164.

7. For an example of the process of pathologizing through schooling, see Carolyn Steedman, "'The Mother-Made-Conscious': The Historical Development of a Primary School Pedagogy," *History Workshop*, 20 (1985), pp. 149–63.

8. For a literary analysis of the romantic construction of childhood, see Peter Coveney, *Poor Monkey: The Child in Literature*, Rockliff, 1957, *passim*.

9. William Labov, *Language in the Inner City*, University of Pennsylvania Press, Philadelphia, 1972, pp. 390–93. In Labov's terms, the child was here orientating Mayhew, setting the scene for an eventual story. But the child does not go on to recount a particular event, as do the children and adolescents whose evidence is used in *Language in the Inner City*. In sociolinguistic terms, there is no label for the personal chronology—the autobiography—of the kind that the little watercress girl imparted.

10. Maria Ramas, "Freud's Dora, Dora's Hysteria," in Judith L. Newton, Mary P. Ryan, Judith R. Walkowitz, (eds.), *Sex and Class in Women's History*, Routledge & Kegan Paul, 1983, pp. 72–113.

11. Freud, "Fragment of an Analysis," p. 66.

12. Ramas, op. cit., p. 73 and n. 5, pp. 107–8.

13. Freud, "Fragment of an Analysis," p. 66.

14. Juliet Mitchell, *Women: The Longest Revolution: Essays in Feminism, Literature and Psychoanalysis*, Virago, 1984, p. 288.

15. Marcus, op. cit., pp. 276–78.

16. ibid., p. 278.

17. Freud, "Fragment of an Analysis," pp. 56, 79.

18. ibid., p. 79.

19. ibid.

20. ibid., p. 163.

21. Sigmund Freud, "From the History of an Infantile Neurosis (the 'Wolf Man')" (1918), The Pelican Freud Library, vol. 9, *Case Histories II*, Penguin, 1979, pp. 287–90.

22. Lewis O. Mink, "Everyman His or Her Own Annalist," *Critical Inquiry*, 7:4 (1981), pp. 777–83.

23. Freud, "Fragment of an Analysis," p. 99.

24. ibid., pp. 104–5.

25. ibid., pp. 105–6.

26. Ramas, op. cit., pp. 88–90.

27. Freud, "Fragment of an Analysis," p. 47.

28. "So in the 'Dora' analysis, in which he unravels the tissues of sexual desire in an eighteen-year-old girl . . . Freud introduces the psychical complex that he is to reveal by the sort of sociological comment on families that would warm the heart of many a radical therapist today." Juliet Mitchell, *Psychoanalysis and Feminism*, Penguin, 1975, pp. 63–64.

29. "Perhaps you do not know that . . . 'Schmuckkästchen' is a favourite expression for the same thing that you alluded to not so long ago . . . for the female genitals, I mean."

"I knew that *you* would say that."

"That is to say, *you* knew that it *was* so." (Freud, "Fragment of an Analysis," p. 105.)

30. Labov, op. cit., pp. 366–70.

31. For a further discussion of nineteenth-century working-class children's understanding of economic selfhood, see Steedman, *The Tidy House,* pp. 110–31.

32. That is, she had paid 6d for them at the wholesale market.

33. The child remembered here her mother's earlier work: "before I had the baby, I used to help mother, who was in the fur trade; and if there was any slits in the fur, I'd sew them up."

34. Jonathan Culler, *The Pursuit of Signs,* Routledge & Kegan Paul, 1981, p. 201.

35. Jane Gallop, *Feminism and Psychoanalysis: The Daughter's Seduction,* Macmillan, 1982, pp. 141–50.

36. Ronald Fraser, *In Search of a Past,* Verso, 1984. History Workshop, "In Search of an Author: A Dialogue with Ronald Fraser," *History Workshop Journal,* 20 (1985), pp. 175–88.

Ideas for Rereading

1. Interpret and apply the quotation from Labov used as the epigraph to Steedman's essay. Write some notes in your reading journal reflecting on the possibility that Dora was mainly intent on avoiding "pointless stories." What does this say about Freud, who seems to have taken her more seriously than Labov might advise?

2. How does the image of Dora both as a controlling narrator and as a mere character in Freud's novel (see Malcolm, pp. 426–27) work alongside Steedman's suggestion that both Dora and the little watercress girl occupy the contradictory and categorically diffuse place between infancy and womanhood" (p. 409)? To what extent might you think of Dora as someone caught between the demands of a man "propelled by the compulsions of scientific inquiry" (p. 411) and the efforts of a woman to expose and escape her subjection to a culturally pervasive "exchange of women" (p. 411)?

Ideas for Writing

1. Steedman's essay gains a large part of its dramatic force from the juxtaposition of Dora's history with the story of the little watercress girl. While the two subjects are very different from one another in terms of human and social circumstances—one a presexual child, one an adolescent; one poor, the other relatively wealthy; one mentally healthy, the other plagued by ailments; one an object of exchange, the other with almost nothing of value—Steedman uses them to draw a number of conclusions that depend on a dynamic understanding of adolescence and how each child's story is put to *historical* use by a culture dominated "by middle-aged men" (p. 411).

Write an essay about the various relationships between Freud's Dora and Mayhew's watercress girl. Consider how each of them inhabits "the contradictory and categorically diffuse place between infancy and womanhood" (p. 409). In what ways does each of them represent uncertainty and failure? How do economic circumstances influence each narrative? In what ways do Dora and the watercress girl live "outside the gate" (p. 417)?

2. Write an essay reconsidering "A Fragment of an Analysis of a Case of Hysteria" in terms of Steedman's argument that "Dora understood two things about her social and sexual worth" (p. 414). As you apply Steedman's theories

about Dora to "A Fragment of an Analysis of a Case of Hysteria," take into account Steedman's conclusions about the source of Dora's hysteria and about how things take on "a universe of meaning" (p. 416). You might also contemplate Freud's efforts to "bring her to reason" (p. 322) in the light of Steedman's suggestion that Dora knew "she might be thought of as an object of exchange between two men" and that her genitals rather than herself were the subject of exchange (p. 414). How is your interpretation of "A Fragment of an Analysis of a Case of Hysteria" confirmed, challenged, or changed by Steedman's suggestion that Dora's illness and cure were rooted in her consciousness that she was socially and sexually positioned as the object of an unreasonable system of exchange? Which episodes in Dora's story seem to be legitimate rejections of unfair, patriarchal ways of positioning and "using" her? You may choose to focus on her relationship with her father, with Herr K., or with Freud.

3. Write an analysis of Steedman's "Histories" by juxtaposing it with the two selections in the Context section in which Freud takes a retrospective view of his work with Dora (pp. 366 and 368). How do these reviews of the Dora case history influence your reading of Steedman? How does Freud's confession of his own mistakes together with his revelation of his own unconscious decision making confirm, complicate, or otherwise resonate with Steedman's perspective? How do these mistakes and revelations influence your understanding of Freud's position in relation to Dora? Develop your essay by returning to places in the case history that come to life in the light of Steedman's essay and Freud's retrospective accounts.

JANET MALCOLM

Janet Malcolm has been a staff writer for The New Yorker *since the early 1970s. In 1980 she published her first book,* Diana and Nikon: Essays on the Aesthetic of Photography. *In this collection of essays previously published in* The New Yorker, *she championed the work of radical photographers, including Robert Frank and Richard Avedon.*

Since 1980, Malcolm has published seven books, three of them specifically addressing the topic of her 1981 book, Psychoanalysis: The Impossible Profession. *In this book, Malcolm puts Freudian practice in a historical context, exposing its follies through a series of dialogues with a working psychoanalyst, "Aaron Green." Not the least interesting line of questioning involves the state of arousal of the doctor as patients reveal their sexual secrets. As this might suggest, Malcolm is notorious among psychologists, particularly those based in New York, but she is widely respected as a journalist and critic outside the circle of psychoanalysis. After an exposé of Freud scholarship in* In the Freud Archives *(1984), Malcolm was sued for libel by the main subject of her attack, Jeffrey Masson (the case was dismissed in 1987). Unabashed, in 1993 Malcolm published* The Purloined Clinic, *a continuation of her skeptical portrayal of Freudian analysis. The essay reprinted here, from that book, is Malcolm's review of a collection of essays on the Dora case.*

"Dora" begins with the provocative assertion that "the chief subject of the psychoanalytic dialogue is not the patient's repressed memories but the analyst's

vacation" (p. 421). Malcolm's irreverent attitude toward Freud appears in her char-
acterization of the Dora case: "After three months spent in complaining angrily
about her dire family situation and listening skeptically to Freud's incredible dream
interpretations and improbable constructions about her infantile sexuality, she
abruptly quit the analysis" (p. 424). Perhaps her scathing skepticism is best seen in
her charge that "the most salient feature" of Freudian therapy is its "erotic poten-
tial" (p. 432).

Malcolm's essay demonstrates the technique of academic summary and cri-
tique. It is an accessible critical review that uses academic sources, a keen eye for
the ridiculous, and a satirist's pen to elucidate and critique Freud's "dour view of
sexuality" (p. 434).

From the beginning, Malcolm calls into question Freud's conception of the un-
conscious mind. As you read "Dora" notice what Malcolm says about the uncon-
scious. How does she characterize Freud's understanding of the unconscious mind?
Why does she dwell on the contradiction between metaphors of "wearing-away"
(p. 422) and metaphors of "construction" (p. 423)? How does Malcolm's work
with In Dora's Case: Freud—Hysteria—Feminism contribute to her debunking of
Freudian analysis? Underline words that reveal Malcolm's disdain for "the new
commentators" (p. 425) and for today's "analysts" (p. 429). What language does
Malcolm use to marginalize Freudian analysis and its apologists? Focus on the fig-
ure of the governess: How does this image reinforce Malcolm's representation of
Freudian understandings of the unconscious mind?

Dora

Today, everyone knows—except possibly a few literary theorists—that
the chief subject of the psychoanalytic dialogue is not the patient's repressed memories but the analyst's vacation. As our therapeutic community grows, as more and more of us participate in the cultural ritual known
as "going to the shrink," the popular view of psychoanalysis as a kind of
surrealistic agon has given way to the less theatrical, more domesticated vision of the analytic encounter as a proving ground for the concept of transference. "The patient does not *remember* anything of what he has forgotten and repressed, but *acts* it out," Freud wrote in "Remembering,
Repeating, and Working-Through" (1914). "He reproduces it not as a
memory but as an action; he *repeats* it, without, of course, knowing that he
is repeating it. For instance, the patient does not say that he remembers
that he used to be defiant and critical towards his parents' authority; instead, he behaves in that way to the doctor." Psychoanalysis is the wary
(ultimately weary) examination by patient and analyst of the patient's behavior toward the analyst. Out of this absurdist collaboration—the tireless
joint scrutiny of the patient's reactions and overreactions to the analyst's
limited repertoire of activity in the sphere of fees, hours, waiting-room etiquette, and, above all, absences—come small, stray self-recognitions that no
other human relationship yields, brought forward under conditions of frustration (and gratification) that no other human relationship could survive.

The patient leaves the analysis older, and wiser about analysis. It is finally borne in on him that the object of analysis is not to make sense of his life but to make nonsense of his neurosis. Through repetitive enactment of the neurosis in the transference, the neurosis loses its edge. Psychoanalysis is a process of blunting. From its earliest period, long before Freud knew what he was doing or where he was going, he used the metaphor of wearing away to express the therapeutic effect of the talking cure. Freud's concept of the unconscious is poised on an opposition between the durable and the mutable. What is unconscious is timeless, of stone, forever, while what is conscious is transient, ephemeral, written in water. Freud's early flounderings with hysterical patients, in which, following Josef Breuer's flounderings with Anna O., he did what he called "cathartic therapy," were posited on the theory that hysteria is caused by "forgotten memories" of trauma, which have "been acting like foreign bodies in the mind." This figure of the oxymoronic irritant appears in Freud's 1897 abstract of earlier writings on hysteria. He continues:

> The memories which are revealed as "pathogenic," as the roots of hysterical symptoms, are regularly "unconscious" to the patient. It seems that by thus remaining unconscious they escape the wearing-away process to which psychical material is normally subject. A wearing-away of this sort is brought about by the method of "abreaction."

In 1909, when Freud wrote his "Notes upon a Case of Obsessional Neurosis," popularly known as the Rat Man case, psychoanalytic theory as we now know it was in place, and clinical practice was a far cry from its earliest manifestation, which has been wonderfully characterized by Leo Stone as "a sort of unwitting, sometimes grudging patient participation, like the bringing of urine to be analyzed, or enduring the expression of pus." But the distinction between what is conscious and what is unconscious remained, and remains, a kind of lodestar of psychoanalytic thought (or, to use Freud's own figure of speech in 1923, "our one beacon-light in the darkness of depth psychology"), and the wearing-away metaphor retained its authority as other figures of pre-psychoanalysis lost theirs. In the Rat Man case, indeed, Freud gave the wearing-away metaphor its fullest and most poetic expression:

> At the next session the patient showed great interest in what I had said, but ventured, so he told me, to bring forward a few doubts. —How, he asked, could the information that the self-reproach, the sense of guilt, was justified have a therapeutic effect? —I explained that it was not the information that had this effect, but the discovery of the unknown content to which the self-reproach was really attached. —Yes, he said, that was the precise point to which his question had been directed. —I then made some short observations upon *the psychological differences between the conscious and the unconscious,* and upon the fact that everything conscious was subject to a process of wearing-away, while what was unconscious was relatively unchangeable; and I illustrated my remarks by

pointing to the antiques standing about in my room. They were, in fact, I said, only objects found in a tomb, and their burial had been their preservation: the destruction of Pompeii was only beginning now that it had been dug up.

However, Freud, with his characteristic refusal to make things easy for his interpreters, elsewhere in his writings uses the analogy of the archaeological relic to make an altogether different and seemingly contradictory point. In his late paper "Constructions in Analysis" (1937), and also in the Dora case, Freud employs the analogy of the archaeological relic not to illustrate the destructive action of psychoanalysis on pathogenic thought, like the corrosive effect of air and light on long-buried objects, but, rather, to legitimate the making of "constructions" — i.e., the analyst's conjectures about fateful events in the patient's psychic life during early childhood:

> Just as the archeologist builds up the walls of the building from the foundations that have remained standing, determines the number and position of the columns from depressions in the floor, and reconstructs the mural decorations and paintings from the remains found in the debris, so does the analyst proceed when he draws his inferences from the fragments of memories, from the associations, and from the behavior of the subject of the analysis.

The apparent contradiction between analysis as destruction and analysis as construction is resolved in the next paragraph in the "Constructions" paper, in which Freud notes that "the main difference" between the analyst and the archaeologist "lies in the fact that for the archaeologist the reconstruction is the aim and end of his endeavors, while for analysis the construction is only a preliminary labor." He continues, "The analyst finishes a piece of construction and communicates it to the subject of the analysis so that it may work upon him." In the case of the Rat Man, Freud's constructions "worked upon" the patient so well that his symptoms were relieved before the whole story of his infantile neurosis could be pieced together. "It was impossible to unravel this tissue of fantasy thread by thread," Freud writes in a footnote, because

> the therapeutic success of the treatment was precisely what stood in the way of this. The patient recovered, and his ordinary life began to assert its claims: there were many tasks before him, which he had already neglected far too long, and which were incompatible with a continuation of the treatment. I am not to be blamed, therefore, for this gap in the analysis. The scientific results of psychoanalysis are at present only a by-product of its therapeutic aims, and for that reason it is often just in those cases where treatment fails that most discoveries are made.

The Rat Man's crippling obsessional neurosis — his tormenting idea that the woman he loved and also his (dead!) father were being subjected to a horrible Turkish torture — was gradually "worn away" during analysis as his unconscious hatred for his father came into consciousness. But, Freud writes, "it was only along the painful road of transference that he was able to reach a conviction that his relation to his father really necessitated the postulation of this unconscious complement," and he goes on to describe the rather comical as-if form of the Rat Man's transference:

> Things soon reached a point at which, in his dreams, his waking fantasies, and his associations, he began heaping the grossest and filthiest abuse upon me and my family, though in his deliberate actions he never treated me with anything but the greatest respect. His demeanour as he repeated these insults to me was that of a man in despair. "How can a gentleman like you, sir," he used to ask, "let yourself be abused in this way by a low, good-for-nothing fellow like me? You ought to turn me out: that's all I deserve." While he talked like this, he would get up from the sofa and roam about the room—a habit which he explained at first as being due to delicacy of feeling: he could not bring himself, he said, to utter such horrible things while he was lying there so comfortably. But soon he himself found a more cogent explanation, namely, that he was avoiding my proximity for fear of my giving him a beating. . . . His father had had a passionate temper, and sometimes in his violence had not known where to stop. Thus, little by little, in this school of suffering, the patient won the sense of conviction which he had lacked—though to any disinterested mind the truth would have been almost self-evident.

Dora, the eighteen-year-old subject of Freud's first major case history (written in 1901 and published in 1905, under the title "Fragment of an Analysis of a Case of Hysteria"), never gained the Rat Man's sense of conviction about the unconscious. After three months spent in complaining angrily about her dire family situation and listening skeptically to Freud's incredible dream interpretations and improbable constructions about her infantile sexuality, she abruptly quit the analysis, her hysteria intact—and thus provided Freud with the instructive failure that he spoke of so wistfully in the Rat Man case. She has also provided our Freud-obsessed age with a kind of marvelous fetish: we cherish the Dora case, because it proves that Freud, who told us such unpleasant truths about ourselves, was himself just another pitiful, deluded, dirty-minded neurotic. The Dora case shows us a Freud out of control, a Freud whose genius has gone awry, a Freud who can be likened to an analytic patient in the grip of a powerful regressive transference. Or, perhaps more to the point of our own transference relationship to Freud, he is like an analyst who has slipped up and at last given the patient something "real" to work with in his desperate struggle against his interlocutor's maddening disinterestedness.

A recently published anthology called *In Dora's Case: Freud—Hysteria—Feminism*, which was edited by Charles Bernheimer and Claire Kahane (Columbia University Press, 1985) and is largely devoted to writings of the past ten years by young and youngish literary critics who teach English and comparative literature at American and English universities, put me in mind of a scene in Virginia Woolf's *The Years*—the scene that forms the novel's symbolic center—where two little girls excitedly dance and leap around a bonfire lit for the older girl's birthday. These new writings—feminist, deconstructive, and Lacanian,* for the most part—have a wild playfulness and a sort of sexual sparkle that flicker through their academic patois and give them an extraordinary verve. (There are also writings from the fifties and sixties by three psychoanalysts—Felix Deutsch, Erik Erikson, and Lacan himself—who form a sort of subdued elder-statesman group, with a transferential agenda different from that of the contemporary lit-crit contributors.) These New Critics of psychoanalysis worry Freud's text as if it were a metaphysical poem and, adroitly using Freud's own weapons against him, find example upon example of unconscious self-betrayal. A telltale passage on which a number of them pounce is the paragraph that follows Freud's interpretation of Dora's nervous cough: it is, he tells her, the hysterical representation of an unconscious fantasy in which she pictures her father's mistress, Frau K., performing fellatio on the father. Freud anticipates the "astonishment and horror" of the reader at his "daring to talk about such delicate and unpleasant subjects to a young girl," and goes on, rather preposterously:

> It is possible for a man to talk to girls and women upon sexual matters of every kind without doing them harm and without bringing suspicion upon himself, so long as, in the first place, he adopts a particular way of doing it, and, in the second place, can make them feel convinced that it is unavoidable. A gynaecologist, after all, under the same conditions, does not hesitate to make them submit to uncovering every possible part of their body. The best way of speaking about such things is to be dry and direct; and that is at the same time the method furthest removed from the prurience with which the same subjects are handled in "society," and to which girls and women alike are so thoroughly accustomed. I call bodily organs and processes by their technical names, and I tell these to the patient if they—the names, I mean—happen to be unknown to her. *J'appelle un chat un chat.*

Jane Gallop, in an essay entitled "Keys to Dora," charmingly points out:

> At the very moment he defines non-prurient language as direct and non-euphemistic, he takes a French detour into a figurative expression. By his terms, this French sentence would seem to be titillating, coy, flirtatious. And to make matters more juicy (less "dry"), *chat* or *chatte* can be used as vulgar (vulvar) slang for the female genitalia. So in this gynecological context, where he founds his innocence upon the direct use of technical terms, he takes a French detour and calls a pussy a pussy.

The fellatio interpretation itself becomes the object of ribald one-upmanship among the new commentators. Toril Moi, in her essay "Representation of Patriarchy: Sexuality and Epistemology in Freud's *Dora*,"

Lacanian: Refers to the most influential critic of Freud in the later part of the twentieth century. Based in Paris, Jacques Lacan is known as a "post-Freudian." He made his name with a collection called *Ecrits* (1966). His fame rests on his demonstration that Freud's conception of the unconscious mind reveals Freud's own unconscious desires, fears, and entanglements.

writes that "it would not be difficult to detect in Freud a defensive reaction-formation." She continues:

> It is little wonder that he feels the need to defend himself against the idea of fellatio, since it is more than probable that the fantasy exists, not in Dora's mind, but in his alone. Freud has informed us that Dora's father was impotent, and assumes this to be the basis of Dora's "repulsive and perverted phantasy." According to Freud, the father cannot manage penetration, so Frau K. must perform fellatio instead. But as Lacan has pointed out, this argument reveals an astonishing lack of logic on Freud's part. In the case of male impotence, the man is obviously much more likely, *faute de mieux,* to perform cunnilingus. As Lacan writes: "Everyone knows that cunnilingus is the artifice most commonly adopted by 'men of means' whose powers begin to abandon them."

Neil Hertz, in his essay "Dora's Secrets, Freud's Techniques," also quotes Lacan's magisterial line, and wryly remarks, "It is hard to guess what Freud would have made of this note of high Parisian *savoir vivre;* whatever everyone else knew, he seems to have taken for granted the more phallic—and phallocentric—option." Hertz goes on to play with the conceit of "oral intercourse in the other sense of that term"—i.e., the verbal one—and to propose that as "Dora refuses to 'know' that when she coughs she is picturing to herself a scene of oral gratification," so "Freud has every reason to deny that his own conversations with girls like Dora are titillating."

Like the perverse fantasies and dreams about Freud and his family that enabled the Rat Man to tell his analyst of his hatred (and love) of him, the sex-playful explications of Gallop, Moi, Hertz, et al. (and also, of course, my own explication of their explications) carry an unmistakable transferential weight. Like the Rat Man's dead father, the dead father of psychoanalysis still "lives" in our imagination as a sort of superstar professor, whose classes are so big that in order to attract his attention we practically have to make public nuisances of ourselves. "I believe that Freud would have been the first to be amused by the observation that in this splendid extended declaration about plain speech . . . he feels it necessary to disappear not once but twice into French," Steven Marcus writes in his anthology essay "Freud and Dora: Story, History, Case History," making manifest what the other commentators carefully leave latent. (We are back in the passage about calling a cat a cat. Freud's second disappearance into French, a paragraph later, is *"Pour faire une omelette il faut casser des oeufs."*)

In addition to the father/naughty-children transference, there are sibling transferences, which carry the book into yet another emotional field. Toril Moi's unpleasant remark about a fellow contributor's essay—that Maria Ramas's "'theoretical' inquiry advances little beyond a scrupulous, somewhat tedious résumé of Freud's text"—has some of the atmosphere of a waiting-room encounter between a departing analytic patient and an arriving one. Claire Kahane, in her introduction, administers a kind of watchful child's justice in pointing out Marcus's (unacknowledged) intellectual debt to Philip Rieff, who "already in 1962 . . . had emphasized . . . the literary nature of the case history as a genre" and had likened "Fragment of an Analysis" — in its labyrinthine narrative structure — to a work of modernist fiction.

Marcus's elaboration of Rieff's suggestion is the matrix of his influential *Freud and Dora: Story, History, Case History* (1974). In it, he characterizes the Dora case as "a great work of literature" and sees Freud as a sort of unwitting modernist master; he writes of the case history's "innovations in formal structure," its "Nabokovian frame," and its "unreliable narrator." But an unwitting modernist is a contradiction in terms, if by modernist literature we mean a certain kind of acutely self-aware writing. In back of every unreliable narrator of modernist fiction stands a reliably artful author. In Dora, however, the Freud who is writing the case history and the Freud who is narrating it are one and the same person. If *Pale Fire* had been *written* by the madman Charles Kinbote as well as narrated by him, there would be an analogy between Nabokov's novel and Freud's case history. Marcus struggles manfully with the contradiction but cannot resolve it: "If Freud communicates in this piece of writing a less than complete understanding of himself . . . like any great writer he provides us with the material for understanding some things that have escaped his own understanding, for filling in some gaps, for restoring certain fragments into wholes." It is in his analysis of Freud as madman rather than as modernist that Marcus makes his most valuable contribution. (As if to blunt his transgression, Marcus constantly calls Freud a "genius" and a "great writer," and wherever he directly challenges Freud he hastens to perform a little caper of propitiation — one recalls the Rat Man's nervous scurryings away from the couch lest Freud hit him — speaking of "this great text," "this passage of unquestionable genius," "an extraordinary piece of writing," "a masterpiece," "a scene that Freud orchestrates with inimitable richness," "the tact and sense of form that one associates with a classical composer of music." The younger siblings who follow in Marcus's footsteps evidently feel none of Marcus's need to appease the father; they attack the father with cool impunity — more confident of his love, perhaps.) Marcus draws attention to the "weirdness and wildness" of Freud's text and notes that it is the analyst rather than the patient who is its true subject: "The case history belongs progressively less to her than it does to him," and by the end "it is his *own* mind that chiefly matters to him."

Following Marcus's cue, the recent commentators place themselves at the head of the couch on which Freud has, so to speak, flung himself in writing the case history and, with an analyst's closely hovering attention, seek to catch the drift of his deeply stirred-up unconscious. Toril Moi performs an arresting feat of interpretation when she connects Freud's recurrent frettings about the fragmentary, incomplete, gap-filled state of his text to his "deeply unconscious patriarchal ideology." She quotes a famous passage from the Dora "Fragment," which contains yet another use by Freud of his beloved archaeological metaphor:

> In the face of the incompleteness of my analytic results, I had no choice but to follow the example of those discoverers whose good fortune it is to bring to the light of day after their long burial the priceless though mutilated relics of antiquity. I have restored what is missing, taking the best models known to me from other analyses; but like a conscientious archaeologist, I have not omitted to mention in each case where the authentic parts end and my construction begins.

She then points out what else it is that Freud is talking about:

> "The priceless though mutilated relics of antiquity" are not only Dora's story: they are Dora herself, her genitals and the feminine epistemological model. Freud makes sure that the message here is clear: "mutilated" is his usual way of describing the effect of castration, and "priceless" also means just what it says: price-less, without value. For how can there be value when the valuable piece has been cut off? The relics are mutilated, the penis has been cut. Freud's task is therefore momentous: he must "restore what is missing"; his penis must fill the epistemological hole represented by Dora.

Neil Hertz's fine-tuned third ear picks up Freud's fear not only of actual sexual entanglement with Dora but of "epistemological promiscuity in which the lines would blur between what Dora knew and what Freud knew, and, consequently, in which the status of Freud's knowledge, and of his professional discourse, would be impugned." This fear, of course, haunts every analysis, enters the transference as well as the countertransference, and is inextricably bound up with the analytic fee. For what the analyst is "selling" is precisely the difference of his psychoanalytic discourse from the discourses of ordinary, conscious life and common sense. If the analyst is to earn his fee, and the talking cure isn't to be mere talk, only the uncommon sense of the patient's symptoms and behaviors may be allowed status in the analysis. Freud seemed to be groping his way toward an understanding of the necessary epistemological inequality between the analytic interlocutors when, in the chapter on the psychotherapy of hysteria in *Studies on Hysteria* (1893–95), he wrote, "It is of course of great importance for the progress of the analysis that one should always turn out to be in the right vis-à-vis the patient, otherwise one would always be dependent on what he chose to tell one."

Jane Gallop examines the lopsided patient-analyst relationship in terms of the analyst's economic dependence on the patient. The starting point of her very original discussion of the analyst as paid servant is the scene in "Dora" where the girl walks into Freud's office and announces that this is her last session. Freud unemotionally asks her when she formed her resolve to quit the analysis. She replies, "A fortnight ago, I think," and he tartly comments, "That sounds just like a maidservant or a governess — a fortnight's warning." Gallop pauses before the comment's manifest ambiguity — "Is the servant giving two weeks' notice before quitting, or is the master giving the servant two weeks' notice" — and opts for the latter reading, an interpretation that one intuitively feels is indeed the one Freud "meant." "Identification between Freud and a governess, maid, or nurse is not restricted to the confines of the Dora case but has a decisive, structural relation to psychoanalysis in general," Gallop writes. She correctly identifies the analytic fee as the fulcrum of transference interpretation — "The money proves that the analyst is only a stand-in" — and continues, "Rather than having the power of life and death like the mother has over the infant, the analyst is financially dependent on the patient. But, in that case, the original 'analyst,' the earliest person paid to replace the mother, is that frequent character in Freud's histories, the nursemaid/governess." In the Dora analysis, however, Freud was not entirely willing to accept the humble role of the servant: he struggled against its alterity; he wanted "in" — he wanted, as Gallop puts it, "to be the Mother (the phallic mother, Lacan's Other, the subject presumed to know, the Doctor) rather than the nurse" — and this was his undoing with Dora, just as every analyst is undone when he wants to move into the patient's family, when he doesn't know his place, which is outside. When we speak of the analyst's countertransference, we refer to some such breaching of "class" lines.

Today, analysts enjoy so much social prestige, have so much money, and are so pompous that the governess/nurse figure — the analyst as Jane Eyre — seems very figurative indeed. But when the metaphor is applied to Freud of the 1880s, 1890s, and early 1900s, it is less farfetched. At the time Freud was doing cathartic and then early analytic therapy, he was such an irregular sort of doctor (according to Peter Swales's recent study *Freud, His Teacher, and the Birth of Psychoanalysis,* he was known as "*der Zauberer,*" the magician, by the children of Anna von Lieben, a rich patient whom he treated at home in the 1880s) that it isn't even certain he was always admitted by the front door when he made house calls. From *Studies on Hysteria* (to which Swales's study forms a valuable pendant), we gain a sense not only of the wild, ad hoc nature of Freud's early therapy but of the marginality of his social position. He was more like one of today's mildly disreputable alternative-medicine men than like a "real" doctor. In the Frau Emmy von N. case, we read of Freud's twice-a-day visits to the sanitarium where his hysterical patient was staying — of his massages, his pacifying hypnotic suggestions, and his nannylike interest in whether she ate her dessert or threw it out the window. Another of his patients — a young Englishwoman, Lucy R. — was actually a governess herself, and one is struck by the tone of cordiality, almost of collegiality, that creeps into Freud's account of his treatment of her. Like him, and in marked contrast to the idle rich women like Emmy von N. and Cäcilie M. (as Freud called Anna von Lieben in *Studies*), Lucy R. had to earn her living and was dependent on the goodwill, and frequently on the whim, of her employer. (In *Studies,* Freud writes with similar friendliness of the eighteen-year-old Katharina, another "service industry" colleague, who waited on table at her mother's mountain inn—Freud stayed there during a vacation—and whose anxiety attacks he traced to an incident of childhood sexual molestation. "I owed her a debt of gratitude for having made it so much easier for me to talk to her than to the prudish ladies of my city practice, who regard whatever is natural as shameful," he wrote.) Lucy R.'s chief hysterical symptom was the loss of her sense of smell, accompanied by a persistent imaginary smell of burnt pudding. Freud traced the latter to a nursery incident in the house where she was working—some pudding had actually burned—and eventually to the fact that she was in love with her employer, the widowed director of a factory in Outer Vienna. Freud writes:

> I said to her, "I cannot think that these are all the reasons for your feelings about the children. I believe that really you are in love with your employer, the Director, though perhaps without being aware of it yourself, and that you have a secret hope of taking their mother's place in actual fact. . . ." She answered in her usual laconic fashion: "Yes, I think that's true." — "But if you knew you loved your employer, why didn't you tell me?" — "I didn't know—or rather I didn't want to know. I wanted to drive it out of my head and not think of it again; and I believe latterly I have succeeded."

In a footnote, Freud remarks of this answer, "I have never managed to give a better description than this of the strange state of mind in which one knows and does not know a thing at the same time . . . that blindness of the seeing eye which is so astonishing in the attitude of mothers to their daughters, husbands to their wives and rulers to their favorites." However, contrary to Freud's expectations, his interpretation did not then and there cure Lucy of her bizarre symptom. In the next few weeks, the smell of burnt pudding gradually receded, only to be replaced by the smell of cigar smoke. "It had been there earlier as well, she thought, but had, as it were, been covered by the smell of the pudding. Now it had emerged by itself." Lucy was one of the first patients on whom Freud tried his "pressure technique," in the place of hypnosis (which he apparently wasn't too adept at), to elicit the desired "forgotten memory"; he would place his hand on the patient's forehead, or take her head in his hands, and say, "You will think of it under the pressure of my hand. At the moment at which I relax my pressure, you will see something in front of you, or something will come into your head. Catch hold of it. It will be what we are looking for." Using this technique, he traced the cigar smoke to a scene at the end of a luncheon at the house of the Director/Mr. Rochester, when the men were smoking cigars and the Director had shouted at a poor accountant for kissing the children. This scene led Freud back to the Ur-scene* of Lucy's hys-

*Ur-scene: Ur refers to an original, primitive drive or moment. In context it refers to the specific impulse and event that created Lucy's hysteria.

teria, a traumatic incident in which the Director, having lashed out at Lucy herself for allowing a visitor to kiss the children on the mouth, had mortifyingly crushed her hopes of his love. This time, the therapy took. Two days later, a radiantly happy Lucy walked into Freud's consultation room. "She was as though transfigured," Freud writes, and continues:

> She was smiling and carried her head high. I thought for a moment that after all I had been wrong about the situation, and that the children's governess had become the Director's fiancée. But she dispelled my notion. "Nothing has happened. It's just that you don't know me. You have only seen me ill and depressed. I'm always cheerful as a rule. When I woke yesterday morning, the weight was no longer on my mind, and since then I have felt well." — "And what do you think of your prospects in the house?" — "I am quite clear on the subject. I know I have none, and I shan't make myself unhappy over it." . . . "And are you still in love with your employer?" — "Yes, I certainly am, but that makes no difference. After all, I can have thoughts and feelings to myself."

As this remarkable passage suggests, Freud's identification with the governess had become so nearly complete that it is he, the doctor, who articulates the fantasy of the governess who becomes the Director's fiancée, and she, the patient, who, in a wonderful kind of reversal, has to remind Freud that when hysterical misery has been transformed into common unhappiness (or, as the case may be, stiff-upper-lip cheerfulness), there is reason enough for rejoicing. *Studies on Hysteria* is full of such reversals; the book as a whole could be characterized as the story of the gradual transformation of a naively blundering hypnotist into the composed founder of psychoanalysis. The Freud who emerges from the book is startlingly young and tentative; if he already exhibits the intellectual agility of the mature Freud, he has none of the latter's magisterial, somewhat grumpy manner. The mature Freud was always defending himself against "the opponents of psychoanalysis"; the young Freud could hardly flatter himself on having opponents, since no one had even heard of him, and he didn't himself yet really know what he was doing. Each of the cases in *Studies* is a humble little progress report on the education of the first psychoanalyst, whose only claim to cleverness was that he didn't pretend to know more than he did, but knew enough to learn from unexpected sources of knowledge. Readers of the mature Freudian texts will recognize what Neil Hertz calls the pose of "the Impressionable Junior Colleague," whose credulity is both a shield against vulgar error and a weapon that penetrates to the truth of things. In "On the History of the Psychoanalytic Movement" (where Freud recounts anecdotes about himself vis-à-vis his mentors Charcot and Breuer, thus giving Hertz his tag), Freud looks back on the period of his "'splendid isolation'" — "those lonely years, away from the pressures and confusions of today" — when "I was not subject to influence from any quarter; there was nothing to hustle me," and "I learnt to restrain speculative tendencies and to follow the unforgotten advice of my master, Charcot: to look at the same things again and again until they themselves begin to speak."

This piece of naive empiricism cannot itself be taken at face value. Freud knew quite as well as we do that nothing "speaks" but men's theories; he opens his paper "Instincts and Their Vicissitudes" (1915) with an almost Kuhnian* discussion of the relationship of theory to observation in scientific method:

> Even at the stage of description it is not possible to avoid applying certain abstract ideas to the material in hand, ideas derived from somewhere or other but certainly not from the new observations alone. Such ideas—which will later become the basic concepts of the science—are still more indispensable as the material is further worked over. They must at first necessarily possess some degree of indefiniteness; there can be no question of any clear delimitation of their content. So long as they remain in this condition, we come to an understanding about their meaning by making repeated references to the material of observation from which they appear to have been derived, but upon which, in fact, they have been imposed. Thus, strictly speaking, they are in the nature of conventions—although everything depends on their not being arbitrarily chosen but determined by their having significant relations to the empirical material, relations that we seem to sense before we can clearly recognize and demonstrate them.

His insistent depiction of himself as a sort of irrepressible stumbler upon solid scientific fact ("There I go, discovering something again!") was a kind of necessary alibi for the promoter of a therapy whose most salient feature was its erotic potential. Freud grasped that if psychoanalysis—with its love-affair-like privacy, intimacy, and intensity—wasn't going to be disreputable it was going to have to be severely depersonalized and firmly relabeled as a science. In their original and underrated book, *The Therapeutic Revolution, from Mesmer to Freud,* Léon Chertok and the late Raymond de Saussure trace a line from the "universal fluid" theory of the eighteenth-century magnetists to the Freudian concept of transference, finding the latter a kind of culminating prophylaxis against the sexual temptations of psychotherapy—a sort of duenna that hovers over the therapeutic pair and keeps them from overstepping the bounds of propriety. But long before Freud developed the full-blown concept of transference he was an adept of the "dry" manner of which he speaks in the Dora case. One has only to compare Freud's cases in *Studies* with Breuer's case of Anna O. to see the distance that Freud had gone beyond his mentor in learning how to play with fire without burning the house down. That the Anna O. case would end as it did—with the frightened doctor fleeing from the lovesick patient—could have been predicted from the start: Breuer's

Kuhnian: A reference to a method developed by Thomas Kuhn in *The Structure of Scientific Revolutions* (1962). Kuhn's governing assumption is that we see what we look for: the model of perception we use to develop our questions determines the answers to those questions.

fondness for the girl, his loverlike attentivenesses, and his admiration of her person were the mechanisms of cure, and once these were withdrawn she could only fall ill again. Freud clearly realized that such a state of affairs had to be avoided at all costs; his tone toward the women in *Studies* is consistently and entirely asexual. But it was Freud's genius to presently see (as none of his predecessors had seen) that for sex to be kept at bay in therapy, only *one* member of the therapeutic pair—namely, the doctor—has to behave himself. When Freud gave his female patients permission to declare their love for him (and his male patients permission to abuse him), psychoanalysis proper was under way. Before that moment, Freud only obscurely understood the newness and bizarreness of the psychoanalytic relationship, its utter unlikeness—in its antinomies of silence and speech, reticence and abandon, veiledness and nakedness—to any other relationship in life. At the time of *Studies,* Freud knew how to behave correctly but didn't yet know how to think analytically; by the time of the Dora case, he was on the verge of becoming a psychoanalyst. He was discovering the devilish complexity of this thing he had "stumbled" upon, and how inadequate the straightforward narrative form of the rudimentary *Studies* cases was for representing cases of more fully developed analysis. "I was trained to employ local diagnoses and electro-prognosis, and it still strikes me myself as strange that the case histories I write should read like short stories and that, as one might say, they lack the serious stamp of science," Freud writes in the Elisabeth von R. case in *Studies*. He goes on, "I must console myself with the reflection that the nature of the subject is evidently responsible for this, rather than any preference of my own. The fact is that local diagnosis and electrical reactions lead nowhere in the study of hysteria, whereas a detailed description of mental processes such as we are accustomed to find in the works of imaginative writers enables me, with the use of a few psychological formulas, to obtain at least some kind of insight into the course of that affection." In the Dora case, this pleasant and easy literary formula no longer suffices, and Freud repudiates it thus:

> I must now turn to consider a further complication, to which I should certainly give no space if I were a man of letters engaged upon the creation of a mental state like this for a short story, instead of being a medical man engaged upon its dissection. The element to which I must now allude can only serve to obscure and efface the outlines of the fine poetic conflict which we have been able to ascribe to Dora. This element would rightly fall a sacrifice to the censorship of a writer, for he, after all, simplifies and abstracts when he appears in the character of a psychologist. But in the world of reality, which I am trying to depict here, a complication of motives, an accumulation and conjunction of mental activities—in a word, overdetermination—is the rule.

The complication that was turning Freud's dry Viennese *Liaisons Dangereuses* into a Swiftian nightmare of bed-wetting, thumb-sucking, fellatio, masturbation, venereal disease, vaginal discharge, and gastric pain was

Freud's libido theory. Writing of the case of Emmy von N., in the *Studies,* Freud recalled that at the time (1889), "I regarded the linking of hysteria with the topic of sexuality as a sort of insult — just as the women patients themselves do." By the time of the Dora case, Freud regarded the linking of hysteria with sexuality as a sine qua non. In the Freud-Fliess letters, we can trace the evolution of Freud's thinking from his idea of the mid-1890s — that hysteria could always be traced to an episode or episodes of sexual abuse in early childhood (the "seduction theory") — to his gradual realizazation that child molesters weren't required for the stunting of a person's psychosexual development; the potential for psychosexual catastrophe lies in wait for us all in the ordinary vicissitudes of infantile life. In the Clark Lectures of 1909, Freud noted, "People are in general not candid over sexual matters. They do not show their sexuality freely, but to conceal it they wear a heavy overcoat woven of a tissue of lies, as though the weather were bad in the world of sexuality." Just how bad this weather was was indicated in *Three Essays on the Theory of Sexuality,* published in 1905 (the same year the Dora case was published). To accomplish the feat of becoming a "normal" sexually active adult was, in Freud's view, about as probable for most people as winning the lottery. The path from the polymorphous perversity of infancy to the missionary position of adulthood is littered with obstacles; in moving from the oral to the anal and on to the genital stages of infancy (and we are talking here about the mewling, puking, sucking, defecating, rhythmically rocking, touching, stroking infant's *imagination* in relation to these activities and to interferences with them), the individual invariably gets a little or very stuck, and in the genital, or Oedipal, period he or she suffers wounds that never heal. Whether one becomes a pervert or a neurotic depends on constitution and circumstance, and is a kind of six-of-one, half-a-dozen-of-the-other "choice," according to the *Three Essays.* When Freud was treating Dora, he was forming this dour view of sexuality and, most daunting of all, the conviction that this misery-filled aspect of the human condition was its central fact. He was coming to see that the scenes he worked so hard to elicit from his patients in the *Studies* — the burnt-pudding scene in Lucy R., or the scene in the Elisabeth von R. case in which she comes to her sister's deathbed and has the "pathogenic" (i.e., morally unacceptable) idea that now that her sister is dead her brother-in-law is free to marry her — were not the final destination of the psychoanalytic journey. He understood that he had to go beyond the novelistic plots and characters of the patient's present life and recent past, cross the river Lethe, and penetrate the obscure, inchoate, shade-populated region of infant sorrow where the patient was still haplessly living. In the Wolf Man and the Rat Man cases, Freud makes this crossing; in the writing of both case histories he eliminates almost everything pertaining to the patient's adult biography and confines himself to the exotic inner world of the Oedipal and pre-Oedipal child. The only fully alive contemporary character in the Wolf Man and Rat Man cases is Freud, the narrator. The patient isn't there; he is like an anesthetized body on which an operation is being performed. The Dora case—where Freud has not yet arrived at his final vision of the psychoanalytic case history and is still rendering the patient as a character in a nineteenth-century novel, and also as the host of a kind of operable cancer—reads like an account of an operation being performed on a fully awake patient. Thus its agony and its horror. Every reader of "Fragment of an Analysis" comes away with the feeling that something awful has been done to the girl. The Dora case is known as the case that illustrates Freud's failure to interpret the transference in time; even more, it illustrates a failure of narration. Freud tells the novelistic story of Dora so well that the psychoanalytic story—the narrative of the analyst's probe into the patient's unconscious being—reads like an assault, almost like a rape; we cannot but feel outraged as Freud describes the girl's desperate attempts to elude him while he obscenely moves in on her. (In the Rat Man and the Wolf Man cases, where we follow the surgeon's movements as he cuts into a small area of flesh surrounded by surgical drapery, we feel no such outrage.)

Moreover, and paradoxically, the superlative telling of the novelistic story of Dora has made Freud more vulnerable to the charges of misogyny and sexism that are regularly leveled at him than he might have been if he had been a less gifted writer. In the standard feminist version of the Dora case, the attractive, spirited, intellectually precocious eighteen-year-old hysterical girl is a victim both of a society that gives women no opportunities to use their minds and of a particularly nasty family constellation—a "charmless circle," as Philip Rieff has memorably described it, of "a sick daughter, [who] has a sick father, who has a sick mistress, who has a sick husband, who proposes himself to the sick daughter as her lover." Dora's father and Herr K., the mistress's husband, have a sinister unspoken pact whereby Dora is to be handed over to Herr K. in exchange for his toleration of the father's affair with Frau K. When Dora refuses to play the game, and slaps Herr K.'s face in answer to a proposition he makes her during a walk beside a lake, Herr K. and the father attempt to browbeat her into admitting that the proposition was never made but was a product of her sexually overheated fancy. Freud is enlisted by the father as an ally in the subduing of the rebellious daughter; the girl is handed over (Freud's term in both cases) to him for indoctrination. Though Freud's natural tendency is to side with respectable grown men against irritating hysterical girls, he is obliged to see that in this instance it is the girl who is telling the truth and the men who are lying to save their reputations. He reluctantly declines to be part of the male plot against the girl.

This gynophilic account, as it happens, is also Freud's own account of Dora's life situation—and, indeed, it is the *only* account of it we have. But such are Freud's narrative powers, and so compelling is the verisimilitude he achieves, that, like the Greek artist Zeuxis, who painted such realistic grapes that birds pecked at them, Freud fools us into believing that we are in the face of unmediated reality. Even a reader as sophisticated as Steven Marcus falls into the trap. Early in his essay, he writes, "It may be helpful for the reader if at the outset I briefly review some of the external facts of the case" — as if such "facts" could be looked up in some archive. But there is no archive. Everything we know about Dora and her father and the K.s is what Freud has chosen to tell us, and everything we think and feel about them is what Freud has directed us to think and feel. The "fact" that Herr K. propositioned Dora and then lied is Freud's "fact." Before writing the case history, Freud had made up his mind that the scene by the lake was not a fantasy, and his "fair-minded" account ("I had resolved from the first to suspend my judgment of the true state of affairs") was written under and shaped by this conviction. For all we know, however, the actual, historical Dora may have invented the scene by the lake, and the actual, historical Herr K. may have been telling the truth. Another writer could have made the episode an illustration of how hysterical, lying women can bring trouble upon innocent, respectable men. But as Freud structured his account of it, the truth and goodness of the girl and the falsity and badness of the father and Herr K. are as unarguable as are the traits of princesses and ogres in fairy stories. The feminists who innocently peck at Freud's grapes (I am not talking about the savvy feminist writers of *In Dora's Case*) — who charge Freud with insufficient understanding of and sympathy for the beleaguered girl's plight at the hands of the creepy men around her — should understand the extent to which their own understanding of and sympathy for the girl are artifacts of Freud's rhetoric.

Ideas for Rereading

1. Make three double-entry notebook entries noting and assessing Janet Malcolm's work with Freud and his critics. In the first entry summarize and critique what she does with the quotations from Freud on pages 423 and 424; in the second entry reconsider your work with specific incidents from "A Fragment of an Analysis of a Case of Hysteria" in the light of Malcolm's portrait of Freud as "more like one of today's mildly disreputable alternative-medicine men than like a 'real' doctor" (p. 429); in the third summarize and analyze how Malcolm uses quotations from the book she is reviewing *(In Dora's Case: Freud — Hysteria — Feminism)*.

2. Write a paragraph beginning, "Janet Malcolm's essay influences my reading of 'A Fragment of an Analysis of a Case of Hysteria' because . . ." Take into account what Malcolm says about Freud's "wild, ad hoc" practices and his marginal social position (p. 429). Develop your paragraph by responding to specific passages where Malcolm expresses disdain for the profession of psychoanalysis and psychoanalytic literary theory.

Ideas for Writing

1. Write an essay assessing Malcolm's use of sources. How does she characterize the work she is reviewing? Obviously you cannot assess how accurate she is in representing these sources (though you might go to the library and examine

the book she is referring to), but how fair is Malcolm in her review? In what ways does she make her own perspective apparent? How does she use references, quotations, and analysis of quotations to characterize the project of psychoanalysis in terms of Freud's "dour view of sexuality" (p. 434)? In what ways does she use the book she is reviewing to demonstrate that "the most salient feature" of Freudian therapy is its "erotic potential" (p. 432)? How does Malcolm use satire, parody, and other comic techniques to express her irreverence for Freudian methods?

2. Malcolm makes a good deal of "the marginality of [Freud's] social position" and of the suggestion that "he was more like one of today's mildly disreputable alternative-medicine men than like a 'real' doctor" (p. 429). While Foucault reads Freud in terms of his contribution to the creation of a scientific approach to storytelling, Malcolm suggests that Freud depicted himself as a "sort of irrepressible stumbler upon solid scientific fact" in order to disguise the fact that the "most salient feature [of psychoanalysis] was its erotic potential" (p. 432).

Write an essay exploring Malcolm's suggestion that Freud was an amateurish bungler whose work had little to do with "solid scientific fact" (p. 432). Explore her proposal that he shared much in common with the figure of the governess. Consider Malcolm's suggestion that "A Fragment of an Analysis of a Case of Hysteria" reveals Freud's effort to define psychoanalysis as a "severely depersonalized" science even as it reveals that his interests involved a high level of "privacy, intimacy, and intensity" (p. 432). In what ways does "A Fragment of an Analysis of a Case of Hysteria" demonstrate that Freud was aware that he would never be taken seriously if he did not downplay the eroticism and seduction that were a necessary part of his work? Use Malcolm's ideas to explore how Freud frames "A Fragment of an Analysis of a Case of Hysteria" in terms of tensions between the cold, hard facts of objective science and the "polymorphous," anecdotal evidence of "novelistic plots" and "the exotic inner world" of subjective consciousness (p. 434).

3. Malcolm and Steedman provide different ways of rethinking what Freud does in "A Fragment of an Analysis of a Case of Hysteria." Each of them gives us a way of revising our understanding of the relationship between Freud and Dora. Write an essay in which you use Malcolm's and Steedman's essays to analyze this relationship. Draw on specific moments from "A Fragment of an Analysis of a Case of Hysteria" to clarify how you see Dora's relationship with Freud, and use specific quotations from Malcolm and Steedman to illustrate how they understand Freud's relationship with Dora. You don't need to insist on one particular reading of the interaction between Freud and Dora; rather you should explore the Dora case history by thinking about what is to be gained and what is lost by framing the relationship between Dora and Freud in particular ways, such as doctor and patient, master figure and maidservant, career-building scientist and object of value/exchange, heterosexual/heterosexist man and sexually ambivalent girl/woman, interpreter of stories and teller of stories.

EXTENDING YOUR WORK

Ideas for Research

1. Find another case history to compare with "A Fragment of an Analysis of a Case of Hysteria." You might find another case history by Freud; the best place to look is *The Standard Edition of the Complete Psychological Works of Sigmund Freud,* published by the Hogarth Press. Or you might look to other psychologists, such as Jean-Martin Charcot, Pierre Janet, Ernest Jones, Carl Jung, Melanie Klein, R. D. Laing, Otto Rank, or Oliver Sacks.

Once you have located and read this second case study, write a comparative analysis of the methods of presentation and interpretation used by each writer. As you compare the two studies, note differences in histoᵣical context: What differences can be explained by differences in the state of psychoanalysis or its forerunners? If the case study precedes the Dora case, what might Freud have learned from it? If the case study was conducted after the Dora case was published, what might the writer have learned from Freud? Where do you see deliberate changes in method? What relationship do you see between the doctor/writer and the patient? Which parts of the patient's story does each writer focus on? What are the sources of healing or suffering in each case? How credible, fanciful, or wrong are each writer's diagnoses, interpretations, and conclusions?

You might choose to work with a different kind of storytelling than that adopted by Freud. Taking a cue from Carolyn Steedman, you might begin with a nineteenth-century "sociological and literary account of nineteenth-century girlhood" — Mayhew and Thackeray would certainly work. An alternative would be to locate a dream narrative from a non-European culture — you might explore how this narrative functions in its cultural context and compare this function with Freud's method for interpreting the dream of a hysteric.

2. Early in "The Clinical Picture" Freud remarks that "it follows from the nature of the facts which form the material of psycho-analysis that we are obliged to pay as much attention in our case histories to the purely human and social circumstances of our patients as to the somatic data and the symptoms of the disorder" (p. 317). In the next sentence Freud writes, "Above all, our interest will be directed towards their family circumstances." That Dora's "human and social circumstances" involved much more than her immediate family is demonstrated by the fact that only twenty years later Hitler used his experience in Vienna to produce *Mein Kampf,* a document instrumental in the Nazi persecution and attempted genocide of the Jewish people and their intellectual and cultural traditions.

Research what it might have been like to be a Jewish girl living in Vienna in 1900. What kinds of social and cultural pressures might Dora have felt that Freud does not take into account? What kinds of sources give us a sense of "human and social" conditions in Vienna in 1885–1905 (newspapers, journals, magazines, books written during the period, books written since 1945, biographies, political histories, feminist accounts)? Which sources specifically discuss young women?

3. Use Ernest Jones's summary of early responses to the publication of the Dora case history (p. 369) as a jumping-off point for exploring immediate reactions to Freud. Begin by looking up the writers and reviewers referred to in Jones's essay, then expand your research to include English and American writers who reviewed or otherwise responded to Freud's work in the years from the publication of "A Fragment of an Analysis of a Case of Hysteria" in 1905 to his death in 1939. Note that English translations of Freud's work often appeared a number of years after their initial publication in German.

4. Explore sites on the World Wide Web that address hysteria, psychoanalysis, and repression. What is the present status of the "talking cure"? From what you can gather, what happened to "hysteria" during the twentieth century? One way to explore the contemporary status of hysteria is to search for uses of the word on Web sites and in the indexes of recently published books of psychology. You might do similar work with the words *repression* and *psychoanalysis:* How are these words used? In what ways do they function in the professional world of psychology? How do contemporary scholars of psychology discuss "repression" and "psychoanalysis"? How central does Freud seem in these discussions? In what ways do Web sites that provide information about psychoanalysis and repression seem indebted to Freud?

5. Use Janet Malcolm's essay as a way to begin an investigation of the current status of Freudian psychoanalysis. Working with sites on the World Wide Web and with library books and articles (you might begin with *In Dora's Case: Freud—Hysteria—Feminism* and Malcolm's *The Purloined Clinic*), assess the accuracy of Malcolm's argument that "the chief subject of the psychoanalytic dialogue is not the patient's repressed memories but the analyst's vacation" (p. 421). How typical is Malcolm's perspective on psychoanalysis? How many writers actively devote time to attacks on Freud and his work? What kinds of things do they attack him for?

6. Search the library and the World Wide Web for "sociological and literary accounts of nineteenth-century girlhood" (p. 408). Once you have located at least two such accounts, use them to write an essay testing Steedman's thesis about how personal histories are transformed into the history of social groups. How do the accounts you located on the Web use their respective subjects for "the construction and writing of history" (p. 409)?

7. Foucault lived a relatively short but highly productive life. When he died in October 1984 at the age of fifty-eight, he was regarded as one of the most important thinkers of his day. But despite his persistence in uncovering and analyzing the structures of thought that shape individual lives, Foucault's own life was mysterious. During the period between 1966 and 1984, after he achieved national and international fame with the publication of *The Order of Things,* Foucault gave numerous interviews for television, radio, newspapers, and journals. But he rarely revealed details about his private life and was disdainful of biography. One result of Foucault's evasiveness about himself is that his personal life has become a matter of contention among scholars, teachers, and critics.

Research Foucault's biography, doing what you can to construct a narrative of his life in the years between 1966 and 1984. While you might pay attention to details about his private life, you should also attend to his intellectual life: How did his ideas evolve during his years as a world-renowned thinker and how might these ideas be connected with what one biographer calls "the lives of Michel Foucault"?

Begin by researching sites on the World Wide Web that provide information about Foucault and his work (the Web site for *Cultural Conversations* includes a list of biographical books and essays about Foucault). What did Foucault do during the last eighteen years of his life? How did he earn money? Who were his acquaintances? Where did he live? How was his research connected with his life? What sorts of things were said about Foucault in the media while he was alive? What did obituaries say about him? What is his reputation *now*? What is he famous for? Who and what is he associated with? How do scholars use the word *Foucaultian*?

8. Use the World Wide Web and other library resources to locate at least one of the models of development that Gilligan's work calls into question and at least one model of development that is somehow influenced by Gilligan. The most obvious place to look for "male-centered" theories of development is Lawrence Kohlberg. But you might also use Gilligan's list of works cited in "Woman's Place in Man's Life Cycle" to locate specific texts that she refers to or other texts by the writers she directly refutes. Searching for writers influenced by Gilligan will be somewhat more difficult, but you might begin by finding a Gilligan text from the 1990s. In most cases these later texts are collaborative and the other editors are a good place to seek Gilligan's influence. You might also search the World Wide Web and library shelves for books published after 1982 that cite *In a Different Voice*.

Once you have located at least one model of psychological development that Gilligan refutes and at least one that is influenced by her, write an essay assessing the impact of Gilligan's work on contemporary understandings of female development.

Ideas for Working across Chapters

1. Consider Freud's "A Fragment of an Analysis of a Case of Hysteria" in light of the ways in which historical narratives function in Chapter 6, "The Frontier: How Do We Imagine the West?" For example, Annette Kolodny exposes the ways in which Frederick Jackson Turner's grand narrative of frontier history runs counter to feminist interests. How does Freud's way of telling the story of Dora compare with Turner's way of narrating the history of the West? How does each of them explain away the fragmented, incomplete facts that they see before them? How does Freud's development of a theory of hysteria in response to a specific case study compare with Turner's development of a theory of American history in response to the study of local history? To what extent does each of these writers go too far in drawing general conclusions from specific events?

2. What happens to Freud's persona when you examine "A Fragment of an Analysis of a Case of Hysteria" in terms of Virginia Woolf's *A Room of One's Own*? In what ways does Freud's work with the case study help you think about the question "Is one born a woman?" What does Freud accomplish, fail

to accomplish, or put in the way of Dora's movement toward a position of economic and social independence? How does Freud contribute to or hinder the development of ways of understanding that promise to overcome what Woolf calls "contrary instincts" (p. 34)? In other words, how does Freud's work with Dora fit in with what Woolf says about the dual pressure women feel as they attempt to reconcile their desires with their possibilities? In what ways is Freud hampered by his inability to see beyond a "manly" paradigm? And how does he facilitate Dora's move toward the kind of educated independence that Woolf, Perkins, and others in Chapter 1 speak of? In what ways does Freud's emphasis on "reason" fit with the work of Woolf and the other writers in Chapter 1?

CHAPTER 5

Nonviolence

A Weapon of Peace?

Nonviolent—so-called passive—resistance to social and political oppression has a history as old as humanity. From ancient Buddhist teachings and the biblical prophet Isaiah's exhortation to "beat swords into ploughshares" to Mahatma Gandhi's *satyagraha* ("truth-force" or "soul-force") and the career of Dr. Martin Luther King Jr., the nonviolent alternative to the armed resolution of conflict has always been available—at least in the view of its advocates. Whether as a pragmatic political strategy or as a sacred way of life, nonviolence has appealed to leaders as diverse as Nelson Mandela, the Dalai Lama, and the late Salvadoran bishop Oscar Romero. Still, the practicality, realism, even the morality of nonviolence have often been disputed.

While proponents of nonviolence find the roots of their belief in the texts of most major religions, their critics also claim the precedent of religious tradition. Nonviolence has often been equated with cowardice, especially by people who perceive military service as a mark of honor and sacrifice. Moreover, even for admirers of people like Gandhi and Martin Luther King Jr., the realities of world history and human nature often seem to contradict the principle of nonviolent resolution of conflict.

The work of Mahatma Gandhi attempts, among other things, to address such objections—positing nonviolence as not only the best but the most innate and natural of human states. Contemporary writers Michael Nagler and Petra Kelly see themselves as continuing Gandhi's work, stressing the potential for a practical and highly organized manifestation of nonviolent action. Susan Griffin focuses instead on the roots of violence, particularly nuclear violence, connecting it to some of the very religious principles that inspired Gandhi's nonviolent worldview. Susanne Kappeler seeks a consensus on the meaning of the term *resistance* and its relationship to violence and nonviolence. As you read the essays in this chapter, consider how Gandhi makes the case for *satyagraha* and how the contemporary writers build on his ideas—both on the nature of violence and on the possibility of a nonviolent future.

TEXT

MAHATMA GANDHI

Born October 2, 1869, in the middle of the long reign of Britain's Queen Victoria—also "Empress of India"—young Mohandas Karamchand Gandhi did not at first seem destined to become India's liberator from British rule. A member of the Vaisya, or merchant caste, and son of a prominent regional politician, Gandhi spent most of his early years becoming educated and enjoying a domestic life (he was married at age thirteen). It was only as a young Westernized law student in London, away from his country and family, that Gandhi first seriously read the text that would bring him closer to his "Indianness"—the Bhagavad Gita. His reading of the Gita planted the seeds for a lifetime commitment to physical renunciation and simplicity—including vegetarianism and, eventually, celibacy.

Gandhi is renowned not only as the "Father of India"—and founder of the home rule movement that freed that country from British control—but also as the originator of the modern nonviolence or passive resistance movement. Gandhi's writings inspired American civil rights leaders such as Martin Luther King Jr.; South Africa's Nelson Mandela; Czechoslovakia's Václav Havel, leader of that country's "Velvet Revolution"; and countless workers for peace and justice around the world. At the same time, Gandhi's ideas were a fusion of the many great religious and philosophical works that inspired him—including the Hindu Bhagavad Gita, Jesus' Sermon on the Mount from the Christian Gospels, elements of the Quran, and the religious writings of Count Leo Tolstoy and others. Gandhi blended all of these concepts into satyagraha *("soul-force"), a way of life combining truth, love, and firmness with an insistence on physical and spiritual courage and sacrifice. Integral to* satyagraha *was the theory and practice of* ahimsa *("no harming"), or nonviolence. That Gandhi came to embody these principles in his own life is evident in the meaning of the name by which he is best known— "Mahatma," or "Great Soul."*

Gandhi's commitment to human rights activism began in South Africa, where he lived and practiced law intermittently from 1893 to 1914. In 1894, seeing the plight of his fellow Indian immigrants, mostly laborers, he founded the Natal Indian Congress to agitate for Indian rights. Gandhi fasted and staged nonviolent protests against the Anti-Asian Laws in South Africa, which was then under British rule. He was imprisoned twice for his activities and had the support of thousands of Indians. Still, throughout these years in South Africa he remained loyal to the British Empire—raising ambulance corps for the British during the Boer War (1899–1901), the Zulu rebellion (1906), and World War I (1914–1918), and almost always sending polite letters to government officials informing them of any of his planned protests.

After returning home to India in 1914, Gandhi would spend the rest of his life working for Indian swaraj, *or "home rule." He sought a humane Indian nation, one that reconciled all of the land's many castes and religious factions, especially Muslims and Hindus. He even fasted and agitated on behalf of India's so-called "untouchables," people outside the country's ancient and hierarchical caste system and perceived by most Indians of the time as socially inferior and "unclean." To the "untouchables" he gave the name* harijan, *or "children of God."*

Gandhi became convinced over time that to be truly free, India must free it-self—always nonviolently—from the British Empire. In 1919 Gandhi became a leader and founder of the Indian National Congress political party and in 1920 began a noncooperation campaign against the British. As part of his work toward home rule, Gandhi wanted his fellow Indians to see themselves as self-sufficient, not dependent on the British Empire for the necessities of life. He encouraged Indians to spin their own cotton rather than depend on British imports—even taking the spinning wheel as his personal symbol and the symbol of satyagraha *and the home rule movement—and urged his people to boycott British goods in protest of the empire's policies. He was imprisoned from 1922 to 1924, and again in 1930 after leading three thousand Indians on a historic march to the sea in protest of the British salt tax. Gandhi's picking up a handful of sea salt at the beach at Dandi is still seen as a pivotal act of defiance and self-determination, and the so-called Salt March stands as a milestone in the home rule movement.*

It would be another seventeen years before India won the independence Gandhi worked so long to realize; but with the establishment of the Muslim state of Pakistan and the accompanying violence between Hindus and Muslims, Gandhi found his longed-for achievement tainted with blood. While India was free, it was not—as he had hoped—united. Yet Gandhi himself was still loved and admired. Upon his assassination by a religious fanatic on January 30, 1948, the "Great Soul" was mourned throughout India and Pakistan, by all cultures and castes of people. As India's first prime minister, Jawaharlal Nehru, proclaimed over All-India Radio: "The light has gone out of our lives and there is darkness everywhere . . . the father of our nation is no more." Today, the image of the spinning wheel, Gandhi's personal symbol and that of the movement he created, can be found on the national flag of India.

The following essays were originally published between 1914 and 1946 and hand-sold as individual pamphlets, easy to produce and occasioned by the political issues and needs of the moment. In these pamphlets, Gandhi sets out to explain the concepts of ahimsa *and* satyagraha *and sometimes to defend and reexplain them to his often critical and impatient correspondents. His tone is often quite personal and genial, perhaps more so than in most of the historical texts in this book. How might Gandhi's fatherly tone and persona have contributed to the success of his cause? Consider the ways in which the immediacy and the "home-grown" nature of the pamphlet form might have affected the course of Gandhi's work, the advancement of his cause.*

The Theory and Practice of Passive Resistance

I shall be at least far away from Phoenix,* if not actually in the Motherland, when this Commemoration Issue is published. I would, however, leave behind me my innermost thoughts upon that which has made

---

Phoenix: A reference to Phoenix farm, a settlement founded in 1910 outside Durban, South Africa. It was modeled on Tolstoy's idea that communities should be based on simplicity and self-sufficiency. Gandhi founded Tolstoy Farms, or "ashrams," throughout South Africa and India.

this special issue necessary. Without Passive Resistance, there would have been no richly illustrated and important special issue of *Indian Opinion,** which has, for the last eleven years, in an unpretentious and humble manner, endeavoured to serve my countrymen and South Africa, a period covering the most critical stage that they will perhaps ever have to pass through. It marks the rise and growth of Passive Resistance, which has attracted world-wide attention. The term does not fit the activity of the Indian community during the past eight years. Its equivalent in the vernacular, rendered into English, means Truth-Force. I think Tolstoy called it also Soul-Force or Love-Force, and so it is. Carried out to its utmost limit, this force is independent of pecuniary or other material assistance; certainly, even in its elementary form, of physical force or violence. Indeed, violence is the negation of this great spiritual force, which can only be cultivated or wielded by those who will entirely eschew violence. It is a force that may be used by individuals as well as by communities. It may be used as well in political as in domestic affairs. Its universal applicability is a demonstration of its performance and invincibility. It can be used alike by men, women, and children. It is totally untrue to say that it is a force to be used only by the weak so long as they are not capable of meeting violence by violence. This superstition arises from the incompleteness of the English expression. It is impossible for those who consider themselves to be weak to apply this force. Only those who realise that there is something in man which is superior to the brute nature in him, and that the latter always yields to it, can effectively be Passive Resisters. This force is to violence and, therefore, to all tyranny, all injustice, what light is to darkness. In politics, its use is based upon the immutable maxim that government of the people is possible only so long as they consent either consciously or unconsciously to be governed. We did not consent to be governed by the Asiatic Act of 1907* of the Transvaal, and it had to go before this mighty force. Two courses were open to us—to use violence when we were called upon to submit to the Act, or to suffer the penalties prescribed under the Act, and thus to draw out and exhibit the force of the soul within us for a period long enough to appeal to the sympathetic chord in the governors or the law-makers. We have taken long to achieve what we set about striving for. That was because our Passive Resistance was not of the most complete type. All Passive Resisters do not understand the full value of the force, nor have we men who always from conviction refrain from violence. The use of this force requires the adoption of poverty, in the sense that we must be indifferent whether we have the wherewithal to

---

Indian Opinion: A newspaper founded by Gandhi in Durban to communicate with the Indian population of South Africa.
Asiatic Act of 1907: A law requiring all Indians and Chinese in the Transvaal region of South Africa to carry certificates of registration at all times. Failure to carry the identification papers resulted in fines and imprisonment and could lead to deportation. Gandhi organized protests against the law.

feed or clothe ourselves. During the past struggle, all Passive Resisters, if any at all, were not prepared to go that length. Some again were only Passive Resisters so-called. They came without any conviction, often with mixed motives, less often with impure motives. Some even, whilst engaged in the struggle, would gladly have resorted to violence but for most vigilant supervision. Thus it was that the struggle became prolonged; for the exercise of the purest soul-force, in its perfect form, brings about instantaneous relief. For this exercise, prolonged training of the individual soul is an absolute necessity, so that a perfect Passive Resister has to be almost, if not entirely, a perfect man. We cannot all suddenly become such men, but, if my proposition is correct—as I know it to be correct—the greater the spirit of Passive Resistance in us, the better men we will become. Its use, therefore, is, I think, indisputable, and it is a force which, if it became universal, would revolutionise social ideals and do away with despotisms and the ever-growing militarism under which the nations of the West are groaning and are being almost crushed to death, and which fairly promises to overwhelm even the nations of the East. If the past struggle has produced even a few Indians who would dedicate themselves to the task of becoming Passive Resisters as nearly perfect as possible, they would not only have served themselves in the truest sense of the term, they would also have served humanity at large. Thus viewed, Passive Resistance is the noblest and the best education. It should come, not after the ordinary education in letters of children, but it should precede it. It will not be denied that a child, before it begins to write its alphabet and to gain worldly knowledge, should know what the soul is, what truth is, what love is, what powers are latent in the soul. It should be an essential of real education that a child should learn that, in the struggle of life, it can easily conquer hate by love, untruth by truth, violence by self-suffering. It was because I felt the force of this truth, that, during the latter part of the struggle, I endeavoured, as much as I could, to train the children at Tolstoy Farm and then at Phoenix along these lines, and one of the reasons for my departure to India is still further to realise, as I already do in part, my own imperfection as a Passive Resister, and then to try to perfect myself, for I believe that it is in India that the nearest approach to perfection is most possible.

Meaning of Satyagraha

In the first leaflet, I hinted that I would consider the meaning of satyagraha in a later number of this series. I feel that the time has now arrived to examine the meaning of satyagraha. The word was newly coined some years ago, but the principle which it denotes is as ancient as time. This is the literal meaning of satyagraha—insistence on truth, and force derivable from such insistence. In the present movement, we are making use of satyagraha as a force: that is to say, in order to cure the evil in the shape of the

Rowlatt legislation,* we have been making use of the force generated by satyagraha, that is, insistence on truth. One of the axioms of religion is, there is no religion other than truth. Another is, religion is love. And as there can be only one religion, it follows that truth is love and love is truth. We shall find too, on further reflection, that conduct based on truth is impossible without love. Truth-force then is love-force. We cannot remedy evil by harbouring ill-will against the evil-doer. This is not difficult of comprehension. It is easy enough to understand. In thousands of our acts, the propelling power is truth or love. The relations between father and son, husband and wife, indeed our family relations are largely guided by truth or love. And we therefore consciously or unconsciously apply satyagraha in regulating these relations.

If we were to cast a retrospective glance over our past life, we would find that out of a thousand of our acts affecting our families, in nine hundred and ninety-nine we were dominated by truth; that in our deeds, it is not right to say we generally resort to untruth or ill-will. It is only where a conflict of interests arises, that there arise the progeny of untruth, viz., anger, ill-will, etc., and then we see nothing but poison in our midst. A little hard thinking will show us that the standard that we apply to the regulation of domestic relations is the standard that should be applied to regulate the relations between rulers and the ruled, and between man and man. Those men and women who do not recognize the domestic tie are considered to be very like brutes are barbarous, even though in form they have the human body. They have never known the law of satyagraha. Those who recognize the domestic tie and its obligations have to a certain extent gone beyond that brute stage. But if challenged, they would say "what do we care though the whole universe may perish so long as we guard the family interest?" The measure of their satyagraha, therefore, is less than that of a drop in the ocean.

When men and women have gone a stage further, they would extend the law of love, i.e., satyagraha, from the family to the village. A still further stage away from the brute life is reached when the law of satyagraha is applied to provincial life, and the people inhabiting a province regulate their relations by love rather than by hatred. And when as in Hindustan we recognize the law of satyagraha as a binding force even between province and province and the millions of Hindustan treat one another as brothers and sisters, we have advanced a stage further still from the brute nature.

In modern times, in no part of the earth have people gone beyond the nation stage in the application of satyagraha. In reality, however, there need be no reason for the clashing of interest between nation and nation, thus arresting the operation of the great law. If we were not in the habit generally of giving no thought to our daily conduct, if we did not accept

---

Rowlatt legislation: The Rowlatt Act was passed by the British viceroy (the King's representative) in Delhi, India, in 1919. It imposed extremely severe punishments for participation in political activities against the government.

local custom and habit as matters of course, as we accept the current coin, we would immediately perceive that to the extent that we bear ill-will towards other nations or at all show disregard for life, to that extent we disregard the law of satyagraha or love, and to that extent we are still not free from the brute nature. But there is no religion apart from that which enables us entirely to rid ourselves of the brute nature. All religious sects and divisions, all churches and temples, are useful only so long as they serve as a means towards enabling us to recognize the universality of satyagraha. In India we have been trained from ages past in this teaching and hence it is that we are taught to consider the whole universe as one family. I do wish to submit as a matter of experience that it is not only possible to live the full national life, by rendering obedience to the law of satyagraha, but that the fullness of national life is impossible without satyagraha, i.e., without a life of true religion. That nation which wars against another has to an extent disregarded the great law of life. I shall never abandon the faith I have that India is capable of delivering this truth to the whole world, and I wish that all Indians, men and women, whether they are Hindus or Mohamedans, Parsis, Christians or Jews will share with me this unquenchable faith.

Religion of Nonviolence

A correspondent writes;

> In the *Harijanbandhu** of the 5th May you have written that your nonviolence contemplates destruction of animals dangerous to mankind, such as leopards, wolves, snakes, scorpions etc.
>
> You do not believe in giving food to dogs etc. Several other people besides the Gujaratis look upon the feeding of dogs as a meritorious act. Such a belief may not be justifiable in times of food shortage like the present. Yet we must remember that these animals can be very useful to man. One can feed them and take work out of them.
>
> You had put 27 questions to Sri Raichandbhai from Durban. One of these questions was: "What should a seeker do when a snake attacks him?" His answer was: "He should not kill the snake and, if it bites, he should let it do so." How is it that you speak differently now?

I have written a lot on this subject in the past. At that time the topic was the killing of rabid dogs. There was much discussion on the subject but all that seems to have been forgotten.

Harijanbandhu: A newspaper founded by Gandhi to discuss issues related to the so-called untouchable caste in India. While the traditional class system shunned this caste, relegating them to the most menial jobs, Gandhi called them *harijan,* or "children of God."

My nonviolence is not merely kindness to all living creatures. The emphasis laid on the sacredness of sub-human life in Jainism* is understandable. But that can never mean that one is to be kind to this life in preference to human life. While writing about the sacredness of such life I take it that the sacredness of human life has been taken for granted. The former has been overemphasized. And, while putting it into practice, the idea has undergone distortion. For instance, there are many who derive complete satisfaction in feeding ants. It would appear that the theory has become a wooden, lifeless dogma. Hypocrisy and distortion are passing current under the name of religion.

Ahimsa is the highest ideal. It is meant for the brave, never for the cowardly. To benefit by others' killing and delude oneself into the belief that one is being very religious and nonviolent, is sheer self-deception.

A so-called votary of nonviolence will not stay in a village which is visited by a leopard every day. He will run away and, when someone has killed the leopard, will return to take charge of his hearth and home. This is not nonviolence. This is a coward's violence. The man who has killed the leopard has at least given proof of some bravery. The man who takes advantage of the killing is a coward. He can never expect to know true nonviolence.

In life it is impossible to eschew violence completely. The question arises, where is one to draw the line? The line cannot be the same for everyone. Although essentially the principle is the same yet everyone applies it in his or her own way. What is one man's food can be another's poison. Meat-eating is a sin for me. Yet, for another person, who has always lived on meat and never seen anything wrong in it, to give it up simply in order to copy me will be a sin.

If I wish to be an agriculturist and stay in the jungle, I will have to use the minimum unavoidable violence in order to protect my fields. I will have to kill monkeys, birds and insects which eat up my crops. If I do not wish to do so myself, I will have to engage someone to do it for me. There is not much difference between the two. To allow crops to be eaten up by animals in the name of ahimsa while there is a famine in the land is certainly a sin. Evil and good are relative terms. What is good under certain conditions can become an evil or a sin under a different set of conditions.

Man is not to drown himself in the well of the shastras* but he is to dive in their broad ocean and bring out pearls. At every step he has to use his discrimination as to what is ahimsa and what is himsa. In this there is

---

Jainism: One of the three major religions of India, along with Hinduism and Buddhism. From the term *Jina* (victor or conqueror), Jainism involves the progression of the individual through increasingly refined stages of consciousness. The ultimate goal is the renunciation of self-interest and worldly concerns.

shastras: A śāstra or shastra is an instructional text book that contains laws and rules. In the Hindu tradition they address specific subjects including logic, grammar, and other scholarly subjects. In the Buddhist tradition they are strongly didactic philosophical interpretations of the sutras, short statements of truth that require lengthy explication.

no room for shame or cowardice. The poet has said that the road leading up to God is for the brave, never for the cowardly.

Finally, Raichandbhai's advice to me was that if I had courage, if I wanted to see God face to face, I should let myself be bitten by a snake instead of killing it. I have never killed a snake before or after receiving that letter. That is no matter of credit for me. My ideal is to be able to play with snakes and scorpions fearlessly. But it is merely a wish so far. Whether and when it will be realized I do not know. Everywhere I have let my people kill both. I could have prevented them if I had wished. But how could I? I did not have the courage to take them up with my own hands and teach my companions a lesson in fearlessness. I am ashamed that I could not do so. But my shame could not benefit them or me.

If Ramanama favours me I might still attain that courage some day. In the meantime, I consider it my duty to act as I have stated above. Religion is a thing to be lived. It is not mere sophistry.

The Law of Suffering

No country has ever risen without being purified through the fire of suffering. Mother suffers so that her child may live. The condition of wheat-growing is that the seed grain should perish. Life comes out of Death. Will India rise out of her slavery without fulfilling this eternal law of purification through suffering?

If my advisers are right, evidently India will realize her destiny without travail. For their chief concern is that the events of April, 1919* should not be repeated. They fear non-cooperation because it would involve the sufferings of many. If Hampden* had argued thus he would not have withheld payment of ship-money, nor would Wat Tyler* have raised the standard of revolt. English and French histories are replete with instances of men continuing their pursuit of the right irrespective of the amount of suffering involved. The actors did not stop to think whether ignorant people would not have involuntarily to suffer. Why should we expect to write our history differently? It is possible for us, if we would, to learn from the mistakes of our predecessors to do better, but it is impossible to do away with the law of suffering which is the one indispensable condition of our being. The way to do better is to avoid, if we can, violence from our

---

events of April, 1919: Protests against the Rowlatt Acts that brought Gandhi international fame. He organized acts of noncooperation on a national scale that involved a total withdrawal from the British structure of government in India.
Hampden: John Hampden (1594–1643), a Puritan statesman who played a major role in the English Civil War. He was a member of the Long Parliament installed by Oliver Cromwell after the overthrow of Charles I. Hampden is famous for his refusal to pay the 1635 ship tax levied to pay for the expansion of the Royal Navy.
Wat Tyler: Tyler (died 1381) was an English revolutionary who led the Peasant's Revolt in 1381. This was the first popular rebellion in English history.

side and thus quicken the rate of progress and to introduce greater purity in the methods of suffering. We can, if we will, refrain, in our impatience, from bending the wrongdoer to our will by physical force as Sinn Feiners* are doing today, or from coercing our neighbours to follow our methods as was done last year by some of us in bringing about hartal.* Progress is to be measured by the amount of suffering undergone by the sufferer. The purer the suffering, the greater is the progress. Hence did the sacrifice of Jesus suffice to free a sorrowing world. In his onward march he did not count the cost of suffering entailed upon his neighbours, whether it was undergone by them voluntarily or otherwise. Thus did the sufferings of a Harishchandra* suffice to re-establish the kingdom of truth. He must have known that his subjects would suffer involuntarily by his abdication. He did not mind because he could not do otherwise than follow truth.

I have already stated that I do not deplore the massacre of Jallianwala Bagh* so much as I deplore the murders of Englishmen and destruction of property by ourselves. The frightfulness at Amritsar* drew away public attention from the greater though slower frightfulness at Lahore* where an attempt was made to emasculate the inhabitants by slow process. But before we rise higher we shall have to undergo such processes many times more till they teach us to take up suffering voluntarily and to find joy in it. I am convinced that the Lahorians never deserved the cruel insults that they were subjected to; they never hurt a single Englishman; they never destroyed any property. But a wilful ruler was determined to crush the spirit of a people just trying to throw off his chafing yoke. And if I am told that all this was due to my preaching satyagraha, my answer is that I would preach satyagraha all the more forcibly for that, so long as I have breath left in me, and tell the people that next time they would answer O'Dwyerean* insolence not by opening shops by reason of threats of forcible sales but by allowing the tyrant to do his worst and let him sell their all but their unconquerable souls. Sages of old mortified the flesh so that the spirit within might be set free, so that their

---

Sinn Feiners: Members of a nationalist-republican political organization in Ireland formed in 1900 by Arthur Griffith to fight British rule in Ireland. The name Sinn Fein translates into English as "Ourselves Alone."

hartal: A general strike against the government.

Harishchandra: A royal and virtuous king who sacrificed his country, his worldly possessions, his family, and himself trying to satisfy the god Visvamitra. The gods took pity on him and raised him and his subjects to heaven.

Jallianwala Bagh: The public square where 379 Indian peasants were killed in the Amritsar massacre.

Amritsar: A city in Northern India. In 1919 a gathering of six thousand peasants at a festival in Amritsar was perceived by the British General Reginald Dyer as a challenge to his authority. Having passed a law banning public meetings following a hartal, he responded by sending troops to fire on the crowd. Three hundred seventy-nine people died; twelve hundred were wounded.

Lahore: A city with three million inhabitants in Northeast Pakistan. Capital of the Punjab, the city is near the River Ravi and close to the border with India.

O'Dwyerean: Presumably a reference to General Dyer.

trained bodies might be proof against any injury that might be inflicted on them by tyrants seeking to impose their will on them. And if India wishes to revive her ancient wisdom and to avoid the errors of Europe, if India wishes to see the Kingdom of God established on earth instead of that of Satan which has enveloped Europe, then I would urge her sons and daughters not to be deceived by fine phrases, the terrible subtleties that hedge us in, the fears of suffering that India may have to undergo, but to see what is happening today in Europe and from it understand that we *must* go through the suffering even as Europe has gone through, but not the process of making others suffer. Germany wanted to dominate Europe and the Allies wanted to do likewise by crushing Germany. Europe is no better for Germany's fall. The Allies have proved themselves to be just as deceitful, cruel, greedy and selfish as Germany was or would have been. Germany would have avoided the sanctimonious humbug that one sees associated with the many dealings of the Allies.

The miscalculation that I deplored last year was not in connection with the sufferings imposed upon the people, but about the mistakes made by them and violence done by them owing to their not having sufficiently understood the message of satyagraha. What then is the meaning of non-cooperation in terms of the Law of Suffering? We must voluntarily put up with the losses and inconveniences that arise from having to withdraw our support from a Government that is ruling against our will. Possession of power and riches is a crime under an unjust government; poverty in that case is a virtue, says Thoreau. It may be that in the transition state we may make mistakes; there may be avoidable suffering. These things are preferable to national emasculation.

We must refuse to wait for the wrong to be righted till the wrongdoer has been roused to a sense of his inequity. We must not, for fear of ourselves or others having to suffer, remain participators in it. But we must combat the wrong by ceasing to assist the wrongdoer directly or indirectly.

If a father does an injustice, it is the duty of his children to leave the parental roof. If the head master of a school conducts his institution on an immoral basis, the pupils must leave the school. If the chairman of a corporation is corrupt, the members thereof must wash their hands clean of his corruption by withdrawing from it; even so, if a government does a grave injustice, the subject must withdraw cooperation wholly or partially, sufficiently to wean the ruler from his wickedness. In each case conceived by me there is an element of suffering whether mental or physical. Without such suffering it is not possible to attain freedom.

The Doctrine of the Sword I

In this age of the rule of brute force, it is almost impossible for anyone to believe that anyone else could possibly reject the law of the final supremacy of brute force. And so I receive anonymous letters advising me that I must not interfere with the progress of non-cooperation even though popular violence may break out. Others come to me and assuming that secretly I must be plotting violence, inquire when the happy moment for declaring open violence will arrive. They assure me that the English will never yield to anything but violence, secret or open. Yet others, I am informed, believe that I am the most rascally person living in India because I never give out my real intention and that they have not a shadow of a doubt that I believe in violence just as much as most people do.

Such being the hold that the doctrine of the sword has on the majority of mankind, and as success of non-cooperation depends principally on absence of violence during its pendancy and as my views in this matter affect the conduct of a large number of people, I am anxious to state them as clearly as possible.

I do believe that where there is only a choice between cowardice and violence I would advise violence. Thus when my eldest son asked me what he should have done, had he been present when I was almost fatally assaulted in 1908, whether he should have run away and seen me killed or whether he should have used his physical force which he could and wanted to use, and defended me, I told him that it was his duty to defend me even by using violence. Hence it was that I took part in the Boer War [1899–1901], the so-called Zulu rebellion and the late War. Hence also do I advocate training in arms for those who believe in the method of violence. I would rather have India resort to arms in order to defend her honour than that she should in a cowardly manner become or remain a helpless witness to her own dishonour.

But I believe that nonviolence is infinitely superior to violence, forgiveness is more manly than punishment. "Forgiveness adorns a soldier." But abstinence is forgiveness only when there is the power to punish; it is meaningless when it pretends to proceed from a helpless creature. A mouse hardly forgives a cat when it allows itself to be torn to pieces by her. I, therefore, appreciate the sentiment of those who cry out for the condign punishment of General Dyer and his ilk. They would tear him to pieces if they could. But I do not believe India to be helpless. I do not believe myself to be a helpless creature. Only I want to use India's and my strength for a better purpose.

Let me not be misunderstood. Strength does not come from physical capacity. It comes from an indomitable will. An average Zulu is any day more than a match for an average Englishman in bodily capacity. But he flees from an English boy, because he fears the boy's revolver or those who will use it for him. He fears death and is nerveless in spite of his burly figure. We in India may in a moment realize that one hundred thousand Englishmen need not frighten three hundred million human beings. A definite forgiveness would therefore mean a definite recognition of our strength. With enlightened forgiveness must come a mighty wave of strength in us, which would make it impossible for a Dyer and a Frank Johnson to heap affront upon India's devoted head. It matters little to me that for the moment I do not drive my point home. We feel too downtrodden not to be angry and revengeful. But I must not refrain from saying that India can gain more by waiving the right of punishment. We have better work to do, a better mission to deliver to the world.

I am not a visionary. I claim to be a practical idealist. The religion of nonviolence is not meant merely for the rishis* and saints. It is meant for the common people as well. Nonviolence is the law of our species as violence is the law of the brute. The spirit lies dormant in the brute and he knows no law but that of physical might. The dignity of man requires obedience to a higher law — to the strength of the spirit.

I have therefore ventured to place before India the ancient law of self-sacrifice. For satyagraha and its off-shoots, non-cooperation and civil resistance, are nothing but new names for the law of suffering. The rishis who discovered the law of nonviolence in the midst of violence were greater geniuses than Newton. They were themselves greater warriors than Wellington. Having themselves known the use of arms, they realized their uselessness and taught a weary world that its salvation lay not through violence but through nonviolence.

Nonviolence in its dynamic condition means conscious suffering. It does not mean meek submission to the will of the evil-doer, but it means the pitting of one's whole soul against the will of the tyrant. Working under this law of our being, it is possible for a single individual to defy the whole might of an unjust empire to save his honour, his religion, his soul and lay the foundation for that empire's fall or its regeneration.

And so I am not pleading for India to practise nonviolence because it is weak. I want her to practise nonviolence being conscious of her strength and power. No training in arms is required for realization of her strength. We seem to need it because we seem to think that we are but a lump of flesh. I want India to recognize that she has a soul that cannot perish and that can rise triumphant above every physical weakness and defy the physical combination of a whole world. What is the meaning of Rama, a mere human being, with his host of monkeys, pitting himself against the insolent strength of ten-headed Ravana surrounded in supposed safety by the raging waters on all sides of Lanka? Does it not mean the conquest of physical might by spiritual strength? However, being a practical man, I do not wait till India recognizes the practicability of the spiritual life in the political world. India considers herself to be powerless and paralysed before the machine-guns, the tanks and the aeroplanes of the English. And she takes up non-cooperation out of her weakness. It must still serve the same purpose, namely, bring her delivery from the crushing weight of British injustice if a sufficient number of people practise it.

I isolate this non-cooperation from Sinn Feinism, for it is so conceived as to be incapable of being offered side by side with violence. But I invite even

---

rishis: A Hindu term (*Ṛṣi*) for seers and inspired poets. It specifically refers to the seven rishis to whom the Vedas, or sacred scriptures, were revealed: they are regarded as the fathers of the human race and the source of all knowledge.

the school of violence to give this peaceful non-cooperation a trial. It will not fail through its inherent weakness. It may fail because of poverty of response. Then will be the time for real danger. The high souled men, who are unable to suffer national humiliation any longer, will want to vent their wrath. They will take to violence. So far as I know, they must perish without delivering themselves or their country from the wrong. If India takes up the doctrine of the sword, she may gain momentary victory. Then India will cease to be the pride of my heart. I am wedded to India because I owe my all to her. I believe absolutely that she has a mission for the world. She is not to copy Europe blindly. India's acceptance of the doctrine of the sword will be the hour of my trial. I hope I shall not be found wanting. My religion has no geographical limits. If I have a living faith in it, it will transcend my love for India herself. My life is dedicated to service of India through the religion of nonviolence which I believe to be the root of Hinduism.

Meanwhile I urge those who distrust me, not to disturb the even working of the struggle that has just commenced, by inciting to violence in the belief that I want violence. I detest secrecy as a sin. Let them give nonviolent non-cooperation a trial and they will find that I had no mental reservation whatsoever.

The Doctrine of the Sword II

I have no dearth of advisers. They send me letters, signed and unsigned and some visit me to proffer their advice in person. Some write to me to say that I am a coward, afraid of the sword, and, therefore, I shall achieve nothing in this world; that it is my fear which makes me prate about nonviolence without knowing what it means. Some others tell me that I have violence enough in my heart, that I approve of killing, but that I am such a "shrewd fellow" and so "cunning" that I do not let people know what I think and, though talking about nonviolence, at heart want to instigate violence. Besides these, there is another class of men who think that I am not a rogue but am only waiting for my opportunity and, when it comes, I shall advise people to use the sword. These people think that the time for this is ripe and that now I should wait no longer.

Ordinarily, it should not be necessary for me to occupy myself with answering the points these advisers make. Where is the harm, or what is there to be exercised about, if some people think me cunning? What right, besides, have I to take up the time of *Navajivan*'s readers with a defence of my saintliness or a rebuttal of the charge of being "cunning"? Certainly, I ought not to enter into any discussion of this matter with a view to defending myself, but I know that, my present position being what it is, the common people are eager to know my views and I know, further, that my actions proceed from my views. I think it necessary, for the sake of these, to clarify my position and so I take the liberty to place once again before readers my views on brute force.

Sword-force is brute force. Killing people requires no intelligence. We may, indeed, by misdirecting our intelligence employ it in the service of brute force but, though aided by intelligence, brute force remains brute force and the law of the sword remains the law of the beast. In the latter, the self is in a state of nescience and can have no knowledge of itself. That is why we know the animal world as enveloped in darkness. The activities of eating, drinking, sleeping, feeling afraid, etc., are common to man and beast. But man has the power of distinguishing between good and evil and can also know the self. One animal subdues another simply by its physical might. Its world is ruled by that law, but not so the human world. The law which is most in harmony with human nature is that of winning over others by the power of love — by soul-force. When, therefore, a man wins over an enemy through love, he simply follows the law of his nature. He has not become a god in doing so. Gods have no physical body. They behave sometimes like beasts and sometimes like men. There are white gods as also black gods. Man is, at times, seen acting like an animal. He is endowed with brute force as well, and so long as he has not developed awareness of his spiritual nature he remains an intelligent animal. Though human in body, instead of obeying the law of his kind he follows the law of the animal. This, however, should not be regarded as his true nature. I believe, therefore, that if we wake up to the consciousness of our true nature, we would, that very moment, renounce the law of the jungle.

But the sages saw that the passions of the beast had not died out in most persons, though they possessed human bodies. They recognized, therefore, that there was scope for the use of brute force even by human beings and showed under what circumstances it could be employed.

When a man submits to another through fear, he does not follow his nature but yields to brute force. He who has no desire to dominate others by brute force will not himself submit to such force either. Recognizing, therefore, that man who fears brute force has not attained self-knowledge at all, our Shastras allowed him the use of brute force while he remains in this state.

A Pathan* made a murderous attack on me in 1908. My eldest son was not present then. He possessed fairly good physical strength. I did not have the Pathan prosecuted since I held the same view then as I do now. I was educating my sons too in the ideas of forgiveness and love, and so at our very first meeting (after the assault), my son said to me: "I want to know what my duty would have been if I had been with you at the time. You have taught us that we may not strike back nor tamely submit to the other man. I understand this principle but I have not the strength to act upon it. I could not remain a silent spectator while you were being beaten to death. I would consider it my duty to protect you if you should be assaulted, but I could not do this by laying down my own life (instead of striking back). I must, therefore, either

Pathan: A member of an ethnic group found throughout Afghanistan and in what is now Pakistan.

protect you by attacking the man who would strike you, or be a passive witness to the attack on you, or run away." I told him: "It would be a sign of cowardice if you ran away or did nothing to protect me. If you could not protect me by taking the danger upon yourself, you should undoubtedly do so by attacking the other man. It is any day better to use brute force than to betray cowardice." I hold this view even now. It is better that India should arm itself and take the risk than that it should refuse to take up arms out of fear. It was for this reason that I had joined the Boer War and did my bit in helping the Government during the Zulu rebellion. It was for this same reason that, during the last War, I gave my help in England and in India, too. I engaged myself in recruiting work.

Forgiveness is the virtue of the brave. He alone who is strong to avenge a wrong knows how to love (and forgive). He alone who is capable of enjoying pleasures can qualify to be a brahmachary* by restraining his desires. There is no question of the mouse forgiving the cat. It will be evidence of India's soul-force only if it refuses to fight when it has the strength to do so.

It is necessary to understand what the phrase "strength to fight" means in this context. It does not mean only physical strength. Everyone who has courage in him can have the strength to fight, and everyone who has given up fear of death has such strength. I have seen sturdy Negroes cowering before white boys, because they were afraid of the white man's revolver. I have also seen weaklings holding out against robust persons. Thus, the day India gives up fear we shall be able to say that she has the strength to fight. It is not at all true to say that, to be able to fight, it is essential to acquire the ability to use arms; the moment, therefore, a man wakes up to the power of the soul, that very moment he comes to know the strength he has for fighting. That is why I believe that he is the true warrior who does not die killing but who has mastered the mantra of living by dying.

The sages who discovered the never-failing law of nonviolence were themselves great warriors. When they discovered the ignoble nature of armed strength and realized the true nature of man, they discerned the law of nonviolence pervading this world all full of violence. They then taught us that the *atman* can conquer the whole world, that the greatest danger to the *atman* comes from itself and that conquest over it brings us the strength to conquer the entire world.

But they did not think, nor have they affirmed or taught anywhere, that because they had discovered that law they alone could live according to it. On the contrary, they declared that even for a child the law is the same, and that it can act upon it too. It is not true that only sannyasis*

brahmachary: In the Hindu tradition a Brahmacarin is a religious seeker who has begun the pursuit of spiritual discipline and self-sacrifice. The related word *Brahmacharya* refers to chastity and is used in both Hinduism and Buddhism to refer to a central principle of the holy life.
sannyasis: In the Hindu tradition the sannyasis (also *Samnyasin*) are those who have renounced the world and live without possessions.

abide by it; all of us do so more or less, and a law which can be followed partially can be followed perfectly.

I have been striving to live according to this law. For many years past, I have been consciously trying to do so and have been exhorting India to do the same.

I believe myself to be an idealist and also a practical man. I do not think that a man can be said to have lived in accordance with this law only if he does so consciously and purposefully. Therefore, like a vaid* (his medicine), I plate it before all, whether or not they have faith in it. To prove that it is not necessary to have the higher knowledge to be able to recognize the importance of this law, I have joined hands with those who hold views contrary to mine. My friend Shaukat Ali seems to attach prime importance to violence, to believe that it is man's dharma* to kill his enemy. Consequently, he follows the law of nonviolence with hatred in his heart. He thinks non-cooperation is a weapon of the weak, and therefore, inferior to resistance by force. Even so, he has joined me because he has seen that except non-cooperation, there is no other effective method of upholding the honour of his faith.

I appeal even to those who have no faith in me to follow my friend Shaukat Ali. They need not believe in the purity of my motives, but must clearly recognize that there can be no violence simultaneously with non-cooperation. The greatest obstacle to the launching of all-out non-cooperation is the fear of violence breaking out. Those who are ready with arms or are eager to be so should also put them by while non-cooperation is going on.

To me, on the day when brute force gains ascendancy in India all distinction of East and West, of ancient and modern, will have disappeared. That day will be the day of my test. I take pride in looking upon India as my country because I believe that she has it in her to demonstrate to the world the supremacy of soul-force. When India accepts the supremacy of brute force, I should no longer be happy to call her my motherland. It is my belief that my dharma recognizes no limits of spheres of duty or of geographical boundaries. I pray to God that I may then be able to prove that my dharma takes no thought of my person or is not restricted to a particular field.

Ideas for Rereading

1. Much of Gandhi's time in these essays is spent explaining, reexplaining, and defending *satyagraha,* or "truth-force." *Satyagraha* is the concept most central to Gandhi's worldview and represents for him a way of life. As you reread

vaid: From the Sanskrit word for knowledge, *veda.*
dharma: A comprehensive term used in Buddhism, Hinduism, and Zen to refer to the essential truth of religion. The basis of all human morality and ethics, of cosmic law, and universal truth, dharma defines and drives all action and thought.

Gandhi's writings, highlight references to *satyagraha,* with the aim of deriving the most complete possible understanding of the concept. List the most important elements of *satyagraha.* How does Gandhi want it to be practiced? To what lengths is he willing to go in his practice of *satyagraha?*

2. In "Religion of Nonviolence," Gandhi suggests occasions when the concept of *ahimsa* ("no harming") can include the killing of animals. What occasions are those? List them. As you reread the essay, note your reaction to Gandhi's assertions concerning animals. How does he attempt to reconcile his nonviolent worldview with the possibility of violence toward animals? In what ways does Gandhi's argument seem to you to be persuasive? Irrelevant? Counterproductive?

3. Paramount to Gandhi's understanding of *satyagraha* is an insistence on the "law of suffering," which he considers "the one indispensable condition of our being" (p. 451). Still, much of contemporary culture is dedicated to the alleviation and prevention of suffering. Reread the short essay "The Law of Suffering," and outline Gandhi's explanation of the necessity and usefulness of suffering. What is your reaction to each of Gandhi's assertions in this essay?

4. In the essay "The Doctrine of the Sword I," Gandhi writes, "I do believe that where there is only a choice between cowardice and violence I would advise violence" (p. 454). What might be the implications of this statement when taken out of context? As you read "The Doctrine of the Sword I and II," trace the ways in which Gandhi justifies and contextualizes his words within his concept of *satyagraha.* In your opinion, how successful is Gandhi in reconciling his statement about cowardice with his overall vision and explanation of *satyagraha?*

Ideas for Writing

1. Gandhi's thought is deeply rooted in the religious teachings of Hinduism, Judeo-Christianity, and Islam. His work is full of religious and spiritual references. At the same time, he is the founder of a movement with political purposes as well as spiritual purposes. Modern Western culture—most notably in the United States, but to varying degrees elsewhere—insists on a separation of politics and religion, "church and state." What do you think are the limitations, benefits, or problems with applying Gandhi's *satyagraha* within the Western social and political context? Write an essay examining how successful Gandhi's ideas can be in a predominantly secular society. In what ways do you think there can be *satyagraha* without a religious worldview? What difficulties or problems could you foresee when applying *satyagraha* in a secular context?

2. Reread "Religion of Nonviolence," focusing on Gandhi's discussion of the potential necessity to harm animals. How does he justify this necessity? Which parts of his argument do you find convincing, questionable, or unacceptable? Write an analysis of Gandhi's attitude toward animals as part of the nonviolent worldview expressed in "Religion of Nonviolence" and, possibly, other Gandhi essays included in this chapter.

CONTEXT

Gandhi wrote of a feeling of "joyful recognition" on reading Jesus' Sermon on the Mount, recognition because these words of the Christian Gospels corresponded so well to his experience of the Hindu Bhagavad Gita and its insistence on pacifism and personal sacrifice. Upon discovering the late religious writing of the Russian Leo Tolstoy, Gandhi began a relationship with the aging author of War and Peace *and thought of him as one of his great mentors. Throughout his life and career as a* satyagrahi *(follower of* satyagraha*) Gandhi would draw the respect and admiration of many of his countrymen, most notably the Nobel Prize–winning poet Rabindranath Tagore—who first dubbed Gandhi "Mahatma," or "Great Soul"— and Jawaharlal Nehru, first prime minister of India, who, though himself an atheist, considered the deeply religious Gandhi a mentor and friend. Sections of the Gita and the Sermon on the Mount are presented in this Context section, along with a letter from Tolstoy, a letter and two poems from Tagore, and Nehru's mournful radio speech following Gandhi's assassination. Two visual images show the evolution of Gandhi's worldview: a photo of Gandhi as a young Westernized lawyer and the iconic image of Gandhi stooping to pick up sea salt on the beach of Dandi.*

MATTHEW

*The Sermon on the Mount, 5.38–39**

38　Ye have heard that it hath been said, An eye for an eye, and a tooth for a tooth:

39　But I say unto you, That ye resist no evil: but whosoever shall smite thee on thy right cheek, turn to him the other also.

From the Bhagavad Gita
The Yoga of Renunciation

1　Arjuna said:

You commend, O Krishna, the renunciation of action and you also praise yoga. Tell me definitely which is the better of the two.

2　The Blessed Lord said:

Both renunciation and the yoga of action lead to the supreme good. But of these two, performance of action is superior to the renunciation of action.

---

*We have chosen to quote from the King James Bible, the standard Bible used throughout the British empire. This is the Bible that Gandhi would have used. —Eds.

3 He who neither hates nor desires is to be known as the everlasting re-nouncer (*sanyasi*); for, free from the dualities, O mighty-armed one, he is easily liberated from bondage.

4 The immature, not the wise, speak of the path of knowledge and the path of action as distinct from each other. He who has perfectly mastered one of them finds the fruit of both.

5 The goal reached by men of renunciation is reached by men of action also. He who sees that the way of renunciation and the way of action are one — he indeed sees!

6 True renunciation is hard to accomplish without the practice of yoga, O mighty-armed one; the sage who is disciplined in the yoga of action quickly reaches Brahman.*

7 He who is devoted to the path of action and is pure in mind, who is master of his self and who has conquered his senses, whose self has become the Self in all beings, he is not tainted even though he acts.

8–9 "I am not doing anything at all," so thinks the yogi, the knower of Truth; for in seeing, hearing, touching, smelling, eating, walking, sleeping, breathing, and in speaking, emptying, grasping, opening and closing the eyes, he believes that the senses are only operating upon the sense objects.

10 He who works, abandoning attachment and resigning his actions to Brahman, is untouched by sin, just as a lotus petal is untouched by muddy water.

11 Having renounced attachment, the yogis perform action with only the body, the mind, the understanding or even merely the senses, for the purifi-cation of the self.

12 He who is disciplined in yoga, having abandoned the fruit of action, at-tains ultimate peace. But the undisciplined person, prompted by desire, is attached to the fruit of action and is therefore bound.

13 The embodied soul, who has mastered the senses and has renounced all actions with the mind, dwells happily in the nine-gated city,* neither acting nor causing action to be done.

Brahman: The eternal, supreme Absolute truth, a truth that is beyond the comprehension of humans and that forms the ultimate level of universal forces. This truth and these forces can be partially glimpsed by pure members of the Brahmin caste, the priestly caste considered to be the highest of the four social classes in Hindu culture.

nine-gated city: Dvaraka, the capital of Krishna's kingdom in western India. Krishna is the most celebrated hero in Indian mythology and is often regarded as a manifestation of the supreme, universal consciousness. Living in Dvaraka is equivalent to living in bliss.

Some texts call Dvaraka the "many-gated city" but the reference to nine is significant in

14 The all-pervading Lord does not create action or the means of action for the people nor the union of action with its fruits. Rather, nature works this out.

15 Nor does the all-pervading Lord partake in anyone's sin or merit. When knowledge is enveloped by ignorance, people are confused.

16 But those whose ignorance is destroyed by the knowledge of the Self find that knowledge illuminates the Supreme Self like the sun.

17 With thought absorbed in That (the Supreme), with the self fixed on That, making That their whole aim, going toward That, they go the way that has no return, for their sins have been washed away by knowledge.

18 The wise see no difference between a learned and humble Brahmin, a cow, an elephant, a dog, or even an outcaste.

19 Even in this world, rebirth is conquered by those whose minds are firmly set in impartiality. Brahman is without flaw and is the same in all. Therefore, they rest in Brahman.

20 Steadfast in his mind and undeluded, he who knows Brahman abides in Brahman. He does not rejoice when experiencing pleasure nor is he perturbed when experiencing pain.

21 He whose self is not attached to the external sense impressions finds happiness in the Self; his heart is one with Brahman through contemplation and he enjoys everlasting bliss.

22 The pleasures that are born of contact with objects are only sources of pain; they have a beginning and an end, O son of Kunti. The wise find no delight in them.

23 He who is able to withstand the upsurge of desire and anger here on earth, before he is liberated from the body, is indeed a yogi. He is a happy man.

24 He who finds happiness within, joy within, inner radiance within, that yogi becomes Brahman and attains freedom in Brahman (*Brahmanirvana*).

25 The sages whose sins have been destroyed, whose doubts have been resolved, who have mastered themselves, and who are dedicated in doing good to all creatures, attain freedom in Brahman (*Brahmanirvana*).

---

this context: in Hindu religious mythology there are nine planets, nine sacred gems, nine sacred plants, nine forms of the goddess Durga, nine childhood diseases, and so on. Gates and doors are often decorated with these symbols as a way of preventing evil from entering.

26 For the austere men (*yatis*), who are delivered from lust and wrath, who have controlled their thoughts and who have realized the Self, the bliss of Brahman lies close at hand.

27–28 Shutting out all outside contacts, fixing the gaze between the eyebrows, inhaling and exhaling evenly within the nostrils, having controlled the senses, the mind and understanding; the sage, who is devoted to liberation as his highest goal, who has cast away desire, fear and anger, is forever liberated.

29 Having known Me as the Lord of sacrifices and austerities, the mighty Lord of all the worlds, the Friend of all beings, he attains peace.

LEO TOLSTOY

Letter to Gandhi   1910

I received your journal and was pleased to learn all contained therein concerning the passive resisters; and I felt like telling you all the thoughts which that reading called up to me.

The longer I live, and especially now, when I vividly feel the nearness of death, I want to tell others what I feel so particularly clearly and what to my mind is of great importance, namely, that which is called "Passive Resistance," but which is in reality nothing else than the teaching of love uncorrupted by false interpretations. That love, which is the striving for the union of human souls and the activity derived from it, is the highest and only law of human life; and in the depth of his soul every human being (as we most clearly see in children) feels and knows this; he knows this until he is entangled by the false teachings of the world. This law was proclaimed by all—by the Indian as by the Chinese, Hebrew, Greek, and Roman sages of the world. I think this law was most clearly expressed by Christ, who plainly said, "In love alone is all the law and the prophets."

But, foreseeing the corruption to which this law of love may be subject, he straightway pointed out the danger of its corruption, which is natural to people who live in worldly interests—the danger, namely, which justifies the defence of these interests by the use of force, or, as he said, "with blows to answer blows, by force to take back things usurped," etc. He knew, as every sensible man must know, that the use of force is incompatible with love as the fundamental law of life; that as soon as violence is permitted, in whichever case it may be, the insufficiency of the law of love is acknowledged, and by this the very law of love is denied. The whole Christian civilization, so brilliant outwardly, grew up on this self-evident and strange misunderstanding and contradiction, sometimes conscious but mostly unconscious.

In reality, as soon as force was admitted into love, there was no more love; there could be no love as the law of life; and as there was no law of love there was no law at all except violence, i.e., the power of the strongest. So lived Christian humanity for nineteen centuries. It is true that in all times people were guided by violence in arranging their lives.

The difference between the Christian nations and all other nations is only that in the Christian world the law of love was expressed clearly and definitely, whereas it was not so expressed in any other religious teaching, and that the people of the Christian world have solemnly accepted this law, whilst at the same time they have permitted violence and built their lives on violence; and that is why the whole life of the Christian peoples is a continuous contradiction between that which they profess and the principles on which they order their lives — a contradiction between love which has been accepted as the law of life and violence which is recognized and praised, being acknowledged even as a necessity in different phases of life, such as the power of rulers, courts, and armies. This contradiction always grew with the development of the people of the Christian world, and lately it reached the ultimate stage.

The question now evidently stands thus: either to admit that we do not recognize any Christian teaching at all, arranging our lives only by power of the stronger, or that all our compulsory taxes, court and police establishments, but mainly our armies, must be abolished.

This year, in spring, at a Scripture examination in a girls' high school at Moscow, the teacher and the bishop present asked the girls questions on the Commandments, and especially on the Sixth, "Thou shalt not kill." After a correct answer the bishop generally put another question, whether killing was always in all cases forbidden by God's law, and the unhappy young ladies were forced by previous instruction to answer, "Not always" — that killing was permitted in war and in execution of criminals. Still, when one of these unfortunate young ladies (what I am telling is not an invention, but a fact told me by an eye-witness), after her first examination was asked the usual question, if killing were always sinful, she became agitated, and, blushing, decisively answered, "Always"; and to all the usual sophisms of the bishop she answered with decided conviction that killing was always forbidden in the Old Testament and not only killing was forbidden by Christ but even every wrong against a brother. Notwithstanding all his grandeur and art of speech, the bishop became silent and the girl remained victorious.

Yes, we can talk in our newspapers of the progress of aviation, of complicated diplomatic relations, of different clubs and conventions, of unions of different kinds, of so-called productions of art, and keep silent about what the young lady said. But it cannot be passed over in silence, because it is felt, more or less dimly, but always felt, by every man in the Christian world, Socialism, Communism, Anarchism, Salvation Army, increasing crime, unemployment, the growing insane luxury of the rich and misery of the poor, the alarmingly increasing number of suicides — all these are the signs of that internal contradiction which must be solved and cannot remain unsolved. And they must be solved in the sense of acknowledging the law of love and denying violence.

Therefore your activity in the Transvaal, as it seems to us at this end of the world, is the most essential work, the most important of all the work now being done in the world, wherein not only the nations of the Christian, but of all the world, will unavoidably take part.

RABINDRANATH TAGORE

Letter to Gandhi and Accompanying Poems   1919

[The following passages are from a letter written to Gandhi at the beginning of the Passive Resistance struggle in April 1919; they show Tagore's wholehearted sympathy with the principle of soul-force and with its practical application by Gandhi.]

Power in all its forms is irrational; it is like the horse that drags the carriage blindfolded. The moral element in it is only represented in the man who drives the horse. Passive Resistance is a force which is not necessarily moral in itself; it can be used against truth as well as for it. The danger inherent in all force grows stronger when it is likely to gain success, for then it becomes temptation.

I know your teaching is to fight against evil by the help of good, but such a fight is for heroes and not for men led by impulses of the moment. Evil on one side naturally begets evil on the other, injustice leading to violence and insult to vengefulness.

In this crisis you, as a great leader of men, have stood among us to proclaim your faith in the ideal which you know to be that of India, the ideal which is both against the cowardliness of hidden revenge and the cowed submissiveness of the terror-stricken. You have said, as Lord Buddha has done in his time and for all time to come:

"Overcome anger by the power of non-anger, and evil by the power of good."

We must know that moral conquest does not insist on success, that failure does not deprive it of its own dignity and worth. Those who believe in the spiritual life know that to stand against wrong, which has overwhelming material power behind it, guarantees a victory of active faith in the idea in the teeth of evident defeat.

I have always felt, and said accordingly, that the great gift of freedom can never come to a people through charity. We must win it before we can own it. And India's opportunity for winning it will come to her when she can prove that she is morally superior to the people who rule her by their right of conquest. She must willingly accept her penance of suffering, which is the crown of the great. Armed with her utter faith in goodness, she must stand unabashed before the arrogance that scoffs at the power of spirit.

And you come to your motherland in the time of her need to remind her of her mission, to lead her in the true path of conquest, to purge her present-day politics of that feebleness which imagines that it has gained its purpose when it struts in the borrowed feathers of diplomatic dishonesty.

This is why I pray most fervently that nothing which tends to weaken our spiritual freedom may intrude into our marching line; that martyrdom for the cause of truth may never degenerate into fanaticism for mere verbal forms, descending into the self-deception that hides itself behind sacred names.

[Tagore's letter also included his translations of two of his poems.]

Let me hold my head high in this faith, that Thou art our shelter, that all fear is mean distrust of Thee.

Fear of man? But what man is there in this world, what king, O King of Kings, that is Thy rival, who holdest me for all time and in all truth?

What power is there in this world to rob me of freedom? For do not Thy arms reach the captive through the dungeon walls, bringing unfettered release to the soul?

And must I cling to this body in fear of death, as a miser to his barren treasure? Has not this spirit of mine the eternal call to the feast of everlasting life?

Let me know that all pain and death are shadows of the moment; that the dark force which sweeps between me and Thy truth is but the mist before the sunrise; that Thou alone art mine for ever and greater than all pride of strength that dares to mock my manhood with its menace.

Give me the supreme courage of love, this is my prayer, the courage to speak, to do, to suffer at Thy will, to leave all or be left alone.

Give me the supreme faith of love, this is my prayer, the faith of the life in death, of the victory in defeat, of the power hidden in the frailness of beauty, of the dignity of pain that accepts hurt, but disdains to return it.

JAWAHARLAL NEHRU

All-India Radio Speech following the Assassination of Gandhi*   1948

Friends and comrades, the light has gone out of our lives and there is darkness everywhere. I do not know what to tell you and how to say it. Our beloved leader, Bapu as we called him, the father of the nation, is no

*Nehru, prime minister of India, made this speech on the evening of Gandhi's assassination, January 30, 1948, without any script. — Eds.

more. Perhaps I am wrong to say that. Nevertheless, we will not see him again as we have seen him for these many years. We will not run to him for advice and seek solace from him and that is a terrible blow not to me only but to millions and millions in this country, and it is a little difficult to soften the blow by any other advice that I or anyone else can give you.

The light has gone out, I said, and yet I was wrong. For the light that shone in this country was no ordinary light. The light that has illumined this country for these many years will illumine this country for many more years and a thousand years later that light will still be seen in this country and the world will see it and it will give solace to innumerable hearts. For that light represented something more than the immediate present; it represented the living truth . . . the eternal truths, reminding us of the right path, drawing us from error, taking this ancient country to freedom.

All this has happened when there was so much more for him to do. We could never think that he was unnecessary or that he had done his task. But now, particularly, when we are faced with so many difficulties, his not being with us is a blow most terrible to bear.

A madman has put an end to his life, for I can only call him mad who did it, and yet there has been enough of poison spread in this country during the past years and months and this poison has had effect on people's minds. We must face this poison, we must root out this poison and we must face all the perils that encompass us and face them not madly or badly but rather in the way that our beloved teacher taught us to face them. The first thing to remember now is that no one of us dare misbehave because we are angry. We have to behave like strong and determined people, determined to face all the perils that surround us, determined to carry out the mandate that our great teacher and our great leader has given us, remembering always that if, as I believe, his spirit looks upon us and sees us, nothing would displease his soul so much as to see that we have indulged in any small behavior or any violence.

So we must not do that. But that does not mean that we should be weak but rather that we should in strength and in unity face all the troubles that are in front of us. We must hold together and all our petty troubles and difficulties and conflicts must be ended in the face of this great disaster. A great disaster is a symbol to us to remember all the big things of life and forget the small things, of which we have thought too much.

It was proposed by some friends that Mahatmaji's body should be embalmed for a few days to enable millions of people to pay their last homage to him. But it was his wish, repeatedly expressed, that no such thing should happen, that this should not be done, that he was entirely opposed to any embalming of his body.

Tomorrow should be a day of fasting and prayer for all of us. Those who live elsewhere out of Delhi and in other parts of India will no doubt also take such part as they can in this last homage. For them also let this be a day of fasting and prayer. And at the appointed time for cremation, that is 4 p.m. tomorrow afternoon, people should go to the river or to the sea and offer prayers there. And while we pray, the greatest prayer that we can offer is to take a pledge to dedicate ourselves to the truth and to the cause for which this great countryman of ours lived and for which he has died.

Young, Westernized Gandhi, 1890

Gandhi picking up salt on the beach at Dandi, 1930

Ideas for Rereading

1. As you reread the verses from the Sermon on the Mount and the Bhagavad Gita, keep in mind Gandhi's dedication to these works—especially the latter. Note the places where you find possible roots or inspiration for Gandhi's thinking. What is your reaction to his interpretation of these works? If you are already familiar with one or both of these texts, consider how you have interpreted them in the past. In what ways does Gandhi's work confirm, modify, or challenge your previous interpretations of these texts?

2. The poet Rabindranath Tagore and Prime Minister Jawaharlal Nehru were contemporaries and admirers of Gandhi. Consider carefully their selections—one a letter, the other a radio eulogy—in the context of Gandhi's writings. Note the two men's perspective on Gandhi's worklife, work, and opinions. Do these writers see Gandhi and his struggle in the same way he does? Note what is important to each man about Gandhi's work, and consider why that is so.

Ideas for Writing

1. Reread the Sermon on the Mount and "The Yoga of Renunciation." Consider your own interpretation of them—whether positive or negative—as well as how Gandhi applies their ideas. Write an essay explaining how you think these religious principles are meant to be practiced—how and if they actually have been practiced—and how Gandhi's work and thought fit into or differ from that practice.

2. Gandhi's rejection of Western dress had symbolic significance for him and for his followers. Examine carefully—that is, "read"—the two photographs in this section—that of the older Gandhi, well known to history, and that of his younger, Westernized self. Write an essay considering the importance of dress and appearance to Gandhi's cause. What does each photograph say about the man and the two cultures in which he participated?

CONTEMPORARY CONVERSATION

MARTIN LUTHER KING JR.

Martin Luther King Jr. (1929–1968) was a fourth-generation Baptist minister and the leader of the civil rights movement of the 1950s and 1960s in the United States. He became acquainted with the philosophy of Gandhi while an undergraduate at Crozer Theological Seminary in Chester, Pennsylvania, but it was not until after he had earned his Ph.D. and had become pastor of Dexter Avenue Baptist Church in Montgomery, Alabama, that he became the leader of a nonviolent political action movement. After Rosa Parks refused to give up her seat to a white passenger on a Montgomery bus in 1955, King led a successful boycott of the local transit system to end segregated seating. He organized the Southern Christian Leadership Conference to extend this success across the southern United States, and over the next decade he led sit-ins, boycotts, and demonstrations that confronted the injustice of segregation with coordinated and massive nonviolent resistance.

King was already a figure of international fame and influence when in the spring of 1963 he was arrested during a demonstration in Birmingham, Alabama, and was jailed along with hundreds of supporters. When eight clergymen published a statement that approved of his ultimate goals but questioned his tactics, King wrote a reply on whatever scraps of paper were available to him in jail. The letter circulated widely before being republished in Christian Century *and the* Atlantic Monthly. *It stands as an essential document of the civil rights movement and of the philosophy of nonviolence. In 1964, King won the Nobel Peace Prize. He was assassinated in Memphis, Tennessee, on April 4, 1968.*

Although King does not mention Gandhi explicitly in the letter, Gandhi's influence is evident not only in King's moral philosophy but also in his tone. As you read "Letter from Birmingham Jail," consider the ways in which King addresses his detractors. List the words he uses to characterize his critics. What do these words tell you about his personality? How do you respond to his suggestion that "we are caught in an inescapable network of mutuality" (p. 473)? How does this attitude help you understand King's ways of addressing his detractors? How does it connect with his call for "negotiation" and "dialogue" (p. 475) and his acknowledgment that his critics have "a legitimate concern" (p. 476)? In what ways does King discuss "the white moderate" (p. 478ff.)? Why do you think he positions himself between "two opposing forces in the Negro community" (p. 480)? Note each place where King discusses his disappointments. Why do you think he uses the idea of disappointment to communicate his criticisms of how people act and think?

Letter from Birmingham Jail

April 16, 1963

My Dear Fellow Clergymen:

While confined here in the Birmingham city jail, I came across your recent statement calling my present activities "unwise and untimely." Seldom do I pause to answer criticism of my work and ideas. If I sought to answer all the criticisms that cross my desk, my secretaries would have little time for anything other than such correspondence in the course of the day, and I would have no time for constructive work. But since I feel that you are men of genuine good will and that your criticisms are sincerely set forth, I want to try to answer your statement in what I hope will be patient and reasonable terms.

I think I should give the reason for my being in Birmingham, since you have been influenced by the argument of "outsiders coming in." I have the honor of serving as president of the Southern Christian Leadership Conference, an organization operating in every southern state, with headquarters in Atlanta, Georgia. We have some eighty-five affiliate organizations all across the South—one being the Alabama Christian Movement for Human Rights. Whenever necessary and possible we share staff, educational and financial resources with our affiliates. Several months ago our local affiliate here in Birmingham invited us to be on call to engage in a nonviolent direct-action program if such were deemed necessary. We readily con-

This response to a published statement by eight fellow clergymen from Alabama (Bishop C. C. J. Carpenter, Bishop Joseph A. Durick, Rabbi Hilton L. Grafman, Bishop Paul Hardin, Bishop Holan B. Harmon, the Reverend George M. Murray, the Reverend Edward V. Ramage, and the Reverend Earl Stallings) was composed under somewhat constricting circumstances. Begun on the margins of the newspaper in which the statement appeared while I was in jail, the letter was continued on scraps of writing paper supplied by a friendly Negro trusty, and concluded on a pad my attorneys were eventually permitted to leave me. Although the text remains in substance unaltered, I have indulged in the author's prerogative of polishing it for publication.—Author's note

sented and when the hour came we lived up to our promises. So I am here, along with several members of my staff, because we were invited here. I am here because I have basic organizational ties here.

Beyond this, I am in Birmingham because injustice is here. Just as the eighth-century prophets left their little villages and carried their "thus saith the Lord" far beyond the boundaries of their hometowns; and just as the Apostle Paul left his little village of Tarsus and carried the gospel of Jesus Christ to practically every hamlet and city of the Graeco-Roman world, I too am compelled to carry the gospel of freedom beyond my particular hometown. Like Paul, I must constantly respond to the Macedonian call for aid.*

Moreover, I am cognizant of the interrelatedness of all communities and states. I cannot sit idly by in Atlanta and not be concerned about what happens in Birmingham. Injustice anywhere is a threat to justice everywhere. We are caught in an inescapable network of mutuality, tied in a single garment of destiny. Whatever affects one directly affects all indirectly. Never again can we afford to live with the narrow, provincial "outside agitator" idea. Anyone who lives in the United States can never be considered an outsider anywhere in this country.

You deplore the demonstrations that are presently taking place in Birmingham. But I am sorry that your statement did not express a similar concern for the conditions that brought the demonstrations into being. I am sure that each of you would want to go beyond the superficial social analyst who looks merely at effects, and does not grapple with underlying causes. I would not hesitate to say that it is unfortunate that so-called demonstrations are taking place in Birmingham at this time, but I would say in more emphatic terms that it is even more unfortunate that the white power structure of this city left the Negro community with no other alternative.

In any nonviolent campaign there are four basic steps: (1) collection of the facts to determine whether injustices are alive, (2) negotiation, (3) self-purification, and (4) direct action. We have gone through all of these steps in Birmingham. There can be no gainsaying of the fact that racial injustice engulfs this community.

Birmingham is probably the most thoroughly segregated city in the United States. Its ugly record of police brutality is known in every section of this country. Its unjust treatment of Negroes in the courts is a notorious reality. There have been more unsolved bombings of Negro homes and churches in Birmingham than any city in this nation. These are the hard,

---

Macedonian call for aid: Macedonia was an ancient kingdom of northern Greece that covered territory now occupied by Bulgaria, Serbia, Kosovo, Greece, and the modern nation of Macedonia. St. Paul (A.D. 5–67) is known as the Apostle to the Gentiles: he took Christianity into places where oppressed subgroups called for his help, into places like Macedonia, that were central to Greco-Roman culture and were thus culturally hostile to Christianity.

brutal and unbelievable facts. On the basis of these conditions Negro leaders sought to negotiate with the city fathers. But the political leaders consistently refused to engage in good faith negotiation.

Then came the opportunity last September to talk with some of the leaders of the economic community. In these negotiating sessions certain promises were made by the merchants—such as the promise to remove the humiliating racial signs from the stores. On the basis of these promises Rev. Shuttlesworth and the leaders of the Alabama Christian Movement for Human Rights agreed to call a moratorium on any type of demonstrations. As the weeks and months unfolded we realized that we were the victims of a broken promise. The signs remained. Like so many experiences of the past we were confronted with blasted hopes, and the dark shadow of a deep disappointment settled upon us. So we had no alternative except that of preparing for direct action, whereby we would present our very bodies as a means of laying our case before the conscience of the local and national community. We were not unmindful of the difficulties involved. So we decided to go through a process of self-purification. We started having workshops on nonviolence and repeatedly asked ourselves the questions, "Are you able to accept blows without retaliating?" "Are you able to endure the ordeals of jail?" We decided to set our direct-action program around the Easter season, realizing that with the exception of Christmas, this was the largest shopping period of the year. Knowing that a strong economic withdrawal program would be the by-product of direct action, we felt that this was the best time to bring pressure on the merchants for the needed changes. Then it occurred to us that the March election was ahead and so we speedily decided to postpone action until after election day. When we discovered that Mr. Connor* was in the run-off, we decided again to postpone action so that the demonstrations could not be used to cloud the issues. At this time we agreed to begin our nonviolent witness the day after the run-off.

This reveals that we did not move irresponsibly into direct action. We too wanted to see Mr. Connor defeated; so we went through postponement after postponement to aid in this community need. After this we felt that direct action could be delayed no longer.

You may well ask, "Why direct action? Why sit-ins, marches, etc.? Isn't negotiation a better path?" You are exactly right in your call for negotiation. Indeed, this is the purpose of direct action. Nonviolent direct action seeks to create such a crisis and establish such creative tension that a community that has constantly refused to negotiate is forced to confront the issue. It seeks so to dramatize the issue that it can no longer be ignored. I just referred to the creation of tension as a part of the work of the nonvi-

---

Mr. Connor: Eugene "Bull" Connor, the commissioner of public safety in Birmingham, Alabama, in 1963. A firm segregationist, he is reputed to have threatened merchants who were willing to remove "Whites Only" and "Colored Only" signs. He gave the order to turn water cannons and police dogs on King's protestors on May 2, 1963.

olent resister. This may sound rather shocking. But I must confess that I am not afraid of the word *tension.* I have earnestly worked and preached against violent tension, but there is a type of constructive nonviolent tension that is necessary for growth. Just as Socrates felt that it was necessary to create a tension in the mind so that individuals could rise from the bondage of myths and half-truths to the unfettered realm of creative analysis and objective appraisal, we must see the need of having nonviolent gadflies to create the kind of tension in society that will help men to rise from the dark depths of prejudice and racism to the majestic heights of understanding and brotherhood. So the purpose of the direct action is to create a situation so crisis-packed that it will inevitably open the door to negotiation. We, therefore, concur with you in your call for negotiation. Too long has our beloved Southland been bogged down in the tragic attempt to live in monologue rather than dialogue.

One of the basic points in your statement is that our acts are untimely. Some have asked, "Why didn't you give the new administration time to act?" The only answer that I can give to this inquiry is that the new administration must be prodded about as much as the outgoing one before it acts. We will be sadly mistaken if we feel that the election of Mr. Boutwell will bring the millennium to Birmingham. While Mr. Boutwell is much more articulate and gentle than Mr. Connor, they are both segregationists, dedicated to the task of maintaining the status quo. The hope I see in Mr. Boutwell is that he will be reasonable enough to see the futility of massive resistance to desegregation. But he will not see this without pressure from the devotees of civil rights. My friends, I must say to you that we have not made a single gain in civil rights without determined legal and nonviolent pressure. History is the long and tragic story of the fact that privileged groups seldom give up their privileges voluntarily. Individuals may see the moral light and voluntarily give up their unjust posture; but as Reinhold Niebuhr* has reminded us, groups are more immoral than individuals.

We know through painful experience that freedom is never voluntarily given by the oppressor; it must be demanded by the oppressed. Frankly, I have never yet engaged in a direct action movement that was "well-timed," according to the timetable of those who have not suffered unduly from the disease of segregation. For years now I have heard the word "Wait!" It rings in the ear of every Negro with a piercing familiarity. This "Wait" has almost always meant "Never." It has been a tranquilizing thalidomide, relieving the emotional stress for a moment, only to give birth to an ill-formed infant of frustration. We must come to see with the distinguished jurist of yesterday that "justice too long delayed is justice denied." We have waited for more than 340 years for our constitutional and God-given rights. The nations of Asia and Africa are moving with jet-like speed

---

Reinhold Niebuhr: A Protestant theologian and progressive social thinker (1892–1971). In 1964 he received the Presidential Medal of Freedom for such works as *Faith and History* and *The Self and the Dramas of History.*

toward the goal of political independence, and we still creep at horse and buggy pace toward the gaining of a cup of coffee at a lunch counter. I guess it is easy for those who have never felt the stinging darts of segregation to say, "Wait." But when you have seen vicious mobs lynch your mothers and fathers at will and drown your sisters and brothers at whim; when you have seen hate-filled policemen curse, kick, brutalize and even kill your black brothers and sisters with impunity; when you see the vast majority of your twenty million Negro brothers smothering in an airtight cage of poverty in the midst of an affluent society; when you suddenly find your tongue twisted and your speech stammering as you seek to explain to your six-year-old daughter why she can't go to the public amusement park that has just been advertised on television, and see tears welling up in her little eyes when she is told that Funtown is closed to colored children, and see the depressing clouds of inferiority begin to form in her little mental sky, and see her begin to distort her little personality by unconsciously developing a bitterness toward white people; when you have to concoct an answer for a five-year-old son asking in agonizing pathos; "Daddy, why do white people treat colored people so mean?"; when you take a cross-country drive and find it necessary to sleep night after night in the uncomfortable corners of your automobile because no motel will accept you; when you are humiliated day in and day out by nagging signs reading "white" and "colored"; when your first name becomes "nigger" and your middle name becomes "boy" (however old you are) and your last name becomes "John," and when your wife and mother are never given the respected title "Mrs."; when you are harried by day and haunted by night by the fact that you are a Negro, living constantly at tiptoe stance never quite knowing what to expect next, and plagued with inner fears and outer resentments; when you are forever fighting a degenerating sense of "nobodiness"; then you will understand why we find it difficult to wait. There comes a time when the cup of endurance runs over, and men are no longer willing to be plunged into an abyss of injustice where they experience the blackness of corroding despair. I hope, sirs, you can understand our legitimate and un-avoidable impatience.

You express a great deal of anxiety over our willingness to break laws. This is certainly a legitimate concern. Since we so diligently urge people to obey the Supreme Court's decision of 1954 outlawing segregation in the public schools, it is rather strange and paradoxical to find us consciously breaking laws. One may well ask, "How can you advocate breaking some laws and obeying others?" The answer is found in the fact that there are two types of laws: there are *just* and there are *unjust* laws. I would agree with Saint Augustine* that "An unjust law is no law at all."

Saint Augustine: Augustine of Hippo (354–430) is considered the greatest of the fathers of the Christian church. From northern Africa, he wrote highly influential books including *The Confessions* and *The City of God*.

Now what is the difference between the two? How does one determine when a law is just or unjust? A just law is a man-made code that squares with the moral law or the law of God. An unjust law is a code that is out of harmony with the moral law. To put it in the terms of Saint Thomas Aquinas, an unjust law is a human law that is not rooted in eternal and natural law. Any law that uplifts human personality is just. Any law that degrades human personality is unjust. All segregation statutes are unjust because segregation distorts the soul and damages the personality. It gives the segregator a false sense of superiority, and the segregated a false sense of inferiority. To use the words of Martin Buber, the great Jewish philosopher, segregation substitutes an "I-it" relationship for the "I-thou" relationship, and ends up relegating persons to the status of things. So segregation is not only politically, economically and sociologically unsound, but it is morally wrong and sinful. Paul Tillich* has said that sin is separation. Isn't segregation an existential expression of man's tragic separation, an expression of his awful estrangement, his terrible sinfulness? So I can urge men to disobey segregation ordinances because they are morally wrong.

Let us turn to a more concrete example of just and unjust laws. An unjust law is a code that a majority inflicts on a minority that is not binding on itself. This is difference made legal. On the other hand a just law is a code that a majority compels a minority to follow that it is willing to follow itself. This is sameness made legal.

Let me give another explanation. An unjust law is a code inflicted upon a minority which that minority had no part in enacting or creating because they did not have the unhampered right to vote. Who can say that the legislature of Alabama which set up the segregation laws was democratically elected? Throughout the state of Alabama all types of conniving methods are used to prevent Negroes from becoming registered voters and there are some counties without a single Negro registered to vote despite the fact that the Negro constitutes a majority of the population. Can any law set up in such a state be considered democratically structured?

These are just a few examples of unjust and just laws. There are some instances when a law is just on its face and unjust in its application. For instance, I was arrested Friday on a charge of parading without a permit. Now there is nothing wrong with an ordinance which requires a permit for a parade, but when the ordinance is used to preserve segregation and to deny citizens the First Amendment privilege of peaceful assembly and peaceful protest, then it becomes unjust.

I hope you can see the distinction I am trying to point out. In no sense do I advocate evading or defying the law as the rabid segregationist would

---

Paul Tillich: A twentieth-century German Protestant theologian, Tillich (1886–1965) believed that religion is the substance of culture and that culture is the formal expression of religion. Tillich sought to redefine the Christian faith as a way of counteracting what he regarded as an increasingly antireligious society.

do. This would lead to anarchy. One who breaks an unjust law must do it *openly, lovingly* (not hatefully as the white mothers did in New Orleans when they were seen on television screaming, "nigger, nigger, nigger"), and with a willingness to accept the penalty. I submit that an individual who breaks a law that conscience tells him is unjust, and willingly accepts the penalty by staying in jail to arouse the conscience of the community over its injustice, is in reality expressing the very highest respect for law.

Of course, there is nothing new about this kind of civil disobedience. It was seen sublimely in the refusal of Shadrach, Meshach and Abednego* to obey the laws of Nebuchadnezzar because a higher moral law was involved. It was practiced superbly by the early Christians who were willing to face hungry lions and the excruciating pain of chopping blocks, before submitting to certain unjust laws of the Roman Empire. To a degree academic freedom is a reality today because Socrates practiced civil disobedience.

We can never forget that everything Hitler did in Germany was "legal" and everything the Hungarian freedom fighters did in Hungary was "illegal." It was "illegal" to aid and comfort a Jew in Hitler's Germany. But I am sure that if I had lived in Germany during that time I would have aided and comforted my Jewish brothers even though it was illegal. If I lived in a Communist country today where certain principles dear to the Christian faith are suppressed, I believe I would openly advocate disobeying these anti-religious laws. I must make two honest confessions to you, my Christian and Jewish brothers. First, I must confess that over the last few years I have been gravely disappointed with the white moderate. I have almost reached the regrettable conclusion that the Negro's great stumbling block in the stride toward freedom is not the White Citizens Counciler or the Ku Klux Klanner, but the white moderate who is more devoted to "order" than to justice; who prefers a negative peace which is the absence of tension to a positive peace which is the presence of justice; who constantly says, "I agree with you in the goal you seek, but I can't agree with your methods of direct action"; who paternalistically feels that he can set the timetable for another man's freedom; who lives by the myth of time and who constantly advised the Negro to wait until a "more convenient season." Shallow understanding from people of good will is more frustrating than absolute misunderstanding from people of ill will. Lukewarm acceptance is much more bewildering than outright rejection.

I had hoped that the white moderate would understand that law and order exist for the purpose of establishing justice, and that when they fail to do this they become dangerously structured dams that block the flow of social progress. I hoped that the white moderate would understand that the present tension of the South is merely a necessary phase of the transition

---

Shadrach, Meshach and Abednego: In the Old Testament Shadrach, Meshach, and Abednego were condemned to the fiery furnace of Babylon by the city's ruler. They called upon God and were rescued by God's command.

from an obnoxious negative peace, where the Negro passively accepted his unjust plight, to a substance-filled positive peace, where all men will respect the dignity and worth of human personality. Actually, we who engage in nonviolent direct action are not the creators of tension. We merely bring to the surface the hidden tension that is already alive. We bring it out in the open where it can be seen and dealt with. Like a boil that can never be cured as long as it is covered up but must be opened with all its pus-flowing ugliness to the natural medicines of air and light, injustice must likewise be exposed, with all of the tension its exposing creates, to the light of human conscience and the air of national opinion before it can be cured.

In your statement you asserted that our actions, even though peaceful, must be condemned because they precipitate violence. But can this assertion be logically made? Isn't this like condemning the robbed man because his possession of money precipitated the evil act of robbery? Isn't this like condemning Socrates because his unswerving commitment to truth and his philosophical delvings precipitated the misguided popular mind to make him drink the hemlock? Isn't this like condemning Jesus because His unique God-consciousness and never-ceasing devotion to his will precipitated the evil act of crucifixion? We must come to see, as federal courts have consistently affirmed, that it is immoral to urge an individual to withdraw his efforts to gain his basic constitutional rights because the quest precipitates violence. Society must protect the robbed and punish the robber.

I had also hoped that the white moderate would reject the myth of time. I received a letter this morning from a white brother in Texas which said: "All Christians know that the colored people will receive equal rights eventually, but it is possible that you are in too great of a religious hurry. It has taken Christianity almost two thousand years to accomplish what it has. The teachings of Christ take time to come to earth." All that is said here grows out of a tragic misconception of time. It is the strangely irrational notion that there is something in the very flow of time that will inevitably cure all ills. Actually time is neutral. It can be used either destructively or constructively. I am coming to feel that the people of ill will have used time much more effectively than the people of good will. We will have to repent in this generation not merely for the vitriolic words and actions of the bad people, but for the appalling silence of the good people. We must come to see that human progress never rolls in on wheels of inevitability. It comes through the tireless efforts and persistent work of men willing to be co-workers with God, and without this hard work time itself becomes an ally of the forces of social stagnation. We must use time creatively, and forever realize that the time is always ripe to do right. Now is the time to make real the promise of democracy, and transform our pending national elegy into a creative psalm of brotherhood. Now is the time to lift our national policy from the quicksand of racial injustice to the solid rock of human dignity.

You spoke of our activity in Birmingham as extreme. At first I was rather disappointed that fellow clergymen would see my nonviolent efforts as those of the extremist. I started thinking about the fact that I stand in the middle of two opposing forces in the Negro community. One is the force of complacency made up of Negroes who, as a result of long years of oppression, have been so completely drained of self-respect and a sense of "somebodiness" that they have adjusted to segregation, and, of a few Negroes in the middle class who, because of a degree of academic and economic security, and because at points they profit by segregation, have unconsciously become insensitive to the problems of the masses. The other force is one of bitterness and hatred, and comes perilously close to advocating violence. It is expressed in the various black nationalist groups that are springing up over the nation, the largest and best known being Elijah Muhammad's Muslim movement. This movement is nourished by the contemporary frustration over the continued existence of racial discrimination. It is made up of people who have lost faith in America, who have absolutely repudiated Christianity, and who have concluded that the white man is an incurable "devil." I have tried to stand between these two forces, saying that we need not follow the "do-nothingism" of the complacent or the hatred and despair of the black nationalist. There is the more excellent way of love and nonviolent protest. I'm grateful to God that, through the Negro church, the dimension of nonviolence entered our struggle. If this philosophy had not emerged, I am convinced that by now many streets of the South would be flowing with floods of blood. And I am further convinced that if our white brothers dismiss as "rabble-rousers" and "outside agitators" those of us who are working through the channels of nonviolent direct action and refuse to support our nonviolent efforts, millions of Negroes, out of frustration and despair, will seek solace and security in black nationalist ideologies, a development that will lead inevitably to a frightening racial nightmare.

Oppressed people cannot remain oppressed forever. The urge for freedom will eventually come. This is what happened to the American Negro. Something within has reminded him of his birthright of freedom; something without has reminded him that he can gain it. Consciously and unconsciously, he has been swept in by what the Germans call the *Zeitgeist,* and with his black brothers of Africa, and his brown and yellow brothers of Asia, South America and the Caribbean, he is moving with a sense of cosmic urgency toward the promised land of racial justice. Recognizing this vital urge that has engulfed the Negro community, one should readily understand public demonstrations. The Negro has many pent-up resentments and latent frustrations. He has to get them out. So let him march sometime; let him have his prayer pilgrimages to the city hall; understand why he must have sit-ins and freedom rides. If his repressed emotions do not come out in these nonviolent ways, they will come out in ominous expressions of violence. This is not a threat; it is a fact of history. So I have not said to my people "get rid of your discontent." But I have tried to say that this normal and healthy discontent can be channelized through the creative outlet of nonviolent direct action. Now this approach is being dismissed as extremist. I must admit that I was initially disappointed in being so categorized.

But as I continued to think about the matter I gradually gained a bit of satisfaction from being considered an extremist. Was not Jesus an extremist in love— "Love your enemies, bless them that curse you, pray for them that despitefully use you." Was not Amos* an extremist for justice— "Let justice roll down like waters and righteousness like a mighty stream." Was not Paul an extremist for the gospel of Jesus Christ— "I bear in my body the marks of the Lord Jesus." Was not Martin Luther* an extremist— "Here I stand; I can do none other so help me God." Was not John Bunyan* an extremist— "I will stay in jail to the end of my days before I make a butchery of my conscience." Was not Abraham Lincoln an extremist— "This nation cannot survive half slave and half free." Was not Thomas Jefferson an extremist— "We hold these truths to be self-evident, that all men are created equal." So the question is not whether we will be extremist but what kind of extremist will we be. Will we be extremists for hate or will we be extremists for love? Will we be extremists for the cause of justice? In that dramatic scene on Calvary's hill, three men were crucified. We must not forget that all three men were crucified for the same crime—the crime of extremism. Two were extremists for immorality, and thusly fell below their environment. The other, Jesus Christ, was an extremist for love, truth and goodness, and thereby rose above his environment. So, after all, maybe the South, the nation and the world are in dire need of creative extremists.

I had hoped that the white moderate would see this. Maybe I was too optimistic. Maybe I expected too much. I guess I should have realized that few members of a race that has oppressed another race can understand or appreciate the deep groans and passionate yearnings of those that have been oppressed and still fewer have the vision to see that injustice must be rooted out by strong, persistent and determined action. I am thankful, however, that some of our white brothers have grasped the meaning of this social revolution and committed themselves to it. They are still all too small in quantity, but they are big in quality. Some like Ralph McGill, Lillian Smith, Harry Golden and James Dabbs have written about our struggle in eloquent, prophetic and understanding terms. Others have marched with us down nameless streets of the South. They have languished in filthy roach-infested jails, suffering the abuse and brutality of angry

---

Amos: Hebrew prophet of the eighth century B.C.; he was the first to have a book of the Bible named after him.

Martin Luther: On October 31, 1517, Luther (1483–1546) nailed his list of ninety-five theses (challenges to Roman Catholic dogma) to the door of the cathedral in Wittenberg, Germany. This act became the catalyst for the Protestant Reformation and the creation of non–Roman Catholic forms of Christianity.

John Bunyan: English Puritan author (1628–1688) regularly jailed for his dissenting views. He wrote his most famous book, *The Pilgrim's Progress*, while in prison. It tells the allegorical story of a man, Christian, who suffers the struggles and temptations of the human soul as he makes his way to the Kingdom of Heaven.

policemen who see them as "dirty nigger-lovers." They, unlike so many of their moderate brothers and sisters, have recognized the urgency of the moment and sensed the need for powerful "action" antidotes to combat the disease of segregation.

Let me rush on to mention my other disappointment. I have been so greatly disappointed with the white church and its leadership. Of course, there are some notable exceptions. I am not unmindful of the fact that each of you has taken some significant stands on this issue. I commend you, Rev. Stallings, for your Christian stance on this past Sunday, in welcoming Negroes to your worship service on a nonsegregated basis. I commend the Catholic leaders of this state for integrating Springhill College several years ago.

But despite these notable exceptions I must honestly reiterate that I have been disappointed with the church. I do not say that as one of the negative critics who can always find something wrong with the church. I say it as a minister of the gospel, who loves the church; who was nurtured in its bosom; who has been sustained by its spiritual blessings and who will remain true to it as long as the cord of life shall lengthen.

I had the strange feeling when I was suddenly catapulted into the leadership of the bus protest in Montgomery several years ago that we would have the support of the white church. I felt that the white ministers, priests and rabbis of the South would be some of our strongest allies. Instead, some have been outright opponents, refusing to understand the freedom movement and misrepresenting its leaders; all too many others have been more cautious than courageous and have remained silent behind the anesthetizing security of the stained-glass windows.

In spite of my shattered dreams of the past, I came to Birmingham with the hope that the white religious leadership of this community would see the justice of our cause, and with deep moral concern, serve as the channel through which our just grievances would get to the power structure. I had hoped that each of you would understand. But again I have been disappointed. I have heard numerous religious leaders of the South call upon their worshippers to comply with a desegregation decision because it is the *law,* but I have longed to hear white ministers say, "Follow this decree because integration is morally *right* and the Negro is your brother." In the midst of blatant injustices inflicted upon the Negro, I have watched white churches stand on the sideline and merely mouth pious irrelevancies and sanctimonious trivialities. In the midst of a mighty struggle to rid our nation of racial and economic injustice, I have heard so many ministers say, "Those are social issues with which the gospel has no real concern," and I have watched so many churches commit themselves to a completely other-worldly religion which made a strange distinction between body and soul, the sacred and the secular.

So here we are moving toward the exit of the twentieth century with a religious community largely adjusted to the status quo, standing as a taillight behind other community agencies rather than a headlight leading men to higher levels of justice.

I have traveled the length and breadth of Alabama, Mississippi and all the other southern states. On sweltering summer days and crisp autumn mornings I have looked at her beautiful churches with their lofty spires pointing heavenward. I have beheld the impressive outlay of her massive religious education buildings. Over and over again I have found myself asking: "What kind of people worship here? Who is their God? Where were their voices when the lips of Governor Barnett* dripped with words of interposition and nullification? Where were they when Governor Wallace* gave the clarion call for defiance and hatred? Where were their voices of support when tired, bruised and weary Negro men and women decided to rise from the dark dungeons of complacency to the bright hills of creative protest?"

Yes, these questions are still in my mind. In deep disappointment, I have wept over the laxity of the church. But be assured that my tears have been tears of love. There can be no deep disappointment where there is not deep love. Yes, I love the church; I love her sacred walls. How could I do otherwise? I am in the rather unique position of being the son, the grandson and the great-grandson of preachers. Yes, I see the church as the body of Christ. But, oh! How we have blemished and scarred that body through social neglect and fear of being nonconformists.

There was a time when the church was very powerful. It was during that period when the early Christians rejoiced when they were deemed worthy to suffer for what they believed. In those days the church was not merely a thermometer that recorded the ideas and principles of popular opinion; it was a thermostat that transformed the mores of society. Wherever the early Christians entered a town the power structure got disturbed and immediately sought to convict them for being "disturbers of the peace" and "outside agitators." But they went on with the conviction that they were "a colony of heaven," and had to obey God rather than man. They were small in number but big in commitment. They were too God-intoxicated to be "astronomically intimidated." They brought an end to such ancient evils as infanticide and gladiatorial contest.

Things are different now. The contemporary church is often a weak, ineffectual voice with an uncertain sound. It is so often the arch-supporter of the status quo. Far from being disturbed by the presence of the church, the power structure of the average community is consoled by the church's silent and often vocal sanction of things as they are.

But the judgment of God is upon the church as never before. If the church of today does not recapture the sacrificial spirit of the early church,

---

Governor Barnett: Ross P. Barnett (1898–1987) was governor of Mississippi from 1960 to 1964.
Governor Wallace: George Corley Wallace (1919–1998) was governor of Alabama 1963–67, 1971–79, and 1983–87. He ran for the presidency in 1968 and 1972.

it will lose its authentic ring, forfeit the loyalty of millions, and be dismissed as an irrelevant social club with no meaning for the twentieth century. I am meeting young people every day whose disappointment with the church has risen to outright disgust.

Maybe again, I have been too optimistic. Is organized religion too inextricably bound to the status quo to save our nation and the world? Maybe I must turn my faith to the inner spiritual church, the church within the church, as the true *ecclesia* and the hope of the world. But again I am thankful to God that some noble souls from the ranks of organized religion have broken loose from the paralyzing chains of conformity and joined us as active partners in the struggle for freedom. They have left their secure congregations and walked the streets of Albany, Georgia, with us. They have gone through the highways of the South on tortuous rides for freedom. Yes, they have gone to jail with us. Some have been kicked out of their churches, and lost support of their bishops and fellow ministers. But they have gone with the faith that right defeated is stronger than evil triumphant. These men have been the leaven in the lump of the race. Their witness has been the spiritual salt that has preserved the true meaning of the gospel in these troubled times. They have carved a tunnel of hope through the dark mountain of disappointment.

I hope the church as a whole will meet the challenge of this decisive hour. But even if the church does not come to the aid of justice, I have no despair about the future. I have no fear about the outcome of our struggle in Birmingham, even if our motives are presently misunderstood. We will reach the goal of freedom in Birmingham and all over the nation, because the goal of America is freedom. Abused and scorned though we may be, our destiny is tied up with the destiny of America. Before the Pilgrims landed at Plymouth we were here. Before the pen of Jefferson etched across the pages of history the majestic words of the Declaration of Independence, we were here. For more than two centuries our foreparents labored in this country without wages; they made cotton king; and they built the homes of their masters in the midst of brutal injustice and shameful humiliation—and yet out of a bottomless vitality they continued to thrive and develop. If the inexpressible cruelties of slavery could not stop us, the opposition we now face will surely fail. We will win our freedom because the sacred heritage of our nation and the eternal will of God are embodied in our echoing demands.

I must close now. But before closing I am impelled to mention one other point in your statement that troubled me profoundly. You warmly commended the Birmingham police force for keeping "order" and "preventing violence." I didn't believe you would have so warmly commended the police force if you had seen its angry violent dogs literally biting six unarmed, nonviolent Negroes. I don't believe you would so quickly commend the policemen if you would observe their ugly and inhuman treatment of Negroes here in the city jail; if you would watch them push and curse old Negro women and young Negro girls; if you would see them slap and kick old Negro men and young boys; if you will observe them, as they did on two occasions, refuse to give us food because we wanted to sing our grace together. I'm sorry that I can't join you in your praise for the police department.

It is true that they have been rather disciplined in their public handling of the demonstrators. In this sense they have been rather publicly "nonviolent." But for what purpose? To preserve the evil system of segregation. Over the last few years I have consistently preached that nonviolence demands that the means we use must be as pure as the ends we seek. So I have tried to make it clear that it is wrong to use immoral means to attain moral ends. But now I must affirm that it is just as wrong, or even more so, to use moral means to preserve immoral ends. Maybe Mr. Connor and his policemen have been publicly nonviolent, as Chief Pritchett was in Albany, Georgia, but they have used the moral means of nonviolence to maintain the immoral end of flagrant racial injustice. T. S. Eliot has said that there is no greater treason than to do the right deed for the wrong reason.

I wish you had commended the Negro sit-inners and demonstrators of Birmingham for their sublime courage, their willingness to suffer and their amazing discipline in the midst of the most inhuman provocation. One day the South will recognize its real heroes. They will be the James Merediths,* courageously and with a majestic sense of purpose facing jeering and hostile mobs and the agonizing loneliness that characterizes the life of the pioneer. They will be old, oppressed, battered Negro women, symbolized in a seventy-two-year-old woman of Montgomery, Alabama, who rose up with a sense of dignity and with her people decided not to ride the segregated buses, and responded to one who inquired about her tiredness with ungrammatical profundity: "My feet is tired, but my soul is rested." They will be the young high school and college students, young ministers of the gospel and a host of their elders courageously and nonviolently sitting-in at lunch counters and willingly going to jail for conscience's sake. One day the South will know that when these disinherited children of God sat down at lunch counters they were in reality standing up for the best in the American dream and the most sacred values in our Judeo-Christian heritage, and thusly, carrying our whole nation back to those great wells of democracy which were dug deep by the Founding Fathers in the formulation of the Constitution and the Declaration of Independence.

Never before have I written a letter this long (or should I say a book?). I'm afraid that it is much too long to take your precious time. I can assure you that it would have been much shorter if I had been writing from a comfortable desk, but what else is there to do when you are alone for days in the dull monotony of a narrow jail cell other than write long letters, think strange thoughts, and pray long prayers?

James Meredith: An American civil rights advocate (b. 1933) whose 1963 registration at the then segregated University of Mississippi prompted a riot. After the Fifth U.S. Circuit Court of Appeals supported his appeal against the University's decision to bar him because of his race, Meredith was escorted to class by federal marshals under President Kennedy's orders.

If I have said anything in this letter that is an overstatement of the truth and is indicative of an unreasonable impatience, I beg you to forgive me. If I have said anything in this letter that is an understatement of the truth and is indicative of my having a patience that makes me patient with anything less than brotherhood, I beg God to forgive me.

I hope this letter finds you strong in the faith. I also hope that circumstances will soon make it possible for me to meet each of you, not as an integrationist or a civil rights leader, but as a fellow clergyman and a Christian brother. Let us all hope that the dark clouds of racial prejudice will soon pass away and the deep fog of misunderstanding will be lifted from our fear-drenched communities and in some not too distant tomorrow the radiant stars of love and brotherhood will shine over our great nation with all of their scintillating beauty.

> Yours for the cause of Peace and Brotherhood,
> Martin Luther King Jr.

Ideas for Rereading

1. As you may know, Martin Luther King Jr. was an accomplished and effective preacher. In his attempt to "answer" his fellow clergymen's public statement in "patient and reasonable terms" (p. 472), King uses a wide range of rhetorical strategies, strategies designed to persuade. As you reread the letter, take note of passages where the rhetorical effect seems to you especially powerful and dramatic. Take some time with these passages and study how King achieved his effect. Notice as many aspects of the rhetoric as you can. In your notes, describe in detail how each of these selected passages works to achieve a desired persuasive effect.

2. King's letter answers a public statement made by eight clergymen of various faiths—Protestant, Catholic, and Jewish—who opposed the demonstrations and civil disobedience actions that King had been leading and organizing. As you reread, try to infer or deduce the nature of the clergymen's arguments. Make notes reconstructing their argument based on King's assertions or answers.

Ideas for Writing

1. King writes: "I would agree with Saint Augustine that 'An unjust law is no law at all'" (p. 476). King then goes on to define and enumerate the elements of an unjust law. Choose a law that you believe to be unjust (or even one that might be considered unjust from a certain reasonable perspective, whether you personally believe it to be unjust or not). Use the elements of King's analysis to argue the injustice of the law. Write an essay that presents your argument.

2. Several of Gandhi's writings in this chapter also take the form of pamphlets that answer readers' objections to the methods and goals of nonviolence. Reread the selections by Gandhi in this chapter, paying close attention to their

rhetorical strategies—that is, how they use language to influence readers' feelings and thoughts and achieve the author's goals. Write an essay on the art of persuasion in the epistolary (i.e., letter) form.

3. King embraced a policy of nonviolence, but he clearly understood how to effect change in the face of powerful, entrenched, and often violent opposition. Civil disobedience and public demonstration were among the instruments he employed, but language—both spoken and written—was no less effective a weapon in his fight against segregation and injustice. Starting with question 1, Ideas for Rereading, select an especially powerful passage from King's letter and examine closely how King achieved his effects. Develop an attentive and detailed analysis of the rhetorical strategies that contribute to the effect of the passage. (Don't be concerned about whether King "intended" to use the strategies in this way; focus on the effect of the passage on the reader, even the effects that may be too subtle for a casual reader to notice consciously.) Write an essay that presents your analysis and illustrates how King used the power of words to change hearts and minds.

SUSAN GRIFFIN

Susan Griffin (b. 1943) is an award-winning poet and feminist philosopher whose writings include Pornography and Silence: Culture's Revolt against Nature *(1981) and the more recent* Bending Home: Selected and New Poems *(1998) and* What Her Body Thought: A Journey into the Shadows *(1999). Since publishing* Woman and Nature: The Roaring Inside Her *in 1978, Griffin's critical writing has centered on problems of dualism. In her early work she focused on the male's drive to separate emotion, desire, and feeling from himself. Analyzing the history of science and philosophy, she exposed the ways in which Euro-American culture has driven a wedge between the mind and the body, between humans and nature, between men and women.*

The following essay, from The Eros of Everyday Life: Essays on Ecology, Gender, and Society *(1995), argues that traditional dualistic ways of thinking have potentially cataclysmic consequences. Tracing a genealogy of the nuclear arms race, Griffin treats nuclear explosions as the manifestation of mental illness, as eruptions that express humanity's pent-up rage. She explains this rage as the product of a denial of the natural self, as the product of repressed instincts and emotions, and suggests that this denial and repression lead to "the suicidal notion of nuclear combat" (p. 490). As you read "Ideologies of Madness" take notes in two columns listing the oppositions and separations that Griffin identifies. Make a further list of the phrases she uses to identify the artificiality of these dualisms. To what extent do you accept Griffin's representation of the "dominant philosophies of this civilization" (p. 490)? How does Griffin's characterization of "consciousness" (p. 490) compare with your own understanding of your ways of thinking? In what ways does her description of "the fascist and authoritarian mentality" (p. 492) resonate with treatments of violence and warfare you have come across in newspapers, magazines, films, and television programs? What is your experience of violence and warfare, and how does it compare with what Griffin describes?*

Ideologies of Madness

Nuclear war has been described as a form of madness. Yet rarely does one take this insight seriously when contemplating the dilemma of war and peace. I wish to describe here the state of mind that has produced nuclear weaponry as a species of socially accepted insanity. This is a state of mind born of that philosophical assumption of our civilization which attempts to divide human consciousness from nature. Exploring the terrain of this state of mind, one will find in this geography, in the subterranean and unseen region that is part of its foundation and history, the hatred of the other in the quite literal forms of misogyny (the hatred of women), racism and anti-Semitism.

If one approaches the explosion of a nuclear weapon as if this were symptomatic of an underlying mental condition, certain facets begin to take on metaphorical meaning. Even the simplest physical aspects of a nuclear chain reaction carry a psychological significance. In order for a chain reaction to be created, the atom must be split apart. The fabric of matter has to be torn asunder. In a different vein, it is important to realize that the first atomic weapons were dropped over a people regarded in the demonology of our civilization as racially inferior. Tangentially, and carrying a similar significance, the first nuclear device exploded over Bikini atoll had a pinup of Rita Hayworth pasted to its surface. And then, speaking of a history that has largely been forgotten or ignored, the prototype of the first missiles capable of carrying nuclear warheads was invented and designed in the Third Reich. And those first rockets, the German V-2 rockets, were produced in underground tunnels by prisoners of concentration camps who were worked to death in this production.

These facets of the existence of nuclear weaponry can lead us to a deeper understanding of the troubled mind that has created our current nuclear crisis. To begin at one particular kind of beginning, with the history of thought, one can see the philosophical roots of our current crisis in the splitting of the atom. In the most basic terms, what occurs when the atom is split is a division between energy and matter. Until this century, modern science assumed matter and energy to be separate. This assumption began not with scientific observation but out of a religious bias. Examining the early history of science, one discovers that the first scientists were associated with and supported by the Church (as was most scholarship at that time) and that they asked questions derived from Christian theology. "What is the nature of light?" A question intimately bound up with the theory of relativity and quantum physics began as a religious question. And the guiding paradigm of the religion that posed this question has been a fundamental dualism between matter and spirit. Matter, or body and earth, were the degraded regions, belonging to the devil and corruption. Spirit, or the realm of pure intellect and heavenly influence, belonged to God, and was, in human experience, won only at the expense of flesh.

Of course, science does not recognize the categories of spirit and matter any longer, except through a process of translation. In the new vocabulary, though, the old dualism has been preserved. Now, matter was conceived of as earthbound and thus subject to gravity, and energy, the equivalent of spirit, was described as a free agent, inspiring and enlivening. Newtonian physics continued the old dualism, but Einsteinian physics does not.

When Einstein discovered the formula that eventually led to the development of the atomic bomb, what he saw was a continuum between matter and energy, instead of a separation. What we call solid matter is not solid, nor is it static. Matter is, instead, a process of continual change. There is no way to divide the energy of this motion from the physical property of matter. What is more, energy has mass. And not only is there no division between matter and energy as such, but to divide any single entity from any other single entity becomes an impossibility. No particular point exists where my skin definitely ends and the air in the atmosphere begins and this atmosphere ends and your skin begins. We are all in a kind of field together. And finally, with the new physics, the old line between subject and object has also disappeared. According to Heisenberg's Principle of Uncertainty, whatever we observe we change through our participation. Objectivity with its implied superiority and control has also vanished.

One might imagine that, with the disappearance of a scientific basis for dualism and the appearance of a physical view that is unified and whole, a different philosophy might arise, one which might help us make peace with nature. But instead what this civilization chose to do with this new insight was to find a way to separate matter from energy (it is spoken of as "liberating" the energy from the atom). And this separation has in turn produced a technology of violence which has divided the world into two separate camps who regard each other as enemies.

The real enemy, however, in dualistic thinking, is hidden: the real enemy is ourselves. The same dualism which imagines matter and energy to be separate also divides human nature, separating what we call our material existence from consciousness. This dualism is difficult to describe without using dualistic language. Actually, the mind cannot be separated from the body. The brain is part of the body and is affected by blood flow, temperature, nourishment, muscular movement. The order and rhythm of the body, bodily metaphors, are reflected in the medium of thought, in our patterns of speech. Yet we conceive of the mind as separate from and above the body. And through a subtle process of socialization since birth, we learn to regard the body and our natural existence as something inferior and without intelligence. Most of the rules of polite behavior are designed to conceal the demands of the body. We excuse ourselves, and refer to our bodily functions through euphemism.

From this dualistic frame of mind two selves are born: one acknowledged and one hidden. The acknowledged self identifies with spirit, with intellect, with what we imagine is free of the influence of natural law. The hidden self is part of nature, earth-bound, inextricable from the matrix of physical existence. We have become very seriously alienated from this denied self. So seriously that our alienation has become a kind of self-hatred, and this self-hatred is leading us today toward the suicidal notion of nuclear combat.

Of course, the body and mind are not separate. And, ironically, the warfare incipient between our ideas of who we are and who we really are is made more intense through this unity. Consciousness cannot exclude bodily knowledge. We are inseparable from nature, dependent on the biosphere, vulnerable to the processes of natural law. We cannot destroy the air we breathe without destroying ourselves. We are reliant on one another for our survival. We are all mortal. And this knowledge comes to us, whether we want to receive it or not, with every breath.

The dominant philosophies of this civilization have attempted to posit a different order of being over and against this bodily knowledge. According to this order of being, we are separate from nature and hence above natural process. In the logic of this order, we are meant to dominate nature, control life, and, in some sense felt largely unconsciously, avoid the natural event of death.

Yet in order to maintain a belief in this hierarchy one must repress bodily knowledge. And this is no easy task. Our own knowledge of our own natural existence comes to us not only with every breath but with hunger, with intimacy, with dreams, with all the unpredictable eventualities of life. Our imagined superiority over nature is constantly challenged by consciousness itself. Consciousness emerges from and is immersed in material experience. Consciousness is not separable from perception, which is to say sensuality, and as such cannot be separated from matter. Even through the process of the most abstract thought we cannot entirely forget that we are part of nature. In the biosphere nothing is ever entirely lost. Death itself is not an absolute end but rather a transformation. What appears to be lost in a fire becomes heat and ash. So, too, no knowledge can ever really be lost to consciousness. It must remain, even if disguised as a mere symbol of itself.

If I choose to bury a part of myself, what I bury will come back to haunt me in another form, as dream, or fear, or projection. This civilization, which has buried part of the human self, has created many projections. Out of the material of self-hatred several categories of otherness have been fashioned. Existing on a mass scale and by social agreement, these categories form a repository for our hidden selves.

The misogynist's idea of women is a fundamental category of otherness for this civilization. In the ideology of misogyny, a woman is a lesser being than a man. And the root cause of her inferiority is that she is closer to the earth, more animal, and hence material in her nature. She is thus described as more susceptible to temptations of the flesh (or devils, or serpents), more emotional and hence less capable of abstract thought than a man. Similarly, in the ideology of racism, those who are perceived as other are, at one and the same time, more sensual and erotic and less intelligent.

During the rise of fascism in Europe a fictitious document was created called the *Protocols of the Elders of Zion*. In this "document" Jewish elders plan to corrupt and eventually seize Aryan bloodlines through the rape and seduction of Aryan women. If one has projected a part of the self upon another, one must always be afraid that this self will return, perhaps even entering one's own bloodstream. But what is equally significant about this myth, and the symbolic life of the racist and anti-Semitic imagination, is that a sexual act, and especially rape, lies at the heart of its mythos.

It was in writing a book on pornography that I first began to understand the ideology of misogynist projection. Since so much in pornography is violent, I began to ask myself why sexual experience is associated with violence. This is a question which poses itself again in the context of nuclear weaponry, not only because Rita Hayworth's image happened to adorn an experimental nuclear bomb, nor simply because of the phallic shape of the missile, nor the language employed to describe the weapons — the first atomic bomb called "little boy," the next "big boy" — but also because of the sexualization of warfare itself, the eroticization of violence in war, the supposed virility of the soldier, the test of virility which is supposed to take place on the battlefield, and the general equivalency between masculine virtues and prowess in battle.

Over time in my study of pornography I began to understand pornographic imagery as an expression of the fear of sexual experience itself. Sexual experience takes one back to a direct knowledge of nature, including mortality, and of one's own body before culture has intervened to create the delusion of dominance. It is part of the nature of sexual pleasure and of orgasm to lose control. And finally the feel of a woman's breast, or of human skin against bare skin at all, must recall infancy and the powerlessness of infancy.

As infants we all experience an understanding of dependence and vulnerability. Our first experience of a natural, material power outside ourselves was through the bodies of our mothers. In this way we have all come to associate nature with the body of a woman. It was our mother who could feed us, give us warmth and comfort, or withhold these things. She had the power of life and death over us as natural process does now.

It was also as infants that we confronted what we have come to know as death. What we call death — coldness, isolation, fear, darkness, despair, trembling — is really the experience of an infant. What death really is lies in the dimension of the unknown. But, from the infantile experience of what we call death, one can see the psychological derivation of civilization's association between women and death. (One sees this clearly in the creation myth from Genesis, as Eve the seductress brings death into the world.) In this sense, too, sexual experience returns one to a primal fear of death. And through this understanding one can begin to see that at the center of the

impulse to rape is the desire to dominate the power of sexual experience itself and to deny the power of nature, including mortality, as this is felt
through sexual experience.

The connection between sexuality and violence exists as a kind of subterranean theme in the fascist and authoritarian mentality. In several places
in Jacobo Timerman's book, *Prisoner Without a Name, Cell Without a
Number,* he points out a relationship between the violence of the dictator
and a pornographic attitude toward sexuality. Imprisoned and tortured
himself, he recalls that those who did not do "a good scrubbing job" when
ordered to clean the prison floors were forced to "undress, lean over with
their index finger on the ground and have them rotate round and round
dragging their finger on the ground without lifting it. You felt," he writes,
"as if your kidneys were bursting." Another punishment was to force prisoners to run naked along the passageway, "reciting aloud sayings dictated"
to them, such as "My mother is a whore, I masturbate, I respect the guard,
the police love me."

That, to the fascist mind, "the other" represents a denied part of the
self becomes clear in the following story about Adolf Hitler. In a famous
passage in *Mein Kampf* he describes the moment when he decided to devote his life's work to anti-Semitism. He recounts that while walking
through the streets of Vienna he happened to see an old man dressed in the
traditional clothes of Jewish men in that city at that time, i.e., in a caftan.
The first question he asked was, "Is this man Jewish?" and then he cor-
rected himself and replaced that question with another, "Is this man German?"

If one is to project a denied self onto another, one must first establish that
this other is different from oneself. Were one to notice any similarity, one
would be endangered by the perception that what one projects may belong to
oneself. The question that Hitler asked himself became a standard part of
German textbooks in the Third Reich. A stereotypical portrait of a Jewish
man's face was shown under the question, "Is this man German?" and the
correct answer the students were taught was, of course, "No." In fact, Germany became a nation rather late. For centuries it existed as a collection of
separate tribes, and one of the oldest tribes in that nation was Jewish.

Hitler's story of the man in the caftan became a standard part of his
orations. He would become nearly hysterical at times telling the story, and
is said to have even vomited once. In the light of this history, a seemingly
trivial story from Hitler's early life becomes significant. As a young art student he bought his clothes secondhand because, like many students, he was
poor. In this period most of those selling secondhand clothing were Jewish
and Hitler bought from a Jewish clothes seller one item of clothing that he
wore so often that he began to be identified with this apparel. And that
was a caftan.

What is also interesting historically is that the caftan was a form of
medieval German dress. Exiled from Germany during a period of persecu-

tion, many Jews, who then lived in ghettos, continued to wear this traditional German dress and were still wearing it when they returned to Germany centuries later. Not only did Hitler fail to recognize an image of himself encountered in the streets of Vienna, but so did an entire generation of Germans. And an entire civilization, that to which we all belong, is in conflict with a part of human nature, which we try to bury and eventually even destroy.

The weapons that now threaten to destroy the earth and life as we know it were developed because the Allied nations feared that the fascist powers were making them. And the missiles which are now part and parcel of nuclear weaponry were first developed in the Third Reich. It is crucial now in our understanding of ourselves and what it is in us that has led to the nuclear crisis that we begin to look at the Nazi Holocaust as a mirror, finding a self-portrait in "the other" who is persecuted and denied, and seeing a part of ourselves too in the fascist dictator who would destroy that denied self.

The illusion this civilization retains, that we are somehow above nature, is so severe that in a sense we have come to believe that we can end material existence without dying. The absurdity of nuclear weaponry as a strategy for defense, when the use of those weapons would annihilate us, would in itself argue this. But if you look closely at the particulars of certain strategies within the overall nuclear strategy you encounter again the same estranged relationship with reality.

An official who was part of Reagan's administration, T. K. Jones, actually proposed that a viable method of civil defense would be to issue each citizen a shovel. It took an eight-year-old boy to point out that this plan cannot work because, after you dig a hole and get into it for protection, someone else must stand outside the hole and shovel dirt on top. The Pentagon refers to its strategies for waging nuclear war as SIOP.* One year the Pentagon actually went through the paces of an SIOP plan. As a literary scholar I found the scenario which the Pentagon wrote for this dramatization very disturbing. The Pentagon was free to write this play in any way that they wished; yet they wrote that the President was killed with a direct hit to Washington, D.C. Any student of tragic drama will tell you that what happens to the king, or the President, is symbolic of what happens to the self. But symbolically this death is not treated as real. Though the earthly self dies, in the Pentagon's version the sky self does not die: the Vice-President goes up in an airplane fully equipped to wage nuclear war by computer. There is such a plane flying above us now, and at every hour of the day and night.

The division that we experience from the natural self, the self that is material and embedded in nature, impairs our perceptions of reality. As Timerman writes:

SIOP: Acronym for Strategic Integrated Operational Plan.

The devices are recurrent in all totalitarian ideology, to ignore the complexities of reality, or even eliminate reality, and instead establish a simple goal and a simple means of attaining that goal.

Through maintaining the supremacy of the idea, one creates a delusion of a supernatural power over nature. Proceeding from an alienation from nature and an estrangement from the natural self, our civilization has replaced reality with an idea of reality.

In the development of this alienation as a state of mind, the delusion of well-being and safety eventually becomes more important than the realistic considerations which will actually effect well-being or safety. Hannah Arendt writes of an illusionary world created by totalitarian movements ". . . in which through sheer imagination uprooted masses can feel at home, and are spared the never-ending shocks which real life and real experience deal to human beings. . . ." Later, in *The Origins of Totalitarianism,* she speaks of the state of mass mind under the Third Reich in which people ceased to believe in what they perceived with their own eyes and ears, preferring the conflicting reports issued by the Führer.

One encounters the same failure to confront reality in Stalin's psychology as it is described by Isaac Deutscher in his biography:

> He [Stalin] was now completely possessed by the idea that he could achieve a miraculous transformation of the whole of Russia by a single *tour de force.* He seemed to live in a half-real and half-dreamy world of statistical figures and indices of industrial orders and instructions, a world in which no target and no objective seemed beyond his and the party's grasp.[1]

During the period of forced collectivization of farms, Stalin destroyed actual farms before the collectivized farms were created. As Deutscher writes, it was as if a whole nation destroyed its real houses and moved "lock, stock and barrel into some illusory buildings."

We are, in fact, now living in such an illusory building. The entire manner in which plans for a nuclear war are discussed, rehearsed, and envisioned partakes of a kind of unreality, an anesthetized and nearly automatic functioning, in which cerebration is strangely unrelated to experience or feeling. The generals imagine themselves conducting nuclear war from a room without windows, with no natural light, choosing strategies and targets by looking at enormous computerized maps. The language they use to communicate their decisions is all in code. No one uses the word "war," the word "bomb," the word "death," or the words "blood," "pain," "loss," "grief," "shock," or "horror." In Siegfried Sassoon's[2] recollection of World War I, he remembers encountering a man, a soldier like himself, who has just learned that his brother was killed. The man is half crazy, tearing his clothes off and cursing at war. As Sassoon passed beyond this man into the dark of the war, he could still hear "his uncouth howlings." It is those "uncouth howlings" that those who are planning nuclear war have managed to mute in their imagination.

But of course that howling is not entirely lost. In the shared imagination of our civilization, it is the "other" who carries emotion, the women who howl. And, far from wishing to protect the vulnerable and the innocent, it is the secret desire of this civilization to destroy those who feel, and to silence feeling. This hidden desire becomes apparent in pornography where women are pictured in a traditional way as weaker than men and needing protection, and yet where erotic feeling is freely mixed with the desire to brutalize and even murder women.

One can find a grim picture of the insane logic of the alienated mind of our civilization in the pornographic film *Peeping Tom*. The hero of this movie is a pornographic film maker. He has a camera armed with a spear. As he photographs a woman's naked body the camera releases the weapon and makes a record of her death agonies. The final victory of the alienated mind over reality is to destroy that reality (and one's experience of it) and replace reality with a record of that destruction. One finds the same pattern in the history of actual atrocities. In California a man lured women into the desert with a promise of work as pornographic models. There, while he tortured and murdered them, he made a photographic record of the event. The Nazis themselves kept the best documentation of atrocities committed in the concentration camps. And the most complete records of the destruction of Native Americans have been kept by the United States military.

Now, the state of conflict in which this civilization finds itself has worsened. The enemy is not simply "the other" but life itself. And it is in keeping with the insane logic of alienation that the Pentagon has found a way that it believes we can win nuclear war. We have situated satellites in space that will record the process of annihilation of life. The Pentagon counts as a future victor that nation which has gathered the best documentation of the destruction.

There is, however, another form of reflection available to us by virtue of our human nature. We are our own witnesses. We can see ourselves. We are part of nature. And nature is not divided. Matter is intelligent. Feeling, sense, the needs of the body, all that has been consigned to the "other," made the province of women, of darkness, contains a deeper and a sustaining wisdom. It remains for us to empower that knowledge and carry it into the world. In insanity and madness, one is lost to oneself. It is only by coming home to ourselves that we can survive.

Notes

1. Isaac Deutscher, *Stalin: A Political Biography* (Oxford, 1961).

2. Siegfried Sassoon, "The Complete Memoirs of George Sherston," as collected in *Sassoon's Long Journey,* ed. Paul Fussell (London, 1983).

Ideas for Rereading

1. Gandhi writes, "Only those who realise that there is something in man which is superior to the brute nature in him, and that the latter always yields to it, can effectively be Passive Resisters" (p. 446). Griffin suggests that the drive toward nuclear violence results from what she sees as a mistaken belief in "a fundamental dualism between matter and spirit" (p. 488). As you reread Griffin's essay, take special note of her critique of dualism, especially in light of Gandhi's statement. What do you notice about the differences between Griffin's and Gandhi's perspectives on nonviolence?

2. Griffin writes, "If one approaches the explosion of a nuclear weapon as if this were symptomatic of an underlying mental condition, certain facets begin to take on metaphorical meaning" (p. 488). As you reread this essay, mark the passages in which Griffin applies the "madness" metaphor to the issue of nuclear proliferation. How, for Griffin, does it reflect and represent human "madness"?

3. As you reread, note Griffin's evaluation of pornography and its uses. Explore her presentation of the relationship between pornography and nuclear "madness." Where does the connection seem right to you? Where and how might you question Griffin's thinking?

Ideas for Writing

1. What is your opinion of Griffin's idea that a nuclear explosion is "symptomatic of an underlying mental condition" (p. 488), that nuclear proliferation is a metaphor for a kind of human madness? Write an essay analyzing Griffin's definition of "madness" and its connection to issues such as nuclear proliferation and pornography. How does Griffin argue for these issues as reflections and representations of human madness?

2. Griffin writes, "The final victory of the alienated mind [the mind separated from the body and nature] over reality is to destroy that reality . . . and replace reality with a record of that destruction" (p. 495). She gives examples such as violent pornographic films and Nazi record keeping during the Holocaust. Pay attention to destructive violence as portrayed by the media—whether the news media or the creative media of film and television fiction. Choose a case that seems to reflect the essence of Griffin's statement. Write an essay illustrating how it does so.

PETRA KELLY

Petra Kelly (1947–1992) was a cofounder (in 1979) of the self-described nonviolent ecological Green Party (Die Grünen), which began in Germany but has since spread to many other European countries and more recently to North America. In 1982 she became the first woman to head a political party in Germany and was elected to the German Parliament in 1983. Kelly concentrated her political efforts on four interrelated themes: peace and nonviolence, ecology, feminism, and human

rights. In addition to becoming Speaker of the German Federation for Social De-
fence, a human-rights organization that addresses issues of environmental pollution
and economic inequity, she chaired the Grace P. Kelly Association for the Support
of Cancer Research in Children from 1973 until her death. In her book Fighting for
Hope *(1984) she asserted that "There is no such thing as a bit of cancer or a little*
bit of malnutrition or a little bit of death or a little bit of social injustice or a little
bit of torture."

In 1989 Kelly organized the first international conference on Tibet and human
rights and in 1983 formed a "war crimes" tribunal at Nuremberg to decry the pos-
session and proliferation of nuclear and other weapons of mass destruction—by
the United States, the Soviet Union, Britain, China, and France—as "a crime of
immense proportions." Her books include Anguish in Tibet *(1991),* Nonviolence
Speaks to Power *(1992), and the posthumously published* Thinking Green! Essays
on Environment, Feminism, and Nonviolence, *from which the following selection is*
taken. Kelly's death from gunshot wounds in October 1992 remains mysterious.
Found dead at her home in Bonn along with her longtime partner, Gert Bastian,
Kelly may have been involved in a double suicide, with Bastian pulling the trigger.
But members of Germany's Green Party have pointed to a conspiracy by govern-
ment agents and to a plot by neo-Nazis.

As we might expect from an activist politician, Kelly uses a number of tech-
niques to communicate the urgency of her ideas. Notice the ways in which she uses
the words must, should, *and* need, *particularly in the first few pages but also*
throughout the essay. How does her detailing of what people must do and should
do contribute to her pervasive argument about "social defense"? How do her ex-
amples of social defense help you understand what she argues? In what ways do the
quotations from Mahatma Gandhi, Jesse Jackson, and Martin Luther King help
Kelly develop her case?

Nonviolent Social Defense

> *People try nonviolence for a week, and when it "doesn't work," they go*
> *back to violence, which hasn't worked for centuries.*
>
> —THEODORE ROSZAK

Young people are our future. It is they who can become peacemakers in
their lives and develop a nonviolent future. We must encourage them
to study peace and to challenge the military-industrial complex that continues to push us into wars and ever-expanding military budgets. The study of
peace analyzes the causes of war, violence, and systematic oppression, and
explores the processes by which conflict and change can be managed in
order to maximize justice and minimize violence. Peace studies encompass
the fields of economics, politics, history, political science, physics, ethics,
philosophy, and religion at the local as well as global levels, showing how
culture, ideology, and technology relate to conflict and change.

War, peace, and justice are the most critical issues we face today, and
they must receive the highest priority. It is important that students debate
peace issues and design research projects on how to conclude arms control
treaties, how to initiate steps toward unilateral disarmament, and how to

protect human rights wherever they are violated. We will not find an instant solution to the nearly half-century of nuclear buildup, so we must make a sustained effort to undertake peace research, action research, and analysis.

Peace studies should also touch the spirituality of politics, talking about the problems of poverty, oppression, and the nature of war, and offering alternatives to war, militarism, and deterrence. Peace studies programs can help develop, through action research, practical methods for the nonviolent resolution of conflicts, including civilian-based defense and social defense. It should also discuss Third World development, ecological planning, human rights, social movements, and grassroots movements. A peace studies program should convey the development of the civil rights and antiwar movements and evaluate the powerful effects of these movements. Students who become involved in looking for nonviolent solutions to military conflicts are on the way to becoming true peacemakers. We need many students to become peacemakers if we want to have hope for the future.

Human dignity is a fundamental value in peace education. Innovative learning to prepare people to act conscientiously in situations in which issues of right or wrong are at stake is sorely needed. This means moving away from the emphasis on competition, achievement, strength, power, profit, and productivity. Peace studies must guide students toward active global citizenship and solving conflicts nonviolently, and must help them acquire the capacity to confront changes and use their personal influence to bring about positive change. Peace studies can, I hope, become truly peacemaking—helping develop an ethic of reverence for life on this Earth, a planet that has no emergency exit. Improving the human social condition is part of peacemaking. I wish our young students the strength and courage to become real peacemakers. The immense task of students and educators is no less than the survival of our planetary home.

"Wars will end when people refuse to fight," expresses the Green approach to peace. The cornerstone of this approach is unilateral disarmament. It is a completely new principle of foreign policy, breaking with the spurious logic of the balance of power and the limits of diplomatic exchange which leads to continual militarism. To embark on a unilateral, nonaligned, and actively neutral departure from the entire military system is to initiate a policy of nonthreatening conduct essential for any real security or peace.

We Greens want to create the conditions for this new way to peace that is completely without the use of military force. Almost everyone in the world thinks that deterrence thinking, stereotypes of the enemy, and belief in the inevitability of war are the only practical ways of operating. But the abolition of slavery once seemed unrealistic, and the abolition of arms, too, can become the norm in international affairs. A disarmed society need not be defenseless. Civilian-based social defense is an alternative to the self-destructive militarism that has been tried again and again and has only brought us more and more suffering. It is time for a fresh new approach, one that is studied and documented and not just naive.

One of the most important advocates of civilian-based defense is Gene Sharp, of the Albert Einstein Institution in Cambridge, Massachusetts. Professor Sharp has studied nonviolent defense worldwide, and has seen that this is a practical and effective strategy, based on the recognition that power derives, first and foremost, from the consent of the governed. Civilian-based defense depends on the highly skilled, coordinated resistance of citizens.

During the Summer of 1968, when nonviolent citizens in Prague were resisting the occupying Soviet forces, my grandmother and I were there in a hotel near Wenceslaus Square, under house arrest. Even after Dubcek* and his close associates were arrested, the people remained steadfast in their resistance. Eventually, by threatening indefinite military occupation, the Soviets were able to reassert their authority and delay the reforms of the Prague Spring by twenty-one years. But through their sacrifice and suffering, the people of Czechoslovakia built up a spirit of positive patriotism, and two decades later did indeed succeed in their "Velvet Revolution." These events demonstrate the power of nonviolent social defense.

Social defense is a way to protect ourselves from foreign invasions or internal *coups* through active, nonviolent resistance and noncooperation, including economic boycotts by consumers and producers, social and political boycotts of institutions, strikes, overtaking facilities and administrative systems important to the opponent, stalling and obstructing, being deliberately inefficient, ostracizing, influencing occupying troops, and other forms of not complying. Military defense seeks to prevent an enemy from invading by threatening battle losses at the border. Social defense sets an unacceptably high price on staying—ceaseless resistance. It spoils the spoils of war and deprives the aggressor of the fruits of victory. The price of aggression becomes so high that occupation is no longer worth it. The opponent is prevented from attaining their aims and their ability to fight is undermined.

Social defense is practical and pragmatic. It requires excellent preparation, organization, and training; a courageous, creative, and determined citizenry; and a radical commitment to democratic values. Independent, resourceful, freedom-loving people that are prepared and organized to resist aggression cannot be conquered. No number of tanks and missiles can dominate a society unwilling to cooperate.

In this century, we have seen several examples of the effectiveness of nonviolent social defense. The home-rule movement led by Gandhi mobilized so much grassroots pressure that the British were forced to withdraw

---

Dubcek: Alexander Dubcek (1921–1992), Czech political leader who led the Prague Spring reforms in 1968. The Soviet Union sent a military force to arrest him and to reverse the moves he had made toward a more open democratic system. He was expelled from the Communist Party in 1970. After the peaceful revolution of 1989, Dubcek became Speaker of Parliament.

from India. The civil rights movement created profound changes in U.S. society. Philippine "people power" overthrew Marcos nonviolently. And in Eastern Europe, it was citizens' movements, not political or military powers, that toppled the state security systems.

Full demilitarization can only come about in a society in which power is shared at the grassroots. In the nineteenth century, Henry David Thoreau called upon free citizens to engage in civil disobedience and nonviolent actions whenever there is injustice. Civil disobedience and nonviolence are an integral part of any democratic society. Even in Western democracies, the state seems invincible, and as individuals we often feel powerless, unable to have much effect. We must remind ourselves that the power of the state derives solely from the consent of the governed. Without the cooperation of the people, the state cannot exist. Even a powerful military state that is nearly invulnerable to violent force can be transformed through nonviolence at the grassroots. Noncooperation, civil disobedience, education, and organization are the means of change, and we must learn the ways to use them. Direct democracies will come into being only when we demand from our leaders that they listen to us. This is fundamental to Green politics. Power is not something that we receive from above. To transform our societies into ones that are peaceful, ecological, and just, we need only to exercise the power we already have.

Like the militaristic mode of defense, social defense demands courage and the willingness to place the interests of the community ahead of individual self-interest, relying as it does on well-organized, tightly bonded affinity groups in every neighborhood prepared to conduct acts of nonviolent resistance on short notice. Every neighborhood must know how to conduct resistance and subversion. This method of democratic security requires little material apparatus but a lot of organization and training.

It is easy to see how economically wasteful, ecologically destructive, immoral, and counter-democratic military defense is, but to criticize militarism is not enough. If we really want to move towards nonviolent societies, we must study and begin to practice some alternatives, and civilian-based defense is the most realistic and effective.

The very fabric of every First World country is woven by militarism. The culture of materialism depends on the use of force. Violence, oppression, and domination are all ways used by the powerful to keep the powerless powerless. In capitalist societies, the social structure depends on the economic exploitation of one group by another, in the form of imperialism abroad and racism at home. Violence is inherent and pervasive, from the nuclear family to the nuclear state.

As long as the world is divided into centralized states in competition for material wealth and political power, war is inevitable, as is the domination of weaker states by stronger ones. SS-20s, Pershing IIs, Tridents, Star Wars "defense" systems, and other weapons do not begin in factories. They begin in our consciousness. We think each other to death. The entire production cycle—from the allocation of funds, to the mining of uranium, to testing—is killing people. American Indian children playing on their reservation lands are breathing radioactive tailings from the waste piles of uranium mines. The radiation poisoning of Pacific Islanders is the result of weapons testing by the French government. Every year, while hundreds of billions of dollars go toward preparation for war, seventeen million children under the age of five die of starvation or inadequate medical care.

The destruction of nature, the militarization of the world, and the exploitation of the disenfranchised all kill life and kill the spirit. We "shut down" and not only numb our fear and pain, we also lose touch with our own innate spiritual resources—compassion, imagination, and the power to respond. As Joanna Macy points out, it is precisely because of our caring, our compassion, and our recognition of our connectedness with life that the pain of the world is so unbearable.[1] These are the qualities that we need most to bring change and healing to our world. We must reclaim our spiritual power.

Satyagraha, "truth force," is the word used by Gandhi to describe the spiritual power of nonviolence. *Ahimsa,* "non-harming," is a value deeply embedded in the Indian religious outlook that shaped Gandhi's thought. The power of nonviolence arises from what is deepest and most humane within ourselves and speaks directly to what is deepest and most humane in others. Nonviolence works not through defeating the opponent but by awakening the opponent and oneself through openness. It is not just a tactic—it embraces life. "Nonviolence that merely offers civil resistance to the authorities and goes no further scarcely deserves the name ahimsa," Gandhi said. "To quell riots nonviolently, there must be true ahimsa in one's heart, an ahimsa that takes even the erring hooligan in its warm embrace."[2]

In acknowledging Gandhi's influence, Dr. Martin Luther King, Jr. made this point: "I had about concluded that the ethics of Jesus were only effective in individual relationships. The 'turn the other cheek' philosophy and the 'love your enemies' philosophy were only valid, I felt, when individuals were in conflict with other individuals; when racial groups and nations were in conflict, a more realistic approach seemed necessary. But after reading Gandhi, I saw how utterly mistaken I was. Gandhi was probably the first person in history to lift the love ethic of Jesus above mere interaction between individuals to a powerful and effective social force on a large scale."[3] Nonviolence extends moral thought beyond individuals and their immediate communities to include the whole of society. It takes the initiative in opposing existing systems of dominance and privilege and addresses the problem of structural violence and the task of structural change.

Faith that we have a natural disposition to love, that we are possessed of moral conscience, and that all life is sacred are at the foundation of nonviolent action, and we can see their power in practical application. The political techniques of nonviolence—noncooperation, civil disobedience, grassroots organizing, fasting, and so forth—derive their power from the faith and confidence that through the integrity and self-sacrifice of our actions, we can awaken our opponent's conscience and bring about a change of heart. Gandhi was uniquely creative in applying nonviolence as an effective force for political and social change. For him, nonviolence was always active, powerful, and dynamic, and had nothing to do with passivity or acceptance of wrongful conditions. He acknowledged the influence of the nineteenth-century Indian women's movement in the development of his approach. Because women's contributions to nonviolence are often unrecognized, this influence is especially encouraging. He was also directly influenced by Jesus' gospel of love and the writings of Tolstoy, Emerson, and Thoreau.

Violence always leads to more violence, hatred to greater hatred. Nonviolence works through communion, never through coercion. We must win over, not defeat, our opponent through openness, dialogue, patience, and love. Our real opponent is not a human enemy, but a system and way of thinking that give some people the power to oppress. Each struggle is part of a larger vision, one of building a society dedicated to the welfare of all. Gandhi felt that India could only become healthy with strong, politically autonomous, economically self-reliant villages. He was critical of industrialism for dehumanizing workers, splitting society into classes, and taking work from humans and giving it to machines. And he saw that any centralized production system requires a state that is restrictive of individual freedom. To him, the spinning wheel represented the dignity of labor, self-sufficiency, and humility needed to guide the people of India in the work of social transformation. Gandhi's influence runs deep in the Green movement. Satyagraha and all it implies have inspired and informed our vision of nonviolent change.

All forms of structural and institutional violence—the arms race, warfare, economic deprivation, social injustice, ecological exploitation, and so forth—are closely linked. Making their interrelationships clear is essential for moving society in a direction that benefits all, not just one nation, class, or even species. Militarism and the culture of militarism are extreme and pervasive examples of structural violence, even in times of relative peace. People assume that militarism at least boosts our economies. But defense spending generates fewer jobs than other areas of public spending. "It produces," as Jesse Jackson has pointed out, "little of utility to our society— no food, no clothes, no housing, no medical equipment or supplies. In short, nothing of social or redemptive value."[4] For the cost of just one jet fighter, 3 million children could be inoculated against major childhood diseases. The cost of one nuclear weapons test could provide enough money to give 80,000 Third World villages access to safe water through the installation of hand pumps. Two billion dollars are spent every day on military weapons. Contrasted with the urgent needs of the world's poor, military expenditures are nothing short of embezzlement.

The ending of the Cold War has brought little change in our militaristic outlook. As old weapons systems are dismantled, they are replaced by new, more sophisticated ones. Weapons research and development continues unabated. Militaries, the arms industry, government leaders, and bureaucrats continue to tell citizens that more refined weapons in larger numbers will bring greater security, and sales of arms and weapons technology continue worldwide.

A nation's policies, values, institutions, and structures comprise the preconditions for violence or for peace. Gandhi said, "Nonviolence is the greatest force mankind has ever been endowed with. Love has more force than a besieging army." Martin Luther King, Jr. added that this power of love is physically passive but spiritually active—that "while the nonviolent resister is passive in the sense that he is not physically aggressive towards his opponent, his mind and his emotions are constantly active, constantly seeking to persuade the opposition." Nonviolence is a spiritual weapon that can succeed where guns and armies never could. "Democracy can only be saved through nonviolence," Gandhi said, "because democracy, so long as it is sustained by violence, cannot provide for or protect the weak. My notion of democracy is that under it the weakest should have the same opportunity as the strongest. This can never happen except through nonviolence."

Now, when the West has more or less won the Cold War, the Warsaw Pact has completely crumbled and NATO is about to move its borders east, a pragmatic, nonideological approach to social defense must be developed and counterposed to all militaristic policies. We spend billions on weapons research and millions training our young people at military academies. Why not invest in peace studies and peace actions? We need training centers, public campaigns, and educational materials. We need to support groups like Peace Brigades International that intervene nonviolently in situations of conflict. We need to work concretely to realize peace and nonviolence in our time.

We also need to support existing nonviolent struggles, such as those of the Tibetans and the Chinese democracy movement. The public is so often ignorant about these nonviolent campaigns, because bombing oneself into history like the IRA, ETA, and others is what receives media and public attention. We can never give peace a chance if we do not even know about the many peaceful movements already in existence.

There are a few hopeful signs. In 1989, 36 percent of the Swiss population voted against having an army, and, though underfunded, small-scale feasibility studies on the same subject were done in Sweden, Denmark, Holland, Austria, and France. I hope that all peace groups will take up the issue of social defense as a main priority. Gandhi said, "Nonviolence is as yet a mixed affair. It limps. Nevertheless, it is there and it continues to work like a leaven in a silent and invisible way, least understood by most. [But] it is the only way."

Notes

1. Joanna Macy, *World as Lover, World as Self* (Berkeley: Parallax Press, 1991), pp. 15–28.

2. Mohandas K. Gandhi, *The Story of My Experiments with Truth* (Boston: Beacon Press, 1957).

3. Martin Luther King, Jr., *Stride Toward Freedom: The Montgomery Story* (New York: Harper & Brothers, 1958), pp. 96–97.

4. Rev. Jesse L. Jackson, *Straight from the Heart* (Philadelphia: Fortress Press, 1987), p. 283.

Ideas for Rereading

1. Kelly explains the Green Party's political approach to peace, the "corner-stone" of which is "unilateral disarmament" (p. 498). She states, "A disarmed society need not be defenseless" (p. 498). As you reread her essay, list Kelly's examples of the practicality of "unilateral disarmament." How does she think it would work? What sacrifices are needed? Take notes concerning what in her argument convinces you and what does not.

2. Kelly states, "The culture of materialism depends on the use of force" (p. 500). What do you think she means by "culture of materialism"? As you reread, mark passages that seem to define or exemplify this concept for Kelly.

3. In discussing the aims of the Green movement, Kelly acknowledges the inspiration of Mahatma Gandhi. Reread the Gandhi essays in this chapter, using quotations and paraphrase to develop a comprehensive definition of *satyagraha*. As you reread Kelly's essay note the ways in which her description of "peace studies" and her idea of "social defense" reflect Gandhi's "truth-force" or "soul-force." Which specific words and phrases does Kelly use that imply there is a religious foundation to her ideas? How do Kelly's thoughts about discipline and self-sacrifice resonate with Gandhi's?

Ideas for Writing

1. Begin with a firm understanding of the elements of Kelly's argument for unilateral disarmament. How does she present the practicality and morality of such a political stance? What evidence does she use? Write an essay exploring your response to Kelly's argument.

2. Beginning with the passages you marked in response to the second Idea for Rereading, write an essay assessing Kelly's assertion that "the culture of materialism depends on the use of force" (p. 500). Use examples from your experience of violence and warfare as they are represented in newspapers, magazines, films, television programs, and on the Internet to explore ways in which materialism and the use of force interact. What kinds of coercion and violence do you see in the media? How are these forces associated with what Kelly calls "the culture of materialism"?

3. Kelly suggests that "like the militaristic mode of defense," nonviolent social defense requires "a lot of organization and training" (p. 500). Write an essay analyzing the practical needs of a nonviolent, nonmilitary social defense strat-

egy and suggesting what special kinds of "organization and training" might be necessary to make such a strategy successful.

SUSANNE KAPPELER

Susanne Kappeler (b. 1949) published her doctoral dissertation, written under the supervision of the renowned literary critic Frank Kermode at Jesus College, Cambridge, under the title Writing and Reading in Henry James *(1980). The analysis of narrative form in this first book left little room for the gender-based analysis of violence and power that has driven Kappeler's professional career since she earned her doctoral degree. But Kappeler has continued to analyze the ways in which things are put together, their form, focusing on narration as a technique that gives order to experience. In her second book,* The Pornography of Representation *(1986), she set out to "build up the concepts . . . necessary for a feminist critique of pornography and patriarchal culture." Arguing that "pornography is the construct of particular discourses," that it is a matter of word- and image-based representational practices rather than a matter of sexuality, she endeavored to shift feminist discussions of pornography from the critique of content to the critique of how this content is presented.*

In the following essay, which is taken from The Will to Violence: The Politics of Personal Behavior *(1995), Kappeler argues that war and militarism are an inherent part of contemporary Euro-American understandings of national community. Kappeler's literary background is evident in her concentration of definitions of terms such as* resistance, defence, *and* violence, *and her work as a critic of narrative structure is evident in her focus on the "reflexively ordered . . . biographical accounting" (p. 507) through which violence is justified. As you read Kappeler's essay, build a definition of* resistance *by taking notes in response to her uses of the term in the first part of her essay. Then think about this definition as you work through the second part of her essay, where she attends to "the growing belligerence of identity politics" (p. 508). Why does Kappeler say "Analysis of violence and discussion of non-violent means of resistance are becoming increasingly rare" (p. 508)? What do you think she means by saying that resistance "is a question of political will and action" (p. 510)? And why does she insist that "resistance to violence . . . cannot consist of violence" (p. 510)?*

Resistance and the Will to Resistance

War—attack, conquest, domination—seems to be the guiding principle of human interaction, in our modern "civilized" times as much as in a projected "barbarian" past. Nation-states, our chosen (or accepted) form of organization into communities, are built on their right to wage war, militarism being a central feature of civil society in "peacetime" around which the *civil* as much as the military order are built.[1] The achievement of European/Western "civilization" seems to consist in the successful exportation of war and militarism to the "rest" of the world, and in having kept military conflict away from home territory since the mid-twentieth century. Its second major achievement is the successful naturalization of war and martiality as a "*civilized*" way of being.

This means that Western society has become thoroughly militarized even in its "civilian" outfit, martiality having been internalized by "individuals" to such an extent that they "naturally" constitute themselves as subject—an entity in opposition—each a warrior at war with an enemy world. Hostility has become the basic constitution of self, not just in relation to recognized enemy forces—an oppressive state, systems of oppression, threatening individuals—but equally in relation to those we consider our nearest and dearest. Hence even resistance tends increasingly to be conceived under the aegis of martiality—a possibility within it rather than a radical refusal of it.

Today, if people are against anything they consider themselves to be in resistance to it. Thus the racist and neo-fascist group of whites in South Africa responsible for murdering Chris Hani call themselves "resistance fighters," a term duly repeated by Western commentators, who merely point out that Black people had given no cause for this particular outburst of anger. The implication is that there might have been a cause for such a murder, only in this case, there happened to be none.[2] If white fascists are against the rights of Black people and thus against *Black people,* we seem to think it fit to describe them as being in resistance to them. Resistance is demoted to a mere synonym for opposition—aggressive enmity—ennobled by the positive connotations of a beleaguered fight against oppression.

A political concept of resistance implies a struggle against a force of power and violence by those who suffer under it, that is, it includes an analysis and recognition of the superiority of that power, and the aim to dismantle that power. Much of what today goes by the name of resistance, however, is retaliation against the enemy (if not indeed attack, as in the example above), a counter-move in what is seen as the chronological sequence of (violent) action and reaction, attack and counter-attack between designated opponents. The aim is not to dismantle power, the aim is victory over the enemy, that is, gathering enough power on one's own side to overpower the other side.

Hence the crucial question is less what the power relations are than where the consideration of history begins, that is, which is the "original" action to which there is re-action, "who began" by making the first move, to which the second is but a counter-move. Thus it was reported in the news that Palestinians were throwing stones and Israeli settlers were shooting, "but it is unclear as yet who began."[3] That is, the concept of "resistance" becomes part of the ideologizing structure of justifying one's own action (or the actions of those with whom the subject identifies), where the other's action preceding ours is said to be the cause of—or to have given us cause for—violent action on our part.

It is why every military force in the world is called a "defence" force, governed by a civil ministry of defence that explains what the current military action is a defence against. Thus a British Falklands war is a defensive war, sinking the Argentinian warship *General Belgrano** a defensive action against its hostile change of course, just as bombing Iraq is but retaliation in defence of an already attacked Kuwait and a justified response to Saddam Hussein's failure to respond to the UN's ultimatum. In fact, consulting history we will find that there never has been an aggressive move in the world, since there always was some previous action or event considered by one or the other party to have been the "cause" for "retaliation."

So the question is really which opponent makes this narrative of self, or from whose subjective point of view we regard an action or sequence of actions (that is, history). Since these selves—be they nations or individuals—by definition are "opponents," each having its "opposite" and thus its enemy, any action then becomes a form of resistance and self-defence. National history—what we also call revisionism—means developing a narrative of the national self understood as a national-biographic accounting with which the national patient feels emotionally comfortable, in fact, a form of nation-psychoanalysis, "the creation of a reflexively ordered narrative" enabling nations "to bring their past 'into line' with exigencies of the present, consolidating an emotional story-line with which they feel relatively content."[4]

For an analysis of *violence,* the violent agent's self-justification for action—the "reflexively ordered narrative" understood as a "biographical accounting" with which that agent feels comfortable—is not the issue, is not what determines whether it was violence or not. Most violent men—like most ministries of defence—provide explanations, that is, rationalizations of why they consider their use of violence justified—say, that their wives had been nagging or otherwise getting on their nerves, or that their victims had provoked them beyond endurance (whether through vulnerability or otherwise). In order to understand what violence is and what may be resistance to violence, we need to analyse the actions in question, to see them within their action context, which includes the power relations of that context.

Violence requires a situation where it can be exerted, a power relation that makes its use possible. Counter-violence, however justifiable we may feel it to be, requires a corresponding reversal of the power relations to enable (counter-)violence to take place. Planning an action of counter-violence, even if conceived as an act of resistance, requires constructing a situation in which those carrying out the action will have the necessary power to succeed, that is, to exert violence. It is therefore an act of violence, carried out from a position of power.

A military intervention in Bosnia, as called for by some peace activists and feminists (at least until recently), would not be an act of resistance to

---

General Belgrano: A ship sunk by the British submarine HMS *Conqueror* on May 2, 1982, after the quiet invasion of the Falkland Islands ("Malvinas") by Argentina. The sinking was controversial because it began bloodshed in the conflict—323 sailors died—and because there is strong evidence that the British navy knew the *General Belgrano* was at least thirty miles outside the two-hundred-mile exclusion zone established by Britain.

war, but an act of aggression with power superior to the power of the Serbian military and paramilitary forces. Similarly, if groups of women in response to incidents of rape decide to beat up men in their neighbourhood, this is less an act of resistance to sexual violence than the construction of a situation in which this group of women will have the power to exert violence against individual men. That is, it is violence, whatever its justification. It is not an act of non-violence simply because men collectively have power over women and because they collectively commit so much violence against women and girls. That is to say, there are different questions involved, namely whether an action—even what we consider an act of resistance or self-defence—is violence, and whether or in what way it is resistance, and resistance to precisely what.

The growing belligerence of identity politics, however, has also brought forth a rhetoric that tends to equate radical resistance with violent resistance. Inversely, one's own violence tends to be presented as non-violence (not really violence) on account of it being resistance. On the "street" level of movements there is talk of women needing to arm ourselves individually, if not indeed to mount a collective armed struggle, while on the "respectable" level of national women's politics there are growing numbers advocating that women join their national military, either to acquire adequate training in the art of war or so as not to leave the military exclusively in the hands of men.[5] Analysis of violence and discussion of non-violent means of resistance are becoming increasingly rare, being thought decidedly "un-radical." Having identified (that is, personified) the enemy, victory over them has become the "natural" aim.

Rather than analysing the violent action proposed (from personal violence through to war) and its adequacy as a means to a defined political end, we tend instead to adduce examples—say, of armed liberation struggles in the Third World, the armed uprising of the Warsaw ghetto, or a woman's self-defence in a life-threatening situation—to prove the justifiability of violent self-defence. Far from clarifying the question at hand, namely how we propose to act, why, and to what end, in which situation, such comparisons suggest the self-evident comparability of our own situation (oppression) with the situations (oppressions) in these historical precedents.

Questioning the usefulness of women arming ourselves here and now or of beating up select men in the park thus becomes equivalent to suggesting that the Jews in the Warsaw ghetto should have non-violently awaited their destruction. Such comparisons, however, mean abusing the suffering (and the resistance) of other people in the interests of justifying our own actions. Our situation is alleged to be comparable to that in the examples, the analogy having to stand in for an analysis of our own situation. The proposal to use violence is derived not from an analysis of our situation and a definition of our political aims; rather, violence is the chosen means, for which justification is now being sought.

Similarly, the notion seems to be gaining ground that, as members of oppressed groups, our violence cannot be violence like the violence of the oppressors, just as white women's power within the system of slavery was said to be "false power," not power "in the sense" that male tyrants and patriarchal despots have it, and white women's contemporary racism is considered to be not really "racism" in the sense of "racism endemic in patriarchy." In the same way our own violence is thought to be "not really" violence, in the sense of the violence of those we oppose. Not only does our being—our identity—apparently soften any violence we may exert, it may make us by definition into resisters. Simply by virtue of not belonging to the (chief) oppressors, we seem to constitute some "kind" of resistance to power.

Resistance, however, like oppression, is not a nebulous climate we vaguely inhabit, move into by coming "home" to our identity. Much less is it a quality which we have *qua* our (oppressed) identity, so that anything we do by definition becomes "resistance." "There is something in each lesbian," Sarah Hoagland writes, "that questions the norm at some level. . . . That is, there is something within each lesbian of the spirit I consider crucial to the sort of ethical concepts I am interested in working on. It is a certain ability to resist and refocus, and it is this ability in all lesbians which draws me."[6] The lesbian herself may neither question the norm(s), nor resist or refocus, yet there "is something within her" that questions the norm (whether she wants it or not). It is an *ability* to resist and refocus, regardless of whether she uses her ability to do so. And there is a spirit crucial to ethical concepts in her—if not like Lévinas's* ethics falling on top of us from outside, still pushing through from within.

It is each and every and "all lesbians" who are blessed with such abilities and spirit—we need not meet or know them individually to know what spirit possesses them and what ethical concepts they are living by. For these are qualities and spirits that come with identity, factors of these "kinds" of people. Other "kinds" of people, if they have them at all, have them to a lesser degree, even if they do resist and refocus or question social norms. Perhaps it is something they happen to do, yet not something which they *are* and *have*. In the same way it used to be whites or white men who were blessed with abilities, whether they showed any by using them or not, whereas whatever ability or spirit Black people or women might have shown, it was never, in the eyes of white men, what they really did and what showed what Black people or women could do; it was something they happened to do in spite of what they *are*.[7]

Lévinas: Emmanuel Lévinas (1906–1995). Born in Lithuania, Lévinas made his home in France after the extermination of his family during the Holocaust. He is famous for the statement that "ethics precedes ontology": he opposed the existentialist obsession with ontology, the study of Being, with the insistence that moral reasoning should be a philosopher's central concern.

Resistance, I would suggest, does not come with any identity. It is a question of political will and action. It requires the political analysis of systems of oppression through to individual acts of oppression and violence — in terms of agency and its consequences, in terms of agents and beneficiaries and victims — and a corresponding analysis of resistance in terms of actions and their consequences.[8] Only once we know what we are doing, and what our actions actually effect, and what we mean them to achieve, can we begin to act in resistance, knowing what it is resistance to; and only then will we be able to identify and co-operate with those acting for the same political goals.

Resistance to *violence* however cannot consist of violence. Violence may change the direction of violence, invert the roles of violator and victim, but it necessarily affirms the principle of violence, whatever else it may achieve. And it adds new victims to the world — victims of our own making, not to mention more violent perpetrators, whose ranks we have decided to join. While in extremity and under the threat of our lives we may not have any means other than violence to secure our survival, most of us most of the time are not in such situations, though we glibly speak of "survival." Instead, we would have ample opportunity in situations of no such threat to challenge the legitimacy of violence and to practise alternatives — above all by deciding not to use violence ourselves.

Notes

1. Cynthia Enloe, *Does Khaki Become You? The Militarization of Women's Lives* (London: Pandora Press, 1988; first published in 1983).

2. See also Patricia Williams's discussion of the racist murders of Howard Beach and the so-called Bernhard Goetz murders in the New York underground [subway] and their public media justifications, in Patricia J. Williams, *The Alchemy of Race and Rights* (London: Virago Press, 1993), pp. 58–79.

3. German television ARD, "Tagesschau," 16 May 1994.

4. Anthony Giddens, *The Transformation of Intimacy: Sexuality, Love and Eroticism in Modern Societies* (Cambridge: Polity Press, 1992), p. 31.

5. Discussed e.g. by Cynthia Enloe in "The Right to Fight: A Feminist Catch-22," *Ms.* 4, no. 1 (July/August 1993), pp. 84–87. Ruth Seifert, in an interview in *taz,* 17 February 1993, argues in favour of women entering the military, as this could perhaps "break open the social construction of masculinity and femininity."

6. Sarah Lucia Hoagland, *Lesbian Ethics: Toward New Value* (Palo Alto: Institute of Lesbian Studies, 1988), p. 6.

7. See e.g. Joanna Russ, *How to Suppress Women's Writing* (London: The Women's Press, 1984); Toni Morrison, *Playing in the Dark: Whiteness and the Literary Imagination* (London: Picador, 1993).

8. Women's resistance often seems to disappear when the focus remains (exclusively) on oppression. Thus Adrienne Rich's essay "Compulsory Heterosexuality and Lesbian Existence," for example, seems to have been received more as a confirmation of the oppression of lesbians than as a brilliant example of how to read, that is, perceive, the resistance of (heterosexual as well as lesbian) women to compulsory heterosexuality.

Ideas for Rereading

1. In what ways does Kappeler consider contemporary use of the term *resistance* to be problematic? What would she consider the proper use of that term? As you reread her essay, outline Kappeler's critique of the contemporary use of the term. Relate her critique to what she calls "identity politics" (p. 508).

2. As you reread Kappeler's essay, take note of her often ironic tone as well as her qualified use of words like *civilized*. List instances where Kappeler uses irony to make her point. What purpose is served by this rhetorical strategy?

Ideas for Writing

1. What according to Kappeler is "identity politics" (p. 508)? Start by making note each time of Kappeler's definition of the concept and its relation to "resistance." How does your perception of "identity politics" relate to Kappeler's? Keeping in mind Kappeler's ideas, write an essay analyzing the relation between resistance and "identity politics" in a specific contemporary situation.

2. Verbal irony is a difficult rhetorical strategy to master but it has a particular power in the setting forth of political ideas and arguments. With Kappeler's essay as a model, write an essay, opinion article, or letter to the editor that uses irony as one of its principal rhetorical strategies. (You might look to Martin Luther King's "Letter from Birmingham Jail" for an example of another essay that uses irony effectively. Perhaps the classic example of sustained irony for political purpose is Jonathan Swift's "A Modest Proposal," which you can find in your library or on the Internet.) Then write a second essay reflecting on how irony works as a rhetorical strategy. How does irony function? What are the necessary elements to make it work? What is the difference between effective irony and ineffective irony? How can a writer be sure that the reader will recognize and understand his or her use of irony?

MICHAEL NAGLER

Michael Nagler has been a professor of classics and comparative literature at Berkeley since 1966. He retired in 1991, but has taught part-time since 1991 as an emeritus professor.

In 1967, after "graduating" from the Free Speech Movement, he met Sri Eknath Easwaran, founder of the Blue Mountain Center of Meditation and author of Gandhi the Man. *Nagler has been a student and resident at the Blue Mountain Center since 1969, and a workshop and retreat leader for the center's numerous programs around the United States and Canada.*

At the University of California, Berkeley, he founded in 1984 the Peace and Conflict Studies Program (PACS), where he continues to teach. His books include America Without Violence: Why Violence Persists and How You Can Stop It *(1982),* The Upanishads *(with Sri Eknath Easwaran, 1987), and* Gandhi for Beginners *(1998). He is also the author of numerous articles on classical literature, peace, and mysticism. Nagler has spoken and written widely on the subject of peace and nonviolence for over twenty-five years. He has consulted for the U.S. Institute of*

Peace and many other organizations. His most recent book, Is There No Other Way: The Search for a Nonviolent Future, *will be published in 2001.*

The following essay, which first appeared in ReVision *magazine in the fall of 1997, sets out to define* peace studies. *As you read, take notes listing the different kinds of violence that Nagler refers to. Underline the key words and phrases in his definition of violence. How does Nagler's work with the word* violence *help you understand his explanation of "nonviolence"? Use your notebook to trace connections between violence, nonviolence, and human nature. How does Nagler connect these concepts? How do you connect them?*

Nonviolence and Peacemaking Today

If passive resistance could conquer racial hatred . . . Gandhi and Negroes like King would have shown the world how to conquer war itself.
—W. E. B. Du Bois

Traditionally, peace studies has tried to look at four distinct levels of violence. First, some kind of intrapersonal violence must exist within the psyche itself, we surmise; human beings are not at peace even when external conditions do not threaten them. Peace psychology studies this sometimes difficult to access level of violence, which is still far from being widely understood. Second, proceeding "outward," we come to interpersonal violence, the harm one person does another for whatever reason. There is a great deal of this kind of violence in today's world, but this form of violence, too, is understudied. Phenomena like racism attract a great deal of attention, but much interpersonal violence has little to do with race, gender, or other kinds of group division; people trapped in an industrial culture hurt one another all the time, with unkind thoughts, words, and deeds. Racism and the like are only specific ways that interpersonal violence is organized and expressed—not a source of the violence per se.[1]

Third, groups of people do violence to others within every society, notoriously in the patterns of structural violence like the exploitation of the poor and powerless, which can be the hardest kind of violence to eradicate or even detect. It was primarily the great peace scholar Johan Galtung who coined the term *structural violence,* and made this pervasive disorder of all societies a topic for peace science (e.g., Galtung and Hivik 1971). Finally, beyond this intrasocial violence is the form of violence that is most dramatic in its periodic devastations, intersocial violence, or war.

Today, two other kinds of violence demand attention. In this neocolonial era, there is increasing structural violence in the international community; globalization threatens to bring with it the globalization of greed and exploitation along with, if not faster than, other modes of trade and exchange. Intersocial structural violence bids to outdo other levels of violence in the sheer weight of devastation it will inflict on humanity. This is partly because scale adds a complicating factor to the structural violence already present within states, since it is always easier to victimize structurally those at a distance than those with whom one directly interacts (even though it is the latter who can make us most passionately irritated). Selling cigarettes to the Third World, and exporting garbage or toxic substances we do not allow in our country, provide examples of this.

Another new wrinkle—new in terms of our awareness—is violence done by humanity as a whole to the interlocking life-support systems of planet earth. Environmental devastation is carried out at practically all levels of organization, by individuals, groups, corporations, and states in their respective capacities.

These additional wrinkles do not substantially alter the serviceable four-level model of peace studies, but they do tend to show that it is not absolute, underneath all forms of violence is the force of violence itself. The sheer scale of the devastation and suffering and the catastrophic disruptions of history caused by wars has made them the most absorbing level of violence about which to inquire. And yet their prominence in our gaze may mislead us. It is a truism, and like many truisms often ignored or forgotten, that "wars begin in the minds of men." An undivided, perfectly happy mind doesn't cause wars; the possessor of such a mind would not even participate in one.

The Nature of Violence

What is violence? One very simple way into that bedeviled question is through the Sanskrit word for violence which has passed somewhat into currency, thanks to Gandhi. This word *himsa* is derived from the root *han,* meaning "to strike," or "to slay." It is not so much the root meaning, however, as the form of the word itself that nonviolence scholars have found so suggestive. *Himsa* is what linguists call a "desiderative," a word that denotes not an action per se but the desire to do it. *Himsa* could be translated as "the intent to harm." The genius embodied in this word was already a step more precise than the "minds of men" formulation arrived at by the founders of UNESCO several thousand years later. The violence is in the wanting to hurt others that can come about in the disordered mind; as Augustine reflected, "Imagine thinking that our enemy could do us as much damage as the enmity we harbor against him" (*Confessions* I. 29, my translation).

With this definition we can avoid two misunderstandings. One can say by extension that "there was a violent storm" or that "my car got a violent jolt when I hit the pothole," but the phenomenon under study in this issue of *ReVision*—and one which cries out for such study—is violence, a human phenomenon that involves us as conscious beings, wrestling with will and desire. Similarly, an accident is not an act of violence. One person can injure another accidentally and they can remain friends; it happens all the time. But if one person injures another purposely, one or both of them is going to have to do some work so that they can get back to being friends. (That very work is what we call nonviolence—but I anticipate my later discussion.)

A second misunderstanding is related to a seeming exception that sometimes bedevils this psychological and ethical approach to violence and nonviolence. Gandhi (in his newspaper *Young India,* 4 November 1926) allowed that in certain extreme emergencies one might be called upon to use injurious force to stop a person from harming others:

> Taking life may be a duty. . . . Suppose a man runs amuck and goes furiously about, sword in hand, and killing anyone that comes in his way, and no one dares capture him alive. Anyone who dispatches this lunatic will earn the gratitude of the community and be regarded as a benevolent man.

Again, this rare necessity to inflict injury or death is not technically violence according to our definition; it is not the extent of the harm but the intent to inflict harm as such that makes for a violent state of mind, and in these theoretical cases the primary intent is not to injure, but to stop the dangerous person. To the extent that one could actually do such a thing without feeling rancor or fear (and we are verging on the ideal here), it would involve no "wish to harm," and thus no violence.

Let us quickly add: this exception is only valid under specific conditions. It cannot be used, as it often is, to excuse the preparations for violence, which means that it can never be made an excuse for war. War requires vast preparation, and as we will see, that time and effort could go into preparations to hold off war by other means. While there are almost no practical cases in which the "madman with the sword" exception would really apply—Gandhi never faced such a circumstance in fifty years of active work—it is theoretically interesting in revealing that external circumstances alone do not tell us whether someone or something was violent.

The Latin word from which violence derives, *violare,* means to "bear in on with force," and this adds another dimension to the inward, psychological focus of the Sanskrit, such that by putting them together we can build up a rich construct with important practical implications:

> Violence is the state of wanting another's harm, and that very state is itself a violation, a forcing, namely of the implicit unity of life. Violence, in this view, is a tearing of the web of life.

This should be borne in mind whenever we are trying to solve a problem of violence on any of its levels: violence is a failure to perceive the living web of unity that binds attacker and victim, hence a forming of the intention to harm, be it in disrupting the intimacy between friend and friend, institutionalizing abuse into the social fabric, or a society directing a large-scale threat system against "foreigners." Absent that malevolent intention, domestic violence would never occur, exploitation would be handily exposed and disestablished, and war would be a nightmare of the past.

That having been said about violence we can now, to paraphrase Dante, hoist our sails for calmer waters. What is nonviolence? We can go back to the ancient Sanskrit for that question too.

Nonviolence

Nonviolence has long been recognized as a poor and misleading term, especially in comparison to or as a translation of the term Gandhi made known to the world: *ahimsa.* The problem here—as much cultural as linguistic—arises from the significance of such negative compounds. The Sanskrit word, like its modern equivalents, is technically a negation, to be sure *a* means "not" just as in *amoral* or *anorexic* (from, respectively, Latin and Greek). But in Sanskrit, some of these negative compounds can work differently. Sanskrit abstract nouns sometimes denote a fundamental positive quality by negating its opposite rather than naming the thing directly. Thus "courage" is expressed by *abhaya,* literally, "nonfear"; or we encounter *akrodha* (nonanger) for kindness, and the Buddha's *avera* (nonhatred), meaning "love."² The reason for this apparently odd, oblique way of speaking may well lie in the fact that human beings have an inveterate tendency to see certain things only when they break down. "I had my back to the sun," Plotinus says, "and everything to which I turned I cast into my own shadow" (*Enneads* 5.5.7.16–19). This is painfully true with regard to peace and nonviolence, or anything that positive. Gandhi spared no words in his condemnation of the discipline of "history" (as the record of power struggles and war) when he wrote his manifesto, *Hind Swaraj,* aboard the S.S. *Rajputana* in 1909:

> Hundreds of nations live in peace. History does not and cannot take note of this fact. History is really a record of the interruption of the even working of the force of love or the soul. . . . History, then, is a record of the interruptions of the course of nature. Soul-force [*satyagraha*], being natural, is not noted in history. (Gandhi 1938, 70)

No wonder that Vedantic India, which perfected the *via negativa* as a means of spiritual inquiry, preferred that we "back into" the awareness of the Real by negating its surrounding conceptual veils: any word for anything as real as nonviolence is only another veil itself.

In short, then, the word *ahimsa* is no more negative than "infinite," but literal translation makes it so, because in general English does not have that habit of referring to positive concepts by trimming away what is not there. To moderns, nonviolence (and especially the older spelling, non-violence) does not sound like a phenomenon existing in its own right. We have had our backs to the sun of nonviolence for so long that we cast everything about it into the shadow of our own negative thinking.

Policy, inevitably, follows vision. What should we do about crime? Obviously, wage a "war on crime" especially on those dangerous youth (our own children, remember). How can we bring peace? By waging a "war to end all wars"; and so it goes on. We let violence take the lead, then react to it with more violence.[3]

It has taken peace research a long time to overcome the idea of "negative peace"; furthermore, the notion that meaningful peace is considerably more than the absence of war has not yet gained wide currency in the public or, alas, policy circles. But nonviolence is even harder. Nonviolence is the subtle side of the coin of peace. Nonviolence is much more recent as a subject of study than peace is, and much more unfamiliar to the general public and, of course, there is the handicap of the word itself. This has made it still more difficult to come to grips with nonviolence as a positive phenomenon.

How does one develop, or mobilize, this positive force of nonviolence? Nonviolence comes from a mind that harbors no intention to harm. But no mind is free of such whims and intentions; at least none is born that way. In practical terms, nonviolence arises from the process of converting negative states, which I believe are part of our animal inheritance, into their positive counterparts.[4] Fear and anger are turned back by some kind of inner struggle to emerge as courage and compassion: this is nonviolence. Gandhi (1960, 111ff.) writes:

> It is not that I am incapable of anger, for instance, but I succeed on almost all occasions to keep my feelings under control. Whatever may be the result, there is always in me conscious struggle for following the law of nonviolence deliberately and ceaselessly. Such a struggle leaves one stronger for it. The more I work at this law, the more I feel the delight in my life, the delight in the scheme of the universe. It gives me a peace and a meaning of the mysteries of nature that I have no power to describe.

Just as the yen to harm arises in the mind of the individual person and propagates throughout the larger human community, even the international community and its institutions, so could nonviolence. Once we realize that nonviolence is not an absence-of-something-else, but what Gandhi frequently called the greatest force mankind has been endowed with, we must also realize that such a law, or force, cannot be limited to only one application. Electricity does not work only in radios; gravity does not work differently on heavy objects than on light ones: so it is with nonviolence. That word makes most of us think of a sit-in, a freedom struggle like India's, the Civil Rights movement of an oppressed minority fighting back for its rights. This is of course one way that nonviolence manifests, but hardly the only one. Once we accept that violence tears the fabric of life (and nonviolence repairs it), it becomes clear that there are endless ways nonviolent energy could be brought to bear on almost any relationship.

So revolutionary are the implications of the nonviolent potential in human consciousness in each and every one of us, waiting to be tapped that when we begin to contemplate the mobilization of that potential on any scale, the term *paradigm shift* inevitably comes to mind. If we could mobilize nonviolence the way we do violence, it would alter beyond recognition the way we create "entertainment" forms, the way we manage the economy, beginning with our relationship as human beings to the planet on whose bounty and serene beauty we live, the way we construct education, the way we respond to crime and war. Virtually every institution we know would be put on a different basis. And that is exactly the revolution Gandhi set in motion:

> Between the two world wars, at the heyday of Colonialism, force reigned supreme. It had a suggestive power, and it was natural for the weaker to lie down before the stronger. Then came Gandhi, chasing out of his country, almost singlehanded, the greatest military power on earth. He taught the world that there are higher things than force, higher even than life itself; he proved that force had lost its suggestive power. (Szent-Gyorgyi, quoted in Shirer 1979, 12)

Note that in this description Albert Szent-Gyorgyi, like most of us, is somewhat vague about those higher things that overcome power-as-we-know-it. Shirer himself is a little less so: Gandhi's *satyagraha,* he explains, "taught us all that there was a greater power in life than force, which seemed [note the use of *seemed*] to have ruled the planet since men first sprouted on it. That power lay in the spirit, in Truth and Love, in nonviolent action" (Shirer 1979, 245).

Because what both these writers say is true, we live in an era of intense ambiguity. Violence is getting worse all the time; it is becoming a norm. By definition a *violatio* cannot be a norm, cannot be normal; yet the word *violent* has become a selling point, for example in ads for computer games, films, and popular novels. At the same time, however, and because of this very strain in our conception of the normal, a true nonviolent revolution is just waiting to happen in the world.

I have come to believe that peace, and hence Gandhi and nonviolence, are not merely involved in but are the key to this hoped-for, this indispensable transition to a new paradigm (see Nagler 1981). Space here doesn't allow more than a brief suggestion as to why I have come to hold that claim. The most dramatic and in a way the most substantial area of modern life in which a new paradigm has begun to occur is of course in the new physics, very remote, it would seem, from the ethical sector of life where we have usually located issues like nonviolence. But for theoretical physicists who have left behind the reductionist, material-based "classical" physics we grew up on, the implications of a science that restores consciousness to the center of reality are quite similar to the world vision I've just been describing:

> Man can no longer be seen as a deterministically controlled cog in a giant machine. He [or she] appears, rather, as an aspect of the fundamental process that gives form and definition to the universe. . . . The assimilation of this quantum conception of man into the cultural environment of the 21st century must inevitably produce a shift in values conducive to human survival. The quantum conception gives an enlarged sense of

self . . . [from which] must flow lofty values that extend far beyond the confines of narrow personal self interest. (Stapp 1989, 6, 8)

The problem, though, is how will the "assimilation of this quantum conception of man" take place? The new physics has definitely got its nose under the Newtonian tent; some scientists routinely work within that startling new worldview. Yet where is the lofty new vision of the human being? The answer is, alas, buried under a barrage of mass media propaganda—the powerful tools of a popular-commercial culture that relentlessly degrade and trivialize human nature.

Nonviolence is centrally concerned with this question of the human image. Violence is dehumanization (Nagler 1982, 23–25). The intention to harm carries with it the profound denial of the humanity of the victim, as we have seen luridly in the killing fields of modern conflicts. Nonviolence first and foremost restores this perspective. In a great British Broadcasting Corporation documentary called *Gandhi's India* (which seems all but unobtainable at present), a woman who worked closely with Gandhi was asked, "Don't you think he was unrealistic—that he didn't take into account the limitations of human nature?" Flashing an unforgettable smile she shot back, "There are no limits to our nature."

Turning to Peace

With this background, I would like to describe a recent development in nonviolence that may be the most important—and is almost certainly the least recognized one: organized nonviolent substitutes for war.

As early as 1913, when Gandhi became aware what power nonviolence could command in the hands of trained, committed volunteers, he began referring to the volunteers working under his inspiration as an "army." Each Satyagrahi was a "soldier" of peace (Gandhi 1950, 199, 204, 272, 281). It was just a metaphor, of course, but from this metaphor grew, decades after Gandhi's assassination, the worldwide movement of unarmed volunteers that has today become a silent presence in Central America, Sri Lanka, Northern Ireland, the Caucasus, Bosnia, and elsewhere.

Gandhi had begun to midwife his idea from metaphor to reality shortly after his return to India, when he called for regional or neighborhood "peace armies" (*shanti sena's*) that would control local, often communal conflicts, and he continued to develop the concept until the end of his life. At no time was he swayed by the argument that nonviolence could not be used against war as well as it had been used to rescue Indian indentured laborers in South Africa and to move to the verge of wresting India from the mighty imperial system imposed over two hundred years ago by the British. He said, "It is blasphemy to say that non-violence can be practised by individuals and never by nations which are composed of individuals" (in *Harijan,* a newspaper published by Gandhi, 12 November 1928). At first, the Mahatma saw "peace armies" as having intrasocial application:

The Congress [his political party] should be able to put forth a non-violent army of volunteers numbering not a few thousands but lakhs [hundreds of thousands] who would be equal to every occasion where the police and the military are required. . . . They would be constantly engaged in constructive activities that make riots impossible. . . . Such an army should be ready to cope with any emergency, and in order to still the frenzy of mobs should risk their lives in numbers sufficient for the purpose. . . . Surely a few hundred young men and women giving themselves deliberately to mob fury will be any day a cheap and braver method of dealing with such madness than the display and use of the police and the military. (Gandhi 1951, 86)

It was a short step, however, from replacing the military in civil unrest to replacing the military in war, and in 1942, when Indians and British alike were cowering before the prospect of a Japanese invasion, he took that step, startling even his own Congressmen by seriously proposing that India could defend herself against the Japanese nonviolently, if necessary by putting up a "living wall" of men, women, and children who would outlast the fury of the invader.

Gandhi was never given a chance to put his bold vision to the test; the British put him in prison, and even most Congress Party members could not follow him that far. But it was too late to stifle the vision.

Two people, about as different as possible, had already taken Gandhi at his word. Twelve years earlier in, of all places, the "wild" Northwest Frontier Province (now part of Pakistan) the great leader Khan Abdul Ghaffar Khan persuaded nearly a hundred thousand Pathan fighters—all devout Muslims—to put on uniforms, form brigades, including the usual marching band, and resist the British all without weapons in their hands or, as far as possible, hate in their hearts. The "Servants of God," as they were called, kept their vow under unbelievable provocation and added immeasurable strength to the freedom struggle. For long an unsung story, Badshah ("royal") Khan, dubbed the "Frontier Gandhi," and the harrowing descriptions of the brutal assaults borne without retaliating by the "Servants of God" have passed into history (Easwaran 1984).

While all this was happening in the Northwest Frontier Province, the Japanese invaded Shanghai in 1932. And as Western powers debated the merits of interfering militarily or doing nothing—either of which was sure to lead to another war—an Anglican clergy-woman named Maude Royden made the daring proposal that tens of thousands of volunteers should interpose themselves between the Chinese and the Japanese armies. Royden, a former suffragist who, like Badshah Khan, had met Gandhi in the twenties, was anticipating the complementary possibility in Gandhi's peace vision: if cadres of nonviolent citizens could use nonviolence within their own country, why could they not also interpose themselves between hostile parties elsewhere in the world; why not, if you will, take the offensive for peace?

Royden's grandiose scheme (which did not gain the Mahatma's approval) never came to fruition, but the vision has continued and it is important to realize why she failed. It was partly because of the enormous logistical difficulties of "parachuting" peacekeepers into another country halfway round the world, partly because no one there had asked for them, but mainly because she did not realize that peace takes more training than war. As one critic had to remind her, "You pacifists are trying to use a weapon you have not got," namely, nonviolent capacities.

In the "rich but little known history" of nonviolent peacemaking (Weber 1993, 52), a history which is only now progressing from the infantile stage of out-of-print pamphlets and photocopied anthologies to actual books (cf. Weber 1996, Mahoney and Eguren 1997), dreamers and idealists are bound to repeat the mistakes of the past as they grope their way forward, because the dream of peace armies to do away with war refuses to die. Sixty years after Maude Royden's scheme of unarmed "shock troops" failed to materialize, a small, better-prepared team tried to interpose itself in 1990 between ground forces on the Iraq-Kuwait border; shortly thereafter a number of organizations sent no small number of people into the Balkan inferno. One such organization, Mir Sada (Seed of Peace), deployed three thousand volunteers, all but ignored by the mainstream media.

While these dramatic interventions have sometimes been little more than an unwanted interference and sometimes rendered a great deal of moral and material support to parties caught in the storm of violence, things have also been happening in very practical and effective ways on a smaller scale. Small groups of relatively well-trained persons from many countries have been going to Central America, Sri Lanka, the Middle East, and elsewhere to offer "protective accompaniment" to individuals or groups, typically human rights groups, who would otherwise be all but incapacitated by death threats. The success of these "unarmed bodyguards" in protecting individual life and creating a political space in regimes otherwise paralyzed by oppressive terror has been impressive. One of the Witness for Peace volunteers who serendipitously discovered that the volunteer nonviolent presence stopped Contra attacks on the villages of Nicaragua during a fact-finding mission back in 1981 was Sue Severin, a health professional from Northern California. I would like to quote what she told me because it answers fairly well to the process described by Gandhi as the psychological conversion which unleashes nonviolent power:

> While I was there I never felt fear . . . I found—much to my surprise— that I became very calm in danger. I'm a Quaker and don't go very much with "God" language, but the only way I can explain it is, I felt I was in the hands of God: not safe—not that I wouldn't be hurt—but that I was where I was supposed to be, doing what I was supposed to be doing. And this can be addictive. Maybe that's why we kept going back.

Today, something like forty nongovernmental organizations are in the business of peace intervention, some of them nominally secular like Peace Brigades International (PBI), some completely ad hoc, like the Gulf

Peace Team, quite a few faith-based like Witness for Peace and Christian Peacemaker Teams. Activists and armchair scholars have been contemplating some kind of global coordinating body to recruit, train, and field nonviolent peace teams and have begun to realize that it's essential to acquaint the general public with their accomplishments and significance (part of the purpose of this article). As with earlier decades' interest in Civilian Based Defense (the Badshah Khan model, where one mobilizes one's own society rather than intervene somewhere else), a government or two is flirting with the idea of a nonviolent peacemaking service that would be parallel to, but utterly different in principle from, the conventional armed force.[5]

They have good reason. The fact is that small numbers of people have gone into extremely dangerous areas and accomplished significant reductions in conflict with almost no equipment while at the same time suffering very minimal personal casualties. Three PBI workers were stabbed in Guatemala and many have received death threats, but the fact is that almost no one has been killed while praying with Nicaraguan villagers, while monitoring a demonstration in Sri Lanka, or even while interposing her- or himself between hostile parties without the "protection" of arms. Peace teams of one kind or another have resettled refugees on Cyprus, restored order among populations terrorized by the threat of war, and negotiated a settlement to the long-standing Nagaland succession conflict in Northern India. In Sri Lanka, Guatemala, and Haiti, workers with PBI and other groups have provided shields consisting of little more than their presences that not only protected individuals who would certainly have been killed, but made it possible for forces of peace and justice to consolidate and expand—the first thing repressive regimes try to prevent. And they have done remarkably well at protecting local communities. When Ernesto Cardenal was Minister of Culture in the Sandinista government, I had occasion to ask him during a visit to Berkeley whether he thought the Witness for Peace groups operating out in the villages were helping. Cardenal—himself far from dedicated to nonviolence—told me with considerable passion that, "We need more of these groups and we need them quickly. Wherever they have been there has been no violence." Later his translator repeated that statement for the gathering, but unconsciously "cleaned it up," saying, "there has been almost no violence." Furious at this distortion (with which all nonviolence advocates are familiar), Cardenal practically pounded the table, insisting, "I said absolutely no violence."

And all this has been done, as a yet-to-be-published study of Yeshua Moser points out, with a "chronic lack of resources, . . . inadequate infrastructure, poor communications, and limited training opportunities," not to mention the near-total cold-shoulder from the mass media and "little popular understanding of the dynamics and history of . . . nonviolent action."

All these disabilities could change. As Marrack Goulding, recently called the world's peacekeeper-in-chief, has put it, "The United Nations can cajole, argue, bluster . . . but it cannot compel" (*Economist* 1992, 57).

Nonviolent peacekeeping would turn this supposed weakness of the U.N. into its greatest strength. Nonviolence is that form of power specifically designed to operate in situations where you cannot compel or do not wish to, because you are among those who know that humankind is on the verge of discovering a better form of power.

Notes

1. Menand (1974, 74) writes: "We've started to understand every human encounter as a symbolic clash of group interests, and this is misleading. Violence can be talked about in the abstract, but violence, like sex, never occurs in the abstract.... Groups are essentially imaginary. Souls are real, and they can be saved, or lost, only one at a time."

2. As Roshi Jiyu Kennett put it, "Buddhism states what the Eternal is not. (I use the term *Eternal* rather than *God*. *God* has the implication of being a deity with a beard and a long stick.) It does not state what it is because if it did we would be stuck with a concept. Buddhism states specifically what we know for certain. It will not state that which is taken on faith. We can find this out for ourselves . . . but we cannot state what it is". (quoted in Friedman 1987, 168).

3. My book *America without Violence* (1982) was routinely labelled *Violence in America* one semester in the campus bookstore at Berkeley.

4. Whatever may have been the adaptive value of these drives in animals to help gain food, stake out territory, or compete for mating privileges, I take it that they are no longer suited in their raw form to the human condition.

5. At the time of this writing, the regional government of Nordrhein-Westphalen in Germany has funded fourteen volunteers to go to Bosnia for reconstructive peacemaking.

Works Cited

Easwaran, E. 1984. *A man to match his mountains: Badshah Kahn, nonviolent soldier of Islam.* Petaluma, Calif.: Nilgiri Press.

Friedman, L. 1987. *Meetings with remarkable women: Buddhist teachers in America.* Boston: Shambhala.

Galtung, J., and T. Hivik. 1971. Structural and direct violence: A note on operationalization. *Journal of Peace Research* 8 (1): 73–76.

Gandhi, M. 1938. *Hind Swaraj, or Indian Home Rule.* Ahmedabad, India: Navajivan.

———. 1950. *Satyagraha in South Africa.* Ahmedabad, India: Navajivan.

———. 1951. *Non-violent resistance.* New York: Schocken Books.

———. 1960. *All men are brothers.* Ahmedabad, India: Navajivan.

Mahoney, L., and L. Eguren. 1997. *Unarmed bodyguards: International accompaniment for the protection of human rights.* Westwood, Conn.: Kumarian Press.

Menand, L. 1974. The war of all against all. *The New Yorker* (March 14): 74–78.

Nagler, M. 1981. Peace as a paradigm shift. *Bulletin of the Atomic Scientists* 37 (December): 49–52.

———. 1982. *America without violence: Why violence persists and how you can stop it.* Covelo, Calif.: Island Press.

Shirer, W. 1979. *Gandhi: A memoir.* New York: Simon & Schuster.

Stapp, H. 1989. *Quantum physics and human values.* Lawrence Berkeley Laboratory paper LBL-27738 (22 September).

The United Nations: Mr. Human Rights. 1992. *The Economist,* 26 December–January 1993: 57–60.

Weber, T. 1993. From Maude Royden's peace army to the Gulf peace team: An assessment of unarmed interpositionary peace forces. *Journal of Peace Research* 30 (1): 45–64.

———. 1996. *Gandhi's peace army: The Shanti Sena and unarmed peacekeeping.* Syracuse: Syracuse University Press.

Ideas for Rereading

1. Of American society, Nagler contends, "Violence is getting worse all the time; it is becoming a norm. . . . At the same time, however, and because of this very strain in our conception of the normal, a true nonviolent revolution is just waiting to happen in the world" (p. 517). Consider this statement in terms of the commonly held belief that violence is inherent in human beings, and thus quite "normal." As you reread Nagler's essay, mark passages that put forward his argument against the "normalcy" of violence. List the elements of his argument and decide which ones convince you.

2. Nagler gives an etymology of Gandhi's word *ahimsa* ("no harm") suggesting that "the word *ahimsa* is no more negative than [the word] 'infinite'" (p. 515). Take this statement into account as you reread Nagler's essay. Take notes outlining his argument for "nonviolence as a positive phenomenon" (p. 516). List the specific ways in which Nagler uses his understanding of language and the roots of certain words to strengthen his political argument.

Ideas for Writing

1. Nagler asserts that the increase of violence in society is a "strain in our conception of the normal" (p. 517), that violence itself is not (as often said) normal or innate in human beings. As you reread Nagler's essay, take note of how he makes this argument. Write an essay responding to Nagler's contentions. Use examples from television, newspapers, the Internet, film, or personal observation to support your position.

2. Gandhi, Nagler, and Kelly all insist, in varying degrees, on the practicality of nonviolence as a political strategy. Reread each writer's arguments on the practicality of nonviolence and write an essay evaluating each of these arguments. Though at first they may seem to be making substantially the same argument, a closer reading may uncover subtle but significant differences. How might their arguments on the practical application of nonviolence be used to complement or extend one other? Your essay should use ideas from Gandhi, Nagler, and Kelly to develop an argument about their combined approach. What kinds of ethical, religious, and political assumptions do these three writers have in common? What are the larger implications of these assumptions for the world as *you* experience it? In what ways are specific ideas expressed by these three writers relevant to your world? As you develop your essay be sure to use direct quotations (words, phrases, and sentences) from all three writers. Also be sure to explain how the quotations you have selected fit in with the argument you are developing.

EXTENDING YOUR WORK

Ideas for Research

1. Using the Internet, make a survey of the Web sites for groups that promote nonviolence. Write an essay that considers the language of these Web sites. Where do they acknowledge—either explicitly or implicitly—the influence of Gandhi? Where do these groups seem to build on or diverge from Gandhi's ideas?

2. Look into the histories of recent self-described "resistance" movements. Include those that have often accepted violence as a pragmatic political strategy—such as the Irish Republican Army (IRA), the Palestine Liberation Organization (PLO), certain animal rights groups—and those—such as Philippine "People Power," Gandhi's *swaraj* movement, and the Tibetan resistance movement—that insist on nonviolence. Choose at least one of each kind of movement. Write an essay exploring how each group's use of violent or nonviolent action has affected the course of its history, the process of its cause toward success or failure. Some issues to consider: What do these groups consider to be an adequate rationale for the use of violence? Under what circumstances? Is it possible to reconcile the opposing groups—those who insist on nonviolence and those who see circumstances that justify it?

3. Conduct research into Petra Kelly's life. Do the same with Gandhi. What in Kelly's upbringing and education do you think led to the views she expresses in her essay? Write an essay comparing Kelly's formation in nonviolence with that of Gandhi.

4. Kappeler writes, "Much of what today goes by the name of resistance . . . is retaliation against the enemy . . . a counter-move in . . . the chronological sequence of . . . attack and counter-attack between designated opponents" (p. 506). Choose a specific area of the world where a violent conflict is occurring or has recently occurred. Narrow your area as much as possible. Then conduct research into the history of the conflict, making notes about the different perspectives associated with the different parties to this situation. How do different people explain the events that created the current state of affairs in this particular area of the world? Find relevant examples of the rhetoric common to each side in the conflict, examining speeches, pamphlets, interviews, official literature, and so on. Write an essay using Kappeler's statement about resistance to analyze the rhetoric, the strategies of persuasion, used by the different participants in your chosen conflict. Focus on specific words, phrases, and examples that demonstrate, complicate, and disprove Kappeler's argument about the process of "attack and counter-attack."

Ideas for Working across Chapters

1. Consider Gandhi's assertion of the supremacy of the human "Soul-Force" over our "brute nature" (p. 446), along with Nagler's parallel statement, "In practical terms, nonviolence arises from the process of converting negative

states [such as fear and anger], which I believe are part of our animal inheritance, into their positive counterparts [such as courage and compassion]" (p. 516). Both writers seem to suggest that true humanity does not admit of violence, that violence is a regression to an animalistic state. Test this idea in the context of Chapter 6. In what ways does Turner assume the necessity of violence as part of social progress? Select examples from the Turner chapter that complicate Gandhi's and Nagler's arguments. Use these examples to write an essay about the interactions between "brute nature" and "nonviolence."

2. Reread Du Bois's "Of Our Spiritual Strivings" in Chapter 2 of this volume, taking careful note of Du Bois's concept of "double-consciousness." Develop good working definitions of both "double-consciousness" and Griffin's concept of "dualism." Write an essay exploring the connections and differences between the two concepts.

CHAPTER 6

The Frontier
How Do We Imagine the West?

Depending on your point of view, the movement of Americans beyond the Mississippi in the nineteenth century is a history of manifest destiny and legitimate conquest; brutal slaughter and systematic denial; open opportunity and good fortune; disappointed dreams and broken promises; lost culture and territorial dispossession; the building of shining "cities on the hill" and the discovery of the promised land; or the destruction of an ecosystem and an unavoidable chapter in the unfolding of America's destiny. For some, "the West" might be characterized as a series of relentless plagues, droughts, dust bowls, and farm failures, studded with incidents of brutality and lawlessness, selfishness and greed, lying, cheating, and deception. For others, it represents all that is good about America: the West is "God's country," "the breadbasket of the world," "the land of opportunity," the place where everyone is free to live as he or she chooses in a dreamland of fresh democratic possibility.

How we define "the West" depends in part on which perspectives we take into account. Some might say that there are two basic points of view on the North American West: the point of view of the European colonizers and the point of view of the Native American colonized. Without denying this fundamental opposition, we can, however, develop more complex understandings of America's frontier.

We might begin to complicate matters by recognizing that each of us is positioned somewhat differently in relation to this cultural, historical, personal place: how we perceive relations between Europeans and Indians depends on where we are from, where we have been, and what we know. Individuals who grew up in New Jersey, North Dakota, or Missouri will think about the trans-Mississippi West differently from one another. Furthermore, within any state there will be differences in perspective as we move from east to west, from farm to town to city, from condominium to reservation to apartment building. Differences in perspective will also be shaped by differences in ethnic and religious background: Irish Catholics, Swedish Lutherans, African American Baptists, and Oglala Christians are likely to differ in their views not just because "everyone has his or her own opinion" but because individual points of view form against a background of cultural experiences and assumptions. The same is true as we take into account the perspectives of the vast array of different nations and tribes that lived on the American continent before Columbus and the other European colonizers and that continue to live in America right now. If we assume homogeneity among the forces of colonization, and if we assume homogeneity among the people who were colonized, we do an injustice to those who made the North American West what it is today and what it might be tomorrow.

When we open discussion of the West, it quickly becomes apparent that experiences and assumptions formed by cultural, ethnic, communal, ritual, and family life are supplemented and transformed by personal experiences and beliefs. While it is certainly important that someone involved in the discussion is, say, English from the agricultural East Midlands, our sense of what this cultural background might mean shifts when we ask questions about where he or she has been in the North American West: Have you driven from coast to coast? Have you been to Elko, Nevada? Have you been east of Las Vegas or west of the Poconos? Have you been to Africa, Asia, or Europe? Do you consider Kansas City to be part of "the West"? How about St. Louis? Denver? Houston? How do you define "civilization"? What is the most protracted, most "uncivilized" experience you have had? What did you learn from this experience? How do you imagine the life of a descendant of Geronimo, Crazy Horse, or Sitting Bull? What do you think about farming practices in western Kansas? Have you ever stood on a piece of unplowed prairie? Have you ever grown a garden that is deliberately perennial and polycultural?

Whatever our experience with, and our beliefs about, the West as an example of "civilization" and "the civilizing process," it is undeniable that the history of the West is the history of an expansion (sometimes self-motivated, sometimes pressured by economic circumstances, sometimes forced through enslavement) by people with European, Asian, and African ancestries into a land populated by people with very different (even if distantly related) ancestries. As Europeans, Asians, and Africans were forced or tempted west beyond the Mississippi, or east beyond the Rockies, technological and numeric advantage held sway over an Indian population that adapted quickly enough to put up a good fight.

Once we have recognized that our own perspectives are different from one another's, we can begin to imagine meaningful differences between and among the descendants of pre-Columbus North Americans. And with these differences in mind we might also begin to imagine differences among those who settled the West and those who write about it. This chapter is organized around the most famous argument about Western expansion, Frederick Jackson Turner's "The Significance of the Frontier in American History." Turner's perspective is built on assumptions about different stages of the civilizing process, and his conclusion is that the frontier "closed" when the West had achieved a certain level of civilization. Patricia Nelson Limerick and Eric Gary Anderson respond directly to Turner, using his arguments to formulate counterarguments by introducing mythologies that Turner ignored (the desert and the outlaw) and thus demonstrating the limitations of Turner's perspective.

While Anderson works with literary representations of two American heroes, Billy the Kid and Geronimo, Jane Tompkins discusses specific material representations, describing and interpreting paintings by Remington, a display of animal memorabilia, a disappointing exhibit on Plains Indians, and a gun collection, before speculating on what Buffalo Bill says about North American civilization: Turner's thesis was deliberately designed to counter Buffalo Bill's version of Western history. Annette Kolodny's rewriting of Western "herstory" shows how the dominant metaphors used to characterize Western expansion are both sexist and destructive. In a challenging essay, "The American West and the Burden of Belief," the Native American writer N. Scott Momaday explores the profound differences between Native American ways of knowing and those of European Americans, focusing especially on their relationships with the land and with language. This essay articulates a point of view that has too often been neglected or silenced, but it also reminds us (like Tompkins's essay) of the enormous difficulty of communicating across such deep divides. Finally, in "America's Debt to the Indian Nations: Atoning for a Sordid Past" and "The Border Patrol State," Leslie Marmon Silko shows how the legacy of the past expresses itself in the troubled and troubling relationship between the power of the state and the rights of Native Americans.

TEXT

FREDERICK JACKSON TURNER

Frederick Jackson Turner was born in Portage, Wisconsin, in 1861. His mother taught in the local school and his father edited a newspaper. Turner's first job was as a typesetter working alongside his father, but eventually he followed his mother's profession. In 1880 he went to the University of Wisconsin to study history and used archival manuscripts to focus on local history. After graduating, Turner worked for two years on newspapers in Chicago and Milwaukee before enrolling in the master's program in Madison, Wisconsin. His master's thesis on the Indian trade in Wisconsin formed the basis of the doctoral dissertation he wrote at Johns Hopkins University: "The Character and Influence of the Indian Trade in Wisconsin: A Study of the Trading Post as an Institution."

In 1889 Turner became an assistant professor of history at the University of Wisconsin. After reading "The Significance of the Frontier in American History" at the 1893 Chicago meeting of the American Historical Association, Turner achieved national recognition. Over the next few years he was offered jobs at Princeton,

Stanford, and the University of Chicago, but he remained loyal to Wisconsin. In 1908, however, the regents of the University of Wisconsin criticized his 1906 book The Rise of the New West *for its assertion of socialist provincialism as an antidote to the damaging effects of pioneer individualism. Coming on the heels of years of complaints by the administration about his "interference" in the running of the university, this criticism spurred Turner to take a job at Harvard University in Massachusetts, where he taught until his retirement in 1924. During a professional career that spanned more than forty years, Turner published many articles and books, including* The Frontier in American History *(1920) and, in the year he died,* The Significance of Sections in American History *(1932), which won a Pulitzer Prize in 1932.*

Turner's name continues to be associated with the argument presented in his 1893 address: historians of the North American West return to this argument with perennial regularity. The argument is complex, but we might summarize it thus: an analysis of the frontier experience as a series of local historical events allows us to define America's difference from Europe and to generalize about the role of the frontier in the civilizing process. Focusing on the "return to primitive conditions on a continually advancing frontier line," Turner characterizes America in terms of a "perennial rebirth" (p. 531). He identifies four main phases in this cycle of rejuvenation: "the trader's frontier, the rancher's frontier, . . . the miner's frontier, and the farmer's frontier" (p. 536). And he reads these phases as a booklike "record of social evolution." Then he shows how the frontier provided "a consolidating agent" (p. 537) for "the formation of a composite nationality for the American people" (p. 541), decreased American dependence on England, stimulated unique ways of distributing land, changed the North–South dynamic by creating a "mediating" Middle region (p. 544), and promoted "democracy here and in Europe" (p. 546). As you read, notice the distinct phases in Turner's argument, marking sentences or passages that connect each of these sections to his main thesis about the significance of the frontier. In the margins or on a separate page, list all the main headings that he covers in his argument. Later, you might construct an outline of his argument that includes all the important claims he makes under each heading. But you'll also want to weigh his argument carefully as you read: What are Turner's overriding values and priorities? Who and what are the major actors in the drama as he sees it? Who and what plays a relatively minor role?

The Significance of the Frontier in American History[1]

In a recent bulletin of the Superintendent of the Census for 1890 appear these significant words: "Up to and including 1880 the country had a frontier of settlement, but at present the unsettled area has been so broken into by isolated bodies of settlement that there can hardly be said to be a frontier line. In the discussion of its extent, its westward movement, etc., it can not, therefore, any longer have a place in the census reports." This brief official statement marks the closing of a great historic movement. Up to our own day American history has been in a large degree the history of the colonization of the Great West. The existence of an area of free land, its continuous recession, and the advance of American settlement westward, explain American development.

Behind institutions, behind constitutional forms and modifications, lie the vital forces that call these organs into life and shape them to meet changing conditions. The peculiarity of American institutions is the fact that they have been compelled to adapt themselves to the changes of an expanding people — to the changes involved in crossing a continent, in winning a wilderness, and in developing at each area of this progress out of the primitive economic and political conditions of the frontier into the complexity of city life. Said Calhoun* in 1817, "We are great, and rapidly — I was about to say fearfully — growing!"[2] So saying, he touched the distinguishing feature of American life. All peoples show development; the germ theory of politics has been sufficiently emphasized. In the case of most nations, however, the development has occurred in a limited area; and if the nation has expanded, it has met other growing peoples whom it has conquered. But in the case of the United States we have a different phenomenon. Limiting our attention to the Atlantic coast, we have the familiar phenomenon of the evolution of institutions in a limited area, such as the rise of representative government; the differentiation of simple colonial governments into complex organs; the progress from primitive industrial society, without division of labor, up to manufacturing civilization. But we have in addition to this a recurrence of the process of evolution in each western area reached in the process of expansion. Thus American development has exhibited not merely advance along a single line, but a return to primitive conditions on a continually advancing frontier line, and a new development for that area. American social development has been continually beginning over again on the frontier. This perennial rebirth, this fluidity of American life, this expansion westward with its new opportunities, its continuous touch with the simplicity of primitive society, furnish the forces dominating American character. The true point of view in the history of this nation is not the Atlantic coast, it is the Great West. Even the slavery struggle, which is made so exclusive an object of attention by writers like Professor von Holst,* occupies its important place in American history because of its relation to westward expansion.

In this advance, the frontier is the outer edge of the wave — the meeting point between savagery and civilization. Much has been written about the frontier from the point of view of border warfare and the chase, but as a field for the serious study of the economist and the historian it has been neglected.

Calhoun: John Caldwell Calhoun (1782–1850), vice president from 1825 to 1832, first under John Quincy Adams and then under Andrew Jackson. As a congressman Calhoun had introduced the declaration of war against Great Britain in 1812. As senator for South Carolina from 1832 to 1850, he championed states' rights and slavery.

von Holst: Herman Eduard von Holst (1841–1904), author of *The Constitutional and Political History of the United States,* 8 vols. (Chicago: Callaghan and Co., 1876–1892). He was head of the history department at the University of Chicago between 1892 and 1902.

The American frontier is sharply distinguished from the European frontier — a fortified boundary line running through dense populations. The most significant thing about the American frontier is that it lies at the hither edge of free land. In the census reports it is treated as the margin of that settlement which has a density of two or more to the square mile. The term is an elastic one, and for our purposes does not need sharp definition. We shall consider the whole frontier belt, including the Indian country and the outer margin of the "settled area" of the census reports. This paper will make no attempt to treat the subject exhaustively; its aim is simply to call attention to the frontier as a fertile field for investigation, and to suggest some of the problems which arise in connection with it.

In the settlement of America we have to observe how European life entered the continent, and how America modified and developed that life and reacted on Europe. Our early history is the study of European germs developing in an American environment. Too exclusive attention has been paid by institutional students to the Germanic origins, too little to the American factors. The frontier is the line of most rapid and effective Americanization. The wilderness masters the colonist. It finds him a European in dress, industries, tools, modes of travel, and thought. It takes him from the railroad car and puts him in the birch canoe. It strips off the garments of civilization and arrays him in the hunting shirt and the moccasin. It puts him in the log cabin of the Cherokee and Iroquois and runs an Indian palisade around him. Before long he has gone to planting Indian corn and plowing with a sharp stick; he shouts the war cry and takes the scalp in orthodox Indian fashion. In short, at the frontier the environment is at first too strong for the man. He must accept the conditions which it furnishes, or perish, and so he fits himself into the Indian clearings and follows the Indian trails. Little by little he transforms the wilderness, but the outcome is not the old Europe, not simply the development of Germanic germs, any more than the first phenomenon was a case of reversion to the Germanic mark. The fact is, that here is a new product that is American. At first, the frontier was the Atlantic coast. It was the frontier of Europe in a very real sense. Moving westward, the frontier became more and more American. As successive terminal moraines result from successive glaciations, so each frontier leaves its traces behind it, and when it becomes a settled area the region still partakes of the frontier characteristics. Thus the advance of the frontier has meant a steady movement away from the influence of Europe, a steady growth of independence on American lines. And to study this advance, the men who grew up under these conditions, and the political, economic, and social results of it, is to study the really American part of our history.

In the course of the seventeenth century the frontier was advanced up the Atlantic river courses, just beyond the "fall line," and the tidewater region became the settled area. In the first half of the eighteenth century another advance occurred. Traders followed the Delaware and Shawnese Indians to the Ohio as early as the end of the first quarter of the century.[3] Gov. Spotswood, of Virginia, made an expedition in 1714 across the Blue

Ridge. The end of the first quarter of the century saw the advance of the Scotch-Irish and the Palatine Germans up the Shenandoah Valley into the western part of Virginia, and along the Piedmont region of the Carolinas.[4] The Germans in New York pushed the frontier of settlement up the Mohawk to German Flats.[5] In Pennsylvania the town of Bedford indicates the line of settlement. Settlements had begun on New River, a branch of the Kanawha, and on the sources of the Yadkin and French Broad.[6] The King attempted to arrest the advance by his proclamation of 1763,[7] forbidding settlements beyond the sources of the rivers flowing into the Atlantic; but in vain. In the period of the Revolution the frontier crossed the Alleghanies into Kentucky and Tennessee, and the upper waters of the Ohio were settled.[8] When the first census was taken in 1790, the continuous settled area was bounded by a line which ran near the coast of Maine, and included New England except a portion of Vermont and New Hampshire, New York along the Hudson and up the Mohawk about Schenectady, eastern and southern Pennsylvania, Virginia well across the Shenandoah Valley, and the Carolinas and eastern Georgia.[9] Beyond this region of continuous settlement were the small settled areas of Kentucky and Tennessee, and the Ohio, with the mountains intervening between them and the Atlantic area, thus giving a new and important character to the frontier. The isolation of the region increased its peculiarly American tendencies, and the need of transportation facilities to connect it with the East called out important schemes of internal improvement, which will be noted farther on. The "West," as a self-conscious section, began to evolve.

From decade to decade distinct advances of the frontier occurred. By the census of 1820[10] the settled area included Ohio, southern Indiana and Illinois, southeastern Missouri, and about one-half of Louisiana. This settled area had surrounded Indian areas, and the management of these tribes became an object of political concern. The frontier region of the time lay along the Great Lakes, where Astor's American Fur Company operated in the Indian trade,[11] and beyond the Mississippi, where Indian traders extended their activity even to the Rocky Mountains; Florida also furnished frontier conditions. The Mississippi River region was the scene of typical frontier settlements.[12]

The rising steam navigation[13] on western waters, the opening of the Erie Canal, and the westward extension of cotton[14] culture added five frontier states to the Union in this period. Grund, writing in 1836, declares: "It appears then that the universal disposition of Americans to emigrate to the western wilderness, in order to enlarge their dominion over inanimate nature, is the actual result of an expansive power which is inherent in them, and which by continually agitating all classes of society is constantly throwing a large portion of the whole population on the extreme confines of the State, in order to gain space for its development. Hardly is a new State or Territory formed before the same principle manifests itself again and gives rise to a further emigration; and so is it destined to go on until a physical barrier must finally obstruct its progress."[15]

In the middle of this century the line indicated by the present eastern boundary of Indian Territory, Nebraska, and Kansas marked the frontier of the Indian country.[16] Minnesota and Wisconsin still exhibited frontier conditions,[17] but the distinctive frontier of the period is found in California, where the gold discoveries had sent a sudden tide of adventurous miners, and in Oregon, and the settlements in Utah.[18] As the frontier had leaped over the Alleghanies, so now it skipped the Great Plains and the Rocky Mountains; and in the same way that the advance of the frontiersmen beyond the Alleghanies had caused the rise of important questions of transportation and internal improvement, so now the settlers beyond the Rocky Mountains needed means of communication with the East, and in the furnishing of these arose the settlement of the Great Plains and the development of still another kind of frontier life. Railroads, fostered by land grants, sent an increasing tide of immigrants into the Far West. The United States Army fought a series of Indian wars in Minnesota, Dakota, and the Indian Territory.

By 1880 the settled area had been pushed into northern Michigan, Wisconsin, and Minnesota, along Dakota rivers, and in the Black Hills region, and was ascending the rivers of Kansas and Nebraska. The development of mines in Colorado had drawn isolated frontier settlements into that region, and Montana and Idaho were receiving settlers. The frontier was found in these mining camps and the ranches of the Great Plains. The superintendent of the census for 1890 reports, as previously stated, that the settlements of the West lie so scattered over the region that there can no longer be said to be a frontier line.

In these successive frontiers we find natural boundary lines which have served to mark and to affect the characteristics of the frontiers, namely: the "fall line"; the Alleghany Mountains; the Mississippi; the Missouri where its direction approximates north and south; the line of the arid lands, approximately the ninety-ninth meridian; and the Rocky Mountains. The fall line marked the frontier of the seventeenth century; the Alleghanies that of the eighteenth; the Mississippi that of the first quarter of the nineteenth; the Missouri that of the middle of this century (omitting the California movement); and the belt of the Rocky Mountains and the arid tract, the present frontier. Each was won by a series of Indian wars.

At the Atlantic frontier one can study the germs of processes repeated at each successive frontier. We have the complex European life sharply precipitated by the wilderness into the simplicity of primitive conditions. The first frontier had to meet its Indian question, its question of the disposition of the public domain, of the means of intercourse with older settlements, of the extension of political organization, of religious and educational activity. And the settlement of these and similar questions for one frontier served as a guide for the next. The American student needs not to go to the "prim little townships of Sleswick" for illustrations of the law of continuity and development. For example, he may study the origin of our land policies in the colonial land policy; he may see how the system grew by adapting the statutes to the customs of the successive frontiers.[19] He may see how the mining experience in the lead regions of Wisconsin, Illinois, and Iowa was applied to the mining laws of the Sierras,[20] and how our Indian policy has been a series of experimentations on successive frontiers. Each tier of new States has found in the older ones material for its constitutions.[21] Each frontier has made similar contributions to American character, as will be discussed farther on.

But with all these similarities there are essential differences, due to the place element and the time element. It is evident that the farming frontier of the Mississippi Valley presents different conditions from the mining frontier of the Rocky Mountains. The frontier reached by the Pacific Railroad, surveyed into rectangles, guarded by the United States Army, and recruited by the daily immigrant ship, moves forward at a swifter pace and in a different way than the frontier reached by the birch canoe or the pack horse. The geologist traces patiently the shores of ancient seas, maps their areas, and compares the older and the newer. It would be a work worth the historian's labors to mark these various frontiers and in detail compare one with another. Not only would there result a more adequate conception of American development and characteristics, but invaluable additions would be made to the history of society.

Loria,[22] the Italian economist, has urged the study of colonial life as an aid in understanding the stages of European development, affirming that colonial settlement is for economic science what the mountain is for geology, bringing to light primitive stratifications. "America," he says, "has the key to the historical enigma which Europe has sought for centuries in vain, and the land which has no history reveals luminously the course of universal history." There is much truth in this. The United States lies like a huge page in the history of society. Line by line as we read this continental page from West to East we find the record of social evolution. It begins with the Indian and the hunter; it goes on to tell of the disintegration of savagery by the entrance of the trader, the pathfinder of civilization; we read the annals of the pastoral stage in ranch life; the exploitation of the soil by the raising of unrotated crops of corn and wheat in sparsely settled farming communities; the intensive culture of the denser farm settlement; and finally the manufacturing organization with city and factory system.[23] This page is familiar to the student of census statistics, but how little of it has been used by our historians. Particularly in eastern States this page is a palimpsest. What is now a manufacturing State was in an earlier decade an area of intensive farming. Earlier yet it had been a wheat area, and still earlier the "range" had attracted the cattleherder. Thus Wisconsin, now developing manufacture, is a State with varied agricultural interests. But earlier it was given over to almost exclusive grain-raising, like North Dakota at the present time.

Each of these areas has had an influence in our economic and political history; the evolution of each into a higher stage has worked political transformations. But what constitutional historian has made any adequate attempt to interpret political facts by the light of these social areas and changes?[24]

The Atlantic frontier was compounded of fisherman, fur-trader, miner, cattle-raiser, and farmer. Excepting the fisherman, each type of industry was on the march toward the West, impelled by an irresistible attraction. Each passed in successive waves across the continent. Stand at Cumberland Gap and watch the procession of civilization, marching single file—the buffalo following the trail to the salt springs, the Indian, the fur-trader and hunter, the cattle-raiser, the pioneer farmer—and the frontier has passed by. Stand at South Pass in the Rockies a century later and see the same procession with wider intervals between. The unequal rate of advance compels us to distinguish the frontier into the trader's frontier, the rancher's frontier, or the miner's frontier, and the farmer's frontier. When the mines and the cow pens were still near the fall line the traders' pack trains were tinkling across the Alleghanies, and the French on the Great Lakes were fortifying their posts, alarmed by the British trader's birch canoe. When the trappers scaled the Rockies, the farmer was still near the mouth of the Missouri.

Why was it that the Indian trader passed so rapidly across the continent? What effects followed from the trader's frontier? The trade was coeval with American discovery. The Norsemen, Vespuccius, Verrazani, Hudson, John Smith, all trafficked for furs. The Plymouth pilgrims settled in Indian cornfields, and their first return cargo was of beaver and lumber. The records of the various New England colonies show how steadily exploration was carried into the wilderness by this trade. What is true for New England is, as would be expected, even plainer for the rest of the colonies. All along the coast from Maine to Georgia the Indian trade opened up the river courses. Steadily the trader passed westward, utilizing the older lines of French trade. The Ohio, the Great Lakes, the Mississippi, the Missouri, and the Platte, the lines of western advance, were ascended by traders. They found the passes in the Rocky Mountains and guided Lewis and Clark,[25] Frémont, and Bidwell. The explanation of the rapidity of this advance is connected with the effects of the trader on the Indian. The trading post left the unarmed tribes at the mercy of those that had purchased fire-arms—a truth which the Iroquois Indians wrote in blood, and so the remote and unvisited tribes gave eager welcome to the trader. "The savages," wrote La Salle, "take better care of us French than of their own children; from us only can they get guns and goods." This accounts for the trader's power and the rapidity of his advance. Thus the disintegrating forces of civilization entered the wilderness. Every river valley and Indian trail became a fissure in Indian society, and so that society became honeycombed. Long before the pioneer farmer appeared on the scene, primitive Indian life had passed away. The farmers met Indians armed with guns. The trading frontier, while steadily undermining Indian power by making the tribes ultimately dependent on the whites, yet, through its sale of guns, gave to the Indian increased power of resistance to the farming frontier.

French colonization was dominated by its trading frontier; English colonization by its farming frontier. There was an antagonism between the two frontiers as between the two nations. Said Duquesne to the Iroquois, "Are you ignorant of the difference between the king of England and the king of France? Go see the forts that our king has established and you will see that you can still hunt under their very walls. They have been placed for your advantage in places which you frequent. The English, on the contrary, are no sooner in possession of a place than the game is driven away. The forest falls before them as they advance, and the soil is laid bare so that you can scarce find the wherewithal to erect a shelter for the night."

And yet, in spite of this opposition of the interests of the trader and the farmer, the Indian trade pioneered the way for civilization. The buffalo trail became the Indian trail, and this became the trader's "trace"; the trails widened into roads, and the roads into turnpikes, and these in turn were transformed into railroads. The same origin can be shown for the railroads of the South, the Far West, and the Dominion of Canada.[26] The trading posts reached by these trails were on the sites of Indian villages which had been placed in positions suggested by nature; and these trading posts, situated so as to command the water systems of the country, have grown into such cities as Albany, Pittsburgh, Detroit, Chicago, St. Louis, Council Bluffs, and Kansas City. Thus civilization in America has followed the arteries made by geology, pouring an ever richer tide through them, until at last the slender paths of aboriginal intercourse have been broadened and interwoven into the complex mazes of modern commercial lines; the wilderness has been interpenetrated by lines of civilization growing ever more numerous. It is like the steady growth of a complex nervous system for the originally simple, inert continent. If one would understand why we are to-day one nation, rather than a collection of isolated states, he must study this economic and social consolidation of the country. In this progress from savage conditions lie topics for the evolutionist.[27]

The effect of the Indian frontier as a consolidating agent in our history is important. From the close of the seventeenth century various intercolonial congresses have been called to treat with Indians and establish common measures of defense. Particularism was strongest in colonies with no Indian frontier. This frontier stretched along the western border like a cord of union. The Indian was a common danger, demanding united action. Most celebrated of these conferences was the Albany congress of 1754, called to treat with the Six Nations, and to consider plans of union. Even a cursory reading of the plan proposed by the congress reveals the importance of the frontier. The powers of the general council and the officers were, chiefly, the determination of peace and war with the Indians, the regulation of Indian trade, the purchase of Indian lands, and the creation and government of new settlements as a security against the Indians. It is evident that the unifying tendencies of the Revolutionary period were facilitated by the previous cooperation in the regulation of the frontier. In this connection may be mentioned the importance of the frontier, from that day to this, as a military training school, keeping alive the power of resistance to aggression, and developing the stalwart and rugged qualities of the frontiersman.

It would not be possible in the limits of this paper to trace the other frontiers across the continent. Travelers of the eighteenth century found the "cowpens" among the canebrakes and peavine pastures of the South, and the "cow drivers" took their droves to Charleston, Philadelphia, and New York.[28] Travelers at the close of the War of 1812 met droves of more than a thousand cattle and swine from the interior of Ohio going to Pennsylvania to fatten for the Philadelphia market.[29] The ranges of the Great Plains, with ranch and cowboy and nomadic life, are things of yesterday and of to-day. The experience of the Carolina cow pens guided the rangers of Texas. One element favoring the rapid extension of the rancher's frontier is the fact that in a remote country lacking transportation facilities the product must be in small bulk, or must be able to transport itself, and the cattle raiser could easily drive his product to market. The effect of these great ranches on the subsequent agrarian history of the localities in which they existed should be studied.

The maps of the census reports show an uneven advance of the farmer's frontier, with tongues of settlement pushed forward and with indentations of wilderness. In part this is due to Indian resistance, in part to the location of river valleys and passes, in part to the unequal force of the centers of frontier attraction. Among the important centers of attraction may be mentioned the following: fertile and favorably situated soils, salt springs, mines, and army posts.

The frontier army post, serving to protect the settlers from the Indians, has also acted as a wedge to open the Indian country, and has been a nucleus for settlement.[30] In this connection mention should also be made of the government military and exploring expeditions in determining the lines of settlement. But all the more important expeditions were greatly indebted to the earliest pathmakers, the Indian guides, the traders and trappers, and the French voyageurs, who were inevitable parts of governmental expeditions from the days of Lewis and Clark.[31] Each expedition was an epitome of the previous factors in western advance.

In an interesting monograph, Victor Hehn[32] has traced the effect of salt upon early European development, and has pointed out how it affected the lines of settlement and the form of administration. A similar study might be made for the salt springs of the United States. The early settlers were tied to the coast by the need of salt, without which they could not preserve their meats or live in comfort. Writing in 1752, Bishop Spangenburg says of a colony for which he was seeking lands in North Carolina, "They will require salt & other necessaries which they can neither manufacture nor raise. Either they must go to Charleston, which is 300 miles distant . . . Or else they must go to Boling's Point in V^a on a branch of the James & is also 300 miles from here . . . Or else they must go down the Roanoke—I know not how many miles—where salt is brought up from the Cape Fear."[33] This may serve as a typical illustration. An annual pilgrimage to the coast for salt thus became essential. Taking flocks or furs and ginseng root, the early settlers sent their pack trains after seeding time each year to the coast.[34] This proved to be an important educational influence, since it was almost the only way in which the pioneer learned what was going on in the East. But when discovery was made of the salt springs of the Kanawha, and the Holston, and Kentucky, and central New York, the West began to be freed from dependence on the coast. It was in part the effect of finding these salt springs that enabled settlement to cross the mountains.

From the time the mountains rose between the pioneer and the seaboard, a new order of Americanism arose. The West and the East began to get out of touch of each other. The settlements from the sea to the mountains kept connection with the rear and had a certain solidarity. But the over-mountain men grew more and more independent. The East took a narrow view of American advance, and nearly lost these men. Kentucky and Tennessee history bears abundant witness to the truth of this statement. The East began to try to hedge and limit westward expansion. Though Webster* could declare that there were no Alleghanies in his politics, yet in politics in general they were a very solid factor.

The exploitation of the beasts took hunter and trader to the west, the exploitation of the grasses took the rancher west, and the exploitation of the virgin soil of the river valleys and prairies attracted the farmer. Good soils have been the most continuous attraction to the farmer's frontier. The land hunger of the Virginians drew them down the rivers into Carolina, in early colonial days; the search for soils took the Massachusetts men to Pennsylvania and to New York. As the eastern lands were taken up migration flowed across them to the west. Daniel Boone, the great backwoodsman, who combined the occupations of hunter, trader, cattle-raiser, farmer, and surveyor — learning, probably from the traders, of the fertility of the lands of the upper Yadkin, where the traders were wont to rest as they took their way to the Indians, left his Pennsylvania home with his father, and passed down the Great Valley road to that stream. Learning from a trader of the game and rich pastures of Kentucky, he pioneered the way for the farmers to that region. Thence he passed to the frontier of Missouri, where his settlement was long a landmark on the frontier. Here again he helped to open the way for civilization, finding salt licks, and trails, and land. His son was among the earliest trappers in the passes of the Rocky Mountains, and his party are said to have been the first to camp on the

Webster: Daniel Webster (1782–1852), the great lawyer and orator. As a congressman for Boston (1823–27) and senator for Massachusetts (1827–41 and 1845–50), he was a champion of American nationalism, defending the Union against supporters of states' rights. He opposed the annexation of Texas in 1845 and the war with Mexico. In the interest of preserving the Union, he supported the Compromise of 1850 with its provisions for returning fugitive slaves to their owners. As secretary of state (1850–52) under President Fillmore, he supervised the enforcement of this law.

present site of Denver. His grandson, Col. A. J. Boone, of Colorado, was a power among the Indians of the Rocky Mountains, and was appointed an agent by the government. Kit Carson's mother was a Boone.[35] Thus this family epitomizes the backwoodsman's advance across the continent.

The farmer's advance came in a distinct series of waves. In Peck's New Guide to the West, published in Boston in 1837, occurs this suggestive passage:

> Generally, in all the western settlements, three classes, like the waves of the ocean, have rolled one after the other. First comes the pioneer, who depends for the subsistence of his family chiefly upon the natural growth of vegetation, called the "range," and the proceeds of hunting. His implements of agriculture are rude, chiefly of his own make, and his efforts directed mainly to a crop of corn and a "truck patch." The last is a rude garden for growing cabbage, beans, corn for roasting ears, cucumbers, and potatoes. A log cabin, and, occasionally, a stable and corn-crib, and a field of a dozen acres, the timber girdled or "deadened," and fenced, are enough for his occupancy. It is quite immaterial whether he ever becomes the owner of the soil. He is the occupant for the time being, pays no rent, and feels as independent as the "lord of the manor." With a horse, cow, and one or two breeders of swine, he strikes into the woods with his family, and becomes the founder of a new county, or perhaps state. He builds his cabin, gathers around him a few other families of similar tastes and habits, and occupies till the range is somewhat subdued, and hunting a little precarious, or, which is more frequently the case, till the neighbors crowd around, roads, bridges, and fields annoy him, and he lacks elbow room. The preemption law enables him to dispose of his cabin and cornfield to the next class of emigrants; and, to employ his own figures, he "breaks for the high timber," "clears out for the New Purchase," or migrates to Arkansas or Texas, to work the same process over.
>
> The next class of emigrants purchase the lands, add field to field, clear out the roads, throw rough bridges over the streams, put up hewn log houses with glass windows and brick or stone chimneys, occasionally plant orchards, build mills, schoolhouses, court-houses, etc., and exhibit the picture and forms of plain, frugal, civilized life.
>
> Another wave rolls on. The men of capital and enterprise come. The settler is ready to sell out and take the advantage of the rise in property, push farther into the interior and become, himself, a man of capital and enterprise in turn. The small village rises to a spacious town or city; substantial edifices of brick, extensive fields, orchards, gardens, colleges, and churches are seen. Broadcloths, silks, leghorns, crapes, and all the refinements, luxuries, elegancies, frivolities, and fashions are in vogue. Thus wave after wave is rolling westward; the real Eldorado* is still farther on.

Eldorado: Originally, Eldorado (Spanish for "the gilded man") was the legendary ruler of an Indian town in modern Colombia, who would coat himself in gold dust for religious festivals. For European explorers and conquistadores it came to refer to a whole mythical country of gold which, though of course never found, nevertheless often appeared on seventeenth-century maps of South America.

A portion of the two first classes remain stationary amidst the general movement, improve their habits and condition, and rise in the scale of society.

The writer has traveled much amongst the first class, the real pioneers. He has lived many years in connection with the second grade; and now the third wave is sweeping over large districts of Indiana, Illinois, and Missouri. Migration has become almost a habit in the West. Hundreds of men can be found, not over 50 years of age, who have settled for the fourth, fifth, or sixth time on a new spot. To sell out and remove only a few hundred miles makes up a portion of the variety of backwoods life and manners.[36]

Omitting those of the pioneer farmers who move from the love of adventure, the advance of the more steady farmer is easy to understand. Obviously the immigrant was attracted by the cheap lands of the frontier, and even the native farmer felt their influence strongly. Year by year the farmers who lived on soil whose returns were diminished by unrotated crops were offered the virgin soil of the frontier at nominal prices. Their growing families demanded more lands, and these were dear. The competition of the unexhausted, cheap, and easily tilled prairie lands compelled the farmer either to go west and continue the exhaustion of the soil on a new frontier, or to adopt intensive culture. Thus the census of 1890 shows, in the Northwest, many counties in which there is an absolute or a relative decrease of population. These States have been sending farmers to advance the frontier on the plains, and have themselves begun to turn to intensive farming and to manufacture. A decade before this, Ohio had shown the same transition stage. Thus the demand for land and the love of wilderness freedom drew the frontier ever onward.

Having now roughly outlined the various kinds of frontiers, and their modes of advance, chiefly from the point of view of the frontier itself, we may next inquire what were the influences on the East and on the Old World. A rapid enumeration of some of the more noteworthy effects is all that I have time for.

First, we note that the frontier promoted the formation of a composite nationality for the American people. The coast was preponderantly English, but the later tides of continental immigration flowed across to the free lands. This was the case from the early colonial days. The Scotch-Irish and the Palatine Germans, or "Pennsylvania Dutch," furnished the dominant element in the stock of the colonial frontier. With these peoples were also the freed indented servants, or redemptioners, who at the expiration of their time of service passed to the frontier. Governor Spotswood of Virginia writes in 1717, "The inhabitants of our frontiers are composed generally of such as have been transported hither as servants, and, being out of their time, settle themselves where land is to be taken up and that will produce the necessarys of life with little labour."[37] Very generally these redemptioners were of non-English stock. In the crucible of the frontier the immigrants were Americanized, liberated, and fused into a mixed race, English in neither nationality nor characteristics. The process has gone on from the early days to our own. Burke and other writers in the middle of the eighteenth century believed that Pennsylvania[38] was "threatened with the danger of being wholly foreign in language, manners, and perhaps even inclinations." The German and Scotch-Irish elements in the frontier of the South were only less great. In the middle of the present century the German element in Wisconsin was already so considerable that leading publicists looked to the creation of a German state out of the commonwealth by concentrating their colonization.[39] Such examples teach us to beware of misinterpreting the fact that there is a common English speech in America into a belief that the stock is also English.

In another way the advance of the frontier decreased our dependence on England. The coast, particularly of the South, lacked diversified industries, and was dependent on England for the bulk of its supplies. In the South there was even a dependence on the Northern colonies for articles of food. Governor Glenn, of South Carolina, writes in the middle of the eighteenth century: "Our trade with New York and Philadelphia was of this sort, draining us of all the little money and bills we could gather from other places for their bread, flour, beer, hams, bacon, and other things of their produce, all which, except beer, our new townships begin to supply us with, which are settled with very industrious and thriving Germans. This no doubt diminishes the number of shipping and the appearance of our trade, but it is far from being a detriment to us."[40] Before long the frontier created a demand for merchants. As it retreated from the coast it became less and less possible for England to bring her supplies directly to the consumer's wharfs, and carry away staple crops, and staple crops began to give way to diversified agriculture for a time. The effect of this phase of the frontier action upon the northern section is perceived when we realize how the advance of the frontier aroused seaboard cities like Boston, New York, and Baltimore, to engage in rivalry for what Washington called "the extensive and valuable trade of a rising empire."

The legislation which most developed the powers of the national government, and played the largest part in its activity, was conditioned on the frontier. Writers have discussed the subjects of tariff, land, and internal improvement, as subsidiary to the slavery question. But when American history comes to be rightly viewed it will be seen that the slavery question is an incident. In the period from the end of the first half of the present century to the close of the Civil War slavery rose to primary, but far from exclusive, importance. But this does not justify Dr. von Holst (to take an example) in treating our constitutional history in its formative period down to 1828 in a single volume, giving six volumes chiefly to the history of slavery from 1828 to 1861, under the title *Constitutional History of the United States*. The growth of nationalism and the evolution of American political institutions were dependent on the advance of the frontier. Even so recent a writer as Rhodes, in his *History of the United States since the Compromise of 1850,* has treated the legislation called out by the western advance as incidental to the slavery struggle.

This is a wrong perspective. The pioneer needed the goods of the coast, and so the grand series of internal improvement and railroad legislation began, with potent nationalizing effects. Over internal improvements occurred great debates, in which grave constitutional questions were discussed. Sectional groupings appear in the votes, profoundly significant for the historian. Loose construction increased as the nation marched westward.[41] But the West was not content with bringing the farm to the factory. Under the lead of Clay* — "Harry of the West" — protective tariffs were passed, with the cry of bringing the factory to the farm. The disposition of the public lands was a third important subject of national legislation influenced by the frontier.

The public domain has been a force of profound importance in the nationalization and development of the government. The effects of the struggle of the landed and the landless States, and of the Ordinance of 1787, need no discussion.[42] Administratively the frontier called out some of the highest and most vitalizing activities of the general government. The purchase of Louisiana was perhaps the constitutional turning point in the history of the Republic, inasmuch as it afforded both a new area for national legislation and the occasion of the downfall of the policy of strict construction. But the purchase of Louisiana was called out by frontier needs and demands. As frontier States accrued to the Union the national power grew. In a speech on the dedication of the Calhoun monument Mr. Lamar explained: "In 1789 the States were the creators of the Federal Government; in 1861 the Federal Government was the creator of a large majority of the States."

When we consider the public domain from the point of view of the sale and disposal of the public lands we are again brought face to face with the frontier. The policy of the United States in dealing with its lands is in sharp contrast with the European system of scientific administration. Efforts to make this domain a source of revenue, and to withhold it from emigrants in order that settlement might be compact, were in vain. The jealousy and the fears of the East were powerless in the face of the demands of the frontiersmen. John Quincy Adams was obliged to confess: "My own system of administration, which was to make the national domain the inexhaustible fund for progressive and unceasing internal improvement, has failed." The reason is obvious; a system of administration was not what the West demanded; it wanted land. Adams states the situation as follows: "The slaveholders of the South have bought the cooperation of the western country by the bribe of the western lands, abandoning to the new Western States their own proportion of the public property and aiding them in the design of grasping all the lands into their own hands. Thomas H. Benton was the

Clay: Henry Clay (1777–1852) was three times elected congressman and four times elected senator for Kentucky. He was known as the "great compromiser" for his support of the Missouri Compromise of 1820 and the Compromise of 1850, both of which aimed to reconcile the conflict between free states and slave states.

author of this system, which he brought forward as a substitute for the American system of Mr. Clay, and to supplant him as the leading states-man of the West. Mr. Clay, by his tariff compromise with Mr. Calhoun, abandoned his own American system. At the same time he brought for-ward a plan for distributing among all the States of the Union the proceeds of the sales of the public lands. His bill for that purpose passed both Houses of Congress, but was vetoed by President Jackson, who, in his an-nual message of December, 1832, formally recommended that all public lands should be gratuitously given away to individual adventurers and to the States in which the lands are situated.[43]

"No subject," said Henry Clay, "which has presented itself to the pres-ent, or perhaps any preceding, Congress, is of greater magnitude than that of the public lands." When we consider the far-reaching effects of the gov-ernment's land policy upon political, economic, and social aspects of American life, we are disposed to agree with him. But this legislation was framed under frontier influences, and under the lead of Western statesmen like Benton and Jackson. Said Senator Scott of Indiana in 1841: "I consider the preemption law merely declaratory of the custom or common law of the settlers."

It is safe to say that the legislation with regard to land, tariff, and inter-nal improvements — the American system of the nationalizing Whig party — was conditioned on frontier ideas and needs. But it was not merely in legislative action that the frontier worked against the sectionalism of the coast. The economic and social characteristics of the frontier worked against sectionalism. The men of the frontier had closer resemblances to the Middle region than to either of the other sections. Pennsylvania had been the seed-plot of frontier emigration, and, although she passed on her settlers along the Great Valley into the west of Virginia and the Carolinas, yet the industrial society of these Southern frontiersmen was always more like that of the Middle region than like that of the tide-water portion of the South, which later came to spread its industrial type throughout the South.

The Middle region, entered by New York harbor, was an open door to all Europe. The tide-water part of the South represented typical English-men, modified by a warm climate and servile labor, and living in baronial fashion on great plantations; New England stood for a special English movement — Puritanism. The Middle region was less English than the other sections. It had a wide mixture of nationalities, a varied society, the mixed town and county system of local government, a varied economic life, many religious sects. In short, it was a region mediating between New England and the South, and the East and the West. It represented that com-posite nationality which the contemporary United States exhibits, that jux-taposition of non-English groups, occupying a valley or a little settlement, and presenting reflections of the map of Europe in their variety. It was de-mocratic and nonsectional, if not national; "easy, tolerant, and contented"; rooted strongly in material prosperity. It was typical of the modern United

States. It was least sectional, not only because it lay between North and South, but also because with no barriers to shut out its frontiers from its settled region, and with a system of connecting waterways, the Middle region mediated between East and West as well as between North and South. Thus it became the typically American region. Even the New Englander, who was shut out from the frontier by the Middle region, tarrying in New York or Pennsylvania on his westward march, lost the acuteness of his sectionalism on the way.[44]

The spread of cotton culture into the interior of the South finally broke down the contrast between the "tide-water" region and the rest of the State, and based Southern interests on slavery. Before this process revealed its results the western portion of the South, which was akin to Pennsylvania in stock, society, and industry, showed tendencies to fall away from the faith of the fathers into internal improvement legislation and nationalism. In the Virginia convention of 1829–30, called to revise the constitution, Mr. Leigh, of Chesterfield, one of the tide-water counties, declared:

> One of the main causes of discontent which led to this convention, that which had the strongest influence in overcoming our veneration for the work of our fathers, which taught us to contemn the sentiments of Henry and Mason and Pendleton, which weaned us from our reverence for the constituted authorities of the State, was an overweening passion for internal improvement. I say this with perfect knowledge, for it has been avowed to me by gentlemen from the West over and over again. And let me tell the gentleman from Albemarle (Mr. Gordon) that it has been another principal object of those who set this ball of revolution in motion, to overturn the doctrine of State rights, of which Virginia has been the very pillar, and to remove the barrier she has interposed to the interference of the Federal Government in that same work of internal improvement, by so reorganizing the legislature that Virginia, too, may be hitched to the Federal car.

It was this nationalizing tendency of the West that transformed the democracy of Jefferson into the national republicanism of Monroe and the democracy of Andrew Jackson. The West of the War of 1812, the West of Clay, and Benton and Harrison, and Andrew Jackson, shut off by the Middle States and the mountains from the coast sections, had a solidarity of its own with national tendencies.[45] On the tide of the Father of Waters, North and South met and mingled into a nation. Interstate migration went steadily on—a process of cross-fertilization of ideas and institutions. The fierce struggle of the sections over slavery on the western frontier does not diminish the truth of this statement; it proves the truth of it. Slavery was a sectional trait that would not down, but in the West it could not remain sectional. It was the greatest of frontiersmen* who declared: "I believe this

---

greatest of frontiersmen: Abraham Lincoln. The quotation is from Lincoln's speech of June 16, 1858, accepting the Republican Party's nomination to run for senator from Illinois.

Government can not endure permanently half slave and half free. It will become all of one thing or all of the other." Nothing works for nationalism like intercourse within the nation. Mobility of population is death to localism, and the western frontier worked irresistibly in unsettling population. The effect reached back from the frontier and affected profoundly the Atlantic coast and even the Old World.

But the most important effect of the frontier has been in the promotion of democracy here and in Europe. As has been indicated, the frontier is productive of individualism. Complex society is precipitated by the wilderness into a kind of primitive organization based on the family. The tendency is anti-social. It produces antipathy to control, and particularly to any direct control. The tax-gatherer is viewed as a representative of oppression. Prof. Osgood, in an able article,[46] has pointed out that the frontier conditions prevalent in the colonies are important factors in the explanation of the American Revolution, where individual liberty was sometimes confused with absence of all effective government. The same conditions aid in explaining the difficulty of instituting a strong government in the period of the confederacy. The frontier individualism has from the beginning promoted democracy.

The frontier States that came into the Union in the first quarter of a century of its existence came in with democratic suffrage provisions, and had reactive effects of the highest importance upon the older States whose peoples were being attracted there. An extension of the franchise became essential. It was *western* New York that forced an extension of suffrage in the constitutional convention of that State in 1821; and it was *western* Virginia that compelled the tide-water region to put a more liberal suffrage provision in the constitution framed in 1830, and to give to the frontier region a more nearly proportionate representation with the tide-water aristocracy. The rise of democracy as an effective force in the nation came in with western preponderance under Jackson and William Henry Harrison, and it meant the triumph of the frontier—with all of its good and with all of its evil elements.[47] An interesting illustration of the tone of frontier democracy in 1830 comes from the same debates in the Virginia convention already referred to. A representative from western Virginia declared:

> But, sir, it is not the increase of population in the West which this gentleman ought to fear. It is the energy which the mountain breeze and western habits impart to those emigrants. They are regenerated, politically I mean, sir. They soon become *working politicians;* and the difference, sir, between a *talking* and a *working* politician is immense. The Old Dominion has long been celebrated for producing great orators; the ablest metaphysicians in policy; men that can split hairs in all abstruse questions of political economy. But at home, or when they return from Congress, they have negroes to fan them asleep. But a Pennsylvania, a New York, an Ohio, or a western Virginia statesman, though far inferior in logic, metaphysics, and rhetoric to an old Virginia statesman, has this advantage, that when he returns home he takes off his coat and takes hold of the

plow. This gives him bone and muscle, sir, and preserves his republican principles pure and uncontaminated.

So long as free land exists, the opportunity for a competency exists, and economic power secures political power. But the democracy born of free land, strong in selfishness and individualism, intolerant of administrative experience and education, and pressing individual liberty beyond its proper bounds, has its dangers as well as its benefits. Individualism in America has allowed a laxity in regard to governmental affairs which has rendered possible the spoils system and all the manifest evils that follow from the lack of a highly developed civic spirit. In this connection may be noted also the influence of frontier conditions in permitting lax business honor, inflated paper currency and wild-cat banking. The colonial and revolutionary frontier was the region whence emanated many of the worst forms of an evil currency.[48] The West in the War of 1812 repeated the phenomenon on the frontier of that day, while the speculation and wild-cat banking of the period of the crisis of 1837 occurred on the new frontier belt of the next tier of States. Thus each one of the periods of lax financial integrity coincides with periods when a new set of frontier communities had arisen, and coincides in area with these successive frontiers, for the most part. The recent Populist agitation is a case in point. Many a State that now declines any connection with the tenets of the Populists, itself adhered to such ideas in an earlier stage of the development of the State. A primitive society can hardly be expected to show the intelligent appreciation of the complexity of business interests in a developed society. The continual recurrence of these areas of paper-money agitation is another evidence that the frontier can be isolated and studied as a factor in American history of the highest importance.[49]

The East has always feared the result of an unregulated advance of the frontier, and has tried to check and guide it. The English authorities would have checked settlement at the headwaters of the Atlantic tributaries and allowed the "savages to enjoy their deserts in quiet lest the peltry trade should decrease." This called out Burke's splendid protest:

> If you stopped your grants, what would be the consequence? The people would occupy without grants. They have already so occupied in many places. You can not station garrisons in every part of these deserts. If you drive the people from one place, they will carry on their annual tillage and remove with their flocks and herds to another. Many of the people in the back settlements are already little attached to particular situations. Already they have topped the Appalachian Mountains. From thence they behold before them an immense plain, one vast, rich, level meadow; a square of five hundred miles. Over this they would wander without a possibility of restraint; they would change their manners with their habits of life; would soon forget a government by which they were disowned; would become hordes of English Tartars; and, pouring down upon your unfortified frontiers a fierce and irresistible cavalry, become

masters of your governors and your counselers, your collectors and comp-trollers, and of all the slaves that adhered to them. Such would, and in no long time must, be the effect of attempting to forbid as a crime and to suppress as an evil the command and blessing of Providence, "Increase and multiply." Such would be the happy result of an endeavor to keep as a lair of wild beasts that earth which God, by an express charter, has given to the children of men.

But the English Government was not alone in its desire to limit the advance of the frontier and guide its destinies. Tidewater Virginia[50] and South Carolina[51] gerrymandered those colonies to insure the dominance of the coast in their legislatures. Washington desired to settle a State at a time in the Northwest; Jefferson would reserve from settlement the territory of his Louisiana Purchase north of the thirty-second parallel, in order to offer it to the Indians in exchange for their settlements east of the Mississippi. "When we shall be full on this side," he writes, "we may lay off a range of States on the western bank from the head to the mouth, and so range after range, advancing compactly as we multiply." Madison went so far as to argue to the French minister that the United States had no interest in seeing population extend itself on the right bank of the Mississippi, but should rather fear it. When the Oregon question was under debate, in 1824, Smyth, of Virginia, would draw an unchangeable line for the limits of the United States at the outer limit of two tiers of States beyond the Mississippi, complaining that the seaboard States were being drained of the flower of their population by the bringing of too much land into market. Even Thomas Benton, the man of widest views of the destiny of the West, at this stage of his career declared that along the ridge of the Rocky Mountains "the western limits of the Republic should be drawn, and the statue of the fabled god Terminus should be raised upon its highest peak, never to be thrown down."[52] But the attempts to limit the boundaries, to restrict land sales and settlement, and to deprive the West of its share of political power were all in vain. Steadily the frontier of settlement advanced and carried with it individualism, democracy, and nationalism, and powerfully affected the East and the Old World.

The most effective efforts of the East to regulate the frontier came through its educational and religious activity, exerted by interstate migration and by organized societies. Speaking in 1835, Dr. Lyman Beecher declared: "It is equally plain that the religious and political destiny of our nation is to be decided in the West," and he pointed out that the population of the West "is assembled from all the States of the Union and from all the nations of Europe, and is rushing in like the waters of the flood, demanding for its moral preservation the immediate and universal action of those institutions which discipline the mind and arm the conscience and the heart. And so various are the opinions and habits, and so recent and imperfect is the acquaintance, and so sparse are the settlements of the West, that no homogeneous public sentiment can be formed to legislate immediately into being the requisite institutions. And yet they are all needed immediately in their utmost perfection and power. A nation is being 'born in a day.' . . . But what will become of the West if her prosperity rushes up to such a majesty of power, while those great institutions linger which are necessary to form the mind and the conscience and the heart of that vast world. It must not be permitted. . . . Let no man at the East quiet himself and dream of liberty, whatever may become of the West. . . . Her destiny is our destiny."[53]

With the appeal to the conscience of New England, he adds appeals to her fears lest other religious sects anticipate her own. The New England preacher and school-teacher left their mark on the West. The dread of Western emancipation from New England's political and economic control was paralleled by her fears lest the West cut loose from her religion. Commenting in 1850 on reports that settlement was rapidly extending northward in Wisconsin, the editor of the *Home Missionary* writes: "We scarcely know whether to rejoice or mourn over this extension of our settlements. While we sympathize in whatever tends to increase the physical resources and prosperity of our country, we cannot forget that with all these dispersions into remote and still remoter corners of the land the supply of the means of grace is becoming relatively less and less." Acting in accordance with such ideas, home missions were established and Western colleges were erected. As seaboard cities like Philadelphia, New York, and Baltimore strove for the mastery of Western trade, so the various denominations strove for the possession of the West. Thus an intellectual stream from New England sources fertilized the West. Other sections sent their missionaries; but the real struggle was between sects. The contest for power and the expansive tendency furnished to the various sects by the existence of a moving frontier must have had important results on the character of religious organization in the United States. The multiplication of rival churches in the little frontier towns had deep and lasting social effects. The religious aspects of the frontier make a chapter in our history which needs study.

From the conditions of frontier life came intellectual traits of profound importance. The works of travelers along each frontier from colonial days onward describe certain common traits, and these traits have, while softening down, still persisted as survivals in the place of their origin, even when a higher social organization succeeded. The result is that to the frontier the American intellect owes its striking characteristics. That coarseness and strength combined with acuteness and inquisitiveness; that practical, inventive turn of mind, quick to find expedients; that masterful grasp of material things, lacking in the artistic but powerful to effect great ends; that restless, nervous energy;[54] that dominant individualism, working for good and for evil; and withal that buoyancy and exuberance which comes with freedom—these are traits of the frontier, or traits called out elsewhere because of the existence of the frontier. Since the days when the fleet of Columbus sailed into the waters of the New World, America has been another name for opportunity, and the people of the United States have taken their tone from the incessant expansion which has not only been open but has even been forced upon them. He would be a rash prophet who should assert that the expansive character of American life has now entirely ceased. Movement has been its dominant fact, and, unless this training has no effect upon a people, the American energy will continually demand a wider field for its exercise. But never again will such gifts of free land offer themselves. For a moment, at the frontier, the bonds of custom are broken and unrestraint is triumphant. There is not *tabula rasa*. The stubborn American environment is there with its imperious summons to accept its conditions; the inherited ways of doing things are also there; and yet, in spite of environment, and in spite of custom, each frontier did furnish a new field of opportunity, a gate of escape from the bondage of the past; and freshness, and confidence, and scorn of older society, impatience of its restraints and its ideas, and indifference to its lessons, have accompanied the frontier. What the Mediterranean Sea was to the Greeks, breaking the bond of custom, offering new experiences, calling out new institutions and activities, that, and more, the ever retreating frontier has been to the United States directly, and to the nations of Europe more remotely. And now, four centuries from the discovery of America, at the end of a hundred years of life under the Constitution, the frontier has gone, and with its going has closed the first period of American history.

Notes

1. Since the meeting of the American Historical Association, this paper has also been given as an address to the State Historical Society of Wisconsin, December 14, 1893. I have to thank the Secretary of the Society, Mr. Reuben G. Thwaites, for securing valuable material for my use in the preparation of the paper.

2. Abridgment of Debates of Congress, V, p. 706.

3. Bancroft (1860 ed.), III, pp. 344, 345, citing Logan MSS.; [Mitchell] Contest in America, etc. (1752), p. 237.

4. Kercheval, History of the Valley; Bernheim, German Settlements in the Carolinas; Winsor, Narrative and Critical History of America, V, p. 304; Colonial Records of North Carolina, IV, p. xx; Weston, Documents Connected with the History of South Carolina, p. 82; Ellis and Evans, History of Lancaster County, Pa., chs. III, XXVI.

5. Parkman, Pontiac, II; Griffis, Sir William Johnson, p. 6; Simms's Frontiersmen of New York.

6. Monette, Mississippi Valley, I, p. 311.

7. Wis. Hist. Cols., XI, p. 50; Hinsdale, Old Northwest, p. 121; Burke, "Oration on Conciliation," Works (1872 ed.), I, p. 473.

8. Roosevelt, Winning of the West, and citations there given; Cutler's Life of Cutler.

9. Scribner's Statistical Atlas, xxxviii, pl. 13; McMaster, Hist. of People of U.S., I, pp. 4, 60, 61; Imlay and Filson, Western Territory of America (London, 1793); Rochefoucault-Liancourt, Travels Through the United States of North America (London, 1799); Michaux's "Journal," in Proceedings American Philosophical Society, XXVI, No. 129; Forman, Narrative of a Journey Down the Ohio and Mississippi in 1780–90 (Cincinnati, 1888); Bartram, Travels Through North Carolina, etc. (London, 1792); Pope, Tour Through the Southern and Western Territories, etc. (Richmond, 1792); Weld, Travels Through the States of North

America (London, 1799); Baily, Journal of a Tour in the Unsettled States of North America, 1796–97 (London, 1856); Pennsylvania Magazine of History, July, 1886; Winsor, Narrative and Critical History of America, VII, pp. 491, 492, citations.

10. Scribner's Statistical Atlas, xxxix.

11. Turner, Character and Influence of the Indian Trade in Wisconsin (Johns Hopkins University Studies, Series IX), pp. 61 ff.

12. Monette, History of the Mississippi Valley, II; Flint, Travels and Residence in Mississippi; Flint, Geography and History of the Western States; Abridgment of Debates of Congress, VII, pp. 397, 398, 404; Holmes, Account of the U.S.; Kingdom, America and the British Colonies (London, 1820); Grund, Americans, II, chs. i, iii, vi (although writing in 1836, he treats of conditions that grew out of western advance from the era of 1820 to that time); Peck, Guide for Emigrants (Boston, 1831); Darby, Emigrants' Guide to Western and Southwestern States and Territories; Dana, Geographical Sketches in the Western Country; Kinzie, Waubun; Keating, Narrative of Long's Expedition; Schoolcraft, Discovery of the Sources of the Mississippi River, Travels in the Central Portions of the Mississippi Valley, and Lead Mines of the Missouri; Andreas, History of Illinois, I, 86–99; Hurlbut, Chicago Antiquities; McKenney, Tour to the Lakes; Thomas, Travels through the Western Country, etc. (Auburn, N.Y., 1819).

13. Darby, Emigrants' Guide, pp. 272 ff.; Benton, Abridgment of Debates, VII, p. 397.

14. DeBow's Review, IV, p. 254; XVII, p. 428.

15. Grund, Americans, II, p. 8.

16. Peck, New Guide to the West (Cincinnati, 1848), ch. IV; Parkman, Oregon Trail; Hall, The West (Cincinnati, 1848); Pierce, Incidents of Western Travel; Murray, Travels in North America; Lloyd, Steamboat Directory (Cincinnati, 1856); "Forty Days in a Western Hotel" (Chicago), in Putnam's Magazine, December 1894; Mackay, The Western World, II, ch. II, III; Meeker, Life in the West; Bogen, German in America (Boston, 1851); Olmstead, Texas Journey; Greeley, Recollections of a Busy Life; Schouler, History of the United States, V, 261–67; Peyton, Over the Alleghanies and Across the Prairies (London, 1870); Loughborough, The Pacific Telegraph and Railway (St. Louis, 1849); Whitney, Project for a Railroad to the Pacific (New York, 1849); Peyton, Suggestions on Railroad Communication with the Pacific, and the Trade of China and the Indian Islands; Benton, Highway to the Pacific (a speech delivered in the U.S. Senate, December 16, 1850).

17. A writer in The Home Missionary (1850), p. 239, reporting Wisconsin conditions, exclaims: "Think of this, people of the enlightened East. What an example, to come from the very frontiers of civilization!" But one of the missionaries writes: "In a few years Wisconsin will no longer be considered as the West, or as an outpost of civilization, any more than western New York, or the Western Reserve."

18. Bancroft (H. H.), History of California, History of Oregon, and Popular Tribunals; Shinn, Mining Camps.

19. See the suggestive paper by Prof. Jesse Macy, The Institutional Beginnings of a Western State.

20. Shinn, Mining Camps.

21. Compare Thorpe, in Annals American Academy of Political and Social Science, September, 1891; Bryce, American Commonwealth (1888), II, p. 689.

22. Loria, Analisi della Proprieta Capitalista, II, p. 15.

23. Compare Observations on the North American Land Company, London, 1796, pp. xv, 144; Logan, History of Upper South Carolina, I, pp. 149–51; Turner, Character and Influence of Indian Trade in Wisconsin, p. 18; Peck, New Guide for Emigrants (Boston, 1837), ch. IV; Compendium Eleventh Census, I, p. xl.

24. See pages 220, 221, 223, *post,* for illustrations of the political accompaniments of changed industrial conditions.

25. But Lewis and Clark were the first to explore the route from the Missouri to the Columbia.

26. Narrative and Critical History of America, VIII, p. 10; Sparks' Washington Works, IX, pp. 303, 327; Logan, History of Upper South Carolina, I; McDonald, Life of Kenton, p. 72; Cong. Record. XXIII, p. 57.

27. On the effect of the fur trade in opening the routes of migration, see the author's Character and Influence of the Indian Trade in Wisconsin.

28. Lodge, English Colonies, p. 152 and citations; Logan, Hist. of Upper South Carolina, I, p. 151.

29. Flint, Recollections, p. 9.

30. See Monette, Mississippi Valley, I, p. 344.

31. Coues' Lewis and Clark's Expedition, I, pp. 2, 253–59; Benton, in Cong. Record, XXIII, p. 57.

32. Hehn, Das Salz (Berlin, 1873).

33. Col. Records of N.C., V, p. 3.

34. Findley, History of the Insurrection in the Four Western Counties of Pennsylvania in the Year 1794 (Philadelphia, 1796), p. 35.

35. Hale, Daniel Boone (pamphlet).

36. Compare Baily, Tour in the Unsettled Parts of North America (London, 1856), pp. 217–19, where a similar analysis is made for 1796. See also Collot, Journey in North America (Paris, 1826), p. 109; Observations on the North American Land Company (London, 1796), pp. xv, 144; Logan, History of Upper South Carolina.

37. "Spotswood Papers," in Collections of Virginia Historical Society, I, II.

38. [Burke], European Settlements, etc. (1765 ed.), II, p. 200.

39. Everest, in Wisconsin Historical Collections, XII, pp. 7 ff.

40. Weston, Documents Connected with History of South Carolina, p. 61.

41. See, for example, the speech of Clay, in the House of Representatives, January 30, 1824.

42. See the admirable monograph by Prof. H. B. Adams, Maryland's Influence on the Land Cessions; and also President Welling, in Papers American Historical Association, III, p. 411.

43. Adams Memoirs, IX, pp. 247, 248.

44. Author's article in The Ægis (Madison, Wis.), November 4, 1892.

45. Compare Roosevelt, Thomas Benton, ch. I.

46. Political Science Quarterly, II, p. 457. Compare Sumner, Alexander Hamilton, chs. II–VII.

47. Compare Wilson, Division and Reunion, pp. 15, 24.

48. On the relation of frontier conditions to Revolutionary taxation, see Sumner, Alexander Hamilton, ch. III.

49. I have refrained from dwelling on the lawless characteristics of the frontier, because they are sufficiently well known. The gambler and desperado, the regulators of the Carolinas and the vigilantes of California, are types of that line of scum that the waves of advancing civilization bore before them, and of the growth of spontaneous organs of authority where legal authority was absent. Compare Barrows, United States of Yesterday and To-morrow; Shinn, Mining Camps; and Bancroft, Popular Tribunals. The humor, bravery, and rude strength, as well as the vices of the frontier in its worst aspect, have left traces on American character, language, and literature, not soon to be effaced.

50. Debates in the Constitutional Convention, 1829–1830.

51. [McCrady] Eminent and Representative Men of the Carolinas, I, p. 43; Calhoun's Works, I, pp. 401–06.

52. Speech in the Senate, March 1, 1825; Register of Debates, I, 721.

53. Plea for the West (Cincinnati, 1835), pp. 11 ff.

54. Colonial travelers agree in remarking on the phlegmatic characteristics of the colonists. It has frequently been asked how such a people could have developed that strained nervous en-

ergy now characteristic of them. Compare Sumner, Alexander Hamilton, p. 98, and Adams's History of the United States, I, p. 60; IX, pp. 240, 241. The transition appears to become marked at the close of the war of 1812, a period when interest centered upon the development of the West, and the West was noted for restless energy. Grund, Americans, II, ch. I.

Ideas for Rereading

1. Identify and define the main phases that Turner describes in the progress of the frontier. Describe in your own words the various forces that Turner sees at work in the movement of the frontier. You might begin by attending to what he says about Indian trade and resistance, "natural boundary lines" (p. 534), the "various intercolonial congresses" (p. 537), East–West relations, bad farming practices, and salt.

2. Once you have developed a fuller sense of what Turner calls "the various kinds of frontiers, and their modes of advance, chiefly from the point of view of the frontier itself" write a list of the influences that he enumerates "on the East and on the Old World" (p. 541). In what ways do the related ideas of "liberation" and "dependence" work for Turner? How does Turner describe the effect of the advancing frontier on governmental legislation and the definition of America as a nation? In what ways does "individualism" function for Turner? What does Turner mean by saying that "up to our own day American history has been in a large degree the history of the colonization of the Great West" (p. 530)? What, according to Turner, were the effects of westward expansion on American history in general?

3. Late in the essay, Turner suggests that "the most important effect of the frontier has been in the promotion of democracy here and in Europe" (p. 546). How does Turner advance this theory? Note the ways in which he characterizes the frontier as a promoter of democracy. And note the arguments and evidence that he provides for America's influence on Europe. According to Turner, what are the "dangers" and "benefits" of "democracy born of free land" (p. 547)?

Ideas for Writing

1. Turner asserts that "to the frontier the American intellect owes its striking characteristics" (p. 549). Both of the key terms here, *frontier* and *American intellect,* take on richness and complexity through Turner's argument. As you reread the essay, take notes that help you develop a full understanding of the meaning of these terms in this context. What is it about the "American intellect" that he sees as developing out of the frontier? Now turn to considering America today: more than a hundred years later, can you see elements of Turner's frontier in the "American intellect" of our times? Do contemporary intellectual trends like feminism, multiculturalism (the view that every culture can make a valuable contribution to the country or the community), perspectivism (the view that absolute certainty is unattainable because only partial perspectives are available), or others that you may have noticed mean that the

Turner thesis is no longer valid? Write an essay that reassesses the Turner thesis in the light of the "American intellect" of today.

2. Turner writes of "winning a wilderness" (p. 531), of the frontier as "the meeting point between savagery and civilization" (p. 531). What does this language reveal about Turner's attitudes toward both the natural environment and the indigenous peoples encountered by Euro-Americans as they moved westward? Write an essay analyzing Turner's characterization of the "winning" of the West. Can you suggest some other ways to characterize the events Turner describes? In what ways does Turner's use of language reveal his distance from the frontier life he describes?

3. Turner's argument about the role of "the primitive" in the formation of America has two parts. The first part maintains:

> This perennial rebirth, this fluidity of American life, this expansion westward with its new opportunities, its continuous touch with the simplicity of primitive society, furnish the forces dominating American character. (p. 531)

And the second part claims:

> Thus the advance of the frontier has meant a steady movement away from the influence of Europe, a steady growth of independence on American lines. And to study this advance, the men who grew up under these conditions, and the political, economic, and social results of it, is to study the really American part of our history. (p. 532)

Write an essay in which you respond to both parts of this argument. You might begin by thinking about your own contacts with and understanding of "primitive society." In what ways is your own understanding of "American character" formed by thinking about its difference from Europe and its "fluidity"? Where do you see evidence of American difference from Europe? Where does America continue European traditions? Where do you see evidence of the American frontier?

CONTEXT

Theodore Roosevelt and Woodrow Wilson knew Frederick Jackson Turner long before they became presidents of the United States. Their keen interest in Turner's work suggests the importance they attached to the West in their understanding of America's past, present, and future: in the 1890s these future leaders of the nation recognized that Turner's frontier thesis had the potential to consolidate America's national identity. Wilson was persistent but unsuccessful in his efforts to lure Turner to Princeton University. Roosevelt embraced the Turner thesis with enthusiasm: "I think you have struck some first-class ideas, and have put into definite shape a good deal of thought which has been floating around rather loosely."[1]

C. W. Dana's rhapsodic article treats the "Great West" as "the Canaan of our time." By contrast, Roosevelt's "Ranch Life in the Far West," with its illustration by the famous artist and recorder of western culture Frederic Remington, shows frontier living in a cruder, though highly attractive and optimistic light. The photographs of how people often actually lived in Kansas in the 1880s and 1890s provide a certain antidote to this romanticism.

Plenty Coups (1849–1932), the great chief of the Mountain Crow in Montana, gives an account of the first of his many trips to Washington in "Plenty Coups Travels to Washington" (1880). A rancher and farmer, Plenty Coups took a conciliatory attitude to the white man, believing throughout his life that through negotiation and compromise, friendly relations were possible. (Today his ranch and house in Montana, which he donated to the State of Montana, are a park and museum.) While the conferences described by Plenty Coups ended amicably, "We Want to Tell You Something," written fourteen years later, tells a different story. This petition suggests that among the Hopi, friendly relations have deteriorated into mutual suspicion and mistrust. But this petition, introduced by Albert Yava from First Mesa in Arizona, also demonstrates how articulate and organized Indians could be. The map of Native American removals to Oklahoma, to what was then called "Indian Territory," is a powerful image of the colonizing process. The photograph of Leadville, Colorado, from 1890 gives an idea of the mining phase referred to in Turner's essay.

Note

1. From a letter to Turner written on February 10, 1894. The letter is in the Turner collection at the Henry E. Huntington Library in Sacramento, California (box 1). Allan Bogue quotes from the letter on page 113 of *Frederick Jackson Turner: Strange Roads Going Down* (Norman: University of Oklahoma Press, 1998).

C. W. DANA

From *The Great West; or The Garden of the World*   *1857*

The *Land of Promise*, and the *Canaan** of our time, is the region which, commencing on the slope of the Alleghanies, broadens grandly over the vast prairies and mighty rivers, over queenly lakes and lofty mountains, until the ebb and flow of the Pacific tide kisses the golden shores of the El Dorado.

With a soil more fertile than human agriculture has yet tilled; with a climate balmy and healthful, such as no other land in other zones can

Canaan: The "land flowing with milk and honey" (Ex. 3:8), promised to the Israelites when they escaped from slavery in Egypt. After the Israelites had wandered in the desert for forty years, Joshua (Moses' successor) led them in the conquest of this region, which lies in modern-day Israel. See the Book of Exodus and the Book of Joshua in the Bible.

claim; with facilities for internal communication which outrival the world in extent and grandeur,—it does indeed present to the nations a land where the wildest dreamer on the future of our race may one day see actualized a destiny far outreaching in splendor his most gorgeous visions.

To the New England man, who has been nurtured among the bleak hills and the rough, rocky valleys of his native section, where land is scant and food scantier, where the farmer laboriously cultivates his little patch of ground, and gets therefrom but a small return for his toilsome labors, let him turn his gaze to the broad fields of the West, and there behold the *ne plus ultra** of farming—an agriculture worthy of the name. There will he see the field where his busy brain and thinking hand can find space and material to work, and an opportunity to rear from its virgin civilization institutions which shall bless generations yet to be.

O, the soul kindles at the thought of what a magnificent empire the West is but the germ, which, blessed with liberty and guaranteeing equal rights to all, shall go on conquering and to conquer, until the whole earth shall resound with its fame and glory!

The hardy yeomanry of New England are peopling by thousands on thousands this land of "milk and honey," carrying with them the indomitable Anglo-Saxon energy, and the stern virtues of their fathers, and more than all, minds which the common school has trained into strong intellectual growth, thus fitting them to be the master spirits of the new era.

The old world, cursed with despotism, is pouring out its oppressed millions into the lap of the West, and they will furnish the hardy sinews which, directed by New England minds, shall lay the untold bounties of nature under contribution, and swell the tide of wealth.

When a Pacific railway shall connect the farthest east and the farthest west within a few days' travel, and the now almost limitless deserts shall "blossom as the rose," inhabited by teeming millions pursuing their avocations peacefully, and each contributing his part to the good of all, it will be a consummation which the mind is lost in contemplating, and of which the imagination is powerless to form an adequate conception.

The rapid strides which the West has made in civilization and in wealth are marvellous. Every body is acquainted with them, from the child who goes to school to the patriarch with the snows of eighty winters on his brow,—how Cincinnati, Chicago, and St. Louis, the spots on which they stand, but a few years since unbroken forests, have sprung into existence and grown with such rapidity and power that they now outrival in wealth and population the older cities of the East, with two centuries of growth on their record; how new States, like Ohio, are wresting the rod of empire from their eastern sisters, and are overshadowing the rest with their power and influence.

The subjects which we shall treat on in this work are of lasting and deep interest to every man, woman, and child on the continent. They need

---

ne plus ultra: Latin for "no further beyond," i.e., the highest point.

no apology. No one who has a spark of patriotism animating his bosom will turn away from the glowing annals of the West.

With resources such as Nature has vouchsafed to no other clime, blessed with a race of men who are no idlers in their vineyard, but chaining all the elements into their service until there seems no limit to their acquisitions, there cannot fail to be set up along its mighty rivers and over its broad prairies a pavilion of human progress which shall bless mankind. This structure is yet in process of erection: the materials of construction, workmen ascending and descending, mar its present appearance; but when the work is finished the scaffolding will fall, and the noble edifice will start in its wondrous beauty before an astonished world!

We will not enlarge upon this topic here. Our province lies with things as they now exist, and the reader will pardon us for indulging in these remarks upon the future of THE GARDEN OF THE WORLD.

THEODORE ROOSEVELT

From *Ranch Life in the Far West*   1888

The country throughout this great Upper Missouri basin has a wonderful sameness of character; and the rest of the arid belt, lying to the southward, is closely akin to it in its main features. A traveler seeing it for the first time is especially struck by its look of parched, barren desolation; he can with difficulty believe that it will support cattle at all. It is a region of light rainfall; the grass is short and comparatively scanty; there is no timber except along the beds of the streams, and in many places there are alkali deserts where nothing grows but sage-brush and cactus. Now the land stretches out into level, seemingly endless plains or into rolling prairies; again it is broken by abrupt hills and deep, winding valleys; or else it is crossed by chains of buttes, usually bare, but often clad with a dense growth of dwarfed pines or gnarled, stunted cedars. The muddy rivers run in broad, shallow beds, which after heavy rainfalls are filled to the brim by the swollen torrents, while in droughts the larger streams dwindle into sluggish trickles of clearer water, and the smaller ones dry up entirely, but in occasional deep pools.

All through the region, except on the great Indian reservation, there has been a scanty and sparse settlement, quite peculiar in its character. In the forest the woodchopper comes first; on the fertile prairies the granger is the pioneer; but on the long stretching uplands of the far West it is the men who guard and follow the horned herds that prepare the way for the settlers who come after. The high plains of the Upper Missouri and its tributary rivers were first opened, and are still held, by the stockmen, and the whole civilization of the region has received the stamp of their marked and individual characteristics. They were from the South, not from the

"An Episode in the Opening Up of a Cattle Country," by Frederic Remington

East, although many men from the latter region came out along the great transcontinental railway lines and joined them in their northern migration.

They were not dwellers in towns, and from the nature of their industry lived as far apart from each other as possible. In choosing new ranges, old cow-hands, who are also seasoned plainsmen, are invariably sent ahead, perhaps a year in advance, to spy out the land and pick the best places. One of these may go by himself, or more often, especially if they have to penetrate little known or entirely unknown tracts, two or three will go together, the owner or manager of the herd himself being one of them. Perhaps their herds may already be on the border of the wild and uninhabited country: in that case they may have to take but a few days' journey before finding the stretches of sheltered, long-grass land that they seek. For instance, when I wished to move my own elkhorn steer brand on to a new ranch I had to spend barely a week in traveling north among the Little Missouri Bad Lands before finding what was then untrodden ground far outside the range of any of my neighbors' cattle. But if a large outfit is going to shift its quarters it must go much farther; and both the necessity and the chance for long wanderings were especially great when the final overthrow of the northern Horse Indians opened the whole Upper Missouri basin at one sweep to the stockmen. Then the advance-guards or explorers, each on one horse and leading another with food and bedding, were often absent months at a time, threading their way through the trackless wastes of plain, plateau, and river-bottom. . . .

At last, after days of excitement and danger and after months of weary, monotonous toil, the chosen ground is reached and the final camp pitched. The footsore animals are turned loose to shift for themselves, out-lying camps of two or three men each being established to hem them in. Meanwhile the primitive ranch-house, out-buildings, and corrals are built, the unhewn cottonwood logs being chinked with moss and mud, while the roofs are of branches covered with dirt, spades and axes being the only tools needed for the work. Bunks, chairs, and tables are all home-made, and as rough as the houses they are in. The supplies of coarse, rude food are carried perhaps two or three hundred miles from the nearest town, ei-ther in the ranch-wagons or else by some regular freighting outfit, whose huge canvas-topped prairie schooners are each drawn by several yoke of oxen, or perhaps by six or eight mules. To guard against the numerous mishaps of prairie travel, two or three of these prairie schooners usually go together, the brawny teamsters, known either as "bull-whackers" or as "mule-skinners," stalking beside their slow-moving teams.

The small outlying camps are often tents, or mere dug-outs in the ground. But at the main ranch there will be a cluster of log buildings, in-cluding a separate cabin for the foreman or ranchman; often another in which to cook and eat; a long house for the men to sleep in; stables, sheds, a blacksmith's shop, etc.,—the whole group forming quite a little settle-ment, with the corrals, the stacks of natural hay, and the patches of fenced land for gardens or horse pastures. This little settlement may be situated right out in the treeless, nearly level open, but much more often is placed in the partly wooded bottom of a creek or river, sheltered by the usual back-ground of somber brown hills.

When the northern plains began to be settled, such a ranch would at first be absolutely alone in the wilderness, but others of the same sort were sure soon to be established within twenty or thirty miles on one side or the other. The lives of the men in such places were strangely cut off from the outside world, and, indeed, the same is true to a hardly less extent at the present day. Sometimes the wagons are sent for provisions, and the beef-steers are at stated times driven off for shipment. Parties of hunters and trappers call now and then. More rarely small bands of emigrants go by in search of new homes, impelled by the restless, aimless craving for change so deeply grafted in the breast of the American borderer: the white-topped wagons are loaded with domestic goods, with sallow, dispirited-looking women, and with tow-headed children; while the gaunt, moody frontiermen slouch alongside, rifle on shoulder, lank, homely, uncouth, and yet with a curious suggestion of grim strength underlying it all. Or cowboys from neighboring ranches will ride over, looking for lost horses, or seeing if their cattle have strayed off the range. But this is all. Civiliza-tion seems as remote as if we were living in an age long past. The whole ex-istence is patriarchal in character: it is the life of men who live in the open, who tend their herds on horseback, who go armed and ready to guard their lives by their own prowess, whose wants are very simple, and who call no man master. Ranching is an occupation like those of vigorous, primitive pastoral peoples, having little in common with the humdrum, workaday business world of the nineteenth century; and the free ranchman in his manner of life shows more kinship to an Arab sheik than to a sleek city merchant or tradesman.

By degrees the country becomes what in a stock-raising region passes for well settled. In addition to the great ranches smaller ones are established, with a few hundred, or even a few score, head of cattle apiece; and now and then miserable farmers straggle in to fight a losing and desperate battle with drought, cold, and grasshoppers. The wheels of the heavy wagons, driven always over the same course from one ranch to another, or to the remote frontier towns from which they get their goods, wear ruts in the soil, and roads are soon formed, perhaps originally following the deep trails made by the vanished buffalo. These roads lead down the river-bottoms or along the crests of the divides or else strike out fairly across the prairie, and a man may sometimes travel a hundred miles along one without coming to a house or camp of any sort. If they lead to a shipping point whence the beeves are sent to market, the cattle, traveling in single file, will have worn many and deep paths on each side of the wheel-marks; and the roads between important places which are regularly used either by the United States Government, by stage-coach lines, or by freight teams become deeply worn landmarks—as, for instance, near us, the Deadwood and the old Fort Keogh trails.

Cattle-ranching can only be carried on in its present form while the population is scanty; and so in stock-raising regions, pure and simple, there are usually few towns, and these are almost always at the shipping points for cattle. But, on the other hand, wealthy cattlemen, like miners who have done well, always spend their money freely; and accordingly towns like Denver, Cheyenne, and Helena, where these two classes are the most influential in the community, are far pleasanter places of residence than cities of five times their population in the exclusively agricultural States to the eastward.

A true "cow town" is worth seeing,—such a one as Miles City, for instance, especially at the time of the annual meeting of the great Montana Stock-raisers' Association. Then the whole place is full to overflowing, the importance of the meeting and the fun of the attendant frolics, especially the horse-races, drawing from the surrounding ranch country many hundreds of men of every degree, from the rich stock-owner worth his millions to the ordinary cowboy who works for forty dollars a month. It would be impossible to imagine a more typically American assemblage, for although there are always a certain number of foreigners, usually English, Irish, or German, yet they have become completely Americanized; and on the whole it would be difficult to gather a finer body of men, in spite of their numerous shortcomings. The ranch-owners differ more from each other than do the cowboys; and the former certainly compare very favorably with similar classes of capitalists in the East. Anything more foolish than the demagogic

A *"dugout"* home in Norton County, Kansas. Exterior.

outcry against "cattle kings" it would be difficult to imagine. Indeed, there are very few businesses so absolutely legitimate as stock-raising and so beneficial to the nation at large; and a successful stock-grower must not only be shrewd, thrifty, patient, and enterprising, but he must also possess qualities of personal bravery, hardihood, and self-reliance to a degree not

A *"dugout"* home in Norton County, Kansas, 1905. Interior.

demanded in the least by any mercantile occupation in a community long settled. Stockmen are in the West the pioneers of civilization, and their daring and adventurousness make the after settlement of the region possible. The whole country owes them a great debt.

PLENTY COUPS

Plenty Coups Travels to Washington   1880

They said they were going to take me to Washington. I thought it over for a while. I thought it was a wise thing. I told them I would go. This was my first trip east. I also told them that I wanted some other chiefs to go with me. I asked Two-Belly. At first he didn't want to go, but finally he said he would. The others were Old Crow, Pretty Eagle, Long Elk, and Medicine Crow. Three white men also accompanied us: A. M. Quivey, Tom Stewart, and J. R. Keller.

It was during the spring. There was no railroad yet in our country, and we had to travel by stagecoach which carried a light at night. We traveled in two coaches. Snow was still lying on the ground. We set out from the old agency, near Flesh Scraper Mountain. The horses were relayed, but we had no rest during these changes of horses. We traveled toward Butte, which took us four nights and five days. The further we came into the mountains, the deeper lay the snow. At Butte we rested for the first time. We slept a whole day and night. And I combed my hair for the first time since leaving our camp.

Early the next morning we were told to dress quickly and eat. The teams were ready and we traveled down the mountain, following Flathead River. Again we were relayed. We continued until we came close to another mountain, and we saw an Indian driving some horses. We called him to us. He was a Bannock. We asked him where the Bannocks were. He told us that they were on the other side of the mountain, in the valley. He also told us that their chief, Comes Out of the Grease, had gone to Washington. . . .

Early the next morning we took a sweatbath with the Bannocks. They told us that the road from their camp to the next station was hard and rough, and that it was better to travel by daytime. At that station, however, we should see the Fast Wagon [train]. They described it as a big black horse with his belly nearly touching the ground. This horse had a big bell on his back. He ran so fast that everytime he stopped, he puffed.

We left about noon and came to a big barn after dark where we slept. Early the next morning we started again and found the snow deep. Soon it started to rain which made the roads even worse. It was again after dark before we stopped at a dugout town, where they were building the railroad. Here we had supper. A white man with us pointed to a clock and told us that when the hands should be in a certain position we should start again. We did not know what he meant. Next morning we were awakened, took our bundles, and were taken to the train. We walked into the cars and sat down. We placed our bundles on shelves and looked out of the window. The train followed the river. Through the windows we could see many horses, game, and mountains. Stewart, who was traveling with us, acted as interpreter. We arrived at the Bannock Agency, and many Indians were there. As soon as the train stopped, we wanted to get off, but we were told to stay. That black horse was panting so hard that the bell on his neck was ringing.

We thought the train journey was grand. I realized, however, that it was not a horse that pulled it, and I wondered what made it go so fast. Birds would fly along outside our windows. They were swift, but before long we outdistanced them.

We had often been told that the Sioux were a numerous tribe. But it seemed to me that the Bannock was even larger. We halted at a junction, and another train passed going in a different direction. I saw a lake with a mountain rising from its center. We saw many white man's places, and passed many freshly skinned elk and buffalo carcasses. . . .

We came to a big forest and passed it and finally we arrived at the Missouri. Here we met a white man called Wood Frost who had been our agent. He invited us to dinner and gave us some red paint and shells. We had not even finished our meal when we had to leave for the train. We crossed the Missouri and were told that we were going to Chicago.

It was the first time that I had seen so many white people together. It was strange to see so many tall black houses. Here we left the train. There was a big lake and we spent much time there watching the ice bump against the shore and break into pieces. It was the biggest ice breakup I had ever seen, and the waves were very high.

There was more travel by train and finally we arrived in Washington. Here wagons were ready waiting for us. They took us to our lodging, and we were told to sleep until the next morning when we should be taken to President Hayes. The next day we were escorted to the President, who shook hands with us and told us that he was glad to see us. The President said that he had sent for us to talk concerning the future of our people. He said that he wanted us to send our children to school and that they would build a house and barn for each of us. He wanted us to learn how to farm. He said they were going to build a railroad through the Yellowstone Valley, but that they wanted us to make peace with the other tribes in our part of the country.

My companions told me to make some reply so I said that we were also glad to see him and that we wished to speak with him too. I said that he had asked us to do many things, but that before we could give him our answer, we would like time to talk it over among ourselves. The President gave us two days to consider his requests. Two days later we returned and again met with him. I said that we agreed to send our children to school and to let the Government build houses for us. I said that as far as stopping the fighting with other tribes, we wanted to fight them for about two more years and then we would reconsider this question. I added that we did not want a railroad built through our country because it was our hunting ground.

When we said this, the President kept us in Washington for over a month. We had several conferences with him in which he tried to overrule our objections, but he failed. The President suggested giving us another hunting ground, in North Dakota, but I refused because we did not wish to leave our country. When the President asked my reasons I said that in North Dakota the mountains are low and that I wanted to live where the mountains are high and where there are many springs of fresh water.

Then the President asked how we had treated the soldiers, and I said that we had been friendly to them. When their horses' feet were sore, so were ours. When they had to drink alkali, we shared their misfortune. When they suffered, we suffered, and I said we would continue to have friendly relations. Then the President said that he would grant our request to remain in the country where we lived, but that in return he expected us to let them build a railroad through the valley of the Yellowstone.

I said that when I returned to my people I would talk with them and hear their objections. I said then he could send us one of his servants and we would hold a council with him and he would tell the President of the results.

We were in Washington a long time. I became anxious to return home and see my people again. The President told us that we could return home in two Sundays. Although we dreaded the long journey, we were glad. When the day arrived, we again walked into the cars and traveled for a long time. It was late summer when we finally reached home, but the trees were still in full leaf.

Soon after we returned, we had a conference with the railroad and Government officials. We finally agreed to let them build the railroad through our country, and they agreed to give us free transportation. This was done at first, but soon this agreement was not lived up to and since then we have had to pay for our own transportation. A few years later the Government began to build homes for the Crows on the Big Horn River. I then went to Pryor [the westernmost town on the Crow Indian reservation]. I donated the use of four head of horses and had a log house built on the land where I live today.

ALBERT YAVA

We Want to Tell You Something   1894

I don't know where [Senator] Dawes got his knowledge of Indian ways, but he was dead set against a tribe or clan owning communal lands. The 1890 law said that clan lands and tribal lands should be abolished and every individual given a plot for himself. A couple of years after that the

Government began to survey the Hopi lands to divide them up, and they did all this without any consultations with responsible Hopi leaders. They started around Oraibi and ran into difficulties when they tried to allot one clan's land to individuals outside that clan. They only stirred up confusion and resentment by what they were doing.

Old Tom Keam was very concerned about the whole land question, the lack of an officially designated Hopi reservation and the carving up of the clan lands as well. He thought that the Hopis had better get together and do something to keep their lands and landholding system intact. In 1894 he went around urging the village and ceremonial leaders to unite and write a petition asking that the Government protect the Hopi claims. He talked with the leaders a good long time before he convinced them that it was important to put up a solid front. The villages had never had a tradition of working together. Each one considered itself to be an independent group. The Hopis had never seen themselves as a single tribe that could act in a unified way, but rather as separate village communities, you might say separate political entities.

Tom Keam persuaded them to send an appeal from the Hopi people to Washington. He drew up the letter in his own handwriting and had it taken to all the important men in the villages and read to them. After that they signed. On First Mesa, representatives of Walpi, Sichomovi and Tewa Village signed. On Second Mesa he got signatures of people living in Shongopovi, Shipaulovi and Mishongnovi, and on Third Mesa from Oraibi. Practically every clan and family was represented. One hundred and twenty-three men in all signed by making their clan marks.

The petition went into great detail explaining the traditional system of clan landholding, and why so much land was required by a family to keep it alive in this desert country. Although the petition was received in Washington, there never was a reply to it, and on the Hopi side there was no follow-up. The Government continued to carve up the clan lands, but finally, about fifteen or sixteen years later, it gave up on this because there was so much confusion and resistance. However, there are still some fields over in Oraibi and Moencopi that are known as allotment lands.

Moqui Villages
Arizona March 27 & 28, 1894

To the Washington Chiefs:

During the last two years strangers have looked over our land with spy-glasses and made marks upon it, and we know but little of what it means. As we believe that you have no wish to disturb our Possessions, we want to tell you something about this Hopi land.

None of us wer[e] asked that it should be measured into separate lots, and given to individuals for they would cause confusion.

The family, the dwelling house and the field are inseparable, because the woman is the heart of these, and they rest with her. Among us the

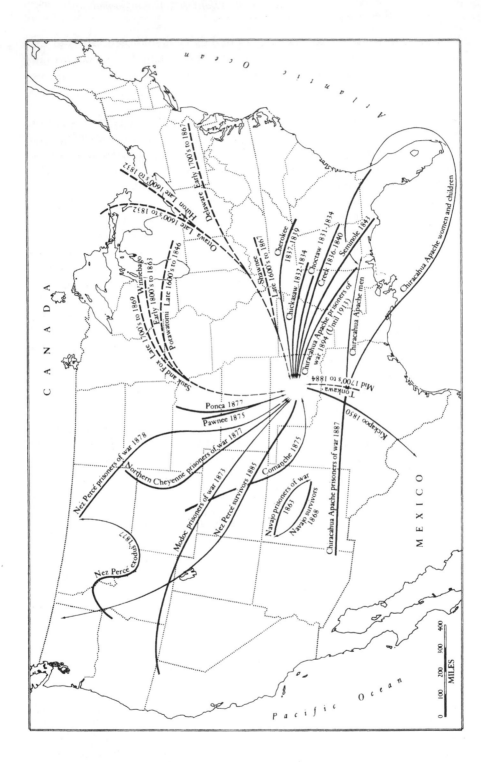

Chiracahua Apache women and children

Delaware Early 1700's to 1867

Huron Late 1600's to 1832

Ottawa Late 1600's to 1832

Shawnee Late 1600's to 1867

Cherokee 1837-1839

Chickasaw 1832-1834

Choctaw 1831-1834

Creek 1836-1840

Seminole 1841

Winnebago Early 1800's to 1863

Pottawatomi Late 1600's to 1846

Sauk and Fox Late 1700's to 1869

Chiracahua Apache prisoners of war 1804 (Until 1913)

Chiracahua Apache men

Tonkawa Mid 1700's to 1884

Kickapoo 1850

Ponca 1877

Pawnee 1875

Nez Percé prisoners of war 1878

Northern Cheyenne prisoners of war 1877

Modoc prisoners of war 1873

Comanche 1875

Nez Percé survivors 1885

Navajo prisoners of war 1863

Navajo survivors 1868

Chiracahua Apache prisoners of war 1887

Nez Percé exodus 1877

CANADA

MEXICO

Atlantic Ocean

Pacific Ocean

MILES

0   100   200   300   400

family traces its kin from the mother, hence all its possessions are hers. The man builds the house but the woman is the owner, because she repairs and preserves it; the man cultivates the field, but he renders its harvest into the woman's keeping, because upon her it rests to prepare the food, and the surplus of stores for barter depends upon her thrift.

A man plants the fields of his wife, and the fields assigned to the children she bears, and informally he calls them his, although in fact they are not. Even of the field which he inherits from his mother, its harvests he may dispose of at will, but the field itself he may not. He may permit his son to occupy it and gather its produce, but at the father's death the son may not own it, for then it passes to the father's sister's son or nearest mother's kin, and thus our fields and houses always remain with our mother's family.

According to the number of children a woman has, fields for them are assigned to her, from some of the lands of her family group, and her husband takes care of them. Hence our fields are numerous but small, and several belonging to the same family may be close together, or they may be miles apart, because arable localities are not continuous. There are other reasons for the irregularity in size and situation of our family lands, as interrupted sequence of inheritance caused by extinction of families, but chiefly owing to the following condition, and to which we especially invite your attention.

In the Spring and early Summer there usually comes from the Southwest a succession of gales, oftentimes strong enough to blow away the sandy soil from the face of some of our fields, and to expose the underlying clay, which is hard, and sour, and barren; as the sand is the only fertile land, when it moves, the planters must follow it, and other fields must be provided in place of those which have been devastated. Sometimes generations pass away and these barren spots remain, while in other instances, after a few years, the winds have again restored the desirable sand upon them. In such event its fertility is disclosed by the nature of the grass and shrubs that grow upon it. If these are promising, a number of us unite to clear off the land and make it again fit for planting, when it may be given back to its former owner, or if a long time has elapsed, to other heirs, or it may be given to some person of the same family group, more in need of a planting place.

Native American diasporas (facing page). Many Native American peoples were displaced from their ancestral homelands through wars, treaties, and takeovers of their lands by white settlers. The map shows the approximate routes and dates of some of these removals; the broken lines indicate a few of the more gradual displacements that took place over a period of time. Indian Territory, which consisted of most of the present-day state of Oklahoma, became a gigantic resettlement camp for tribes from every corner of the United States. Peter Nabokov, Native American Testimony: A Chronicle of Indian-White Relations from Prophecy to Present, 1492–1992 *(New York: Penguin Books, 1991), 146–47.*

Leadville, Colorado, ca. 1890

These limited changes in land holding are effected by mutual discussion and concession among the elders, and among all the thinking men and women of the family groups interested. In effect, the same system of holding, and the same method of planting, obtain among the Tewa, and all the Hopi villages, and under them we provide ourselves with food in abundance.

The American is our elder brother, and in everything he can teach us, except in the method of growing corn in these waterless sand valleys, and in that we are sure we can teach him. We believe that you have no desire to change our system of small holdings, nor do we think that you wish to remove any of our ancient landmarks, and it seems to us that the conditions we have mentioned afford sufficient grounds for this requesting to be left undisturbed.

Further it has been told to us, as coming from Washington, that neither measuring nor individual papers are necessary for us to keep possession of our villages, our peach orchards and our springs. If this be so, we should like to ask what need there is to bring confusion into our accustomed system of holding corn fields.

We are aware that some ten years ago a certain area around our land, was proclaimed to be for our use, but the extent of this area is unknown to us, nor has any Agent, ever been able to point it out, for its boundaries have never been measured. We most earnestly desire to have one continuous boundary ring enclosing all the Tewa and all the Hopi lands, and that it shall be large enough to afford sustenance for our increasing flocks and herds. If such a scope can be confirmed to us by a paper from your hands, securing us forever against intrusion, all our people will be satisfied.

[The above Hopi petition was signed in clan symbols by 123 principals of kiva societies, clan chiefs, and village chiefs of Walpi, Tewa Village, Sichomovi, Mishongnovi, Shongopovi, Shipaulovi, and Oraibi.]

Ideas for Rereading

1. The Context section for this chapter is designed to heighten awareness of the importance of point of view in discussions of the North American West. How do Dana and Roosevelt, for example, look at the West? How do they see the process of settlement and "civilization"? What points of view are suggested by the various images included in the section? What changes in the Native American attitude toward the U.S. government can you identify in "Plenty Coups Travels to Washington" and "We Want to Tell You Something"?

2. As you reread "We Want to Tell You Something," consider the implications of Turner's use of a biological analogy when he considers expansion as "like the steady growth of a complex nervous system for the originally simple, inert continent" (p. 537). How do the Native American perspectives represented in the Context section complicate Turner's idea that the continent was "simple"

and "inert" before the westward expansion? Or his statement about the revitalizing power of the frontier's contact with "the simplicity of primitive society" (p. 531)? How does the photograph of Leadville, Colorado, in 1890 influence your understanding of Turner's biological analogy?

Ideas for Writing

1. Carefully study and note your reactions to the engraving by Frederic Remington reproduced in this chapter. Make further notes comparing Remington's illustration with the photograph of a Kansas family in front of its dugout home and the 1890 photograph of Leadville, Colorado. What does each of these images tell you about life in the American West in the late nineteenth century? How would you characterize Remington's point of view and how does this point of view resonate with the image of Western life captured in the two photographs? Write an essay analyzing the Remington illustration in the context of the three photographs in the Context section.

2. Write an essay responding to the different perspectives represented in the selections by Dana, Albert Yava and the Hopi, Plenty Coups, and Roosevelt. Identify and analyze specific words, phrases, and passages that reflect the character and worldview of each writer. What kinds of experiences and beliefs underpin the views that each piece expresses? What are the main goals of each? For whom is each piece written, and what effects is it intended to produce in the reader (so far as you can tell from the ways in which language is used)? You may choose to take into account the various images in this section as a way of extending and developing your essay.

3. Reread Turner's essay in light of two of the four written accounts in the Context section. Identify those places where these other perspectives help you to see Turner's particular perspective. You may find that Turner's perspective is entirely different from those represented in the selections; or you may find that his perspective extends, complicates, ignores, or refutes the two writers you have chosen to work with. As you explore Turner's essay in terms of his perspective toward his subject, you should focus on the ways in which Turner accounts for points of view other than his own. Pay particular attention to the ways in which his responses to other people's views reveal his own observational bias.

The following questions might help you draft your essay: What qualities does Turner associate with "Americanization"? How do these qualities differ from the traits he associates with Europe and with "the primitive"? In what senses does Turner use the word "civilization"? How would you characterize Turner's vision of "social evolution"? How do the two perspectives you are working with help you to read, interpret, and critique Turner's use of such interdependent ideas as "American life" and "the American intellect," "free land" and the "public domain," "independence" and "regulation," "the wilderness" and "exploitation," "composite nationality" and "the rise of democracy," "civilization" and "primitive society"?

CONTEMPORARY CONVERSATION

Patricia Nelson Limerick

Patricia Nelson Limerick is the recipient of numerous awards in the humanities, including the prestigious MacArthur Fellowship (1995–2000). She received her Ph.D. in American studies from Yale University in 1980, and she has taught history at Harvard University and, since 1984, at the University of Colorado at Boulder. Her books include Something in the Soil: Field-Testing the New Western History *(2000) and* The Real West *(1996). But it was* The Legacy of Conquest: The Unbroken Past of the American West *(1988) that established her as one of the leading figures in the "new western history," a movement that strives to examine neglected aspects of American history and seek out the more complicated truth behind the romanticized legends of the "old West." The* Legacy of Conquest *was especially noted for demonstrating the many ways in which the West's past—both as myth and as reality—continues to shape the politics, economics, and culture of modern America.*

Following a symposium titled "Trails: Toward a New Western History," Limerick composed a one-page statement in response to a participant who wanted to know what "new western history" was all about ("What on Earth Is the New Western History?" in Trails: Toward a New Western History, 1991*). We reprint it here to offer a sense of the larger project to which the essay that follows belongs.*

New Western Historians define "the West" primarily as a place—the trans-Mississippi region in the broadest terms, or the region west of the hundredth meridian. The boundaries are fuzzy because nearly all regional boundaries are.

New Western Historians do see a "process" at work in this region's history, a process that has affected other parts of the nation as well as other parts of the planet. But they reject the old term "frontier" for that process. When clearly and precisely defined, the term "frontier" is nationalistic and often racist (in essence, the area where white people get scarce); when cleared of its ethnocentrism, the term loses an exact definition.

To characterize the process that shaped the region, New Western Historians have available a number of terms—invasion, conquest, colonization, exploitation, development, expansion of the world market. In the broadest picture, the process involves the convergence of diverse people—women as well as men, Indians, Europeans, Latin Americans, Asians, Afro-Americans—in the region, and their encounters with each other and with the natural environment.

New Western Historians reject the notion of a clear-cut "end to the frontier," in 1890, or in any other year. The story of the region's sometimes contested, sometimes cooperative, relations among its diverse cast of characters and the story of human efforts to "master" nature in the region are both ongoing stories, with their continuity unnecessarily ruptured by attempts to divide the "old West" from the "new West."

New Western Historians break free of the old model of "progress" and "improvement," and face up to the possibility that some roads of western development led directly to failure and to injury. This reappraisal is not meant to make white Americans "look bad." The intention is, on the contrary, simply to make it clear that in western American history, heroism and villainy, virtue and vice, and nobility and shoddiness appear in roughly the same proportions as they appear in any other subject of human history (and with the same relativity of definition and judgment). This is only disillusioning to those who have come to depend on illusions.

> *New Western Historians surrender the conventional, never-very-convincing claim of an omniscient, neutral objectivity. While making every effort to acknowledge and understand different points of view, New Western Historians admit that it is OK for scholars to care about their subjects, both in the past and the present, and to put that concern on record.*

As you read the following selection from The Legacy of Conquest, *notice how Limerick uses brief historical examples and narratives to support the larger argument of her essay. After you have read the selection once, you may want to come back to her statement on the new western history to assess how the selection contributes to Limerick's broader objectives.*

Denial and Dependence

During any week, some Western politician or businessman will deliver a speech celebrating the ideal of regional independence. Westerners, the speaker will say, should be able to choose a goal and pursue it, free of restriction and obstacle. They should not have other people telling them what to do. If authority must be used, it should be their own authority imposed on those who try to block the path toward progress. In a one-to-one correspondence between nature and politics, the wide open spaces were meant to be the setting for a comparable wide open independence for Westerners. This independence, the speaker will assume, is the West's legitimate heritage from history.

In our era of global interdependence, that traditional speech seems to be out of place, for other people's actions affect our lives in an infinite number of ways. The repeated invocation of the Westerner's right to independence begins to sound anachronistic, opposed to the reality of a more complex time. In fact, the times were always complex. At any period in Western history, the rhetoric of Western independence was best taken with many grains of salt.

In 1884 Martin Maginnis, the delegate to Congress from Montana Territory, geared up for a classic denunciation of a travesty against Western independence. Territorial delegates could speak, but not vote, in Congress, and a sense of oppression did not make Maginnis shy about exercising his right to speak. "The present Territorial system," he said, ". . . is the most infamous system of colonial government that was ever seen on the face of the globe." Territories "are the colonies of your Republic, situated three thousand miles away from Washington by land, as the thirteen colonies were situated three thousand miles away from London by water. And it is a strange thing that the fathers of our Republic . . . established a colonial government as much worse than that which they revolted against as one form of government can be worse than another."[1]

The colonies and the Revolution gave Westerners an irresistible analogy. Denouncing the territorial system required no originality. One simply matched up the parallels: London and Washington, D.C.; George III's ministers and the secretaries of the interior; appointed royal governors and appointed territorial governors; and beyond that, many terms did not even need translation—inadequate representation, violated sovereignty, unrecognized rights.

In fact, there were parallels between British colonies and American territories; the framers of the Northwest Ordinance had the colonial precedent in mind. It is still not easy to think of an alternative way to manage a newly occupied region. Maginnis's stridency aside, he was right in thinking that the territory, the primal political reality of most early Western development, did involve a limit on local sovereignty. But the difference between a British colony and an American territory was so enormous, and of such practical and philosophical significance, that it put something of a dent in Delegate Maginnis's argument. Colonies were to remain colonies, but territories were to become states, and thus, as the historian Howard Lamar has summed it up, the problems of liberty and empire were reconciled.[2]

Territories were transitional, even if the transition came in all lengths—no time at all in California, four years in Nevada, and sixty-three years in Arizona and New Mexico. Before statehood, even though they had elected representatives, residents in territories were under the authority of federally appointed governors and judges. Some of those men were perfectly competent; others were party hacks of limited charm and skill, to whom the office was only a reward for political services and not an opportunity to serve the nation, much less the territory. In Congress, a territory had only a solitary delegate, entitled merely to speak, and no senators or representatives.

"Citizens resented the territorial status," the historian Earl Pomeroy has pointed out, "not only because they were Westerners, but also because recently they had been Easterners." They had vivid memories of what it was to be citizens in an established state, and from that point of view the move to a Western territory did not heighten one's independence, but lessened it.[3]

An arbitrarily appointed governor, descending from outside, brought to mind other wars of independence besides the Revolution. The term "carpetbagger" became almost as much a favored epithet in the West as in the South. The imposed governments of Southern Reconstruction did resemble the territorial system, and that resemblance could make it look as if the West was receiving gratuitously what the South earned as punishment—a forced cutback in state sovereignty.

Were Westerners truly at the mercy of these appointed invaders? Were they, as a Dakota paper put it, "not even wards of the government, but a party subject to the whims of political leaders, the intrigues of schemers and the mining of party rats"?[4]

In territorial histories, one plot repeats. The territorial governor arrives. He is not a talented man, but he has some hopes of doing his job. He has a modest salary, less modest expenses, and some interest in his own political and economic advancement. He knows the territory's affairs are not in good order, and he would like it to be to his credit that he restored order and created a climate conducive to investment and prosperity.

In six months the fray is on. Petitions travel regularly to Washington, demanding the governor's removal. He has been pulled by one group of residents into a scheme for local development that will benefit them to the exclusion of others, and those others prove to be a resourceful group of opponents. Factions and feuds preceded the governor and will outlast him; in the meantime, though, he provides the handiest target for the discontented. With a salary limited by an economy-minded Congress and with living expenses inflated by territorial isolation, the governor's economic dilemma is soon a moral one. If the governors "starved," Earl Pomeroy has pointed out, "they showed that they were driven West by their incompetence; if they prospered, they showed they were dishonest." Under these pressures, "nearly all tried to retain business connections in the states or to invest in the territories." Territorial legislators were not unaware of the governor's financial vulnerability; it was a frequent strategy to supplement the official's salary with "increased compensation," a gesture of less than pure altruism. When one adds up the opportunities for Westerners to resist or to counterattack, the picture of appointed tyrants bullying the vulnerable, authentic Westerners appears to be a bit overdrawn. In 1862, the New Mexico legislature printed the "governor's message with a preamble referring to the 'false erroneous absurd and ill-sounding ideas therein contained.'" Victimized Westerners evidently retained a few powers of self-defense.[5]

Given little respect from their constituents, territorial governors could not hope for much more from Washington. Because authority was split between the Department of the Treasury, in charge of funds, and the Department of State and, after 1873, the Department of the Interior, it was not always clear who was in charge. No department went to much trouble to consolidate authority over the territories or to direct their operations with any guiding philosophy. Appointed officials found their supervisors reluctant to give advice; governors were often dispatched without instructions, and the Washington office was even known to refuse advice on particular matters. Even when the supervising department had a policy to pursue, its enforcement over the Western distances was hard; until the arrival of the telegraph, it was difficult to discover — much less prevent — absenteeism in officials. The standing rhetoric of the oppressed West aside, the territorial system's methods were more "ineffective" than "tyrannical."[6]

To say that the system was inefficient is not to say that it was insignificant. The territory guaranteed that a degree of dependence on the federal government would be central to every Western state's first years. This was a matter not simply of power but of its cousin, money.

In the early development of the Far West, five principal resources lay ready for exploitation: furs, farmland, timber, minerals, and federal money. Territorial experience got Westerners in the habit of asking for federal subsidies, and the habit persisted long after other elements of the Old West had vanished.

Nothing so undermines the Western claim to a tradition of independence as this matter of federal support to Western development. The two key frontier activities—the control of Indians and the distribution of land—were primarily federal responsibilities, at times involving considerable expense. Federal subsidies to transportation—to freighting companies and to railroads, to harbor improvement and to highway building—made the concept of private enterprise in transportation an ambiguous one. Even apparent inaction could in a way support development. Failing to restrain or regulate access to the public grazing lands or to the timber lands, the federal government in effect subsidized private cattle raisers and loggers with unlimited access to national resources.

Within the territorial framework, the significance of federal money was often dramatic. Federal office provided a valued form of patronage; appropriations for public buildings offered another route to local income. Official government printing, entrusted to a local newspaper of the proper political orientation, could determine a publisher's failure or success. Territorial business involving Indians was another route to federal money. Volunteers in Indian campaigns would expect federal pay. Local Indian hostilities were a mixed blessing; forts and soldiers meant markets for local products and business for local merchants. Similarly, once conquered and dependent on rations, Indians on reservations became a market for local grain and beef.

In its early years, Dakota Territory gave the purest demonstration of this economic dependence. With the delayed development of farming and mining, Dakota settlers rapidly grasped the idea "of the federal government not only as a paternalistic provider of land and governmental organization but also as a subsidizing agency which furnished needed development funds in the form of offices, Indian and army supply orders, and post and land office positions." When Indian troubles increased, white settlement became risky, and hard times came to Dakota, "the federal government remained the only source of revenue and sustenance." In those rough times, "Washington was in essence subsidizing a government which had few citizens, no income, and a highly questionable future." Agricultural development and the mining boom of the Black Hills later relieved the pressure on federal resources, but in the meantime the precedent had been well set. It had become an "old Dakota attitude that government itself was an important paying business."[7]

Nonetheless, Dakotans also took up the standard cry of the oppressed colony. "We are so heartily disgusted with our dependent condition, with being snubbed at every turn in life, with having all our interest subjected to the whims and corrupt acts of persons in power that we feel very much as the thirteen colonies felt," a Dakota newspaper declared in 1877. As they asserted their rights to statehood, Dakota residents did not give much support to the idea that political innovation emanated from the frontier. They used the familiar states' rights arguments; their political ideas were "so much those of the older sections" that "they had not developed any indigenous ones of their own since coming to Dakota." After a close study, Howard Lamar found in the Dakota activists "a singular lack of political originality."[8]

Frederick Jackson Turner's idea that the frontier had been the source of American democracy did receive some support from pioneer rhetoric. Politically involved residents were often gifted speechmakers and petition writers, even if they lacked originality. Western settlers were so abundantly supplied with slogans and democratic formulas that putting our trust in their recorded words alone would be misleading. Only close archival research can reveal what those gifted speakers and writers were actually doing. An early event in Dakota history demonstrates the problem.

In 1857, in unorganized territory to the west of Minnesota, American citizens took part in what appeared to be a classic exercise in frontier democracy. Having moved beyond Minnesota's limits, the settlers in Sioux Falls organized their own government, elected officials, and began to petition Congress for territorial status. Acting to protect their lives and their property, they had fashioned a temporary political order to suit their unique needs. The whole exercise would surely have warmed the heart of Frederick Jackson Turner, and a number of local historians happily took the Sioux Falls "squatter government" at their word.

The risk came with a closer look, provided by Howard Lamar. Those self-reliant squatters were, it turns out, agents of a land company, financed and organized by Minnesota Democrats. Their plan was to get to Dakota early, create paper towns, organize a government, persuade Congress to ratify their legitimacy, and then enjoy the benefits of dominating a new and developing region. They were, at least, willing to work for the appearance of political legitimacy. "Electing" their first legislature, "the citizens of Sioux Falls split into parties of three or four and traveled over the countryside near the settlement. Every few miles each party would halt, take a drink of whiskey, establish a voting precinct, and then proceed to vote several times themselves by putting the names of all their relatives or friends on the ballots. After a reasonable number of fictitious voters had cast their ballots, the party would travel to the next polling place and repeat the process."[9]

The lesson of the Sioux Falls squatter government, of Dakota Territory, and of the other territories as well, was a simple one: in Western affairs, business and government were interdependent and symbiotic, and only a pathologically subtle mind could find a line dividing them. Petitioned to grant a railroad charter, the first Dakota Assembly members were cautious and reserved—until the railroad agreed to make "every member of the Assembly a partner!" True to their insight into government as a paying business, "the assemblymen had not hesitated to use their office to get in on the ground floor of what they considered a very good business deal."[10]

It does not take much exposure to Western political history to lead one to a basic fact: "conflict of interest" has not always been an issue of political sensitivity. The career of Senator William Stewart of Nevada has al-

ready provided us with a case study in overlapping loyalties in public officials—in Stewart's case—to the railroads and mining companies. Other
Nevada senators of the same era could hardly criticize Stewart on this
count. They were themselves officials and owners of banks and mines. Similarly, New Mexico Territory underwent years of domination by the Santa
Fe Ring, a combination of lawyers, businessmen and politicians prospering
from the territory's abundance of land. In Montana, politics paralleled the
fortunes of copper, leaving Anaconda by 1915 in a position that "clearly
dominated the Montana economy and political order."[11]

There was, of course, a difference between the sporting and energetic
use of government in Dakota, and the corporate domination of Montana,
between the individual initiative shown by Horace C. Wilson, territorial
secretary of Idaho, who departed in 1866 with $33,550 of the territorial
legislature's funds (he "seems to have been of a very selfish nature," as a
contemporary put it), and the coordinated, legally sanctioned enterprises of
the Santa Fe ring. But it was a difference of scale, not of kind. Companies
as well as individuals followed narrow self-interest, failing to perceive "any
separation between government and private enterprise." In every newly
settled area, one of the first political questions concerned the location of
the territorial capital or, one level below, of the county seat. These
struggles came out of a full recognition on the part of the contestants that
securing the seat of government also meant securing financial opportunity
through a guaranteed population and a reliable market.[12]

Looking over his political history of Nevada, Gilman Ostrander
summed up its message: "Actually, almost everyone knows that businessmen are out to make money and that politicians are out to gain office and
that much history has been made in this nation by businessmen and politicians helping each other out." Ostrander's only error of phrasing was the
suggestion that businessmen and politicians were different people; in fact,
they were often the same. This interpenetration of business and government is too easily defined as "corruption." Like "speculation," "corruption" suggests that a practice, actually the product of an obvious
opportunity and overlap of interests, is an anomaly or social illness. The
essential project of the American West was to exploit the available resources. Since nature would not provide it all, both speculation and the
entrepreneurial uses of government were human devices to supplement nature's offerings.[13]

Consider the dominant political figure of Wyoming, before and after
statehood. The imagination supplies a tough and self-reliant rancher—a
Cincinnatus* in this case leaving his horse, not his plow, to go to the aid of

---

Cincinnatus: Lucius Quinctius Cincinnatus (b. ca. 519 B.C.E.) was a farmer who was appointed dictator of Rome in 458 B.C.E. in order to rescue a Roman army surrounded on
Mount Algidus. After defeating the enemy in one day, he resigned his dictatorship and returned to his farm. Legend has it that he was appointed dictator again in 439 B.C.E. and once
again ended the crisis, resigned, and returned to his farm.

his homeland. The picture is partly true. Francis Warren did invest in ranching, but also in utilities, banks, railroads, and, at first, merchandising. Like many Westerners, he pursued two interchangeable goals—"his own enrichment and the development of Wyoming." What made him a leader in the territory, governor for a time and senator after statehood? "His ability to construct a political machine dedicated to the efficient acquisition of federal subsidies," the historian Lewis Gould has explained, "set him apart from his colleagues." Wyoming "could not rely solely on its own economic resources for growth." Aridity and a short growing season limited agriculture, and cattle raising did not lead to either stable or widely distributed prosperity. Compensating for nature's shortages, Warren's pursuit of federal money—for forts, public buildings, and other improvements—met the hopes of his constituents, who "were more concerned with economic development than with social protest and as a result favored policies designed to increase their stake in society."[14]

Warren and Wyoming were beneficiaries of the Great Compromise of 1787, by which the American Constitution gave "equal representation to all states, regardless of the disparity of their populations." Proclamations of powerlessness aside, Western states had huge areas of land, few people, and two senators apiece. Given equal standing with their colleagues from more populous states, Western senators had the additional "advantage of representing relatively few major economic interests. They were therefore in a position to trade votes advantageously, in order to pass the relatively few measures which the interests they represented wanted badly." Senator Warren of Wyoming, as his biographer has put it, "left scant positive imprint on American life. He rarely looked up from his pursuit of influence for himself and riches for his state to consider the pressing questions of his time." The opportunity to take up a concern for national affairs always existed for Warren and his Western counterparts, but the workings of Western politics did not push them to it.[15]

Western dependence on federal resources did not end with the territories. Neither did the accepting of help—with resentment. Far from declining in the twentieth century, federal participation in the Western economy expanded. The Reclamation Act of 1902 put the national government in the center of the control and development of water, the West's key resource. President Theodore Roosevelt and Chief Forester Gifford Pinchot pressed the cause of expert management of the national forests, using federal powers to guide resource users toward a longer-range version of utility. The Taylor Grazing Act of 1934 finally centralized the control of grazing on the public domain. Beyond the Taylor Act, many New Deal measures framed to address the national problems of the Great Depression were especially rewarding for the West.

In early June 1933, Wyoming was proud of its status as "the only state or territory which had not asked for or received any federal assistance for its needy." In late June 1933, the state changed course and took its first federal relief check. Wyoming's "late start," T. A. Larson has pointed out, "proved to be no deterrent. . . . The federal government's nonrecoverable relief expenditures in Wyoming between July 1, 1933, and June 30, 1937, amounted to $330.64 per capita compared with $115.18 in the United States. Meanwhile, per capita internal revenue collected in Wyoming for the years 1934–1937 amounted to $28.94 compared with $109.43 in the United States." This was not an imbalance unique to Wyoming; Colorado "received twice as much as it sent to a government which it considered meddlesome and constitutionally threatening." The New Deal, Leonard Arrington has found, "benefited the West more than other sections of the nation. Indeed, when one lists the states in the order of the per capita expenditures of the federal economic agencies, the top fourteen states in benefits received were all in the West." The West got "sixty percent more" on a per capita basis than the impoverished regions of the South. "Per capita expenditures of federal agencies in Montana from 1933 to 1939, for example, were $710, while they were only $143 in North Carolina."[16]

The New Deal was a good deal for the West. The Civilian Conservation Corps did much of its finest work in the West; the farm credit programs saved numerous farmers and cattlemen from bankruptcy; the Soil Conservation Service tried to keep the West from blowing away; the Farm Security Administration built camps to house the impoverished migrant workers of California. And yet many Western political leaders complained. They took advantage of programs that helped their local interests, and they spent much of their remaining time denouncing the spread of bureaucracy and the give-away quality of the New Deal. The case of the cattlemen was representative: hit by drought, the consequences of overgrazing and of dropping prices, Western cattlemen needed help. But aid "brought regulation, and regulation the cattlemen could not abide." In 1934, in a Drought Relief Service program, the federal government began buying cattle. The sellers "had to agree to any future production-control plans which might be started," and "the prices paid were not high." Still, federal money to the amount of "nearly $525 million" went "to save cattlemen from ruin and starvation," the historian John Schlebecker has written. "For this salvation, many cattlemen never forgave the government. Large numbers of them resented the help."[17]

New Deal assistance went against a number of Western values. T. A. Larson's description of Wyoming residents applied to many other Westerners: "Although they had always been dependent on various types of federal aid, they wanted as little government as possible, and preferred most of that to be in state or local hands. Professing independence, self-reliance, and dedication to free enterprise, they served as vocal, aggressive custodians of what remained of the frontier spirit." In fact, a fair amount of that "frontier spirit" lived on. Parading their independence and accepting federal money, Westerners in the 1930s kept faith with the frontier legacy.[18]

It is common to associate the American West with the future, one of independence and self-reliance. The future that was actually projected in the Western past is quite a different matter. It was in the phenomenon of dependence—on the federal government, on the changeability of nature, on outside investment—that the West pulled ahead. In the course of American history, the central government and its role in the economy grew gradually; years of nonintervention were succeeded by the growing power of the federal government in the Progressive Era, the New Deal, and World War Two. In the West, in land policy, transportation, Indian affairs, border regulation, territorial government, and public projects, it has been possible to see the future and to see that it works—sometimes. Heavy reliance on the federal government's good graces, the example of the West suggests, does expose the two principals to substantial risk—to inefficiency and mismanagement on the part of the benefactor and to resentment and discontent on the part of the beneficiaries. To a striking degree, the lessons of the problems of the American welfare state could be read in the nation's frontier past.

As powerful and persistent as the fantasy that the West set Americans free from relying on the federal government was the fantasy that westward movement could set one free from the past. The West, for instance, was once a refuge for people who had trouble breathing. Sufferers from asthma, bronchitis, and even tuberculosis believed they chose a therapeutic environment when they chose the clean, dry air of the West.

Respiratory refugees particularly favored Arizona. Tucson's population jumped from 45,454 in 1950 to 330,537 in 1980, in large part an accretion of people who liked the climate—the clear air, the direct sunlight. Understandably, many of these new arrivals missed their homelands. Ill at ease with the peculiar plants and exposed soil of the desert, they naturally attempted to replicate the gardens and yards they had left behind. One popular, familiar plant was the magnificently named fruitless mulberry, the male of the species, which does not produce messy berries. What the fruit-free mulberry produces is pollen.

Re-creating a familiar landscape, Tucson immigrants had also re-created a familiar pollen count. Allergies reactivated. Coping with all the problems of Sun Belt growth, the Tucson City Council found itself debating in 1975 a resolution to ban the fruitless mulberry.[19]

Tucson citizens with allergies had taken part in a familiar Western exercise: replicating the problems they had attempted to escape. It was a twentieth-century version of the Boone paradox. Daniel Boone found civilization intolerable and escaped to the wilderness. His travels blazed trails for other pioneers to follow, and Boone found himself crowded out. His fresh start turned rapidly stale.

Of all the meanings assigned to Western independence, none had more emotional power than the prospect of becoming independent of the past. But Western Americans did what most travelers do: they took their problems with them. Cultural baggage is not, after all, something one retains or discards at will. While much of the Western replication of familiar ways was voluntary and intentional, other elements of continuity appear to have caught Westerners by surprise—as if parts of their own character were specters haunting them despite an attempt at exorcism by migration. No wonder, then, that emigrants made so much of their supposed new identity; no wonder they pressed the case of their supposed adaptations to the new environment, their earned status as real Westerners. Accenting the factor of their migration and new location, Westerners tried to hold the ghosts of their old, imported identities at bay.

The West had no magic power for dissolving the past, a fact that Americans confronted at all levels, from the personal to the national. A tragic demonstration of this came in the pre–Civil War relations of North, South, and West. The West might have seemed to be a route of escape from the struggles between the two other sections; in fact, the West brought those struggles to their most volatile peak. The process came to a focus in the life of Stephen Douglas, portrayed in a telling biography by Robert W. Johannsen.[20]

Widely remembered for his debates with Abraham Lincoln, Douglas was a congressman and then a senator from Illinois. He made his first great impact on the national scene by responding to the crisis posed by the acquisition of new Western territories in the Mexican War. The open question of slavery in the new territories had brought a congressional deadlock, which Douglas's maneuvering managed to break.

Douglas succeeded because he broke the compromise into pieces and passed these individually. Reassembled, the Compromise of 1850 gave, to the North, California as a free state and restrictions on slavery in the district of Columbia; to the South, it gave a tighter Fugitive Slave Law and the federal assumption of Texas's debts, left over from the republic. And, in a plank that was officially neutral and a concession to no one, Utah and New Mexico were organized as territories—with the right to make their own decisions before statehood on whether they would have slavery. This doctrine of "popular sovereignty," with which Douglas was particularly associated, played a political version of "hot potato," removing the inflammatory issue of slavery from Congress and tossing it to the territories; they would make a decision on slavery before statehood, but Congress gave no indication of just when, or by what mechanism, that decision would be made.

Senator Douglas was so delighted with the peace he thought he had achieved in the Compromise of 1850 that he declared a determination "never to make another speech on the slavery question." Douglas, like many Americans, cared more about making a living than about slavery. And he, like many other Americans, had some of his economic hopes attached to the project of a railroad to the Pacific.[21]

Douglas loved the American West and the possibilities for economic expansion and profit it presented. In various set speeches given throughout his career, he compared America to a young and growing giant. "I tell you," he would say, increase, and multiply, and expand, is the law of this nation's existence. You cannot limit this great Republic by mere boundary lines, saying, "Thus far shalt thou go, and no further." Any one of you might as well say to a son twelve years old that he is big enough, and must not grow any larger, and in order to prevent his growth put a hoop around him to keep him to his present size. What would be the result? Either the hoop must burst and be rent asunder, or the child must die. So it would be with this great nation.[22]

It no doubt added to the effectiveness of this speech that Douglas's own appearance complemented the metaphor. He was very short—and did not grow longitudinally over time—but he did, through the 1850s, encapsulate the drama of national expansion through the middle. No one put a hoop around Stephen Douglas; no one said, "Thus far and no further," and, judging from the photographs, a hardworking tailor evidently performed for Douglas's waistlines the same function Douglas performed for the nation—freeing it of the constrictions and boundaries of earlier compromises.

A good Illinois man, Douglas wanted Chicago to enjoy the prosperity of becoming the Eastern terminus of the Western railroad. To support this patriotic project, Douglas had invested in Chicago real estate. But the Pacific railroad and the related increases in Chicago real estate had to face their first obstacle in the territory immediately west of Missouri and Iowa, the area known as Permanent Indian Territory. In 1830, with the Indian Removal Act, the federal government had relocated Eastern tribes in the areas that would become Kansas, Nebraska, and Oklahoma, and the proper promises were made that all this was a permanent arrangement. Thus, in the early 1850s, as Pacific railroad fantasies proliferated, it looked as if the United States might have hemmed itself in.

Douglas began introducing bills to organize Nebraska Territory. By the conventional pattern of territorial organization, there would be an accumulation of white settlers in a new region; they would call Congress's attention to themselves; and then they would receive territorial status. Douglas's efforts thus were, from the beginning, peculiar, because there were hardly any white people in what would become Kansas and Nebraska, and the ones who were there—a few missionaries, traders, and advance squatters—were not much concerned with their official status.

Douglas wanted the new territory in order to do away with the lingering fiction of a permanent Indian territory. "The idea of arresting our progress in that direction," he said, "has become so ludicrous that we are amazed, that wise and patriotic statesmen ever cherished the thought. . . . How are we to develop, cherish and protect our immense interests and possessions on the Pacific, with a vast wilderness fifteen hundred miles in breadth, filled with hostile savages, and cutting off all direct communication. The Indian barrier must be removed."[23]

To get Nebraska and a railroad route, Douglas had to conciliate the South. That turned out to mean creating two territories, so that one territory could be a free state and one a slave state. Nonetheless, the Kansas-Nebraska Act of 1854 left that decision, by the doctrine of popular sovereignty, to the settlers themselves.

Douglas thought in 1854 that he had arranged for peace and prosperity again. Instead, he became a widely hated man as the struggle over Kansas became a national nightmare. Douglas was vilified so often, he said, that he "could travel from Boston to Chicago by the light of [his] own effigy." Without realizing it, Douglas had selected the best possible stage to make national melodrama out of the slavery controversy, as Northerners and Southerners contested—both in Congress and on the site—for control of Kansas. Newspapers made the most of the violent events, in which the issue of slavery and the acquisition of land together created the worst social tinder.[24]

The frontier, far from being a refuge from the problems of "civilization," became the symbolic source of disunion. In Kansas, Americans made the prewar transition to the dehumanization of opponents, to the preparation to wage a justified war against savages and barbarians, and the creation of a climate where verbal violence could suddenly turn into physical violence.

Douglas had just wanted peace and a railroad and a decent return on his real estate investments. He thought he had found a way to maximize the profits of American expansion and to minimize, or even dispose of, the costs.

On June 3, 1861, only forty-eight years old and deeply in debt, Douglas died of causes that are hard to figure out from the terms of nineteenth-century medicine: "rheumatism 'of a typhoid character,'" an "ulcerated sore throat," and "'torpor of the liver.'" Just before his death, Kansas was finally admitted to statehood, in one of those congressional acts that had to await the removal of Southern opposition—through secession. Douglas's very enthusiasm for the future of the Union had led to its collapse.[25]

A troubling decade of history taught Douglas the cruel but common lesson of Western history: postponements and evasions catch up with people. An apparently successful evasion, more often than not, turns out to be a greater obligation contracted to the future. Douglas's personal act of evasion reenacted in miniature a national attempt at postponement. Planning the future of the Republic, Thomas Jefferson had hoped that America could avoid the problems of mature or declining societies by developing through space, not through time. Westward expansion would keep Americans in possession of property, agrarian, independent, and responsible. To maintain the vision, Jefferson looked away from crucial aspects of expansion. The dreams of the Jeffersonians aside, Drew McCoy has written, "the system of commercial agriculture that expanded westward across space entailed an exploitative cast of mind that could not be eradicated—a cast of mind well revealed in the rampant land speculation and profiteering of nonslaveholding Americans in the West, but undoubtedly best exemplified in the most vicious form imaginable of exploiting both land and people, the institution of slavery."[26] The price of the Jeffersonian evasion would finally have to be paid, and Douglas, going about his business in the happy faith that personal improvement and national improvement ran on parallel tracks, found himself presented with the bill.

The Civil War posed no permanent obstacle to fantasies of Western independence and fresh starts. Into our own time, they have continued to appeal to Westerners at all positions on the political spectrum. Ernest Callenbach's popular utopian novel, published in 1975, sketched life in Ecotopia. Innovative in detail, *Ecotopia* was nothing if not traditional in its basic motif: the West as a place secure from the corruptions and decadence of the East. The familiar faith in boundaries persisted; Callenbach had his Ecotopians fight a war of independence and then maintain a policed border, protecting them from the moral, economic, and ecological contagions emanating from the East. The Ecotopians, and Callenbach, were well advised to select the well-watered Pacific Northwest for their nation; drawing their borders carefully, they eliminated the troubling problem of Western aridity. Feminists ruled Ecotopia; patriarchy and all its futile dreams of mastery and conquest, the narrator discovered to his initial alarm, had been put in their place—and that place was outside Ecotopia's well-policed borders. Economic freedom and fulfillment had risen to fill their place. In sensuality and personal development, Ecotopians had at last found an unending frontier. With the contagions of the East suppressed, Ecotopians could make the West what it was supposed to be in centuries of imaginings: a place where nature would restore Euro-Americans to their senses.[27]

Other strains of Western utopianism in the 1960s and 1970s showed a similar debt to the past. In college in 1971, in a class in American history, we were treated to guest speakers from a New Mexico alternative community. For half an hour, our two visitors bragged to us of their freedom from the corruptions of modern industrial society. While the two men spoke, we couldn't help noticing that their women stayed on the side with the children. In the classic Western fashion, the commune had replicated a few old traditions. The community, the speakers told us, had declared its independence from a sick society and now celebrated its self-sufficiency. A member of the audience, interested in their farming methods, asked how they had achieved their self-sufficiency in food. They were, it turned out, a little short of the goal. And what did they get by with in the meantime? Food stamps.

The hippies from the New Mexico commune were secure participants in Western tradition: living in a rugged environment, putting on magnificent verbal displays on the subject of fresh starts and autonomy, and still solidly connected to the system they had supposedly left behind. Independent living is hard work, after all; one needs all the help one can get.

There is nothing wrong with human interdependence; it is, among other things, a fact of life. A recognition that one is not the sole captain of one's fate is hardly an occasion for surprise. Especially in the American West, where the federal government, outside capital, and the market have always been powerful factors of change, the limits on personal autonomy do not seem like news. And yet humans have a well-established capacity to meet facts of life with disbelief. In a region where human interdependence has been self-evident, Westerners have woven a net of denial. That net, it is clear in our times, can entrap as well as support.

Notes

1. Martin McGinnis quoted in Earl Pomeroy, *The Territories and the United States, 1861–1890: Studies in Colonial Administration* (1947; Seattle: Univ. of Washington Press, 1969), 104.

2. Howard R. Lamar, *The Far Southwest, 1846–1912: A Territorial History* (1966; New York: W. W. Norton, 1970), 9.

3. Pomeroy, *Territories,* 106.

4. *Vermillion Republican* quoted ibid., 104.

5. Ibid., 36, 101, *Santa Fe Gazette* quoted on 101.

6. Ibid., 106.

7. Howard R. Lamar, *Dakota Territory, 1861–1889: A Study of Frontier Politics* (New Haven: Yale Univ. Press, 1956), 40, 94, 98, 276.

8. Ibid., 225, *Press and Dakotan* quoted on 205.

9. Ibid., 46.

10. Ibid., 88, 130.

11. Michael Malone and Richard B. Roeder, *Montana: A History of Two Centuries* (Seattle: Univ. of Washington Press, 1976), 176.

12. Pomeroy, *Territories,* 30; Lamar, *Dakota,* 79.

13. Gilman M. Ostrander, *Nevada: The Great Rotten Borough, 1859–1964* (New York: Alfred A. Knopf, 1966), xii.

14. Lewis Gould, *Wyoming: A Political History, 1866–1896* (New Haven: Yale Univ. Press, 1968), 80, ix.

15. Ostrander, *Nevada,* 162; Gould, *Wyoming,* 268.

16. T. A. Larson, "The New Deal in Wyoming," 254, 257; James V. Wickens, "The New Deal in Colorado," 284; Leonard Arrington, "The New Deal in the West: A Preliminary Statistical Inquiry," 311, 312, all in "The New Deal in the West," *Pacific Historical Review* (Aug. 1969).

17. John T. Schlebecker, *Cattle Raising on the Plains, 1900–1961* (Lincoln: Univ. of Nebraska Press, 1963), 133, 141.

18. Larson, "New Deal in Wyoming," 249.

19. Calvin Trillin, "U.S. Journal: Tucson, Ariz.: Under the Fruitless Mulberry," *New Yorker,* July 19, 1982, 62–65.

20. Robert W. Johannsen, *Stephen A. Douglas* (New York: Oxford Univ. Press, 1973).

21. Stephen Douglas quoted ibid., 303.

22. Robert W. Johannsen, ed., *The Lincoln-Douglas Debates* (New York: Oxford Univ. Press, 1965), 92.

23. Stephen Douglas quoted in Johannsen, *Douglas,* 399.

24. Stephen Douglas quoted ibid., 451.

25. Ibid., 871.

26. Drew McCoy, *The Elusive Republic: Political Economy in Jeffersonian America* (New York: W. W. Norton, 1982), 252.

27. Ernest Callenbach, *Ecotopia* (1975; New York: Bantam Books, 1977).

Ideas for Rereading

1. As you reread this essay, notice how Limerick works as a historian. Identify the chief components of her argument, and note the themes of each of the four major divisions of her essay. Note in the margins of your text where and how she relies on the work of other historians to build her argument. What claims does she make on the basis of their work and what lessons does she draw from the stories they tell? What is Limerick's contribution? How would you describe the work that Limerick is doing? Why does she need to work selectively and anecdotally? What are the risks of this method?

2. Tone and voice in written work can be difficult to analyze. There are, however, clues to an author's tone and voice throughout any text, and noticing and following these clues is necessary for the fullest understanding of the work. Note the different voices Limerick adopts. Where does she write at length in what appears to be her own, "natural" voice—one that is conversational rather than academic? How does this voice differ from the voice she adopts to summarize or paraphrase the work of another writer? Where does she use irony—even sarcasm—and to what purpose? At what points does she write feelingly and with urgency? What can you conclude from a careful reading of Limerick's tone in this essay about her methods and goals as a historian?

Ideas for Writing

1. Limerick's argument ranges widely across time and space and subject matter as it exposes or deconstructs the "fantasies" of Western "independence" and "fresh starts." She draws several explicit connections between the West's past and the politics of the present day, but to a great extent she leaves the reader to work out the full implications of her argument. In certain respects, her essay aims to dispel some commonly held illusions, but you may find that positive or hopeful ideas and possibilities also emerge from it. What does Limerick's argument mean for the America of today? What image or idea of America emerges from her writing? How does it differ from the familiar, conventional one? Write an essay that presents your interpretation of the significance of Limerick's argument for contemporary America.

2. How does Limerick's argument influence your reading of Frederick Jackson Turner's "The Significance of the Frontier in American History"? Reread Turner's essay with Limerick's argument in mind, and write an essay that presents your view of how Limerick's critique shifts your reading of Turner. Does the vaunted "tradition of independence" (p. 575) stand up against the tradition of federal subsidy? What difference does it make to your understanding of the meaning of the "frontier" in American history when you start to take seriously the lessons that Limerick draws in her essay? How do these lessons alter your

understanding of the West and the relationship between Western states and the federal government?

3. The concept of borders meant different things to different inhabitants of the West. It would be fair to say that in general borders (when they existed at all) for the natives of America were more fluid than those created by Euro-American settlement. Read Leslie Marmon Silko's essays in this chapter (p. 616), paying attention to her concept of borders as it compares with those that Limerick describes. How do borders figure in each writer's work? Write an essay on borders in the works by Silko and Limerick.

JANE TOMPKINS

Jane Tompkins's West of Everything: The Inner Life of Westerns *(1992), from which the following essay is an excerpt, was nominated for the 1992 Pulitzer Prize for nonfiction. Most recent among her many published works are* Private Voices, Public Lives *(1995) and* A Life in School *(1996), a record of her experience as a teacher. She is now a professor of education at the University of Illinois at Chicago. She has taught and written extensively on the history and cultural legacy of the American West, and yet, as the following essay demonstrates, she often prefers the role of thoughtful amateur to that of expert. As you read this essay, note how her reactions to the exhibits reflect a process of self-questioning and self-conscious revision. The last section, with its dramatic shift in perspective, might at first seem to represent a reversal in her views, but you will need to consider — especially in light of her final paragraph — why Tompkins chose to structure her essay in this way, why she chose to include this reversal in her account of a visit to the Buffalo Bill Historical Center. How does this exemplify the philosophical problems inherent in the representation of the West?*

At the Buffalo Bill Museum, June 1988

The video at the entrance to the Buffalo Bill Historical Center says that Buffalo Bill was the most famous American of his time, that by 1900 more than a billion words had been written about him, and that he had a progressive vision of the West. Buffalo Bill had worked as a cattle driver, a wagoneer, a Pony Express rider, a buffalo hunter for the railroad, a hunting guide, an army scout and sometime Indian fighter; he wrote dime novels about himself and an autobiography by the age of thirty-four, by which time he was already famous; and then he began another set of careers, first as an actor, performing on the urban stage in wintertime melodramatic representations of what he actually earned a living at in the summer (scouting and leading hunting expeditions), and finally becoming the impresario of his great Wild West show, a form of entertainment he invented and carried on as actor, director, and all-around idea man for thirty years. Toward the end of his life he founded the town of Cody, Wyoming, to which he gave, among other things, two hundred thousand dollars. Strangely enough, it was as a progressive civic leader that Bill Cody wanted to be remembered. "I don't want to die," the video at the entrance quotes him as saying, "and have people say—oh, there goes another old showman. . . . I would like people to say—this is man who opened Wyoming to the best of civilization."

"The best of civilization." This was the phrase that rang in my head as I moved through the museum, which is one of the most disturbing places I have ever visited. It is also a wonderful place. It is four museums in one: the Whitney Gallery of Western Art, which houses artworks on Western subjects; the Buffalo Bill Museum proper, which memorializes Cody's life; the Plains Indian Museum, which exhibits artifacts of American Indian civilization; and the Winchester Arms Museum, a collection of firearms historically considered.

The whole operation is extremely well designed and well run, from the video program at the entrance that gives an overview of all four museums, to the fresh-faced young attendants wearing badges that say "Ask Me," to the museum shop stacked with books on Western Americana, to the ladies room—a haven of satiny marble, shining mirrors, and flattering light. Among other things, the museum is admirable for its effort to combat prevailing stereotypes about the "winning of the West," a phrase it self-consciously places in quotation marks. There are placards declaring that all history is a matter of interpretation, and that the American West is a source of myth. Everywhere, except perhaps in the Winchester Arms Museum, where the rhetoric is different, you feel the effort of the museum staff to reach out to the public, to be clear, to be accurate, to be fair, not to condescend—in short, to educate in the best sense of the term.

On the day I went, the museum was featuring an exhibition of Frederic Remington's works. Two facts about Remington make his work different from that of artists usually encountered in museums. The first is that Remington's paintings and statues function as a historical record. Their chief attraction has always been that they transcribe scenes and events that have vanished from the earth. The second fact, related to this, is the brutality of their subject matter. Remington's work makes you pay attention to what is happening in the painting or the piece of statuary. When you look at his work you cannot escape from the subject.

Consequently, as I moved through the exhibit, the wild contortions of the bucking broncos, the sinister expression invariably worn by the Indians, and the killing of animals and men made the placards discussing Remington's use of the "lost wax" process seem strangely disconnected. In the face of unusual violence, or implied violence, their message was: what is important here is technique. Except in the case of paintings showing the battle of San Juan Hill, where white Americans were being killed, the material accompanying Remington's works did not refer to the subject matter of the paintings and statues themselves. Nevertheless, an undertone of disquiet ran beneath the explanations; at least I thought I detected one. Someone had taken the trouble to ferret out Remington's statement of horror at the slaughter on San Juan Hill; someone had also excerpted the judgment of art critics commending Remington for the lyricism, interiority, and mystery of his later canvasses—pointing obliquely to the fascination with bloodshed that preoccupied his earlier work.

The uneasiness of the commentary, and my uneasiness with it, were nothing compared to the blatant contradictions in the paintings themselves. A pastel palette, a sunlit stop-action haze, murderous movement arrested under a lazy sky, flattened onto canvas and fixed in azure and ochre—two opposed impulses nestle here momentarily. The tension that keeps them from splitting apart is what holds the viewer's gaze.

The most excruciating example of what I mean occurs in the first painting in the exhibit. Entitled *His First Lesson,* it shows a horse standing saddled but riderless, the white of the horse's eye signaling his fear. A man using an instrument to tighten the horse's girth, at arm's length, backs away from the reaction he clearly anticipates, while the man who holds the horse's halter is doing the same. But what can they be afraid of? For the horse's right rear leg is tied a foot off the ground by a rope that is also tied around his neck. He can't move. That is the whole point.

His First Lesson. Whose? And what lesson, exactly? How to stand still when terrified? How not to break away when they come at you with strange instruments? How to be obedient? How to behave? It is impossible not to imagine that Remington's obsession with physical cruelty had roots somewhere in his own experience. Why else, in statue after statue, is the horse rebelling? The bucking bronco, symbol of the state of Wyoming, on

"His First Lesson," by Frederic Remington, 1903. Oil on canvas.

every licence plate, on every sign for every bar, on every belt buckle, mug, and decal—this image Remington cast in bronze over and over again. There is a wild diabolism in the bronzes; the horse and rider seem one thing, not so much rider and ridden as a single bolt of energy gone crazy and caught somehow, complicatedly, in a piece of metal.

In the paintings, it is different—more subtle and bizarre. The cavalry on its way to a massacre, sweetly limned, softly tinted, poetically seized in mid-career, and gently laid on the two-dimensional surface. There is about these paintings of military men in the course of performing their deadly duty an almost maternal tenderness. The idealization of the cavalrymen in their dusty uniforms on their gallant horses has nothing to do with patriotism; it is pure love.

Remington's paintings and statues, as shown in this exhibition, embody everything that was objectionable about his era in American history. They are imperialist and racist; they glorify war and the torture and killing of animals; there are no women in them anywhere. Never the West as garden, never as pastoral, never as home. But in their aestheticization of violent life, Remington's pictures speak (to me, at least) of some other desire. The maternal tenderness is not an accident, nor is the beauty of the afternoons or the warmth of the desert sun. In them Remington plays the part of the preserver, as if by catching the figures in color and line he could save their lives and absorb some of that life into himself.

In one painting that particularly repulsed and drew me, a moose is outlined against the evening sky at the brink of a lake. He looks expectantly into the distance. Behind him and to one side, hidden from his view and only just revealed to ours, for it is dark there, is a hunter poised in the back of a canoe, rifle perfectly aimed. We look closer; the title of the picture is *Coming to the Call.* Ah, now we see. This is a sadistic scene. The hunter has lured the moose to his death. But wait a moment. Isn't the sadism really directed at us? First we see the glory of the animal; Remington has made it as noble as he knows how. Then we see what is going to happen. The hunter is one up on the moose, but Remington is one up on us. He makes us feel the pain of the anticipated killing, and makes us want to hold it off, to preserve the moose, just as he has done. Which way does the painting cut? Does it go against the hunter—who represents us, after all—or does it go against the moose who came to the call? Who came, to what call? Did Remington come to the West in response to it—to whatever the moose represents or to whatever the desire to kill the moose represents? But he hasn't killed it; he has only preserved an image of a white man about to kill it. And what call do we answer when we look at this painting? Who is calling whom? What is being preserved here?

That last question is the one that for me hung over the whole museum.

The Whitney Gallery is an art museum proper. Its allegiance is to art as academic tradition has defined it. In this tradition, we come to understand a painting by having in our possession various bits of information. Something about the technical process used to produce it (pastels, watercolors, woodblock prints, etc.); something about the elements of composition (line and color and movement); something about the artist's life (where born, how educated, by whom influenced, which school belonged to or revolted against); something about the artist's relation to this particular subject, such as how many times the artist painted it or whether it contains a favorite model. Occasionally there will be some philosophizing about the themes or ideas the paintings are said to represent.

The problem is, when you're faced with a painter like Remington, these bits of information, while nice to have, don't explain what is there in front of you. They don't begin to give you an account of why a person should have depicted such things. The experience of a lack of fit between the explanatory material and what is there on the wall is one I've had before in museums, when, standing in front of a painting or a piece of statuary, I've felt a huge gap between the information on the little placard and what it is I'm seeing. I realize that works of art, so-called, all have a subject matter, are all engaged with life, with some piece of life no less significant, no less compelling than Remington's subjects are, if we could only see its force. The idea that art is somehow separate from history, that it somehow occupies a space that is not the same as the space of life, seems out of whack here.

I wandered through the gallery thinking these things because right next to it, indeed all around it, in the Buffalo Bill Museum proper and in the Plains Indian Museum, are artifacts that stand not for someone's expertise or skill in manipulating the elements of an artistic medium, but for life itself; they are the residue of life.

The Buffalo Bill Museum is a wonderful array of textures, colors, shapes, sizes, forms. The fuzzy brown bulk of a buffalo's hump, the sparkling diamonds in a stickpin, the brilliant colors of the posters—the mixture makes you want to walk in and be surrounded by it, as if you were going into a child's adventure story. For a moment you can pretend you're a cowboy too; it's a museum where fantasy can take over. For a while.

As I moved through the exhibition, with the phrase "the best of civilization" ringing in my head, I came upon certain objects displayed in a section that recreates rooms from Cody's house. Ostrich feather fans, peacock feather fans, antler furniture—a chair and a table made entirely of antlers—a bearskin rug. And then I saw the heads on the wall: Alaska Yukon Moose, Wapiti American Elk, Muskox (the "Whitney," the "DeRham"), Mountain Caribou (the "Hyland"), Quebec Labrador Caribou (the "Elbow"), Rocky Mountain Goat (the "Haase," the "Kilto"), Woodland Caribou (world's record, "DeRham"), the "Rogers" freak Wapiti, the "Whitney" bison, the "Lord Rundlesham" bison. The names that appear after the animals are the names of the men who killed them. Each of the animals is scored according to measurements devised by the Boone and Crockett Club, a big-game hunters' organization. The Lord Rundlesham bison, for example, scores 124⅞, making it number 25 in the world for bison trophies. The "Reed" Alaska Yukon Moose scores 247. The "Witherbee" Canada moose holds the world's record.

Next to the wall of trophies is a small enclosure where jewelry is displayed. A buffalo head stickpin and two buffalo head rings, the heads made entirely of diamonds, with ruby eyes, the gifts of the Russian crown prince. A gold and diamond stickpin from Edward VII; a gold, diamond, and garnet locket from Queen Victoria. The two kinds of trophies — animals and jewels — form an incongruous set; the relationship between them compelling but obscure.

If the rest of the items in the museum — the dime novels with their outrageous covers, the marvelous posters, the furniture, his wife's dress, his daughter's oil painting — have faded from my mind it is because I cannot forget the heads of the animals as they stared down, each with an individual expression on its face. When I think about it I realize that I don't know why these animal heads are there. Buffalo Bill didn't kill them; perhaps they were gifts from the famous people he took on hunts. A different kind of jewelry.

After the heads, I began to notice something about the whole exhibition. In one display, doghide chaps, calfskin chaps, angora goathide chaps, and horsehide chaps. Next to these a rawhide lariat and a horsehair quirt. Behind me, boots and saddles, all of leather. Everywhere I looked there was tooth or bone, skin or fur, hide or hair, or the animal itself entire — two full-size buffalo (a main feature of the exhibition) and a magnificent stone sheep (a mountain sheep with beautiful curving horns). This one was another world's record. The best of civilization.

In the literature about Buffalo Bill you read that he was a conservationist, that if it were not for the buffalo in his Wild West shows the species would probably have become extinct. (In the seventeenth century 40 million buffalo roamed North America; by 1900 all the wild buffalo had been killed except for one herd in northern Alberta.) That the man who gained fame first as a buffalo hunter should have been an advocate for conservation of the buffalo is not an anomaly but typical of the period. The men who did the most to preserve America's natural wilderness and its wildlife were big-game hunters. The Boone and Crockett Club, founded by Theodore Roosevelt, George Bird Grinnell, and Owen Wister, turns out to have been one of the earliest organizations to devote itself to environmental protection in the United States. *The Reader's Encyclopedia of the American West* says that the club "supported the national park and forest reserve movement, helped create a system of national wildlife refuges, and lobbied for the protection of threatened species, such as the buffalo and antelope." At the same time, the prerequisites for membership in the club were "the highest caliber of sportsmanship and the achievement of killing 'in fair chase' trophy specimens [which had to be adult males] from several species of North American big game."

The combination big-game hunter and conservationist suggests that these men had no interest in preserving the animals for the animals' sake but simply wanted to ensure the chance to exercise their sporting pleasure. But I think this view is too simple; something further is involved here. The men who hunted game animals had a kind of love for them and a kind of love for nature that led them to want to preserve the animals they also desired to kill. That is, the desire to kill the animals was in some way related to a desire to see them live. It is not an accident, in this connection, that Roosevelt, Wister, and Remington all went west originally for their health. Their devotion to the West, their connection to it, their love for it are rooted in their need to reanimate their own lives. The preservation of nature, in other words, becomes for them symbolic of their own survival.

In a sense, then, there is a relationship between the Remington exhibition in the Whitney Gallery and the animal memorabilia in the Buffalo Bill Museum. The moose in *Coming to the Call* and the mooseheads on the wall are not so different as they might appear. The heads on the wall serve an aesthetic purpose; they are decorative objects, pleasing to the eye, which call forth certain associations. In this sense they are like visual works of art. The painting, on the other hand, has something of the trophy about it. The moose as Remington painted it is about to become a trophy, yet in another sense it already is one. Remington has simply captured the moose in another form. In both cases the subject matter, the life of a wild animal, symbolizes the life of the observer. It is the preservation of that life that both the painting and the taxidermy serve.

What are museums keeping safe for us, after all? What is it that we wish so much to preserve? The things we put in safekeeping, in our safe-deposit boxes under lock and key, are always in some way intended finally as safeguards of our own existence. The money and jewelry and stock certificates are meant for a time when we can no longer earn a living by the sweat of our brows. Similarly, the objects in museums preserve for us a source of life from which we need to nourish ourselves when the resources that would normally supply us have run dry.

The Buffalo Bill Historical Center, full as it is of dead bones, lets us see more clearly than we normally can what it is that museums are for. It is a kind of charnel house that houses images of living things that have passed away but whose life force still lingers around their remains and so passes itself on to us. We go and look at the objects in the glass cases and at the paintings on the wall, as if by standing there we could absorb into ourselves some of the energy that flowed once through the bodies of the live things represented. A museum, rather than being, as we normally think of it, the most civilized of places, a place most distant from our savage selves, actually caters to the urge to absorb the life of another into one's own life.

If we see the Buffalo Bill Museum in this way, it is no longer possible to separate ourselves from the hunters responsible for the trophies with their wondering eyes or from the curators who put them there. We are not, in essence, different from Roosevelt or Remington or Buffalo Bill, who killed animals when they were abundant in the Wild West of the 1880s. If in doing so those men were practicing the ancient art of absorbing the life of an animal into their own through the act of killing it, realizing themselves through the destruction of another life, then we are not so different from them, as visitors to the museum, we stand beside the bones and skins and nails of beings that were once alive, or stare fixedly at their painted images. Indeed our visit is only a safer form of the same enterprise as theirs.

So I did not get out of the Buffalo Bill Museum unscathed, unimplicated in the acts of rapine and carnage that these remains represent. And I did not get out without having had a good time, either, because however many dire thoughts I may have had, the exhibits were interesting and fun to see. I was even able to touch a piece of buffalo hide displayed especially for that purpose (it was coarse and springy). Everyone else had touched it too. The hair was worn down, where people's hands had been, to a fraction of its original length.

After this, the Plains Indian Museum was a terrible letdown. I went from one exhibit to another expecting to become absorbed, but nothing worked. What was the matter? I was interested in Indians, had read about them, taught some Indian literature, felt drawn by accounts of native religions. I had been prepared to enter this museum as if I were going into another children's story, only this time I would be an Indian instead of a cowboy or a cowgirl. But the objects on display, most of them behind glass, seemed paltry and insignificant. They lacked visual presence. The bits of leather and sticks of wood triggered no fantasies in me.

At the same time, I noticed with some discomfort that almost everything in those glass cases was made of feathers and claws and hide, just like the men's chaps and ladies' fans in the Buffalo Bill Museum, only there was no luxury here. Plains Indian culture, it seemed, was made entirely from animals. Their mode of life had been even more completely dedicated to carnage than Buffalo Bill's, dependent as it was on animals for food, clothing, shelter, equipment, everything. In the Buffalo Bill Museum I was able to say to myself, well, if these men had been more sensitive, if they had had a right relation to their environment and to life itself, the atrocities that produced these trophies would never have occurred. They never would have exterminated the Indians and killed off the buffalo. But the spectacle before me made it impossible to say that. I had expected that the Plains Indian Museum would show me how life in nature ought to be lived: not the mindless destruction of nineteenth-century America but an ideal form of communion with animals and the land. What the museum seemed to say instead was that cannibalism was universal. Both colonizer and colonized had had their hands imbrued with blood. The Indians had lived off animals and had made war against one another. Violence was simply a necessary and inevitable part of life. And a person who, like me, was horrified at the extent of the destruction was just the kind of romantic idealist my husband sometimes accused me of being. There was no such thing as the life lived in harmony with nature. It was all bloodshed and killing, an unending cycle, over and over again, and no one could escape.

But perhaps there was a way to understand the violence that made it less terrible. Perhaps if violence was necessary, a part of nature, intended by the universe, then it could be seen as sacramental. Perhaps it was true, what Calvin Martin had said in *Keepers of the Game:* that the Indians had a sacred contract with the animals they killed, that they respected them as equals and treated their remains with honor and punctilio. If so, the remains of animals in the Plains Indian Museum weren't the same as those left by Buffalo Bill and his friends. They certainly didn't look the same. Perhaps. All I knew for certain was that these artifacts, lifeless and shrunken, spoke to me of nothing I could understand. No more did the life-size models of Indians, with strange featureless faces, draped in costumes that didn't look like clothing. The figures, posed awkwardly in front of tepees too white to seem real, carried no sense of a life actually lived, any more than the objects in the glass cases had.

The more I read the placards on the wall, the more disaffected I became. Plains Indian life apparently had been not only bloody but exceedingly tedious. All those porcupine quills painstakingly softened, flattened, dyed, then appliqued through even more laborious methods of stitching or weaving. Four methods of attaching porcupine quills, six design groups, population statistics, patterns of migration. There wasn't any glamour here at all. No glamour in the lives the placards told about, no glamour in the objects themselves, no glamour in the experience of looking at them. Just a lot of shriveled things accompanied by some even drier information.

Could it be, then, that the problem with the exhibitions was that Plains Indian culture, if representable at all, was simply not readable by someone like me? Their stick figures and abstract designs could convey very little to an untrained Euro-American eye. One display in particular illustrated this. It was a piece of cloth, behind glass, depicting a buffalo skin with some marks on it. The placard read: "Winter Count, Sioux ca. 1910, after Lone Dog's, Fort Peck, Montana, 1877." The hide with its markings had been a calendar, each year represented by one image, which showed the most significant event in the life of the tribe. A thick pamphlet to one side of the glass case explained each image year by year: 1800–1801, the attack of the Uncapoo on a Crow Indian Fort; 1802–1803, a total eclipse of the sun. The images, once you knew what they represented, made sense, and seemed poetic interpretations of the experiences they stood for. But without explanation they were incomprehensible.

The Plains Indian Museum stopped me in my tracks. It was written in a language I had never learned. I didn't have the key. Maybe someone did, but I wasn't too sure. For it may not have been just cultural difference that made the text unreadable. I began to suspect that the text itself was corrupt, that the architects of this museum were going through motions whose purpose was, even to themselves, obscure. Knowing what event a figure stands for in the calendar doesn't mean you understand an Indian year. The deeper purpose of the museum began to puzzle me. Wasn't there an air of bad faith about preserving the vestiges of a culture one had effectively extinguished? Did the museum exist to assuage our guilt and not for any real educational reason? I do not have an answer to these questions. All I know is that I felt I was in the presence of something pious and a little insincere. It had the aura of a failed attempt at virtue, as though the curators were trying to present as interesting objects whose purpose and meaning even they could not fully imagine.

In a last-ditch attempt to salvage something, I went up to one of the guards and asked where the movie was showing which the video had advertised, the movie about Plains Indian life. "Oh, the slide show, you mean," he said. "It's been discontinued." When I asked why, he said he didn't know. It occurred to me then that that was the message the museum was sending, if I could read it, that that was the bottom line. Discontinued, no reason given.

The movie in the Winchester Arms Museum, *Lock, Stock, and Barrel,* was going strong. The film began with the introduction of cannon into European warfare in the Middle Ages, and was working its way slowly toward the nineteenth century when I left. I was in a hurry. Soon my husband would be waiting for me in the lobby. I went from room to room, trying to get a quick sense impression of the objects on display. They were all the same: guns. Some large drawings and photographs on the walls tried to give a sense of the context in which the arms had been used, but the effect was nil. It was case after case of rifles and pistols, repeating themselves over and over, and even when some slight variation caught my eye the differences meant nothing to me.

But the statistics did. In a large case of commemorative rifles, I saw the Antlered Game Commemorative Carbine. Date of manufacture: 1978. Number produced: 19,999. I wondered how many antlered animals each carbine had killed. I saw the Canadian Centennial (1962): 90,000; the Legendary Lawman (1978): 19,999; the John Wayne (1980–81): 51,600. Like the titles of the various sections of the museum, these names had a message. The message was: guns are patriotic. Associated with national celebrations, law enforcement, and cultural heroes. The idea that firearms were inseparable from the march of American history came through even more strongly in the titles given to the various exhibits: Firearms in Colonial America; Born in America: The Kentucky Rifle; The Era of Expansion and Invention; The Civil War: Firearms of the Conflict; The Golden Age of Hunting; Winning the West. The guns embodied phases of the history they had helped to make. There were no quotation marks here to indicate that expansion and conquest might not have been all they were cracked up to be. The fact that firearms had had a history seemed to consecrate them; the fact that they had existed at the time when certain famous events had occurred seemed to make them not only worth preserving but worth studying and revering. In addition to the exhibition rooms, the museum housed three "study galleries": one for hand arms, one for shoulder arms, one for U.S. military firearms.

As I think back on the rows and rows of guns, I wonder if I should have looked at them more closely, tried harder to appreciate the workmanship that went into them, the ingenuity, the attention. Awe and admiration are the attitudes the museum invites. You hear the ghostly march of military music in the background; you imagine flags waving and sense the implicit reference to feats of courage in battle and glorious death. The place had the air of an expensive and well-kept reliquary, or of the room off the transept of a cathedral where the vestments are stored. These guns were not there merely to be seen or even studied; they were there to be venerated.

But I did not try to appreciate the guns. They were too technical, too foreign. I didn't have their language, and, besides, I didn't want to learn. I rejoined my husband in the lobby. The Plains Indian Museum had been incomprehensible, but in the Winchester Arms Museum I could hardly see the objects at all, for I did not see the point. Or, rather, I did see it and rejected it. Here in the basement the instruments that had turned live animals into hides and horns, had massacred the Indians and the buffalo, were being lovingly displayed. And we were still making them: 51,600 John Waynes in 1980–81. Arms were going strong.

As I bought my books and postcards in the gift shop, I noticed a sign that read "Rodeo Tickets Sold Here," and something clicked into place. So that was it. *Everything* was still going strong. The whole museum was just another rodeo, only with the riders and their props stuffed, painted, sculpted, immobilized and put under glass. Like the rodeo, the entire museum witnessed a desire to bring back the United States of the 1880s and 1890s. The American people did not want to let go of the winning of the West. They wanted to win it all over again, in imagination. It was the ecstasy of the kill, as much as the life of the hunted, that we fed off here. The Buffalo Bill Historical Center did not repudiate the carnage that had taken place in the nineteenth century. It celebrated it. With its gleaming rest rooms, cute snack bar, opulent museum shop, wooden Indians, thousand rifles, and scores of animal trophies, it helped us all reenact the dream of excitement, adventure, and conquest that was what the Wild West meant to most people in this country.

This is where my visit ended, but it had a sequel. When I left the Buffalo Bill Historical Center, I was full of moral outrage, an indignation so intense it made me almost sick, though it was pleasurable too, as such emotions usually are. But the outrage was undermined by the knowledge that I knew nothing about Buffalo Bill, nothing of his life, nothing of the circumstances that led him to be involved in such violent events. And I began to wonder if my reaction wasn't in some way an image, however small, of the violence I had been objecting to. So when I got home I began to read about Buffalo Bill, and a whole new world opened up. I came to love Buffalo Bill.

"I have seen him the very personification of grace and beauty . . . dashing over the free wild prairie and riding his horse as though he and the noble animal were bounding with one life and one motion." That is the sort of thing people wrote about Buffalo Bill. They said "he was the handsomest man I ever saw." They said "there was never another man lived as popular as he was." They said "there wasn't a man woman or child that he knew or ever met that he didn't speak to." They said "he was handsome as a god, a good rider and a crack shot." They said "he gave lots of money away. Nobody ever went hungry around him." They said "he was way above the average, physically and every other way."

These are quotes from people who knew Cody, collected by one of his two most responsible biographers, Nellie Snyder Yost. She puts them in the last chapter, and by the time you get there they all ring true. Buffalo Bill was incredibly handsome. He was extremely brave and did things no other scout would do. He would carry messages over rugged territory swarming with hostile Indians, riding all night in bad weather and get through, and then take off again the next day to ride sixty miles through a blizzard. He was not a proud man. He didn't boast of his exploits. But he did do incredible things, not just once in a while but on a fairly regular basis. He had a great deal of courage; he believed in himself, in his abilities, in his strength and endurance and knowledge. He was very skilled at what he did — hunting and scouting — but he wasn't afraid to try other things. He wrote some dime novels, he wrote his autobiography by age thirty-four, without very much schooling; he wasn't afraid to try acting, even though the stage terrified him and he knew so little about it that, according to his wife, he didn't even know you had to memorize lines.

Maybe it was because he grew up on the frontier, maybe it was just the kind of person he was, but he was constantly finding himself in situations that required resourcefulness and courage, quick decisions and decisive action and rising to the occasion. He wasn't afraid to improvise.

He liked people, drank a lot, gave big parties, gave lots of presents, and is reputed to have been a womanizer (Cody, 16). When people came to see him in his office tent on the show grounds, to shake his hand or have their pictures taken with him, he never turned anyone away. "He kept a uniformed doorman at the tent opening to announce visitors," writes a biographer. "No matter who was outside, from a mayor to a shabby woman with a baby, the Colonel would smooth his mustache, stand tall and straight, and tell the doorman to 'show 'em in.' He greeted everyone the same" (Yost, 436).

As a showman, he was a genius. People don't say much about *why* he was so successful; mostly they describe the wonderful goings-on. But I get the feeling that Cody was one of those people who was connected to his time in an uncanny way. He knew what people wanted, he knew how to entertain them, because he *liked* them, was open to them, felt his kinship with them, or was so much in touch with himself at some level that he was thereby in touch with almost everybody else.

He liked to dress up and had a great sense of costume (of humor, too, they say). Once he came to a fancy dress ball, his first, in New York, wearing white tie and tails and a large Stetson. He knew what people wanted. He let his hair grow long and wore a mustache and beard, because, he said, he wouldn't be believable as a scout otherwise. Hence his Indian name, Pahaska, meaning "long hair," which people loved to use. Another kind of costume. He invented the ten-gallon hat, which the Stetson company made to his specifications. Afterward, they made a fortune from it. In the scores of pictures reproduced in the many books about him, he most often wears scout's clothes—usually generously fringed buckskin, sometimes a modi-fied cavalryman's outfit—though often he's impeccably turned out in a natty-looking three-piece business suit (sometimes with overcoat, some-times not). The photographs show him in a tuxedo, in something called a "Mexican suit" which looks like a cowboy outfit, and once he appears in Indian dress. In almost every case he is wearing some kind of hat, usually the Stetson, at exactly the right angle. He poses deliberately, and with dig-nity, for the picture. Cody didn't take himself so seriously that he had to pretend to be less than he was.

What made Buffalo Bill so irresistible? Why is he still so appealing, even now, when we've lost, supposedly, all the illusions that once sup-ported his popularity? There's a poster for one of his shows when he was traveling in France that gives a clue to what it is that makes him so pro-foundly attractive a figure. The poster consists of a huge buffalo galloping

"Je Viens," ca. 1900. Color lithograph.

across the plains, and against the buffalo's hump, in the center of his hump, is a cutout circle that shows the head of Buffalo Bill, white-mustachioed and bearded now, in his famous hat, and beneath, in large red letters, are the words "Je viens."

Je viens ("I am coming") are the words of a savior. The announcement is an annunciation. Buffalo Bill is a religious figure of a kind who makes sense within a specifically Christian tradition. That is, he comes in the guise of a redeemer, of someone who will save us, who will through his own actions do something for us that we ourselves cannot do. He will lift us above our lives, out of the daily grind, into something larger than we are.

His appeal on the surface is to childish desires, the desire for glamour, fame, bigness, adventure, romance. But these desires are also the sign of something more profound, and it is to something more profound in us that he also appeals. Buffalo Bill comes to the child in us, understood not as that part of ourselves that we have outgrown but as the part that got left behind, of necessity, a long time ago, having been starved, bound, punished, disciplined out of existence. He promises that that part of the self can live again. He has the power to promise these things because he represents the West, that geographical space of the globe that was still the realm of exploration and discovery, that was still open, that had not yet quite been tamed, when he began to play himself on the stage. He not only represented it, he *was* it. He brought the West itself with him when he came. The very Indians, the very buffalo, the very cowboys, the very cattle, the very stagecoach itself which had been memorialized in story. He performed in front of the audience the feats that had made him famous. He shot glass balls and clay pigeons out of the air with amazing rapidity. He rode his watersmooth silver stallion at full gallop. "Jesus he was a handsome man," wrote e. e. cummings in "Buffalo Bill's Defunct."

"I am coming." This appearance of Buffalo Bill, in the flesh, was akin to the apparition of a saint or of the Virgin Mary to believers. He was the incarnation of an ideal. He came to show people that what they had only imagined was really true. The West really did exist. There really were heroes who rode white horses and performed amazing feats. e. e. cummings was right to invoke the name of Jesus in his poem. Buffalo Bill was a secular messiah.

He was a messiah because people believed in him. When he died, he is reputed to have said, "Let my show go on." But he had no show at the time, so he probably didn't say that. Still, the words are prophetic because the desire for what Buffalo Bill had done had not only not died but would call forth the countless reenactments of the Wild West, from the rodeo—a direct descendant of his show—to the thousands of Western novels, movies, and television programs that comprise the Western genre in the twentieth century, a genre that came into existence as a separate category right about the time that Cody died. Don Russell maintains that the way the West exists in our minds today is largely the result of the way Cody presented it in his show. That was where people got their ideas of what the characters looked like. Though many Indian tribes wore no feathers and fought on foot, you will never see a featherless, horseless Indian warrior in the movies, because Bill employed only Sioux and other Plains tribes which had horses and traditionally wore feathered headdresses. "Similarly," he adds, "cowboys wear ten-gallon Stetsons, not because such a hat was worn in early range days, but because it was part of the costume adopted by Buffalo Bill for his show" (Russell, 470).

But the deeper legacy is elsewhere. Buffalo Bill was a person who inspired other people. What they saw in him was an aspect of themselves. It really doesn't matter whether Cody was as great as people thought him or not, because what they were responding to when he rode into the arena, erect and resplendent on his charger, was something intangible, not the man himself, but a possible way of being. William F. Cody and the Wild West triggered the emotions that had fueled the imaginative lives of people who flocked to see him, especially men and boys, who made up the larger portion of the audience. He and his cowboys played to an inward territory; a Wild West of the psyche that hungered for exercise sprang into activity when the show appeared. *Je viens* was a promise to redeem that territory, momentarily at least, from exile and oblivion. The lost parts of the self symbolized by buffalo and horses and wild men would live again for an hour while the show went on.

People adored it. Queen Victoria, who broke her custom by going to see it at all (she never went to the theater, and on the rare occasions when she wanted to see a play she had it brought to her), is supposed to have been lifted out of a twenty-five-year depression caused by the death of her husband after she saw Buffalo Bill. She liked the show so much that she saw it again, arranging for a command performance to be given at Windsor Castle the day before her Diamond Jubilee. This was the occasion when four kings rode in the Deadwood stagecoach with the Prince of Wales on top next to Buffalo Bill, who drove. No one was proof against the appeal. Ralph Blumenfeld, the London correspondent for the New York *Herald*, wrote in his diary while the show was in London that he'd had two boyhood heroes, Robin Hood and Buffalo Bill, and had delighted in Cody's stories of the Pony Express and Yellow Hand:

> Everything was done to make Cody conceited and unbearable, but he remained the simple, unassuming child of the plains who thought lords and ladies belonged in the picture books and that the story of Little Red Riding Hood was true. I rode in the Deadwood coach. It was a great evening in which I realized a good many of my boyhood dreams, for there was Buffalo Bill on his white rocking horse charger, and Annie Oakley behind him. (Weybright, 172)

Victor Weybright and Henry Blackman Sell, from whose book on the Wild West some of the foregoing information has come, dedicated their book to Buffalo Bill. It was published in 1955. Nellie Snyder Yost, whose 1979 biography is one of the two scholarly accounts of Cody's life, dedicates her book "to all those good people, living or dead, who knew and liked Buffalo Bill." Don Russell's *The Lives and Legends of Buffalo Bill* (1960), the most fact-filled scholarly biography, does not have a dedication, but in the final chapter, where he steps back to assess Cody and his influence, Russell ends by exclaiming, "What more could possibly be asked of a hero? If he was not one, who was?" (Russell, 480).

Let me now pose a few questions of my own. Must we throw out all the wonderful qualities that Cody had, the spirit of hope and emulation that he aroused in millions of people, because of the terrible judgment history has passed on the epoch of which he was part? The kinds of things he stands for—courage, daring, strength, endurance, generosity, openness to other people, love of drama, love of life, the possibility of living a life that does not deny the body and the desires of the body—are these to be declared dangerous and delusional although he manifested some of them while fighting Indians and others while representing his victories to the world? And the feelings he aroused in his audiences, the idealism, the enthusiasm, the excitement, the belief that dreams could become real—must these be declared misguided or a sham because they are associated with the imperialistic conquest of a continent, with the wholesale extermination of animals and men?

It is not so much that we cannot learn from history as that we cannot teach history how things should have been. When I set out to discover how Cody had become involved in the killing of Indians and the slaughter of buffalo, I found myself unable to sustain the outrage I had felt on leaving the museum. From his first job as an eleven-year-old herder for an army supply outfit, sole wage earner for his ailing widowed mother who had a new baby and other children to support, to his death in Colorado at the age of seventy-one, there was never a time when it was possible to say, there, there you went wrong, Buffalo Bill, you should not have killed that Indian. You should have held your fire and made your living some other way and quit the army and gone to work in the nineteenth-century equivalent of the Peace Corps. You should have known how it would end. My reading made me see that you cannot prescribe for someone in Buffalo Bill's position what he should have done, and it made me reflect on how eager I had been to get off on being angry at the museum. The thirst for moral outrage, for self-vindication, lay pretty close to the surface.

I cannot resolve the contradiction between my experience at the Buffalo Bill Historical Center with its celebration of violent conquest and my response to the shining figure of Buffalo Bill as it emerged from the pages of books—on the one hand, a history of shame; on the other, an image of the heart's desire. But I have reached one conclusion that for a while will have to serve.

Major historical events like genocide and major acts of destruction are not simply produced by impersonal historical processes or economic imperatives or ecological blunders; human intentionality is involved and human knowledge of the self. Therefore, if you're really, truly interested in not having any more genocide or killing of animals, no matter what else you might do, if you don't first, or also, come to recognize the violence in yourself and your own anger and your own destructiveness, whatever else you do won't work. It isn't that genocide doesn't matter. Genocide matters, and it starts at home.

Works Cited

Cody, Iron Eyes. *Iron Eyes: My Life as a Hollywood Indian,* as told to Collin Perry. New York, Everest House, 1982.

Lamar, Howard R., ed. *The Reader's Encyclopedia of the American West.* New York: Crowell, 1977.

Russell, Donald B. *The Lives and Legends of Buffalo Bill.* Norman, Okla.: University of Oklahoma Press, 1960.

Weybright, Victor, and Henry Blackman Sell. *Buffalo Bill and the Wild West.* New York: Oxford University Press, 1955.

Yost, Nellie Snyder. *Buffalo Bill, His Family, Friends, Fame, Failure, and Fortunes.* Chicago: Sage Books, 1979.

Ideas for Rereading

1. In the first half of her essay, Tompkins records and evaluates her experience of the Buffalo Bill Historical Center, calling it "one of the most disturbing places I have ever visited" but "also a wonderful place" (p. 588). As you reread Tompkins's essay, outline the essential elements of her experience at the center. What are her principal reactions to each of the center's four museums? Why does she react in the ways she does? Taken together, how do her reactions to the four museums explain her contradictory experience of the Buffalo Bill Historical Center as both "disturbing" and "wonderful"?

2. Tompkins writes, "The Buffalo Bill Historical Center, full as it is of dead bones, lets us see more clearly than we normally can what it is that museums are for" (p. 593). What, according to Tompkins, are museums for? As you reread, mark passages in which Tompkins relates her experience of the center to an analysis of the purpose of museums. Note also your own reaction to that analysis.

3. In the second half of her essay, Tompkins writes that her disturbing experience at the Buffalo Bill Historical Center left her with a need to read about Buffalo Bill the man: "I began to read about Buffalo Bill, and a whole new world opened up. I came to love Buffalo Bill" (p. 597). As you reread this part of the essay, outline the process by which Tompkins comes to love Buffalo Bill. What aspects of his character attract her? Why? How does she eventually reconcile the attractiveness of Buffalo Bill's character with her earlier negative reaction to the Buffalo Bill Historical Center.

Ideas for Writing

1. Near the end of the essay, Tompkins writes, "It is not so much that we cannot learn from history as that we cannot teach history how things should have been"

(p. 602). How does Tompkins explain this statement? What is it about Tompkins's reading of the life of Buffalo Bill that leads her to this conclusion? Write an essay exploring your reaction to Tompkins's statement—both in relation to the ideas and events she describes in her essay and, if possible, to your own understanding of some other specific historical or legendary figure (some possibilities: King Arthur, Joan of Arc, St. Francis of Assisi, Johnny Appleseed, Paul Bunyan, John Henry, Sacagawea, Christopher Columbus, Robin Hood, Paul Revere).

2. Reread a section of Tompkins's essay in which she relates her experience of one of the four museums in the Buffalo Bill Historical Center: the art museum, the Buffalo Bill Museum, the Plains Indian Museum, or the gun museum. Write an essay analyzing Tompkins's reaction to the museum you choose. Based on the experience she describes, what can you discern about Tompkins's opinions, life experience, interests, and character?

3. After reading several works about Buffalo Bill Cody, Tompkins poses some hard questions of her own—about the qualities that Cody embodied and stood for, and about the feelings he inspired. These questions remain unanswered as she admits that she cannot "resolve the contradiction" between her response to the Buffalo Bill Historical Center and her response to the biographies of Cody. Clearly this contradiction represents more than just indecisiveness: perhaps none of us can easily pass judgment on those who acted in a different time according to a different set of values, yet none of us can easily abandon our convictions, however modern they might be. Reread the final section of Tompkins's essay and take notes to fill out your understanding of the ethical dilemma that she presents here. Equipped with this understanding, reread Turner's "The Significance of the Frontier in American History," taking notes that consider his essay in the light of this ethical dilemma. Without attempting to resolve the contradiction, write an exploratory essay that raises Tompkins's questions in relation to Turner's argument. What are the key questions that emerge? What aspects of Turner's argument arouse your "moral outrage"? What arouses you to feel inspired and idealistic? How might a modern historian reassess Turner's argument in the light of this ethical dilemma? Offer a reading of Turner's essay as seen through the lens of Tompkins's dilemma.

4. This Idea for Writing builds on the first Idea for Writing following the Context section in this chapter (p. 570). After you have studied the Remington engravings and the photographs of the dugout home and the photograph of Leadville, Colorado, in 1890, reread Tompkins's essay, focusing especially on her analysis of the Remington paintings at the Buffalo Bill Historical Center.
     Write an essay analyzing the Remington illustrations in the context of the three photographs in the Context section and in response to Tompkins's critique of Remington. How do the photographs and Tompkins's analysis affect your reaction to the paintings? In what ways does your analysis reflect Tompkins's ideas, and in what ways is Remington's representation of Western life complicated by the photographs?

ANNETTE KOLODNY

Annette Kolodny (b. 1941) is the author of The Lay of the Land: Metaphor as Experience and History in American Life and Letters *(1975),* The Land Before Her: Fantasy and Experience of the American Frontiers, 1630–1860 *(1984), and "Dancing through the Minefield" (1980), a work of feminist literary criticism. Kolodny earned a B.A. from Brooklyn College in her native New York City, and master's and doctoral degrees in English literature from the University of California, Berkeley. She received her Ph.D. in 1969 and taught at the University of British Columbia and at the University of New Hampshire before moving to the University of Arizona, where she is a professor of English. She is a recipient of awards and grants from the Modern Language Association and the Ford, Guggenheim, and Rockefeller foundations.*

Kolodny has dedicated herself to the task of developing productive relationships between ecology and feminism. When asked to describe what motivates her work, she responded:

> *I fear that the human species is hell-bent on self-annihilation, with the United States rather blindly leading the way. We pollute our minds with trivia and our environment with carcinogens. The political and moral awakenings of the nineteen-sixties are now being dismissed—to our peril; and the current women's movement may run out of energy before it achieves the changes it envisions. The nation as a whole is in the hands of the blind, the selfish, and the mediocre.*

In the following essay from The Ecocriticism Reader: Landmarks in Literary Ecology, *edited by Cheryll Glotfelty and Harold Fromm (1996), Kolodny explores how the landscape of the American West has been imagined as "gendered"—viewed as essentially feminine. As you read, consider how this gendered conception of the American landscape (and, by extension, the settlers who "conquered" and "subdued" the land) may have influenced both our thinking about the environment and our thinking about what it means to be a woman or to be a man.*

Unearthing Herstory

> You don't know what you've got 'til it's gone,
> They paved Paradise and put up a parking lot.
> —JONI MITCHELL, "Big Yellow Taxi"

For the brief space of perhaps two weeks at the end of May 1969, a small plot of deserted ground just south of the University of California campus at Berkeley dominated headlines and news broadcasts across the country. That such an apparently local incident as the "Battle for People's Park" could so quickly and so effectively capture a nation's attention suggests that it had touched off a resonant chord in the American imagination. If the various legal, political, moral, and ecological issues involved in the controversy are as confused and confusing today as they were in 1969, they do at least all seem to cohere around a single unifying verbal image that appeared in almost all of the leaflets, handbills, and speeches printed during the uproar:

The earth is our Mother
   the land
The University put a fence around
   the land — our Mother.[1]

In what has since been partially paved over and designated a parking lot, the advocates of People's Park dared fantasize a natural maternal realm, in which human children happily working together in the spontaneous and un-alienated labor of planting and tilling might all be "sod brothers."[2] So pow-erful was the fantasy, in fact, that many seriously believed that, armed "with sod, lots of flowers, and spirit," those evicted from the park might return and "ask our brothers in the [National] Guard to let us into our park."[3]

If the wished-for fraternity with the National Guard was at least errati-cally realized, the return to "the land — our Mother," the place, they in-sisted, "where our souls belong,"[4] was thwarted completely. The disposition of the land through "proper channels" — including city council and university officials — was characterized variously as "the rape of People's Park" or, more graphically, as a case of "The University . . . / fucking with our land."[5] For many, hurt and angered at the massive repres-sion their fantasy had engendered, People's Park became "a mirror in which our society may see itself," a summing up of American history: "We have constituted ourselves socially and politically to conquer and trans-form nature."[6]

In fact, the advocates of People's Park had asserted another version of what is probably America's oldest and most cherished fantasy: a daily real-ity of harmony between man and nature based on an experience of the land as essentially feminine — that is, not simply the land as mother, but the land as woman, the total female principle of gratification — enclosing the individual in an environment of receptivity, repose, and painless and integral satisfaction.[7] Such imagery is archetypal wherever we find it; the soul's home, as the People's Park Committee leaflet and three hundred years of American writing before it had asserted, is that place where the conditions of exile — from Eden or from some primal harmony with the Mother — do not obtain; it is a realm of nurture, abundance, and unalien-ated labor within which all men are truly brothers. In short, the place America had long promised to be, ever since the first explorers declared themselves virtually "ravisht with the . . . pleasant land" and described the new continent as a "*Paradise* with all her Virgin Beauties."[8] The human, and decidedly feminine, impact of the landscape became a staple of the early promotional tracts, inviting prospective settlers to inhabit "valleyes and plaines streaming with sweete Springs, like veynes in a naturall bodie," and to explore "hills and mountaines making a sensible proffer of hidden treasure, neuer yet searched."[9]

As a result, along with their explicit hopes for commercial, religious, and political gains, the earliest explorers and settlers in the New World can be said to have carried with them a "yearning for paradise." When they ran across people living in what seemed to them "the manner of the golden age," and found lands where "nature and liberty affords vs that freely, which in *England* we want, or it costeth vs dearely," dormant dreams found substantial root.[10] When, for instance, Arthur Barlowe's account of his "First Voyage Made to the Coasts of America . . . Anno 1584," described the Indian women who greeted him and his men as uniformly beautiful, gracious, cheerful, and friendly, with the wife of the king's brother taking "great pains to see all things ordered in the best manner she could, making great haste to dress some meat for us to eat," he initiated a habit of mind that came to see the Indian woman as a kind of emblem for a land that was similarly entertaining the Europeans "with all love and kindness and . . . as much bounty." Not until the end of the seventeenth century, when the tragic contradictions inherent in such experience could no longer be ignored, were the Indian women depicted more usually as hag-like, ugly, and immoral. The excitement that greeted John Rolfe's marriage to Pocahontas, in April of 1614, may have been due to the fact that it served, in some symbolic sense, as a kind of objective correlative for the possibility of Europeans' actually possessing the charms inherent in the virgin continent. Similarly, the repeated evocation of the new continent as "some delicate garden abounding with all kinds of odoriferous flowers," and the sometimes strident insistence that early explorers had "made a Garden vpon the top of a Rockie Ile . . . that grew so well,"[11] tantalizes with the suggestion that the garden may in fact be "an abstraction of the essential femininity of the terrain." Paul Shepard undoubtedly has a point when he claims that "we have yet to recognize the full implication of the mother as a primary landscape,"[12] especially since, as psychiatrist Joel Kovel has argued, "the life of the body and the experiences of infancy, . . . are the reference points of human knowledge and the bedrock of the structures of culture."[13]

If the initial impulse to experience the New World landscape, not merely as an object of domination and exploitation, but as a maternal "garden," receiving and nurturing human children, was a reactivation of what we now recognize as universal mythic wishes, it had one radically different facet: *this* paradise really existed, "Whole" and "True," its many published descriptions boasting "the *proofe* of the present benefit this Countrey affoords"[14] (italics mine). All the descriptions of wonderful beasts and strangely contoured humans notwithstanding, the published documents from explorers assured the reader of the author's accuracy and unimpeachable reliability. No mere literary convention this; an irrefutable fact of history (the European discovery of America) touched every word written about the New World with the possibility that the ideally beautiful and bountiful terrain might be lifted forever out of the canon of pastoral convention and invested with the reality of daily experience. In some sense, the process had already begun, as explorer after explorer claimed to have "personally . . . wth diligence searched and viewed these contries" before concluding them to be "the fairest, frutefullest, and pleasauntest of all the worlde."[15] Eden, Paradise, the Golden Age, and the idyllic garden, in short, all the backdrops for European literary pastoral, were subsumed in the image of an America promising material ease without labor or hardship, as opposed to the grinding poverty of previous European existence; a frank, free affectional life in which all might share in a primal and noncompetitive fraternity; a resurrection of the lost state of innocence that the adult abandons when he joins the world of competitive self-assertion; and all this possible because, at the deepest psychological level, the move to America was experienced as the daily reality of what has become its single dominating metaphor: regression from the cares of adult life and a return to the primal warmth of womb or breast in a feminine landscape. And when America finally produced a pastoral literature of her own, that literature hailed the essential femininity of the terrain in a way European pastoral never had, explored the historical consequences of its central metaphor in a way European pastoral had never dared, and, from the first, took its metaphors as literal truths. The traditional mode had embraced its last and possibly its most uniquely revitalizing permutation.

As Joel Kovel points out, of course, "It is one thing to daydream and conjure up wishful images of the way things ought to be in order that one's instinctually-based fantasies may come true"; at the time of America's discovery, this had become the province of European pastoral. "It is quite another matter, and a more important one in cultural terms,"[16] he continues, to begin experiencing those fantasies as the pattern of one's daily activity — as was the case in sixteenth- and seventeenth-century America. For only if we acknowledge the power of the pastoral impulse to shape and structure experience can we reconcile the images of abundance in the early texts with the historical evidence of starvation, poor harvests, and inclement weather.[17] To label such an impulse as "mere fantasy" in order to dismiss it ignores the fact that fantasy is a particular way of relating to the world, even, as R. D. Laing suggests, "part of, sometimes the essential part of, the meaning or sense . . . implicit in action."[18] In 1630 Francis Higginson, "one of the ministers of Salem," claimed that "Experience doth manifest that there is hardly a more healthfull place to be found in the World" and boasted that "since I came hither . . . I thanke God I haue had perfect health, and . . . whereas beforetime I cloathed my self with double cloathes and thicke Wastcoats to keepe me warme, euen in the Summer time, I doe now goe as thin clad as any, onely wearing a light Stuffe Cassocke vpon my Shirt and Stuffe Breeches and one thickness without Linings."[19] The fact that he died the next year of pneumonia, or, as Governor Dudley phrased it, "of a feaver," in no way negates what the good minister claimed his "Experience doth manifest." American pastoral, unlike European, holds at its very core the promise of fantasy as daily reality. Implicit in the call to emigrate, then, was the tantalizing proximity to a happiness that had heretofore been the repressed promise of a better future, a call to act out what was at once a psychological and political revolt against a culture based on toil, domination, and self-denial.

But not many who emigrated yearning for pastoral gratifications shared Higginson's "Experience." Colonization brought with it an inevitable paradox: the success of settlement depended on the ability to master the land, transforming the virgin territories into something else—a farm, a village, a road, a canal, a railway, a mine, a factory, a city, and finally, an urban nation. As a result, those who had initially responded to the promise inherent in a feminine landscape were now faced with the consequences of that response: either they recoiled in horror from the meaning of their manipulation of a naturally generous world, accusing one another, as did John Hammond in 1656, of raping and deflowering the "naturall fertility and comelinesse," or, like those whom Robert Beverley and William Byrd accused of "slothful Indolence," they succumbed to a life of easeful regression, "spung[ing] upon the Blessings of a warm Sun, and a fruitful Soil" and "approach[ing] nearer to the Description of Lubberland than any other."[20] Neither response, however, obviated the fact that the despoliation of the land appeared more and more an inevitable consequence of human habitation—any more than it terminated the pastoral impulse itself. The instinctual drive embedded in the fantasy, which had first impelled men to emigrate, now impelled them both to continue pursuing the fantasy in daily life, and, when that failed, to codify it as part of the culture's shared dream life, through art—there for all to see in the paintings of Cole and Audubon, in the fictional "letters" of Crevecoeur, the fallacious "local color" of Irving's Sleepy Hollow, and finally, the northern and southern contours clearly distinguished, in the Leatherstocking novels of James Fenimore Cooper and in the Revolutionary War romances of William Gilmore Simms. "Thus," as Joel Kovel argues, "the decisive symbolic elements [of a culture's history] will be those that represent not only repressed content, but ego activity as well."[21]

Other civilizations have undoubtedly gone through a similar history, but at a pace too slow or in a time too ancient to be remembered. Only in America has the entire process remained within historical memory, giving Americans the unique ability to see themselves as the wilful exploiters of the very land that had once promised an escape from such necessities. With the pastoral impulse neither terminated nor yet wholly repressed, the entire process—the dream and its betrayal, and the consequent guilt and anger—in short, the knowledge of what we have done to our continent, continues even in this century, as Gary Snyder put it, "eating at the American heart like acid."[22] How much better might things have turned out had we heeded the advice of an earlier American poet, Charles Hansford, who probably wrote the following lines about the middle of the eighteenth century:

> To strive with Nature little it avails.
> Her favors to improve and nicely scan
> Is all that is within the reach of Man.
> Nature is to be follow'd, and not forc'd,
> For, otherwise, our labor will be lost.[23]

From accounts of the earliest explorers onward, then, a uniquely American pastoral vocabulary began to show itself, releasing and emphasizing some facets of the traditional European mode and all but ignoring others. At its core lay a yearning to know and to respond to the landscape as feminine, a yearning that I have labeled as the uniquely American "pastoral impulse." Obviously, such an impulse must at some very basic level stem from desires and tensions that arise when patterns from within the human mind confront an external reality of physical phenomena. But the precise psychological and linguistic processes by which the mind imposes order or even meaning onto the phenomena—these have yet to be understood. Let us remember, however, that gendering the land as feminine was nothing new in the sixteenth century; Indo-European languages, among others, have long maintained the habit of gendering the physical world and imbuing it with human capacities. What happened with the discovery of America was the revival of that linguistic habit on the level of personal experience; that is, what had by then degenerated into the dead conventions of self-consciously "literary" language, hardly attended to, let alone explored, suddenly, with the discovery of America, became the vocabulary of everyday reality. Perhaps, after all, the world *is* really gendered, in some subtle way we have not yet quite understood. Certainly, for William Byrd, topography and anatomy were at least analogous, with "a Single Mountain [in the Blue Ridge range], very much resembling a Woman's breast" and a "Ledge that stretch't away to the N.E. . . . [rising] in the Shape of a Maiden's Breast."[24]

Or, perhaps, the connections are more subtle still: was there perhaps a *need* to experience the land as a nurturing, giving maternal breast because of the threatening, alien, and potentially emasculating terror of the unknown? Beautiful, indeed, that wilderness appeared—but also dark, uncharted, and prowled by howling beasts. In a sense, to make the new continent Woman was already to civilize it a bit, casting the stamp of human relations upon what was otherwise unknown and untamed. But, more precisely still, just as the impulse for emigration was an impulse to begin again (whether politically, economically, or religiously), so, too, the place of that new beginning was, in a sense, the new Mother, her adopted children having cast off the bonds of Europe, "where mother-country acts the stepdame's part."[25] If the American continent was to become the birthplace of a new culture and, with it, new and improved human possibilities, then it was, in fact as well as in metaphor, a womb of generation and a provider of sustenance. Hence, the heart of American pastoral—the only pastoral in which metaphor and the patterns of daily activity refuse to be separated.

All of which indicates how bound we still are by the vocabulary of a feminine landscape and the psychological patterns of regression and violation that it implies. Fortunately, however, that same language that now appalls us with its implications of regression or willful violation also supplies a framework, open to examination, within which the kinds of symbolic functioning we have examined here get maximum exposure. It gives us, to begin with, at least some indication of *how* those peculiar intersections of human psychology, historical accident, and New World geography combined to create the vocabulary for the experience of the land-as-woman. And it gives us, more importantly, another vantage point from which to understand those unacknowledged but mutually accepted patterns by which Americans have chosen to regulate their lives and interactions for over three hundred years now. Our continuing fascination with the lone male in the wilderness, and our literary heritage of essentially adolescent, presexual pastoral heroes, suggest that we have yet to come up with a satisfying model for mature masculinity on this continent; while the images of abuse that have come to dominate the pastoral vocabulary suggest that we have been no more successful in our response to the feminine qualities of nature than we have to the human feminine. But such speculations are only the beginning: the more we understand how we use language and, conversely, how (in some sense) language uses us, the stronger the possibility becomes that we may actually begin to choose more beneficial patterns for labeling and experiencing that mysterious realm of phenomena outside ourselves and, hopefully, with that, better our chances for survival amid phenomena that, after all, we know only through the intercession of our brain's encodings.

We must begin by acknowledging that the image system of a feminine landscape was for a time both useful and societally adaptive; it brought successive generations of immigrants to strange shores and then propelled them across a vast uncharted terrain. For it is precisely those images through which we have experienced and made meaning out of the discrete data of our five senses (and our cerebral wanderings) that have allowed us to put our human stamp on a world of external phenomena and, thereby, survive in the first place in a strange and forbidding wilderness. And the fact that the symbolizations we chose have now resulted in a vocabulary of destructive aggression and in an active expression of frustration and anger should not make us assume that they may not yet again prove useful to us, or, if not, that we have only to abandon them altogether in order to solve our ecological problems. The habits of language are basically conservative, representing what Benjamin Lee Whorf characterizes as "the mass mind." As he points out, language may indeed be "affected by inventions and innovations, but affected little and slowly."[26] The habits of image-laden language such as we have looked at here, especially, inhibit change because they contain within them an extension, in adult mental processes, of experiential and perceptual configurations inherited from infancy; and, because of the various coincidences through which such configurations got projected out onto the American continent, they have come to reflect not only the integration of universal human dilemmas into cultural patterns, but also the psychic content of the group's shared fantasies—however unacknowledged or unconscious these may have been. Students of language, following Whorf and Edward Sapir, are coming more and more to assert the intimate interaction between language, perception, and action, even going so far, as Whorf does, to argue that once particular "ways of analyzing and reporting experience . . . have become fixed in the language as integrated 'fashions of speaking,'" they tend to influence the ways in "which the personality not only communicates, but also analyzes nature, notices or neglects types of relationship and phenomena, channels . . . reasoning, and builds the house of . . . consciousness."[27] "And once such a system of meanings comes into being, it is never simply abandoned or superseded, as Freud and all other developmental psychologists have repeatedly demonstrated."[28]

Still, if this study has suggested anything, it must be that what we need is a radically new symbolic mode for relating to "the fairest, frutefullest, and pleasauntest [land] of all the worlde";[29] we can no longer afford to keep turning "America the Beautiful" into *America the Raped*. The tantalizing possibility that metaphor, or symbolizing in general, both helps to give coherence to the otherwise inchoate succession of discrete sense data and, also, helps us explore the *possibilities* of experience, suggests that we might, on a highly conscious level, call into play once more our evolutionary adaptive ability to create and re-create our own images of reality. The magic, and even salvation, of man may, after all, lie in his capacity to enter into and exit from the images by which, periodically, he seeks to explore and codify the meaning of his experience. Which suggests that the will to freedom and the will to community, the desire for self-fulfillment, and the attractions of passive acceptance, which were always at the base of the pastoral impulse, might, in some other metaphor, prove finally reconcilable.

Notes

1. Poem credited to Book Jones, printed in a leaflet issued in Berkeley during the last week of May 1969, by the People's Park Committee (hereafter cited as "People's Park Committee leaflet"). For one of the better detailed accounts of this event, see Sheldon Wolin and John Schaar, "Berkeley: The Battle of People's Park," *New York Review of Books,* 19 June 1969, pp. 24–31. A full collection of pamphlets, leaflets, and newspaper articles about People's Park is available in the Bancroft Library, University of California, Berkeley.

2. A red and black sign printed with the words "sod brother" appeared on shop windows and doors in the south campus area to identify their owners as sympathetic to the demands for a People's Park. The words were also lettered on windows and doors of private homes and became a means of protection from damage by angry and frustrated demonstrators.

3. "People's Park Committee leaflet." While most of the law enforcement groups brought into the area were regarded with hostility both by the student and local communities, the National Guard, which bivouacked on park grounds for two weeks, were more cordially tolerated. Rumors flew that guardsmen were watering the plants behind the fence, and both the underground and establishment local press frequently printed photographs of guardsmen accepting flowers from demonstrators.

4. "People's Park Committee leaflet."

5. Joanna Gewertz, "culturevulture," *Berkeley Monitor,* 31 May 1969, p. 3; "People's Park Committee leaflet."

6. Quoted from leaflet entitled "Ecology and Politics in America," distributed 26–27 May 1969, in Berkeley, by American Federation of Teachers locals 1474 and 1795.

7. The Freudian argument for this approach, with which I only partly concur, but by which my remarks are influenced, is best put forth by Herbert Marcuse, *Eros and Civilization* (1955; reprint ed., New York: Random House, Vintage Books, 1961), pp. 246–47.

8. Robert Johnson, "Nova Britannia: Offering Most Excellent fruites by Planting In Virginia. Exciting all such as be well affected to further the same" (London, 1609), p. 11; Robert Mountgomry, "A Discourse Concerning the design'd Establishment of a New Colony To The South of Carolina In The Most delightful Country of the Universe" (London, 1717), p. 6. Both papers are in *Tracts and Other Papers, Relating Principally to the Origin, Settlement, And Progress of the Colonies in North America, From The Discovery Of The Country To The Year 1776*, comp. Peter Force, 3 vols. (Washington, D.C., 1836–38), vol. 1 (hereafter cited as *Force's Tracts*). All of the papers in *Force's Tracts* are paginated separately.

9. Johnson, "Nova Britannia," p. 11, in *Force's Tracts*, vol. 1.

10. "The First Voyage Made To The Coasts Of America With Two Barks, Wherein Were Captains M. Philip Amadas And M. Arthur Barlowe Who Discovered Part Of The Country Now Called Virginia, Anno 1584. Written By One Of The Said Captains [probably Barlowe, who kept the daily record], And Sent To Sir Walter Raleigh, Knight, At Whose Charge And Direction The Said Voyage Was Set Forth," in *Explorations, Descriptions, and Attempted Settlements of Carolina, 1584–1590*, ed. David Leroy Corbitt (Raleigh: State Department of Archives and History, 1948), pp. 19–20 (hereafter cited as *Explorations of Carolina*); John Smith, "A Description of New England; or, The Observations, and Discoueries of Captain John Smith (Admirall of the Country) in the North of America, in the year of our Lord 1614" (London, 1616), p. 21, in *Force's Tracts*, vol. 2.

11. [M. Arthur Barlowe], "The First Voyage Made to the Coasts of America," in *Explorations of Carolina*, pp. 19, 13; Smith, "A Description of New England," p. 9, in *Force's Tracts*, vol. 2.

12. Paul Shepard, *Man in the Landscape* (New York: Alfred A. Knopf, 1967), pp. 108, 98.

13. Joel Kovel, *White Racism* (New York: Random House, Pantheon Books, 1970), p. 7.

14. Smith, "A Description of New England," title page, in *Force's Tracts*, vol. 2.

15. Richard Hakluyt, "Discourse of Western Planting . . . 1584, in *The Original Writings and Correspondence of the Two Richard Hakluyts*, ed. E. G. R. Taylor, 2d ser. (London: Hakluyt Society, 1935), 77:222 (hereafter cited as *Hakluyt Correspondence*). Hakluyt's note identifies "the work alluded to" as John Ribault's *"The whole and true discouerye of Terra Florida . . . Prynted at London . . . 1563."*

16. Kovel, *White Racism*, p. 99.

17. Most of the original settlers of Jamestown died of either disease or starvation, while only about half of the Pilgrims who landed at Plymouth in December 1620 survived the first winter; of the 900 settlers led by Winthrop to Massachusetts Bay, 200 died during the first year. Howard Mumford Jones has surveyed these materials and pointed out that "it took many years for investors and home officials to learn that you could not found a plantation by dumping a few men on a New World shore. . . . A high percentage of sickness and death accompanied the process of acclimatization" (*O Strange New World* [1952; reprint ed., London: Chatto & Windus, 1965], p. 277).

18. R. D. Laing, *The Politics of Experience* (New York: Random House, Pantheon Books, 1967), pp. 14–15.

19. Thomas Dudley, "Gov. Thomas Dudley's Letter To The Countess of Lincoln, March, 1631," p. 10, in *Force's Tracts*, vol. 2; Francis Higginson, "New-Englands Plantation; or, A Short And Trve Description of The Commodities and Discommodities of that Countrey" (London, 1630), pp. 9, 10, in *Force's Tracts*, vol. 1.

20. John Hammond, "Leah and Rachel; or, The Two Fruitfull Sisters Virginia and Maryland," in *Narratives of Early Maryland, 1633–1684*, ed. Clayton Colman Hall (New York:

Charles Scribner's Sons, 1910), p. 300; Robert Beverley, *The History and Present State of Virginia*, ed. Louis B. Wright (Chapel Hill: University of North Carolina Press, 1947), p. 319; William Byrd, *William Byrd's Histories of the Dividing Line Betwixt Virginia and North Carolina*, ed. William K. Boyd (Raleigh: North Carolina Historical Commission, 1929), p. 92.

21. Kovel, *White Racism*, p. 99. For a fuller discussion, see chap. 5, "The Symbolic Matrix," pp. 93–105.

22. Gary Snyder, *Earth House Hold* (New York: New Directions, 1969), p. 119.

23. Charles Hansford, "My Country's Worth," in *The Poems of Charles Hansford*, ed. James A. Servies and Carl R. Dolmetsch (Chapel Hill: University of North Carolina Press, 1961), p. 52. Probably born about 1685, Hansford lived in York County, Virginia, and was by trade a blacksmith; when he died, in 1761, he left in manuscript several poems which he called "A Clumsey Attempt of an Old Man to turn Some of his Serious Thoughts into Verse." The poems are printed here for the first time, with titles supplied by the editors.

24. Byrd, *Histories of the Dividing Line*, pp. 214(*H*), 249(*SH*).

25. Philip Freneau, "To Crispin O'Conner, a Back-Woodsman," in *The Poems of Philip Freneau, Poet of the American Revolution*, ed. Fred Lewis Pattee, 3 vols. (Princeton, N.J.: University Library, 1902–7), 3:74–75. The poem was first published in 1792; the text is from the 1809 edition of Freneau's collected *Poems*. Unless otherwise noted, all quotations from Freneau's poems are from the Pattee edition.

26. Benjamin Lee Whorf, *Language, Thought and Reality* (1956; reprint, Cambridge, Mass.: MIT Press, 1969), p. 156.

27. Ibid., pp. 158, 252.

28. Richard M. Jones, *The New Psychology of Dreaming* (New York: Grune and Stratton, 1970), p. 161.

29. Richard Hakluyt, "Discourse of Western Planting . . . 1584," in *Hakluyt Correspondence*, 77:222.

Ideas for Rereading

1. Kolodny writes of what she calls "America's oldest and most cherished fantasy: a daily reality of harmony between man and nature based on an experience of the land as essentially feminine—that is, not simply the land as mother, but the land as woman" (p. 606). She quotes many historical documents that use the imagery of the "land-as-woman." As you reread, mark passages where Kolodny interprets this tendency to characterize the American landscape as female. According to Kolodny, what is the "vocabulary for the experience of the land-as-woman" (p. 611)? What are the purposes of such a vocabulary? What are its positive and negative effects?

2. In the essay, Kolodny refers to the American "pastoral impulse." As you reread "Unearthing Herstory," take notes outlining in detail what she means by that term. What are the elements of her definition of the "pastoral impulse" (p. 610)? How does she characterize and evaluate it? What, for Kolodny, are the contradictions inherent in the pastoral impulse?

Ideas for Writing

1. After exploring language and symbolism that treat "the land" as "our Mother," Kolodny writes, "we need . . . a radically new symbolic mode for relating to 'the fairest, frutefullest, and pleasauntest [land] of all the worlde'; we

can no longer afford to keep turning 'America the Beautiful' into *America the Raped"* (p. 612). Kolodny argues that we need to develop new ways of imagining the history of the American West that do not depend on "decidedly feminine" (p. 606) metaphors and symbols.

Write an essay in response to Kolodny that tests different ways of thinking about American history and landscape. While you may assess the value of "gendering the land as feminine" (p. 610), responding directly to Kolodny's criticisms of this "image system" (p. 611), you should also develop ways of thinking about the land and the history of the American West that are not centered on ideas of motherhood and feminine beauty. In what ways is the symbolism of "land-as-woman" still valid and powerful for you? Taking your cue from Kolodny, and keeping in mind what she says about woman-centered ways of thinking about the land, propose and assess your own "radically new symbolic mode" of relating to the American landscape. One way of extending and developing your ideas about alternative image systems would be to peruse this chapter's Context section and the other essays in the Contemporary Conversation section.

2. Reread Turner's essay in this chapter, keeping in mind Kolodny's analysis of the vocabulary of "land-as-woman." Mark passages where you find Turner using such a vocabulary, paying attention to his use of Kolodny's "image system of a feminine landscape" and his use of what Kolodny calls "American pastoral" and the "pastoral impulse" (p. 610). In what ways does Turner's thesis confirm, challenge, or refute Kolodny's idea that "the nation as a whole is in the hands of the blind, the selfish, and the mediocre" (p. 605)?

Write an essay applying Kolodny's argument about the images and ideas that have dominated North American ways of thinking about the land to Turner's thesis about the frontier. How does Turner's use of such vocabulary and imagery reflect Kolodny's analysis? How does Turner's writing seem to diverge from that analysis? Which specific parts of Turner's essay seem to confirm, challenge, or refute Kolodny's argument?

LESLIE MARMON SILKO

Leslie Marmon Silko (b. 1948), a poet, novelist, and essayist of Pueblo, Laguna, Mexican, and European descent, grew up on the Laguna Pueblo reservation and attended a Bureau of Indian Affairs school in Albuquerque. On one side of her family, Silko is related to Walter and Robert Marmon, Protestant governors of Old Laguna who banished the guardians of crucial tribal customs and destroyed Laguna's main kivas (circular meeting places); on the other, she is related to people like her "Grandma A'mooh," who was deeply versed in Laguna ceremonies and traditions of storytelling. In 1969, Silko graduated with honors from the University of New Mexico. After studying law briefly, she turned to writing as a career and published her first book, a collection of poems entitled Laguna Woman, *in 1974. Her first novel, the highly acclaimed* Ceremony *(1977), was the first novel published by a Native American woman. Since then Silko has published nine books, including* Storyteller *(1981),* Almanac of the Dead: A Novel *(1991), and* Yellow Woman and a Beauty of the Spirit: Essays *(1996), from which the following essays are taken. Her most recent work is* Gardens in the Dunes *(1999). She was the recipient of a MacArthur Foundation Fellowship in 1981.*

Silko's work focuses on relationships between Laguna and Euro-American cultures and reflects a personal and familial commitment to community affairs and to the adaptation of Laguna traditions to twentieth-century America. Her novels are rooted in her Laguna experience but, like Storyteller, *they mix photographs, art, and different genres of writing to produce an effect that is decidedly postmodern. Controversy has surrounded Silko's career since the mid-1970s when she published the essay "An Old-Time Attack Conducted in Two Parts," expressing anger over the ways in which Euro-American writers such as Gary Snyder (specifically in* Turtle Island, *1974) assume the right to steal Native American stories and point of view. Silko attacked such writers as imperialists who appropriate American Indian art and perspectives instead of land and resources. The two essays included here convey some of Silko's frustration over the treatment of Native Americans in contemporary culture. In the first, she calls attention to a report published by the U.S. Commission on Civil Rights in 1981 that details "the deplorable tactics that federal and state governments have used to plunder Indian land, water, and energy resources" (p. 617). In the second, an account of being stopped and searched by U.S. border guards, she analyzes the racist and other implications of police "profiles" of suspects and the powers invested in those who patrol the U.S.-Mexican border.*

America's Debt to the Indian Nations
Atoning for a Sordid Past

Until Indian activists occupied Alcatraz Island, marched across the country on the Trail of Broken Treaties, and occupied the Bureau of Indian Affairs Building in Washington, the general public was content to think the Indian nations had gone out with the buffalo. But the occupation and siege at Wounded Knee in 1973 forced America to acknowledge shameful chapters in American history that had been conveniently whitewashed for so long. Unfortunately, the history lessons supplied in 1973 by the media were often simplistic and inaccurate, and they failed to report the validity of Indian claims of treaty violations and the legitimacy of other Indian grievances. The old Hollywood stereotypes of the hostile Indian uprisings were generally reinforced.

Eight years after the siege of Wounded Knee, the U.S. Commission on Civil Rights has issued a report entitled "Indian Tribes: A Continuing Quest for Survival." Although the report is long overdue, it is a landmark for two reasons: it was compiled and written largely by a staff of American Indian lawyers and Indian legal specialists who advance a unique perspective of American history and jurisprudence, and it provides the general public with detailed information that documents the history of Indian tribes and the American legal system. The basic findings — that "civil rights violations are prompted by public ignorance of Indian rights and by the failure of appropriate parties to respond promptly to any infringement of Indian rights" — will surprise no one. But the report does not hesitate to identify the "appropriate parties" or to document the deplorable tactics that federal and state governments have used to plunder Indian land, water, and energy resources.

Resulting from nearly a decade of hearings and study, the report, among other recommendations, urges Congress to recognize Indian tribes on the same basis as it recognizes states and their subdivisions for distribution of federal funds, recommends a joint congressional oversight committee on Indian affairs, and asks for "impact statements" when contemplated federal action might affect Indian rights. The Civil Rights Commission included no details, however, of what new legislation might be required, nor did it offer many specifics on changes in such matters as federal funding.

But by detailing the long history of the Indian nations' principles of international law in the fourteenth century to pending land-claims lawsuits in the 1980s, the Civil Rights Commission takes an important first step in wiping out public ignorance of Indian rights. Any questions about the unique legal status of American Indian tribes as sovereign nations or about the legal basis for Indian treaty rights and claims are answered in this document. The report addresses many of the topics most controversial to non-Indians: Indian fishing rights in the Pacific Northwest, Indian land claims on the East Coast, and the legal status of Indian tribes and their members vis-à-vis federal and state jurisdictions.

If you've ever wondered, "What right do those Washington and Oregon Indians have to 50 percent of the salmon and steelhead runs?" or, "What makes those Indians think they own all of Maine and half of Massachusetts?" then read this report. Arthur S. Flemming, chairman of the Civil Rights Commission, has observed, "There are a great many adults who do not have any understanding of the treaties, of tribal government and the implications of it . . . and they are reacting from a position of no knowledge." This report should be required reading in high school history classes, although the report notes that a basic understanding of Indian rights is lacking even in law-school curricula: "An entire volume of the U.S. Code is devoted to Indian Law. . . . Yet until the past decade, any treatment of Indian law in law schools was a rare exception."

One of the more original and controversial views to emerge from this document is that greed, not racism per se, accounts for the apparent anti-Indian backlash: "The non-Indian interests, both governmental and private, that have been unfairly profiting at Indian expense have found their individual advantages disrupted by Indian legal and political victories and have organized to recapture their preferential position," the report states. The majority of Americans are not necessarily "anti-Indian," but profiteers know how to manipulate the ignorance of the American public and the racism that is generated, not as an end in itself, but as a means to ensure continued profiteering by special interests at the expense of Indian tribes.

As the report clearly indicates, the stakes are high: Indian water rights to the Colorado, Rio Grande, San Juan, Gila, and Salt Rivers will have far-reaching effects on the growth and quality of life in Los Angeles, Phoenix,

Tucson, and El Paso. Indian tribes control 3 percent of the total national oil and gas reserves and 7 to 13 percent of U.S. coal deposits. Indian tribes control a large number of extensive uranium deposits. In Washington and Oregon, enforcement of treaty provisions governing salmon and steelhead fishing rights of the Puyallup, Nisqually, Yakima, and other northwestern tribes involves millions of dollars each season. Land-claim lawsuits filed in 1975 by the Passamaquoddy and Penobscot tribes cast a cloud over the legal title to more than 10.5 million acres of land in the state of Maine. Other East Coast states face similar lawsuits. Thus, in the decades to come, it is imperative that the American public have a basic understanding of the history and legal status of Indian tribes.

From the beginning, the European governments viewed the Indian tribes of the Western Hemisphere as sovereign nations, and international law and protocol dictated that all dealings with the Indian nations (even as conquered sovereign nations) be legitimized in formal treaties. This, of course, did not save those Indian tribes from mass extermination, torture, or slavery, but it did require that the Europeans clothe these criminal activities with legal procedures so that, from the beginning, the bloody business was legitimized or justified by formal treaties that were acknowledged by all other Western European governments. Similarly, the British veiled their brutal colonization with formal treaties.

Bound by preexisting international treaties, America's founders found it necessary to acknowledge Indian tribes as distinct political entities in the constitutional clause giving Congress the powers "to regulate Commerce with Foreign Nations, and among the several states, and with the Indian Tribes." Thus the Civil Rights Commission report emphasizes that Indian tribes have had a unique, separate legal and political status in American jurisprudence from the very beginning. This clarifies a most damaging and prevalent misconception: that Indian tribes demand fishing rights and other treaty rights solely on the basis of race, in violation of the Fourteenth Amendment to the U.S. Constitution.

The report cites the U.S. Ninth Circuit Court of Appeals, which found that "race was only a factor in determining who was a member of the specific political group that had a treaty agreement with the U.S. Indians who were not members of treaty tribes, had no special rights and, as a race, were subject to fishing laws of the state just like anyone else." As the report goes on to explain, negotiations of treaties with tribes of Washington and Oregon were conducted during peacetime. No wars were fought. The treaties negotiated then were, basically, contracts in which northwest coastal tribes and others gave non-Indians land to settle in exchange for promises of protection from the onslaught of non-Indian settlers and protection of their traditional fishing and hunting practices. Simply stated, the tribes of the northwest kept their part of the bargain and it is high time the federal and state governments kept theirs.

Despite the overwhelming legitimacy and strength of the Indian fishing rights, the commission found that

- The federal government as guarantor of Indian fishing rights has not effectively protected and assured these rights.
- Throughout this century, the state of Washington has utilized its governmental authority in such a manner as to deprive Indians of their fishing rights.
- Indian tribes have been blamed erroneously for the crisis concerning the scarcity of fish.

The commission findings on land claims, law enforcement, and civil rights for Indian tribes, while they will come as no surprise to Indians, spell out similar violations of Indian rights by federal and state governments. For a carefully documented, step-by-step example of such an outrage, read, on page 95 of the commission's report, how the solicitor general of the United States very nearly lost treaty rights that the Puyallup Indians had spent forty years asserting and defending. This, perhaps, has always been the greatest outrage: that for American Indians, the worst violations came not at the hands of private individuals acting out racist perversions, but from the federal government itself.

Most Americans, while they may not know much about Indian cultures or Indian treaty rights, tend to harbor a special sentiment for American Indians that is not held for other minority groups in America. Whether this is a dim recognition of the fact that Indians were here first or whether it is merely a romantic American notion is difficult to determine. The American public has difficulty believing such injustice continues to be inflicted upon Indian people because Americans assume that the sympathy or tolerance they feel toward Indians is somehow felt or transferred to the government policy that deals with Indians. This is not the case.

For American Indians, injustice has been institutionalized and is administered by federal and state governments. In this regard, the United States is not so different from the racist governments of South Africa and the former Rhodesia. The report observes: "Without wealth or political power, Indian tribes have to rely upon the constitutional-legal system and the moral conscience of society for survival. . . . If this society, through its government, does not live up to its promises and commitments to Indian people, then no rights are secure."

The Border Patrol State

I used to travel the highways of New Mexico and Arizona with a wonderful sensation of absolute freedom as I cruised down the open road and across the vast desert plateaus. On the Laguna Pueblo reservation, where I was raised, the people were patriotic despite the way the U.S. government had treated Native Americans. As proud citizens, we grew up believing the freedom to travel was our inalienable right, a right that some Native Americans had been denied in the early twentieth century. Our cousin old Bill Pratt used to ride his horse three hundred miles overland from Laguna, New Mexico, to Prescott, Arizona, every summer to work as a fire lookout.

In school in the 1950s, we were taught that our right to travel from state to state without special papers or threat of detainment was a right that citizens under Communist and totalitarian governments did not possess. That wide open highway told us we were U.S. citizens; we were free. . .

Not so long ago, my companion Gus and I were driving south from Albuquerque, returning to Tucson after a book promotion for the paperback edition of my novel *Almanac of the Dead*. I had settled back and gone to sleep while Gus drove, but I was awakened when I felt the car slowing to a stop. It was nearly midnight on New Mexico State Road 26, a dark, lonely stretch of two-lane highway between Hatch and Deming. When I sat up, I saw the headlights and emergency flashers of six vehicles—Border Patrol cars and a van were blocking both lanes of the highway. Gus stopped the car and rolled down the window to ask what was wrong. But the closest Border Patrolman and his companion did not reply; instead, the first agent ordered us to "step out of the car." Gus asked why, but his question seemed to set them off. Two more Border Patrol agents immediately approached our car, and one of them snapped, "Are you looking for trouble?" as if he would relish it.

I will never forget that night beside the highway. There was an awful feeling of menace and violence straining to break loose. It was clear that the uniformed men would be only too happy to drag us out of the car if we did not speedily comply with their request (asking a question is tantamount to resistance, it seems). So we stepped out of the car and they motioned for us to stand on the shoulder of the road. The night was very dark, and no other traffic had come down the road since we had been stopped. All I could think about was a book I had read—*Nunca Más*—the official report of a human rights commission that investigated and certified more than twelve thousand "disappearances" during Argentina's "dirty war" in the late 1970s.

The weird anger of these Border Patrolmen made me think about descriptions in the report of Argentine police and military officers who became addicted to interrogation, torture, and the murder that followed. When the military and police ran out of political suspects to torture and kill, they resorted to the random abduction of citizens off the streets. I thought how easy it would be for the Border Patrol to shoot us and leave our bodies and car beside the highway, like so many bodies found in these parts and ascribed to drug runners.

Two other Border Patrolmen stood by the white van. The one who had asked if we were looking for trouble ordered his partner to "get the dog," and from the back of the van another patrolman brought a small female German shepherd on a leash. The dog apparently did not heel well enough to suit him, and the handler jerked the leash. They opened the doors of our car and pulled the dog's head into it, but I saw immediately from the expression in her eyes that the dog hated them and that she would not serve them. When she showed no interest in the inside of our car, they brought her around back to the trunk, near where we were standing. They half-dragged her up into the trunk, but still she did not indicate any stowed-away human beings or illegal drugs.

Their mood got uglier; the officers seemed outraged that the dog could not find any contraband, and they dragged her over to us and commanded her to sniff our legs and feet. To my relief, the strange violence the Border Patrol agents had focused on us now seemed shifted to the dog. I no longer felt so strongly that we would be murdered. We exchanged looks — the dog and I. She was afraid of what they might do, just as I was. The dog's handler jerked the leash sharply as she sniffed us, as if to make her perform better, but the dog refused to accuse us; she had an innate dignity that did not permit her to serve the murderous impulses of those men. I can't forget the expression in the dog's eyes; it was as if she were embarrassed to be associated with them. I had a small amount of medicinal marijuana in my purse that night, but she refused to expose me. I am not partial to dogs, but I will always remember the small German shepherd that night.

Unfortunately, what happened to me is an everyday occurrence here now. Since the 1980s, on top of greatly expanding border checkpoints, the Immigration and Naturalization Service and the Border Patrol have implemented policies that interfere with the rights of U.S. citizens to travel freely within our borders. INS agents now patrol all interstate highways and roads that lead to or from the U.S.-Mexico border in Texas, New Mexico, Arizona, and California. Now, when you drive east from Tucson on Interstate 10 toward El Paso, you encounter an INS check station outside Las Cruces, New Mexico. When you drive north from Las Cruces up Interstate 25, two miles north of the town of Truth or Consequences, the highway is blocked with orange emergency barriers, and all traffic is diverted into a two-lane Border Patrol checkpoint — ninety-five miles north of the U.S.-Mexico border.

I was detained once at Truth or Consequences, despite my and my companion's Arizona driver's licenses. Two men, both Chicanos, were detained at the same time, despite the fact that they too presented ID and spoke English without the thick Texas accents of the Border Patrol agents. While we were stopped, we watched as other vehicles — whose occupants were white — were waved through the checkpoint. White people traveling with brown people, however, can expect to be stopped on suspicion they work with the sanctuary movement, which shelters refugees. White people who appear to be clergy, those who wear ethnic clothing or jewelry, and women with very long hair or very short hair (they could be nuns) are also frequently detained; white men with beards or men with long hair are likely to be detained, too, because Border Patrol agents have profiles of "those sorts" of white people who may help political refugees. (Most of the political refugees from Guatemala and El Salvador are Native American or mestizo because the indigenous people of the Americas have continued to resist efforts by invaders to displace them from their ancestral lands.) Alleged increases in illegal immigration by people of Asian ancestry mean that the Border Patrol now routinely detains anyone who appears to be Asian or part Asian, as well.

Once your car is diverted from the interstate highway into the checkpoint area, you are under the control of the Border Patrol, which in practical terms exercises a power that no highway patrol or city patrolman possesses: they are willing to detain anyone, for no apparent reason. Other law-enforcement officers need a shred of probable cause in order to detain someone. On the books, so does the Border Patrol; but on the road, it's another matter. They'll order you to stop your car and step out; then they'll ask you to open the trunk. If you ask why or request a search warrant, you'll be told that they'll have to have a dog sniff the car before they can request a search warrant, and the dog might not get there for two or three hours. The search warrant might require an hour or two past that. They make it clear that if you force them to obtain a search warrant for the car, they will make you submit to a strip search as well.

Traveling in the open, though, the sense of violation can be even worse. Never mind high-profile cases like that of former Border Patrol agent Michael Elmer, acquitted of murder by claiming self-defense, despite admitting that as an officer he shot an illegal immigrant in the back and then hid the body, which remained undiscovered until another Border Patrolman reported the event. (Last month, Elmer was convicted of reckless endangerment in a separate incident, for shooting at least ten rounds from his M-16 too close to a group of immigrants as they were crossing illegally into Nogales in March 1992.) Never mind that in El Paso, a high school football coach driving a vanload of his players in full uniform was pulled over on the freeway and a Border Patrol agent put a cocked revolver to his head. (The football coach was Mexican-American, as were most of the players in his van; the incident eventually caused a federal judge to issue a restraining order against the Border Patrol.) We've a mountain of personal experiences like that that never make the newspapers. A history professor at UCLA told me she had been traveling by train from Los Angeles to Albuquerque twice a month doing research. On each of her trips, she had noticed that the Border Patrol agents were at the station in Albuquerque scrutinizing the passengers. Since she is six feet tall and of Irish and German ancestry, she was not particularly concerned. Then one day when she stepped off the train in Albuquerque, two Border Patrolmen accosted her, wanting to know what she was doing, and why she was traveling between Los Angeles and Albuquerque twice a month. She presented identification and an explanation deemed suitable by the agents and was allowed to go about her business.

Just the other day, I mentioned to a friend that I was writing this article and he told me about his seventy-three-year-old father, who is half Chinese and had set out alone by car from Tucson to Albuquerque the week before. His father had become confused by road construction and missed a turnoff from Interstate 10 to Interstate 25; when he turned around and circled back, he missed the turnoff a second time. But when he looped back for yet another try, Border Patrol agents stopped him and forced him to open his trunk. After they satisfied themselves that he was not smuggling Chinese immigrants, they sent him on his way. He was so rattled by the event that he had to be driven home by his daughter.

This is the police state that has developed in the southwestern United States since the 1980s. No person, no citizen, is free to travel without the scrutiny of the Border Patrol. In the city of South Tucson, where 80 percent of the respondents were Chicano or Mexicano, a joint research project by the University of Wisconsin and the University of Arizona recently concluded that one out of every five people there had been detained, mistreated verbally or nonverbally, or questioned by INS agents in the past two years.

Manifest Destiny may lack its old grandeur of theft and blood—"lock the door" is what it means now, with racism a trump card to be played again and again, shamelessly, by both major political parties. "Immigration," like "street crime" and "welfare fraud," is a political euphemism that refers to people of color. Politicians and media people talk about "illegal aliens" to dehumanize and demonize undocumented immigrants, who are for the most part people of color. Even in the days of Spanish and Mexican rule, no attempts were made to interfere with the flow of people and goods from south to north and north to south. It is the U.S. government that has continually attempted to sever contact between the tribal people north of the border and those to the south.[1]

Now that the "Iron Curtain" is gone, it is ironic that the U.S. government and its Border Patrol are constructing a steel wall ten feet high to span sections of the border with Mexico. While politicians and multinational corporations extol the virtues of NAFTA and free trade (in goods, not flesh), the ominous curtain is already up in a six-mile section at the border crossing at Mexicali; two miles are being erected but are not yet finished at Naco; and at Nogales, sixty miles south of Tucson, the steel wall has been all rubber-stamped and awaits construction, likely to begin in March. Like the pathetic multimillion-dollar antidrug border surveillance balloons that were continually deflated by high winds and made only a couple of meager interceptions before they blew away, the fence along the border is a theatrical prop, a bit of pork for contractors. Border entrepreneurs have already used blowtorches to cut passageways through the fence to collect "tolls" and are doing a brisk business. Back in Washington, the INS announces a $300 million computer contract to modernize its record keeping and Congress passes a crime bill that shunts $255 million to the INS for 1995, $181 million earmarked for border control, which is to include seven hundred new partners for the men who stopped Gus and me in our travels, and the history professor, and my friend's father, and as many as they could from South Tucson.

It is no use; borders haven't worked, and they won't work, not now, as the indigenous people of the Americas reassert their kinship and solidarity with one another. A mass migration is already under way; its roots are not simply economic. The Uto-Aztecan languages are spoken as far north as Taos Pueblo near the Colorado border, all the way south to Mexico City. Before the arrival of the Europeans, the indigenous communities throughout this region not only conducted commerce; the people shared cosmologies, and oral narratives about the Maize Mother, the Twin Brothers, and their grandmother, Spider Woman, as well as Quetzalcoatl, the benevolent snake. The great human migration within the Americas cannot be stopped; human beings are natural forces of the earth, just as rivers and winds are natural forces.

Deep down the issue is simple: the so-called Indian Wars from the days of Sitting Bull and Red Cloud have never really ended in the Americas. The Indian people of southern Mexico, of Guatemala, and those left in El Salvador, too, are still fighting for their lives and for their land against the cavalry patrols sent out by the governments of those lands. The Americas are Indian country, and the "Indian problem" is not about to go away.

One evening at sundown, we were stopped in traffic at a railroad crossing in downtown Tucson while a freight train passed us, slowly gaining speed as it headed north to Phoenix. In the twilight I saw the most amazing sight: dozens of human beings, mostly young men, were riding the train; everywhere, on flatcars, inside open boxcars, perched on top of boxcars, hanging off ladders on tank cars and between boxcars. I couldn't count fast enough, but I saw fifty or sixty people headed north. They were dark young men, Indian and mestizo; they were smiling and a few of them waved at us in our cars. I was reminded of the ancient story of Aztlán, told by the Aztecs but known in other Uto-Aztecan communities as well. Aztlán is the beautiful land to the north, the origin place of the Aztec people. I don't remember how or why the people left Aztlán to journey farther south, but the old story says that one day, they will return.

Note

1. The Treaty of Guadalupe Hidalgo, signed in 1848, recognizes the right of the Tohano O'Odom (Papago) people to move freely across the U.S.-Mexico border without documents. A treaty with Canada guarantees similar rights to those of the Iroquois nation in traversing the U.S.-Canada border.

Ideas for Rereading

1. While Silko writes of the "kinship and solidarity" of the indigenous people of the Americas (p. 624), she writes of governments and borders with the skepticism of an outsider. In what ways does Silko's legal status as both an American citizen and a Laguna Indian complicate her understanding of American political geography? How does her point of view on America, the way that she

imagines the political geography of "the Americas," differ from your own, or the one you are familiar with from maps and geography classes? What legal and historical facts support her point of view? How does Silko's treatment of the report by the U.S. Commission on Civil Rights titled "Indian Tribes: A Continuing Quest for Survival" (p. 616) influence your sense of Silko's insider/outsider status?

2. Reread "The Border Patrol State," paying careful attention to the story Silko tells about being stopped on New Mexico State Road 26 (p. 620). What aspects of Silko's story do you find disturbing? How does Silko gain your empathy? Underline specific words and phrases that she uses to characterize the Border Patrol agents. How do you respond to Silko's references to the practices of the Argentine police? How do these references and this story help explain Silko's analysis of what she calls "the police state"? Do you find her position persuasive? Explain.

Ideas for Writing

1. Write an essay about Silko's dual status as a U.S. citizen who swears allegiance to a nation that precedes the creation of the United States. Consider the ways in which she thinks about the border between the United States and Mexico, taking into account her argument about "America's debt to the Indian nations." Analyze the moments in the two essays when Silko assumes a specific national, tribal, cultural, or other form of identity. Does she change her identity according to circumstances, and if so, how, and how successfully?

2. In the final paragraphs of his essay, Frederick Jackson Turner writes stirringly of the influence of the frontier experience on American character. In the late nineteenth century the frontier closed, "and with its going," Turner concludes, "has closed the first period of American history" (p. 550). But Silko suggests that the frontier has not yet finally closed, and she states that the "Indian Wars . . . have never really ended" (p. 624). How does her point of view on America differ from Turner's? What counterarguments to Turner are offered by her essays? Develop an essay that uses Silko as the basis for a response or counterargument to Turner.

N. Scott Momaday

N. Scott Momaday, Ph.D. (b. 1934) was born in Lawton, Oklahoma, and spent his first year on the Kiowa Indian reservation. His father, a Kiowa, and his mother, English and Cherokee, both were teachers on reservations; his father was a visual artist and his mother authored children's books. It is little surprise, then, that Momaday was brought up with full awareness of Kiowan and Cherokee traditions. His parents also exposed him to the Navajo, Apache, and Pueblo cultures of the Southwest.

Momaday graduated from the University of New Mexico, taught on an Apache reservation in Jicarilla, and won a poetry fellowship to Stanford University. He worked with the famous poet and critic Yvor Winters and, in 1963, earned his doctorate in English Literature. After a stint at the University of California, Santa Barbara, Momaday published his first book, House Made of Dawn *(1969). This earned him the Pulitzer Prize for Fiction and landed him a job at the University of California, Berkeley. At Berkeley he designed one of the first courses in American Indian literature and mythology and did research into the Kiowa oral tradition. This research led to a collection of folktales, illustrated by his father,* The Way to Rainy Mountain *(1972). It also produced an influential essay about Native American attitudes toward the land, "The American Land Ethic" (1971).*

From 1973 to 1982 Momaday taught at Stanford University. He then moved to the University of Arizona, Tucson, where he is Regent's Professor of English. Since the mid-1970s he has illustrated his own books of poems and novels. His autobiographical work, The Names: A Memoir, *appeared in 1976 and was reprinted in 1987 and 1996. Recent books include* The Ancient Child *(1989) and* Circle of Wonder: A Native American Christmas Story *(1993).*

The following essay is from The Man Made of Words: Essays, Stories, and Passages *(1997). It uses the medium of writing to describe the gulf that separates literate from preliterate ways of thinking. As you read, consider the difficulties posed by this separation. How does Momaday handle these difficulties? Consider Momaday's use of the stage as a way of illustrating what he means by "a burden of belief, a kind of ambiguous exaggeration" (p. 627). How does this image of the stage assist your understanding of the difference between literate and preliterate ways of thinking? In what ways did figures like Cody and Custer treat the Indian country as a stage? How did this attitude help to turn them into mythic heroes?*

The American West and the Burden of Belief

I

West of Jemez Pueblo there is a great red mesa, and in the folds of the earth at its base there is a canyon, the dark red walls of which are sheer and shadow stained; they rise vertically to a remarkable height. You do not suspect that the canyon is there, but you turn a corner and the walls contain you; you look into a corridor of geologic time. When I went into that place I left my horse outside, for there was a strange light and quiet upon the walls, and the shadows closed upon me. I looked up, straight up, to the serpentine strip of the sky. It was clear and deep, like a river running across the top of the world. The sand in which I stood was deep, and I could feel the cold of it through the soles of my shoes. And when I walked out, the light and heat of the day struck me so hard that I nearly fell. On the side of a hill in the plain of the Hissar I saw my horse grazing among sheep. The land inclined into the distance, to the Pamirs, to the Fedchenko Glacier. The river which I had seen near the sun had run out into the endless ether above the Karakoram range and the Plateau of Tibet.

When I wrote this passage in *The Names,* some years ago, it did not seem strange to me that two such landscapes as that of northern

New Mexico and that of Central Asia should become one in the mind's eye and in the confluence of image and imagination. Nor does it seem strange to me now. Even as we look back, the partitions of our experience open and close upon each other; disparate realities coalesce into a single, integrated appearance.

This transformation is perhaps the essence of art and literature. Certainly it is the soul of drama, and historically it is how we have seen the American West. Our human tendency is to concentrate the world upon a stage. We construct proscenium arches and frames in order to contain the thing that is larger than our comprehension, the plane of boundless possibility, that which reaches almost beyond wonder. Sometimes the process of concentration results in something like a burden of belief, a kind of ambiguous exaggeration, as in the paintings of Albert Bierstadt, say, or in the photographs of Ansel Adams, in which an artful grandeur seems superimposed upon a grandeur that is innate. Or music comes to mind, a music that seems to pervade the vast landscape and emanate from it, not the music of wind and rain and birds and beasts, but Virgil Thomson's *The Plow That Broke the Plains,* or Aaron Copland's *Rodeo,* or perhaps the soundtrack from *The Alamo* or *She Wore a Yellow Ribbon.* We are speaking of overlays, impositions, a kind of narcissism that locates us within our own field of vision. But if this is a distorted view of the West, it is nonetheless a view that fascinates us.

And more often than not the fascination consists in peril. In *My Life on the Plains,* George Armstrong Custer describes a strange sight:

> I have seen a train of government wagons with white canvas covers moving through a mirage which, by elevating the wagons to treble their height and magnifying the size of the covers, presented the appearance of a line of large sailing vessels under full sail, while the usual appearance of the mirage gave a correct likeness of an immense lake or sea. Sometimes the mirage has been the cause of frightful suffering and death by its deceptive appearance.

He goes on to tell of emigrants to California and Oregon who, suffering terrible thirst, were deflected from their route by a mirage, "like an *ignis fatuus,*" and so perished. Their graves are strewn far and wide over the prairie.

This equation of wonder and peril is for Custer a kind of exhilaration, as indeed it is for most of those adventurers who journeyed westward, and even for those who did not, who escaped into the Wild West Show or the dime novel.

For the European who came from a community of congestion and confinement, the West was beyond dreaming; it must have inspired him to formulate an idea of the infinite. There he could walk through geologic time; he could see into eternity. He was surely bewildered, wary, afraid. The landscape was anomalously beautiful and hostile. It was desolate and unforgiving, and yet it was a world of paradisal possibility. Above all, it was wild, definitively wild. And it was inhabited by people who were to him altogether alien and inscrutable, who were essentially dangerous and deceptive, often invisible, who were savage and unholy—and who were perfectly at home.

This is a crucial point, then: the West was occupied. It was the home of peoples who had come upon the North American continent many thousands of years before, who had in the course of their habitation become the spirit and intelligence of the earth, who had died into the ground again and again and so made it sacred. Those Europeans who ventured into the West must have seen themselves in some way as latecomers and intruders. In spite of their narcissism, some aspect of their intrusion must have occurred to them as sacrilege, for they were in the unfortunate position of robbing the native peoples of their homeland and the land of its spiritual resources. By virtue of their culture and history—a culture of acquisition and a history of conquest—they were peculiarly prepared to commit sacrilege, the theft of the sacred.

Even the Indians succumbed to the kind of narcissism the Europeans brought to bear on the primeval landscape, the imposition of a belief—essentially alien to both the land and the peoples who inhabited it—that would locate them once again within their own field of vision. For the Indian, the mirage of the Ghost Dance—to which the concepts of a messiah and immortality, both foreign, European imports, were central—was surely an *ignis fatuus,* and the cause of frightful suffering and death.

II

George Armstrong Custer had an eye to the country of the Great Plains, and especially to those of its features which constituted a "deceptive appearance." In November 1868, as he stealthily approached Black Kettle's camp on the Washita River, where he was to win his principal acclaim as an Indian fighter, he and his men caught sight of a strange thing. At the first sign of dawn there appeared a bright light ascending slowly from the skyline. Custer describes it sharply, even eloquently:

> Slowly and majestically it continued to rise above the crest of the hill, first appearing as a small brilliant flaming globe of bright golden hue. As it ascended still higher it seemed to increase in size, to move more slowly, while its colors rapidly changed from one to the other, exhibiting in turn the most beautiful combinations of prismatic tints.

Custer and his men took it to be a rocket, some sort of signal, and they assumed that their presence had been detected by the Indians. Here again is the equation of fascination and peril. But at last the reality is discovered:

> Rising above the mystifying influences of the atmosphere, that which had appeared so suddenly before us and excited our greatest apprehensions developed into the brightest and most beautiful of morning stars.

In the ensuing raid upon Black Kettle's camp, Custer and his troopers, charging to the strains of "Garry Owen," killed 103 Cheyennes, including Black Kettle and his wife. Ninety-two of the slain Cheyennes were women, children, and old men. Fifty-three women and children were captured. Custer's casualties totaled one officer killed, one officer severely and two more slightly wounded, and eleven troopers wounded. After the fighting, Custer ordered the herd of Indian ponies slain; the herd numbered 875 animals. "We did not need the ponies, while the Indians did," he wrote.

In the matter of killing women and children, Custer's exculpatory rhetoric seems lame, far beneath his poetic descriptions of mirages and the break of day:

> Before engaging in the fight orders had been given to prevent the killing of any but the fighting strength of the village; but in a struggle of this character it is impossible at all times to discriminate, particularly when, in a hand-to-hand conflict such as the one the troops were then engaged in, the squaws are as dangerous adversaries as the warriors, while Indian boys between ten and fifteen years of age were found as expert and determined in the use of the pistol and bow and arrow as the older warriors.

After the fighting, Black Kettle's sister, Mah-wis-sa, implored Custer to leave the Cheyennes in peace. Custer reports that she approached him with a young woman, perhaps seventeen years old, and placed the girl's hand in his. Then she proceeded to speak solemnly in her own language, words which Custer took to be a kind of benediction, with appropriate manners and gestures. When the formalities seemed to come to a close, Mah-wis-sa looked reverently to the skies and at the same time drew her hands slowly down over the faces of Custer and the girl. At this point Custer was moved to ask Romeo, his interpreter, what was going on. Romeo replied that Custer and the young woman had just been married to each other.

It is said that Mah-wis-sa told Custer that if he ever again made war on the Cheyennes, he would die. When he was killed at the Little Bighorn, Cheyenne women pierced his eardrums with awls, so that he might hear in the afterlife; he had failed to hear the warning given him at the Washita.

In the final paragraph of *My Life on the Plains,* Custer bids farewell to his readers and announces his intention "to visit a region of country as yet unseen by human eyes, except those of the Indian—a country described by the latter as abounding in game of all varieties, rich in scientific interest, and of surpassing beauty in natural scenery." After rumors of gold had made the Black Hills a name known throughout the country, General (then Lieutenant Colonel) George Armstrong Custer led an expedition from Fort Abraham Lincoln into the Black Hills in July and August, 1874. The Custer expedition traveled six hundred miles in sixty days. Custer reported proof of gold, but he had an eye to other things as well. He wrote in his diary:

> Every step of our march that day was amid flowers of the most exquisite colors and perfume. So luxuriant in growth were they that men plucked

them without dismounting from the saddle . . . It was a strange sight to glance back at the advancing columns of cavalry and behold the men with beautiful bouquets in their hands, while the headgear of the horses was decorated with wreaths of flowers fit to crown a queen of May. Deeming it a most fitting appellation, I named this Floral Valley.

In the evening of that same day, sitting at mess in a meadow, the officers competed to see how many different flowers could be picked by each man, without leaving his seat. Seven varieties were gathered so. Some fifty different flowers were blooming in Floral Valley.

Imagine that Custer dreamed that night. In his dream he saw a man approaching on horseback, approaching slowly across a meadow full of wildflowers. The man drew very close and stopped, sitting straight up on the horse, holding Custer fast in his gaze. There could be no doubt that he was a warrior, and fearless, though he flourished no scalps and made no signs of fighting. His unbound hair hung below his waist. His body was painted with hail spots, a white bolt of lightning ran down one of his cheeks, and on his head he wore the feathers of a red-backed hawk. Except for moccasins and breechcloth he was naked.

"I am George Armstrong Custer," Custer said, "called Yellowhair, called Son of the Morning Star."

"I am Curly," the man said, "called Crazy Horse."

And Custer wept for the nobility and dignity and greatness of the man facing him. And through his tears he perceived the brilliance of the meadow. The wildflowers were innumerable and more beautiful than anything he had ever seen or imagined. And when he thought his heart could bear no more, a thousand butterflies rose up, glancing and darting and floating around him, to spangle the sky, to become prisms of the sun. And he awoke serene and refreshed in his soul.

George Armstrong Custer sees the light upon the meadows of the plains, but he does not see disaster lurking at the Little Bighorn. He hears the bugles and the band, but he does not hear or heed the warning of the Cheyenne women. All about there is deception; the West is other than it seems.

III

In 1872, William Frederick Cody was awarded the Medal of Honor for his valor in fighting Indians. In 1913, army regulations specified that only enlisted men and officers were eligible to receive the Medal of Honor, and Cody's medal was therefore withdrawn and his name removed from the records. In 1916, after deliberation, the army decided to return the medal, having declared that Cody's service to his country was "above and beyond the call of duty."

Ambivalence and ambiguity, like deception, bear upon all definitions of the American West. The real issue of Cody's skill and accomplishment as an Indian fighter is not brought into question in this matter of the Medal of Honor, but it might be. Beyond the countless Indians he "killed" in the arena of the Wild West Show, Cody's achievements as an Indian fighter are suspect. Indeed, much of Cody's life is clouded in ambiguity. He claimed that in 1859 he became a Pony Express rider, but the Pony Express did not come into being until 1860. Even the sobriquet "Buffalo Bill" belonged to William Mathewson before it belonged to William Frederick Cody.

Buffalo Bill Cody was an icon and an enigma, and he was in some sense his own invention. One of his biographers wrote that he was "a man who was so much more than a western myth." One must doubt it, for the mythic dimension of the American West is an equation much greater than the sum of its parts. It would be more accurate, in this case, to say that the one dissolved into the other, that the man and myth became indivisible. The great fascination and peril of Cody's life was the riddle of who he was. The thing that opposed him, and perhaps betrayed him, was above all else the mirage of his own identity.

If we are to understand the central irony of Buffalo Bill and the Wild West Show, we must first understand that William Frederick Cody was an authentic western hero. As a scout, a guide, a marksman, and a buffalo hunter, he was second to none. At a time when horsemanship was at its highest level in America, he was a horseman nearly without peer. He defined the Plainsman. The authority of his life on the plains far surpassed Custer's.

But let us imagine that we are at Omaha, Nebraska, on May 17, 1883, in a crowd of eight thousand people. The spectacle of the "Wild West" unfolds before us. The opening parade is led by a twenty-piece band playing "Garry Owen," perhaps, or "The Girl I Left Behind Me." Then there comes an Indian in full regalia on a paint pony. Next are buffalo, three adults and a calf. Then there is Buffalo Bill, mounted on a fine white horse and resplendent in a great white hat, a fringed buckskin coat, and glossy thigh boots. He stands out in a procession of cowboys, Indians, more buffalo, and the Deadwood Stage, drawn by six handsome mules; the end is brought up by another band, playing "Annie Laurie" or "When Johnny Comes Marching Home." Then we see the acts—the racing of the Pony Express, exhibitions of shooting, the attack on the Deadwood Stage, and the finale of the great buffalo chase. Buffalo Bill makes a stirring speech, and we are enthralled; the applause is thunderous. But this is only a modest beginning, a mere glimpse of things to come.

What we have in this explosion of color and fanfare is an epic transformation of the American West into a traveling circus and of an American hero into an imitation of himself. Here is a theme with which we have become more than familiar. We have seen the transformation take place numberless times on the stage, on television and movie screens, and on the pages of comic books, dime novels and literary masterpieces. One function of the American imagination is to reduce the American landscape to size, to fit that great expanse to the confinement of the emigrant mind. It is a way to persist in our cultural being. We photograph ourselves on the rim of Monument Valley or against the wall of the Tetons, and we become our own frame of reference. As long as we can transform the landscape to accommodate our fragile presence, we can be saved. As long as we can see ourselves on the picture plane, we cannot be lost.

Arthur Kopit's play *Indians* is a remarkable treatise on this very subject of transformation. It can and ought to be seen as a tragedy, for its central story is that of Buffalo Bill's fatal passage into myth. He is constrained to translate his real heroism into a false and concentrated reflection of itself. The presence of the Indians is pervasive, but he cannot see them until they are called to his attention.

BUFFALO BILL: THANK YOU, THANK YOU! A GREAT show lined up tonight! With all-time favorite Johnny Baker, Texas Jack and his twelve-string guitar, the Dancin' Cavanaughs, Sheriff Brad and the Deadwood Mail Coach, Harry Philamee's Trained Prairie Dogs, the Abilene County Girl's Trick Roping and Lasso Society, Pecos Pete and the—
VOICE: *Bill.*
BUFFALO BILL (*startled*): Hm?
VOICE: Bring on the Indians.
BUFFALO BILL: What?
VOICE: The *Indians.*
BUFFALO BILL: Ah . . .

Solemnly the Indians appear. In effect they shame Buffalo Bill; they tread upon his conscience. They fascinate and imperil him. By degrees his desperation to justify himself—and by extension the white man's treatment of the Indians in general—grows and becomes a burden too great to bear. In the end he sits trembling while the stage goes completely black. Then all lights up, rodeo music, the glaring and blaring; enter the Roughriders of the World! Buffalo Bill enters on his white stallion and tours the ring, doffing his hat to the invisible crowd. The Roughriders exit, and the Indians approach, and the lights fade to black again.

At five minutes past noon on January 10, 1917, Buffalo Bill died. Western Union ordered all lines cleared, and, in a state of war, the world was given the news at once. The old scout had passed on. Tributes and condolences came from every quarter, from children, from old soldiers, from heads of state.

In ambivalence and ambiguity, Cody died as he had lived. A week before his death, it was reported that Buffalo Bill had been baptized into the Roman Catholic Church. His wife Louisa was, however, said to be an Episcopalian, and his sister Julia, to whom he declared, "Your church suits me," was a Presbyterian. Following his death there was a controversy as to where Cody should be buried. He had often expressed the wish to be buried on Cedar Mountain, Wyoming. Nonetheless, his final resting place is atop Mount Lookout, above Denver, Colorado, overlooking the urban sprawl.

IV

DECEMBER 29, 1890
Wounded Knee Creek

In the shine of photographs
are the slain, frozen and black

on a simple field of snow.
They image ceremony:

women and children dancing,
old men prancing, making fun.

In autumn there were songs, long
since muted in the blizzard.

In summer the wild buckwheat
shone like fox fur and quillwork,

and dusk guttered on the creek.
Now in serene attitudes

of dance, the dead in glossy
death are drawn in ancient light.

On December 15, 1890, the great Hunkpapa leader, Sitting Bull, who had opposed Custer at the Little Bighorn and who had toured for a time with Buffalo Bill and the Wild West Show, was killed on the Standing Rock Reservation. In a dream he had foreseen his death at the hands of his own people.

Just two weeks later, on the morning of December 29, 1890, on Wounded Knee Creek near the Pine Ridge Agency, the 7th Cavalry of the United States Army opened fire on an encampment of Big Foot's band of Miniconjou Sioux. When the shooting ended, Big Foot and most of his people were dead or dying. It has been estimated that nearly three hundred of the original 350 men, women, and children in the camp were slain. Twenty-five soldiers were killed and thirty-nine wounded, most of them caught in their own fire.

Sitting Bull is reported to have said, "I am the last Indian." In some sense he was right. During his lifetime the world of the Plains Indians had changed forever. The old roving life of the buffalo hunters was over. A terrible disintegration, demoralization, had set in. If the death of Sitting Bull marked the end of an age, Wounded Knee marked the end of a culture.

> I did not know then how much was ended. When I look back now from the high hill of my old age, I can still see the butchered women and children lying heaped and scattered all along the crooked gulch as plain as when I saw them with eyes still young. And I can see that something else died there in the bloody mud, and was buried in the blizzard. A people's dream died there. It was a beautiful dream.   —Black Elk

In the following days there were further developments. On January 7, 1891, nine days after the massacre at Wounded Knee, a young Sioux warrior named Plenty Horses shot and killed a popular army officer, Lieutenant Edward W. Casey, who wanted to enter the Sioux village at No Water for the purpose of talking peace. The killing appeared to be unprovoked. Plenty Horses shot Casey in the back at close quarters.

On January 11, two Sioux families, returning to Pine Ridge from hunting near Bear Butte, were ambushed by white ranchers, three brothers named Culbertson. Few Tails, the head of one of the families, was killed, and his wife was severely wounded. Somehow she made her way in the freezing cold a hundred miles to Pine Ridge. The other family—a man, his wife, and two children, one an infant—managed to reach the Rosebud Agency in two weeks. This wife, too, was wounded and weak from the loss of blood. She survived, but the infant child had died of starvation on the way.

On January 15 the Sioux leaders surrendered and established themselves at Pine Ridge Agency. The peace for which General Nelson A. Miles had worked so hard was achieved. The Indians assumed that Plenty Horses would go free, and indeed General Miles was reluctant to disturb the peace. But there were strong feelings among the soldiers. Casey had been shot in cold blood while acting in the interest of peace. On February 19, Plenty Horses was quietly arrested and removed from the reservation to Fort Meade, near Sturgis, South Dakota.

On March 27, General Miles ordered Plenty Horses released to stand trial in the federal district court at Sioux Falls. Interest ran high, and the courtroom was filled with onlookers of every description. The Plenty Horses trial was one of the most interesting and unlikely in the history of the West. Eventually the outcome turned upon the question of perception, of whether or not a state of war existed between the Sioux and the United States. If Plenty Horses and Casey were belligerents in a state of war, the defense argued, then the killing could not be considered a criminal offense, subject to trial in the civil courts.

General Miles was sensitive to this question for two reasons in particular. First, his rationale for bringing troops upon the scene—and he had amassed the largest concentration of troops in one place since the Civil War—was predicated upon the existence of a state of war. When the question was put to him directly, he replied, "It was a war. You do not suppose that I am going to reduce my campaign to a dress-parade affair?" Second, Miles had to confront the logically related corollary to the defense argument that, if no state of war existed, all the soldiers who took part in the Wounded Knee affair were guilty of murder under the law.

Miles sent a staff officer, Captain Frank D. Baldwin, to testify on behalf of Plenty Horses' defense. This testimony proved critical, and decisive. It is a notable irony that Baldwin and the slain Casey were close friends. Surely one of the principal ironies of American history is that Plenty Horses was very likely to have been the only Indian to benefit in any way from the slaughter at Wounded Knee. Plenty Horses was acquitted. So too—a final irony—were the Culbertson brothers; with Plenty Horses' acquittal, there was neither a logical basis nor a practical possibility to hold them accountable for the ambush of Few Tails and his party.

We might ponder Plenty Horses at trial, a young man sitting silent under the scrutiny of curious onlookers, braving his fate with apparent indifference. Behind the mask of a warrior was a lost and agonized soul.

As a boy Plenty Horses had been sent to Carlisle Indian School in Pennsylvania, the boarding school founded in 1879 by Richard Henry Pratt, whose obsession was to "kill the Indian and save the man." Carlisle was the model upon which an extensive system of boarding schools for Indians was based. The schools were prisons in effect, where Indian children were exposed to brutalities, sometimes subtle, sometimes not, in the interest of converting them to the white man's way of life. It was a grand experiment in ethnic cleansing and psychological warfare, and it failed. But it exacted a terrible cost upon the mental, physical, and spiritual health of Indian children.

Plenty Horses was for five years a pupil at Carlisle. Of his experience there he said:

> I found that the education I had received was of no benefit to me. There was no chance to get employment, nothing for me to do whereby I could earn my board and clothes, no opportunity to learn more and remain with the whites. It disheartened me and I went back to live as I had before going to school.

But when Plenty Horses returned to his own people, they did not fully accept him. He had lost touch with the old ways; he had lived among whites, and the association had diminished him. He rejected the white world, but he had been exposed to it, and it had left its mark upon him. And in the process he had been dislodged, uprooted from the Indian world. He could not quite get back to it. His very being had become tentative; he lived in a kind of limbo, a state of confusion, depression, and desperation.

At the trial Plenty Horses was remarkably passive. He said nothing, nor did he give any sign of his feelings. It was as if he were not there. It came later to light that he was convinced beyond any question that he would be hanged. He could not understand what was happening around him. But in a strange way he could appreciate it. Indeed he must have been fascinated. Beneath his inscrutable expression, his heart must have been racing. He was the center of a ritual, a sacrificial victim; the white man must dispose of him according to some design in the white man's universe. This was perhaps a ritual of atonement. The whites would take his life, but in the proper way, according to their notion of propriety and the appropriate. Perhaps they were involving him in their very notion of the sacred. He could only accept what was happening, and only in their terms. With silence, patience, and respect he must await the inevitable. He said later:

> I am an Indian. Five years I attended Carlisle and was educated in the ways of the white man . . . I was lonely. I shot the lieutenant so I might make a place for myself among my people. Now I am one of them. I shall

be hung and the Indians will bury me as a warrior. They will be proud of me. I am satisfied.

But Plenty Horses was not hanged, nor did he make an acceptable place for himself among his people. He was acquitted. Plenty Horses lived out his life between two worlds, without a place in either.

Perhaps the most tragic aspect of Plenty Horses' plight was his silence, the theft of his language, and the theft of meaning itself from his ordeal. At Carlisle he had been made to speak English, and his native Lakota was forbidden—thrown away, to use a term that indicates particular misfortune in the plains oral tradition. To be "thrown away" is to be negated, excluded, eliminated. After five years Plenty Horses had not only failed to master the English language, he had lost some critical possession of his native tongue as well. He was therefore crippled in his speech, wounded in his intelligence. In him was a terrible urgency to express himself—his anger and hurt, his sorrow and loneliness. But his voice was broken. In terms of his culture and all it held most sacred, Plenty Horses himself was thrown away.

In order to understand the true nature of Plenty Horses' ordeal—and a central reality in the cultural conflict that has defined the way we historically see the American West—we must first understand something about the nature of words, about the way we live our daily lives in the element of language. For in a profound sense our language determines us; it shapes our most fundamental selves; it establishes our identity and confirms our existence, our human being. Without language we are lost, "thrown away." Without names—and language is essentially a system of naming—we cannot truly claim to be.

To think is to talk to oneself. That is to say, language and thought are practically indivisible. But there is complexity in language, and there are many languages. Indeed, there are hundreds of Native American languages on the North American continent alone, many of them in the American West. As there are different languages, there are different ways of thinking. In terms of worldview, there are common denominators of experience which unify language communities to some extent. Although the Pueblo peoples of the Rio Grande Valley speak different languages, their experience of the land in which they live and have lived for thousands of years is by and large the same. And their worldview is the same. Other peoples—Europeans, for example—also have common denominators which unify them. But the difference between Native American and European worldviews is vast. And that difference is crucial to the story of the American West. We are talking about different ways of thinking, deeply different ways of looking at the world.

The oral tradition of the American Indian is a highly developed realization of language. In certain ways it is superior to the written tradition. In the oral tradition words are sacred; they are intrinsically powerful and beautiful. By means of words, by the exertion of language upon the unknown, the best of the possible—and indeed the seemingly impossible—is accomplished. Nothing exists beyond the influence of words. Words are the names of Creation. To give one's word is to give oneself, wholly — to place a name, than which nothing is more sacred, in the balance. One stands for his word; his word stands for him. The oral tradition demands the greatest clarity of speech and hearing, the whole strength of memory, and an absolute faith in the efficacy of language. Every word spoken, every word heard, is the utterance of prayer.

Thus, in the oral tradition, language bears the burden of the sacred, the burden of belief. In a written tradition, the place of language is not so certain.

Those European immigrants who ventured into the Wild West were of a written tradition, even the many who were illiterate. Their way of seeing and thinking was determined by the invention of an alphabet, the advent of the printed word, and the manufacture of books. These were great landmarks of civilization, to be sure, but they were also a radical departure from the oral tradition and an understanding of language that was inestimably older and closer to the origin of words. Although the first Europeans venturing into the continent took with them and held dear the Bible, Bunyan, and Shakespeare, their children ultimately could take words for granted, throw them away. Words, multiplied and diluted to inflation, would be preserved on shelves forever. But in this departure was also the dilution of the sacred, and the loss of a crucial connection with the real, that plane of possibility that is always larger than our comprehension. What follows such loss is overlay, imposition, the distorted view of the West of which we have been speaking.

V

My children, when at first I liked the whites,
My children, when at first I liked the whites,
I gave them fruits,
I gave them fruits.

— Arapaho

Restore my voice for me.
— Navajo

The landscape of the American West has to be seen to be believed. And perhaps, conversely, it has to be believed in order to be seen. Here is the confluence of image and imagination. I am a writer and a painter. I am therefore interested in what it is to see, how seeing is accomplished, how the physical eye and the mind's eye are related, how the act of seeing is or can be expressed in art and in language, and how these things are sacred in nature, as I believe them to be.

Belief is the burden of seeing. And language bears the burden of belief rightly. To see into the heart of something is to believe in it. In order to see to this extent, to see and to accomplish belief in the seeing, one must be prepared. The preparation is a spiritual exercise.

In order to be perceived in its true character, the landscape of the American West must be seen in terms of its sacred dimension. *Sacred* and *sacrifice* are related. Something is made sacred by means of sacrifice; that which is sacred is earned. I have a friend who wears on a string around his neck a little leather pouch. In the pouch is a pebble from the creekbed at Wounded Knee. Wounded Knee is sacred ground, for it was purchased with blood. It is the site of a terrible human sacrifice. It is appropriate that my friend should keep the pebble close to the center of his being, that he should see the pebble and beyond the pebble to the battlefield and beyond the battlefield to the living earth.

The history of the West, that is, the written story that begins with the record of European intervention, is informed by tensions which arise from a failure to see the West in terms of the sacred. The oral history, the oral tradition that came before the written chronicles, is all too often left out of the equation. Yet one of the essential realities of the West is centered in this still-living past. When Europeans came into the West they encountered a people who had been there for untold millennia, for whom the landscape was a kind of cathedral of their spiritual life, the home of their deepest being. It had been earned by sacrifice forever. But the encounter was determined by a distortion of image and imagination and language, by a failure to see and believe.

George Armstrong Custer could see and articulate the beauty of the plains, but he could not see the people who inhabited them. Or he could see them only as enemies, impediments to the glory for which he hungered. He could not understand the sacred ceremony, the significance of the marriage he was offered, nor could he hear the words of warning, or comprehend their meaning.

Buffalo Bill was a plainsman, but the place he might have held on the picture plane of the West was severely compromised and ultimately lost to the theatrical pretensions of the Wild West Show. Neither did he see the Indians. What he saw at last was a self-fabricated reflection of himself and of the landscape in which he had lived a former life.

The vision of Plenty Horses was that of reunion with his traditional world. He could not realize his vision, for his old way of seeing was stolen from him in the white man's school. Ironically, just like the European emigrants, Plenty Horses attempted by his wordless act of violence to persist in his cultural being, to transform the landscape to accommodate his presence once more, to save himself. He could not do so. I believe that he wanted more than anything to pray, to make a prayer in the old way to the old deities of the world into which he was born. But I believe too that he had lost the words, that without language he could no longer bear the burden of belief.

> The sun's beams are running out
> The sun's beams are running out
> The sun's yellow rays are running out
> The sun's yellow rays are running out

We shall live again
We shall live again

— Comanche

They will appear—may you behold them!
They will appear—may you behold them!
A horse nation will appear.
A thunder-being nation will appear.
They will appear, behold!
They will appear, behold!

— Kiowa

Ideas for Rereading

1. Reread Momaday's discussions of General Custer (p. 628), of Buffalo Bill Cody (p. 630), of Plenty Horses (p. 633). What lessons does Momaday draw from each? To reach a fuller understanding, work back from the brief recapitulations at the end of the essay (p. 638) to the lengthy stories in the body. What does each story reveal about the myths and realities of the American West? About language? About the challenges that a historian faces?

2. As you reread, note the various different instances of "transformation" that Momaday works with in this essay. What do we learn from these transformations? What do they have in common? What joins them together? How do these transformations relate to the "narcisissism" of the European tradition?

Ideas for Writing

1. At the end of section IV, Momaday writes of the "loss of a crucial connection with the real" (p. 637) in the written tradition. What are the consequences of this loss? Need such a loss be total? Does Momaday's essay help to bridge the gap between the written tradition and the oral? Although Momaday explains that the oral tradition of the American Indian is "in certain ways . . . superior to the written tradition" (p. 636), his own essay, of course, is a written document. But does his writing bear traces or echoes of the oral tradition, of other ways of using language? What role do poetry, narrative, and metaphor play in his argument? Write an essay analyzing how Momaday uses writing— both prose and poetry—to help readers understand the oral tradition.

2. How does the essay make sense of its title, "The American West and the Burden of Belief"? How do you understand Momaday's statement that the West "has to be believed in order to be seen" (p. 637)? Follow Momaday's argument closely. Write an essay on the meaning of what Momaday means by "belief."

3. In "At the Buffalo Bill Museum, June 1988," Jane Tompkins describes her visit to the Plains Indian Museum as a "terrible letdown" (p. 594): the artifacts "spoke to me of nothing I could understand" (p. 595). At last, she questions whether perhaps Plains Indians culture "was simply not readable by someone like me" (p. 595). Momaday's essay affords some insight into this other way of

seeing—this other point of view that Tompkins found so distant. What answer does Momaday provide to Tompkins's question? How and why is our understanding of this other way of seeing necessarily limited?

4. Jane Tompkins also discusses Buffalo Bill and General Custer in "At the Buffalo Bill Museum, June 1988." Reread Tompkins's essay in light of Momaday's discussion of Buffalo Bill and Custer. On what points do their accounts agree and on what points do they differ? How does each writer use these figures to serve a larger argument? How does your reading of one author affect your understanding of the other? Write an essay that compares Tompkins's use of these figures with Momaday's.

ERIC GARY ANDERSON

Eric Gary Anderson (b. 1960) is the author of American Indian Literature and the Southwest: Contexts and Dispositions *(1999), from which the following essay is excerpted, along with numerous articles and reviews. A two-time recipient of the Oklahoma Foundation for the Humanities Research Grant, he is a professor of English at Oklahoma State University. Anderson has studied and taught with Calvin Martin at Rutgers University in New Brunswick; it was from Martin, author of the influential book* Keepers of the Game: Indian-Animal Relationships and the Fur Trade *(1978), that he learned to mediate between historical and literary ways of thinking and between American Indian and European conceptions of language and the landscape. In the book that includes the chapter "Unsettling Frontiers," Anderson engages with a number of different ways of understanding literature and the history of the American Southwest. He sees them as products of the dynamic exchange among the various civilizations that interact in the so-called desert, in a place that teems with life and culture despite its reputation. Anderson's work addresses visual art by Georgia O'Keeffe and George Herriman (the cartoonist who created* Krazy Kat*), novels and poems by Euro-American authors including Willa Cather, T. S. Eliot, and Frank Norris, and American Indian writers including N. Scott Momaday and Leslie Marmon Silko. Focusing in the following essay on Billy the Kid as an example of the western outlaw, Anderson shows how Frederick Jackson Turner's desire to close the frontier led him to ignore the erratic, unpredictable role of an unruly, unsettling, and large group of violent criminals and petty thieves, a group that actively worked to prevent the closing of the frontier.*

Unsettling Frontiers
Billy the Kid and the Outlaw Southwest

Toward the close of "The Significance of the Frontier in American History," Frederick Jackson Turner banishes the western outlaw to footnote 49:

> I have refrained from dwelling on the lawless characteristics of the frontier, because they are sufficiently well known. The gambler and desper-

ado, the regulators of the Carolinas and the vigilantes of California, are types of that line of scum that the waves of advancing civilization bore before them, and of the growth of spontaneous organs of authority where legal authority was absent. (pp. 32–33)

About a dozen years before Turner first publicized his frontier thesis in 1893, Pat Garrett shot and killed perhaps the most famous southwestern outlaw, Billy the Kid, in a Fort Sumner, New Mexico Territory, bedroom. This transaction, one of a vast number of violent acts in the territorial American Southwest, underscores that it was still, in 1881, very much a frontier zone. As Robert Utley describes it, for example, the territory of New Mexico (still more than thirty years away from statehood)

> was a land of vast distances; of rugged mountains, parched deserts, and grassy plains; and of a cultural medley of Hispanic, Anglo, and Indian that did not always mix well. . . . New Mexico was also a land of rudimentary transportation, of isolation and parochialism, of poverty and privation relieved by only nominal prosperity, of centuries-old cultural institutions and infant political and economic institutions, of ineffective government, and of endemic violence. (*Billy the Kid,* 3)

Like New Mexico Territory, Mexico and the territory of Arizona were border zones punctuated by multicultural encounters and violence. In their autobiographies, Geronimo and his relative, Jason Betzinez, recount frequent border crossings and recrossings by both Apaches and Mexicans on raids and war parties against each other.[1] Another Apache autobiographer, James Kaywaykla, remarks that "Until I was about ten years old [approximately 1883] I did not know that people died except by violence. This is because I am an Apache" (xiii). Into this already dangerous environment came mobile "adventurers" such as Billy the Kid, who were able to blend in, finding or making room to practice a sort of uneven recklessness, an often unpremeditated violence that nonetheless helped keep the western outback unsettled. Witness, for example, their "casual view of suffering and death," their often unreflective responses to confusing social arrangements, and their use of the territory's formidable terrain for hiding out and for numerous "accidental" killings (Utley, *Billy the Kid,* 4).

This alliance of the physical frontier and the frontier criminal kicked up a problem for Turner, whose faith in the steady progress of American civilization westward rested on the assumption that outlaws would not survive that migration for long, that each successive region's savageries and barbarisms would yield to the inevitable, inexorable waves of civilization. But, to Turner's distaste and disappointment, these waves hurled up a freakish realm of "scum" and stopgap "spontaneous organs of [dubious] authority," some of which had acquired national celebrity status even before he presented his paper. The forces of civilization and the natural laws envisioned by Turner and others would have to be strong indeed to tame biology and sanitize this barely mentionable environment; that he writes little about the Southwest suggests, for one thing, that its natural frontiers and mix of inhabitants might not cooperate so readily with his metaphorical frontier's closing.

In Utley's words, the outlaws "rocked New Mexico with violence and lawlessness" (*Billy the Kid*, 4). Turner sees these unspeakable figures as uncivilized, ungendered, borderline traitorous forces who actively obstruct and disrupt the steady westward advance of American civilization; in a sense, he groups outlaws with Indians while inviting speculation about how the westering migrations of "scum" compete against the Indian-hating migrations of "law-abiding" Americans. As Richard Drinnon argues, in Turner's writings, American Indians "subsisted as natural objects, extensions of the nature that had to be subdued, impediments that had to be removed from the irresistible march to the West" (462). Euro-American residents in the territorial Southwest frequently regarded Indians as outlaws or worse and bestialized them: "There is a royalty for wolf scalps and why not Indian scalps," the *Las Vegas (New Mexico) Daily Optic* asked its readers; "let them be hunted to death. . . . We kill mad dogs and mountain lions on sight. Of the beast and the Indian which is the worst?" (Weigle and White, 288). Similarly, Turner's quasi-biological metaphors for outlawry seem to suggest that the frontier process, in which even the lawless participate, has been naturalized rather than fully understood as an ideologically charged cultural process. All in all, local and national debate about Indians, outlaws, and emigrants was of course much more complex than these quotations from Turner and the *Daily Optic* let on. . . . This chapter . . . will focus on the physical and textual mobility of territorial outlaws like Billy the Kid and Indians like Geronimo, in part by discussing some of the ways in which this mobility is transformed into legends that are themselves highly elastic and capable of demonizing, romanticizing, and otherwise recirculating the figures of the outlaw, the Apache, and the places they inhabit—the very frontier that Turner declared closed.

The outlaws of the Southwest were no more completely bad than the lawmen were completely virtuous: just as the outlaws often vacillated between deviltry and more "civilized" occupations, the agents of law and order raised hell and broke their own laws, and members of both groups worked, hid, and rioted in a variety of "uncivilized" environments. In the Lincoln County, New Mexico Territory, wars of the 1870s, in which Billy the Kid participated, both "sides claimed to be instruments of the law," both sides deputized allies illegally, and both sides committed cold-blooded murders. "Under color of law, both sides, . . . engage[d] in a great deal of unlawful activity" (Utley, *Billy the Kid*, 56). Both sides fell in and out of favor with local and federal authorities, including territorial governor Lew Wallace, who, when he wasn't working on *Ben Hur*, was first bargaining with Billy the Kid and then signing his death warrant.

Geronimo, of course, was only captured—as distinct from surrendering—once, and that, as Angie Debo points out, by a ruse (107). Soldiers and Indian agents varied in ability and ethics; some, like General

O. O. Howard, treated the Apaches fairly and earned their respect, while others, like General George Crook, received Geronimo's scorn: "I think that General Crook's death was sent by the Almighty as a punishment for the many evil deeds he committed" (Geronimo, 139–140). But Betzinez, who later came to terms with much of Euro-American culture, writes of the same man, "We actually loved General Crook, and even today think of him, and talk about him, with genuine affection" (121). Kaywaykla takes more of a middle ground, saying that Crook "was an enemy, yes, but he was an honorable enemy. His promise was good; his understanding of Apaches was fair" (150). As Betzinez understates to his predominantly Euro-American readership, "All was not harmony at all times in the Apache tribe" (67–68). In fact, S. M. Barrett interpolates a chapter into *Geronimo's Story of His Life* (1906) in which he explains that Apaches banished from the tribe for crimes often came to be regarded as outlaws: "Frequently these outlaw Indians banded together and committed depredations which were charged against the regular tribe. . . . [T]hese bands frequently provoked the wrath of the tribe and secured their own destruction" (Geronimo, 30). And Theodore Roosevelt contends in "Across the Navajo Desert,"

> The lawless Indians are the worst menace to the others among the Navajos and Utes; and very serious harm has been done by well-meaning Eastern philanthropists who have encouraged and protected these criminals. I have known some startling cases of this kind. (209)

Outlawry in the Southwest was not necessarily contingent on Euro-Americans or on simple polarizations of "Indian" and "white" as racialized cultural stances. The point is obvious but important to rearticulate precisely because it warns against constructing historiographical master narratives of the places and the peoples in question.

To turn away from Billy the Kid and the Apaches for a moment,

> [t]he celebrated Wyatt Earp, stern-eyed guardian of law and order in so many Westerns, had once been an outlaw himself, indicted by a grand jury on a horse-stealing charge. [In 1881] Wyatt and his brothers were hired to keep the peace in Tombstone, Arizona, a task they conducted with a certain light-fingered permissiveness toward the roaring trades of gambling and prostitution. Their opponents referred to them as the Fighting Pimps. (Brownlow, 280)

As Kevin Brownlow remarks, "The dividing line between lawmen and outlaws in the West was, to put it mildly, blurred" (280)—as was the line between, for example, "renegade" Apaches and the Apache scouts who pursued and sometimes guarded them. These shifting, hazy borderlands of law and disorder are well captured in western films such as *My Darling Clementine,* John Ford's 1946 treatment of the Wyatt Earp story. In this film, Doc Holliday embodies a complex, confusing mixture of virtues and vices; Doc, though clearly a thief and a killer who intimidates the Tombstone citizenry, seems equally at home as a medical and civic hero, struggling to save the life of his mortally wounded Mexican lover and accompanying the lawman Earp to the OK Corral. Earp's fictional character has more than one dimension, too: he is played by Henry Fonda, familiar to movie audiences as a versatile yet characteristically homespun actor who also portrayed Gil Carter (*The Ox-Bow Incident,* 1943), Charles Pike (*The Lady Eve,* 1941), Tom Joad (*The Grapes of Wrath,* 1940), Abraham Lincoln (*Young Mr. Lincoln,* 1939), and the outlaw Frank James (twice). When the bare beams of the first Tombstone church go up in *My Darling Clementine,* silhouetted against the Arizona desert sky, the church-raising is celebrated not with a sermon but with a dance attended by the entire community—including Earp, the avenging lawman who, for a little while, exchanges gun battles for awkward, comic dance steps.

At the very least, the range and complexity of many western outlaws, lawmen, soldiers, Indians, actors, and territories—in both actual and fictionalized manifestations—represent and embody an argument against the Turner thesis. Even in the late nineteenth century, when Turner was preparing and delivering his ideas, these often disruptive, unpredictable forces were complicating the inexorable advance of civilization as Turner understood and theorized it and were helping to maintain an unruly frontier rather than participating in its closing. The western presence of such "scum" before the official "closing of the frontier" (1890) could of course be used to back up Turner's contentions; outlaws, vigilantes, and "savages" were to be expected in "precivilized" places, and the vanquishing of these "bad" people was typically seen as indisputable proof of civilization's advance. But the continued activities of actual western outlaws after 1890, as well as the lingering presence of outlaws as icons, of ghostly, fictionalized Billy the Kids and Wyatt Earps, of Geronimo riding in President Theodore Roosevelt's inaugural parade and agreeing to present himself to white spectators as a commercial property, badger Turner's thesis; for in another sense, the persistence of crime and criminal legends gives powerful evidence of post-1890 frontier conditions.

Put another way, Turner offers a strong explanation of westward expansion and settlement, seeing it as a clear, steady, sequential process; western outlaws such as Billy the Kid, many of whose actions are still hotly debated and thoroughly unclear, unwittingly point up the disorderly, random, still-unsettled side of much frontier experience. And Indians such as Geronimo, although captured and exhibited (in part) as evidence of U.S. imperialism, also continue to disrupt the easy binaries of "civilization" and "savagery" long after their capture. They do so in part by producing autobiographical texts that register their continuing resistance to U.S. policies and in part by helping to encourage resistance in the hearts and minds of those who come after, including American Indian writers such as Jimmie Durham and, most notably, Leslie Marmon Silko.

• • •

The Billy the Kid legend often seems more open-ended than the frontier thesis. Rather than turning predictable and closing things down, Billy the Kid usually surprises as he is reinvented over and over again; a decade or two older than Turner's essay, the Kid as icon has been much more flexible and adaptable than the frontier thesis as paradigm. His legend, based in part on his early death (he was twenty-two) combined with his unusually bad temper, was coming into being at about the same time Turner was declaring the frontier closed. In the same year that the census marked the official, statistical closing of the frontier, Francis W. Doughty published, in the New York Detective Library, one of many dime novels about the outlaw, *Old King Brady and Billy the Kid; or, the Great Detective's Chase* (1890). Books such as Doughty's, published in the wake of Billy the Kid's death, dramatized and debated what Turner theorized: the contest between civilization and frontier. Generally promoting the forces of law and domesticity while interpreting American history in the Turner/Roosevelt manner, these books nonetheless also reproduced and perpetuated the frontier that historians were declaring closed, civilized, eradicated. These books provided their readers, many of them easterners, with neither a peaceful agrarian West nor a successful, urbanizing, "civilized" West; instead, they focused on precisely the qualities that Turner pronounced dead. Sometimes Billy the Kid was painted as the archfiend and Garrett glamorized as the hero; sometimes their roles were reversed. Sometimes the iconographers complicated such polarizations. But typically, the frontier was glamorized as an exciting, unruly spectacle, sometimes mythic, often romanticized, and generally, in its capacity for imaginative reconstruction and its transformation of local history into legend and national concerns into marketable appetites, a fit prototype for the Southwest as aesthetic spectacle.[2]

Billy the Kid's long and varied afterlife, then, bears witness to a powerful popular image of an active, open frontier. His malleable frontier rides alongside the more monumental metaphorical frontier of Turner's, harrying and disrupting the historian's claims about American character and American history. Further, these conflicting readings of the West and Southwest, more so than either narrative considered separately and thus out of context, are signally important to the gradual development of a southwestern frontier aesthetic that typically combines and blurs elements of outlawry and settlement, among other things. As richly as Silko works with Indian history and Indian prophecy in *Almanac of the Dead,* she also bases her representation of southwestern outlawry in part on these shifting, blurred Euro-American cultural processes of constructing and deconstructing frontiers.

Clearly, a great many other writers more than compensate for Turner's refusal to elaborate on Wild West outlaws and territorial violence. His thesis is predicated on his decision that "scum" taint a history assumed to be already magisterially in progress; he does not theorize a frontier in which a variety of people move cross-culturally toward the construction of multiple, arrhythmic histories. As Richard White explains,

> The nationally imagined West depended on the mass media, and the popularity of western stories with the mass media was in part serendipitous. Anglo American settlement of the West happened to take place simultaneously with the rise of penny newspapers, dime novels, and sensationalist journals such as the *National Police Gazette*. . . . [M]ass media, a mass audience, and mass western migration all bumped into each other, as it were, at a given historical moment. (620)

What results is a frontier condition characterized by its unpredictable cultural collisions and exchanges. Just as Roosevelt, Frederic Remington, and others were popularizing a bracing and upright West in prose works and paintings, a whole industry of dime novels depicted and sometimes romanticized the corruption, chaos, and outlawry of the same region; between 1881 and 1906, for example, some 270 dime novels appeared in the James gang series alone (Tatum, 44; see also G. Edward White). Other western figures, among them Billy the Kid, were well represented in all their satanic attractiveness in the dime novels: there were approximately fifteen Billy the Kid dime novels between 1881 and 1906. By 1965, conservative estimates place the Billy the Kid bibliography at more than eight hundred items, including more than forty movies (Tatum, 5). Moreover, contemporary commentators on the death of Billy the Kid were much more forthcoming than Turner about addressing western outlawry. As Kent Steckmesser observes, "The Kid's death was national news" (71); amplifying this statement, Richard White points out that "The actual Billy the Kid was a relatively inconsequential gunman and stock thief. . . . He was, however, by the time of his death a national figure of sorts because the *National Police Gazette* and mass-circulation eastern papers reported the story of his crimes. In New York City eight newspapers published notices of the Kid's death" (625). Alleged by some to have migrated from New York City to New Mexico as a youth, Billy the Kid continues to migrate after his death; as one result of this process, ideas of the Southwest, along with southwestern texts, become more visible, more prominent, and more understandable as part of the American nation.

The multitude of newspaper reports, with their already hazy combinations of fact and legend, paved the way for the variety of "pseudo-biographical dime novels" (Steckmesser, 75) as well as an aggressively fictionalized work titled *The Authentic Life of Billy, the Kid* (1882). Credited on the title page to none other than Pat Garrett himself, this account was in fact mostly written by the local postmaster, Ash Upson, whom Utley describes as "a restless journalist who loved words, people, and the bottle, in reverse order" (*Billy the Kid*, 20). From very early on, "authentic" advertises not historiographical "fact" but a merging and mixing of fact and fiction, with each pressurizing and validating the other. Precisely because he was and is so mobile, so able and ready to cross and blur the boundaries of fact and fiction, history and legend, Billy as cultural icon takes on complex significance and aesthetic potentiality. Even the circumstances of his death remain uncertain, and indeed the fact of his death was, within more or less reasonable limits, disputed; as late as 1950, the Texas codger "Brushy Bill" Roberts claimed to be Billy the Kid (Tatum, 123–24). Did the Kid conspire in inventing the stories of his own death? In March 1882, some eight months after Pat Garrett's bedroom ambush, a posted notice in Las Vegas, New Mexico, warned away "thieves, thugs, fakirs, and bunco steerers" (Steckmesser, 70) and named, among other badmen, Billy the Kid. As Steckmesser remarks, "The good citizens sought to banish him even in death" (70). Or was their error a tacit acknowledgment of his imaginable presence?

Though *Authentic Life* attempts to soften the Kid's image as a satanically villainous wretch, most of Turner's contemporaries agreed with him that such outlaws were, not to mince words, scum. Writing at approximately the same time as Turner, Frank Hall describes Billy as "the most desperate and bloody-minded civilized white man that ever cursed the border with his crimes" and concluded, "The earth was well rid of him" (Steckmesser, 81). Heinous as Billy the Kid clearly is, he nonetheless qualifies as "civilized," his whiteness duly noted and mobilized in his defense even as he is otherwise vilified as indefensible: "civilized white man" implies, in the logic of racialized polarities, "uncivilized" or "savage" Indian. In two books, written in 1897 and 1901, the popular western historian Emerson Hough—a friend of Garrett's—calls upon other polarizations when he characterizes the Kid as an animal and, as Steckmesser puts it, an "archfiend" (81). The very quotable Hough embellished the "animal" tag by explaining that "the soul of some fierce and far-off carnivore got into the body of this little man" (Tatum, 56). Even so, the energy expended on these lurid statements suggests that "this little man" is interestingly fiendish, as compelling as he is repulsive.

Despite Turner's footnoted refusal to speak of outlaws, then, the outlaw as satanic antihero was a well-known and very popular figure, and as the "archfiend" of them all, Billy the Kid was fast attaining the status of national legend. Readers were fascinated, for example, by the psychopathic energy of an outlaw who was both so very bad and so very young. Soon after his death at age twenty-two, the legends began to take shape; Billy was said to have boasted that he killed one man for each of those twenty-two years. (In fact, the best estimates credit him with four killings of his own, as well as complicity in five other murders [Tatum, 34; Utley, *Billy the Kid*, 203–04]. From early on, the legend and its makers have interesting conversations with the facts and fact mongers.) The early popular interest in Billy the Kid, from his death in 1881 until around 1910, lingered over his exaggerated deviltry and defiance of social proprieties, the Mansonesque, fictive "dipping his finger into the blood of his victims" and a wavering between male and female clothing (Tatum, 45, 46, 48). Stephen Tatum writes that "the Kid was generally perceived [in these years] as the romance story's villainous foil to the hero's progress through a depraved landscape" (55), and as such, he appears to stand in the way of manifest destiny and the workings of westward expansion as theorized by Turner. But at the same time, the stories about Billy the Kid draw attention to and illuminate (however distortedly) a region, the Southwest, that Turner pays little attention to, with or without outlaws. In other words, the writers who attempt to come to terms with unruly southwestern outlaw elements also help integrate the Southwest itself into America. Even the early popular historians of the Kid, who agree with Turner that such outlaws were bad sorts indeed, propose at the same time the beginnings of a more open-ended and disorderly (though exaggerated) Southwest. The quick translations of Billy the Kid into a type, a metaphor, even an icon mark the origins of a legend very successful at persuading American readers to imagine, remake, and in some way participate in the previously disregarded American Southwest.

Given this emerging national public interest in outlaws and their regional environs, it is not entirely surprising to find the satanic Billy transforming into a saintlier and more sentimentalized hero beginning early in the twentieth century. Arizona and New Mexico were granted statehood in 1912, and at about the same time dime novel Westerns began to make their way to Hollywood, where often-romanticized backward glances at the more violent years of settlement were quickly gaining in popularity. The Southwest becomes in these years still more visible to still more audiences. John Cawelti notes the Western's "unique adaptability to film" (42); more specifically, Tatum argues that "the movies did the most to establish the Kid as a figure in popular culture" (107). Indeed, the book most influential and important in reshaping the Billy the Kid legend was compared to and made into a movie. Chicago newspaperman Walter Noble Burns's *Saga of Billy the Kid,* published in 1926, became a best-seller; selecting it for the Book of the Month Club, a judge remarked that it conveyed "the vivid reality of the moving pictures without the infusion of false sentiment" (Tatum, 102). Four years later, in 1930, it was reworked into the MGM movie *Billy the Kid,* directed by King Vidor. In his reshaping of the legend, Burns paints Billy as an American Robin Hood, actively blurs history and fiction, and plays up the local Mexican and New Mexican folklore, in part so that he can align Robin Hood with the locals who believed in Billy (Steckmesser, 86–87). In the process, Burns makes intriguing cross-cultural connections between the Kid and some of the frontier cultures he inhabits; Billy's alliance with the local Mexican population has in fact become a strong part of the legend. At the same time, Burns powerfully defamiliarizes the notorious outlaw by reconstituting him as attractively heroic and even virtuous, although he does so by reversing rather than dismantling readily available binaries.

Richard White, working closely with Tatum, argues that this

new Kid, too, eventually became a means to revitalize rather than undermine [1920s–1930s American] society. In the thirties, with the country in the midst of the Depression, it was easy to make the Kid a Robin Hood defending ordinary Americans against corrupt capitalists who were driving the country to ruin. He is, however, if not a conservative, at least a New Deal liberal; he destroys evil bankers but not banks. The Kid becomes Pat Garrett; he becomes the Virginian. He defends American ideals. (626)

Burns's *Saga* performs a crucial role in reworking not only the outlaw but also the American Southwest, not only in reaffirming that the Southwest can be reworked and re-created but also in dramatizing and popularizing yet another revision and reopening of the frontier Turner deemed closed nearly two generations earlier. For one thing, Burns demonstrates and confirms Billy the Kid's ability to change over time, to be a "flexible container" (Tatum, 11) and a complex aesthetic property. All in all, the frontier, allied with its favorite outlaw son, functions from the early 1880s on as a metaphor, a fiction, a myth, a place where history and legend, fact and fiction, law and order, settlement and open space blur in the imagination—a place, in short, reproduced yet reinvented, aesthetically valued, and characterized by the literal and figurative mobility of its occupants. Problematic as it certainly is, this frontier is nonetheless, in some ways, energetically created and sustained in a variety of American popular-culture discourses, enabling region and nation to make limited yet volatile contact.

Writes Tatum, "Discovering the Kid throughout the years since his death in 1881 has usually meant discovering the appeals of the West and the Western, the historical landscape and the aesthetic context within which the Kid both resides and rides. Such appeals continue to preoccupy us and beckon to us, even though we no longer confront the conditions of frontier existence" (13). Tatum replicates and supports, perhaps more than he realizes, the Turner thesis; though the various reinventions of Billy the Kid certainly point up contrasts between frontier and contemporary conditions, they also encourage comparisons.[3] Images of the Kid reopen and perpetuate frontier conditions because frontier conditions are as subject to redefinition as is the Kid; Turner, insisting that the process of westward expansion closes the frontier, leaves no room for such redefinitions, even though his metaphor of the frontier is itself an act of great imaginative power and redefinition. Perhaps there is something teasingly criminal about not only frontier conditions but also frontier redefinitions. Whether these white outlaws come to seem safer and somehow more appealing than Indian "outlaws" such as Geronimo is a tricky question. Clearly, though, the aesthetic careers of the white outlaw and the American Southwest get under way in large part because of the imaginableness and, ironically, the cooperation of its most visible outlaw as his mythic incarnations tangle with the mythic movements of the frontier thesis.

Notes

1. Both Geronimo and Betzinez write extensively about hostilities between Apaches and Mexicans. In *Geronimo's Story of His Life*, Geronimo gives an entire section (Chapters 6–12) to

these battles and their consequences. Betzinez is less interested in elaborating on Apache-Mexican relations, but he does begin *I Fought with Geronimo* by discussing them, and his attitude toward the Mexicans is clear and very similar to Geronimo's (see 1–9, 14–17, 93–96).

2. Limerick reads the desert as "aesthetic spectacle" in *Desert Passages,* especially 6–7, 91–94. Readers interested in Billy the Kid's academic career should begin with Tatum, *Inventing Billy the Kid.* Written for the centennial of Billy the Kid's death, this text studies both the formation of an iconic American outlaw and the various transformations this icon has undergone. Tatum both updates and usefully supplements Steckmesser's chapters on Billy the Kid in *Western Hero.* Utley, *Billy the Kid,* is a solid, more straightforwardly biographical work. Finally, see Tuska, *Billy the Kid,* which includes inconsistently persuasive critiques of rival scholars.

3. In *Billy the Kid,* 231–236, Tuska rightly notes Tatum's Turneresque assumptions, but readers should note in turn Tuska's disciplinary biases and blind spots.

Works Cited

Barrett, S. M. *Geronimo's Story of His Life.* New York: Duffield and Company, 1906.

Betzinez, Jason, with Wilbur Sturtevant Nye. *I Fought with Geronimo.* Harrisburg, Pa.: Stackpole, 1959.

Brownlow, Kevin. *The War, the West, and the Wilderness.* New York: Alfred A. Knopf, 1979.

Burns, Walter Noble. *The Saga of Billy the Kid.* Garden City, N.Y.: Doubleday, Page & Co., 1926.

Cawelti, John. *Adventure, Mystery, and Romance: Formula Stories as Art and Popular Culture.* Chicago: University of Chicago Press, 1976.

Debo, Angie. *Geronimo: The Man, His Time, His Place.* Norman: University of Oklahoma Press, 1976.

Doughty, Francis W. *Old King Brady and Billy the Kid; or, the Great Detective's Chase.* New York Detective Library, No. 411. New York: Frank Tousey, 1890.

Drinnon, Richard. *Facing West: The Metaphysics of Indian-Hating and Empire-Building.* 1980. New York: Schocken, 1990.

Garrett, Pat F. *The Authentic Life of Billy, the Kid.* 1882. Norman: University of Oklahoma Press, 1954.

Geronimo, with S. M. Barrett. *Geronimo's Story of His Life.* New York: Duffield and Company, 1906.

Hough, Emerson. "Billy the Kid, the True Story of a Western 'Bad Man.'" *Everybody's Magazine,* 5 (September 1901): 302–10.

———. *The Story of the Outlaw.* New York: D. Appleton, 1897.

Kaywaykla, James, and Eve Ball. *In the Days of Victorio: Recollections of a Warm Springs Apache.* Tucson: University of Arizona Press, 1970.

Limerick, Patricia Nelson. *Desert Passages: Encounters with the American Deserts.* Albuquerque: University of New Mexico Press, 1985.

Roosevelt, Theodore. "Across the Navajo Desert." In *The Works of Theodore Roosevelt,* national ed., 3:204–24. New York: Scribner's, 1926.

Silko, Leslie Marmon. *Almanac of the Dead.* New York: Simon and Schuster, 1991.

Steckmesser, Kent Ladd. *The Western Hero in History and Legend.* Norman: University of Oklahoma Press, 1965.

Tatum, Stephen. *Inventing Billy the Kid: Visions of the Outlaw in America, 1881–1981.* Albuquerque: University of New Mexico Press, 1982.

Turner, Frederick Jackson. *The Frontier in American History.* New York: Henry Holt and Company, 1920.

Tuska, Jon. *Billy the Kid: His Life and Legend.* Westport, Conn.: Greenwood Press, 1994.

Utley, Robert M. *Billy the Kid: A Short and Violent Life.* Lincoln: University of Nebraska Press, 1989.

Weigle, Marta, and Peter White. *The Lore of New Mexico.* Albuquerque: University of New Mexico Press, 1988.

White, G. Edward. *The Eastern Establishment and the Western Experience: The West of Frederic Remington, Theodore Roosevelt, and Owen Wister.* New Haven: Yale University Press, 1968.

White, Richard. *"It's Your Misfortune and None of My Own": A New History of the American West.* Norman: University of Oklahoma Press, 1991.

Ideas for Rereading

1. Eric Gary Anderson writes, "The range and complexity of many western outlaws, lawmen, soldiers, Indians, actors, and territories . . . represent and embody an argument against the Turner thesis" (p. 644). What, according to Anderson, is the "Turner thesis"? As you reread Anderson's essay, mark passages that explain his definition of Turner's thesis as put forward in Frederick Jackson Turner's "The Significance of the Frontier in American History."

2. Begin with as full an understanding as possible of the "Turner thesis" as it is defined by Anderson. In what ways—for Anderson—do the career and myth of Billy the Kid undermine Turner's assertion that the frontier ceased to exist in 1890? As you reread, mark passages in which Anderson uses Billy the Kid and other outlaws to disprove Turner's thesis. What is your reaction to Anderson's assertions? How does Anderson's work with outlaws resonate with your own understanding of "the West" as a place?

Ideas for Writing

1. Anderson suggests that the legends of figures like Geronimo and Billy the Kid are "capable of demonizing, romanticizing . . . the figures of the outlaw, the Apache, and the places they inhabit" (p. 642). Use your reading of Anderson as a basis for an essay exploring the relationship between "demonizing" and "romanticizing." In what ways are these terms mutually exclusive and in what ways can they sometimes be used synonymously? Apply Anderson's discussion of the "demonizing" and "romanticizing" of Billy the Kid and others to a legendary or semilegendary figure of your choice (whether of the "old West" or not) such as Sitting Bull, Christopher Columbus, Buffalo Bill, General Custer, Joan of Arc, Genghis Khan, Attila the Hun, or another.

2. Anderson's essay is designed to challenge and complicate Turner's thesis about the American West by showing the crucial role played by a group that Turner "banishes" to a footnote. Write an essay analyzing the effectiveness of Anderson's argument that Turner and subsequent historians have made a mistake. What kinds of sources does Anderson cite to substantiate his argument about the outlaw Southwest? How convincing do you find these sources? Why do you think he chooses to list a number of western films that were released between 1939 and 1946? How do you explain his references to dime novels

and newspaper reports from the 1880s and 1890s? As you work on your essay, take into account your own ways of thinking about Turner's thesis and such "heroic" figures as Billy the Kid.

EXTENDING YOUR WORK

Ideas for Research

1. How does the rhetoric of "western independence" and "fresh starts" manifest itself in political controversies and popular culture today? Explore print media or the Internet to find a case in which the rhetoric of western independence is in evidence—debates over such issues as gun control or states' rights, for example, or the portrayal of this rhetoric in music, films, literature, or advertising. Whose interests does this rhetoric serve? To what uses is it put? You'll need to examine the rhetoric—whether visual or verbal—carefully and relate it to Limerick's themes. Examine how this rhetoric works, what it aims to accomplish, what its goals are, what its effects are, and what they mean to be.

2. The image of the American West as a utopia of freedom and opportunity is part of its art and literature up to the present day. Gather a number of representations of the West in film, literature, music, or other media (a few starting points: the novels of Louis L'Amour and Zane Grey; John Ford's western films, such as *The Searchers* and *My Darling Clementine;* Owen Wister's *The Virginian*). Analyze how these works treat the West—do they portray the West as a "utopia" or as something more complicated? Do idealized concepts of the West and the reality of experience in the West come into conflict in these works? Write an essay on utopianism in the representation of the West in selected works of art.

3. Leslie Marmon Silko writes that "Manifest Destiny may lack its old grandeur of theft and blood—'lock the door' is what it means now, with racism a trump card to be played again and again" (p. 623). How and when did the belief in Manifest Destiny arise? What role has it played in American history? Using the Internet and traditional sources, conduct research into the origins and influence of the concept of Manifest Destiny. What alternative to this belief does Silko offer?

4. Start with as full as possible an understanding of Jane Tompkins's perspective on the purpose of museums (that is, "what museums are for"). Then visit a small to medium-sized museum, perhaps one with a stated unifying theme (for example, the home of a famous person, or a museum dedicated to a particular culture or craft). Keeping in mind Tompkins's evaluation of "what museums are for," write an essay analyzing your experience at the museum. Where does your understanding of your museum's purpose coincide with Tompkins's ideas? How might your experience add to or modify Tompkins's perspective?

5. Buffalo Bill can be seen as an icon of Western history. History has lifted him to a mythic, heroic status through which he symbolizes much more than a normal human. He is, somehow, larger than life, inspiring fascination, even veneration. Using the Internet and traditional paper sources, conduct research into the history and myth surrounding some other historical icon. With Jane Tompkins's essay as a model, develop a biographical reading of this mythic figure that indicates why this person inspires fascination, veneration, celebration. Why has this person become legendary? What did s/he do to achieve this iconic status? As you write your essay be sure to include factual details as well as suggestions about why history has elevated this person to the level of the extraordinary.

While you might work with a figure associated with Western expansion, such as General Custer, Geronimo, Soapy Smith (of Skagway, Alaska), or a figure associated with the American Civil War, such as General Lee or President Lincoln, you might also look to such icons as Joan of Arc, Kurt Cobain, Florence Nightingale, President John F. Kennedy, and Martin Luther King Jr.

6. Annette Kolodny suggests that the American fantasy of relating to the earth as a woman is codified "as part of the culture's shared dream life, through art" (p. 609). She mentions as examples the paintings of Cole and Audubon and the writings of Crevecoeur, Washington Irving, and James Fenimore Cooper. Choose one of these artists or writers to research. Write an essay on one of your subject's paintings or fictional pieces from the point of view of Kolodny's analysis. Use the terms and ideas provided by Kolodny to explore your writer's or artist's work. In what ways does your chosen piece of work reflect Kolodny's argument about the "vocabulary for the experience of the land-as-woman" (p. 611)? In what ways do you see the piece outside of or diverging from that argument?

7. Find several essays or book chapters about a historical figure of the "old West" who has also become a figure of myth and legend, such as Wyatt Earp, Buffalo Bill, Annie Oakley, Calamity Jane, Sitting Bull, Geronimo, Crazy Horse, Belle Starr, or General Custer. If possible, watch one or more of the many films about the figure you've chosen. What facts do we have about him or her? What are the myths and legends? And what lies somewhere between the two, in the realm of interpretation? How might a historian go about making decisions about how to determine the truth about this person's role and importance in history? What problems emerge in the attempt to do so?

8. Eric Gary Anderson writes that, from the early 1880s on, the frontier functions as "a metaphor, a fiction, a myth" (p. 649). Keeping in mind Anderson's discussion of dime novels and other literary representations of the myth of the West, choose and view two or three western films. Write an essay exploring the ways in which those films represent a fictional, metaphorical, mythical West. (Consider the fact that there are differences between those three terms.) If you wish, relate your analysis to Anderson's discussion of Billy the Kid.

9. Conduct your own research into the actual life and career of Billy the Kid, with an aim to developing as complete as possible a picture of the outlaw. Write an essay analyzing Eric Gary Anderson's depiction of Billy the Kid from the point of view of your own research.

Ideas for Working across Chapters

1. Frederick Jackson Turner writes with enthusiasm about the process of colonizing, "civilizing," the American West. In Chapter 5 of this book, "Nonviolence: A Weapon of Peace?" Mahatma Gandhi outlines the means by which his people can and must resist colonization by an outside force, Britain. Reread Gandhi's writings in Chapter 5, taking special note of his explanation of noncooperation and resistance. Write an essay analyzing Turner's work — especially the vocabulary of "civilizing the wilderness" — from Gandhi's perspective. What might Gandhi have to say about Turner's theories?

2. W. E. B. Du Bois describes "double-consciousness" — at once an affliction and an opportunity for the African Americans of his day — in his essay, "Of Our Spiritual Strivings" (p. 130). It might be considered a double point of view, one that combines that of the insider and that of the outsider. How might this concept be used to analyze the perspective of Leslie Marmon Silko? In what respects is "double-consciousness" (as described by Du Bois) a useful term for describing the way Silko understands her position in relation to the majority culture? And at what point does this concept cease to be useful? Write an essay that extends the concept of "double-consciousness" to Silko's point of view. As a further elaboration of this project, you might consider extending this concept to the point of view of one of the writers in Chapter 3, "Disabled Persons: How Do Individuals Form a Culture?" such as Simi Linton or Harlan Lane.

Acknowledgments (continued from copyright page)

Hazel Carby. "Lethal Weapons and City Games." From *Race Men* by Hazel Carby, pp. 169–91. Copyright © 1998 by The President and Fellows of Harvard College. Reprinted by permission of Harvard University Press.

W. E. B. Du Bois. "I, Of Our Spiritual Strivings" and "XIV, The Sorrow Songs." From *The Souls of Black Folk* by W. E. B. Du Bois. Copyright © 1983 by W. E. B. Du Bois. Reprinted by permission of Alfred A. Knopf, Inc. "Criteria of Negro Art" from *The Crisis,* October 1926. The editors wish to thank The Crisis Publishing Co., Inc., the publisher of the magazine of the National Association for the Advancement of Colored People, for the use of this work.

Michel Foucault. "Scientia Sexualis." From *The History of Sexuality* by Michel Foucault, pp. 53–73. Copyright © 1978 by Michel Foucault. Reprinted by permission of Georges Borchardt Literary Agency, on behalf of the author.

Sigmund Freud. "The Clinical Picture," "The Second Dream," and "Postscript to Dora Case." Published in *The Standard Edition of the Complete Psychological Works of Sigmund Freud.* Edited and translated by James Strachey. Sigmund Freud © Copyrights, The Institute of Psycho-Analysis and The Hogarth Press. Reprinted by permission of The Random House Archive & Library, a Division of the Random House Group Ltd.

Marcus Garvey. "Motive of the NAACP Exposed." Editorial letter to *Negro World,* August 31, 1923. Published in *Marcus Garvey: Marcus Garvey and Universal Negro Improvement Association Papers,* 9 volumes. Edited and translated by Robert Hill. Copyright © 1983–1995 Regents of the University of California. Courtesy of the University of California Press.

Carol Gilligan. "Woman's Place in Man's Life Cycle." From *In a Different Voice: Psychological Theory and Women's Development* by Carol Gilligan, pp. 5–23. Copyright © 1982, 1993 by Carol Gilligan. Reprinted by permission of Harvard University Press.

Charlotte Perkins Gilman. "The New Generation of Women." Excerpt from *Charlotte Perkins Gilman: A Non-Fiction Reader* edited by Larry Ceplair, pp. 276–79. Copyright © 1991 Columbia University Press. Reprinted by permission of the publisher.

Susan Griffin. "Ideologies of Madness." From *Eros of Everyday Life* by Susan Griffin, pp. 223–35. Copyright © 1995 by Susan Griffin. Used by permission of Doubleday, a division of Random House, Inc.

bell hooks. "Feminism: A Movement to End Sexist Oppression." From *Feminist Theory: From Margin to Center* by bell hooks, pp. 147–63. Copyright © 1984 by bell hooks. Reprinted by permission of South End Press.

Langston Hughes. "The Negro Speaks of Rivers." From *Collected Poems* by Langston Hughes. Copyright © 1994 by the Estate of Langston Hughes. Reprinted by permission of Alfred A. Knopf, a division of Random House, Inc.

Ernest Jones. "Summary of Early Responses to the Dora Analysis." From *The Life and Work of Sigmund Freud,* Volume 2: *Years of Maturity 1901–1919* by Ernest Jones, pp. 110–13. Copyright © 1955 by Ernest Jones. Copyright renewed © 1983 by Mervyn Jones. Reprinted by permission of Basic Books, a member of Perseus Books, L.L.C.

Susanne Kappeler. "Resistance and the Will to Resistance." From *The Will to Violence: The Politics of Personal Behavior* by Susanne Kappeler, pp. 253–80.

Joan Morgan. "From Fly-Girls to Bitches and Hos." Originally published in *Vibe*. Reprinted by permission.

Michael Nagler. "Nonviolence and Peacemaking Today." From *ReVision 20, 2*, pp. 12ff. Copyright © 1997. Published by Heldref Publications, 1319 Eighteenth Street, NW, Washington, D.C. 20036-1802. Reprinted with permission of the Helen Dwight Reid Educational Foundation.

Punch, vol. 177 (December 25, 1929). Review of *A Room of One's Own* by Virginia Woolf. Reproduced by permission of Punch, Ltd.

Oliver Sacks. "Protest at Gallaudet." Chapter 3 from *Seeing Voices: A Journey into the World of the Deaf* by Oliver Sacks. Copyright © 1989 by Oliver Sacks. Reprinted with permission of The Wylie Agency, Inc.

Eve Kosofsky Sedgwick. "Gender Criticism." From *Redrawing the Boundaries: The Transformation of English and American Literary Studies*, pp. 271–99. Reprinted by permission of the Modern Language Association of America.

Leslie Marmon Silko. "America's Debt to the Indian Nations: Atoning for a Sordid Past" and "The Border Patrol State." From *Yellow Woman and a Beauty of the Spirit: Essays on Native American Life Today* by Leslie Marmon Silko, pp. 73–79, 115–23. Copyright © 1996 by Leslie Marmon Silko. Reprinted with the permission of Simon & Schuster, Inc. "America's Debt to the Indian Nations: Atoning for a Sordid Past" originally appeared in the *Los Angeles Times*. "The Border Patrol State" originally appeared in *The Nation*.

Carolyn Steedman. "Histories." From *Landscape for a Good Woman: A Story of Two Lives* by Carolyn Steedman, pp. 125–39. Copyright © 1986 by Carolyn Steedman. Reprinted by permission of Rutgers University Press.

The *Times Literary Supplement*. Review of *A Room of One's Own* by Virginia Woolf, October 31, 1929. Reprinted by permission.

Jane Tompkins. "At the Buffalo Bill Museum, June 1988." From *West of Everything: The Inner Life of Westerns* by Jane Tompkins. Copyright © 1992 by Jane Tompkins. Used by permission of Oxford University Press, Inc.

Alice Walker. "In Search of Our Mothers' Gardens." From *In Search of Our Mothers' Gardens: Womanist Prose* by Alice Walker. Copyright © 1983 by Alice Walker. Reprinted by permission of Harcourt, Inc.

Patricia Williams. "Owning the Self in a Disowned World." From *The Alchemy of Race and Rights* by Patricia Williams, pp. 181–201; notes pp. 253–54. Copyright © 1991 by the President and Fellows of Harvard College. Reprinted by permission of the publisher, Harvard University Press.

Monique Wittig. "The Category of Sex" and "One Is Not Born a Woman." From The *Straight Mind and Other Essays* by Monique Wittig, pp. 2–8, 9–20. Copyright © 1992 by Monique Wittig. Reprinted by permission of Beacon Press, Boston.

Fritz Wittels. "Veiling and Unveiling Psychotherapy." Edited extract from *Freud and His Time* by Fritz Wittels, pp. 320–23. Copyright © 1931 by Fritz Wittels. Horace Liveright, Publisher. Reprinted by permission.

Elisabeth Woodbridge. Review of *A Room of One's Own* by Virginia Woolf. From *The Yale Review*, vol. 19, 1930. Reprinted by permission.

Virginia Woolf. Excerpts from *Orlando* and *A Room of One's Own* by Virginia Woolf. Copyright © 1928; 1929 by Harcourt, Inc. Renewed 1956; 1957 by Leonard Woolf. Reprinted by permission of Harcourt, Inc.

Illustrations

Chapter 1
Picture of Orlando on her return from England. Reproduced with permission of The Society of Authors.
Dust jacket design by Vanessa Bell for *A Room of One's Own*. Reproduced with permission of Henrietta Garnett.
Virginia Woolf studio portrait, 1925. Reproduced with permission of the Harvard Theatre Collection.

Chapter 2
Portrait of W. E. B. Du Bois, used by permission of the National Portrait Gallery, Smithsonian Institution/Art Resource, NY.

Chapter 3
Photo of the water-pump scene from *The Miracle Worker* reproduced with permission of Bettmann/Corbis.
Photo of Helen Keller and Anne Sullivan reproduced by permission of the Alexander Graham Bell Association.
Photo of Helen Keller with Alexander Graham Bell and Annie Sullivan reproduced by permission of the Alexander Graham Bell Association.
Photo of Helen Keller with the Nike of Samothrace reproduced by permission of Corbis.
Photo of twelve-year-old Helen Keller with John Hitz reproduced by permission of the Alexander Graham Bell Association.

Chapter 4
Photo of Jean-Martin Charcot reproduced by permission of Bettmann/Corbis.
Drawing of electric brush and probe used to treat hysteria adapted with the permission of The Free Press, a Division of Simon & Schuster, Inc., from *Freud, Dora, and Vienna 1900* by Hannah S. Decker. Copyright ©1991 by Hannah S. Decker.
Photo of Freud's consulting room in Vienna © Edmund Engelman. Used with permission.
Photo of Freud reproduced by permission of the Library of Congress.

Chapter 5
Photo of Gandhi as a young lawyer reproduced by permission of the Gandhi National Museum, Delhi; print courtesy of Amrit Singh.
Photo of Gandhi gathering salt on the beach reproduced by permission of the Gandhi National Museum, Delhi; print courtesy of Amrit Singh.

Chapter 6
An Episode in the Opening Up of a Cattle Country by Frederic Remington, reproduced with permission of the North Wind Picture Archives.
Photo of the exterior of a "dugout" home in Norton County reproduced by permission of the Kansas State Historical Society.
Photo of the interior of a "dugout" home, 1905, reproduced by permission of the Kansas State Historical Society.

Photo of Leadville, Colorado, ca. 1890, reproduced by permission of the Denver, Colorado, Public Library.

His First Lesson by Frederic Remington, reproduced with permission of the North Wind Picture Archives.

"Je Viens" reproduced by permission of The Buffalo Bill Museum and Grave.

Index of Authors and Titles